THE AGE OF HIROSHIMA

The Age of Hiroshima

EDITED BY MICHAEL D. GORDIN
AND G. JOHN IKENBERRY

PRINCETON UNIVERSITY PRESS
PRINCETON & OXFORD

Copyright © 2020 by Princeton University Press

Published by Princeton University Press
41 William Street, Princeton, New Jersey 08540
6 Oxford Street, Woodstock, Oxfordshire OX20 1TR

press.princeton.edu

All Rights Reserved

Library of Congress Control Number 2019931721
Cloth ISBN 978-0-691-19345-8
Paperback ISBN 978-0-691-19344-1
Ebook ISBN 978-0-691-19529-2

British Library Cataloging-in-Publication Data is available

Editorial: Eric Crahan and Thalia Leaf
Production Editorial: Jill Harris
Cover Design: Layla Mac Rory
Production: Merli Guerra and Brigid Ackerman
Publicity: Alyssa Sanford and Julia Hall
Copyeditor: Anita O'Brien

Cover art: Kiyoshi Tsukishita (1920–2012), "Fifty Years after the End of World War II, a Prayer for Peace Dedicated to Hiroshima," 1995. 91" × 117". Collection of the Hiroshima Peace Memorial Museum.

This book has been composed in Arno Pro

Printed on acid-free paper. ∞

Printed in the United States of America

10 9 8 7 6 5 4 3 2 1

CONTENTS

Acknowledgments ix

1 Introduction: Hiroshima's Legacies   1
  Michael D. Gordin and G. John Ikenberry

PART I. DECISIONS AND CHOICES

2 The Atom Bomb as Policy Maker: FDR and the Road
  Not Taken   19
  Campbell Craig

3 The Kyoto Misconception: What Truman Knew, and
  Didn't Know, about Hiroshima   34
  Alex Wellerstein

4 "When You Have to Deal with a Beast": Race, Ideology,
  and the Decision to Use the Atomic Bomb   56
  Sean L. Malloy

5 Racing toward Armageddon? Soviet Views of Strategic
  Nuclear War, 1955–1972   71
  David Holloway

6 The Evolution of Japanese Politics and Diplomacy under the
  Long Shadows of Hiroshima and Nagasaki, 1974–1991   89
  Takuya Sasaki

PART II. MOVEMENTS AND RESISTANCES

7   The Bandung Conference and the Origins of Japan's Atoms for Peace Aid Program for Asian Countries   109
    Shinsuke Tomotsugu

8   India in the Early Nuclear Age   129
    Srinath Raghavan

9   The Unnecessary Option to Go Nuclear: Japan's Nonnuclear Policy in an Era of Uncertainty, 1950s–1960s   144
    Wakana Mukai

10 Nuclear Revolution and Hegemonic Hierarchies: How Global Hiroshima Played Out in South America   164
    Matias Spektor

11 Remembering War, Forgetting Hiroshima: "Euroshima" and the West German Anti–Nuclear Weapons Movements in the Cold War   179
    Holger Nehring

12 Hiroshima, Nanjing, and Yasukuni: Contending Discourses on the Second World War in Japan   201
    Kiichi Fujiwara

PART III. REVOLUTIONS AND TRANSFORMATIONS

13 The End of the Beginning: China and the Consolidation of the Nuclear Revolution   221
    Avery Goldstein

14 Data, Discourse, and Disruption: Radiation Effects and Nuclear Orders   243
    Sonja D. Schmid

15 Nuclear Harms and Global Disarmament   259
    Shampa Biswas

16 The Legacy of the Nuclear Taboo in the Twenty-First Century   276
    Nina Tannenwald

17 History and the Unanswered Questions of the Nuclear Age: Reflections on Assumptions, Uncertainty, and Method in Nuclear Studies 294
Francis J. Gavin

Notes 313
List of Contributors 395
Index 399

ACKNOWLEDGMENTS

THIS VOLUME HAS BEEN A long time in the making, and both editors have accumulated a number of debts. Without the assistance—personal and financial—of dozens of individuals (beyond the contributors themselves), we would not have been able to present this project, and this array of interpretations of the Age of Hiroshima, to readers. It is a pleasure to acknowledge them here.

The journey to this book began with a conference at Princeton University on October 1–2, 2015, commemorating the seventieth anniversary of the dropping of the atomic bombs at the end of World War II. Many of the essays began in the discussions that took place there. Nothing at all would have happened without the organizational acumen of Cynthia Ernst—she deserves our special thanks. Generous support was provided by Princeton's Center for International Security Studies, the Future of Multilateralism Fund of the Woodrow Wilson School, the McCosh-Orita Fund of the East Asian Studies Program, the Princeton-University of Tokyo Research Partnership, the University Center for Human Values, and the Princeton Institute for International and Regional Studies (PIIRS). We are especially grateful to the successive directors of PIIRS, Mark Beissinger and Stephen Kotkin, for their continued financial support of this project into its next stage.

We owe a particular debt of gratitude to Hidehiko Yuzaki, governor of Hiroshima Prefecture, for his vision and his support for the second conference, "The Legacies of Hiroshima," which took place on August 3–4, 2017, immediately after Governor Yuzaki's important Hiroshima Round Table, an expert panel focused on nuclear arms control and disarmament. Kiichi Fujiwara was indispensable in engaging with Governor Yuzaki and serving as a pivotal supporter and consultant of the project—this volume would not exist without him. The governor's office, and especially Takuya Tazawa, provided invaluable advice and organization for the meeting in Hiroshima, Japan. We are also grateful for financial support from PIIRS and the International Fund; Anastasia Vrachnos was immensely helpful in navigating the latter.

Over the course of these years, many participants in one or both conferences were unable to continue their involvement with this volume. Their earlier drafts and contributions to the discussions helped make the end result as rich as it is. We thank Dan Deudney, Robert Jervis, Yukiko Koshiro, Scott Sagan, Mark Walker, and Vladislav Zubok for their time and thoughtful advice.

Princeton University Press was willing to see this ambitious venture into print, and they have guided it through the shoals of the refereeing process, a difficult undertaking with a diverse and interdisciplinary collection like this one. Al Bertrand and Eric Crahan were part of the early discussions, and Eric has shepherded it expertly to its final form. Connor Mills provided both his expert copyediting and his knowledge of Japanese and American sources in preparing the manuscript for submission. Scott Sagan was an enthusiastic participant in both conferences, and we were delighted to learn that he was one of the (no longer) anonymous referees for the Press. We thank him and the other anonymous referee for their very helpful comments on the chapters, which have strengthened the whole.

THE AGE OF HIROSHIMA

1

Introduction

HIROSHIMA'S LEGACIES

Michael D. Gordin and G. John Ikenberry

HIROSHIMA IS A NAME that everyone has heard of, and most people can identify something of what it means. It was the first city ever to suffer nuclear destruction, when the United States Army Air Forces dropped the Little Boy uranium fission bomb on the center of the city at 8:15 in the morning of August 6, 1945. (A second bomb—the last nuclear attack to date—followed on the city of Nagasaki on August 9.) This meaning of Hiroshima is relatively widespread and uncontroversial: the city stands as a metonym for the destructiveness of nuclear weapons. Yet from the very earliest days the meanings of Hiroshima multiplied and dispersed, and it has become almost impossible to grasp all its various significations at one glance. This book is an attempt to do just that.

The chapters that follow trace different strands of Hiroshima's legacies around the globe and across the decades since that fateful morning. Our collective goal is to represent the diversity of approaches to what we might still call the Nuclear Age—or the Age of Hiroshima—without reducing the many stories to a simplified and reductionist narrative. The first and most salient characteristic of these chapters is their interdisciplinary character. Among scholars, nuclear matters have been addressed with great depth and sophistication by both historians and political scientists, but rarely have those communities gathered in the same place. At two conferences convened by the editors—the first in Princeton, New Jersey, in October 2015 and the second in Hiroshima, Japan, in August 2017—a heterogeneous group of scholars from various disciplines, working on different parts of the world, and with divergent and sometimes clashing interpretations of the matters at hand, met and debated these issues. The resultant chapters, composed and heavily revised in the light of these discussions, represent some of the best contemporary work in international relations, political theory, science and technology studies, and intellectual and cultural history.

We strove to deepen the engagement not just across disciplines, but also to address as many parts of the world as we could, and to understand the Age of Hiroshima as a matter not just of states and scientists—though, to be sure, those actors are important in the ensuing pages—but also of peace activists, cultural commentators, and Geiger counters. The majority of the essays focus on either Japan or the United States, which were, after all, the intertwined contexts for the origin point of August 6, 1945, but the reverberations extend across South America, South Asia, the Soviet Union, Europe, and beyond. The result is greater than the sum of its parts. What you have in your hands is neither a disparate volume of disconnected essays nor an (almost certainly futile) attempt to provide a be-all, end-all snapshot of Hiroshima's legacies. Rather, we intend these essays to continue the vibrant renaissance in nuclear scholarship at seventy-five years after its inception. Such a renewal has been under way in the past decade, a slow reemergence from a period of intense controversy and confusion that followed in the wake of the end of Cold War and an often unconscious reconsideration of the role of nuclear weapons in global history, and especially in American history.

As a point of comparison, it is worth reflecting on the multiple scholarly commemorations of the fiftieth anniversary of the bombings of Hiroshima and Nagasaki in 1995. In a series of monographs and edited collections[1]— many of them of the highest scholarly standards and bringing together the luminaries of especially the historical discipline of the day—one was introduced to a very specific meaning of "Hiroshima," a narrow legacy that it is the objective of this book to unsettle.

The reasons for that restrictive vision were multiple. Some of it had to do with the end of the Cold War and the way that event highlighted the end of the Second World War as another instantiation of American victory (in the eyes of triumphalists). In addition, a proposed exhibit at the Smithsonian in 1994 that adopted a critical approach to the decision to use atomic weapons against Japan prompted a backlash from angry veterans, championed by congressional Republicans, who interpreted the suggested presentation of the *Enola Gay* (the plane that had dropped the Little Boy on Hiroshima) as exonerating Japan of war crimes while accusing the United States of the same. The exhibit was canceled, and the upshot was to simultaneously polarize and constrain discussion of this complex event, chilling a late 1980s efflorescence of original scholarship.[2]

The nature of the restrictive interpretation of the legacy that emerged in 1995 was highly constrained in both time frame and geography. In terms of the former, attention was tightly focused on the summer of 1945 and the endgame of the Pacific theater of the Second World War. Geographically, this meant that almost the only countries' histories explored were those of Japan and the United States. Historians of Japan concentrated on the terrible destruction that followed the atomic bombings, often in the context of the violence committed by Japanese troops and the suffering of civilians both in the home islands and in Japanese-occupied lands. For the United States, the discussion emphasized the development and preparation of the atomic bombs, and how the bombing fit into President Harry S. Truman's end-of-war strategy.[3]

These were, and remain, valuable approaches to the historical issues surrounding Hiroshima's legacies. The chapters below demonstrate, however, the benefits of following recent pioneers who have pursued strands of research set aside in 1995 in favor of radically expanding our understanding of the Age of Hiroshima—an expansion that, in turn, forces us to reevaluate the implications of August 1945. One direct consequence of allowing a broader swath of legacies is that the vast debate about the existence and implications of a so-called nuclear revolution is essential to any present-day historical evaluation.

The nuclear revolution is hard to define precisely—scholars will disagree about whether a particular feature is essential or only contingent—but easy to recognize in aggregate. It did not settle in immediately after the destruction of Hiroshima and Nagasaki, as though someone had flipped a light switch. Rather, over the two decades following those bombings, innovations in weapons design, decisions about arsenals, and geopolitical crises had cohered into a rethinking not only of the status of nuclear weapons but of the entire geopolitical order. The transformations happened in parallel and reinforced each other. In the early 1950s both the United States and the Soviet Union developed thermonuclear weapons ("hydrogen bombs"), massively increasing the destructive potential of a nuclear attack. These were soon added to the inexorably growing arsenals of fission bombs on both sides of the Iron Curtain, joined by those of nuclear newcomers the United Kingdom and then France. Later in that same decade, heralded by the launch of the Sputnik satellite by the Soviet Union in 1957, ballistic missiles were developed, which matched seamlessly with the lighter thermonuclear warheads to promise the delivery of apocalyptic devastation across the globe in a matter of thirty minutes. The escalation of destructive potential, the compression of time, and the inability to recall a missile (unlike a bomber) once an attack was launched began to reshape how political and military leaders understood a future superpower conflict. The purpose of these weapons was *not* to be used. Both Soviet and

American planners focused on how to strengthen deterrence and build stability in crises—the latter point underscored in the terrifying standoffs in Berlin in 1961 and Cuba in 1962. An enormous apparatus grew up around how to manage diplomacy and (limited, conventional) warfare in lieu of unleashing nuclear Armageddon. Political scientists were the first to point out the characteristics of this era, and historians followed suit by tracing the implications in every area from military strategy to the social sciences.[4]

In addition to coming to terms with those insights, the consequences of a revised view of Hiroshima for time frame and geography are fairly dramatic. Understanding the end of World War II is of course essential to any complete history of the twentieth century, but to evaluate Hiroshima's legacy only in those terms is to view the age through the smallest of filters. One of the most fascinating revelations of the chapters in this book is how tremendously divergent the legacies of Hiroshima have become as the mushroom cloud itself recedes into the past. At no point in the history of international relations, energy generation through nuclear power, or protests for world peace has the image of the nuclear devastation of two Japanese cities vanished. It is always present, but what that image represents varies depending on whether you look at the early Cold War, the 1960s, the era of détente, the last days of the Cold War, or after the bipolar geopolitical stalemate had evaporated. In each section of this book, we have arranged the chapters roughly chronologically, but there are necessarily resonances and shuttling back-and-forth as one reads across them. You can skip around, double back, and go through the chapters one after the other: choosing your own path—aided by multiple cross-references within each chapter—will make this book valuable for your own interests and at the same time open up potentially new areas that you had not thought to explore. This temporal oscillation and progression is essential for renewing our understanding of the nuclear era.

It stands to reason that Hiroshima's legacies change depending not only on *when* you are looking but also on *where*. "Hiroshima" has always had a special symbolism for Japan and for the United States, but it bears a further set of significations for all who live in the shadow of nuclear weapons—and that means everyone on the globe. All the states that have developed nuclear weapons (and those that have not) stand in relation to the United States as the first nuclear weapons state, and thus in relation to the use of those weapons in 1945. One of the most important fronts in recent research concerns how Soviet (and Russian), Indian, European, Latin American, Middle Eastern, and African reactions have themselves become formative in the propagation of Hiroshima's legacies, and the most recent nuclear crises in North Korea and Iran have only reconfirmed that finding.[5] The chapters portray a wide range of these geographical variations, in many instances showing the temporal changes within one region or state. It is a testament to the worldwide vibrancy of Hiroshima as a cultural symbol that this book is unable to be comprehensive; as many places as there are in the world, and as long as history continues to unfold, Hiroshima will go on to generate even more interpretations that deepen our understanding of the past and the present.

An additional theme that runs through this book marking the seventy-fifth anniversary of the bombings is an expansion of what we mean when we talk about nuclear "use."[6] One way in which nuclear weapons have been (and could always be) used is, of course, as weapons of war to destroy on a massive scale. This has happened only twice so far in human history, and it is those two uses that pick Hiroshima and Nagasaki out from the dozens of cities brought to ruin in the Second World War (not to mention before and since). In the 1990s, scholarship tended to focus on "use" understood in this sense of the detonation over and destruction of cities in wartime. But nuclear weapons are usable not only in this way, and expanding the notion of use demands a different sort of attention to events by both historians and political scientists. Seen more broadly, nuclear weapons have been routinely used all the time: as threats, through deployment, through testing. Many people now argue that we should look at nuclear accidents, environmental destruction in uranium mining, and weapons proliferation (as well as "latency") as different forms of nuclear use.[7]

These transformations in the intellectual conversation might seem to diminish the uniqueness of Hiroshima and its legacies, but in fact they demonstrate how Hiroshima has become more central than ever. Since Hiroshima and Nagasaki remain the only evidence of what a detonation will do to a city and its inhabitants, any threat or invocation of using nuclear weapons is necessarily a legacy of Hiroshima. Scientists' data about the effects of nuclear exposure are made on the baseline of the records of the Atomic Bomb Casualty Commission (ABCC), an organization set up by the American Occupation in Japan to monitor the health consequences of the nuclear explosions.[8] Those data have never gone stale. When we think about civil-society mobilization against the atomic bomb—as in the ICAN movement resulting in the Treaty on the Prohibition of Nuclear Weapons in 2017, recognized by a Nobel Peace Prize later that same year—alongside the brinksmanship of state governments such as North Korea and the United States, we are also always reactivating the legacy of Hiroshima. So too did President Obama reactivate this legacy when, in May 2016, he became the first sitting U.S. president to visit Hiroshima, where, in front of a world audience, he laid a wreath at the Hiroshima Peace Memorial and called for a "moral revolution" in response to the growing dangers of nuclear war. We also participate in the transformation of that legacy with this volume, whose cover art by Kiyoshi Tsukishita, a survivor of the

Hiroshima bombing, is drawn from the extensive collections of the Hiroshima Peace Memorial Museum.

This book is organized into three parts: "Decisions and Choices," "Movements and Resistances," and "Revolutions and Transformations." Rather than presenting the material in terms of strict chronology or organized by geography—the typical choice of the historian—we have adapted an approach from political science to highlight different scales of activity.

In part 1, "Decisions and Choices," the essays focus on the actions and thinking of individuals and groups—leaders, strategists, diplomats, politicians, scientists—as they grappled with war, peace, and the bomb. Here the stories are told from the viewpoint of individuals and groups in positions of power—making military decisions, charting grand strategy, operating in rapidly shifting wartime and postwar settings. Personalities and specific historical moments take on great importance. On the American side, we revisit President Truman's fateful decisions in the summer of 1945, as well as President Franklin Delano Roosevelt's consequential choices even before there was an atomic bomb. In the aftermath of the war, Japan debated about its postwar identity and diplomatic paths forward. Meanwhile, the Soviet Union contemplated the geopolitical meaning of Hiroshima and its implications within a quickly unfolding Cold War.

One of the important unifying themes within this section is a reckoning with what we mean when we talk about politicians or military officers making "decisions." There is a straightforward sense of the term, of course: facing a set of options, an actor makes a choice in favor of one and not others. But how does that list of options get determined in the first place? Truman was responsible, both de jure and de facto, for the atomic bombing of Hiroshima and Nagasaki, but circumstances were so arrayed, and information funneled to him was so curated, in the summer of 1945 that it is hard to conceive of him facing an unconstrained "choice." He could not choose to undo past decisions made by Roosevelt to lock the Soviets out of negotiations over the forthcoming nuclear age, nor could he (or the foreign policy apparatus of the United States) simply change assumptions that had shaped American policy toward other ethnicities or races for centuries. The classical model of decision making requires one to be aware of one's options, and many of these actors found various channels foreclosed in advance. Nor could Soviet planners or Japanese politicians choose freely in a world where American nuclear weapons already set the terms of engagement. There are many decisions and choices chronicled in this part, but they are not all free. Science and technology, knowledge and uncertainty, morality and the national interest, and great-power politics in the nuclear age created the shifting landscape for a multitude of unfolding choices and decisions.

Beginning with the second chapter, "The Atom Bomb as Policy Maker," Campbell Craig takes the story of Hiroshima back *before* the city was attacked—years before. Craig notes that the tremendous scholarly attention on Truman's decision making in August 1945 has left a significant issue by the wayside: Truman had inherited the atomic bomb from his predecessor, Roosevelt, and perhaps had also inherited some assumptions about how the bomb was to be used as well as options that had been foreclosed by those assumptions and actions. Concentrating in particular on FDR's decisions *not* to explicitly share information about the atomic bomb project with Joseph Stalin, Craig suggests a fundamental transformation of how one should view the classic "orthodox/revisionist" debate about the decision to use the bombs in the first place. At a minimum, Craig provocatively forces the reader to consider that the fork in the road between engaging and shutting out the Soviets, and setting up a nuclearized Cold War, took place years earlier than generally recognized.

Building on the geopolitical background presented by Craig, chapter 3, Alex Wellerstein's "The Kyoto Misconception," takes the reader to the heart of the classic scholarship about the atomic bombings of Hiroshima and Nagasaki: President Truman's decision process. Wellerstein crafts a careful narrative, emphasizing the evidence we have available for what Truman knew about the prospective targets for nuclear weapons—specifically, whether he considered Hiroshima as a "purely" military base or knew that it was in fact a populous city with a large civilian population—and how Truman's perplexingly contradictory statements in later years about his actions in August 1945 can be attributed to honest confusion about the details in the midst of a tumultuous presidential transition. What came next mattered enormously: Truman asserted control over nuclear weapons, stopping all bombings after Nagasaki, and this laid the framework for presidential control over nuclear weapons ever since.

In chapter 4, "'When You Have to Deal with a Beast,'" Sean Malloy continues the focus on the United States but turns it away from the White House and toward radical critiques of the bomb. Malloy locates the dropping of atomic bombs on Japan within a larger debate about racialized violence in American foreign policy. Was race a facilitating factor in Truman's decision? If the atomic bomb had been ready, would the United States have used it against Germany? Malloy argues that this way of narrowly posing the question distorts our view of what it means to consider race as a factor shaping international relations and political structures. At the time, many observers in Asia and the colonial and postcolonial world made sense of Hiroshima and Nagasaki through the prism of Western racial and imperial hierarchies. With the coming of the Vietnam War, many critics of American foreign policy both at home and abroad made connections between domestic racism and racial violence and use of force overseas. Malloy surveys the historiographical debates on American foreign policy, identifying major positions and scholarly silences on questions of race, the bomb, and American postwar power, and how thinking through Hiroshima can highlight this broader context.

David Holloway, in chapter 5, "Racing toward Armageddon?," shifts the focus to the nuclear policies and strategies of the other nuclear superpower of the Cold War: the Soviet Union. The narrative here spans from 1955—with the advent of thermonuclear weapons and a realization by both the Americans and the Soviets that a global atomic war was not winnable (though sadly still possible)—to the Anti-Ballistic Missile and Strategic Arms Limitation accords of the early 1970s. Holloway carefully describes the evolution of Soviet nuclear planning, which necessarily provides, as a mirror image, the parallel transformations in Washington. The staggering growth of nuclear arsenals in this period and their corresponding predicted death tolls ("a hundred Holocausts") show how quickly the destruction of Hiroshima and Nagasaki had become normalized within the thinking that was later characterized as the nuclear revolution. Hiroshima itself remained a benchmark on both sides of the Iron Curtain, even as the Soviets and Americans attempted arms control to tame the Golem that they had themselves brought into existence.

In chapter 6, "The Evolution of Japanese Politics and Diplomacy under the Long Shadows of Hiroshima and Nagasaki," Takuya Sasaki picks up the chronology where the previous chapter left off but changes the geographical focus to Japan. In this comprehensive survey of Japanese-American relations from the 1970s to the end of the Cold War, with extensive attention to economic and other regional-security issues, Sasaki shows how the issue of a potentially nuclear-armed Japan was always present in the background. There was no question that Japan had the technical capacity to develop such weapons by the 1970s; public and elite sentiments (as well as international pressure) provide the answer for why Japan did not proliferate. Here, at the level of high politics and public relations, we see that the legacy of Hiroshima and Nagasaki within Japan also served as a touchstone for establishing a place for Japan in the postwar geopolitical and economic order.

———

In part 2, "Movements and Resistances," the essays pull back to look at the wider global system. Here we are interested in the multiple ways in which

Hiroshima triggered new political movements, global alignments, and grand shifts in the hierarchy of international order. The nuclear revolution redefined what it meant to be a great power. Like lightning in darkness, Hiroshima illuminated the geopolitical hierarchies of the emerging postwar order. The global system developed new centers and new peripheries. Weak and developing countries were forced to rethink their prospects. Hiroshima and the U.S.-Soviet nuclear arms race came to define the logic and dangers of the Cold War. But, as this part showcases, the nuclear revolution was also experienced in Asia, Latin America, and Africa. Essays look at the dangers and opportunities of atomic weapons and nuclear power as seen from Brazil, India, and West Germany, as well as from the United States and Japan. Race, civilization, colonialism, and hegemonic power were prisms through which countries across the global system made sense of the new era.

This part illuminates the breadth and diversity of the agents—activists, bureaucrats, diplomats, and others—who were drawn into the politics and struggles triggered by Hiroshima. Outside the great-power world, the significance of Hiroshima and the unfolding nuclear revolution was not primarily about deterrence and arms control. It was in the multiplicity of ways the emerging global nuclear order would affect peace and development, hegemony and power alignments, and regional leadership and national projects across the global system. Civil society became the site for new forms of peace activism. State bureaucracies and scientific groups assessed the implications of the new nuclear technology as tools of economic development and national autonomy. Diplomats and strategists explored the new constraints and opportunities for regional order building and security cooperation. These agents and actors unfurled new narratives and discourses to make sense of their actions and agendas. "Hiroshima" became a shorthand for the new technological age, and the emerging world nuclear order became a site in the struggle for modernity.

In chapter 7, "The Bandung Conference and the Origins of Japan's Atoms for Peace Aid Program for Asian Countries," Shinsuke Tomotsugu explores Japan's postwar efforts to rebuild relations with its Asian neighbors under the shadow of the nuclear revolution. The Bandung Conference of 1955 stands as an important moment when countries across Asia and Africa attempted to speak with a collective voice on questions of racial equality, peaceful coexistence, and the grand principles of world order. These countries sought both to proclaim their opposition to nuclear weapons—now in the hands of the postwar great powers—and to gain access to the benefits manifest in the fast-emerging civilian use of atomic energy. As Tomotsugu details, it was in this setting that Japanese scientists, diplomats, and politicians maneuvered to find a leadership role for Japan in Asia, doing so by aligning with the worldwide movement in the development of nuclear energy for peaceful purposes.

Srinath Raghavan, in chapter 8, "India in the Early Nuclear Age," offers a new account of India's fraught response to the emerging Age of Hiroshima and the new nation's journey to its status as a nuclear weapons state. The story is frequently told in teleological terms, reading back from India's first nuclear test in 1974 a coherent sequence of steps driven by the determined efforts of Jawaharlal Nehru and other leaders to establish the country's nuclear weapons capability. In contrast, Raghavan sees a deeper ambivalence in India's postwar journey, with policies and choices tied to wider debates about the country's involvement in the Second World War, decolonization and state-led economic development, and the unfolding Cold War. Indian leaders were genuinely frightened by the destructive power of the atomic bomb and the dangers at the heart of the nuclear revolution, yet they also saw opportunities for harnessing the power of the atom for India's own development and keeping open its options to join the great power nuclear club.

In chapter 9, "The Unnecessary Option to Go Nuclear," Wakana Mukai enters the debate over the sources of Japan's postwar antinuclearism. Some scholars see Japan's decision not to "go nuclear" as an expression of Japanese identity: a deep postwar pacifism forged by the trauma of war and the atomic bombings. Other scholars emphasize a more pragmatic judgment made by Japanese elites to base the country's security on extended deterrence provided by the U.S. nuclear umbrella. Mukai argues that these two narratives—one focused on public opinion and social movements and the other on policy makers and national security doctrine—are seldom brought together. In reexamining Japanese nuclear policy in the 1950s and 1960s, Mukai finds important, if indirect, impacts of the peace movement and antinuclear discourses emerging from civil society on government decisions.

In chapter 10, "Nuclear Revolution and Hegemonic Hierarchies," Matias Spektor explores how elites in Brazil and Argentina experienced Hiroshima and the beginning of the nuclear revolution. As in other parts of the world, elites in these South American countries had complicated reactions. There was the growing danger of catastrophic war inherent in this new escalation of the capability to inflict violence. There was also a new recognition of the realities of the global power hierarchy, with the advanced industrial states, led by the United States, looming over the weak and less developed periphery. But as Spektor shows, the governments of Brazil and Argentina also saw new opportunities. The nuclear revolution was "a new battlefield in the struggle for modernity." The nuclear revolution illuminated a pathway forward, harnessing the forces of science, technology, and the state in pursuit of development. Spektor looks closely at the ways in which the events of 1945 shaped South

American visions of the global nuclear order and the strategies and agendas Brazil and Argentina devised to operate in this new world.

Turning to Germany, in "Remembering War, Forgetting Hiroshima," chapter 11, Holger Nehring provides a portrait of the West German anti–nuclear weapons movement. Across the world, "Hiroshima" became a shorthand term for the power of technology and the looming possibility of human annihilation. But, as Nehring argues, this global vision of Hiroshima as a new moment in the human condition played out within very specific political, social, and cultural settings. Nehring shows how "Hiroshima" was used as a touchstone for West German activists as they developed memories and worldviews to fit together the experiences of the Second World War—the bombing of German cities, interpretations of victimhood—and the building of a new postwar ideology of protest and resistance as it emerged during the Cold War. The German antinuclear movement appropriated "Hiroshima" as a term of commemoration, and together with "Auschwitz" it became a signifier of genocide and technological destruction.

Kiichi Fujiwara brings our attention back to Japanese war memories and the centrality of the "Hiroshima discourse" in postwar Japanese society in chapter 12, "Hiroshima, Nanjing, and Yasukuni." Memories are intrinsically selective, constructed, and collectively held. Japan emerged from war attempting to make sense of itself as both aggressor and victim, and the bombings of Hiroshima and Nagasaki came to dominate public memories of the war. This Hiroshima discourse called attention to the Japanese people as victims, but it also carried with it a more universal rallying cry of opposition to nuclear weapons. With the end of Cold War and the disappearance of nuclear tensions between the United States and the Soviet Union, Fujiwara argues, two other narratives of victimhood have taken hold in Japan. In conservative Japanese circles, a "Yasukuni discourse" has gained prominence, focused on the sacrifices of Japanese soldiers and the recovery of a more traditional Japanese nationalism. Partly in response to this narrative, a "Nanjing discourse" has also appeared, calling attention to non-Japanese victims and the suffering wrought by imperial aggression. As Fujiwara shows, more than seven decades after the end of the war, contestation within Japan over how to remember the conflict continues, although the Hiroshima discourse remains at the center of collective understandings of Japanese identity.

The final part, "Revolutions and Transformations," explores the legacies of Hiroshima as they shaped and reshaped the intellectual frameworks that people employ to make sense of and define the workings of history and politics.

The nuclear revolution altered the way people across the world think about global interdependence. It altered our ideas of anarchy, vulnerability, violence, and the possibilities of human catastrophe. It changed our categories and concepts for talking about war and peace. It forced intellectuals to rethink their arguments about security and public ethics. China, for example, emerged from revolution and rose up as a great power in the shadow of the nuclear revolution, and along the way it discovered what security and strategy meant in this Age of Hiroshima. At the same time, campaigns for nuclear arms control and disarmament have captured world attention, giving new significance to the international peace movement. In these various ways, the chapters in this part grapple with Hiroshima's impact on international society and our visions of global order.

These chapters illuminate the decades of thinking and rethinking that have accompanied the nuclear revolution. It had become urgent to discern the complex logic of the new technology of violence. A basic question has shadowed the nuclear revolution: Is the atomic bomb useful or useless? In think tanks, universities, and defense ministries, assumptions about the bomb's usefulness were continuously debated and rethought. Scientists and strategists also found themselves searching for knowledge and data to evaluate their theories and public claims. What counts as data and what data should be counted? Communities of experts—military, scientific, health-related, international relations theorists—took shape and became centers for the production of ideas and policies. Within the wider sphere of global civil society, opinion leaders and political groups debated the meaning of the nuclear revolution and promulgated strategies and norms for controlling nuclear weapons and preventing new Hiroshimas.

In chapter 13, "The End of the Beginning," Avery Goldstein explores China's experience with the nuclear revolution. The first thirty years after Hiroshima can be seen as a period of learning and discovery by states about the character and significance of these new weapons for international relations. China played an important role in this drama. After emerging from political revolution in 1949, China again shook the world in the mid-1960s when it became a nuclear-armed state. During these formative decades, ideas began to crystallize among scholars and strategic thinkers about how these new weapons and technologies would matter in the real world. Looking back at China's nuclear experience, Goldstein identifies these emerging ideas about nuclear proliferation, deterrence, coercive diplomacy, and military conflict. It is the story of the rise of strategic thought for the nuclear age.

In chapter 14, "Data, Discourse, and Disruption," Sonja Schmid explores another facet of knowledge as it emerged out of the Hiroshima experience and played a role in shaping the postwar "nuclear order." Soon after the atomic bombings, scientists from Japan and the United States began to gather data and study the medical consequences of radiation exposure. Schmid argues that this "production of knowledge" took shape in a way that facilitated a nuclear order that simultaneously condemned the use of nuclear weapons and approved civilian nuclear programs. In the aftermath of Hiroshima, distinctive epistemic communities emerged, separating the worlds of nuclear weapons and nuclear power. The Chernobyl and Fukushima nuclear reactor accidents provide important moments for Schmid in illuminating the interaction among professional knowledge communities, power structures, and social orders.

Shampa Biswas, in "Nuclear Harms and Global Disarmament," chapter 15, shifts the focus to competing visions of "the global" that lie behind campaigns for nuclear disarmament. Biswas argues that the leading approaches to nuclear disarmament remain tied to Western narratives of the state and international order. This can be seen in the ideas of the "gang of four" appeal for nuclear arms reductions—led by Henry Kissinger and George Shultz—and the sweeping abolitionist manifesto of Jonathan Schell, which are simultaneously parochial and universalist in character, and therefore disconnected from the diverse and lived experiences of "nuclear harms" across the world. Drawing on Edward Said's idea of "contrapuntalism," Biswas advances an alternative approach to constructing a global disarmament ethic, one that constructs a vision of "the global" through the interplay among unique, distinct, and interconnected histories. Through a focus on the nuclear harms experienced by people at the bottom and the edges of the world, Biswas points toward a more authentic ethic of survival and security in the nuclear age.

In chapter 16, "The Legacy of the Nuclear Taboo in the Twenty-First Century," Nina Tannenwald brings the reader to today's global nuclear moment. In the seven decades since the bombing of Hiroshima and Nagasaki, nuclear weapons have not been used in war. There are many explanations for this surprising—and welcome—outcome, including the logic of deterrence and fears of escalation. In an important book published a decade ago, Tannenwald argued that something more is at work in inhibiting the use of nuclear weapons: the rise of a global norm, or taboo, against the first use of nuclear weapons. State leaders are not simply making rational calculations about nonuse of these weapons; rather, there has emerged a widespread normative sense of obligation not to do so. Tannenwald returns to this argument, and, although it is difficult to determine the strength or status of a norm of this sort, she finds the nuclear taboo under challenge today but still operating as a constraint on the nuclear behavior of states.

In the final chapter, "History and the Unanswered Questions of the Nuclear Age," Francis Gavin reflects on seven decades of historical inquiry into the nuclear revolution. It is remarkable that seventy-five years after the dawn of the Age of Hiroshima, the scholarly world still has more questions than answers about nuclear weapons and their impact on the modern world. As Gavin notes, the challenge is partly epistemological: scholars are trying to understand an event that has not happened. They operate in a hall of mirrors, attempting to understand the way nuclear-age leaders think, calculate, and render judgments. Certainty about cause and effect is elusive, a situation that seems to be inherent in the very nature of the nuclear revolution. Gavin brings us to the end of the book by returning to the core questions of the study of the nuclear age. How close have we come to a nuclear war? What are nuclear weapons good for? Why do states want nuclear weapons, and why do so few states have them? And how many is enough? Gavin reminds us that our understanding of the meaning of the Age of Hiroshima—how it has been lived and understood across generations and places—is always incomplete, even as we respond to a moral obligation to search for understanding.

This book illuminates the legacies of Hiroshima by tracing multiple strands across time and space, scholarly disciplines, and angles of observation. It is not a collection of disparate essays, nor does it propose a single, unified historical narrative. The chapters are designed to work together to bring to life a richly textured portrait of the Age of Hiroshima and its global significance. We build on a renewal of interest in "Hiroshima" as a moment in time and as the starting point for a nuclear revolution that is—quite ominously—still with us. The approaching seventy-fifth anniversary of the August bombings will be an important moment, and we hope this book will provide a foundation for an expanded dialogue about Hiroshima and its many legacies.

Hiroshima emerges in these pages as both an "event" and a "phenomenon." Hiroshima, understood as an event, is captured in portraits of the moment itself within the grand flow of history—in the actions of people, in the war and its aftermath, and in the human experiences surrounding the dropping of the bomb. The bombing occurred at a specific time and place. We hope to make sense of its causes and consequences, placing it in the context of unfolding dramas of war and peace, science and technology, empire and liberation, and geopolitics and world society. We try to reconstruct the chain of events that culminated in the bombing and that, in turn, triggered reactions around the world. We explore the memories and legacies of Hiroshima and how they became woven into the postwar world.

But as the bombing recedes further into the past, Hiroshima is increasingly seen less as an event than as a phenomenon. We think of Hiroshima as a turning point in human affairs: the end of one age and the beginning of another. As Michael Mandelbaum puts it, August 1945 appears to be "one of those rare moments when a new world could be seen being born, when a great transformation seemed to occur palpably and almost instantaneously."[9] Indeed, this is implied in the term nuclear *revolution*, which suggests a manifold and ongoing world-historical process. Hiroshima marked the beginning of a revolution that remains multifaceted and unfinished. Very few aspects of life have been left untouched by the political, technological, intellectual, and cultural fallout of the nuclear revolution. New frameworks for thinking about security and peace were invented. New conceptions of the world and its precarious interconnectedness emerged. Notions of justice, race, and hierarchy all were reshaped by the nuclear revolution, and we continue to rethink them today.

The portrait of the Age of Hiroshima that emerges from these chapters also reflects multiple disciplinary orientations, particularly those of history and international relations. Each brings its own sensibilities. The historian's eye sees the diplomatic, intellectual, and political events and movements that marked the unfolding story of Hiroshima, manifest in its many and divergent plots and dramas. International relations scholars bring abstractions and theories about power, order, and complex interdependence to their own scholarship of the same material. The historian sees complexity and multiple causal pathways shaping the events of Hiroshima and the postwar world. The international relations scholar sees states, great-power rivalry, and logics of international order. Some of the chapters in this book tilt in the direction of history, others in the direction of international relations. But as a whole, they show that the viewpoint of the historian and that of the international relations scholar complement each other, providing a richer and fuller portrait of Hiroshima and the world than would exist otherwise.

These dual sensibilities help illuminate the complexities of the postwar international order that emerged in the aftermath of Hiroshima. We see the great breadth and diversity of ways that peoples and societies experienced the bombing and the nuclear revolution. In the various regions of the world, the bomb represented a new technology—atomic energy—that might be harnessed in pursuit of economic development and national autonomy. Meanwhile, the peace movement raised its voice in countries such as Japan and the United States, but also in Cold War Europe and in the quieter efforts of atomic scientists and arms-control advocates. This is the global history of Hiroshima, which reveals a world that was shifted off its old axis by the bombing of Hiroshima. The activities of governments, civil society, and epistemic communities were reshaped and redirected in its wake. But Hiroshima was also a jolt to the realms of order explored by international relations scholars. Starting with FDR, Truman, and Stalin, government leaders made calculations about the atomic bomb based on the old logic of power and national advantage. The Cold War quickly overran—although it did not extinguish—the "one world" aspirations of idealists and activists. Power remained the coin of the realm, even if it was now denominated in a new and frightening currency. These multiple and divergent impulses and patterns, captured by historians and international relations theorists, coexist and create the Age of Hiroshima.

Finally, we turn to the future. Thankfully, the horrific violence of the destruction of Hiroshima and Nagasaki has never been repeated, but the dangers of the nuclear revolution have not abated. Indeed, the strange duality that has marked the nuclear age—war and peace, Cold War and détente, the nuclearized state and the antinuclear movement—has continued into the twenty-first century. Nuclear weapons and technology continue to spread to more countries, nuclear modernization programs are under way in the United States, Russia, and China, and nuclear violence threatens to erupt on the Korean peninsula. Yet, at the same time, the peace movement has won a victory at the United Nations with the passage of the Nuclear Weapons Ban Treaty. This duality suggests that the future has not yet been written or determined. New dangers are afoot, but so too are efforts to roll back the nuclear revolution. The chapters in this volume reinforce this view that the future is still open. They show the fluidity and richness of the global response to Hiroshima. There is not just one story line to the nuclear age.

This view of the past—of the last seventy-five years—gives us a hint about the future. It tells us that people and ideas continue to matter. It tells us that the work of scholars and activists will persist. We learn that the risks, dangers, and possibilities of the nuclear revolution are not obvious, and so experts and public intellectuals need to educate the public. Jeffrey Lewis's evocative recent "speculative novel," *The 2020 Commission Report on the North Korean Nuclear Attacks against the United States*, reflects this sort of effort. It is a cautionary tale of missed signals, misperception, organizational failure, hubris, and other human frailties.[10] It is also deeply researched and based on a mixture of international relations theory and the actual history of the past seventy-five years of the Age of Hiroshima. As Robert Jervis—one of the early interpreters of the nuclear revolution—shows in his review of Lewis's novel, there are actually quite a few pathways to an inadvertent nuclear war, and he too relies on a mixture of history and political science.[11] There is no other way to grapple with the phenomenon that is Hiroshima, and we intend this volume to be a guide to help readers come to their own terms with the present-day nuclear era. In showing us the violence and human catastrophe that can be unleashed in complex and unintended chains of action and reaction, Lewis and Jervis teach us about one possible future, doing so in the hope that a different future is possible. This is the fundamental insight of the Age of Hiroshima.

PART I

Decisions and Choices

2

The Atom Bomb as Policy Maker

FDR AND THE ROAD NOT TAKEN

Campbell Craig

IN OUR ASSESSMENT OF RESPONSIBILITY for the U.S. decision to drop the atomic bomb on Japan, where does Franklin Delano Roosevelt fit in? The majority of work on the American bombardment of Hiroshima and Nagasaki, a topic that rivals the Cuban Missile Crisis in terms of scholarly attention and easily surpasses it in contentiousness, focuses on Harry Truman's policies during the spring and summer of 1945.[1] FDR of course established the Manhattan Project, oversaw total war against Japan, developed the policy of unconditional surrender, and died with the bomb just about to be tested: no one can argue that he did not leave Truman in a position in which the bomb could be used. But it was Truman who carried out the bombing, accepting the military logic of using the bombs when ready, rather than considering other alternatives proposed by senior officials during the spring and summer of 1945 (such as a demonstration bombing or modification of unconditional surrender) to which FDR might have turned.[2] (On Truman's familiarity, or lack thereof, with these debates, see Alex Wellerstein's essay in chapter 3.)

The fact that Roosevelt set the stage for Truman's decision obviously goes undisputed in the historical literature. Where FDR tends to recede from the picture, however, is in the debate about *why* the United States dropped two atomic bombs on Japan in early August 1945. This debate is of course quite familiar and will not be discussed here at length. It is necessary, though, to frame it in a general way because the argumentation on both sides tends to diminish FDR's responsibility, an omission that this chapter will argue may be unwarranted.

The first historical approach to the decision, normally called "traditional" or "orthodox," stresses that the United States bombed Hiroshima and Nagasaki in order to end the war as quickly as possible, to avoid the massive Allied (and Japanese) casualties that would have resulted from a direct invasion of the main islands, which was scheduled to begin later in 1945. Advocates of this position concentrate on several specific historical claims: the absence of serious Japanese peace overtures, despite Japan's hopeless situation; the disinclination of U.S. policy makers to regard the bomb as a revolutionary weapon, given the strategic bombing of cities that had been taking place throughout the war; the risks inherent in alternative options such as a demonstration bombing; Truman's own determination to shorten the war for reasons of populism and his identification with the common American soldier; and the simple inertia of using weapons that were available.[3]

I am not interested in dealing with these particular arguments here. Rather, I want to make the broader point that the first approach removes *strategy* from U.S. decision making about the bombardment. In this depiction, American leaders did not have the kind of larger, ulterior motivations that are routinely ascribed to leaders of other states; the decision, whether for good or for ill, was made for the nonstrategic reason of casualty avoidance, and the (again nonstrategic) absence of practical alternatives.

To be clear: my point is not to argue (here) that this interpretation is wrong. It is to make the larger assertion that the first approach effectively rejects the question of *responsibility* from the outset, in the sense of being responsible for a political strategy that culminated in a particular action. According to this way of thinking, neither Truman nor Roosevelt regarded the bomb in a strategically instrumental way: they built it, and then used it, to defeat America's enemies and avoid casualties.[4]

The second approach, normally called "revisionist," argues that the U.S. bombardment of Hiroshima and Nagasaki was indeed shaped by ulterior motives, primarily those of ending the Pacific War before the Soviet Union could participate in it and/or demonstrating U.S. power to its emerging Soviet rival. Again, revisionists point to other historical events to support their case, including the unwillingness of the United States and the United Kingdom to tell Stalin about the atomic project; the rejection of alternatives to bombing in the late spring and summer of 1945; the postponement of the Potsdam Conference to wait for the Trinity test in July; and the decision not to oppose the Japanese retention of the imperial throne after the second bombing in August.[5]

On the whole, revisionists have tended to focus on the Truman presidency.[6] Their accusation that the United States bombed Japan for reasons other than those articulated is largely an indictment of Truman and his advisers (particularly James Byrnes) and much less of FDR. I would suggest that there are two probable reasons for this. The first is the counterfactual possibility that Roosevelt, had he lived, would have found some alternative to the bombing.[7] Truman, a less liberal and less sophisticated leader, resorted to the most brutal option. As Sean Malloy demonstrates in this volume (chapter 4), some revisionist scholarship suggests that the Truman administration's disinclination to look for alternatives to the bombing was driven by anti-Japanese racism.

Second, and much more important and persuasive: revisionists cannot easily attribute strategic responsibility to FDR because there is almost no evidence for them to use. On the question of the atomic bombing, the job of the revisionist has been much harder than that of the traditionalist. To put it in legal terms, the traditionalists have had to demonstrate only "reasonable doubt" that the United States had ulterior motives to bomb Hiroshima and Nagasaki, while the revisionists have to provide real evidence that the official, and commonsense, justification of casualty avoidance is fallacious. Otherwise the jury must conclude not guilty.

With Truman, there is some circumstantial evidence. His secretary of state James Byrnes strongly opposed modifying unconditional surrender in the Interim Committee debates in May and June, ostensibly for domestic political reasons, but perhaps, as Tsuyoshi Hasegawa suggests, because maintaining unconditional surrender was the best way to ensure that the bomb would indeed be dropped and the USSR thus intimidated. Truman postponed the Potsdam Conference until the time of the Trinity test, and he and Byrnes consciously sought to exclude the USSR from the "Potsdam Declaration" to Japan even though the Soviet delegation to that conference was in the same building, the United States had previously (i.e., before Trinity) pressed Moscow to commit to entering the war, and Soviet delegates at Potsdam clearly wanted and expected to be part of the declaration and had even drawn up a Soviet version whose terms were remarkably similar to the American ones.[8] Finally, the Truman administration ended up accepting the Japanese retention of their emperor following the week of negotiation after Nagasaki, even though, as we have just seen, Byrnes had explicitly opposed offering Japan any assurance on the emperor before the bombing in the name of unconditional surrender. This shift indicates that the United States may have now been more interested in a *rapid* surrender after the bombing rather than an unconditional one, again for reasons of keeping the Soviets away from Japan. All this suggests that, as Barton Bernstein has argued, Truman's determination to contend with the USSR was at least a secondary motivation behind the bombings.[9]

So with Truman, there is some evidence for the prosecution. With FDR, however, there is almost nothing. This is for three reasons. First, FDR was notoriously secretive about his actual intentions with respect to almost every policy. The "Juggler" routinely told different things to different advisers, made decisions in his own mind rather than as a consequence of formal (and recorded) meetings, and died before writing memoirs that might have at least retrospectively explained his real views. Second, his normal secretiveness was magnified several-fold by the top-secret nature of the atomic project. Only a handful of people in Washington even knew about it before 1945: FDR never held any official government meetings on the bomb nor even mentioned it to most of his key aides. Unlike most domestic policies, and indeed most foreign ones during peacetime, there was no public debate about the bomb at all until after it was dropped; FDR was never forced to explain his position to anyone, much less engage in the normal policy struggles with Congress that would have pushed him to justify his views. Third, and most obvious, for Roosevelt the bomb remained a prospect until his death, never an actuality. He did not know when, or whether, the Manhattan Project would produce a workable bomb; nor could he precisely foresee how and when the United States might use it.[10] As Warren Kimball, writing about this absence of evidence, puts it, "who knows about FDR?"[11]

All this means that the revisionists cannot make much of a case against FDR by means of conventional historical argumentation. They cannot point to substantial documentary evidence to show that Roosevelt also had ulterior motives about the bomb that can be connected to Hiroshima and Nagasaki. If one wants to make the revisionist case, it is easier to concentrate on Truman.

In this chapter I will present a brief argument that FDR can be seen as responsible for Hiroshima and Nagasaki, not at all because he specifically wished to see those (or any) cities bombarded, but because he made a basic policy decision, in response to two new conditions raised by the prospect of atomic warfare, that paved the way for the bombings. I substantiate this claim by providing a historical overview of his policy making with respect to his postwar vision of an American-led international order and the conflict this created with the Soviet Union, his decision on the question of international atomic control in 1944, and his disinclination to resolve key problems with the USSR during the final months of his life.

The Atom Bomb as Policy Maker

In an underappreciated *Foreign Affairs* essay in 1948, Bernard Brodie develops a kind of structural argument *avant la lettre* about the effect of the bomb on foreign policy. The revolutionary potential of atomic bombs, he argues, lies not simply in the new and horrible destruction they could wreak, as had recently been seen in Hiroshima and Nagasaki. It also lies in their transformation of geopolitics.

Brodie discusses a book written near the end of the war by William T. R. Fox, *The Super-Powers*, to make this point. Fox foresaw a postwar order of stalemate, between the United States and the United Kingdom on one side and the Soviet Union on the other, as neither side would be able to militarily challenge the other. Given the Anglo-American naval domination of the great oceans, the Soviet Union would never be able to threaten the New World; given Soviet land domination of Eurasia, the United States and the UK would never be able to threaten the USSR. The West might have an advantage in strategic bombing, such as was used during the war. But Germany and Japan, nations far smaller than the USSR, withstood such attacks for years.

"The atomic bomb," Brodie argues, "has changed all that." "Unless the number of atomic bombs which it is possible for any nation to make in, say, 10 years' time," Brodie asserts, "is far smaller than the most restrained estimates would indicate, there can no longer be any question of the 'decisiveness' of a strategic bombing campaign waged primarily with atomic bombs."[12]

Because a relatively small number of atomic bombs can destroy a large nation's major cities quickly, and because they are (in 1948) deliverable with long-range bombers to almost anywhere on the planet, atomic technology permits decisive intercontinental war.[13] This technological reality creates two new geopolitical conditions. On the one hand, Brodie argues, it means that the United States will eventually be deprived of the free security it had enjoyed over the previous century.[14] The bomb "has in military effect translated the United States into a European Power": in a third world war, the United States would be vulnerable to total destruction just as European powers were in the second.[15] On the other hand, however, it gives the United States, as long as it continues to possess an atomic monopoly, a short-term qualitative advantage over the Soviet Union. It makes it possible, in the abstract, for the United States to overcome the geopolitical stalemate Fox had identified by technological means.[16]

These two new geopolitical conditions each raise the possibility of new kinds of foreign policy that would have been unrecognizable before the atomic age. The first condition portends, over the longer term, a third world war, which the United States might not survive, and indeed which could threaten the human race generally.[17] This suggests a policy, if for no other reason than U.S. national interest, of global war-avoidance—of the development of some kind of international body or other set of radical policies that could reliably prevent atomic war. As we shall see, several advisers to Roosevelt were already raising this issue, and it became a popular cause for a short time after Hiroshima.[18]

The second condition, on the other hand, permits the United States to project war-winning power across the globe, the first time any state had attained such capability. This enables a policy of American, or Anglo-American, primacy: of using this revolutionary military innovation to seek strategic victories on a planetary scale. Of course, states have tried to use innovations in military technology to seek such advantage throughout recorded history, but their geopolitical ambitions have always been constrained by the destructive and delivery capacities of their new weapons.[19] Now, the strategic advantage could be realized at the global level, as Brodie stresses. A few officials in Washington and London were already raising this issue as well, with talk of preventative war and cornering the market on uranium.[20]

In 1944 President Roosevelt was presented with a choice between these two conditions: between regarding the bomb, as Michael Gordin puts it, as a "world shaking event or a tactical tool."[21] I do not wish to suggest that FDR necessarily regarded it in this way, but that, from Brodie's structural perspective, these were essentially the alternatives in front of him. In that year, the overarching political question facing FDR was whether it would still be possible to realize his postwar vision of a cooperative and effective regime of collective security in the face of Soviet *Machtpolitik*. The president regarded a conventional means of achieving this goal—coercion, or conciliation, of the USSR—as impossible. It was in this context that he rejected the first option, of international control, a move that effectively shifted American atomic policy toward the second. As I have already suggested, this latter claim is difficult to substantiate with traditional historical methods, so I use a deductive argument about his diplomacy during the final several months of his life to bolster it.

FDR's Postwar Vision and the Soviet Union

To show how, and why, Roosevelt made this decision, it is first necessary to provide a general overview of his primary objectives for world order after the war, and to show how it became evident to the president in 1944 and early 1945 that Soviet policy in Eastern Europe, and with respect to plans for postwar collective security, fundamentally threatened these objectives. Over the space of several months, FDR had to confront the fact that unless he took radical action, the USSR would reject the postwar regime he had developed and so doom it to the same fate as the League of Nations after the First World War.

Roosevelt's conception of the postwar world was, in broad terms, fairly coherent and (unlike atomic policy) well documented. Above all, he was determined to avoid repeating the error of his predecessor Woodrow Wilson.[22] Wilson had made the grave mistake of believing that he could *persuade* European states to give up their antiquated system of empire, autarky, and realpolitik, and to adopt his American plan of economic integration and international cooperation. The horrors of the Great War and its obvious origins in the broken European international system made it self-evident to Wilson that the Europeans would adopt his vision. But when they rejected it in Paris, he had no other course of action. Despite the destruction of the Great War, the United States was in no position to impose Wilsonianism on the European states, and the president had to return to America empty-handed.

To avoid repeating the failure of Versailles, Roosevelt understood that the United States must emerge from the Second World War in a preponderant position, able to coerce recalcitrant nations to accept the new order rather than simply trying to persuade them. By the middle of 1944 the United States was on the verge of attaining this kind of power. It was dominant in the Pacific, about to become preponderant in Western Europe, and its economy was out-producing the rest of the war's belligerents combined. FDR had successfully pushed Great Britain into a subordinate position.[23] The policy of unconditional surrender portended a postwar settlement where the victors could dictate terms on the broadest of scales.

As Warren Kimball argues, it is difficult to pin down exactly what these "terms" were for FDR. Early on in the war he expressed idealistic aims in the Atlantic Charter and his "Four Freedoms" speech. Certainly, he agreed with Wilson that an ideal international order ought to incorporate the American goals of free trade and self-determination, at least in some parts of the world. But by 1944 he began to emphasize the broader objective of establishing a full security collaboration of the major powers, with the aim of policing the world and preventing regional conflicts from escalating toward major war. These powers, a "family of nations," as he put it, would use force to dominate international politics from the top down, thus providing a comprehensive form of international security that had never emerged in the abortive League of Nations after 1918. By late 1944 this collaboration was taking the form of a Security Council in the nascent United Nations Organization, which would eventually be composed of the United States, the United Kingdom, France, China, and the Soviet Union.[24]

During that year, however, the Soviet leader Stalin was making it clear that the USSR was disinclined to go along with American plans. At the Bretton Woods Conference, the Soviet delegation declined to open the USSR's borders to free trade or to participate in international economic institutions based on capitalist principles and undergirded by the new global currency, the American dollar, despite U.S. promises of massive financial inducements. In Eastern Europe, and most notably Poland, the USSR imposed communist regimes in the territories it conquered en route to Germany, brutally suppressed anticommunist forces, and rejected demands from Britain and the United States that it hold free elections. Finally, and perhaps most important, it insisted on maintaining a veto in the Security Council, which meant that the latter could act only given unanimity of the five permanent members.[25]

By the time of the Yalta Conference in early 1945, Roosevelt and his senior foreign policy advisers understood well how seriously these Soviet policies threatened his vision of a comprehensive international security order. Stalin's cynical domination of Eastern Europe threatened to undermine public support for cooperation with the USSR and, even worse, demonstrated to smaller states what subordination to the "family of nations" might actually portend. A regime of collective security to prevent further war could not work if any of the permanent members could veto Security Council action against itself: who would believe in collective security if the world's most powerful states could commit aggression with impunity?[26]

As many officials in the U.S. State Department, and elsewhere, had long been arguing, none of this should have come as a surprise.[27] How shocking was it that the USSR would seek to dominate the states between it and Germany, given what had just happened during the war? Why would anyone with knowledge of Stalinism be surprised by Soviet brutality in Eastern Europe? And why on earth would Stalin agree to majority rule on the Security Council, when it was composed of the United States and three of its allies? With such a majority, the United States could engineer a resolution to attack the USSR, and Stalin could do nothing about it.

Moscow was not going to just accept the American plan because it was a good idea. If FDR wanted his postwar vision to succeed, he had two conventional means of achieving that in early 1945, neither of them appealing. On the one hand, he could organize a new coalition to compel the USSR to ease its repression in Eastern Europe and abandon the veto, a move that almost certainly would mean war against an erstwhile ally dominating much of the Eurasian landmass. There were several hawkish officials, in the United States and Britain, who were suggesting such a move. On the other hand, he could try to accommodate the USSR, perhaps by offering it financial incentives, modifying U.S. global economic policies, and—as many advisers had been suggesting since 1943—informing it of the Manhattan Project and inviting its central involvement in a regime to develop international control of atomic energy.

This brings us to a puzzle about Roosevelt's foreign policy during the final few months of his life. The president knew that Soviet recalcitrance threatened to destroy his postwar plans. He knew that their success demanded either a much more belligerent approach to the USSR or a much more accommodating one. Yet he chose neither course of action during late 1944 and early 1945. Why?

Early historiography on this question tended to divide along conventional right-left lines. Conservative critics of FDR characterize his late foreign policy, and especially the "sell-out" at Yalta, as excessively acquiescent to Soviet aggression; critics from the left accuse the president of undermining the grand alliance with the USSR in favor of an American-led capitalist order. More recent work stresses the limited options available to the president, especially given the constraints of U.S. electoral politics, and also FDR's seriously declining health in late 1944 and early 1945.[28]

None of these interpretations, however, satisfactorily answers the question asked: if the achievement of his postwar vision was as important as we have hypothesized, why did Roosevelt maintain a policy during his final months that seemed clearly to avoid dealing with the fundamental obstacles to it posed by Soviet power?

To be sure, the dilemma facing Roosevelt was politically dire. The idea of developing a much harder line toward the Soviet Union—of presenting it with demands to integrate into the world economy, allow self-determination in Eastern Europe, and accept majority rule on the Security Council, or else—was close to politically impossible in the United States. He could not plausibly ask the American people to consider waging another land war, this time against an erstwhile ally: not only would this alienate average Americans, it would also antagonize the left wing of the Democratic Party, still a major component of the Roosevelt coalition.

At the same time, a policy of systematic accommodation of the USSR was equally foreboding. It was difficult for FDR to know exactly what it would take to secure Stalin's agreement to go along with his postwar vision, but it would have to have required any number of territorial and financial incentives, and a proposal to cooperate on international atomic control, which (as detailed further below) would have at the very least entailed telling Stalin about the bomb and setting up an international agency with heavy Soviet participation. As Mary Glantz shows, this would have met with intense opposition in the U.S. State Department and among political opponents on the right, as well as triggering massive protest by the large Polish-American community.[29] Moreover, it would have meant running the risk of altering his plans to the point of rendering them impotent, the mistake that Wilson made after the First World War and which FDR was determined not to repeat.[30]

Given such a grim choice, FDR (or any putative U.S. president) would naturally have grasped at a third option, no matter how implausible we might regard it in retrospect. What if the atomic bomb, which FDR knew by late 1944 was likely to be tested in the near future, would so intimidate Stalin with the image of overwhelming American power that he would relent on the core issues? Could the simple prospect of overarching American economic might, now combined with a revolutionary weapon, persuade Stalin to accede to Roosevelt's security order?

As Sergey Radchenko and I have written, there is no way that this would have actually worked.[31] Stalin would not have relented, at least not in the fundamental ways FDR needed him to, in a million years. But, for the purposes of this essay, that is not at all the point. Roosevelt could not know what the Soviets would do. What he did know is that he might have an "ace up the sleeve" that could solve his problems in a much easier way than otherwise.

The Pattern of FDR's Diplomacy on the Bomb, 1944–1945

My hypothesis, then, is as follows. Roosevelt was confronted with the fact that the Soviet rejection of Western demands to permit self-determination in Eastern Europe, and to accept majority rule on the Security Council, likely foretold the failure of his postwar order. Stalin was making it clear that the USSR would not agree to being incorporated into an American-defined global system, and such was the scale of Soviet power by the end of 1944 that this meant the system would be incomplete. If there was any lesson to take from the failure of Versailles, it was that new world orders that exclude large and powerful nations do not work. Harry Truman got it: "without Russia there would not be much of a world organization," he said only a few days after becoming president.

The two ways Roosevelt could have solved this problem—direct confrontation, or major conciliation—were politically unattractive, to say the least. His response to this dilemma, I suggest, was to use the prospect of an American, or Anglo-American, monopoly over the atomic bomb as a way of *persuading himself* that he could still make Stalin back down, this terrible dilemma could be finessed, and his postwar vision could still succeed.

As discussed above, we have little direct evidence that this was Roosevelt's plan. Therefore, to support my hypothesis, I will show two things. First, in the summer of 1944, and again in the spring of 1945, Roosevelt rejected the advice of key advisers that he inform the USSR of the bomb and initiate talks on international control. Second, during this same period, and most notably at Yalta, he took no action to either coerce or conciliate Stalin in his negotiations over Poland and the Security Council, even though he recognized that these problems threatened the very existence of his postwar order.

In the late summer of 1944, following a second U.S.-UK summit in Quebec—where atomic matters were pointedly avoided—Roosevelt and Churchill traveled to the president's residence in Hyde Park, New York. The two leaders agreed that their two nations would seek to maintain a monopoly over atomic technology. They would not inform other nations (that is, the USSR) about the Manhattan Project; they would decline to pursue a regime of international control. Both leaders also concluded that the bomb might be dropped on a target in Japan if it was ready and the war had not ended. FDR told none of his aides of the agreement, and indeed there was no written record of it on the American side. That makes it clear that the president regarded the decision as both crucially important and requiring absolute internal secrecy.[32]

FDR had been informed well before the Hyde Park deal that spies had infiltrated the atomic project and relayed information about it to Moscow.[33] Therefore he was undeniably aware that by not informing Stalin about the bomb, he was communicating to the Soviet leader the implicit message that Washington and London regarded the atomic project as their own, and that they were knowingly deciding not to involve their wartime ally in matters atomic. Espionage is important to this story, because Roosevelt and Churchill could not claim that they were choosing not to tell Stalin for normal reasons of secrecy. They knew that Stalin knew: everyone concerned could see that the decision not to inform was made for another purpose.

Moreover, Roosevelt and Churchill made an explicit point of ruling out international control. Rather than designating the bomb as a revolutionary weapon that demanded a new form of politics lest it be unleashed on a world of warring states, they decided that it must be controlled by the United States and Great Britain. For the remaining nine months of his life, Roosevelt did not waver from this agreement.

This cannot be described as anything other than a conscious and deliberate decision. Key figures in the American atomic project, including FDR's two main advisers on the project, Vannevar Bush and James Conant, and the Danish physicist Niels Bohr, expressed to the president, before and immediately after the Hyde Park meeting, in clear detail, their convictions that the secret could not be kept forever and that the United States should consider initiating some kind of international regime that would have to include the Soviet Union. They argued (recalling our first option) that the world could not forever withstand a bomb let loose among rival states and spelled out how the United States might proceed in this direction.[34]

The evidence we have about FDR and the bomb in 1944 and 1945, then, is conclusive with respect to four specific points. The president certainly had come to believe that the United States should not cooperate with the Soviet Union on atomic matters; that it should retain a monopoly with Great Britain rather than pursue full international control; that it was agreeable that Stalin would be aware of this; and that the view of key advisers that more radical action was necessary was to be rejected. These were all decisions that Roosevelt made. He could have followed the advice of Bush and Conant and argued strongly for an overture to Moscow: by the summer of 1944 the invasion of France was already on, and he no longer had to worry about Churchill tacitly threatening that disagreement on the atomic question could lead him to postpone the second front, as he had done the year before.³⁵ An initial approach to the USSR could (and would) have been done secretly, with little political risk at home. It would have done no damage to the objective (which Michael Dobbs attributes to Roosevelt) of saving the bomb for the purpose of avoiding later U.S. casualties in Japan. Yet FDR declined. Why?

If FDR regarded, however vaguely, the bomb as a strategic instrument of U.S. power rather than a problem demanding new forms of international cooperation, then the puzzle introduced above becomes explicable. Why did Roosevelt take no decisive steps to resolve the problems of Poland and the Security Council? As we have seen, throughout 1944 Stalin had been rebuffing demands from Washington and London that he allow noncommunist political parties to participate in a postwar Polish government and had made little attempt to disguise the brutal repression of anyone opposed to communist rule there, as well as elsewhere in Eastern Europe. He also, in careful and crafted language, insisted on rejecting majority rule on the Security Council and giving each permanent member a veto. It is "essential," Stalin wrote to Roosevelt just after the Hyde Park meeting, "that the Council should base its work on the principle of agreement and unanimity between the four leading powers on all matters, *including those which directly concern one of those powers*."³⁶

Roosevelt corresponded directly with Stalin on both of these questions at the end of 1944 and early 1945, and then, of course along with Churchill, at the Yalta Conference in early February. On February 6 the veto and Poland arose as the two main issues of contention at Yalta, and on both matters Roosevelt neither acceded to nor rejected Stalin's position (he apparently also agreed with George Marshall's rejection of a proposal to tell Stalin about the bomb there).³⁷ He and Churchill left Yalta with a vague agreement to reconsider the Security Council veto, a loosely worded commitment by Stalin to consider noncommunist participation in the Polish government, and a "Declaration on Liberated Europe" that committed all three powers to respect political pluralism but contained no means of enforcement. Stalin, as we know, left Yalta with no intention of living up to any of these vague agreements; FDR returned to America and told Congress that he had secured the "Four Freedoms" for the postwar world.³⁸

Roosevelt knew that Poland and the veto threatened to undermine his plans for the postwar world.³⁹ His failure to contend with it demands explanation. I suggest that the bomb helps explain it. To be clear, I am not arguing that the prospect of an American, or Anglo-American, monopoly over the atomic bomb was, for the president, some kind of magic pill that would effortlessly resolve this dilemma. He had other reasons, moreover, for avoiding confrontation, including the absence of other viable options and his own increasingly infirm health.

The claim here is more subtle and modest. It is to argue, using circumstantial evidence and deductive logic, that Roosevelt developed a kind of strategic attitude toward the prospective bomb. He allowed himself to believe that this strategy could permit him to continue to pursue his grand postwar vision despite Soviet recalcitrance, and that this new strategy, delusional as it actually was, helps to explain why he made no attempt to resolve the outstanding issues of Poland and the Security Council veto in late 1944 and early 1945. Roosevelt was an exhausted and, by the time of Yalta, dying man. He was having to confront the prospect of the failure of his plans to save the world for democracy, to succeed where Wilson had failed, after four years of horrific war. The bomb provided him with a potential means of escaping that disappointment.

How, then, does this connect to the bombing of Hiroshima and Nagasaki? There is no way to know what FDR would have done were he still alive in August, and this essay will not speculate about that question.

But we can identify two leading figures in Washington who were quite close to both Roosevelt and Truman, and so represented a kind of "human link," as Robert Messer puts it, between the atomic policies of both presidents: Henry Stimson and James Byrnes.

Stimson's views on the atomic problem, particularly as expressed to Truman, provide us with an original and vivid historical articulation of Brodie's first condition. The secretary of war had been exposed to the arguments for international control expressed by Bush, Conant, and Bohr during the war, but we have no evidence that he made the case for it himself to FDR. To Truman, however, Stimson was more forthright. On the April 25 Stimson stated clearly to the president that the secret of the bomb could not be held indefinitely and that the question of sharing these secrets spoke to the core of U.S. postwar foreign policy and indeed the possible formation of a "world peace organization." Were the bomb to be let loose on an anarchic world, "modern civilization might be completely destroyed." An attempt to establish some kind of international control, the secretary of war insisted, might ensure a long-term "peace of the world." Stimson made similar arguments in May when proposing the formation of the Interim Committee, again in June, and most memorably, in a kind of farewell address in September, after the bombs had been dropped.[40]

Byrnes, on the other hand, pushed Truman toward Brodie's second condition. Here, the evidence is murkier. Byrnes formed a close relationship with FDR during the war, styling himself as his "assistant president," and was informed of the bomb project in 1943. We do not know whether he advised Roosevelt on atomic matters before his death, much less whether FDR gave him specific guidance on his preferred atomic policies, though neither is likely as Byrnes's job under Roosevelt was primarily to deal with domestic politics. However, Byrnes did accompany the president to Yalta, when Marshall advised Roosevelt against informing Stalin about the atomic project.

Like Stimson, Byrnes spoke much more authoritatively to Truman on the question. On the day after FDR's death, he informed Truman of the Manhattan Project and told him (according to Truman's memoirs) that the bomb "might well put us in a position to dictate terms at the end of the war." As we have seen, Byrnes was decisive in steering the Interim Committee away from discussion about international control in May and June and certainly played the central role in defeating any attempts to modify the policy of unconditional surrender. If, after the war, Stimson made his final act as secretary of war a plea for international control, Byrnes talked about using the American monopoly to coerce the USSR at the postwar conferences in London and Moscow.

Truman was wholly unversed in atomic politics when he became president and felt a strong obligation to follow through on FDR's wartime policies such as he could discern them. He could not know exactly what Roosevelt intended with respect to the bomb and so was completely reliant on the information and arguments he received from senior officials who had advised FDR on the matter. Stimson and Byrnes clearly understood this, which is why they hastened to lobby the new president immediately.

Whom to believe? Truman did not know what FDR really wanted, but what he did know is that his predecessor took no steps toward the novel aim of international control. Truman "knew," in the sense of having no evidence to the contrary, that Roosevelt's decision in 1944 to reject the idea of international cooperation to control atomic technology and favor instead an Anglo-American monopoly meant that FDR wanted to maintain the bomb as an instrument of American policy. In other words, Truman had no reason to doubt that FDR had decided to treat atomic weaponry as all weaponry had been treated before: as a means toward U.S. ends, rather than as a new problem that was too dangerous to leave in national hands.[41]

It is in this regard that Roosevelt's decision to reject international control in 1944 and 1945 looms large in our consideration of responsibility for Hiroshima and Nagasaki. Had FDR openly signaled an interest in atomic control before his death, he would have been communicating to his successor the message that the atom bomb was not just another weapon, and that the larger interests of not only American foreign policy but also civilization as a whole, as Stimson put it, demanded something new. Truman, in that case, would have been much harder pressed to avoid larger decision making about postwar atomic policy, and he would have found it more difficult to reject alternatives to the straightforwardly military decision to drop the bombs when they were ready. Because Truman received no such message, he could continue to treat the bomb as a "tactical tool" without any qualms, as the course of least resistance, an approach that conflicted far less with his own political interests and sensibilities.

Truman, to put it another way, could therefore regard Stimson's argument as the eccentric one, as a dissenting view, even though it reflected the opinions of the top atomic officials in the American project and many key atomic scientists and had not been overtly repudiated by FDR. Once Truman chose this path, the trajectory of postwar U.S. atomic policy veered irretrievably toward Brodie's second condition. This meant not only an imminent Cold War with the USSR but also the effective disappearance of an idea, that atomic bombs necessitate a new form of international politics, that Stimson, Conant, Bush, and others regarded as a perfectly reasonable response to the atomic age.

Was this Truman's decision? As with everything on the atomic question, it is difficult to be certain. But in July, after postponing the Potsdam Conference in order to make sure that it would take place while the bomb was tested, Truman set sail for Germany. Accompanying him on his journey was James Byrnes, now his secretary of state. Before leaving, Truman and Byrnes had agreed that Stimson, the secretary of war, was to be left behind. Uninvited, Stimson nevertheless eventually made his way to Potsdam.

3

The Kyoto Misconception

WHAT TRUMAN KNEW, AND DIDN'T KNOW, ABOUT HIROSHIMA

Alex Wellerstein

IT IS NO UNDERSTATEMENT to say that the final days of World War II, and the atomic bombings of Japan in particular, are an archival corpse that historians have picked to the bones. For over seven decades, these events and their protagonists have been dissected, scrutinized, and interpreted. Arguments as to their meaning have come into and gone out of favor, and while the flames of controversy in the field today burn several degrees cooler when compared to the situation ten or fifteen years ago, the events of August 1945 still command our attention and can provoke acrimonious debate.[1]

Despite all this scholarly attention, there are still some mysteries. Separate from the apparently eternal questions (Did the atomic bombings end the war? Were they necessary?), there is at least one major archival puzzle that several historians have noted in passing, without a complete resolution: *How can we explain President Harry Truman's vastly disparate recorded reactions to the atomic bomb?* The most notable puzzler is Truman's Potsdam journal entry of July 25, 1945, in which he noted that the atomic bomb's first target was a "purely military one" so that "soldiers and sailors," and "not women and children," would be the victims.[2] This is obviously at odds with the facts: while Hiroshima contained a Japanese Army headquarters, it was clearly a city populated mainly by civilians, and likely fewer than 10 percent of the dead were soldiers. While one might quibble over who Truman believed the *intended* victims of the bombing of Hiroshima might have been, calling Hiroshima a "purely military" target is by any standard incorrect.[3]

It is also at odds with Truman's own later statements, despite his generally adopting a resolute postwar position with respect to the necessity and propriety of the bombings. After getting news of the success of the weapon, he described it as "the greatest thing in history,"[4] but a day after the attack on Nagasaki, he put a stop to atomic bombing, claiming that he didn't like the idea of killing "all those kids."[5] In December 1945, in a speech entirely of his own writing, he described the atomic bomb as "the most terrible of all destructive forces for the wholesale slaughter of human beings."[6] On the day he left office, he wrote privately that the atomic bomb "affects the civilian population and murders them by the wholesale."[7] And yet he never expressed explicit regret at the atomic bombings, and in fact he took on a far larger burden of the responsibility than the historical record shows him to perhaps deserve, in the sense that he was actually quite peripheral to most of the decisions that led to the use of the weapons.[8]

Scholars have noted these apparent discrepancies, and they have provided fodder for divergent interpretations. For example, Truman's July 25 journal entry, which notes that the target will be "purely military," has been variously described as Truman's "self-deception in order to block out troubling facts,"[9] or indicative of a "schizophrenic"[10] attitude toward the targeting of noncombatants, or even "writing with an eye to 'history' "—which is to say, doctoring the record.[11] Either Truman was deceiving himself or he is deceiving history.

In this chapter, I suggest another possibility, one that seems more straightforward and can, despite its apparent counterintuitiveness, be shown as fitting with other aspects of the archival record. It is a relatively simple idea, but one that has far-reaching implications: that Truman's diary is an *accurate representation* of his understanding at the time, but *he was himself in error*. That is, it may be possible that Truman thought Hiroshima was, in fact, a "purely military" target and that he did not understand that it was a city full of noncombatants. The broader context of the July 25 journal entry, which concerns targeting discussions about the city of Kyoto, gives a plausible narrative for how this confusion might have occurred.

My argument is easily summarized. As historians have long known, Truman's connection to the practical planning of the atomic bombing operations was minimal. The one decision he actually made on the matter concerned the sparing of Kyoto, the ancient capital of Japan. In discussions with his secretary of war, Henry Stimson, about the Kyoto question, Truman may have become confused as to the nature of Hiroshima as a target. If true, this gives us a profoundly different interpretation of his actions not only in the days immediately prior to and after the atomic bombing of Hiroshima and Nagasaki, but also with regard to the atomic weapons policies he undertook during the rest of his presidency.

Methodologically, I call explicit attention to the available evidence and the types of interpretations that might be plausible. This may sound like a shifting of the epistemic status of the argument, from "what is true" to "what is plausible," but it is not clear to me that we can do much better (if we are being honest) when engaging in an endeavor as essentially quixotic as trying to uncover what another human being, long dead, actually had within his or her mind. Of course, there may be several plausible interpretations. In the end, I think we also need to more explicitly acknowledge what we get out of adopting one interpretation over another. I do not suggest that this reading of the archival record is the only *allowable* one, but I do hazard that it may be a *productive* one: it "fits the facts," and its explanatory power can be more impressive than the other possible interpretations, especially for the postwar.

In our focus on the final days of World War II, we often overlook Truman's policies toward atomic weapons in the postwar. Truman was not only the first president to use an atomic bomb in war—he was also the *last* president (so far) to have done so. Truman's role in the establishment of the so-called nuclear taboo, the *belief* that nuclear weapons should not be used again, has been noted in discussions about American nuclear strategy.[12] Truman's postwar attitudes toward nuclear weapons are important but understudied, and I believe that with a deep look at his mindset just before and after the bombings of Hiroshima and Nagasaki, one can see the roots of this aversion.

Further, Truman's postwar policies were crucial in the development of the modern American approach to nuclear command and control, which in principle has a strict separation of military and civilian authorities. During Truman's terms, this separation was physically enforced: Truman repeatedly refused to authorize the military to have access to complete nuclear weapons, making *physical* what in later administrations was a primarily *legal* differentiation. Truman furthermore established that the use decision for nuclear weapons was vested exclusively in the presidency, something that has continued to this day. I believe Truman's postwar attitudes toward the military and the bomb can also be better understood with a closer reading of his wartime experience.

Last, I should say something explicit about my approach, which might be described as "epistemological." Historians of science, like myself, use the term in a variety of ways. In this instance, I invoke it to frame my interests in what was known, what was not known, and when these various knowledges changed over time. It is a banal observation to point out that there are many types and ways of "knowing," beyond a simple dichotomy of salience and ignorance.

There are things not fully understood, and there are things misunderstood, and there are places where the knower may not realize his or her ignorance. They often involve, explicitly or implicitly, questions of a counterfactual nature: What mattered and what did not, what choices were real choices and which were not? (As Francis Gavin's chapter 17 in this volume indicates, these are questions hardly limited to the wartime years.) Limited as our sources are, and being appropriately mistrustful of later recollections, we latter-day analysts are always going to face gaps in what we can say about these things. However, this approach can lead to fruitful observations and new insights, as evidenced by a number of important recent pieces on early nuclear history by historians of science.[13]

Decisions to Use the Bomb

As essentially all serious historians of the bomb have acknowledged in recent decades, there was no single "decision" to use the atomic bomb. By streamlining numerous, cumulative, and often subtle decisions into a single life-or-death moment in postwar depictions of their wartime experiences, the historical actors sought to make their wartime activities seem more reasoned, rational, and carefully weighed than they appear to have been, whether to deflect criticism or to secure what they felt was the appropriate legacy for their wartime contributions.[14] This narrative was explicitly created to bias judgment in favor of the bombings: if the only alternatives offered were "use two atomic bombs, on cities, within three days of each other" versus "a full land invasion," then it becomes very easy to accept the former. (While casualty estimates of the land invasion vary dramatically, even the low estimates that were shown to Truman in 1945 would certainly have struck him, and present-day readers, as unpleasantly high.)[15]

In reality, the decision-making process was broken into a large number of parallel committees and conversations and telegrams, the future was unknown, and the many uncertainties involved in the atomic bomb's development, much less the end of the war, meant that top-down, overly strategic planning was difficult. The results of the many contingent choices were difficult for the historical actors to anticipate; to ascribe too much prescience or rationality to many of these choices is to fall into a trap of memory.[16]

That the atomic bombs would be used in some way (if successfully developed in time for use in the war, which was not a sure thing until the spring of 1945) was taken for granted by most top-level administrators or officials who knew about them;[17] the exact manner of their use was a more complicated issue.[18] The most relevant parts for our purposes are that while there were some vague discussions of targeting early in the Manhattan Project, actual, concrete planning for targets did not begin in earnest until the spring of 1945, when the schedule for the deployment of the bomb had become much more solidified.

Two secret committees within the War Department and Manhattan Project infrastructure were largely responsible for finalizing the idea that cities would be the targets of the first atomic bomb. The Interim Committee was created at the behest of Secretary of War Henry L. Stimson, who was the highest-level official in the Truman administration with sustained participation in the bomb project.[19] The committee's name referred to its handling of "interim" matters that would need to at least be planned, if not settled, between the use of the bomb and the creation of a postwar organization to take over the nation-spanning wartime nuclear complex. This proved to be a massively expansive remit, including, importantly, questions relating to the use of the weapons themselves. The Interim Committee wrestled with whether the bombs should be "demonstrated" first (rejected), whether Japan should be warned (no explicit warning was issued), and the nature of the targets (cities containing some kind of military or industrial infrastructure).[20]

The other committee, the Target Committee, concerned itself with mostly operational matters, such as the specific target cities and technical aspects of the bombs' use. Matters relevant to policy were, to be sure, discussed—for example, it confirmed that a psychological impact was of primary importance, and that the weapon should explicitly be used against cities—but its meetings were about specifics, not broad political questions.[21] Several of these meetings were heavily attended by scientists, and, as Sean Malloy has argued, many of the options for how to use the first atomic bombs were determined by technological choices made earlier by weapons designers who were far removed from the strategic discussions. Cities were targeted, in part, because the bombs that were built were not very good at doing much else.[22]

Thus there were precious few decisions reserved for the commander in chief. We should not be surprised by this: the bomb was developed in a military context and was being treated as a military weapon. It was Stimson's heavy involvement that was unusual. He did not intervene so personally in any other weapon developments or military tactics. Stimson was even absent from decisions on many broad matters of wartime strategy, like the switch from precision bombing to area bombing in the Pacific theater. In one case, it is clear he learned about a firebombing campaign's results from the newspapers, like everyone else (to his anger).[23] While there were high-level consultations on certain major war policy matters, such as the question of authorizing the invasion of Japan in June 1945, during World War II the military generally operated with considerable autonomy with respect to operational details.[24]

Truman did make one important decision with regard to the use of the bomb while at Potsdam. It wasn't *whether* to use it at all: his role on this, as General Leslie R. Groves, the military head of the Manhattan Project, put it later, was "one of noninterference—basically, a decision not to upset the existing plans."[25] But he did make himself the final authority on *where* it would be used: he made a positive assertion in favor of Hiroshima rather than Kyoto as the target of the first bomb. The Kyoto decision has largely been relegated to a footnote to the existing bomb literature but should be more closely scrutinized.

Choosing Hiroshima—and Not Kyoto

At its second meeting the Target Committee produced a shortlist of targets, ranked by priority: Kyoto, Hiroshima, Yokohama, and Kokura.[26] On May 15 three cities—Kyoto, Hiroshima, and Niigata—were placed on a list of "Reserved Areas" not to be bombed by the massive incendiary raids that were being waged against Japan by the U.S. Army Air Forces; Kokura was added to the list in late June.[27] Nagasaki was not considered as a serious atomic target until much later and was never placed on the "reserved" list.[28]

The question of whether Kyoto would be targeted, as the Target Committee desired most of all, became a site for contestation on two fronts. One was the surface issue about the morality and justification in targeting civilian populations. Underlying this, however, was another concern: whether that decision was one for military decision makers or for civilian policy makers. In a story that is often briefly mentioned in histories of the atomic bombing, Kyoto went from being the first-priority target for the atomic bomb to a spared city owing to the personal intervention of Secretary of War Stimson.[29] Stimson had visited Kyoto in the 1920s, when he was secretary of state for President Herbert Hoover, and knew it as a great center of Japanese culture.[30] For reasons known only to him, he adopted its survival of the war as a personal crusade: not only would Kyoto be spared the atomic bomb, it avoided virtually *all* bombing, the only Japanese city of appreciable size (with a wartime population of a million) to do so.[31]

On May 29, 1945, Stimson and Chief of Staff George Marshall discussed the nature of the bombing campaign; the question of the morality of the firebombing of Tokyo appears to have become relevant to Stimson's thinking about the targeting of the atomic bombs. The next day he called Groves to his office to discuss targeting. Groves had not intended to get the secretary's approval of his targets—he planned to submit them directly to Marshall for action. A showdown of sorts occurred, where Stimson, the top civilian authority on the handling of the war, demanded to know what targets were being considered from a military general who essentially asserted that this was not a civilian matter. "This is a question I am settling myself," Groves much later recounted Stimson declaring, "Marshall is not making that decision."[32] In a later interview, Groves would say that Kyoto was the only time in which Stimson "interfered with a military matter that I know of."[33] Stimson carried the day... for the moment.

Two days after his meeting with Groves, Stimson met with General Henry "Hap" Arnold, the head of the Army Air Forces and architect of U.S. strategic bombing policy, to discuss the progress of the war in the Pacific.[34] He confronted Arnold on the bombing of Tokyo—he thought he had received a guarantee that the Army Air Forces would limit itself to precision bombing, and that "the press yesterday had indicated a bombing of Tokyo which was very far from that."[35] Stimson was likely referring to a statement by General Curtis E. LeMay about the success of the bombing campaign, in which he bragged that 46 percent of Tokyo had been burned.[36] Arnold told Stimson that the policy had arisen out of tactical considerations owing to Japanese dispersal of industrial facilities among civilian areas; Stimson recorded in his diary that Arnold had told him "it was practically impossible to destroy the war output of Japan without doing more damage to civilians connected with the output than in Europe." Arnold gave Stimson an assurance of restraint, and in response Stimson asserted that "there was one city that they must not bomb without my permission and that was Kyoto."[37] Stimson again drew the line at Kyoto, and drawing a line at all seems an important power play for civilian authority over military tactics.

Stimson had been trying to convince Truman since at least mid-May that they ought to conduct only "precision" bombing over Japan in order to preserve the "reputation of the United States for fair play and humanitarianism." He felt the "rule of sparing the civilian population should be applied as far as possible to the use of any new weapons"—certainly a reference to the atomic bomb.[38] On June 6 Stimson met with Truman to report on his unease about the strategic bombing campaigns. This passage in Stimson's diary is worth quoting in its entirety:

> I told him I was anxious about this feature of the war for two reasons: first, because I did not want to have the United States get the reputation of outdoing Hitler in atrocities; and second, I was a little fearful that before we could get ready the Air Force might have Japan so thoroughly bombed out that the new weapon would not have a fair background to show its strength. He laughed and said he understood. Owing to the shortness of time I did not get through any further matters on my agenda.[39]

Stimson appears to have been trying to play both sides, appealing first to Truman's humanitarianism (or, at least, his legacy and reputation), and second to the more tactical question of being able to "demonstrate" the power of the atomic bomb when it was ready. Truman's laughter is a curious response, presumably acknowledging the irony of preserving cities in order to later destroy them, rather than the suggestion that the actions of his military might get him compared to Hitler.

Truman saying he "understood" did not end the discussion. In mid-June Groves received information on the proposed targets, including a map of Kyoto. In the copy in Groves's files, someone has drawn an asterisk on the Kyoto roundhouse, a prominent railroad structure, and a circle with a radius of around 1.5 miles has been drawn around it, which corresponds well with their rough understanding of the area of maximum damage for a 15-kiloton bomb.[40] On July 2 Groves received more information on the value of Kyoto as a military target, information that identified a large number of strategic industries, including plants to produce machine tools, ordnance and aircraft parts, explosives manufacture, and a new aircraft engine factory that was judged to be the second-largest in Japan, able to produce four hundred units monthly.[41] This framing of Kyoto appears to have been a deliberate move toward accommodating the moral framing that Stimson was giving it: showing that Kyoto was a worthy military or industrial target. One can compare this with the original justification given by the Target Committee in May:

> Kyoto—This target is an urban industrial area with a population of 1,000,000. It is the former capital of Japan and many people and industries are now being moved there as other areas are being destroyed. From the psychological point of view there is the advantage that Kyoto is an intellectual center for Japan and the people there are more apt to appreciate the significance of such a weapon as the gadget.[42]

After the Trinity test, while Stimson was at Potsdam, Groves sent several messages to confirm the final target list. On July 21 Stimson received word from an assistant back in Washington that the military advisers still "favored your pet city and would like to feel free to use it as first choice if those on ride select it out of 4 possible spots in the light of local conditions at the time."[43] Stimson soon replied: "Aware of no factors that change my decision. On the contrary, new factors confirm it."[44] The new factors may have included the fact that the Soviets were being intransigent allies. Stimson had begun to think that the crew in Washington "may have been thinking in a vacuum," assuming that the postwar situation with the Soviets could be managed on trust.[45]

Stimson met with Truman on July 22. They spoke of the Soviet situation and news from Washington that the bomb would be ready sooner than anticipated. Stimson recorded in his diary that Truman was "immensely pleased." He then noted: "As to the matter of the special target which I had refused to permit, he strongly confirmed my view and said he felt the same way."[46] The next day, Stimson also met with General Arnold and discussed the matter with him, recording in his diary that Arnold had voiced agreement "about the target which I had struck off the program."[47] Thus fortified, Stimson cabled Washington with a request to "give name of place or alternate places, always excluding the particular place against which I have decided." He concluded: "My decision has been confirmed by highest authority."[48]

Note Stimson's repetition and vehemence. He appears to have felt that the Kyoto decision was still reversible despite his apparent victory on the matter. On July 23 he received the news that the new target list was "Hiroshima, Kokura, Niigata in order of choice here,"[49] and yet he still instigated a discussion with Truman about the matter on July 24. Stimson recorded the exchange in his diary as follows:

> We had a few words more about the S-1 program, and I again gave him my reasons for eliminating one of the proposed targets. He again reiterated with the utmost emphasis his own concurring belief on that subject, and he was particularly emphatic in agreeing with my suggestion that if elimination was not done, the bitterness which would be caused by such a wanton act might make it impossible during the long post-war period to reconcile the Japanese to us in that area rather than to the Russians. It might thus, I pointed out, be the means of preventing what our policy demanded, namely a sympathetic Japan to the United States in case there should be any aggression by Russia in Manchuria.[50]

In his diaries, Stimson repeatedly portrayed Truman as a complete convert to his way of thinking, in which Stimson had transmuted a moral problem into a political one: the nonbombing of Kyoto was, in this framing, as much about the Soviets as it was about the citizens of Japan. It is worth emphasizing that Groves would have challenged Stimson's portrayal of Kyoto as a "civilian" target had Groves been in the room at Potsdam. He clearly thought Kyoto was at least as legitimate a target as any other on the list. Stimson's distinction between Hiroshima and Kyoto was, from the perspective of a military planner, nonobvious. Both were cities, one with a military base and the other with weapon factories. Choosing the former over the latter is an ambiguous resolution to the moral hazard of targeting noncombatants—at the very least, one must admit it is a fairly subtle distinction.[51]

It may have been too subtle for Truman. This is not meant as an insult; Truman's activities at Potsdam were dominated by many other matters relating to the Soviet Union, the Potsdam Declaration, and internal disagreements among his staff. (Stimson was not even explicitly invited to attend, in an effort by others, notably James Byrnes, to monopolize the president; Stimson showed up on his own initiative.) Truman was still relatively new to the job, and as many have noted before (and as he noted himself) he was in considerably over his head, helped in no way by the fact that his predecessor had never brought him into his circles of trust.[52] Compare Truman's account of the same July 24 meeting with Stimson, as written in a journal he kept at Potsdam:

> I have told the Sec. of War, Mr. Stimson, to use it so that military objectives and soldiers and sailors are the target and not women and children. Even if the Japs are savages, ruthless, merciless and fanatic, we as the leader of the world for the common welfare cannot drop that terrible bomb on the old capital or the new. He and I are in accord. The target will be a purely military one and we will issue a warning statement asking the Japs to surrender and save lives. I'm sure they will not do that, but we will have given them the chance.[53]

The apparent contradiction of this passage with the truth has often been noted. None of the cities on the target list fit the definition of "purely military" in the sense that "women and children" would not make up the bulk of the casualties. "Purely" is a peculiarly strong modifier. Did Truman really believe that this was the case? Was he deceiving himself, was he creating a doctored historical record, or was it something else?

In fact, he could have been genuinely confused, and specifically *confused by the discussions involved in the Kyoto decision*. Stimson went to Truman repeatedly with arguments he thought would persuade him. These included appeals to morality, to national reputation, and to postwar politics. All centered on the notion that Kyoto was a wholly "civilian" target, whereas any other target chosen, such as Hiroshima, was implicitly "military" by contrast. Stimson was trying to split a pretty fine moral line. It seems entirely possible (and to be sure, this is an interpretive leap) that he portrayed the contrast between targets as much starker than it was in reality: that Kyoto was a "city" and that Hiroshima, the other primary target under discussion, was a "military base."

It seems unlikely that Stimson would have tried to *intentionally* deceive Truman. Stimson appears to have believed that the distinction was real and important, and indeed in later years, including when he worked in 1946 to develop his famous article on the decision to use the atomic bomb, he repeated many of the same distinctions—to the frustration of some of his early readers connected to the armed forces, who convinced him to acknowledge that Kyoto also had a military nature.⁵⁴ There is no indication that anyone *other than* Truman was truly confused over the status of Hiroshima.

Truman never accused Stimson of having misled him or made himself out to be anything but in control of the situation. This is fully compatible with my interpretation: Truman clearly thought in the postwar that the story to tell about the bombings was one of his total control, of being the ultimate deliberator. To admit his own errors in understanding would strongly undermine the moral and political argument he felt the bomb deserved, and to displace responsibility for the decision onto subordinates would go against his "the buck stops here" philosophy of presidential responsibility.

We might pose an opposite question: Is there any positive evidence that Truman *did* understand that Hiroshima was a city? Hiroshima was not a household name in America during the war (Nagasaki was better known, both because of its prominence on the southwestern end of Kyushu and because of its long history as an international port); it almost never appeared in newspapers prior to the atomic bombings. There is only one document that was verifiably taken to Potsdam that, to an alert reader, would have indicated its status: a report on the targets developed by Colonel John N. Stone at the request of Groves, sent to General Arnold, which became the basis for the final bombing strike order. The Stone memo, sent on July 24, describes Hiroshima as follows: "Hiroshima (population 350,000) is an 'Army' city; a major POE [point of embarkation]; has large QM [quartermaster] and supply depots; has considerable industry and several small shipyards."⁵⁵ Though it emphasizes its strategic value, the report makes clear that Hiroshima is a city of considerable size. All four of the targets under consideration (Hiroshima, Kokura, Niigata, and Nagasaki, the latter having been added to the list of targets just that day), are at one point in the memo listed as "cities."

Did Truman read and understand this memo? The archival record on its travel and provenance, while unusually detailed, does not conclusively answer the question. It was not cabled to Potsdam; it was sent as an original copy along with other materials and arrived only on July 26. Stimson had already left Potsdam and was making his way first through Germany and then back to the United States. Generals Marshall and Arnold determined that there was nothing in the materials that needed to be immediately forwarded to Stimson.⁵⁶ The next day two telegrams were received in Washington from a colonel who was handling the transmitted material: one said that "the booklet and the original of Stone's Memorandum to General Arnold have been turned over to the President" while the next, sent two hours later, noted that the memo was "recovered from the President and burned."⁵⁷

How long did Truman actually have the memo? Did he read it? Did he comprehend it? If he had a mistaken view of the targets, would he have noticed material that had contradicted it? As someone notoriously uninterested in detailed reports, would he have, barring a compelling reason, paid it any attention in the two hours it might have been available to him, having already made his "decision"? There appears to be no archival confirmation either way. The day before, Truman had been traveling and quite busy; according to the log of his Potsdam trip, the only notation for July 27 is that "the President worked on his mail during the forenoon" and then had meetings during the rest of the day.[58]

When Would Truman Have Learned That Hiroshima Was a City?

Other than the Stone memo, there is no other indication that these targets were discussed as "cities." There are, however, other indications that Truman may have misunderstood them to be something else: "purely" military bases. This same language was initially part of the drafts of Truman's August 10 address to the nation about the Potsdam Conference, which, unlike the press release sent out after the Hiroshima bombing (which was largely written by Stimson's friend, Arthur Page, vice president for public relations for AT&T), Truman had a direct hand in creating.[59] The published version of Truman's radio address contained a brief note about the atomic bombs:

> The world will note that the first atomic bomb was dropped on Hiroshima, a military base. That was because we wished in this first attack to avoid, insofar as possible, the killing of civilians. But that attack is only a warning of things to come. If Japan does not surrender, bombs will have to be dropped on her war industries and, unfortunately, thousands of civilian lives will be lost. I urge Japanese civilians to leave industrial cities immediately, and save themselves from destruction.[60]

These passages have been frequently criticized as misleading. It is even more interesting, however, to consider that in the first draft of this speech, the atomic bomb was scarcely mentioned, perhaps indicating that the speech was drafted prior to the Hiroshima attack.[61] On the original copy in the holdings of the Truman Library, someone has handwritten "why we dropped bomb on Hiroshima" on part of the first draft, and language very similar to the final version was added to the next draft at that spot:

> The world will note that the first atomic *bombs* were dropped on Hiroshima which is *purely* a military base. That was because we did not want to

destroy the lives of women and children and innocent civilians in this first attack. But it is only a warning of things to come. If Japan does not surrender, bombs will have to be dropped on war industries and thousands of civilian lives will be lost. I urge the Japanese civilians to leave industrial cities and save themselves from destruction. [Emphasis added.][62]

Several language changes from the final version are worth noting. First is a pluralizing of atomic bombs. This was rectified by the next draft of the speech but shows a remarkable lack of specificity about the operation it is describing. Second and third are the assertion that Hiroshima was "purely" a military base, and language about "killing civilians" that was far more florid ("destroy the lives of women and children and innocent civilians"). Both mirror very closely the kind of language Truman used in his July 25 journal entry ("purely a military one ... not women and children"). This suggests that perhaps the journal entry was used in the process of crafting this language, or Truman himself provided it. It seems too close to his own, peculiar wording to be purely coincidental.

So when, exactly, would Truman have definitively learned that Hiroshima was not "purely" a military target and thus changed the language? We can put a definitive date and even time on the final point at which Truman could have no longer been ignorant about the nature of Hiroshima: August 8, 1945, when Truman had a meeting with Stimson at the White House in the midmorning, in which they discussed the consequences of the attack. As Stimson wrote in his diary:

> I showed the President the teletype report from Guam showing the extent of the damage; also, the Wire Service bulletin showing the damage as reported by Tokyo at nine A.M. August 8th. I showed him the photograph showing the total destruction and also the radius of damage which Dr. Lovett had brought me from the Air Corps just before I went. He mentioned the terrible responsibility that such destruction placed upon us here and himself.[63]

Newspaper front pages on the same day were similarly concerned with damage: Hiroshima, clearly named as a "city," was reported to have been 60 percent destroyed.[64] By the next day, huge numbers of casualties were being reported in the same papers: "200,000 Believed Dead in Inferno That Vaporized City of Hiroshima."[65] The issue was acute enough from a propaganda standpoint that "high authorities" in the War Department apparently urged the Office of War Information to stress that the targets possessed "sufficient military character to justify attack under the rules of civilized warfare."[66] To be sure, nobody involved in the planning, even those who knew that Hiroshima was a city, would have known in advance exactly the number of dead from the attack. Arthur Compton would later recall that J. Robert Oppenheimer had believed that only twenty thousand would die in the first attack, which is a large number though several multiples smaller than reality. Stimson would have heard this number at the Interim Committee meeting of May 31; there is no indication that other detailed estimates were made. There is no indication whatsoever that any such estimates made it to Truman's ears.[67]

If my interpretation is correct, one might expect August 8 to be an important demarcation in how Truman spoke about the bomb. And indeed, in the drafts of his Potsdam address, August 8 is the date at which the language on the atomic bomb started getting a considerable overhaul. Assistant Secretary of State Archibald MacLeish sent Samuel Rosenman, the speechwriter tasked with editing the statement, several paragraphs on the atomic bomb that were integrated into the final draft, specifically the first language making a strong justification for the use of the weapon: "Its production and its use were not lightly undertaken by this Government.... Only the certainty that the terrible destructiveness of this would will shorten the agony of the war and will save American lives has persuaded us to use it against our enemies."[68] These were integrated into a fifth and near-final version of the speech, along with language reinforcing the idea that the atomic bomb was a carefully considered, deliberative action designed to save American lives: "We have used it in order to shorten the agony of war, in order to save the lives of thousands and thousands of young Americans."[69] Before Truman delivered it, and without any record in Rosenman's papers, the "purely" language and the phrase about women and children being spared were both removed.

Let us also look at one other piece of evidence often used to assess Truman's mindset from this period, a letter written to Senator Richard B. Russell. Russell had sent Truman a telegram on August 7 advocating a brutal path:

> Permit me to respectfully suggest that we cease our efforts to cajole Japan into surrendering in accordance with the Potsdam Declaration. Let us carry the war to them until they beg us to accept the unconditional surrender.... If we do not have available a sufficient number of atomic bombs with which to finish the job immediately, let us carry on with TNT and fire bombs until we can produce them.... We should cease our appeals to Japan to sue for peace. The next plea for peace should come from an utterly destroyed Tokyo.[70]

Truman's response, dated August 9, contains characteristic language:

> I know that Japan is a terribly cruel and uncivilized nation in warfare but I can't bring myself to believe that, because they are beasts, we should

ourselves act in the same manner. For myself, I certainly regret the necessity of wiping out whole populations because of the "pigheadedness" of the leaders of a nation and, for your information, I am not going to do it unless it is absolutely necessary. It is my opinion that after the Russians enter into war the Japanese will very shortly fold up. My object is to save as many American lives as possible but I also have a humane feeling for the women and children of Japan.[71]

The reference to the Soviet Union having not yet entered into the war against Japan implies that the letter was written prior to August 9,[72] either sometime late on August 7 (after Truman had returned to the White House from the USS *Augusta*) or August 8 prior to 3 p.m. (when he announced the USSR had entered the war). This leaves open two interesting possibilities: the letter was either written prior to or after his meeting with Stimson about the damage done to Hiroshima.[73] It is interesting to consider how each of these situations would change our interpretation of the letter. If he wrote about it in ignorance of the damage done to the "women and children" of Japan, then it might be further evidence of his confusion. If he wrote it shortly after learning about the damage to Japan, it might be read in a more rueful tone: a "humane feeling" toward those whom he recently learned were dead. Either way, it is an interesting response: a rejection of slaughter for its own sake, and a refrain about "women and children" that was already then becoming a common phrase of his for talking about the atomic bombs.

There appears to be sufficient documentary evidence to support the plausibility of the idea that Truman legitimately did not understand, prior to August 8, that the atomic bombs were in fact being dropped on cities and that their primary casualties would be civilians. If he did have such a misunderstanding, there is a very likely explanation for it: his discussion of the nontargeting of Kyoto with Stimson, his primary engagement with the use of atomic bomb while at Potsdam. To be sure, there is evidence for variable depths of Truman's confusion, ranging from total ignorance (truly believing the target to be "purely a military base") to something more mixed and self-deceptive ("lying to himself"). This is not the only interpretation made possible by the evidence, but it suggests that, if we have other reasons to think this interpretation is useful, then it is worthy of serious consideration.

Truman's Atomic Trajectory

If Truman was genuinely confused as to the nature of the target of the first atomic bombing, then his Potsdam journal entry, and his apparent contributions to his radio announcement after Potsdam, would reflect this confusion and not deception (self- or otherwise). Let us now imagine Truman on August 8, when he learns, for sure, that the bomb has done damage to a *city*, killing the "women and children" he thought would be largely spared. Reports from the Japanese, on August 8 and 9, further emphasized the civilian toll, to the point of overstatement. Truman's initial feelings of elation, his initial reaction that the atomic bomb was "the greatest thing in history," might now become more ambiguous. It is in this context that Truman and others started to talk about the need to justify the atomic bombs: to contrast the lives saved to those lost, to talk about them as a Faustian bargain, as a matter of ends (which had not yet materialized) justifying means.

The day after Truman definitively learned of Hiroshima's true nature and fate, another atomic bomb was dropped on another city—Nagasaki. This was within the language of the original strike order but would have been a surprise to Truman if he were not aware that another bomb would be ready so soon. Would Truman have known about the pending second strike? Nothing in his journals or press statements indicates that he conceptualized the atomic bomb as anything more than a singular entity.[74] The actual schedule of both atomic bombs was determined on the island of Tinian in any event, a consequence of the weather, which moved the Hiroshima attack later than it had been projected, and the Nagasaki attack earlier.[75] In any case, in marked contrast to the Hiroshima strike, neither Stimson nor Truman was forewarned about Nagasaki.[76] Its bombing may have come as a rude shock to Truman, only three days following the Hiroshima attack and just after the Soviet invasion of Manchuria. Nagasaki was as much of a city as Hiroshima, if not more so: it was not a military base that was hit but a dense urban area with military factories on the fringes of the damage area.[77]

Truman was a president out of the loop, shouldering political burdens imposed by a military operating with its own priorities and agenda, with little civilian oversight on their day-to-day operations. The possibility of the Soviets staying out of the Pacific theater was dashed as Stalin moved his invasion operation schedule up, but, more positively, on August 10 Japan sent a note of a preliminary willingness to surrender, one that provoked considerable discussion over its reserved role for the emperor.[78]

In this context, Groves sent a message to General Marshall on August 10, indicating that another atomic bomb might be ready for use "on the first suitable weather after 17 or 18 August." The response was immediate and decisive: General Marshall replied back that the next bomb "is not to be released over Japan without express authority from the President."[79] At a cabinet meeting that morning, Truman took credit for the action, saying "he had given orders to stop atomic bombing." Henry Wallace, the former vice president and then secretary of commerce, recorded in his diary that Truman had professed that "the thought of wiping out another 100,000 people was too horrible. He didn't like the idea of killing, as he said, 'all those kids.' "[80]

Truman did so, in part, because the discussions with the Japanese were getting delicate. There are several diary accounts of the cabinet meeting of August 10, and few of them put much attention on the atomic bomb; the issue of the day was what to do about the Japanese conditional surrender offer. James Forrestal noted that it was Stimson who initially raised the question of halting the bombing: "The Secretary of War made the suggestion that should now cease sending our bombers over Japan; he cited the growing feeling of apprehension and misgivings as to the effect of the atomic bomb even in our own country." Toward the end of the meeting, Forrestal related: "The President observed that we would keep up the war in its present intensity until the Japanese agreed to these terms, with the limitation however that there would be no further dropping of the atomic bombs."[81]

Framing the matter, as did Wallace, in terms of killing innocents makes for a strong contrast with Truman's earlier statements, which seemed to deny consequences for noncombatants. By August 10 Truman appeared to be reclaiming his authority over any future use. This is not to suggest that he would definitely not have used the third bomb had the war continued. On August 14, in a midmorning meeting with British officials, he "remarked sadly" that since unconditional Japanese surrender had not yet been achieved, "he had no alternative but to order an atomic bomb be dropped on Tokyo."[82] Whether he would have actually done so is unknown, but in any event it would have been *his* choice, rather than being delegated.[83]

If Truman had been ignorant of the likely noncombatant casualties for the atomic bomb, and ignorant about the fact that two were to be dropped in rapid succession, what psychological effect would this have produced? Truman's actions might fit into this rough psychological interpretation: a rapid movement from elation to something more ambivalent, and then a feeling of lack of control of the situation, accompanied by a rapid assertion of authority to regain that sense of control.[84] His attitudes toward the atomic bombings, in general, became more intricate and less unambiguously positive. He simultaneously took on responsibility for the use of the bomb (above and beyond his actual, literal role) and was, for a time, willing to acknowledge its horrors even as he unequivocally defended its use.

Thus Truman's letter of August 11 to Samuel Cavert of the Federal Council of the Churches of Christ in America, in which he claimed that while "nobody is more disturbed over the use of the Atomic bombs" than he was, the Japanese behavior toward POWs and at Pearl Harbor warranted bombardment: "When you have to deal with a beast you have to treat him as a beast. It is most regrettable but nevertheless true."[85] Or, for example, his handwritten notes from his Gridiron Dinner speech of December 1945, in which an early version of the "decision" narrative was coalescing:

> You know the most terrible decision a man ever had to make was made by me at Potsdam. It had nothing to do with Russia or Britain or Germany. It was a decision to loose the most terrible of all destructive forces for the wholesale slaughter of human beings. The Secretary of War, Mr. Stimson, and I weighed that decision most prayerfully. But the President had to decide. It occurred to me that a quarter of a million of the flower of our young manhood was worth a couple of Japanese cities, and I still think that they were and are. But I couldn't help but think of the necessity of blotting out women and children and non-combatants. We gave them fair warning and asked them to quit. We picked a couple of cities where war work was the principle [sic] industry, and dropped bombs. Russia hurried in and the war ended.[86]

This passage is remarkable for several reasons: the acknowledgment of the "necessity of blotting out women and children and non-combatants," the honest assessment of the bomb's use as "the wholesale slaughter of human beings" even while veering back between these horrors and an inflated "decision" narrative, exaggerated casualty estimates (well beyond those being discussed by the military commanders at the time), the misleading statement about the Potsdam Declaration being a "fair warning" (it was an ultimatum, not an actionable warning), the noting of the targets as "a couple of cities," and the sidelining of the issue of Soviet entry into the Pacific War. It has the germ of the later decision narrative that Stimson, Truman, and others would develop in the face of mounting criticism of the bombings, but in a rawer, less clinical, less strictly "rational" presentation.[87] It also places much of the "decision" around the question of his meetings with Stimson—which as we have seen largely revolved around the question of Kyoto versus Hiroshima. That Truman himself (and not a speechwriter) clearly wrote these words—they are handwritten, and have all the hallmarks of his characteristic phrasing—adds additional weight to them as evidence of his internal state.

One counterpoint that can be raised is that if Truman really was disturbed about the killing of noncombatants, why didn't he question the firebombing campaign? As far as can be determined, Truman never attempted to intervene with the military with regard to any of its conventional campaigns: either they did not bother him, or he did not want to micromanage a conventional military campaign that had been ongoing since before he became president.[88] That Truman, and many others, considered there to be political and moral differences between the firebombing and the atomic bombings seems evident: while not *all* parties saw them as being different, both Stimson and Truman did seem to consider the atomic bombs to have a "special" nature that made deliberations about them of a different quality from those on conventional attacks.[89] One can speculate as to *why* that was the case (e.g., by the time Truman was president, firebombing raids had become common practice), but Truman plainly did not see them as equivalent and never felt the need to justify or explain the firebombings in the way he did the atomic bombings.

Would Truman have done anything *differently* if he had completely understood the nature and timing of the two bombings? There are several possible outcomes. The least likely is that he would have called off the atomic bombing. Perhaps he would have looked into alternative targets or strategy, or the timing of the attacks. One can wonder, as Campbell Craig does in chapter 2 of this volume about Roosevelt, about whether some less "brutal" option might have been found if the full brutality of the choice were known to Truman, but I find it hard to believe, given the brutality of the time and Truman's (arguably mistaken) belief that the decision to use the atomic bomb was a continuation of past policy. He would have simply found a justification for it, as many of his advisers clearly had done. At the very least, it seems he would not have been quite so unprepared for the news of the casualties and would not have had such a jarring difference in his pre- and postdamage assessment narratives.

When considering Truman and the atomic bomb, discussions (including mine) largely center on the events of 1945. Truman's atomic legacy after the war is arguably more important. The years 1945–1953 saw immensely consequential decisions: domestic and international control of atomic energy, the custody dispute over the atomic bomb, the nonuse of nuclear weapons in the Korean War, and the development of thermonuclear weapons.[90] Truman's stances on these matters were not always consistent, but certain themes emerge.

Throughout Truman's presidency, he and his advisers framed the question of domestic control as being about the appropriate balance between military and civilian oversight. Truman emphasized that division, in particular in ways that reduced the capacities of the military, along stronger lines than any president afterward. For example, over the course of his presidency, while the American stockpile of atomic bombs climbed from dozens to hundreds to thousands, he explicitly rejected calls from the military to give them physical possession of the weapons (the "custody dispute"). Under Truman, the United States did not even have any formal policy on the employment of nuclear weapons until September 1948, when the National Security Council, upon recognizing that there was no policy, finally created a determination that reinforced what Truman had established as the status quo: "The decision as to the employment of atomic weapons in the event of war is to be made by the Chief Executive when he considers such decision to be required."[91] Toward the end of his administration, in 1951, he eventually allowed the military to have nine completed nuclear bombs (around 1 percent of the arsenal), to be stationed in Guam; this is in marked contrast to his successor, Dwight D. Eisenhower, who gave the military control over 90 percent of the ever more massive stockpile, and whose successors made this transfer of weapons from civilian to military possession automatic.[92]

Which is to say, Truman went out of his way, contrary to the recommendations of his military advisers, to ensure that in the United States nuclear weapons were a matter of exclusively presidential authority for use; he made sure that legal control was enforced through a strict physical division of the weapons. In 1948, at a meeting with Truman and several military and civilian officials, David Lilienthal, chairman of the civilian Atomic Energy Commission, recorded a telling interaction. The discussion was on the custody dispute, and military representatives were explaining that they required physical possession of the weapons. Secretary of the Air Force W. Stuart Symington had just related, with an air of skepticism, that some of the scientists at Los Alamos had remarked that the military ought not have the bombs, and not be able to use them. As Lilienthal recorded:

> The President was giving this line of irrelevant talk a very fishy eye; at this point he said, poker-face, "I don't either. I don't think we ought to use this thing unless we absolutely have to. It is a terrible thing to order the use of something that" (here he looked down at his desk, rather reflectively) "that is so terribly destructive, destructive beyond anything we have ever had. You have got to understand that this isn't a military weapon." (I shall never forget this particular expression.) "It is used to wipe out women and children and unarmed people, and not for military uses. So we have got to treat it differently from rifles and cannons and ordinary things like that."[93]

This Truman sounds like the same man we've seen since the end of the war— ambivalence about the weapon with a frank admission that it is something that can "wipe out women and children and unarmed people." The language echoes a refrain that goes back to the journal entry of July 25, 1945, when he asserted that the atomic bomb would *not* target "women and children," or his regret of killing "all those kids," expressed the day after Nagasaki. This is a Truman dedicated to a level of control that he had not exhibited during the war.

Truman did, of course, make one more major, individual decision in 1945 when it came to the atomic bomb: the decision to *halt* atomic bombing. That transformed the Nagasaki attack from the *second* use of the atomic bomb in war to the *final* use of the atomic bomb in war (so far).[94] During his presidency, there were several instances to reconsider, such as the Berlin Crisis of 1948 or the Korean War. Truman's attitude toward the bomb, that it was "not for military uses," played a role in keeping the weapon out of the latter conflict. As Nina Tannenwald has argued: "If Eisenhower had been president before Truman, or if nuclear weapons had been used in the Korean War, the development of the nuclear taboo might have proceeded quite differently, or not at all."[95] There are other examples (Truman's role in the Atomic Energy Act of 1946, his endorsement of the H-bomb program), but the two consistent themes in Truman's postwar atomic policies are being suspicious about the military intentions and the insistence that the weapons were not meant to be used.

It seems clear that Truman, despite his public protestations, harbored some regrets about the use of nuclear weapons during the war.[96] I posit that some of this regret came out of a fundamental misunderstanding (on the nature of the targets) and a subsequent feeling of loss of control (exemplified by the second bombing). Truman's later actions can be seen as an about-face on both matters: after World War II, he never again ceded control over nuclear matters to his military advisers, and he never again admitted the weapon was anything other than a slaughterer of noncombatants. Both of these were not at all what one might expect given someone of his position. While Truman always took responsibility, even blame, for the use of the weapons and never expressed any regrets over the use of the bombs during the war, his actions speak of someone who realized, after the fact, that weighty decisions were made in his midst that came with serious consequences.

I will conclude with the reasons why this interpretation appeals to me as an interpreter of the past, despite the fact that, as I have acknowledged, it is not the only interpretation allowed by the evidence and it does require some care in making the evidence "fit." First, it strikes me as being very "in character" with the Truman who has emerged out of the historiography of the past several decades. I see Truman neither as a truly steely strategist nor as a self-deceiver. I see him as someone out of his league in the early presidency and overly dependent on advisers lobbying for their positions. That this lobbying confused Truman on several important points seems quite possible given Truman's own inattentiveness to many of these details and the fact that his advisers generally presented him with the final products of processes that had taken them weeks if not months or years to develop. For Truman to have an incomplete understanding of Stimson's views on Kyoto, for example, would be understandable.

Second, I think that this interpretation better grasps Truman's atomic trajectory. This is the criterion that most appeals to me in discerning between rival interpretations that are equally plausible: What *else* do they inform us on? Truman's later pushes for civilian control and the establishment of the nuclear taboo point to deeply held responses to the bombings of Japan that are specifically rooted in feelings of a lack of control and a lack of understanding about the civilian consequences of nuclear attacks. It strikes me as intuitively plausible that such feelings could be rooted in an early ignorance and sudden revelation, a stark misunderstanding made brutally clear over a very stressful period.

Ultimately, there seems to be considerable evidence to suggest that Truman's understanding of the nature of the atomic bomb's first targets was flawed and incomplete. Truman would certainly have agreed that this did not absolve him of responsibility—he was the commander in chief. But it changes our view of him, and our sense of the meaning of the atomic bombs and their implications for what came next (as Francis Gavin explores in chapter 17). Truman the man, and the president, had many flaws. Perhaps he should have been more invested in these decisions. While no one would begrudge him for sparing Kyoto, to do so while dooming Hiroshima without understanding the consequences until several days after the fact is more problematic. Truman's decision after Nagasaki to *stop* the bombing, and his decisions in the postwar to keep atomic bombs from becoming regular weapons of war, are perhaps even more important to our understanding of his presidency and its legacy than the decisions made about the use of the bombs themselves.

4

"When You Have to Deal with a Beast"

RACE, IDEOLOGY, AND THE DECISION
TO USE THE ATOMIC BOMB

Sean L. Malloy

ON MAY 2, 1967, Bobby Seale and members of the Black Panther Party for Self-Defense marched on the state capitol in Sacramento, California. The Panthers had been founded less than a year earlier as a neighborhood group primarily concerned with police brutality directed at the African American residents of Oakland. The march was intended to protest a bill, soon to be signed into law by then California governor Ronald Reagan, aimed at disarming the party by prohibiting the public brandishing of firearms. In response, Seale, conspicuously carrying a loaded shotgun, stood on the steps of the capitol building and read a statement by the Panthers' cofounder and minister of defense, Huey P. Newton:

> The enslavement of Black people from the very beginning of this country, the genocide practiced on the American Indians and the confining of the survivors on reservations, the savage lynching of thousands of Black men and women, the dropping of atomic bombs on Hiroshima and Nagasaki, and now the cowardly massacre in Vietnam, all testify to the fact that towards people of color the racist power structure of America has but one policy[:] repression, genocide, terror, and the big stick.[1]

The Sacramento demonstration provoked a flurry of public attention and transformed the Panthers into a national sensation. The party soon grew to encompass sixty-eight chapters scattered across the United States. The Panthers also reached out internationally with an embassy in Algeria and visits to Sweden, Germany, North Korea, North Vietnam, China, and Japan, where they met and collaborated with a number of Japanese radical groups, including Beheiren and the Tokyo-based Sanya Liberation Committee.[2]

This chapter takes at its starting point the analysis offered by Newton, which located the use of the atomic bomb against Japan as part of a history of racialized violence that went back to the European colonization of the Americas and the genocide and slavery that followed in its wake. In the single sentence quoted above, Newton, then a twenty-five-year-old community college graduate and ex-convict, offered a more coherent and illuminating analysis of race and the bomb than have the vast majority of scholarly works in diplomatic history, political science, and international relations in the past fifty years. In this chapter, I will briefly survey the dominant thinking within that literature, highlighting gaps that are revealing about the nature of contemporary scholarship on race and international relations. I will also begin to offer some alternative ways of thinking about nuclear weapons in the context of race and colonialism. This analysis is focused on the United States and does not necessarily offer a transferable explanation of how, for example, German leaders thought about race, violence, and nuclear (or conventional) weapons during World War II. However, in foregrounding race and colonialism, it offers a natural link to the British and French nuclear programs as well as opportunities to connect with scholarship that examines the bomb and its history from non-Western perspectives, as exemplified by Shampa Biswas's "contrapuntal" reading of nuclear harms in chapter 15 of this volume.

Race and the Decision to Use the Bomb: A Historiographical Overview

As early as mid-August 1945 some observers were questioning whether racism played a factor in President Harry S. Truman's willingness to use nuclear weapons against people of color in Asia. As chronicled by historian Matthew Jones, an editorial in a Calcutta newspaper asked:

> What were the considerations that weighed with the Allies in not using [the bomb] against the Germans? Is it because that would have shocked "white humanity" all over the world as a barbarity? . . . Was the bomb used against the Japanese simply because it was produced at the psychological moment when Japan remained the only enemy to be dealt with? Or was it because there would not be so much a horror at the atrocity, the victims being mere Asiatics?[3]

Some African American activists voiced similar sentiments in 1945, more than two decades before Huey Newton and the Black Panthers, linking the use of the bomb against Japan to the long American tradition of employing indiscriminate violence against people of color.[4] Even after it became clear that the bomb had not been ready in time for use in the war in Europe, the counterfactual question remains whether it *would have been* used in that context, along with the more concrete issue of what role, if any, race played in facilitating the decision to use it against Japanese cities and civilians. Historian Vincent J. Intondi has traced the ways in which black leftists such as Paul Robeson and W.E.B. Du Bois continued to raise these charges during the early Cold War, efforts that dovetailed with campaigns by Communist Party USA–affiliated organizations such as the Civil Rights Congress (CRC) and Council on African Affairs (CAA) to link American treatment of people of color both at home and around the world to racialized colonialism.[5] The race argument gained particular traction within Japan. On August 14, 1945, Kiyose Ichiro of the Greater Japanese Political Association argued in the *Asahi shimbun* that American racism was a major motivating factor in the bombings. While the U.S. Occupation kept such views of out official media for years after the bombings, images of American atrocities in Vietnam during the 1960s reawakened the issue in Japan, and the notion that race played a factor in the A-bomb decision remains popular in Japan into the twenty-first century.[6]

Despite the fact that contemporary observers suggested racial motives within days of Hiroshima, scholarly interest in this question in the United States was slow to develop. In part this was undoubtedly because the academic and popular consensus was long dominated by the official government (or "orthodox") account of the bombings, which stressed the need to end the war speedily and with a minimum loss of life as the one and only reason for the decision.[7] But even after Gar Alperovitz's *Atomic Diplomacy* (1965) shattered that consensus and popularized a "revisionist" account of the bombings, the general absence of serious consideration of race and racism as factors in U.S. foreign policy within academic circles contributed to an ongoing silence on race and the bomb. John Dower's landmark work *War without Mercy* (1986) raised the issue of race in the larger context of the conflict in the Pacific but did not wrestle with the specific issues surrounding the development and use of the atomic bomb. Dower did address Hiroshima and Nagasaki in his later work *Cultures of War* (2010), but in doing so he largely downplayed racial motives, instead stressing "power politics" and "the simple fact that, by this stage in the war, reliance on overwhelming force was both gospel and second nature."[8]

The most comprehensive examination of race and the bomb in Western scholarship remains ethnic studies scholar Ronald Takaki's *Hiroshima: Why America Dropped the Atomic Bomb* (1995). Takaki did not claim that racism played the sole or even determining role in the decision, acknowledging both the pressure to end the war in the Pacific as well as the international implications for postwar relations with the Soviet Union as important factors. He did, however, suggest that the history of racial prejudice against Asians, going back to the 1882 Chinese Exclusion Act and the rise of anti-Chinese and later anti-Japanese sentiment on America's West Coast, played an important role in facilitating the use of the bomb. "Truman," he wrote, "had grown up and lived in a society where racial stereotypes were ubiquitous. He had little opportunity in school or in his community to acquire an accurate understanding of peoples of different races and cultures. Consequently Truman succumbed to the raging hate rooted in a long history of animosity against the Japanese, as well as the fierce memory of Pearl Harbor" in deciding to employ nuclear weapons against Japanese cities in August 1945.[9]

Nuclear weapons scholars are a notoriously contentious group, and few historiographical questions have been as fiercely debated as the decision to use the bomb against Japan. One of the few things that has traditionally united so-called orthodox defenders of Truman and his revisionist critics has been a rejection of even Takaki's relatively mild assertions about the role of race in the bombings. Revisionists have largely ignored or downplayed Takaki's claims, preferring to focus on anti-Soviet motives or other diplomatic, military, and political calculations rather than on race. While conceding the existence of "racial stereotypes and virulent anti-Japanese sentiment," arch-revisionist Gar Alperovitz concluded that "it is all but impossible to find specific evidence that racism was an important factor in the decision to attack Hiroshima and Nagasaki."[10] Orthodox defenders of Truman's decision have been equally dismissive of the role of race in the decision to use the bomb. Some, such as Robert P. Newman, have rejected race entirely as a motive.[11] A more novel argument was employed by those such as Michael Kort, Stephen Ambrose, and Brian Loring Villa, who attributed anti-Japanese sentiment among American leaders not to any inherent sense of white supremacy or history of racial discrimination but rather to the attack on Pearl Harbor and the tenor of the ensuing conflict in the Pacific. As Kort put it, "the readiness of American leaders to resort to atomic weapons in 1945 can only be understood in terms of what this country experienced in four years of bitter fighting during which Japanese soldiers consistently fought to the last man."[12] This argument is an attempt to deracialize American hatred of the Japanese, removing it from the long history of anti-Asian sentiments and thus eliminating race from the possible calculus of U.S. decision making in August 1945. Dower himself employed a version of this argument in *Cultures of War*. While acknowledging the history of racial animosity toward the Japanese, he concluded that, "in immeasurable part, too, however, this particularly virulent hatred toward the Japanese as a collectivity... was triggered by the particularly shocking and unforgettably iconic, almost cinematic, nature of the Pearl Harbor attack."[13]

A final rebuke to the notion of race motivating use of the bomb, and one that can be found across the spectrum of A-bomb scholars, draws on the conduct of the war against Germany. In addition to pointing out that the Manhattan Project was initiated in response to threats of a Nazi bomb, numerous scholars have suggested that the fury of the Allied air offensive against Germany, including the targeting of cities and the mass killing of civilians, demonstrates that racism was not needed to explain similar assaults on Japanese civilians with either conventional or nuclear weapons. As Richard Frank concluded in his discussion of the American bombing of Japanese cities, "Race might have eased the switch in tactics [to mass killing], but it did not cause it. Strategic bombing in the Pacific, including the atomic bombs, marked the culmination of strategic thinking, not an abrupt departure."[14] This "moral threshold" argument suggests that there is, in fact, little to explain when it comes to the use of the bomb, which was the natural culmination of six years of increasing violence against civilians, and hence that factors such as race played at best a tangential role in American decision making. As Dower put it in *Cultures of War*, "Modern war breeds its own cultures, and incinerating civilians is one of them."[15]

Taken on their own terms, the various arguments employed against Takaki's thesis, and more broadly against the salience of race in the A-bomb decision, have a convincing internal logical consistency. The problem with this debate, however, is that *all* these analyses, including Takaki's, rely on a way of thinking about race and racism that is extraordinarily narrow and ahistorical. That narrowness is in part a result of the way in which most scholars have approached the evidentiary record on this question. Diplomatic and military historians have traditionally been rooted in archival research and government documents, and there is, at least on the face of it, little in the official record that gives scholars much traction on the issue of race and the bomb. As chronicled by Dower and others, popular media in the United States was filled with virulently racist and eliminationist sentiments directed at the Japanese. The government materials relevant to the A-bomb decision, however, seldom if ever address the issue of race. A May 1943 document from the Military Policy Committee suggested that, once ready, the bomb should be used against the Japanese as "they would not be so apt to secure knowledge from it as would the Germans." This could be read as a racialized assumption about Japanese scientific and technical capabilities, but there is an equally plausible argument that this admittedly tentative decision flowed out of an objective intelligence assessment of the state of the two countries' respective nuclear programs at the time.[16] There was also some disturbing language in the reports of the Targeting Committee in April–May 1945 (where it was suggested that Kyoto was "an intellectual center for Japan and the people there are more apt to appreciate the significance of such a weapon") but nothing that directly suggests that race played a motivating factor in the actual decision to use the atomic bomb.[17]

Given the lack of direct evidence in the documentary record, scholars looking for a racial aspect to the bombings have instead turned to the personal utterances and musings of the individuals involved in the decision making. Takaki, for example, traced Truman's attitudes prior to the presidency, when he wrote unflatteringly about African Americans, Asians, and various immigrant groups.[18] More contemporary evidence came from Truman's August 11 letter to a clergyman concerned about the use of the bomb against Japan in which he declared: "The only language they [the Japanese] seem to understand is the one we have been using to bombard them. When you have to deal with a beast you have to treat him as a beast. It is most regrettable but nevertheless true."[19] Truman's defenders have countered with examples from his writings that show him expressing what appears to be genuine sympathy for the Japanese as well as pointing to his later progressive actions, such as desegregating the U.S. military in 1948, as evidence that whatever racial sentiments he might have harbored were not strong enough to serve as a primary motivating factor in his decision to use the bomb. There have also been a few similar debates about the individual prejudices and motives of other figures in the decision, such as Henry L. Stimson.[20]

Race, Racism, and Ideology in U.S. Foreign Relations

A major problem with the scholarly debate with respect to the use of the atomic bomb against Japan is that it has proceeded under flawed premises about what race and racism are and how they operate in the realm of policy. To contextualize the role of race and racism in thinking about the use of the atomic bomb, as well as in the subsequent history of the Cold War nuclear arms race, it is necessary to step back for a moment to consider what we mean when we use these terms.

In the aftermath of World War II, and particularly the Holocaust, the notion that race was a biologically meaningful concept was largely discredited, at least among American policy-making elites. This shift was perhaps best exemplified by the statement in 1950 by the United Nations Educational, Scientific and Cultural Organization (UNESCO), which concluded that "the scientific material available to us at the present does not justify the conclusion that inherited genetic differences are a major factor in producing the differences between the cultures and cultural achievements of different peoples or group [*sic*]."²¹ But even as biological definitions of race faded from elite discourse, cultural explanations arose that ended up serving much the same purpose. This was exemplified in the domestic context by the so-called Moynihan Report (1965), which blamed African American poverty at least in part on the "cultural pathologies" of the black family. Internationally, modernization theory and area studies frequently portrayed the emerging nations of Asia, Africa, and Latin America as being held back not by the legacy of colonialism and imperialism or their ongoing economic and political exploitation by the West but rather by their own "backward" cultures.²² These cultural explanations were often propounded by well-meaning liberals who saw them as a more progressive way of understanding racial and national differences. Such explanations did at least have the virtue of recognizing that what we call "race" is not based in the iron laws of biology but rather socially constructed and hence susceptible to change over time. But this model also frequently assumed culture to be monolithic and hierarchical, with the United States as the cultural pinnacle of development that all nations and cultures should strive to emulate. It is not surprising, then, that it has often been used to simply replicate discredited notions of racial or national inferiority or superiority under the guise of culture rather than biology. Perhaps the best example of this lamentable trend is the notion of a "clash of civilizations" promoted by Harvard political scientist Samuel P. Huntington, which recycled the old race war fantasies of overt white supremacists and eugenicists such as Lothrop Stoddard and Madison Grant in the new clothes of cultural and civilizational discourse.²³

There is another major problem with the cultural model in thinking about race that is more directly relevant to explaining the use of the atomic bomb against Japan. Once one attributes race to the realm of culture, it makes it relatively easy to divorce it from thinking about policy. Race, and more particularly racism, is frequently invoked as a cultural pathology that has somehow poisoned the otherwise pure American experiment in democracy and undermined U.S. leadership of the free world. Takaki, for example, declared that "America, despite its history of racism, stood for certain great principles that had been forged in the American Revolution and the crucible of the Civil War." Truman's racism and prejudice were thus rooted not in rational policy frameworks that had long used race as a tool by which to exploit and expropriate the land and labor of people of color but rather in the fact that he "had little opportunity in school or in his community to acquire an accurate understanding of peoples of different races and cultures."²⁴ Even in the age of President Donald Trump, racism is frequently portrayed as either an individual pathology or an unfortunate cultural artifact confined to the uneducated and unenlightened segments of the population and destined to fade over time under the weight of a cosmopolitan liberal multiculturalism.

In much of academic writing on race and international relations, concepts such as "national interest" and "balance of power" are treated as important, objective, and real, while race, when mentioned at all, is cast as an irrational outside force that occasionally intrudes in unpredictable ways into the otherwise rational world of policy making. This dismissal of racism as an inconvenient cultural atavism was visible in both government documents and academic writings throughout the Cold War. U.S. foreign policy elites continually bemoaned the inability of both the American masses and Third World nations and peoples to shed their "irrational" ideas about race to focus on "real" issues such as combating communism or expanding the project of capitalist free trade across borders.[25] Historian Matthew Jones is one of the few scholars to write an extended work examining race and the bomb. But even Jones sometimes falls into the trap of subordinating issues of race and racism to the status of outside forces that cloud the judgment of otherwise rational calculations about national security. In describing the scope of his book *After Hiroshima: The United States, Race and Nuclear Weapons in Asia, 1945–1965*, he writes that "the emphasis throughout has been on the political problems faced by the United States in implementing its evolving nuclear and defense policies in Asia, *and how the issue of race could intrude.*"[26]

At the heart of the cultural explanation of race and racism is a fundamental failure to understand the historical construction and ongoing operation of these ideas in American life. Race, and more specifically the ideology of white supremacy, has not "intruded" into policy making in the United States. Rather, racism has been inextricably embedded in much of the foreign and domestic policy of the United States from the very beginning. While seldom engaged by diplomatic historians or scholars of international relations, there is a rich body of scholarly literature that looks at race and racism not simply as social constructions but as social constructions that are deeply tied to the origins and functioning of the American state, society, and economy at home and abroad from the foundation of the republic to the present day. Rather than hinging on the individual prejudices of those involved or on vague and inchoate notions of culture and attitudes, these works examine white supremacy as an ideological system that shapes both perceptions and policy and is rooted in material interests. Put simply, you do not need to be Nazi, a white-robed Klansman, or a snarling southern sheriff to participate in, benefit from, or even preside over a system that produces and reproduces racial inequalities and racialized violence on a daily basis. Nowhere is this clearer than in American cities such as Los Angeles, Chicago, or New York, which are renowned as bastions of liberalism and multiculturalism even as they are marked by glaring and chronic racial inequalities and injustices that are perhaps most visible in the form of police violence against people of color. As Richard Rothstein recently demonstrated in his history *The Color of Law*, the racial disparities of modern American urban life are neither accidents nor simply the result of personal preference (often lumped under the label "white flight") but rather the deliberate result of racial ideologies enshrined in national, state, and local laws and policies.[27]

There is a large and growing literature that examines the operation of institutional or so-called color-blind racism, but for the purpose of thinking about the atomic bomb I want to turn to an essay by Barbara J. Fields, "Slavery, Race, and Ideology in the United States of America" (1990). Though focused on slavery, at the heart of Fields's essay is an argument about how race works. Race—and racism—she argues, are not timeless or disembodied ideas that pass seamlessly from one generation to the next. "Race is not an element of human biology (like breathing oxygen or reproducing sexually); nor is it even an idea (like the speed of light or the value of π) that can plausibly be imagined to live an external life of its own. Race is an ideology. It came into existence at a discernible historical moment for rationally understandable historical reasons and is subject to change for similar reasons."[28] In the case of the United States, race and racism, or, more precisely, institutionalized white supremacy, arose as a byproduct of the need to explain and justify the existence of slavery as a dominant form of labor in the context of a nominally democratic republic. Slavery in the United States was not a system designed to create racism; it was a system designed to grow tobacco, rice, indigo, and cotton and hence make profits for the planter class. It was in the need to justify this particular arrangement of labor in the context of, first, English and, later, American notions of individual liberty that race became a necessary concept if the system was to survive. Ideas about race and racism were embedded in law, culture, and the practice of daily life in such a way as to naturalize them to those living inside the system (or at least to those who benefited from it). But to the extent that notions of white superiority and black inferiority continued to survive even after the end of slavery, it was not because they had magically "taken on a life of their own," but rather because they continued to serve a useful purpose for those inside the system and were thus continually replicated and enacted on a daily basis.

"Nuclear Apartheid": Framing the Bomb in a Racial Context

What would a race-conscious reading of the A-bomb decision look like from the perspective of Fields's model? Understanding the functioning of racial ideology does not provide us with a magic solution that suddenly illuminates the history of the nuclear age. It does, however, offer a different and much needed perspective on the bomb and its legacy. If we are to follow the rigorous examination of racial ideology called for by Fields, it is not sufficient to simply observe that American leaders have seldom if ever shied away from the indiscriminate killing of people of color (though this is true). We need to try to understand how and why racial ideology functioned for those in charge of the killing and how it has changed and evolved over time. As Fields observes, "Only if *race* is defined as innate and natural prejudice of color does its invocation as a historical explanation do more than repeat the question by way of answer. And there an insurmountable problem arises: since race is not genetically programmed, racial prejudice cannot be genetically programed either but, like race itself, must arise historically."[29] As such, it will not do to declare that Harry Truman, Andrew Jackson, Henry Kissinger, or Dick Cheney were genetically destined to be war criminals or that their callous indifference to the death and suffering of people of color was the result of some sort of ill-defined cultural pathology or poor parenting. Rather, we need to examine the specific ways in which racial ideology intertwined in the context of policy making at particular times and places.

In the case of World War II and the atomic bomb, scholars have frequently invoked the surprise attacks on Hawaii and the Philippines in December 1941 as well as the unwillingness of Japanese leaders to accept unconditional surrender in the face of military defeat in 1945 as explanations for the virulence with which Americans prosecuted the war in the Pacific. But these explanations assume the American occupation of the Philippine Islands, the existence of Hawaii (over 2,000 miles off the West Coast) as a state in the union, the postwar U.S. Occupation of Japan, and the creation of a permanent ring of bases spread across the Pacific as somehow natural and inevitable facts that have nothing to do with ideas about race and racism. In fact, World War II in the Pacific was a colonial war between two empires, American and Japanese, in a contest between different visions of regional hegemony. The pressure to end that conflict with Japan's unconditional surrender was in turn directly related to ensuring American predominance in the region. Similarly, the haste to conclude the fighting before Soviet intervention and to keep Stalin from claiming a piece of postwar Japan was not motivated by an abstract disagreement over the merits of communism, but rather directly linked to the larger American commitment to exercise hegemony over the Pacific in the postwar period.

While perhaps sharply put, neither of the statements above would seem unintelligible to diplomatic historians or theorists of international relations. And yet race seldom if ever figures in these accounts, even among revisionist historians for whom American hegemony looms large in explaining the use of the bomb against Japan. When race does feature in these accounts, it is usually cited as an outside or "additive" factor that exists somehow independently of material calculations of national interest or national security. This is absurd given that it is impossible to understand American policy and practice in the Pacific without reference to a long-standing racial ideology that portrayed the nations and people of that region as immature and incapable of self-government and hence in need of U.S. guidance, tutelage, and, when necessary, discipline.[30] More broadly, as historian Matthew Jones has explored in *After Hiroshima*, the possession and planning for use of nuclear weapons was a crucial underpinning of American strategy for maintaining hegemony in the Pacific in the decades after Hiroshima, a fact that caused considerable tensions with the peoples of the region who would have to live with the literal and metaphorical fallout from their use.

While it is true that the United States also sought to wield postwar influence over Europe, the context in the Pacific was entirely different. The American presence in the Pacific as a hegemonic economic, military, and geopolitical power both before and after World War II was inextricably tied to racialized colonialism that often manifested in massive state-sanctioned violence against people of color, from the Philippines at the turn of the twentieth century to the Vietnam War. Conversely, when the United States unleashed violence against civilians in Europe during World War II, it marked the exception, rather than the rule, to a pattern that tended more toward reciprocity and compromise even when the United States wielded disproportionate power over the countries and governments of the region. Given the context of this history, it strains credulity not to see the use of the atomic bomb as part of a larger effort to protect a racialized American empire from both Japanese and Soviet challenges. As Fields and other scholars have demonstrated, racial ideology sets up white supremacy as a "commonsense" arrangement by which violence against people of color is naturalized, making it possible for renowned scholars to speak of the United States as a restrained "liberal hegemon" while ignoring the millions of dead in wars and covert actions on the so-called periphery.[31] A truly race-conscious analysis of the atomic bomb decision would not focus on individual prejudice but rather situate its use against the backdrop of a particular type of racialized colonialism in which the mass killing of people of color in the service of advancing American economic, political, and national security interests was the norm rather than the exception in Asia.

Thinking about race and policy in a broad historical context also offers us a new way to look at the so-called moral threshold argument. The conventional wisdom on this subject is that the use of the bomb against Japanese cities was facilitated by a slow erosion of moral scruples about the mass killing of civilians that can be traced back to the beginning of World War II with the aerial assaults on Warsaw and Rotterdam through the Allied strategic bombing offensive in Europe and the firebombing of Tokyo and other Japanese cities. But as Huey Newton observed in 1966, the indiscriminate killing of people of color, both at home and abroad, is deeply enshrined in the history of the United States and was inextricably tied to the labor system of slavery, territorial expansion in North America, and the projection of U.S. power into the nonwhite world. Sometimes that killing was state-directed and wholesale, such as the frequent massacres that characterized American policy toward Native Americans or the atrocities committed by U.S. troops in the occupation of the Philippines, sometimes it took the form of individual acts of terror, such as lynching in the American South, and sometimes it has been paired with innovative high-technology weapons such as aerial counterinsurgency practiced by the U.S. Marines in Nicaragua in the 1920s or modern-day drone strikes. In the last year of the Barack Obama presidency, for example, the United States dropped over twenty-six thousand bombs on seven Muslim majority countries in the Middle East and Africa.[32]

In the case of the bombing of Europe during World War II, the exigencies of war were pitted against imperfectly realized but real legal and moral traditions designed to shield civilians in conflicts between so-called civilized nations. Indeed, for the duration of the war in Europe, the U.S. Army Air Forces (AAF) went to great pains to distinguish its efforts at "precision bombing" from the indiscriminate area and firebombing practiced by Britain's Bomber Command. Though the reality was that AAF bombing killed large numbers of European civilians, both in public and in private its leaders continued to assert that they were committed to attacking military targets even if that meant exposing American airmen to greater risk by operating in daylight (as opposed to British nighttime area attacks).[33] No such counterweight existed in the conflict in the Pacific. Indeed, we might invert the typical formulation of this argument to suggest that the strategic bombing of Europe, as well as the later Cold War doctrine of nuclear apocalypse, drew on practices of mass killing that American statesmen and generals had been honing for much of the history of republic in campaigns against people of color.[34]

As Shampa Biswas deftly illustrates in her essay in this volume on "nuclear harms" (chapter 15), much of the nuclear age is embedded in older patterns of racialized colonialism. For all the rhetoric on the use of the bomb as a unique, world-shaping event that ushered in a new era in international relations, nuclear weapons were born into a world shaped by centuries of Western imperialism and white supremacy. The atomic bombs were first used to indiscriminately kill people of color at the end of a colonial war for hegemony in the Pacific. The victims were studied by the American Atomic Bomb Casualty Commission (ABCC) not so they could be better treated but in the service of a form of colonial knowledge that has deep roots in the racialized "tropical medicine" that characterized the American occupations of the Philippines and other territories.[35] The uranium for both the Hiroshima and Nagasaki bombs came largely from mines in the Belgian Congo, and throughout the Cold War significant amounts of the world's uranium came from Africa and were produced under either colonial or neocolonial relations of power.[36] Similarly, much of the West's postwar nuclear testing was conducted in Asia and Africa (with U.S. testing in Nevada the one obvious exception). Efforts at nuclear nonproliferation often resembled what Indian diplomat V. M. Trivedi referred to as "nuclear weapons apartheid," whereby white nations sought to keep the bomb out of the hands of nonwhite nations in the Third World.[37] Even the internal aspects of the U.S. nuclear program had racialized aspects, as a significant amount of U.S. uranium mining was conducted by Navajo who went on to suffer ongoing health impacts.[38]

In surveying the links between colonialism and the bomb, Biswas asks in chapter 15: "Where are the margins of the nuclear world? In what kinds of peripheral places can we find the reach of nuclear power and perspectives on that power that help augment the narratives from the center? What kind of universals can we build from these narratives?" While much of the nuclear age was shaped by older patterns of white supremacy and colonialism, nuclear weapons also featured in anticolonial and antiracist organizing during the second half of the twentieth century, from the efforts of a multinational group of activists to shut down French nuclear testing in the Sahara in the late 1950s and early 1960s to Malcolm X's meeting with a delegation of atomic bomb victims (*hibakusha*) in Harlem in June 1964.[39] It would be a mistake, however, to categorize all such activism as reflexively antinuclear. For example, many in postcolonial nations as well as activist groups in the United States such as the Black Panther Party hailed the Chinese development of the atomic bomb as not only a counterweight to the Western nuclear monopoly but also a positive development for those resisting Western colonialism and neocolonialism.[40] Recovering the racialized history of nuclear weapons is thus not simply an exercise in establishing the ongoing culpability of the West but also crucial to understanding the way that peoples of the periphery and the Global South sought to contest both the nuclear and colonial orders.

All these developments are complicated subjects in their own right and deserve far more attention than the admittedly surface-level gloss that I have given them in this chapter. And yet it is striking how little attention has been paid to the way in which racialized colonialism has shaped the history of nuclear weapons. As Robert Vitalis recently argued, race and colonialism have been largely absent from the post–World War II scholarly literature in international relations despite the fact that the prewar origins of that discipline can be directly traced to efforts to both understand and facilitate the management of America's colonial empire.[41] Diplomatic historians have more forthrightly examined issues of race and colonialism, but all too often this work has been intentionally or unintentionally separated from discussions of nuclear weapons and other policy issues. Thus, while we have literature on civil rights activism and U.S. foreign policy or the role of race in U.S. policy toward Africa, Asia, and Latin America, seldom have diplomatic historians paused to consider the foundational role of racial ideology in both the policy and academic underpinnings of the American approach to national interest and national security. In a different context, Sonja Schmid remind us in chapter 14 of this volume that "what we know, how we know it, and why we care to know originate in the way we perceive the nuclear order and at the same time have the capacity to reshape that order." In this case, the systematic dismissal and silences with respect to race and the atomic bomb speak volumes not only about the foundations of our current nuclear order but also about the role of the academy in cementing those foundations.

It is well past time for scholars to respond to the challenge laid down by generations of scholars and activists of color, ranging from W.E.B. Du Bois to Huey P. Newton, who understood from bitter experience that, in the case of the United States, racial ideology cannot be divorced from the institutions and practices of both domestic and foreign policy making. Doubtless there will be those who are unconvinced by this essay and remain skeptical about the importance of racial ideology as tool for understanding the decision to use the atomic bomb against Japan. There remains a need for a more detailed study of the complicated relationship among American racial ideology, colonialism in the Pacific, and the way in which thinking about nuclear weapons intersected with those long-standing forces during the course of World War II and beyond. As Fields cautions, simply invoking "race" is never adequate to explain historical events. Rather, we must pay close attention to how—and why—racial ideologies operate in the realms of law, policy, and culture at particular times in particular places. This chapter suggests a framework for such an analysis in the case of the atomic bomb, centered around its role in cementing American hegemony in a region long seen as peopled by racial inferiors in need of Western guidance and a time when Western imperial designs were under great external and internal stress, but much work remains to be done to flesh out this argument and the way in which it operated at the level of policy making. Racial ideology is seldom the *only* factor influencing even overtly racist policies, and conscientious scholars must consider how it worked in conjunction with—and sometimes in opposition to—other material and ideological influences on U.S. foreign policy.

But while I am sympathetic to those who demand a more rigorous scholarly examination of the nature of the relationship between race and the decision to use the bomb than is offered in this brief essay, I am considerably less so to those who reflexively dismiss race and racism as critical categories in understanding U.S. foreign policy. Brilliant scholars such as DuBois, Merze Tate, and Alaine Locke spent decades unsuccessfully attempting to convince the academic establishment to take race, and more specifically the ideology of white supremacy, seriously as a tool with which to explain the actions of the United States on the world stage. In the face of hundreds of years of institutionalized white supremacy in the United States, from Native genocide to slavery, Jim Crow, and the more subtle but still insidious policies of racial segregation and racialized economic inequality in the cities of the North and West, as well as the nearly continuous history of overt and covert U.S. military interventions in Latin America, Asia, the Middle East, and Africa, to see racial ideology as anything but a central pillar of the nation's history is a form of malpractice. At a time when white nationalists are operating openly in the streets and the halls of the U.S. government, blindness to the history of white supremacy that brought us to the moment is itself a form of complicity.

5

Racing toward Armageddon?

SOVIET VIEWS OF STRATEGIC
NUCLEAR WAR, 1955–1972

David Holloway

HIROSHIMA HAS MANY LEGACIES: the victims in Japan, most obviously, and the continuing debate in the United States about the decision to use the bomb. The most enduring legacy is that we still live with nuclear weapons, which the bombing of Hiroshima first revealed to the world. Hiroshima has been a key point of reference for understanding the effects of nuclear weapons, not only their ability to damage human health and destroy material objects, but also their impact on international politics. It remains, moreover, a key point of reference, even though thousands of much more powerful nuclear weapons have been deployed since 1945. That is because the bombings of Hiroshima and of Nagasaki are the only times nuclear weapons have been used to destroy targets in war.

This chapter looks at Soviet strategic arms policy in the years from 1955 to 1972 in light of the legacy of Hiroshima. This was a turbulent period, perhaps the most dangerous in the nuclear age. It saw the introduction of thermonuclear warheads of enormous destructive power. In March 1954 a U.S. nuclear weapons test in the Pacific produced a yield of 15 megatons (MT)—more than one thousand times greater than the 13-kiloton explosive yield of the bomb that destroyed Hiroshima. In November 1955 the Soviet Union tested a bomb of a similar type in Kazakhstan. The United States and the Soviet Union produced long-range ballistic missiles that could deliver thermonuclear warheads from one country to the other in thirty minutes. This was also the period of the most intense crises of the nuclear age—the Berlin Crisis of 1961 and the Cuban Missile Crisis of 1962. The Soviet Union made a huge effort in these years to gain strategic parity with the United States. The Anti-Ballistic Missile (ABM) Treaty and the Interim Agreement on Offensive Forces, which Richard Nixon and Leonid Brezhnev signed in Moscow in May 1972, signified a relationship of strategic parity between the two nuclear superpowers.

Hiroshima and the Soviet Union

Like their counterparts in other countries in the early part of the twentieth century, Russian scientists were intrigued by the prospect that the energy locked up inside the atom could be harnessed for human purposes. In the 1920s and 1930s they pursued research into the structure of the atomic nucleus. They greeted with excitement the discovery of nuclear fission at the end of 1938, and, like their foreign colleagues, they conducted research into the conditions under which nuclear fission chain reactions (both controlled and explosive) could take place.[1]

The German invasion of June 22, 1941, brought that research to an end, but during the war the Soviet Union collected a vast amount of intelligence about British and American nuclear research, as well as information about the German atomic project. In October 1941 it obtained a copy of the British government's Maud Committee Report, which laid out the path to the development of the bomb. Intelligence continued to come in, providing information on fundamental physical data, isotope separation, nuclear reactors, and the progress of the Manhattan Project as well as the design of the bombs. Early in 1945 Theodore Hall and Klaus Fuchs reported from Los Alamos on the spontaneous fission problem in plutonium and the implosion method that was being devised to deal with it.[2] All this is now well documented, thanks to Russian declassification policy over the past twenty-five years.[3]

In spite of the remarkable success of Soviet atomic espionage, there is no evidence that the Soviet Union had information about U.S. plans to drop the bomb on Japanese cities. This might of course be an artifact of declassification policy, but there are reasons for thinking that is not the case. First, Russian Foreign Intelligence (Sluzhba vneshnei razvedki, SVR) and Military Intelligence (Glavnoe razvedivatel'noe upravlenie, GRU) have been eager since the collapse of the Soviet Union to publicize their successes; it would be surprising, therefore, if they remained silent about any intelligence they had obtained on the U.S. decision to use the bomb.

Second, there is circumstantial evidence that Hiroshima came as a surprise to Stalin. His daughter Svetlana reports that he was preoccupied with Hiroshima once the bomb had been dropped. "The day I was out at his *dacha* he had the usual visitors. They told him that the Americans had dropped the first atom bomb over Japan," she writes in *20 Letters to a Friend*. "Everyone was busy with that, and my father paid hardly any attention to me." Svetlana was bringing her three-month-old son, Josef, to visit his grandfather for the first time, so it is unlikely she was wrong about the date. "But this was such a little thing compared with the great events going on around us," she writes. "In a word, nobody cared."[4] On August 7, 1945—the day after the bombing of Hiroshima—Stalin decided to advance Soviet entry into the war with Japan by forty-eight hours. This too suggests that Hiroshima came as a surprise to him.[5] On the same day the U.S. ambassador, Averell Harriman, asked Molotov "what news he had from Japan about the effect of the atomic bomb. Molotov said that they had no news yet, and commented, 'You Americans can keep a secret when you want to.'"[6] Harriman later interpreted this as a snide reference to the success of Soviet atomic espionage, but perhaps it was in fact a grudging acknowledgment that the United States had managed to keep secret its plan to use the bomb against Japan.[7]

Stalin regarded Hiroshima as an atomic gauntlet thrown down by Truman, a challenge he had to respond to. On August 20, two weeks to the day after Hiroshima, he signed a decree setting up a Special Committee of the State Defense Committee to be chaired by Lavrentii Beria. This converted the small atomic project into a crash program to build the bomb as quickly as possible. The decree also established the First Chief Directorate, which was to create and manage the research institutes, design bureaus, and production plants of the new atomic industry. The Special Committee reported directly to Stalin.[8] Building the bomb came to be known in official documents as "Problem No. 1."[9]

It may seem surprising that Stalin gave the bomb such high priority immediately after Hiroshima. The first reports from the Soviet Embassy in Tokyo noted that the bomb had had an "enormous effect on the population of Japan," but they also commented that the Japanese press was going out of its way "to exaggerate the destructive power of the bomb and the duration of the effects of the explosion."[10] These assessments, which came after the August 20 decree, did not affect Stalin's judgment. He had told Harriman and George Kennan on the evening of August 8 that the bomb might give the Japanese the "pretext" to replace the current government with one that would be qualified to surrender.[11] He seems to have concluded, from the very beginning, that Truman would endeavor to use the bomb as an instrument of political pressure. The decision to build the bomb was, moreover, one of a series of decisions to develop the new military technologies that had appeared during the war in the United States, Britain, and Germany—rocketry, radar, and jet propulsion. It was important for the Soviet Union to develop those technologies for the future great war that Stalin regarded as inevitable.

In Moscow, as in Washington and in London, Hiroshima appeared to mark a radical shift in the balance of power that had taken shape three months earlier with the final defeat of Germany. Stalin told Andrei Gromyko, then ambassador to the United States, that Washington and London would try to use their atomic monopoly to impose their plans on Europe and the rest of the world.[12] "They are killing the Japanese and intimidating us," Stalin remarked to Molotov, according to Gromyko.[13] Stalin now had two goals. The first was to eliminate the American monopoly by building a Soviet bomb as quickly as possible. The second was to deprive the United States of any possible advantage it might seek from that monopoly in shaping the postwar world. The monopoly ended on August 29, 1949, when the Soviet Union detonated a plutonium bomb based on the design of the bomb that destroyed Nagasaki. It was a major undertaking to produce that bomb, even though the Soviet Union had a detailed description of the design. The main challenge was to build a production reactor and separate the plutonium for the bomb from the spent fuel.

During the Cold War Moscow presented the use of the bomb against the Japanese cities as an unnecessary act. Japan, it claimed, would have surrendered in response to Soviet entry into the war, and the bomb must therefore have been used to intimidate the Soviet Union. It was an anti-Soviet act, a sign of American callousness and perfidy. That is how it is still presented in post-Soviet Russia. In 2007 Vladimir Putin told a meeting of social studies teachers that no one should try to make Russia feel guilty for the Great Purge of 1937: "in other countries worse things happened," such as the use of the atomic bomb against civilian populations in Japan.[14] Putin portrays Hiroshima as a stain on the character of the United States: "We know Stalin now like never before. He was a dictator and a tyrant, but I very much doubt that in the spring of 1945, if he had been in possession of an atomic bomb, he would have used it against Germany."[15]

There is no evidence that Stalin was appalled by the destructiveness of the bomb or that he would have been opposed to its use. What mattered to him was that the Western allies had not forewarned him about the use of the bomb and were clearly, in his mind, intending to use it to put pressure on the Soviet Union. In the United States those who argued in favor of the international control of atomic energy did not necessarily oppose the use of the bomb. What they did advocate—and Niels Bohr was the most pressing on this point—was that Stalin be informed about the Manhattan Project before the bomb was a certainty and before the war was over. Bohr deliberately did not try to spell out the forms cooperation might take. The important thing was to start the discussion and dispel as far as possible the mistrust that the bomb might give rise to.[16] Whether the approach Bohr recommended would have averted an arms race, as he hoped, is open to debate, but what seems clear is that the use of the bomb without any prior discussion gave grounds for suspicions on Stalin's part that he might have harbored in any event about U.S. and

British intentions. For the context of the decision not to inform Stalin about the bomb, see chapter 2 in this volume by Campbell Craig.

Deterrence and War Fighting

There are three reasons why 1955 is an appropriate starting date for this chapter. The first is the development of thermonuclear weapons, which greatly increased the destructive power in the nuclear arsenals of the two countries. After the Cold War, scientists at VNIIEF (Vserossiskii nauchno-issledovatel'skii institut eksperimental'noi fiziki), the Russian equivalent of Los Alamos, calculated what the effects of a U.S. nuclear attack on the Soviet Union in the mid-1950s would have been. Using declassified U.S. figures, they concluded that U.S. nuclear forces in 1953 (1,169 bombs with a total explosive yield of 73 MT) could not have determined the outcome of a large-scale conflict between the Soviet Union and the United States. By 1957, however, the United States had 5,543 nuclear bombs that could deliver 17,500 MT. An attack by those forces would have created an area of destruction measuring 1.5 million square kilometers, an area of fires covering 2 million square kilometers, and levels of radiation exceeding 300 rads over an area of 10 million square kilometers, with the result that the Soviet Union would have been turned into a "radioactive desert."[17]

The second reason is that the political leaders of the three nuclear powers at the time came to understand, as a result of briefings from scientists and the military, that a general nuclear war would be catastrophic for all concerned. They also came to understand that the other leaders understood that too. Dwight Eisenhower returned to Washington from the Geneva summit meeting in July 1955 believing, as he put it in a television broadcast, that "there seems to be a growing realization by all that nuclear warfare, pursued to the ultimate, could be practically race suicide."[18] Harold Macmillan, the British foreign secretary, wrote in his diary during the Geneva meeting: "One of the chief impressions which we all have of Geneva is this. 'War—a modern war—nuclear war, just isn't on.' All the great nations, especially the three nations which are in the nuclear 'game' know this."[19] In his memoirs, Nikita Khrushchev recalled returning from Geneva aware that "our probable adversaries feared us just as we feared them."[20] Eight months later he told Harold Stassen, Eisenhower's adviser on disarmament, that "nearly everyone knew that war was unacceptable and that coexistence was elementary."[21]

The third reason is that the United States and the Soviet Union aimed to continue their conflict without a major war. The Eisenhower administration adopted the idea of "rivalry over the long pull," and the Soviet Union espoused "peaceful coexistence."[22] Neither side believed that war was inevitable, but neither believed that it was impossible. In January 1955 the Eisenhower administration adopted a document on Basic National Security Policy (NSC 5501), which stated that "a central aim of US policy must be to deter the Communists from use of their military power, remaining prepared to fight general war should one be forced upon the US." It also stated that "the United States must make clear its determination to prevail if general war eventuates."[23] In February 1956 the Twentieth Party Congress in Moscow adopted similar principles. It declared that war was no longer "fatalistically inevitable," because the Soviet Union now had nuclear weapons. This was a significant shift from V. I. Lenin's view, which Stalin had reaffirmed after World War II, that war was inevitable as long as imperialism existed. But the Party Congress also declared that a new world war would mean the end of imperialism.[24] Preparations had therefore to be made to ensure that the Soviet Armed Forces would defeat the imperialist powers in the event of war.

Soviet Military Strategy for Nuclear War to the Mid-1960s

The Soviet Union lagged far behind the United States in the development of its strategic nuclear forces. Before 1956 it lacked intercontinental bombers and had no overseas bases close to the continental United States. In the mid-1950s it took the decision to give priority to the development of long-range nuclear-armed missiles, and in December 1959 it created the Strategic Rocket Forces as a separate service. Those forces consisted of all land-based ballistic missiles with a range of over 1,000 kilometers. The Soviet Union had few such missiles at the time, but by 1963 it had built up a force of about 600 MRBMs and IRBMs armed with 1 MT warheads; the deployment of ICBMs proceeded at a slower pace.[25] In the late 1950s there was a campaign in the United States trumpeting the existence of a "missile gap" in the Soviet Union's favor. Khrushchev added fuel to the fire by boasting about Soviet missile strength, and Soviet successes in space gave his claims some plausibility. It was only in 1961 that the United States began to get from satellite photography a clearer picture of the real size of Soviet strategic forces.[26]

Along with the creation of the Strategic Rocket Forces, the Soviet military began to develop a new strategy for nuclear war. Already in the mid-1950s, after Stalin's death, Soviet military thinkers had begun to emphasize the danger of a surprise attack and the need to prepare to preempt such an attack. In 1960 the General Staff Academy published a secret study written under the guidance of Marshal V. D. Sokolovskii, chief of the General Staff, under the title *Modern War*.[27] A new world war would start with massed strategic nuclear strikes. The Strategic Rocket Forces would have the decisive role, with two main missions: first, to destroy the most important targets in enemy countries with the aim of quickly knocking those countries out of the war, and, second, to crush the enemy coalition's forces and destroy its offensive nuclear forces—in the first instance to "strike the enemy's offensive nuclear forces and in particular his missiles and strategic aviation." The Air Defense Forces would have the second most important role: "defending the homeland against missile and bomber nuclear strikes." Ballistic missile defense was one of the cardinal problems facing the Soviet Union, according to Sokolovskii, and unless it could be solved "it would be impossible to count on successful attainment of the goals of the war." Sokolovskii asserted that the ABM problem would soon be solved.[28]

After the Cold War, Russian military historians confirmed that Soviet military strategy in the late 1950s and the 1960s had placed a heavy reliance on preemption in the event of war: "Both the theory and the practice of strategic planning regarded the delivery by the Soviet Armed Forces of a preemptive rocket-nuclear blow against the aggressor as the main variant of operation. That variant was conditioned not only by the unpredictably severe consequences of a sudden first nuclear strike by the U.S., but also by the fact that the nuclear forces of the USSR were simply not ready for any other mode of operation."[29] According to David Rosenberg, "the idea of a single war-winning blow was an irresistible temptation" for U.S. Strategic Air Command planners in the 1950s."[30] By the same token, the idea of an American first strike was an unavoidable preoccupation for Soviet planners, because they worried that they might not be able to retaliate: hence their interest in preemption.

The chiefs of the General Staff in the early 1960s—Marshals S. S. Biryuzov and M. V. Zakharov, as well as Sokolovskii—shared this view of military strategy as nuclear blitzkrieg.[31] A 1964 study under the direction of Defense Minister Marshal R. Ya. Malinovskii seems to have marked a high point of thinking about nuclear war in this way. Entitled *The Strategy of Nuclear War*, it stressed that "the conditions of nuclear war ... present us with the alternative: either the offensive or defeat."[32] It paid particular attention to the first strategic nuclear strike, which would aim to weaken as far as possible the adversary's military and economic might, to seize the strategic initiative at the beginning of the war, to eliminate countries or groups of states from the opposing coalition in the first hours of the war, and to create favorable conditions for successful strategic operations in the theaters of war and for attaining the political goals of the war in the shortest possible time. "It follows from what has been said," the book continued, "that the first strategic nuclear strike is the chief method for attaining strategic goals and the chief form of nuclear war fighting."[33]

The Sokolovskii and Malinovskii books should not be taken as descriptions of Soviet war plans at the time. For one thing, the Soviet Union did not have the forces that could carry out the missions outlined. Those studies should be regarded rather as Kriegsbilder, images of a future war, which could potentially play a role in military plans and decisions on force structure. There was apparently in this period a prevailing assumption that nonmilitary as well as military factors would enable the Soviet Union to win a world war: the moral and political character of the Soviet state; the vast territory of the Soviet Union; the higher concentration of population and industry in the United States. According to the judgment of later Russian military historians, the military overestimated the effect of Soviet nuclear strikes and underestimated the effects of enemy strikes.[34]

Khrushchev's Attitude toward Nuclear War

In a speech to the Soviet High Command in December 1959, Khrushchev underlined the importance of striking first in a nuclear war, but he warned that no surprise attack, no preemptive strike, could put out of action all the adversary's launch sites. "Our adversary," he said, "will always have the possibility of delivering a retaliatory strike against us." He underlined the terrible destructiveness of nuclear weapons. "America cannot wage war without Britain, France, and Germany, that is where its bases are," he said. "And those countries are like hostages, attached to a chain. And they know it." If you launch 300 missiles, he told his audience, it means exploding the equivalent of 300 million tons of TNT "over France, over West Germany mainly, and over Britain. What will remain of those countries? These are terrible things, comrades. These missiles are so far impossible to intercept. Neither we, nor they have defenses against missiles. Therefore, this is a terrible weapon."[35]

Khrushchev then told the senior officers that the party leadership had no intention of getting into a war. "I do not know how you military people think," he said, "but we in the Presidium think and abide by a firm rule, that we ourselves are not intending to go to war, no matter what the situation (kon"iunktura). We are not looking for the situation to start a war, we simply reject war." Why? Because even victory brought disaster and destruction, as the Soviet Union knew from the last war. "That is why we reject war."[36]

This statement points to the importance of taking both the political and the military dimensions of military strategy into account. This duality of the prevention or deterrence of war and preparation for victory in war is a complex and often confusing aspect of nuclear history. Bernard Brodie claimed in his 1959 book, *Strategy in the Missile Age*, that "a plan and a policy which offers a good promise of deterring war is ... by orders of magnitude better in every way than one which depreciates the objective of deterrence in order to improve somewhat the chances of winning. Of future total wars we can say that winning is likely to be less ghastly than losing, but whether it will be by much or by little we cannot know." Brodie asserted that military strategy in the sense of "seizing the initiative and carrying the fight to the enemy" was no longer the right way to think about national security.[37] That was not a view that Soviet (or American) military planners accepted in the early 1960s.

The Shift in Soviet Military Strategy

Following Khrushchev's removal from power in October 1964, a process of reassessment began that led to a shift in Soviet thinking about the relationship between deterrence of major war and preparation to fight and win such a war. This was only dimly understood in the West at the time, and even now there is much that is unclear. A number of factors contributed to the shift, among them the changing balance of strategic nuclear forces with the United States and the introduction of operations research and systems analysis into the decision-making process. These led to a more sober appreciation by the military of the effects of nuclear weapons and the consequences of nuclear war. But American ideas about the stability of deterrence and about the relationship between offensive and defensive strategic systems also played a role. Matthew Evangelista has provided a revealing analysis of the role of the Pugwash movement, which brought Soviet and Western scientists together to discuss nuclear weapons and international security, as a channel through which Western ideas could enter the Soviet policy debates.[38]

President John F. Kennedy, who had made much of the "missile gap" during the 1960 presidential election campaign, launched a rapid buildup of ICBMs and SLBMs, leaving the Soviet Union far behind in the early and mid-1960s. The air force and the navy were pressing for more, forcing the administration to address the question: "How much is enough?" The first Strategic Integrated Operational Plan (SIOP-62), which had been initiated under the Eisenhower administration, stressed the advantages of preemption. The growth of Soviet forces and growing intelligence about targets in the Soviet Union boosted the military's claims for more missiles. The systems analysts Robert McNamara brought into the Pentagon developed what they called a "theory of requirements—a conceptual framework for measuring the need and adequacy of our strategic forces." The two criteria they came up with were "assured destruction" and "damage limitation."[39] These corresponded roughly to the missions laid out in the Basic National Security Policy of 1955, with "prevailing" replaced by the less confident notion of "damage limitation."

The criteria of "assured destruction" and "damage limitation" were designed to provide guidance for deciding on the size of U.S. strategic forces. The capacity to inflict assured destruction in a retaliatory strike became the most important criterion for judging the adequacy of U.S. strategic forces for deterrence.

Various quantitative criteria were adopted for defining it: the ability to destroy a certain percentage of population (30 percent) and industry (50 percent), or a particular number of cities (150), in a retaliatory strike.[40] Assured destruction was in some ways a very misleading concept. It implied that deterrence was to be achieved solely by targeting the adversary's population and industry, but the military planners continued to focus their attention also on the destruction of military forces and other military targets in line with the criterion of damage limitation, though of course it was understood that that would involve the targeting of cities.

In 1965 the Military-Industrial Commission, which coordinated Soviet defense production, asked two research institutes for a joint study of the development of the Strategic Rocket Forces from 1971 to 1975.[41] These institutes were TsNIIMash (Tsentral'nyi nauchno-issledovatel'skii institut mashinostroeniia) and 4 TsNII MO (4th Tsentral'nyi nauchno-issledovatel'skii institut Ministerstva oborony).[42] The second generation of ICBMs (SS-9s and SS-11s) was being deployed at the time, so the focus of the study by the institutes was the third generation. The first question that arose concerned the silos in which the second generation of ICBMs was being deployed. The institutes calculated that a Minuteman III ICBM with multiple independently targeted reentry vehicles (MIRVs), which the United States was developing, would pose a significant threat to those silos; they proposed therefore that the silos be significantly hardened.[43]

The Ministry of Defense disliked this proposal. Yu. A. Mozzhorin, the director of TsNIIMash from 1961 to 1990, reports that at a meeting in the summer of 1966, "some of the top brass began to express the thought that there was no urgent need to strengthen the protection of the silo launch complexes. Because no one intends to sit and wait until we are struck by missiles; a retaliatory counterstrike will be employed and our missiles will leave the silos before the aggressor's warheads arrive, so protection will in general not be needed." The Military-Industrial Commission nevertheless ordered work on new launch complexes.[44]

TsNIIMash and 4 TsNII MO conducted computer simulations of nuclear exchanges and came to the conclusion that a preemptive attack against an enemy that possessed a strategic triad (ICBMs, SLBMs, and heavy bombers) would lead only to the mutual destruction of the warring states. They became very interested in the concept of assured destruction in a retaliatory strike as the criterion by which to judge the adequacy of Soviet strategic forces. One of the definitions they advanced of assured destruction was the capability to destroy no fewer than 150 of the largest U.S. administrative-political and military-industrial centers in a retaliatory strike—which was also one of McNamara's criteria for assured destruction. The two institutes were also interested in strikes against military targets—"damage limitation"—and recommended the rapid development of a new generation of highly accurate MIRVed ICBMs with better protection in silos.

It was not only the Ministry of Defense that opposed the ideas coming from the two institutes. The Ministry of General Machine Building (the missile production industry) did not like the thought of rebuilding missile silos because that would interfere with its plans for the production of new missiles. There were, moreover, doubts about the ability of Soviet industry to produce the onboard digital computers needed for MIRVed warheads. The net result of these disagreements was a prolonged but intense bureaucratic battle involving different missile design bureaus, different ministries, and different senior figures in the military-industrial complex. The intensity of this conflict is attested to by the names given to it in the Soviet Union at the time: the "little civil war" and the "argument of the century."[45]

The "little civil war" also involved questions of military strategy. In March 1969 the director of TsNIIMash wrote to Brezhnev, arguing, as he recalled in his memoirs:

> In my report I expressed concern at the absence of a concrete and precise formulation of defense doctrine with respect to the state's missile-nuclear arms. Some leading military chiefs were interpreting defense doctrine willfully and inconsistently. I briefly made the case that only the doctrine of a guaranteed retaliatory strike would deter aggression and ensure stability and peace. I showed that the doctrine of a preemptive strike against an aggressor preparing to attack or a retaliatory counterstrike would not ensure the defense of the country and would lead only to the mutual destruction of the conflicting states. I cited the results of modeling all those methods of using rocket-nuclear forces in defending the country and the dependence of the doctrine of the retaliatory strike on the degree of protection of the missile complexes.[46]

The issue was not resolved until August 1969, at a meeting in the Crimea of the Defense Council, which consisted of the top political and military leaders as well as weapons designers and science advisers.[47]

The Defense Council decided that the third generation of ICBMs should enable the Soviet Union to inflict assured destruction in a retaliatory strike. New ICBMs should be better protected, MIRVed, and highly accurate; work should start on a rail-mobile system. Two Strategic Rocket Force officers later wrote:

> At the end of the 1960s and in the 1970s the Strategic Rocket Forces had a scientifically grounded conception of deterrence, based on the inevitability

of delivering an assured retaliatory strike, with damage deliberately unacceptable to the aggressor. The material embodiment of this conception was the highly defended and effective stationary complexes with powerful single-warhead missiles, and from the middle of the 1970s—MIRVed warheads.[48]

The echo of McNamara is clear, and it appears that his ideas did indeed influence Soviet thinking about nuclear war. The 1969 Defense Council meeting decided that the Soviet Union should have secure, survivable strategic nuclear forces, but forces that were also capable of limiting damage to the Soviet Union through counterforce attacks. In 1974 the Soviet Union began to test the ICBMs whose development and production the Defense Council had approved in the summer of 1969—the SS-17, SS-18, and SS-19. These were powerful systems, MIRVed, and much more accurate than the previous generation, and they caused alarm in the United States, where they precipitated a sharp debate about the nature of Soviet military strategy.

By 1969 key elements of the strategy elaborated by Sokolovskii in 1960 had changed. Most important, the Soviet Union backed away from reliance on preemption to adopt a policy of building a secure retaliatory force. It is interesting to note that Soviet analyses of the German attack on the Soviet Union began to change in the late 1960s and early 1970s. In 1956 Khrushchev had taken the failure to heed warnings of the German attack as one of the major points in his indictment of Stalin. "Everything was ignored," he said, implying that the warnings presented Stalin with a clear decision. A more complex picture was presented in *The Initial Period of War* (*Nachal'nyi period voiny*), published by the Ministry of Defense in 1974. This pointed to German efforts at disinformation, to faulty assumptions made by Stalin in his assessment of intelligence, and to the General Staff's misconceptions about the way in which a war would start. This new analysis made it clear that the problem of surprise attack—and of preempting such an attack—was far from simple. It may be that the new understanding of the complexity of preemption played a role in the decision to move away from a strategy of preemption in nuclear war.[49]

Ballistic Missile Defense

Another major shift in Soviet thinking resulted from a growing realization that an effective ABM system was not possible. By the mid-1950s, both the United States and the Soviet Union were doing serious R&D on missile defense. In the United States this led to the development of the advanced Nike-X system, which had two interceptor missiles: the Spartan for exo-atmospheric interception, and the Sprint for close-in interception. McNamara opposed deployment on the grounds that the Soviet Union could defeat the system, at a lesser cost, by increasing the number of warheads or adopting countermeasures of different kinds. As a result, the deployment of missile defenses would stimulate the development of offensive forces on the other side. McNamara took the view that it would be impossible to reduce offensive forces unless ABM systems were limited in some way. The Joint Chiefs of Staff favored deployment of a system to defend twenty-five cities. Lyndon Johnson was under pressure to do something: in January 1967 he asked for contingency funds to be allocated for use if there was no agreement with the Soviet Union to limit ABM.[50]

Soviet work on ABM was even more intense: in March 1961 a Soviet interceptor missile destroyed the warhead of an SS-4 MRBM in flight.[51] There was a strong belief in the Soviet technical and military communities that a solution could be found to the problem of missile defense. In October Malinovskii told the Twenty-second Party Congress that "the problem of destroying rockets in flight has been successfully solved."[52] A start was made under Khrushchev on an ABM system around Moscow, and Khrushchev approved a proposal for a nationwide system. This latter project was abandoned when Khrushchev was removed from office in 1964, but in 1965 the Defense Council accepted a new proposal for a nationwide system known as *Avrora*. By the summer of 1967 the design for this system was ready.[53]

At just this point, in June 1967, an unexpected opportunity arose to discuss ABM limits when the Soviet premier, Aleksei Kosygin, met President Johnson at Glassboro, New Jersey. McNamara tried to persuade Kosygin that a freeze on ABM deployment was essential if the arms race in offensive systems was to be restrained. Kosygin did not share this view. He had said some months earlier in London that "a defensive system which prevents attack is not a cause of the arms race," and he had not changed his view.[54] The conceptual gap was wide and significant.

Three months later, in September, two key events took place. The first was that an interagency committee in Moscow, which had been set up to review the design of the *Avrora* ABM system, concluded that it would not work and that, at the current stage of science and technology, defense against a massed attack was impossible. The Military-Industrial Commission confirmed this assessment in the following month and canceled the project.[55] Soviet optimism about the effectiveness of ABM systems had waned in the face of MIRV technology and countermeasures. This conclusion was not made public, and there is no evidence that U.S. intelligence was aware of it.

The second event in September was a speech McNamara gave in San Francisco in which he laid out all the reasons why ABM did not make sense and then, at the end, announced the deployment of a thin ABM system ("Sentinel") to protect American cities against a future threat from China.[56] This decision led in the United States to an intense public debate about ABM. In the Soviet Union "complete uncertainty" reigned after the cancelation of the *Avrora* project in October 1967; there was no consensus on how to move forward.[57] McNamara's speech contributed to the uncertainty, for it persuaded some influential Soviet weapons scientists that the United States must have found a way of dealing with exo-atmospheric target discrimination—a fundamental problem in missile defense.[58] Early in 1970, however, Dmitrii Ustinov, the Central Committee secretary in charge of the defense sector, convened a meeting of the key ABM people. This concluded that an effective ABM system could not be created in the near future. A serious R&D program should be maintained with limited upgrading of the Moscow system.[59] By contemporary Soviet estimates, the Moscow system at the time could intercept one simple ICBM and 6 to 8 single-warhead MRBMs. It could not intercept even one Minuteman III.[60]

SALT

Ustinov's ABM meeting in early 1970 took place after the first, preliminary round of the Strategic Arms Limitation Talks (SALT). The United States had proposed the idea of limits on strategic arms in 1964, but it was only in November 1969 that negotiations began, after many delays. They ended in May 1972 with the signing of the ABM Treaty and the Interim Agreement on offensive missiles.

The initial exploratory round of talks had proved "exceptionally useful," in the words of V. S. Semenov, the chief Soviet negotiator. It had become clear, he wrote in his memoirs, that ABM systems would have to be severely limited if the arms race in strategic offensive weapons were to be brought under control.[61] Ustinov's ABM meeting in January 1970 had concluded that it made no sense to press ahead with an ineffective ABM system, but that it did make sense to keep the Moscow system and engage in an active R&D program. It also made sense to negotiate a treaty that would ensure that American ABM deployments were limited too. These conclusions laid the basis for the Soviet position on the ABM Treaty, just as the decisions taken at the Crimean meeting of the Defense Council in the summer of 1969 laid the basis for the Soviet position in negotiating limits on offensive systems.

In May 1972 Nixon and Brezhnev signed the ABM Treaty, which imposed severe limits on the deployment of ABM systems. Those limits were strengthened two years later, and in fact neither side built what it was allowed to build under the terms of the treaty. The Interim Agreement on offensive missiles was much less satisfactory. It set limits on the number of launchers but not on the number of warheads each side could deploy. SALT was a very mixed result.

It showed that strategic arms control was possible, but it left the way open to further intense competition in offensive systems.

Assessment

In the years from 1955 to 1972, the United States and then the Soviet Union built up very large nuclear forces capable of inflicting death and destruction on a massive scale. They also began to engage in a dialogue about managing their nuclear relationship and took the first faltering steps toward creating institutions—in this case arms control—for that purpose. Brodie was right to say that deterrence was more important than preparing for war fighting, and by the end of the 1960s both the United States and the Soviet Union had adopted policies that created a relationship of mutual assured destruction. But neither side adopted a policy of assured destruction alone, for they both developed and deployed strategic nuclear weapons capable of destroying at least some part of the retaliatory forces of the other side.

It is no surprise that the Soviet Union paid attention to U.S. thinking about nuclear weapons and military strategy. What perhaps *is* surprising is the strong influence that the ideas coming from McNamara's Pentagon had on Soviet thinking about nuclear weapons and military strategy. That may be because the Soviet Union faced the same questions as the United States, but a little bit later: What are strategic nuclear forces for? How much is enough? In the 1960s there were two highly contentious issues in Soviet military strategy: How important was it to have secure retaliatory forces? And should there be limits on ABM defenses? In both of these disputes, arguments advanced by the McNamara Pentagon played a role. "Our theoreticians were armed with McNamara's arguments," according to Boris Chertok, a leading rocket designer. "Our military had to pay heed to McNamara's conception."[62] It is not only the spread of science and technology that plays an important role in nuclear history but the diffusion of ideas and concepts as well. Soviet military strategy was in some respects a reflection of American thinking. Diffusion does not always take place, however. China has not built up its strategic nuclear forces in the way in which the United States and the Soviet Union did during the Cold War. Avery Goldstein's discussion in chapter 13 tracks the different path China has followed in creating strategic nuclear forces.

This chapter has focused on the debates about strategic weapons policy in the military and technical communities. What was the relationship between those debates and the discussions between Soviet and American scientists in Pugwash and other nongovernmental fora? In their well-informed book, *The Big Five*, Aleksandr Savelyev and Nikolai Detinov offer two different answers. First, they discount the role of American ideas, arguing that it was the Soviet leaders' recognition that, in spite of earlier hopes, an effective ABM defense could not be created that made them willing to sign the ABM Treaty. Second, they argue—more persuasively to my mind—that it was the combination of American arguments and Soviet technical assessments that led them to the treaty.[63]

M. V. Keldysh, president of the Soviet Academy of Sciences from 1961 to 1975, was a key point of contact between the Pugwash channel and the debates and controversies discussed in this chapter. He was a mathematician who had played a key role in the nuclear, missile, and space programs, and he was also a close adviser to Ustinov. He did not himself attend Pugwash meetings, but M. D. Millionshchikov, head of the Soviet Pugwash Committee in those years, was vice president of the academy and thus in close contact with Keldysh. Keldysh spoke at the August 1969 Defense Council meeting to make the point that the disagreement over which missile designs to choose was not so much about technology but at heart a disagreement about doctrine. One designer assumed that the missiles would have left their silos by the time the attacking warheads arrived; the other wanted to provide the capability to retaliate after an attack. Keldysh backed the latter.[64]

By the late 1960s the Soviet image of a future war, as presented by Sokolovskii and Malinovskii in the early 1960s, had changed in fundamental ways. First, there was a greater understanding of just how destructive a nuclear war would be, which called into question the meaning of victory in such a war. Second, Sokolovskii had written in 1960 that, unless the problem of missile defense was solved, one could not count on achieving the goals of the war. During the 1960s it became clear that there was no prospect of solving it, at least for the time being. Third, as the Soviet Union built up an assured retaliatory force, it had less need to rely on preemption. "From the end of the 1960s," according to an authoritative history of Russian military strategy, "methods of delivering preemptive strikes against the adversary ceased to be considered in military-strategic drafts and plans."[65] Military planners began to show increasing interest in launch on warning. Fourth, military planners no longer assumed that a general war would begin with massed missile strikes; they developed the idea of a war in stages, with nuclear weapons brought into use after a conventional stage.[66]

Several sources indicate that in 1969 the Soviet Union adopted, as part of its military doctrine, the principle that military plans and preparations should be based on the idea that the Soviet Union would not be the first to use nuclear weapons.[67] It is likely that this decision was made in connection with the Defense Council meeting in the summer of 1969. On October 10, 1969, in a speech summing up a major military exercise, Marshal A. A. Grechko, the minister of defense, said it was essential to take both nuclear war and nonnuclear war into account. "In this respect," he said, "we are guided by the principle, which our party adheres to, not to be the first to use nuclear weapons. But that does not mean," he added, "that in a given military-political situation, when the enemy has revealed his aggressive intentions, we would not use our might to frustrate the threat of an attack."[68]

Conclusion

This sketchy outline of the U.S.-Soviet strategic arms competition from the 1950s to the 1970s raises issues for reflection. What was the impact of Hiroshima on Soviet policy? The legacies of Hiroshima endure, but they are shaped by the way in which the dropping of the atomic bomb was first experienced. The attainment of strategic nuclear parity, as symbolized by the SALT agreements, was an important achievement in the eyes of the Soviet leaders. It could be seen as righting the balance of power that the bomb had upset at the end of World War II. It gave to the Soviet Union the place in world politics that it believed it deserved above all by virtue of its role in defeating Nazi Germany.

In making the case for the ABM Treaty, Brezhnev warned the Central Committee, just before Nixon's visit in May 1972, that if the United States created a "more or less reliable" ABM system covering a large part of the country, it "would once again restore to itself the strategic invulnerability it lost when we created intercontinental missiles. The effectiveness of our retaliatory nuclear strike in the event of an attack by the U.S. would be seriously weakened." There could be no doubt, he continued, "that a return to such a position would encourage the growth of aggression and adventurism in American foreign policy toward socialist countries and liberation movements in the world."[69]

How relevant was the legacy of Hiroshima once thermonuclear weapons were developed? The U.S. military estimated in 1949 that an atomic air offensive against the Soviet Union would result in 2.7 million Soviet deaths. In 1955 the estimate was 60 million deaths in the Soviet Union and its allied countries. If the first Strategic Integrated Operational Plan had been implemented in 1961, the estimated number of immediate deaths in the Soviet Union and China was judged likely to be 285 million.[70] Six months later, it was judged, that number would reach 325 million, as a result of deaths from initial injuries and radioactive fallout. Another 300 million might die from fallout in Europe and in countries close to the Soviet Union. Daniel Ellsberg, who was then a senior consultant to the government and involved in drafting the SIOP, later wrote: "the total death toll as calculated by the Joint Chiefs, from a U.S. first strike aimed primarily at the Soviet Union, its Warsaw Pact satellites, and China, would be roughly six hundred million dead. A hundred Holocausts."[71]

Even in the face of such unimaginable numbers (which do not include estimates of those who would be killed by Soviet nuclear weapons), Hiroshima has provided a kind of benchmark. The effects of the bomb were embodied in photographs of death and destruction, in medical studies of the effects of radiation, and above all in the experience of the survivors. The gulf between the Hiroshima bomb, whose effects we can observe, and thermonuclear war, whose effects we can only try to calculate, in an odd way enhances our understanding of how terrible a nuclear war might be.

The early history of nuclear weapons has been described as both exciting and repellent: a race to create the bomb, and then its use on Hiroshima and Nagasaki. In the mid-1960s Andrei Sakharov, the nuclear weapons designer who became a campaigner for human rights in the Soviet Union, took part in conferences on military strategy where nuclear strikes were discussed. The "unthinkable and monstrous" was transformed into "a subject for detailed examination and calculation," he wrote. "It became *a part of daily existence*—still imagined, but already seen as something possible."[72] It may seem strange that Sakharov, who had taken part in the design of the most powerful bomb ever built, should have had this reaction to discussions of military strategy. And yet it is hard to look at doctrines and plans for the use of nuclear weapons without having a similar reaction. Planning and preparing for thermonuclear war are more disturbing to think about than the development of weapons (exciting technological races) or even the nuclear crises over Berlin and Cuba (we know how they ended). Doctrines and plans for the use of thermonuclear weapons bring to the fore the issue of intention. What does it say about our societies that in order to be secure we have felt the need to build immensely destructive weapons, create vehicles capable of delivering them to any point in the world, select targets, train troops to launch the weapons, and finally convince our adversaries (and ourselves) that we are prepared to implement strategies that would make Hiroshima look like a picnic?

6

The Evolution of Japanese Politics and Diplomacy under the Long Shadows of Hiroshima and Nagasaki, 1974–1991

Takuya Sasaki

WHEN THE SURRENDER OF JAPAN was announced on August 15 and formally signed on September 2, 1945, on the USS *Missouri*, bringing the hostilities of World War II to an end, the homeland of Japan lay in ruins. Japan had lost nearly three million people and a third of its national wealth. More than sixty major cities, which had been subjected to an extensive strategic bombing campaign efficiently executed by the United States, had been heavily damaged or completely destroyed; Japan's economy was in a complete shambles, and the specter of mass starvation loomed large. The atomic bombings of Hiroshima and Nagasaki, as well as Soviet entry into the war against Japan, capped three and a half years of hostilities that Japan had begun by attacking Pearl Harbor. Japan was made to pay dearly for its egregious misdeeds. The bitter wartime experience and its memory significantly shaped the trajectory of postwar Japan both at home and abroad.

This chapter provides a critical overview of the evolution of Japanese internal politics and diplomacy under the shadows of Hiroshima and Nagasaki in the latter half of the Cold War years. It places emphasis on the analyses of major policy makers and discusses how and in what ways they interacted with the so-called peace constitution, the Yoshida Doctrine, and the U.S.-Japan security system in the development of Japanese domestic politics and foreign policy in this critical period.

The Institutionalization of the Yoshida Doctrine

Probably no other politician was more responsible for concluding the 1951 U.S.-Japan Security Pact and the San Francisco Peace Treaty that terminated the Allied Occupation of Japan than Yoshida Shigeru. Twice prime minister (from 1946 to 1947 and 1948 to 1954), Yoshida formulated the basics of postwar Japanese foreign and defense policy by pursuing an economic recovery while relying on U.S. military guarantees for its security. Scholars in the field have termed Yoshida's policy of pro–U.S., modest rearmament and economic development the Yoshida Doctrine.[1]

Although Article 9 of the Japanese Constitution renounced war as an instrument of solving international conflict, Yoshida reinterpreted it in a way to allow Japan to maintain defense forces strictly for its own protection. His reinterpretation was made in the wake of the Korean War and the American decision to rearm Japan. General Douglas MacArthur, supreme commander for the Allied Powers in Japan, who had been instrumental in the adoption of Article 9 in 1947, directed Yoshida in July 1950 to form the National Police Reserve, which ultimately became the Self-Defense Forces (SDF) four years later. Yoshida accepted the directive, although he succeeded in limiting the Japanese rearmament program, deflecting the repeated requests for an overall rearmament program by John Foster Dulles, President Harry S. Truman's special envoy in charge of the Japanese peace settlement. In refusing Dulles's proposal, Yoshida cited Article 9, the devastated Japanese economy, and suspicion in the region over a possible revival of Japanese militarism.

Yoshida was able to rely on his party's parliamentary majority to pass the San Francisco Peace Treaty and the U.S.-Japan Security Pact through the Diet by comfortable margins. The Japanese public, albeit without evident enthusiasm, accepted his decisions, which they regarded as both realistic and desirable in the context of the domestic and international circumstances of the time. They were wary of an expensive rearmament program and anxious to rebuild their own economic lives, having gone through the painful and calamitous wartime years. A deep sense of pacifism and an aversion to anything that smacked of militarism prevailed in the population at large, and Yoshida constantly kept the pacifistic leanings of his constituency in mind.

Internationally, the robust security system that the United States constructed in the Asia-Pacific region worked well for Yoshida's program. With the coming of the Cold War in Asia and the outbreak of the Korean War, the United States embarked on a policy of containment of Soviet and Chinese communism, concluding a number of security pacts with anticommunist allies in the region and providing these nations with enormous military and economic aid. Japan, a former enemy, was the major beneficiary in this altered geopolitical landscape. Yoshida correctly expected that Japan would be able, under the auspices of the United States, to proceed with a domestic and foreign policy focused on the economy without allocating major resources to a defense program. These international and domestic circumstances were decisive in the formulation of the Yoshida Doctrine.

With the encouragement and blessing of the United States, the Liberal Democratic Party (LDP) was established in 1955 after Yoshida stepped down as prime minister, and the Yoshida Doctrine continued to constitute a conceptual framework for his successors in the LDP as they implemented Japanese national security policy. Importantly, Yoshida left behind his own faction in the LDP, a group often called the "Yoshida School," which produced future prime ministers like Ikeda Hayato and Satō Eisaku, both of whom were Yoshida's protégés.[2]

Yoshida's archrival was Kishi Nobusuke, a former member of General Tōjō Hideki's cabinet and a Class-A war crimes suspect. Kishi, who was eventually released without indictment as a result of the beginning of the Cold War in Asia, harbored simmering dissatisfaction with the foreign policy launched by Yoshida but was realistic enough to recognize the enormity of American power and to embrace Yoshida's concept when he came to power in 1957. President Dwight Eisenhower and his secretary of state John Foster Dulles warmly welcomed Kishi's staunch anticommunist political outlook and agreed to his proposal to revise the 1951 security pact on more equal terms. By 1960 Kishi had successfully amended the pact by clarifying the U.S. defense commitment to Japan, introducing a system of prior consultation regarding any significant changes to the deployment and equipment of U.S. military forces in Japan, and stipulating the treaty term (ten years). The new pact also affirmed, like the North Atlantic Treaty, the principles of democracy, individual liberty, and the rule of law as well as the promotion of economic stability and the well-being of the two nations.

Thus the 1960 security pact, by addressing most Japanese grievances against the 1951 pact, contributed immensely to a long-term stable political and security relationship. Ironically for Kishi, then, although his ultimate goal was to institute a new, independent constitution and he regarded the pact revision as the first step toward achieving that goal, the new pact convinced the Japanese people of the appropriateness of focusing on economic policy and security cooperation with the United States and succeeded in garnering support for the Yoshida Doctrine at home. In the 1960s Kishi's successors, Prime Ministers Ikeda (who served from 1960 to 1964) and Satō (who served from 1964 to 1972), two prominent members of the "Yoshida School," further promoted the concept of Japan as a lightly armed nation focused on its economy.[3]

The Yoshida Doctrine and the Nuclear Option

While in office, Yoshida had been cautious about discussing the issue of Japan's potential possession of nuclear weapons. However, in mid-1962, while in retirement from political life, he stated that Japan should not rule out such a possibility. Ikeda, whose constituency was a district of the Hiroshima Prefecture, startled his trusted aide by asserting in 1958 that "Japan has to go nuclear" for self-protection. Satō too told Ambassador Edwin Reischauer that following the Chinese nuclear test in the fall of 1964, it would be "only common sense" for Japan to arm itself with nuclear weapons. Satō even admitted in 1969 that of the three nonnuclear principles he proposed in 1967—that Japan would not (1) possess, (2) manufacture, or (3) permit the introduction of nuclear weapons into the country—the third was a "mistake." He also secretly agreed with President Richard Nixon in the Okinawa reversion treaty of 1971 that the United States could reserve the right to station nuclear weapons on Okinawa in case of emergency. The first Defense Agency White Paper published in 1970 under Nakasone Yasuhiro's directorship stated that although Japan was "jurisprudentially" allowed to possess a small-scale nuclear bomb, it did not do so as a matter of policy.[4]

The ambivalence among a number of powerful conservative politicians toward nuclear weapons is partly explained by the fact that it took six years to ratify the Nuclear Nonproliferation Treaty (NPT) in spite of the fact that the Japanese government had signed it in 1970. Powerful national antinuclear organizations, demanding strict enforcement of the three nonnuclear principles, contended that the NPT did not squarely address prospects for realizing a world without nuclear weapons, while conservative legislators in the LDP complained that by ratifying the treaty Japan would opt out of arming itself with nuclear weapons and argued that the country should not give up the nuclear card. According to a Japanese diplomat who was involved in the NPT negotiations, "As far as the substance is concerned, there is no more unequal treaty for Japan than the NPT."[5]

Furthermore, both the announcement of the Nixon Doctrine indicating U.S. strategic retrenchment in Asia and the Nixon administration's unilateral policy change toward China (without first consulting Japan) cautioned Tokyo against early ratification of the NPT. The apparent U.S. policy shift in Asia made the Japanese government uneasy over the prospect of a U.S. nuclear umbrella that might extend to allies in the region.[6]

The Nixon administration, skeptical of the effectiveness of the NPT in the first place, did not press Japan. While the State Department from time to time called for speedy Japanese ratification of the treaty, President Nixon and his national security adviser, Henry Kissinger, were at best lukewarm about its prospects. When, in a meeting with Nixon in January 1972, Satō inquired about Nixon's view on the timing of ratification, Nixon replied that Japan could take its time. Kissinger also rejected the State Department's requests in 1972 to encourage Japan to sign the treaty. He was ambivalent about Japan's development of nuclear weapons. On the one hand, he advised Nixon to emphasize to the Chinese leadership in early 1972 that "we oppose [a] nuclear Japan" and urged him to explain the American position in opposing Japan's remilitarization. On the other hand, Kissinger repeatedly predicted that Japan's possession of nuclear weapons was inevitable. He told the Australian ambassador in August 1974 that Japan had the ability to build a number of nuclear bombs even without nuclear tests. Secretary of Defense Melvin Laird, in a meeting in Tokyo on July 8, 1971 (exactly when Kissinger was conducting his secret mission in Beijing), even hinted to his Japanese counterpart that Japan might arm itself with nuclear weapons.[7]

Retired admiral Gene La Rocque's testimony in Senate hearings in October 1974 further complicated matters. La Rocque testified that U.S. warships armed with nuclear weapons would not unload them before entering a Japanese port. The remark created a political uproar in Japan as the public viewed it as a violation of the third of Satō's nonnuclear principles. The statement came at an awkward time, just before President Gerald Ford was scheduled to visit Japan in November, the first visit by a sitting American president, and just as the Nobel Committee announced that the Peace Prize was to be awarded to Satō for his pledge of a nonnuclear Japan.

Recently declassified Japanese diplomatic documents illustrate that high-ranking officials in the Foreign Ministry seriously considered modifying the three nonnuclear principles in a way that would allow temporary transit of nuclear warships in Japan. Matsunaga Nobuo, director of the Treaties Bureau and later undersecretary and ambassador to the United States, was gravely concerned that if the La Rocque statement were left to run its course, it would cause popular distrust of government and create domestic political turmoil. Matsunaga proposed an "appropriate measure immediately," to which Undersecretary Tōgō Fumihiko agreed. Nonetheless, Prime Minister Tanaka Kakuei (who was on the verge of resigning owing to his involvement in a financial scandal) and Foreign Minister Ōhira Masayoshi rejected the proposal.

When, some years later, former ambassador Reischauer made a claim similar to that of La Rocque, the Foreign Ministry again considered the same step. The Suzuki Zenkō administration, concerned over possible political turmoil, dismissed the idea. On these occasions, the Japanese government steadfastly denied the credibility of these statements while the U.S. government reiterated the policy to "neither confirm nor deny" (NCND) the location of nuclear weapons. The Japanese public had little faith in the government's explanation:

a poll conducted by the *Asahi shimbun* in the summer of 1975 demonstrated that 67 percent believed the third principle was not being enforced effectively (ten years later, the figure rose to 73 percent). Still, the Japanese public showed little interest in pursuing the issue.[8]

Tokyo's ratification of the NPT was driven by a number of factors, including West Germany's ratification of it, India's nuclear detonation in 1974 (which raised the specter of nuclear proliferation), the International Atomic Energy Agency's guarantee that Japan would be subject to the same safeguard inspection system regarding the civilian use as the European Atomic Energy Community, the First Review Conference of the NPT scheduled to be held in 1975, and the U.S. government's renewed nuclear commitment to Japan. A joint press announcement in August 1975 by President Ford and Prime Minister Miki Takeo confirmed that "they recognized that the U.S. nuclear deterrent is an important contribution to the security of Japan. In this connection, the President reassured the Prime Minister that the United States would continue to abide by its defense commitment to Japan under the Treaty of Mutual Cooperation and Security in the event of armed attack against Japan, whether by nuclear or conventional forces." This was the first public assurance made by a U.S. president regarding the nuclear umbrella over Japan.[9]

While the Japanese government came to be aware of South Korea's clandestine nuclear weapons program probably in late 1975, apparently it did not affect the NPT ratification process, which had already been set in motion; Diet deliberations on the ratification had started in the spring of 1975 and concluded a year later.[10] (On fundamentally contrasting developments that the NPT triggered among U.S. major allies in Latin America, see chapter 10 in this volume by Matias Spektor.)

In addition to ratifying the NPT in 1976, Prime Minister Miki, a center-left politician in the LDP, made four significant defense policy decisions. First, his administration determined in a cabinet meeting that Japan would limit its defense budget to approximately 1 percent of the country's GNP "in the interim period." The decision, reflective of a deep sense of pacifism among the general public, as well as an aversion to any revival of militarism, also aimed to dispel the suspicion in the region that Japan might reemerge as a military power. Second, the Miki administration banned Japan's export of arms to any foreign nation, thus strengthening the principle (laid down by Satō a few years before) of banning arms exports to communist nations and to nations actively participating in conflicts. Third, Miki directed his defense officials to start consultations with the U.S. Defense Department on defense cooperation in the event of an armed attack against Japan, which led to the formulation of the U.S.-Japan Defense Guidelines of 1978. Last, in 1975 Tokyo became an original member in the Nuclear Suppliers' Group (NSG), a brainchild of Kissinger, in order to control the international transfer of nuclear-related materials and technology.[11]

By the mid-1970s the consensus view was that Japan's defense policy should be "nonnuclear and exclusively defense-oriented" (*hikaku senshu bōei*). The public, with memories of Hiroshima and Nagasaki still fresh, firmly rejected Japan's development of nuclear weapons while maintaining steady support for the three nonnuclear principles and a defense budget that was frozen at current levels. At the same time, as political scientist Yoshida Shingo points out, 1975 was a pivotal year, with public polls showing a marked decline of strict antimilitarism and steady support for the SDF and the U.S.-Japan Security Pact.

A memorandum drafted in the summer of 1976 by Undersecretary of the Defense Agency Kubo Takuya, an influential official in the formulation of defense planning in the 1970s, illustrated the dominant view in Japan's defense establishment. He wrote:

> As long as Japan remains a vital ally for the U.S., we have no doubt whatsoever regarding the reliability of the U.S. nuclear umbrella. Still, some theoretical questions can be raised. First, even if we are assured many times by the U.S. about the reliability of U.S. nuclear commitment, some wonder that the U.S. ever dare resort to nuclear retaliation for an ally if it faces risk of having nuclear attack upon New York or Washington, thus facing the danger of suffering millions of residents' deaths. Second, it is meaningless for Japan that the U.S. resorts to nuclear retaliation after Japan is annihilated by nuclear attack. Nevertheless, these questions are premised in an extreme situation where strategic nuclear weapons are employed massively.... Since an adversary will have to consider a number of nuclear options that the U.S. may take, it is be extremely unlikely to initiate a nuclear challenge against the U.S.[12]

The Expansion of Japan's Diplomatic Horizon

Japan, at the invitation of France and West Germany, joined in an economic summit of the G-6 (later the G-7) in 1975. In the late 1970s the position of Japan as a major member of the "Western bloc" had become widely recognized. Japan, which had become the third largest economy by the end of the 1960s, enjoyed a remarkable economic record, with annual GDP growth of 5 percent in the 1970s despite a temporary setback caused by the 1973 oil shock. This figure was higher than that of any other advanced nation. A noted Japan scholar at Harvard, Ezra Vogel, published a book titled *Japan as Number 1: Lessons for America* in 1979. The Japanese translation sold more than seven million copies, becoming an instant best seller. Vogel praised the Japanese economic and social system for the economic success it had produced, thereby flattering Japanese who were proud of their extraordinary economic progress. The book was so popular in Japan that Vogel became "a renowned public figure and eagerly sought-after speaker among Japanese scholars, government officials, and business leaders."[13]

Prime Minister Fukuda Takeo, who had inherited the Kishi faction in the LDP, made several foreign policy decisions that were instrumental in expanding the Japanese diplomatic horizon. First, Fukuda pledged in the so-called Fukuda Doctrine in 1977 that Japan would never become a major military power and would contribute to peace and stability in Southeast Asia through economic assistance. The announcement was generally welcomed in the region, helping to promote reconciliation between Japan and the nations of Southeast Asia, which had suffered from Japan's cruel occupation in the Pacific War.

Second, Fukuda concluded a Treaty of Peace and Friendship with China in August 1978, despite vehement Soviet opposition. President Jimmy Carter's national security adviser, Zbigniew Brzezinski, had dropped by Tokyo in May 1978 on his way home from Beijing, prodding Fukuda to accelerate the conclusion. With the formal establishment of U.S.-Chinese diplomatic relations the following year, an informal entente of the United States, Japan, and China was formed against the Soviet Union, one of the most important events in determining the course of the Cold War in Asia. Third, Fukuda opposed President Carter's plan to withdraw U.S. ground troops from South Korea, a military presence that was historically linked to Japan's security. With the apparently deteriorating international standing of the United States in the Horn of Africa, Nicaragua, and Iran, Carter relented and decided to cease the withdrawal by the summer of 1979.

Fourth, Fukuda won Carter's consent for Japan to operate a facility at Tokai Mura where it could reprocess U.S.-supplied reactor fuel. Initially Carter opposed Fukuda's proposal, having argued against the spread of nuclear weapons in the presidential campaign and having signed Presidential Directive 8: "U.S. non-proliferation policy shall be directed at preventing the development and use of sensitive nuclear power technologies which involve direct access to plutonium, highly enriched uranium, or other weapons useable material in non-nuclear weapons states, *and* at minimizing the global accumulation of these materialism." Nonetheless, Carter grudgingly accepted the Japanese position by the summer of 1977, albeit with some reservations; Ambassador Mike Mansfield and Brzezinski had stressed the importance of ties with an ally in Asia, persuading the president to concur with the compromise.[14]

Japan's proactive foreign policy was accelerated under Ōhira Masayoshi's premiership. Ōhira, a devout Christian, quickly formed a close personal bond with Carter, with whom he had been acquainted since the mid-1970s. Entering office in December 1978, Ōhira organized groups of academics and scholars and charged them with studying important domestic and foreign issues. Kōsaka Masataka of Kyoto University, an influential academic figure in foreign and defense policy, chaired the group in charge of national security. He explained in the report written by his group that

> one of the most basic facts of the changing international situation in the 1970s is the end of clear American predominance in the military and economic fields.... The era was over when we could depend on the international system led by the U.S., whether it might be of military security or security of a political-diplomatic and economic nature. Japan, as a major power in the Free World, will have to contribute to the maintenance and administration of the international system. In summary, the situation has changed from that of Pax Americana to that of Peace through Responsibility Sharing.

According to Kōsaka, the era of Japan as "a free rider" in international affairs, guaranteed by a U.S. security and economic umbrella, had come to an end; Japan would need to play a more active role commensurate with its economic strength to maintain the postwar international system that had been so beneficial to Japan's striking development.[15]

Ōhira started to extend Japan's Official Development Assistance (ODA) to China in 1979 as a sort of compensation to China, which had abandoned its demands for war reparations from Japan in its normalization of diplomatic relations in 1972, as well as to draw China closer to the Western bloc by assisting Deng Xiaoping's policy of economic modernization. Japan's ODA to China was the first of its kind made by any member of the Western bloc. The total amount of aid provided by Japan to China from 1979 to 1995 amounted to almost $10 billion, the largest amount of any major Western bloc nation. The second largest aid package came from West Germany, which provided $2.2 billion.

One of Ōhira's academic groups proposed that Japan should actively promote a Pan-Pacific community, aiming for Asian-Pacific economic integration. The Ōhira administration, concerned that Tokyo's unilateral proposal might raise the specter of the Greater East Asian Co-prosperity Sphere, asked for Australian cooperation. With Australian agreement, Japan initiated the first meeting of a Pacific Community, held in Canberra in 1979, which led to the creation of Asia Pacific Economic Cooperation (APEC) ten years later.

Ōhira was also active in furthering the U.S.-Japan relationship. He dared to refer to the bilateral relationship as an "alliance" in a welcoming ceremony held at the White House in 1979. This marked the first time a Japanese prime minister had ever used the term in this context. Prime ministers had hitherto strictly avoided the term, which implied active military cooperation with the United States

While the Carter administration was preoccupied with the Iranian hostage crisis and the Soviet invasion of Afghanistan from 1979 to 1980, Ōhira, calling on the Japanese people to stand shoulder to shoulder with the United States in these international crises, joined the economic sanctions led by the United States against Iran and the Soviet Union and agreed to boycott the Summer Olympic Games in Moscow in 1980. The Japanese government also steadily increased its defense budget and proceeded to extend "strategic" aid to Pakistan, Turkey, and Thailand, countries that were viewed as strategically important to the West. The U.S. government, increasingly frustrated with the mounting trade deficit with Japan, welcomed these steps.[16]

Following the Soviet invasion of Afghanistan at the end of 1979, and in the face of an apparently growing Soviet military menace, right-wing scholars and intellectuals published numerous articles and books warning that the Soviet Union might invade Hokkaido as early as 1985. Of these pundits, Shimizu Ikutarō, a prominent sociologist and social critic, was the most sensational. He contended that Japan should renounce the pacifist constitution and become militarily independent by increasing defense spending to 3 percent of GDP while considering the nuclear option. His book became an instant best seller as Shimizu had been a well-known intellectual in postwar Japan. However, the book was received more with amusement and even scorn than with seriousness since the author, once an ardent supporter of Japan's "peace constitution" and a vocal opponent of the U.S-Japan Security Pact, now appeared to have converted to a traditional militarist stance.[17]

Toward the U.S.-Japan Alliance

Nakasone Yasuhiro assumed the role of prime minister in November 1982 after his predecessor, Suzuki Zenkō, stumbled over alliance diplomacy with the United States. Suzuki, who became prime minister following Ōhira's untimely death, had failed to deal effectively with rising demands made on Japan by the Ronald Reagan administration in the economic and defense fields.

Nakasone had, since his election to the Diet in 1947 at the age of twenty-eight, been known as a proponent of revising the constitution and developing an independent defense policy. He had voted for the San Francisco Peace Treaty but abstained from voting on the U.S.-Japan Security Pact, citing what he perceived as the pact's infringement on Japanese independence. Although he had joined the LDP at its formation in 1955, he had been one of the "young officers" highly critical of Yoshida's foreign and defense policy. He once called Yoshida "an opportunist" and confessed that he detested "his slyness... his self-protection." He derisively described Yoshida's concept of national security as "one-nation pacifism" (*ikkoku heiwashugi*).

Nakasone was one of the prominent Japanese political leaders interested in the issue of nuclear power. In the early 1950s he was invited to attend a Harvard international seminar organized by an assistant professor named Henry Kissinger. While in the United States, Nakasone grew interested in the peaceful use of atomic power; returning home, he sponsored legislation with fellow Diet members that sought to introduce U.S. nuclear technology into Japan in order to build nuclear power plants.

He remembered that Prime Minister Ikeda had casually confessed to him at one point that "Japan cannot conduct international politics without strengthening its military and developing a strong army. We may need an atomic bomb depending on the international situation." Ikeda apparently made this comment after he returned to Japan from a visit to Western Europe in the fall of 1962, where he was allegedly scoffed at by President Charles de Gaulle as "a transistor radio salesman." As director of the Defense Agency in the early 1970s, Nakasone secretly ordered experts to study the cost in time and money of building a nuclear bomb. They concluded that Japan would be able to construct a bomb within five years at a cost of $500 million, the major problem being that no appropriate site for a nuclear blast was available in territory governed by Japan. Nakasone quietly shelved the report.[18]

Nakasone was not, however, an advocate of Japan's possessing nuclear weapons. During his official visit to Washington, DC, in 1970, he explained in a National Press Club speech that "as long as the U.S.-Japan security system works effectively towards any possible nuclear threat against Japan, there will be absolutely no possibility of arming Japan with nuclear weapons," and he explicitly told his counterpart, Melvin Laird, that "Japan should make clear its intention of not going nuclear in order to avoid an international misunderstanding and to value national consensus." With his steady political rise in the LDP and government, Nakasone grew moderate in his outlook on defense and foreign policy, recognizing the crucial importance of the U.S.-Japan Security Pact in maintaining peace and stability in the region and knowing that a majority of voters remained reluctant to revise Article 9 and its renunciation of war. He too came around to the fundamentals of the Yoshida Doctrine, although he never gave up of his lifelong ambition of adopting a new constitution.[19]

Nakasone turned out to be a staunch pro-U.S. prime minister. He recognized that Japan, as a major economic powerhouse, had to assume an appropriate international burden within the limits of the constitution and within the framework of the security pact with the United States. He lifted the self-imposed principle of banning arms exports to the United States and joined the Strategic Defense Initiative (SDI) research program in 1986. He also decided to increase Japan's defense budget to over 1 percent of GDP in 1987, an important step in augmenting Japan's defense policy.

Nakasone was instrumental in issuing a political communiqué during the Williamsburg G-7 Summit meeting in 1983. Supporting a proposal made by Reagan, he insisted that only a global zero option would eliminate all the Soviet Union's SS-20 missiles and remove the danger of transferring those missiles from the European theater to the Asian mainland. Nakasone emphasized to the leaders that "I should be silent as Japan is not a member of NATO and we have a Peace Constitution and three nonnuclear principles. Still I dare support President Reagan's proposal since I believe that we have to demonstrate the strength of Western solidarity so that we can bring the Soviets to the negotiating table." Secretary of State George Shultz concurred, recalling that "this was Nakasone's doing. It was a strong, bold, and important step for him to take."[20]

The Japanese public, while endorsing Nakasone's overall foreign policy, was uneasy about the increase of Japan's military role overseas and closer military cooperation with the United States. Nakasone was unable to overcome strong resistance from the powerful chief cabinet secretary Gotōda Masaharu, who had the backing of public opinion polls, regarding the SDF's dispatch to the Persian Gulf in 1987 to help clear Iranian mines.

Public opinion in the 1980s showed that approximately 60 percent of respondents supported the current level of the SDF, and almost 90 percent opposed the idea of Japan's possessing nuclear weapons. In response to the Reagan administration's large-scale military buildup and bellicose rhetoric against the USSR, a massive antinuclear movement formed in Japan, the largest and best-organized since the mid-1950s when the *Lucky Dragon* incident occurred. In that incident, a Japanese fishing vessel named *Lucky Dragon No. 5* and its crew were exposed to the radioactive fallout from an American test of its new hydrogen bomb near the Marshall Islands in 1954. (See chapter 9 of this volume by Wakana Mukai.) Almost thirty million people signed the antinuclear petition. Japan's rejection of nuclear weapons led to the declaration of nuclear-free zones by 1,067 local communities, including 7 prefectures and 400 cities, by 1987.[21]

When the Labor government of New Zealand adopted a national policy of strictly barring nuclear-armed American naval vessels from its ports in 1984, the U.S. government watched the development with great concern, obviously afraid of the repercussions it might have on Japan and other U.S. allies. Secretary of Defense Caspar Weinberger termed the policy "an attack on the alliance" and ended military cooperation with New Zealand, which had been part of an alliance treaty with the United States and Australia since 1951. Admiral William Crowe, commander-in-chief, United States Pacific Command (CINPAC), and later chairman of the Joint Chiefs of Staff, warned that "a number of other countries with nuclear sensitivities, notably Japan, Australia and our NATO allies, are watching closely how we handle the situation. Necessarily . . . our ultimate objective is unfettered port access while maintaining our NCND policy."[22]

In the Diet debates, Prime Minister Nakasone insisted that the case of New Zealand was different from that of Japan, repeating the mantra that Japan had a prior consultation formula with the United States regarding any introduction of nuclear-armed vessels into Japanese territory and, since the U.S. government had not raised the subject with the Japanese government, he believed that U.S. vessels had not carried nuclear weapons into Japanese territory.[23]

The End of the Cold War

In the heyday of the Cold War, the U.S. government had made efforts to separate economic from security considerations in conducting foreign policy toward Japan, a tacit assumption inherent in the Yoshida Doctrine. But with the rapid rise of Japan's economic power and the receding Soviet threat in the late 1980s, the boundary between the two began to blur. Japan's trade surplus with the United States in 1981 was $15.8 billion. This soared to $56.3 billion by 1987. While the surplus was somewhat reduced due to the Plaza Accord of 1985 (whereby the G-5 agreed to devalue the dollar against the yen and West German mark) and the Nakasone government took some major steps to open up the Japanese market in agricultural products, the amount still hovered around $50 billion. Japanese ambassador Matsunaga, who was in Washington in the late 1980s, recalled that he was forced to devote "85 percent of his time" as ambassador to dealing with trade issues. The 1980s saw a number of prominent U.S. journalists and politicians warning of the economic threat posed by Japan.

In March 1985, by a unanimous vote of ninety-two to zero, the U.S. Senate adopted a resolution that condemned Japan's "unfair" trade practices and called on the president to retaliate by curtailing Japanese imports. The following month, the *New York Times* ran an editorial titled "Japan-Bashers, on the March." Journalist Theodore White, who had witnessed the ceremony of Japan's surrender aboard the battleship *Missouri* on the September 2, 1945, wrote in the *New York Times Magazine* in the summer of 1985 that the Pacific War was still going on and that Japan was winning. Journalist and former presidential speechwriter James Fallows argued that the United States should "contain" Japan to deal with the huge trade deficit as it had contained Soviet expansion in the Cold War. Senator Paul Tsongas claimed that "the good news is that the Cold War is over. The bad news is that Germany and Japan won." A real estate developer named Donald Trump ran a full-page advertisement in several newspapers in September 1987 calling for the U.S. government to "stop paying to defend countries that can afford to defend themselves" and insisting that "Japan, Saudi Arabia, and others pay for the protection we extend as allies."[24]

A July 1989 poll indicated that 68 percent of Americans viewed the Japanese economic threat as the most serious foreign threat to the United States and only 22 percent viewed the Soviet military threat as similarly challenging. The U.S. Congress initiated the Omnibus Trade Bill of 1988 that urged the president to eliminate unfair trade practices under threat of unilateral retaliation. The primary target, of course, was Japan. Longtime Asia expert Michael Armacost published a memoir entitled *Friends or Rivals?* that detailed his four-year experience of acrimonious trade negotiations with Japan as ambassador to Tokyo from 1989 to 1993. The title suggested deep ambivalence prevailing among American policy makers toward Japan, a longtime ally in the region, in the aftermath of the Cold War.

The Japan threat theory was soon developed in popular fiction. Journalist George Friedman and his wife Meredith Lebard coauthored a book in 1991 called *The Coming of War with Japan*. The following year, best-selling author Michael Crichton published *Rising Sun*, warning about Japanese economic domination of the United States, and Tom Clancy's *Debt of Honor* soon followed.

Meanwhile, Sony purchased Columbia Pictures for $3.4 billion, Mitsubishi Estate purchased the New York landmark Rockefeller Center in 1989, and the following year Matsushita Electric bought Hollywood's MCA for about $6.59 billion. Nintendo became the majority owner of the Seattle Mariners, a Major League Baseball team, in 1992. A newspaper in Hawaii published a cartoon on December 7, 1991, showing that, while Japan had bombed Pearl Harbor fifty years before, it had bought Pearl Harbor fifty years later.

Japan became the largest foreign holder of U.S. government bonds by the early 1990s, while the United States became the largest debtor nation in the world. Japanese politicians' insensitive and arrogant remarks about America's society and people worsened matters. Nakasone, for one, stated in 1986 that Japan's homogenous society was superior in many ways to America's multiracial and multiethnic society. Watanabe Michio, chairman of the LDP's Policy Research Council, made derogatory comments about American blacks and

Hispanics. Speaker Sakurauchi Yoshio of the Lower House boasted that the United States had become a "subcontractor" for Japan. All were forced to make immediate apologies in the face of American protests.

Deep anti-American resentment was also visible in the publication of 1989's *The Japan That Can Say No*, a book coauthored by Morita Akio, president of Sony, and Ishihara Shintarō, a nationalist politician and a proponent of a nuclear Japan. In the book, Ishihara claimed that the United States dropped the atomic bomb on Japan because of racial prejudice and accused the United States of trying to steal Japanese high-tech information, while Morita faulted American business practices for prioritizing short-term profits at the expense of long-term gains.

The overwhelming prowess of the U.S. military that had been demonstrated in the Gulf War, coupled with an apparent lack of appreciation from the U.S. and Kuwaiti governments regarding Japan's enormous financial assistance (totaling $13 billion) to the Allied military efforts, produced an anti-American backlash in Japan. A new word, *kenbei*, or "dislike of the United States," was coined and became popular in Japan.

Issues surrounding the historical interpretation of World War II, which had receded in the background in the Cold War years, reemerged as significant concerns for the bilateral relationship. The fiftieth anniversary of Pearl Harbor might have been an excellent opportunity to put an end to a thorny question involving the two countries, but Prime Minister Miyazawa Kiichi, a loyal adherent of the Yoshida Doctrine, said that he had no intention of apologizing to the United States for the attack, and President George H. W. Bush, who signed the law to provide additional funds to compensate Japanese Americans for their wartime internment, said that he had no plan to invite the Japanese prime minister to the ceremony in Pearl Harbor. In the early 1990s the Smithsonian Museum, to commemorate the fiftieth anniversary of the end of World War II, started to explore a plan to exhibit the *Enola Gay* with the cooperation of Hiroshima City, but this ended in a fiasco.[25]

The unspoken assumption of the U.S.-Japan Security Pact was rudely clarified by a comment made by Major General Henry Stackpole of the U.S. Marine Corps in Okinawa in March 1990. He told the *Washington Post*, echoing Kissinger's advice to Nixon two decades earlier, "No one wants a rearmed, resurgent Japan. So we are a cap in the bottle, if you will." Although the Defense Department explained that the remark did not represent the official view of the U.S. government, Japanese authorities did not hide their displeasure.

When the Defense Department announced its post–Cold War military strategy in the Asia-Pacific region in 1990, it reiterated a significant and implicit objective of the nuclear umbrella: "[The] U.S. nuclear umbrella will remain a critical element. In large measure, it has been our nuclear commitment that has slowed nuclear proliferation in the area. Movement away from this commitment would have disastrous effects and could destabilize the entire region."[26]

President George H. W. Bush announced in September 1991 a new policy of withdrawing nuclear weapons from navy vessels, thus eliminating this simmering issue from an already fraught U.S.-Japan relationship.[27]

Conclusion

Japanese politics and diplomacy in the 1970s and 1980s evolved under the still powerful shadows and legacies of the Pacific War, and the devastation visited on Hiroshima and Nagasaki. Japan basically pursued and implemented a defense policy that was "nonnuclear and exclusively defense-oriented." In spite of its rapid and remarkable economic rise, Japan never really had the option to become an independent, militarily powerful nation free of the security pact with the United States. The basic structure of the Yoshida Doctrine remained surprisingly strong and elastic; political restraints and the popularity of pacifism worked against Japan's assumption of a larger, more active regional military role and prevented a substantial increase of defense spending. Although the Miyazawa administration introduced a law in 1992 that would enable the SDF to be dispatched overseas in UN peacekeeping operations, and the Diet passed it, the law contained strict stipulations.

From time to time a number of Japanese political leaders and intellectuals did argue for going nuclear, and the Japanese government sometimes evaded the issue of a strict application of nonnuclear principles to American vessels. Nonetheless, the majority of the Japanese people opposed nuclear development on moral and ethical grounds and agreed to limit the defense program to the field of conventional forces. In this respect, as former prime minister Miyazawa put it, "The Japan-U.S. Security Pact in a sense has protected Article 9 of the Japanese Constitution."

However, the end of the Cold War, North Korea's nuclear program, China's rapid economic and military progress, increasingly intractable problems involving the shared history of Japan, China, and South Korea and the intensification of U.S.-Japan trade conflicts altered the strategic landscape in the region. To further complicate matters, changes in government that occurred in Tokyo and Washington from 1992 to 1993 saw the end of thirty-eight years of LDP rule with the formation of a new government in Tokyo and the beginning of the administration of President Bill Clinton, which was to downplay the U.S.-Japan Security Pact and place trade at the top of its agenda with Tokyo. President Clinton's apparently high-handed manner of dealing with Japan contributed to the collapse of a summit meeting with Prime Minister Hosokawa Morihiro in February 1994.

In this changing political and diplomatic context, Ozawa Ichirō, a key figure in the political maneuvers to unseat the LDP and establish the Hosokawa coalition government, called in a book published in 1993 for Japan's political, social, and economic reformation to build a "normal nation." Influenced by his own experiences as the powerful secretary-general of the LDP during the Gulf War, Ozawa asserted that, if necessary, Japan should revise the constitution in order to actively contribute to peace and stability by participating in UN-sanctioned peacekeeping operations.[28]

Because of trade disputes, by the mid-1990s the U.S.-Japan relationship had entered its most turbulent period since the end of the Pacific War. How the nuclear legacies of Hiroshima and Nagasaki were to play out in Japanese foreign and defense policy in this new environment is a topic that requires further research.

PART II

Movements and Resistances

7

The Bandung Conference and the Origins of Japan's Atoms for Peace Aid Program for Asian Countries

Shinsuke Tomotsugu

THE CONFERENCE OF ASIAN COUNTRIES was held on a nongovernmental basis in New Delhi, India, between April 6 and 10, 1955. One of its purposes was to bring about a groundswell of sentiment in favor of peaceful coexistence at a forthcoming conference in Bandung. The Conference of Asian Countries called for the prohibition of weapons of mass destruction, including nuclear weapons, and welcomed the peaceful use of nuclear energy while expressing a desire to launch a regional collaboration. At the conference, the Japanese delegation, which consisted of politicians, scientists, literature scholars, and a medical doctor, screened a movie about Hiroshima, Nagasaki, and the fishing vessel *Lucky Dragon No. 5*, highlighting various experiences of suffering from past uses of nuclear weapons.

Two weeks later Japan participated on a governmental basis in the first Asian-African Conference, known as the Bandung Conference, in Bandung, Indonesia. This conference, held from April 18 to 25, was meaningful for Japan as it provided a unique opportunity to reestablish relationships with its neighbors in Asia. The spirit of the Bandung Conference concerned racial equality and peaceful coexistence beyond national systems, and the conference had an appeal for intellectuals and policy makers in Japan, a country that had just recovered its national sovereignty. The conference provided a symbolic opportunity for nations to protest the condition of ex-colonial industrial backwardness. Also, new forms of nuclear energy generation appeared to promise future economic benefits, and the use of nuclear energy for peaceful purposes was included on the agenda at Bandung. As U.S. historian Mara Drogan argues, the Asian and African, or "A.A.," nations expressed high expectations regarding the latter at this historic conference.[1] A.A. nations demanded that nuclear weapons, which the Soviet Union, the United States, and the United Kingdom monopolized, should be abolished, while claiming their right to share in the benefits of nuclear energy for peaceful purposes.

The Japanese antinuclear movement spread nationwide after Kuboyama Aikichi, a crew member on *Lucky Dragon No. 5*, died of radiation-induced illness on September 23, 1954. His illness was brought about by the nuclear fallout from the U.S. Castle Bravo thermonuclear weapon test on Bikini Atoll in March 1, 1954. In response, the United States sponsored the Atoms for Peace campaign in Japan to make Japanese citizens understand U.S. intentions to use science and technology not only for military purposes but also for general welfare.

The United States had to compete with the Soviet Union in the field of nuclear energy for peaceful purposes. The Soviet Union had already developed an operational nuclear power plant, with an initial grid connection in June 1954 in Obninsk. This achievement contrasted starkly with the *Lucky Dragon No. 5* incident. Moscow would make good use of the latter by accusing the United States of being obsessed with expansion of its nuclear arsenal.[2] To neutralize the effect of Soviet propaganda, the United States tried to foster international cooperation for the civilian use of nuclear energy. Such American attempts certainly stimulated public interest in nuclear energy in Asia, and vice versa, but the desire for the peaceful use of nuclear energy was not generated by American public diplomacy alone. Developing countries in Asia and Africa, many of which were nonaligned and newly independent, yearned for the civilian use of nuclear energy, which spurred the United States to promote the Atoms for Peace campaign.

Many Japanese shared this desire despite, or perhaps because of, their nation's experience of the atomic bombings. They hoped such destructive power, which unfortunately already existed, could be used for peaceful purposes. The so-called nuclear allergy did not necessarily apply to the use of nuclear energy for peaceful purposes, and even in Hiroshima and Nagasaki, some residents supported such use. In part this was because, although the Japanese understood that it would be possible to turn military nuclear technology to peaceful purposes, they did not fully recognize that the reverse was also possible. In any event, even as they adopted a strong stance against nuclear weapons, the participating countries at the Bandung Conference made clear that all nations, not just the superpowers, should share equally in the boon of peaceful nuclear energy. Recognizing this, Japan explored ways to help them.

The Bandung Conference proved to be a good starting point for Japan to promote its Atoms for Peace aid program for Asian countries, although the concept did not spring up overnight. As the only country in the world to have been bombed with atomic weapons, Japan thought that it should not be excluded from the benefits of nuclear energy for peaceful purposes and that it should take the initiative to help its Asian neighbors as a leader of "nuclear have-not" countries.

Furthermore, as will be discussed in detail below, Japan mounted a campaign to host the Asian Nuclear Center, which the Eisenhower administration offered member states of the Colombo Plan in October 1955. By offering to provide the location for the nuclear center, and with the use of U.S. financial resources, Japan tried to become the leading nation in Asia in the field of nuclear energy. While Japan showed an interest in collaborating with other Asian nations, the country's bid to host the center failed because the Philippines received America's nomination instead. (Eventually the United States abandoned the proposal entirely.) The Japanese politicians who had enthusiastically supported Japan's bid to host the center felt a great sense of loss at this defeat. Consequently, they came to believe more firmly that Japan would need to strengthen its ties with Asian countries in the peaceful use of nuclear energy. In fact, Japan started accepting trainees from Asian countries in 1957.

The objective of this chapter is to trace the origin and evolution of Japanese ideas in collaborating with Asian nations in the field of nuclear energy around the time of the Bandung Conference. First, I examine how Japanese scientists tried to get involved in the development of nuclear energy, with special attention paid to the Conference of Asian Countries in New Delhi. Second, I analyze the arguments of Japanese diplomats and politicians before and after the Bandung Conference. Finally, I consider how Japanese nuclear cooperation with other Asian countries began.

Prelude: Scientists and the Conference in New Delhi

Japan tried to apply the Atoms for Peace aid campaign to other Asian nations. However, this policy did not develop in a linear manner. The concept of the Japanese international aid policy regarding nuclear energy emerged early on through interactions among scientists, politicians, and diplomats (though, of course, none of these groups was monolithic in its outlook). The Conference of Asian Countries was the first opportunity for these groups to consider the possibility of peaceful coexistence, as well as the reestablishment of ties with Asian nations through the peaceful use of nuclear energy.

The conference was convened only three years after the recovery of Japanese national sovereignty. The Japanese government signed a peace treaty in

San Francisco in 1951 with only the United States, its allies, and a limited number of friendly nations. This was termed "solo peace" (*tandoku kōwa*). Meanwhile, most Japanese intellectuals supported signing a broader peace treaty that included members of the communist bloc. Dozens of prominent Japanese scholars, who organized the Peace Problem Symposium (*Heiwa mondai danwakai*), issued a "Statement on the Peace Problem" in January 1950. By unanimous consent, the symposium advocated "full peace" (*zenmen kōwa*), or the signing of a peace treaty with all members of the international community. This group of intellectuals included not only the famous ethicist Watsuji Tetsuro and political scientists such as Rōyama Masamichi, Shimizu Kitarō, and Maruyama Masao, but also nuclear scientist Nishina Yoshio, who, at the request of the military during World War II, had made an abortive attempt to develop a Japanese atomic bomb.[3] These intellectuals and scientists thought that solo peace would make Japan permanently subordinate to the United States; as a result, Japan would have to provide the United States with military bases indefinitely, which would embroil Japan in the Cold War. In the end, the Japanese government rejected the policy of full peace. When Japan ratified the San Francisco Peace Treaty, many Japanese intellectuals were disappointed at what they perceived as Japan's incorporation into the Western bloc. Under such circumstances, Kaya Seiji, a leading Japanese scientist, asked his colleague Fushimi Kōji to draft a proposal establishing the Japanese Atomic Energy Commission (JAEC) as a public entity.

Fushimi revealed his resulting draft proposal to scholars at the Science Council of Japan in the fall of 1952.[4] Fushimi himself had expressed the view that because of the tragedies caused by the atomic bombings, Japan had a right to enjoy the benefits of peaceful nuclear energy.[5] Yet many scientists considered Kaya and Fushimi's initiative to be impetuous: such a hasty move could pave the way for government intervention, the restructuring of academia, and the military use of science. For their part, Kaya and Fushimi felt that making the first move was the better way to secure academic autonomy.

Japanese politics, however, moved more quickly than Japanese scientists expected. The Liberal Party, Japan Reform Party, and National Liberal Party passed a budget bill on nuclear energy on April 3, 1954. At around the same time, the Japanese fishing vessel *Lucky Dragon No. 5* and its crew were exposed to radiation from a nuclear test near Bikini Atoll. Japanese antinuclear sentiment ran high. Criticizing the Japanese government's anemic response to the incident, the Science Council declared on April 23 that it would reject any research regarding nuclear weapons, and that any nuclear research should be conducted in line with the three principles of autonomy, public accessibility, and democracy. These principles were approved in a resolution in October.

Meanwhile, the Conference for the Relaxation of International Tension was held in Stockholm, Sweden, in June 1954 and attended by Japanese politicians, including Nakasone Yasuhiro (Japan Reform Party) and Matsumae Shigeyoshi (Japan Socialist Party, JSP), both of whom were well-known proponents of nuclear energy.[6] Marxist Hirano Gitaro, prominent physicist Sakata Shōichi, and left-wing political scientist Shimizu Kitarō participated in the conference as well. Importantly, at the Stockholm conference, Rameshwari Nehru, a prominent Indian social activist and wife of Brijlal Nehru (a cousin of Prime Minister Jawaharlal Nehru), proposed assembling the Conference of Asian Countries on a nongovernmental basis in New Delhi the next April to articulate the will of the people, and her proposal was adopted.[7] At the outset, the proposed conference was intended to be private and nonpartisan. Newly elected prime minister Hatoyama Ichiro (Japan Democratic Party) hoped to modify previous prime minister Yoshida Shigeru's diplomacy, which seemed to Hatoyama to be overly dependent on the United States. Hatoyama's preference seemed to reflect the attitude of his coalition government toward the New Delhi conference, although this meeting was nongovernmental. Ikeda Masanosuke (Japan Democratic Party, later the chairman of JAEC) served as the secretary of the Japanese preparatory commission, which included former prime minister Katayama Tetsu (JSP).[8] However, Nakasone did not join the commission, although he attended the Stockholm conference. He may have wanted to take a more cautious attitude toward the earlier conferences, let alone toward a nongovernmental meeting that could adopt a radical attitude toward the "white" powers.

On February 9, 1955, a preliminary meeting was held in New Delhi, with representatives from Burma, Ceylon, India, North Korea, and Syria attending. The agenda for the forthcoming conference included a prohibition on weapons of mass destruction, the exchange of scientific knowledge and information, and the peaceful use of nuclear energy. Five scientists joined the Japanese delegation for the plenary session of the New Delhi conference between April 6 and 10, 1955. Among them, Tominaga Gorō, a scientist at the University of Tokyo, claimed in his speech on April 8 that signing the bilateral agreement with the United States on peaceful uses of nuclear energy would impair Japanese autonomy in the related field. He also argued, "We must get rid of the military nature of atomic energy and pursue the program of atomic energy development independent of foreign intervention," while asserting that "for this purpose it is necessary to promote cooperation among Asian friendly nations."[9] For Tominaga, collaboration with Asian countries would become, as it were, an antidote to being pulled along by American diplomacy.

Finally, the New Delhi conference stated that "the forthcoming United Nations conference in Geneva for the peaceful application of atomic energy is to be heartily welcomed" and demanded that "atomic, thermonuclear, and other weapons of mass destruction should be banned and stocks of these weapons should be dismantled to retrieve nuclear materials for peaceful uses." After returning to Japan, Tominaga repeatedly argued, though in a somewhat milder tone, that "we should not necessarily deny international cooperation [even with the advanced nations]," although "we should be scientifically capable enough to handle it," so that Japanese academia could maintain its independence and Japan could promote solidarity with Asian nations.[10] Scientists generally shared the sentiment that Japan should not import or purchase peaceful nuclear technology without first acquiring scientific knowledge.

The Bandung Conference and Cooperation concerning Nuclear Energy

Having sounded out the U.S. perception of the Bandung Conference, the government of Japan under the Hatoyama cabinet and its Foreign Ministry officially announced that it would participate. The question of the conference was handled with extreme caution before the United States indicated in February 1955 its intention not to prevent Japan's participation. Japanese policy makers worried that the conference would arouse American antipathy. For one thing, conference organizers had invited the People's Republic of China while excluding South Korea and the Republic of China (or Taiwan), in the midst of the First Taiwan Strait Crisis.[11] Under such circumstances, Japanese policy makers thought their participation might breed suspicion in the United States that Japan was seeking a position of neutrality.

In reality, on February 8, 1955, the U.S. State Department argued that "we should no[t] volunteer comment on the conference, we can counteract the effect of certain issues likely to be raised at Bandung by taking public positions on them without making specific reference to the Conference itself," while recognizing that since "only 2 of the 30 invited countries are Communists and 10 may be [counted as] pro-Western, the Bandung Conference will probably avoid issues on which general agreements cannot be reached."[12] In fact, according to historian Yuka Tsuchiya, *Our Time*, a movie provided by the United States Information Agency in 1955, showed only that the participating countries at the Bandung Conference had expressed their support for the idea of Atoms for Peace, a U.S. creation, though the film ignored the concepts of nonalignment and neutrality also favored by A.A. countries.[13]

Whereas Hatoyama never found any critical problem with Japan's participation in the Bandung Conference inasmuch as it did not mean secession from the Western bloc, his foreign minister, Shigemitsu Mamoru, was more cautious. During the Pacific War, Shigemitsu had served as foreign minister in the Tōjō cabinet. He was also in charge of hosting the Greater East Asian Assembly (Dai tōa kaigi) on November 5, 1943. On this occasion, he attempted to lend an air of nobility to the Greater East Asia Co-Prosperity Sphere by preparing the Declaration of the Greater East Asia War. Partly for that reason, he avoided undertaking the role of plenipotentiary to the conference in Bandung, not wanting to provoke the United States even after it had signaled tacit agreement with Japanese participation in the meeting.

Instead of Shigemitsu, therefore, the general director of the Economic Planning Agency, Takasaki Tatsunosuke, served as the chief delegate for the Japanese government. Prior to the end of World War II, Takasaki was chairman of the Manchuria Heavy Industries Development Corporation. After the war he became president of Electric Power Development (from 1952 to 1954), and later (in 1959) general director of the Science and Technology Agency (STA). Before going to Bandung, Takasaki was also vice chairman of the Investigation Committee on the Use of Atomic Energy (Genshiryoku riyo chosakai). Essentially, he was a proponent of the development of nuclear energy for peaceful purposes. At the Bandung Conference he stated: "The world is now entering upon the age of nuclear energy. Whether nuclear energy is to become a deeply [sic] instrument of destruction that will extinguish the human race, or it is turned to peaceful uses to bestow infinite benefits on mankind, will depend solely upon the intelligences [sic] of men."[14] His speech adopted a tone of universalism, downplaying the slogan of the "rise of Asian nations." The Japanese delegation highlighted the importance of economic cooperation, although Japan still lacked the ability to provide large-scale economic aid to neighboring states. In conjunction with this basic policy, the Japanese government had considered it necessary to assert in the thematic session of the conference that the Soviet Union and the United States should not monopolize the benefits of nuclear energy for civilian purposes. The countries attending the conference considered making an appeal regarding the importance and profitability of sharing nuclear energy.[15]

On April 19, 1955, the first day of the conference, delegates were supposed to discuss five topics: cooperation concerning economic development, cooperation to promote trade, mutual help on other issues, the problem of establishing an international organization for future Asian and African economic cooperation, and issues pertaining to nuclear energy. Thus, on April 12, a week before the Bandung Conference, the Third Bureau of International Cooperation at MOFA prepared a package of documents for the conference entitled "Materials for Peaceful Uses of Atomic Energy." One of these documents included a memorandum entitled "2nd Draft of Document for the A.A. Conference No. 2–3: The Attitudes of Our Country toward the Issues Concerning the Peaceful Purpose of Atomic Energy," which suggested what Japan could do for Asia in related fields, presumably in consultation with the Science Council of Japan.[16] Leading scientists pragmatically and cautiously helped MOFA go on with the nuclear program so as not to be exploited by the government's possible military ambitions, although there was in fact no concrete political action toward nuclear armament in Japan after World War II.

Some Japanese officials and conservative politicians sporadically mentioned that Japan should not rule out the possibility of nuclear armament (see, for example, the remarks of Yoshida Shigeru and Ikeda Hayato quoted in chapter 6 of this volume). However, such discourse has never garnered popularity in Japan. Historian Akira Kurosaki argues the Japanese government adopted nonnuclear policy in the 1950s to avoid a situation in which progressive forces would exclusively enjoy the position of speaking for national antinuclear sentiment.[17] Wakana Mukai, in chapter 9 of this volume, discusses how the remaining uncertainty of the governmental stance on nuclear weapons was gradually dissolved and a "nonnuclear resolution" was eventually passed by the Diet in the 1970s.

The MOFA memorandum of April 12 sought to counterbalance Western dominance in Asia. MOFA argued that civilian uses of nuclear energy were secondary considerations outside of Japan, with military uses having been the top priority in developing nuclear energy in the past. Seeing that "the peaceful use of nuclear energy was apt to be swayed by the interests of the great powers," MOFA commented on Japanese attitudes regarding the peaceful use of nuclear energy in A.A. countries (in reality, Japan was usually focused on Asian perspectives, even when it used the term "A.A."):

> Considering that developments and uses of nuclear energy gravely concern themselves with the future of mankind, our state strongly hoped that these developments and uses would be only for human welfare. We welcome that an international program has been promoted at the United Nations and its special organ. Yet we strongly demand continuous consideration of preventing the calamity of nuclear energy use, ardently requesting that nuclear energy should be utilized for improving the living conditions of underdeveloped countries. At the same time, we request that the peaceful use of nuclear energy within the areas of the A.A. countries should be done primarily for cooperation with the United Nations and the improvement of living conditions. Our state is prepared to get fully involved in international cooperation to promote the peaceful uses of nuclear energy from these stands.[18]

Foreseeing that nuclear energy might be extremely significant for long-term regional economic development, MOFA's Third Bureau of the International Cooperation attached reference material entitled "The Possibility of Cooperation concerning the Peaceful Uses of Nuclear Energy among States in A.A. Areas." In this document, MOFA argued that research into nuclear energy was an issue not for the present but rather for the future, because "the fundamental policy and domestic development system were not yet developed"; therefore "it would take at least several years to be able to provide technical assistance." Nevertheless, the ministry argued that "we can provide information regarding the use of isotopes, and if we construct a nuclear reactor it would make it possible to provide an isotope itself."[19] In short, MOFA predicted the possibility of providing aid to Asian countries in the future by constructing a research reactor on Japanese soil, though it did not specify a location. The final communiqué in Bandung reinforced the Japanese government's prediction: it demanded the abolition of nuclear weapons and the peaceful use of nuclear energy for Asian and African welfare. Indeed, the Bandung Conference conveyed the distinct impression that even Japan could do something both for itself and for the other Asian countries.

After returning from Bandung to Tokyo, Takasaki stated the following in a meeting of the Committee of Commerce and Industry at the Diet on May 13, 1955:

> On this occasion, I would like to talk about the Japanese fundamental policy on the issues of nuclear energy. As you know, among the nations, only the Japanese suffered an atomic bombing at the previous war, where nuclear energy was used. If you say you want to use nuclear energy not for wars but for peace, I hope to make the best use of it. Thinking so, I went to Bandung and argued many things. The atmosphere in the whole world is like, if you use it for the peaceful industry, let's make the Japanese do it first. Such an atmosphere naturally prevailed. I do not want to be exclusive but want to accept [nuclear aid from the United States] with an open mind and will conduct research on the use for peaceful industry, this is what I intend to do.[20]

Leading Japanese scientist and socialist sympathizer Taketani Mitsuo took note of the Asian zeal for atomic power and, although he never directly referred to the Bandung Conference, two years after the conference argued:

> To begin with, in the field of atomic power, a certain tendency became clearer in Norway at first, and then in the strong rise of Asian and African nations in more recent years. This was the advancement by small powers themselves against the major powers. Such a powerful advancement by the smaller powers can probably be considered one of the pillars to maintain the world peace, and it is as if it were a Third Force.[21]

In sum, the Bandung Conference was a good starting point for the Japanese to think about the legacy of World War II and consider what Japan had to offer to its Asian neighbors. Indeed, the conference encouraged Japan to look into the possibility of direct collaboration with other Asian nations.

Japanese Campaign to Host the Asian Nuclear Center

The initial Japanese foray into international cooperation with Asian nations regarding nuclear energy was actually an unintended side effect of a U.S. proposal for an Asian Nuclear Center.[22] Before examining Japan's attitudes toward the U.S. proposal, we should touch on how this concept evolved. The origin of the proposal probably dated back to the initial meeting of SEATO in Bangkok in February 1955. At that meeting, Secretary of State John F. Dulles indicated that the United States would not officially oppose the A.A. conference. Instead, Dulles reached for a carrot, offering nuclear aid to the Asian countries. As Li Qianyu argues, the U.S. State Department predicted that Asian and African nations would express a desire for solidarity at the forthcoming conference in Bandung.[23]

At the Bangkok meeting, Dulles also mentioned courses on reactor operation and radioisotopes in which SEATO students would take part.[24] The U.S. offer to provide Atoms for Peace aid to Asian regions might be seen as a calculated attempt to ensure that Asian solidarity would not exclude the United States from the region. The Atoms for Peace program was important to U.S. strategy in Southeast Asia. For instance, U.S. National Security Council document NSC 5405, entitled "United States Objectives and Courses of Action with Respect to Southeast Asia," issued on January 16, 1954, contended that "the loss of Southeast Asia, especially of Malaya and Indonesia, could result in such economic and political pressures in Japan as to make it extremely difficult to prevent Japan's eventual accommodation to communism." Nuclear energy became a crucial agenda item in the document in due course. For instance, NSC 5405 progress reports issued in December 1955 and July 1956 referred to the Asian Nuclear Center as the dominant issue to be tackled.[25] Thus the nuclear center was seen as a tool to draw Asian nations into the orbit of the anticommunist bloc.

In June 1955 President Eisenhower stated in a speech at the University of Pennsylvania that the United States was prepared to assist a group of nations in certain regions to jointly obtain or operate a research reactor.[26] On August 23, 1955, Phillip Farley, deputy to the special assistant to the secretary of state for atomic energy affairs, argued in a memorandum that the United States should project a more accurate image of its desire to expand the Atoms for Peace aid program overseas, as Asian nations were susceptible to Soviet propaganda emphasizing the U.S. obsession with the atomic bomb. As such, in consultation with Britain, the U.S. State Department and the International Cooperation Agency (ICA) made a confidential proposal to establish the Asian Nuclear Center under the Colombo Plan and SEATO, and in October 1955 the proposal was opened to all Asian countries. In 1956 the U.S. Brookhaven

National Laboratory drew up a detailed blueprint regarding budget, staff, organizational structure, and facilities, drawing on the example of the already-launched European Council for Nuclear Research (CERN).[27]

At the outset, the United States considered Ceylon to be the best location for the new center, likely due to its central location in the region, and obtained the informal consent of the UK and Ceylon itself; however, ICA director John B. Hollister strongly recommended Manila in the Philippines, despite the existing secret Anglo-American consensus. Hollister managed to change the site from Ceylon to the Philippines by the end of 1955, and the U.S. government announced that Manila had been selected as the final candidate. However, the UK did not want local communists in Asian countries to regard the Asian Nuclear Center as a SEATO institution.[28] Even Gerald C. Smith, the U.S. special assistant to the secretary of state on atomic energy matters, was seriously cautious. He alerted Undersecretary of State Herbert Clark Hoover that the United States should remember that it had offered to build a reactor while the Bandung Conference was being held.[29] Smith felt that the nomination of Manila might lead other Asian nations to conclude that the competition for the nomination had been rigged. However, Hollister and some pro-Manila staff members at the State Department thought there was theoretically no contradiction between the Colombo Plan and SEATO. The Philippines was a member of both. Thus, even if Manila were chosen as the construction site, there would be no problems of perception. Moreover, the pro-American politician Ramón Magsaysay was president of the Philippines (1953–1957). Hoping that the Philippines might become a success story of American economic and technological aid, a few pro-Manila American policy makers predicted that Magsaysay would pursue democratic reforms. If anything, the fact that the Philippines became a SEATO member was more important for those who advocated for establishing the nuclear center in Manila. SEATO was expected to create a framework within which the United States, other Western powers, and Asian nations could collaborate with one another.

Unaware of the behind-the-scenes Anglo-American talks and the internal disputes in Washington, the Japanese government tried to obtain the nomination. When Hollister, in October 1955, announced the U.S intention to build a regional nuclear center somewhere in Asia, Nakasone requested that the Japanese government make a bid to host the center under the framework of the Colombo Plan.[30] On November 2, 1955, Foreign Minister Shigemitsu officially informed American ambassador John M. Allison of the Japanese government's desire to host the center.[31]

On the morning of December 13 three interested politicians from the newly formed Liberal Democratic Party (LDP), Tomabechi Gizō, Arita Kiichi, and Nakasone, visited Ambassador Allison to request that Japan be chosen as the location for the nuclear center, emphasizing nationwide Japanese support for the development of nuclear energy.[32] This event on the eve of the enactment of Atomic Energy Basic Act on December 19 gained almost unanimous support, from the LDP to the JSP. Meanwhile, Ambassador Iguchi Sadao informed Undersecretary Hoover of the message from Foreign Minister Shigemitsu to the effect that Japan wanted to host the center. Such an all-out campaign reflected Japan's evaluation that it possessed the most advanced science and technology in the Asian region, but that it still needed assistance from other industrial nations such as the United States and the United Kingdom. By the end of 1955, however, it became clear that the Japanese bid to host the Asian Nuclear Center had fallen through.

The Eisenhower administration had initiated the Atoms for Peace campaign with Japan on a bilateral basis: Tokyo and Washington signed the U.S.-Japan Agreement Concerning Civil Uses of Atomic Energy on November 14, 1955. Historian Shingo Tanaka points out that even within the Truman administration, the idea of providing a former enemy with either research or a "power reactor" was viewed with a certain degree of caution.[33] Whereas it did not intend to give a free hand to Japan because of concerns about nuclear proliferation, the United States gradually became tolerant of Japanese attempts to launch research into nuclear energy during the Truman and Eisenhower administrations. This did not necessarily mean that the United States wanted to allow Japan to become a center of Asian regional nuclear cooperation. In fact, the Japanese campaign to host the nuclear center might have aroused American suspicions that Japan aimed to take the lion's share of the money on offer. For example, viewing Japanese intentions cynically, U.S. diplomat and Asia expert Richard Sneider suspected that the Japanese merely wanted to acquire a reputation as good mediators between West and East by hosting a regional nuclear center where scientists from industrially advanced nations in the West could assist students from less developed nations in Asia.[34] Sneider was correct, as the Japanese government was hoping for windfall profits from the arrangement.

The Origins of Japan's Atoms for Peace Aid Program for Asian Countries

After the failure of their bid to host the Asian Nuclear Center damaged the pride of some Japanese politicians, they came to believe in the importance of promoting the Japanese version of the Atoms for Peace aid program for Asian countries. Half a year earlier, in June 1955, the U.S.-Japan nuclear research cooperation agreement had been unofficially signed. Some scientists, such as Taketani, Fushimi, and nuclear physicist Yukawa Hideki, were worried that overly close collaboration with the United States could destroy Japan's three principles regarding nuclear development (autonomy, public accessibility, and democracy), as U.S. technical assistance and the supply of uranium from the United States required a confidentiality pledge. Likewise, some politicians felt that strengthening ties with Asian countries in the nuclear field was the antidote to exclusive ties with the United States. Notably JSP politicians, whether they belonged to the right or the left faction, tended to take such a view. For instance, Oka Ryōichi lamented that the United States deployed nuclear diplomacy "as if all were planned beforehand," while pointing out that "the U.S. is said to be holding [a de facto] regional bloc conference [under the pretext of the proposed] Asian Nuclear Center in Manila to discuss with the countries that have bilateral nuclear agreements." Oka criticized the Japanese government for planning to import the American experimental reactor CP-5 without any requests and reservations, saying, "Like Don Quixote, Japan [recklessly] swallows it that [sic] whole," without any of his colleagues speaking up. He also said, "I even fear the risk that Japan's nuclear research could be under a sort of colonized situation."[35] Regarding the collaboration with Asian countries that could mitigate Japan's overreliance on the United States, Oka, three months before, called on Shōriki Matsutarō, the first chairman of Atomic Energy Commission and owner of *Yomiuri shimbun*, one of Japan's major daily newspapers, to promote Japan's own nuclear diplomacy toward Asian nations:

> The Asian Nuclear Center that Mr. Chairman had ardently desired, as opposed to your expectations, will come to Manila. Nevertheless, the newspaper report recently says, Indian Prime Minister, Jawaharlal Nehru or his proxy announced at the policy board in ECAFE that he would like to hold the conference around July for joint nuclear development in Asia. I think this is very meaningful. I believe you will decisively join it. Mr. Chairman, will you join it if requested by them?

Fully being aware that Japanese technologies were lagging far behind, however, Shōriki did not play up any kind of rivalry with the United States. He simply replied, "We are happy to join it for Asian joint development," saying, "it cannot be helped we were not chosen as the site [for the Asia Nuclear Center] because we were not ready at all." Meanwhile Shōriki boasted of Japan's potential by arguing that "although the final candidate is Manila, Japan intends to be the center and I think it is possible."[36]

An occasion for learning about Japanese cooperation with Asian countries quickly presented itself. Following a tour to Pakistan, India, Ceylon, Burma, Indonesia, and the Philippines, the Brookhaven National Laboratory team visited Japan from June 3 to 11 on the way back to the United States. The team's aims were threefold: to conduct a preparatory study about how to establish the Asian regional nuclear center, to explain what the newly formed center would do for these countries, and to exchange views with Asian counterparts on future nuclear collaboration. After a formal meeting in Tokyo attended by twenty-three Japanese representatives from political, business, and academic circles, twenty-nine scholars from the Science Council of Japan had an informal meeting with the Brookhaven team. In preparation, the Japanese scholars had previously convened a meeting to discuss the impact of the Asian Nuclear Center on Japan.[37] Though a detailed account of what transpired at this meeting does not exist, they almost certainly recognized assistance to Asian nations through nuclear technological cooperation as an important issue on the agenda. However, their attitudes appeared somewhat ambivalent. For example, on October 24, 1956, the Committee on the Atomic Energy Problem under the Science Council of Japan concluded that Japanese staff should not stay at the Asian Nuclear Center for too long, and that their wages should not be lower than those of staff from other countries. Yet they simultaneously confirmed the basic principle that "Japan should cooperate positively."[38] In June 1956 the scientists in the Atomic Nucleus Special Commission took a more suspicious, if still somewhat equivocal, view by arguing:

> The third problem is the principle of equality in case where a variety of countries have mutual relations in international cooperation in science and technology. For example, like Atomic International Agency [sic] in case where many countries are involved, whether they are supplier or recipient countries, the participating countries should hold this equal right to speak, and oppression or ignorance should not be added to specific country. Mutual academic exchange and cooperation would not be developed in real sense, unless each country has its relations and cooperation under the principle of equality. This [cooperation] can be said to be especially harmful when it is "tied" economically, politically, and militarily. This is the point about which we must be cautious, not only in our state's atomic issues but also in forthcoming Atomic Center in Asia.[39]

In short, the commission recognized the necessity of nuclear cooperation in the Asian region in principle but was unenthusiastic about the prospect, especially in cases where the United States or other Western powers took the lead. These Japanese scientists feared a loss of research autonomy.

Although their attitudes showed an ambivalence now and then similar to that of the scientists, some political and industrial elites took a more positive view, even sometimes expressing admiration for the U.S. Atoms for Peace campaign overseas. The Delegation to Investigate Nuclear Energy for Peaceful Purposes was formed in response to an American invitation, and twelve politicians, government officers, and industrialists toured the United States in September 1956. The delegates visited the Brookhaven National Laboratory to ask about the development of nuclear energy in the United States, the present status of the Asian Nuclear Center proposal, the uses of isotopes, and related training programs. This experience nurtured in the delegates the concept of aiding Asian countries.[40]

The following month politicians Maeda Masao (LDP) and Matsumae Shigeyoshi (JSP), both of whom were among the twenty-three Japanese representatives who hosted the meeting with the Brookhaven team as well as the twelve members of the Delegation to Investigate Nuclear Energy for Peaceful Purpose mentioned above, personally toured European and Asian countries to inspect the development of nuclear energy. During this tour, both politicians met with leaders in the nuclear field in India, Thailand, and Burma on October 18, 22, and 23, 1956, respectively, to explore the possibility of Asian collaboration. A few months earlier, on July 23, India had hosted a five-country nuclear conference in Bombay with Burma, Indonesia, Ceylon, and Egypt. Those countries, India and Egypt in particular, had strengthened their ties at the Bandung Conference.[41] During their tour in Asia, Maeda and Matsumae therefore tried to achieve a consensus around the necessity of broader regional cooperation including Japan and Thailand. Moreover, at the Twenty-Fifth Special Committee for the Promotion of Science and Technology in the Diet on November 20, 1956, they suggested that "the government as a leader should promptly talk with India and other countries and make efforts to hold [an] Asian Nuclear Conference."[42] Though not a neutral observer, Matsumae gave the following interpretation of their Asian tour on March 12, 1957:

> I visited Burma with Mr. Maeda the other day. In Burma, Deputy Prime Minister U Kyaw Nyun concurrently serves as Minister for Atomic Energy.... We asked him about whether it would be possible to have an international agreement in which Japan could send a delegation of inquiry for surveying atomic resources to a certain degree in Burma.... However, Nyun instantly replied, "In fact, the investigation team for natural resources for atomic energy will arrive in Burma tomorrow and we will greet them at the airport."... The British took action earlier [than we did], so I think they will take everything.... At the time of the Meiji Restoration, the European and American powers took away all the Asian natural resources. When we opened our eyes, we found there were no natural resources left to be provided to Japan, so we began to call for the redistribution of resources. And then, I think the situation took place where we couldn't get natural resources unless we established the Greater East Asia Co-Prosperity Sphere to expel [the West]. We took such a historical path, and if we don't look at the atomic resources, we will be heading for trouble [again] in the future.[43]

Japanese bureaucrats and scientists preserved their aplomb in the face of the progress of the Asian Nuclear Center. On June 5, 1957, STA, the Japan Atomic Energy Research Institute (JAERI), Ministry of Education, and Nuclear Fuel Corporation held an unofficial meeting on "consultation on the Asian Nuclear Center," which a staff member of the Science Council of Japan attended as an observer. During the meeting, one JAERI official introduced the opinion of its board member Sagane Ryōkichi, a prominent physicist.[44] According to the official, Sagane suggested that Japan should not use its limited domestic resources to join the center in a foreign country. Another participant from STA argued that Japan should make efforts to locate the "Asia Radio Isotope Center," which JAERI officially considered establishing at the time, in "the core of the Asian Nuclear Center" that the United States planned to set up. In the end, the participants concluded that while taking a low profile and passively cooperating with the Asian Nuclear Center, Japan should build up capacity and "eventually take an initiative."[45]

To examine how Japan could promote nuclear aid to Asian countries, Foreign Service officers, bureaucrats of related agencies, as well as scientists entertained close contacts. Following the aforementioned meeting, officials of MOFA, the Ministry of Finance (MOF), JAERI, and STA, along with scientists from the Science Council of Japan, held a second "consultation on the Asian Nuclear Center" at MOFA on June 10, 1957. They confirmed Japan's basic policy line of cooperating with the proposed U.S. initiative. The participants concluded that Japan should prepare to counterpropose two options for the Working Group meeting in Washington, DC: (1) an option favorable not only for donors but also for Asian countries as a whole, and (2) an ideal option most advantageous to Japan.[46]

Subsequently, the Science Council of Japan sent a memorandum to MOFA on June 17 that repeated its basic consent to cooperating with the Asian Nuclear Center. The council, however, added that a few scientists saw no need to actively help the center; that the center should confine itself to peaceful purposes; and that it must not get started with only limited members in the Asian region—participation by at least India was desirable.[47] As Srinath Raghavan indicates in chapter 8 of this volume, the Indian government urged that its own nuclear program progress more decisively after witnessing the Hiroshima and Nagasaki bombings, judging that it would be possible to convert such disastrous energy into a measure for securing Indian economic development and national independence. To some Japanese scientists, Indian participation must have meant internationalization of the Asian Nuclear Center, which could dilute U.S. influence.

Nonetheless, despite the Japanese discussions, the United States ended up abandoning the idea of an Asian Nuclear Center owing to its failure to obtain enthusiastic support from the UK, Australia, Japan, and other Asian countries by October 1958 and sent an official notification of its decision to participating countries on March 25, 1959. Still, it is fair to assume that this American initiative inspired many Japanese to look for their own version of Atoms for Peace cooperation with Asian countries. In sum, Japanese politicians and a few scientists anxiously viewed the Asian Nuclear Center as a U.S. tool to make Asian countries dependent on the United States, while bureaucrats and mainstream scientists cautiously tried to utilize the American initiative for Japan's benefit.

A year and a half earlier, on November 14, 1957, Kenzo Saito, a prominent pronuclear LDP politician and founder of Japanese major electric component manufacturer TDK, referring to EURATOM, had stated that "we should host [an] Asian nuclear conference, and gradually take measures for the future prosperity and peace." Based on Saito's demand, the committee adopted "the resolution on the establishment of the system for nuclear energy cooperation in Asian countries" and submitted it to Prime Minister Kishi Nobusuke on November 18 in the name of the chairman, Kanno Wataro.[48] The objective of the resolution was to convene a conference among Asian nations. However, no appropriation for holding such a conference would be made immediately from the annual budget, presumably because the conference was not feasible.

Instead, Japan's nuclear aid to Asian countries began quietly, with the acceptance of trainees at the Radioisotopes School that JAERI established in 1957, only two years after the Bandung Conference.[49] Historian Angela N. H. Creager argues that the U.S. government, especially after the Atomic Energy Act in 1954 was passed under the Eisenhower administration, considered the distribution of radioisotopes overseas for the medical therapy, physiological research, and scientific purposes as a tool to gain political influence in recipient countries.[50] For Japan, it was not the distribution of radioisotopes but capacity building in related fields that became a political tool to gain good will. From 1957 to 1962, the Radioisotopes School had 1,166 students, 112 of whom came from overseas, including 33 from the Republic of China (Taiwan), 12 from the Republic of Korea, 11 from India, 11 from Thailand, 9 from Malaya, 9 from Pakistan, and 8 from Indonesia.[51] This training for international students was provided at UNESCO's request and was implemented under the framework of the Colombo Plan, with some fellowships offered by ICA in the United States. Japan provided the facilities, equipment, and basic needs, including accommodation. Thus Japan's initial foray into nuclear aid looked quite similar to MOFA's predictions at the Bandung Conference.

In September 1961, at the fifth meeting of the Board of Directors of the IAEA, Miki Takeo (LDP) made a proposal to establish the Radioisotope

Training Center for the Asian Region based on a five-year record of Japanese success in administering training programs. Following this, STA informally negotiated with IAEA staff and confidentially agreed on cost sharing. Simultaneously, the government of Japan started planning to hold the Conference of Countries in Asia and the Pacific for the Promotion of Peaceful Uses of Atomic Energy. Both the training center and the conference represented proposals to raise the standard of Japan's nuclear diplomacy in Asia. Both were adopted as a cabinet decision entitled "The Request on the Cooperation Regarding the Establishment of the Radioisotope Training Center for the Asian Region" on January 30, 1962.

In the end, the Radioisotope Training Center was not realized for "several reasons," according to STA. At MOFA's United Nations Bureau, Ootori Kurino explained that it became difficult to consider the question of Japan's proposal at the IAEA board meeting on February 27 because of the political unease around a discussion concerning a regional isotope center in Cairo proposed by the United Arab Republic (UAR).[52] Since September 1958 the UAR had expressed its interest in establishing a regional nuclear center under the auspices of the IAEA. On May 25, 1960, it wrote to the IAEA director general to discuss the realization of this concept. However, Greece and Turkey, both NATO members, strongly opposed such a center, pointing out the UAR's (mainly Egypt's) hidden political motives. Seeing that its close allies disliked the UAR proposal, the United States became hesitant to express its support for the Cairo center. Meanwhile, the Eastern bloc countries, India, Venezuela, and Ceylon strongly supported the center.[53] The Soviet Union criticized Western countries for intentionally slowing down the Egyptian attempt.[54] The Soviet Union had strengthened ties with Egypt in the nuclear field by installing the first research reactor for isotope production in Cairo and sending technicians. The United States criticized Nasser for opening "the African door to Soviet penetration."[55]

In a series of thorny debates, remarks by the Japanese representative hoping to establish Japan's own Asian regional isotope center got the most attention. Nonetheless, though the UAR was dissolved in 1961, the Middle Eastern Regional Isotope Center began operations in Cairo following an agreement with the IAEA in January 1963. The Asian radioisotope center pushed by Japan was not established as a permanent organ; however, the Japanese government continued talks with the IAEA and reached an "Agreement on Providing Radioisotopes Training Courses by the IAEA" in May 1964.[56] Japan managed to save face by offering the venue for the IAEA to conduct an intensive training program from August 17 to December 24, 1964, at the JAERI Radioisotopes School. This program, offered only once, was supposed to accept up to fifteen trainees from "Asia and Far East countries" via IAEA fellowships, though there is no record of the number of trainees who eventually attended.

In contrast, the Conference of Countries in Asia and the Pacific for the Promotion of Peaceful Uses of Atomic Energy was held as planned for three days beginning on March 11, 1963. The conference was attended by representatives from fourteen countries (Afghanistan, Australia, Ceylon, Taiwan, India, Indonesia, Iran, Japan, South Korea, New Zealand, Pakistan, the Philippines, Thailand, and South Vietnam) and five international organizations (ECAFE, IAEA, ILO, FAO, and WHO), as well as observers from six countries (Canada, France, West Germany, Italy, the United Kingdom, and the United States). The Japanese delegation consisted of four committee members from JAEC, the director and two staff members from JAERI, and an adviser. The conference confirmed the importance of collaboration but did not adopt any concrete projects. Japan and the other conference participants decided to request that the IAEA promote activities in the Asia and Pacific regions and study the possibility of setting up an IAEA regional office in this area.[57] However, when Pakistan suggested establishing a EURATOM-like Asian regional framework, "ASIATOM," Ota Masami, director of the Management Division of the Bureau of the United Nations, reportedly opposed the suggestion on behalf of the Japanese government, saying that it was too early. Ota said that the Japanese government would emphasize cooperation with the IAEA for the time being.[58] Though its true rationale remains unclear, MOFA was apparently exercising caution before deciding to accelerate regional cooperation. Overall, though, the conference was a meaningful experience for Japan in that it strengthened Japan's determination to take the lead in establishing peaceful nuclear cooperation among Asian nations.[59]

Conclusion

Around the time of the Bandung Conference, Japanese scientists, politicians, and government officials became enamored of the idea of providing technological assistance to Asian countries to develop nuclear energy for civilian purposes. Between the nonaligned countries' struggle to strengthen their independence through the development of nuclear energy and the U.S. Atoms for Peace campaign overseas as a countermeasure against the connection of decolonization and communism, Japan tried to locate its own nuclear aid programs for Asian countries. The Conference of Asian Countries in New Delhi, held two weeks before the Bandung Conference, was significant in shaping how Japanese policy makers saw their Asian neighbors' hopes for the future of cooperation in nuclear energy. The New Delhi conference also created a great deal of rhetoric on the issue of the solidarity of Asian nations in the field of nuclear energy. MOFA might have fostered the understanding that the civilian use of nuclear energy should not be monopolized by great powers such as the Soviet Union and the United States.

At Bandung, Japanese diplomats must have recognized the Asian nations' strong desire for nuclear energy and contemplated what Japan might do to satisfy this desire. Their experiences in Bandung spurred scientists and politicians to get involved in future nuclear collaboration with Asian nations. Meanwhile, many scientists were concerned about the possible loss of Japanese autonomy in nuclear development, fearing that Japan was perhaps already too closely partnered with the United States in related areas. For some of the Japanese politicians and scientists who wanted to mitigate Japan's overreliance on the United States, it made sense to strengthen ties with Asian countries.

The failure to win a bid to host the proposed Asian Nuclear Center wounded Japan's pride in its advanced science and technology. This experience made some politicians recognize the need to promote a Japanese version of nuclear diplomacy toward Asian countries. The Japanese delegation, which consisted mainly of members of the ruling party, was dispatched to the United States, European countries, and Asian countries including India, Thailand, and Burma in the fall of 1956. India had already held a nuclear conference in which five Asian countries participated. Japan feared that it might not be able to ride on the Asian "bus" to a bright future filled with the benefits of nuclear energy. Anxious Japanese politicians pushed the Special Committee of Science and Technology to adopt "a resolution on the establishment of the system for nuclear energy cooperation in Asian countries," which was submitted to Prime Minister Kishi on November 18, 1957. However, it took five more years for Japan to convene a conference that Asian and Pacific countries could join.

From 1957 to 1962 Japan accepted trainees from Asian countries at the Radioisotopes School at JAERI. This was what MOFA had predicted when it looked to the future of international cooperation in the field of nuclear energy during the Bandung Conference. The experience of accepting trainees encouraged Japanese politicians to promote nuclear diplomacy. In 1962, as the director of STA, Miki Takeo proposed establishing the Radioisotope Training Center for the Asian Region. Unable to get support from overseas, this endeavor fell through. However, the Japanese government eventually succeeded in hosting the Conference for Asia in 1963. Through the experiences outlined above, Japan gradually came around to the idea that it should maintain nuclear energy aid programs toward Asian countries.

8

India in the Early Nuclear Age

Srinath Raghavan

ON MAY 18, 1974, India conducted its first nuclear test in the deserts of Rajasthan. Prime Minister Indira Gandhi insisted that India had detonated a "peaceful nuclear explosive." The test took the international community by surprise—not least because of the sheer incongruity of India's nuclear status. Over the previous decade and a half, India had been the largest recipient of foreign aid among the developing countries. The fact that a country that had yet to attain self-sufficiency in the production of food grains should test a nuclear device and thumb its nose at the nonproliferation order, especially after having refused to join the Nuclear Nonproliferation Treaty (NPT), was galling even to friends of India.

Among the many consequences of the test of 1974 was the long shadow it cast on the historiography of India in the early nuclear age (from the mid-1940s to the late 1950s). The early nuclear journey of India was cast into a teleological narrative of a quest for nuclear weapons capability that culminated in the "Smiling Buddha" test of 1974. India's avowed declarations in the early years that it would not pursue nuclear weapons were read as a charade that masked its real ambitions. The tendency to write the early nuclear history under the sign of its nuclear test was accentuated in the aftermath of the next tests that India conducted in May 1998, in the process declaring itself an overt nuclear weapons power.

Interestingly, this teleological approach is shared by supporters as well as critics of India's nuclear weapons capability. Thus Bharat Karnad writes approvingly of India's first prime minister, Jawaharlal Nehru, donning a veneer of "moralpolitik" that effectively shielded his realpolitik pursuit of nuclear weapons.[1] From the opposite side of the divide, George Perkovich argues that Nehru was an "ambitious, realist prime minister who recognized nuclear weapon capability could enhance India's status and power," that he "recognized and welcomed from the beginning the options [the nuclear program's] military dimension gave to India," and that he "took India to a unique position of restrained nuclear weapon capability with little regard for particular security concerns."[2] Karnad, an advocate of India's possession of thermonuclear weapons mounted on intercontinental ballistic missiles, and Perkovich, an advocate of nonproliferation, have much the same reading of India's early nuclear history. Their accounts are similar not only in their emplotment of the narrative but also in their treatment of the evidence. On the one hand, both tend to treat Nehru's statements against the bomb as rhetoric masking reality. On the other, Nehru's open acknowledgment of the blurred line between nuclear research and weapons programs is read as a partial admission of his genuine intent—as if a denial of this would have had any credibility in the wake of Hiroshima and Nagasaki. The differences between their accounts are primarily normative and secondarily related to international relations theory: Perkovich is keen to use India as a case study of states pursuing nuclear weapons for prestige rather than security.

This chapter seeks to avoid the tendency to start from the tests of 1974 and work backward in explaining India's nuclear trajectory in the decade or so following the nuclear bombing of Japan. Inspired by the new histories of nuclear physics in early independent India as well as new international histories of the same period, it offers a different framework within which to think about India's first forays in the nuclear domain. These emerging historiographies force us to rethink the established teleology in terms of the substantive issues that animated the early Indian nuclear program as well as the manner in which it was shaped by the wider context.

India's response to the advent of the nuclear age must be understood in the context of the country's involvement in the Second World War; decolonization, state building, and plans for state-led economic development; and the country's position in the emerging Cold War. Only then can we come to grips with the ambivalence toward nuclear power that marked Indian policy during the decade that followed the bombing of Hiroshima and Nagasaki.[3] On the one hand, Indian leaders were appalled at the destruction wrought by the bomb and its portents for the future of world politics. On the other, they were keen to harness the potential of atomic power for India's own development and were averse to foreclosing the possibility of acquiring nuclear weapons in the future.

The Second World War

British India was pulled into the Second World War with no account taken of the opinion of Indian nationalists. Although the nationalists were divided on the role that India should play in the conflict, the bulk of them were prepared to support the Western democracies, provided India was promised its own freedom. Britain's unwillingness to contemplate any such move during the war led to a serious rift between the Raj and the dominant nationalist outfit, the Indian National Congress led by M. K. Gandhi. The manner in which India was drawn into the war would color the postcolonial leadership's thinking about the country's role in any future conflict. Here lay the origins of the idea of nonalignment.

In any event, the Raj managed to mobilize India massively for the war effort. The Indian Army grew over tenfold, recruiting, training, and deploying some 2.5 million men. Even at the time, it was recognized as the largest volunteer force in the war. These soldiers fought in an astonishing range of places: Hong Kong and Singapore; Malaya and Burma; Iraq, Iran, and Syria; North and East Africa; Italy and Greece; Cyprus and Crete. India's material and financial contributions to the war were equally significant. India emerged as a major military-industrial and logistical base for Allied operations in Southeast Asia and the Middle East. Such extraordinary mobilization for war was achieved at great human cost: the Bengal famine was the most extreme manifestation of widespread wartime deprivation. The costs on India's home front must be counted in millions of lives. As far as our story is concerned, the war had three major consequences that impinged on India's subsequent nuclear trajectory.

In the first place, the war at once brought to the fore the enormous challenge of reconstruction and development that lay ahead and highlighted the critical role of the state in postwar development. The British Raj had long fancied itself as a classic "nightwatchman" state that would focus on a set of activities: above all, law and order, taxation, and development of communications. The First World War and the Great Depression had already forced the British Indian state toward a deeper involvement in the management of the economy. The Second World War enormously accelerated this process. At the outbreak of war, India had only a few government-run ordnance factories and no basic industries—private or government—necessary to support a war in the industrial age. The country had been reliant on imports for everything from machine tools to heavy chemicals and optical instruments. In the first two years of the war, the demands on India were not extraordinary, and the Raj attempted to continue business as usual with minimal changes. Thus there was little effort on the part of the government to coordinate the activity of war-related industries. Nor did the government welcome offers by Indian businessmen to collaborate with the war effort provided the government gave them regulatory clearances and firm orders.[4] In the wake of Pearl Harbor and the Japanese advances in Southeast Asia and Burma, India was pulled into the war in a serious manner. The ensuing mammoth demands of manpower and materiel, as well as the disruption of shipping and curtailment of imports, forced the British Indian state to massively expand its footprint.

From early 1942 the Indian economy began moving into a higher gear. GDP in real terms expanded during the war years by 10.6 percent. In fact, from 1943 to 1944 it expanded by 12.3 percent, before contracting a bit over the next two years. The growth in output was comparable to that in countries like the USSR and Britain. The state played an important role in spurring industrial production, especially after 1941. The various government departments and bodies dealing with war supplies began coordinating their activities and reducing multiplication of effort. An Industrial Planning Organization was set up under the supply department and staffed by experts from various sectors. The department established links with industry via a plethora of advisory committees and panels that helped draw on technical expertise and experience. The government also began encouraging industrial production by a variety of means. This included helping industrialists to start new ventures or expand existing ones by providing capital assistance and a promise of protection for those undertakings whose postwar prospects seemed uncertain. Nearly 160 private factories—many of them undertaking heavy engineering—were expanded thanks to government financing. In effect, the government was adopting a policy of import-substituting industrialization—one that would be continued in independent India.[5]

Even before the war ended, there was widespread thinking in India that the state would have to play a leading role in postwar, planned economic development. The Raj's bureaucracy and leading Indian businessmen shared this view with political parties across the spectrum of Indian politics. Even prior to the war, the Congress had established a National Planning Commission, including businessmen and scientists, and its members advanced the agenda of state-led economic development during the war.[6] Perhaps the most famous statement about the need for a developmental state for independent India was the "Bombay Plan" of 1944, drafted by a group of prominent Indian businessmen.[7]

The war not only etched the idea of state-led development in the minds of Indian politicians and publicists, bureaucrats and businessmen, but also established the institutional framework for leveraging scientific and technological research for industrial purposes. In 1940 the Indian government created a Board of Scientific and Industrial Research and appointed the physical chemist Shanti Swarup Bhatnagar as its director. In late 1942 this entity was expanded into a Council on Scientific and Industrial Research (CSIR) that oversaw all civilian research pertaining to the war. Within months the CSIR also drew up plans for a National Physical Laboratory and a National Chemical Laboratory and managed to secure Indian philanthropic funding for the latter from the Tata Trusts. While its functioning was far from smooth owing to the diversity of views held by Indian scientists, businessmen, and bureaucrats, the CSIR emerged as a central body for coordination of scientific research during and after the war.[8]

In late 1943 the Indian government also invited the eminent physiologist Archibald V. Hill to visit India as a representative of the Royal Society and to survey scientific research establishments for their contribution to the war effort. Hill spent five months in India studying various laboratories and institutions with an eye to the aftermath of the war as well. Even before Hill had arrived, the National Institute of Sciences of India (NIS) held a symposium on the "Postwar Organization of Scientific Research in India." Attended by leading Indian scientists, the meeting considered "how should wartime infrastructure in science and technology be assimilated for peacetime civil organization; what should be the organization model for science and technology adopted for postwar and independent India." The NIS continued to deliberate this issue even as it surveyed the Indian scientific scene. Both the NIS and Hill's report spoke of research committees, boards, and national laboratories, but Hill went further in favoring the creation of a centralized government department that would entirely control and coordinate all scientific and industrial research.[9] The importance of state-led scientific research was reinforced when, over the course of five months starting in late 1944, a group of Indian scientists, including Bhatnagar and physicist Meghnad Saha, visited research facilities in Britain, Canada, and the United States.

The war shaped India's subsequent nuclear program in yet a third way. It cast into sharp relief the geopolitical position of independent India in the years ahead. As early as 1940, when the leaders of the Congress Party were grappling with the question of India's attitude toward the war, a sharp rift emerged between Gandhi and other leaders, especially Nehru. Gandhi wanted India to affirm its nonviolent credentials by promising that independent India would dispense with armed forces. Nehru and other senior colleagues held this to be unrealistic in a world of sovereign states and great powers that ruthlessly pursued their interests. These debates also rekindled older differences between them on the need for large-scale industrialization in India. Against Gandhi's idea of an India consisting of self-sustaining village communities, Nehru argued that if independent India had to maintain its independence, both de jure and de facto, then it had to embark on planned industrialization. The geopolitical imperative of going down this path was amply underscored by the war, and there was no escaping it.[10] In the years ahead, too, Nehru would frequently emphasize the geopolitical importance of building an industrial and scientific base in India.

The war also thrust India into a significant geopolitical position in Asia. By 1946 Japan lay prostrate in defeat, and China was enmeshed in a renewed civil war. India stood, therefore, as a potent Asian power. As de facto prime minister of the interim government constituted in September 1946, Jawaharlal Nehru could confidently assert: "Whatever the present position of India might be, she is potentially a Great Power. Undoubtedly in the future she will have to play a very great part in security problems of Asia and the Indian Ocean, more especially of the Middle East and South-East Asia. Indeed, India is the pivot around which these problems will have to be considered.... India is the centre of security in Asia." At the same time, he held that "India should adopt an independent attitude with no marked alignment with any group.... India should play a much more independent role in foreign affairs."[11] In his first speech as the head of the interim government, Nehru declared: "We propose, so far as possible, to keep away from the power politics of groups aligned against one another, which have led in the past to world wars and which may again lead to disasters on an even vaster scale."

Even as Nehru looked forward to independent India playing an important role in Asian and world affairs, he was mindful of the dramatic changes ushered in by the atomic bomb. "Warfare in modern times," he noted, "assumes industrial development of a high order. Tomorrow's army may consist largely of technicians with scientists at their back.... The atom bomb will decide wars in the future."[12] At the same time, Nehru was deeply concerned about an incipient, spiraling nuclear arms race. Following an American nuclear test in July 1946, he observed that the U.S. objective might be coercive: "to announce to the world ... their readiness to blow up any people or country who came in the way of their policy." Yet it was bound to increase insecurity in other countries: "Inevitably that fear will grow and grip nations and peoples and each would try frantically to get this new weapon or some adequate protection from it." Nehru was certain that "the atom bomb is not the way of peace or freedom."[13]

Nehru's thoughts on dangers posed by nuclear weapons echoed those of Gandhi. The apostle of nonviolence had been stunned into silence by the destruction of Hiroshima and Nagasaki. As he wrote to a friend a couple of months later, "The more I think, the more I feel that I must not speak on the atomic bomb. I must act if I can."[14] Almost a year passed before he wrote at length about the bombing of Japan. The use of atomic bombs, he noted, portended limitless escalation of wars. "There used to be the so-called laws of war, which made it tolerable. Now we know the naked truth. War knows no law except that of might." Japanese aggression, he conceded, had been the original crime. Still, it "conferred no right on ... [the Allies] to destroy without mercy men, women and children of Japan in a particular area." The only moral that could be drawn from the "supreme tragedy of the bomb is that it will not be destroyed by counter-bombs [sic] even as violence cannot be by counter-violence."[15]

Nehru and other leaders of the Congress had long ago parted with Gandhi on the question of absolute nonviolence. Yet, while Nehru realized the import of nuclear weapons, he was also loath to take India down that road. His subsequent approach to nuclear research would be shaped by the confluence of the three wartime developments discussed above: ideas of a developmental state, state control over scientific and industrial research, and the geopolitical importance of an indigenous scientific-industrial complex.

State, Development, and Nuclear Science

Even as the Second World War moved toward its denouement, the CSIR began to plan for research on atomic energy. This effort was led by a group of scientists interested in nuclear matters well before August 1945. Leading Indian physicists such as Saha, Bhatnagar, and Homi Bhabha had closely followed the discovery of fission in 1939 and grasped its theoretical import and experimental requirements. In 1941 Saha had already written about the "possibility of a chain reaction" and explosions through the fission of U_{235}. In the wake of the nuclear bombing of Japan, he wrote a series of articles expounding the "Logic of the Atomic Bomb." Saha was, however, more interested in underscoring the opportunities opened up by nuclear energy for the development of poverty-stricken countries like India. The Manhattan Project showed, he wrote, "that if a team of well-chosen scientists be selected for studying a problem in an objective way, and be directed to find out the remedy, and if sufficient funds and power be placed in their hands to execute their plans, they can be trusted to solve problems of [postwar] reconstruction which baffle the politician and centuries of neglect can be compressed into decades."[16]

The physicist K. S. Krishnan similarly wrote in August 1945 that "the discovery of the atomic bomb has made warfare *terrific beyond imagination*." Yet if the "tremendous energy released from atomic explosions is made available to drive machinery, it will bring about an industrial revolution of a far reaching character." The eminent physicist and Nobel laureate C. V. Raman insisted that "the accomplishment of atomic fission on a mass scale and the consequent release of nuclear energy have been the most outstanding by-products of atomic research, having found their application in the so-called Atom Bomb.... The tremendous possibilities of nuclear research cannot be overemphasized and it is truly the 'Problem of the Times.'"[17]

Bhatnagar and Saha had picked up a good amount of information about nuclear research, its organization, and the secrecy around it during their tour from 1944 to 1945. By the end of 1945, nuclear research was on the scientific establishment's radar. As Bhatnagar wrote, "We raised the issue in the last meeting of the Governing Body [CSIR] and I am raising it again. I fully appreciate that India cannot be allowed to completely ignore this research and that we shall have to take some very active steps to do something as it is going to be a very potent factor in industrial development of the world, and India cannot be a cipher in this direction."[18] In the years ahead, this network of experts would drive India's nuclear energy program, emphasizing its developmental possibilities.

Nehru was quick to seize the idea of nuclear energy driving India's development. He had been following debates on planned economic development since the mid-1930s and had well-developed views on the need for scientific expertise in steering the process of planning and industrialization. Nehru was particularly interested in the work of nuclear physicists, having played an important role in procuring the first cyclotron for India some two decades back.

As independence approached, Nehru worked closely with Bhabha and Saha among others to place atomic research in India on a firm institutional footing. "Atomic energy," he argued, "is going to play a vast and dominating part . . . in the future shape of things." While he hoped that India would undertake this research "not to make bombs . . . nevertheless I do not see how we can lag behind in this very important matter."[19] Writing to his defense minister just months after India became independent, he noted that "the future belongs to those who produce atomic energy. That is going to be the chief, noted power of the future. Of course, Defence is intimately connected with this."[20] Interestingly, Nehru was at this time consulting the British physicist Patrick Blackett on matters relating to science and security. He asked Blackett if the knowledge gained in the process of making nuclear piles could be used for building a bomb "even though the present government is averse to such an idea."[21]

This ambivalent note—one that emphasized the developmental aspect of atomic energy while recognizing yet disavowing the military angle—was also evident in Nehru's interventions in the constituent assembly of India, the body that was drawing up a republican constitution for the country. Introducing the Atomic Energy Act in April 1948, Nehru noted that "unfortunately, the first use that atomic energy has been put to has somewhat clouded the other manifold uses that it is likely to be put to in the future." It was imperative for India, with its "vast potential and strength," to work toward channeling atomic energy for developmental purposes. The bill was challenged on the floor of the House for the secrecy that would shroud nuclear research in India. One member of the assembly wanted to know "if secrecy is insisted upon even for research for peaceful purposes. . . . In the United Kingdom secrecy is restricted only for defence purposes." The prime minister tersely replied: "I do not know how you are to distinguish between the two." In subsequent discussion, he added, "We must develop [atomic energy] . . . for peaceful purposes. . . . Of course, if we are compelled as a nation to use it for other purposes, possibly no pious sentiments of any of us will stop the nation from using it that way."[22]

Yet it would be misleading to assume that the military applications of nuclear research were covertly on the agenda of the independent Indian government. The secrecy surrounding the Indian program was neither a cloak for other pursuits nor merely an imitation of the governmental practices adopted by other countries such as the United States and Britain. Rather, as Robert Anderson argues, it was more the consequence of the conditions imposed by foreign agencies on which India was necessarily dependent for negotiation of nuclear power. As Nehru put it in 1954, "Those other countries are more advanced than we are, and if we have any association with them in regard to this work, they would want us to keep it secret, even if we do not."[23]

In its first meeting in the summer of 1948, the new Atomic Energy Commission (AEC) adopted a resolution laying down the general policy guidelines for the nuclear program. The first point in this top-secret document read: "With a view to its future industrial and economic importance for India steps should be taken to set up a small pile as soon as possible. This pile would be used for making radio-active tracer elements for biological, chemical and metallurgical research, for testing materials like graphite and beryllium which might be used in a larger pile, and for training scientific personnel." The fourth and last point noted: "Steps should be taken for processing monazite to thorium nitrate and ultimately to thorium metal, and also for extracting the uranium from the monazite. The possibilities of making heavy water, beryllium metal and pure graphite should be investigated." The two intervening points focused on the need to complete construction of a cyclotron in Calcutta, which would be useful for training, and on providing main support for research in nuclear physics to work on cosmic rays.[24]

When Frederic Joliot-Curie, the high commissioner for Atomic Energy in France, visited India in early 1950, Nehru invited him to a meeting of the AEC and shared the guidelines of 1948. The Indian prime minister opened the meeting by stating that "India's interest in atomic energy is solely for its peaceful uses. Quite apart from the fact that she had not the resources to make atomic bombs and use atomic energy for military purposes, she was not interested in its military use on principle." He was keen to hear Joliot-Curie's views on three key issues: "general scientific possibilities," the "time within which the harnessing of atomic power could be achieved," and "the price at which atomic power could be promoted in the future."

If nuclear power generation was a central concern of the early program, the shaping of scientific research was the other. Recent histories of early nuclear India have persuasively suggested that much of the discussion in the government and the scientific community was actually over the contours of nuclear research laboratories. Questions of scale, location, and financing were far more important in the early nuclear debates than was a potential weapons capability. As Jahnavi Phalkey has argued, it is far more useful to think about the history of the Indian program in the decade following independence as a multicornered debate between key scientific institutions—the Indian Institute of Science (in Bangalore), the Tata Institute of Fundamental Research (in Bombay), and Calcutta University—over the best direction in which to advance nuclear research, with an ensuing tussle over government funding. It was also at times a clash of personalities—especially between Bhabha and Saha—that had very different substantive views and styles of research.

Above all, the history of the Indian nuclear program in these years is best understood in relation to the emergence of an ambitious state. Even as the Nehru government embarked on five-year plans for economic development drawn up by a battery of Indian and foreign economists and experts, the state's control over nuclear research deepened at the expense of university laboratories. As with planned economic development, this dimension of the Indian state developed in line with the views of an international network of nuclear scientists. For instance, at the meeting with Joliot-Curie in 1950, Nehru pointedly asked for his suggestion about the organization of nuclear scientific research in India. The French scientist replied:

> The scale of operations in India is not yet large enough at present to develop atomic energy in a reasonably short time. Larger sums of money will be required to bring the effort up to the appropriate level.... He was strongly of the view that in countries like India or France where there was a great limitation of specialists, both scientists and technicians, it was necessary to establish only one centre for atomic energy and concentrate in it not only the most qualified scientists, but engineers with the requisite knowledge of chemical, mechanical and electrical techniques. This centre should have a character both scientific and industrial. After a time, when the requisite personnel had been developed in sufficient numbers and more scientific means were available, another centre could be established, and then several. But concentration at the beginning was absolutely essential if the effort was not to be frittered away and dissipated.[25]

The move toward such concentration of nuclear research or "big science" under governmental control marked a major step in the evolution of the developmental state in India.

Geopolitics and the Cold War

By the fall of 1946, almost a year before India became independent, Nehru was speaking of India's role as an Asian and global actor and was adumbrating the idea of nonalignment against the backdrop of the souring relationship between the wartime Allies. His views on industrialization and the role of science and technology were strongly shaped by perceived geopolitical necessity. If India's independence and nonalignment were to be substantial, it was imperative to embark on state-led industrialization informed by scientific expertise. Ahead of Indian independence in August 1947, however, Nehru had failed to reckon with the potential consequences of the partition of India. Partition proved to be a colossal human tragedy, with millions killed and displaced. But it had longer-term geopolitical consequences as well.

For one thing, it severed India's geographic, economic, and cultural links with the Middle East and Southeast Asia, thereby shrinking India's ability to project its influence in these regions. India was no longer the "pivot" of Asian security, as Nehru had believed in the wake of the Second World War. On the contrary, its geopolitical position had been circumscribed. For another, India was soon locked into a bitter rivalry with Pakistan—one that opened up the subcontinent to the continued involvement of the great powers. Nehru saw Pakistan's decision in 1954 to enter into military alliance with the United States as bringing the Cold War to India's doorstep.[26] Nehru did not believe that the U.S.-Pakistan alliance portended an immediate security threat to India. Rather, he saw it as pulling India deeper into the geopolitics of the Cold War with potential implications for its ability to play an independent role in world politics. India, he insisted, had to adopt a longer view on building up its strength and not get bogged down in the immediate machinations of the great powers: "The equation of defence is your defence forces plus your industrial and technological background, plus, thirdly, the economy of the country, and fourthly, the spirit of the people."[27]

The early Cold War did, however, impinge on India's nuclear policy in at least two important ways. From the outset, it was evident to Nehru and Indian scientists that, while India would be heavily dependent on Western assistance to bootstrap its nuclear program, such assistance would not be easy to secure. As early as mid-1945 Bhatnagar had observed that the fact that "the USA is not prepared to share the scientific knowledge regarding the atomic bomb with the rest of the world is indicative of how statesmen and politicians, even in advanced countries, can hamper science in solving international problems."[28] Nor was securing such assistance from the Soviet Union even a remote possibility, owing to both the poor state of bilateral relations until the mid-1950s and India's avowed desire to stay nonaligned. Nehru and his scientists initially hoped that India's decision to remain in the Commonwealth would enable it to access some of Britain's scientific and technological expertise, but these fell short of expectations.

Yet India was able to find some room for maneuver in the nuclear politics of the Cold War. In particular, it was able to establish a relationship with France that proved crucial in the early years of the Indian program. Even more so than India, postwar France chafed under the Anglo-American (composed of the three Manhattan Project powers of the United States, United Kingdom, and Canada) dominance of the emerging nuclear order. The quest for recovering French grandeur inevitably led to an emphasis on establishing a nuclear program. It was in this context that France forged a nuclear tie with India, supplying nuclear technology while receiving mineral resources. India had, in fact, jealously guarded its deposits of strategic minerals, especially beryl and monazite, resisting attempts by Britain and the United States to access them. More significantly, the French and Indian nuclear establishments collaborated on equal terms in conducting research and undertaking technical studies of beryllium-moderated research reactors—a frontier technology at that point in time. In short, notwithstanding the dynamics of the Cold War, India found important ways to advance its nuclear program.[29]

As the Cold War deepened in the late 1940s, India was concerned about its more problematic nuclear dimension. The testing of the bomb by the Soviet Union and Britain suggested that a serious nuclear arms race was now under way. Equally worrying was the awesome destructive power of thermonuclear bombs. The Korean War drove home to Nehru the persisting danger of a major conflict in Asia—one that would draw India into the vortex and end its plans for peaceful economic growth. As an interlocutor between China and the United States in the early stages of the war, Nehru had followed its escalation, including the threat of nuclear attack, with mounting concern. As he noted in late 1952, "If atomic and hydrogen bombs are used in warfare it means complete giving up of civilization.... Wars are fought presumably to attain certain objectives. But these objectives themselves are destroyed in the process of war."[30]

Nehru was clear, however, that banning the bomb was easier said than done: "Who is to bell the cat?" It might have been easier had there been no superpower rivalry. "Nobody is going to be controlled till he is quite certain that the other is controlled; and nobody is going to be certain till there is much more confidence in each other than there is at present." Unless such confidence were built between the superpowers—"some agreement to live and let live and not to try to destroy others"—the nuclear arms race would continue apace. Nehru was equally skeptical about President Eisenhower's "Atoms for Peace" proposal calling for international control and supervision of nuclear research and production: "It would be to the advantage of the countries who have adequate power resources to restrain and restrict the use of atomic energy.... It would be to the disadvantage of a country like India that is restricted or stopped."[31]

Even as India was determined not to allow its nuclear program to be crimped, Nehru sought to take the lead in slowing down the nuclear arms race. In November 1953 India spearheaded a UN General Assembly resolution on disarmament calling for the "elimination and prohibition of atomic, hydrogen, bacterial, chemical and other weapons of mass destruction and for the attainment of these ends through effective means." In the wake of the Bikini Atoll test of March 1, 1954, Nehru advanced a specific proposal regarding thermonuclear weapons. He advocated a "Standstill Agreement" with respect to testing them, "even if arrangements about the discontinuance of production and stockpiling must await more substantial agreements amongst those principally concerned." He also called for a concerted international effort to raise public awareness of the enormous destructive capacities of the hydrogen bomb.[32]

Writing to Winston Churchill ahead of a British parliamentary debate on the subject, Nehru said that his proposal was "feasible of immediate achievement and without prejudice to matters of acute difference between the parties principally concerned." The "Standstill Agreement" was very like a ceasefire in war. He believed that if the superpowers agreed to a moratorium on testing, "we would have made a beginning in stopping the dangerous drift to disaster."[33] Nehru also urged a meeting of Southeast Asian leaders to adopt a resolution to this effect. Although the Colombo Conference issued a statement calling for a moratorium on hydrogen bomb testing, it fell on stony ground. Neither superpower deigned to take notice of the resolution, let alone acted on it. (On the broader "Third World" context in which India's efforts unfolded, see Shinsuke Tomotsugu's discussion in chapter 7 of this volume.)

In the following years, Nehru was tireless in his public advocacy for a ban on nuclear testing. At the same time, he ensured that the Indian nuclear research program continued to progress—notwithstanding the latent possibility of weaponization in the future. Visiting Hiroshima in October 1957, Nehru received a rapturous welcome. The Indian prime minister described the trip as a "pilgrimage." Speaking to an audience of over thirty thousand residents, he stated, "We must strive towards the goal of abolition of nuclear devices and disarmament, and through mutual trust we must realize One World."[34]

It was characteristic of the distinctive Indian stance during this period that these attempts at and calls for nuclear disarmament did not imply that India was willing either to accept intrusive international controls over its own program or to foreclose the possibility that the country could possess a nuclear bomb at some point in the future. Thus India stood up against U.S.-led efforts to establish tight safeguards on states' abilities to acquire and use nuclear fuels and facilities under the new International Atomic Energy Agency. In particular, India opposed the provision in the draft statute that plutonium and other special fissionable materials were to be deposited with the IAEA—barring what the agency would allow countries to hold for specified nonmilitary purposes under safeguards. Speaking at the IAEA statute conference in September 1956, Homi Bhabha maintained: "We consider it to be the inalienable right of States to produce and hold fissionable material required for the peaceful power programmes." He went on to argue that technologically advanced states would not need assistance from the IAEA; hence they would dispense with the safeguards being imposed on states that were not technologically independent. "We will stand on the brink of a dangerous era," he warned, "sharply dividing the world into atomic 'haves' and 'have nots' dominated by the Agency."[35]

Bhabha's argument carried the day. It also anticipated India's stance toward the nonproliferation regime that would be crafted by the United States in subsequent years—especially its refusal to sign the Nuclear Nonproliferation Treaty of 1968. Yet it would be erroneous to find too strong a continuity between India's position in the mid-1950s and that of a decade later. The latter was shaped more strongly by India's immediate security concerns, especially in the wake of the war with China in 1962, the Chinese nuclear tests of 1964, and the war with Pakistan in 1965, during which the Chinese aligned themselves with Pakistan to put pressure on India. All this could barely have been foreseen in the mid-1950s when India-China relations were at a high point. (On China's nuclear trajectory during this period, see Avery Goldstein's analysis in chapter 13 of this volume.) India's position on safeguards was continuous with its early tryst with nuclear research.

During the decade following independence, India's nuclear trajectory was shaped by the impact of the Second World War on the Indian state, the turn toward creating a strong developmental state with scientific expertise, and the need to secure India's geopolitical independence and its developmental aspirations in the context of the Cold War. These meant creating institutions and adopting policies that could potentially give India the option to build a bomb. Nehru and his scientists acknowledged this openly while also disavowing their intent to go down that route. It is reductive to flatten the many, and at times competing, priorities and considerations of the Indian nuclear program into a fig leaf for the pursuit of nuclear weapons. It is also ahistorical. Hindsight is necessary and often invaluable for the historian. But its flat glare can also distort our understanding of the past, especially by suggesting that things had to turn out the way they did. In the early nuclear age India had a rather different set of priorities, considerations, and constraints than those in the following years. The early 1960s marked a rupture in this early history, and the ensuing break led India down a different, although equally jagged, path over the next decade and beyond.

9

The Unnecessary Option to Go Nuclear

JAPAN'S NONNUCLEAR POLICY IN AN
ERA OF UNCERTAINTY, 1950S–1960S

Wakana Mukai

WHY DID JAPAN DECIDE not to develop or possess nuclear weapons? Scholars engaged in the study of nuclear issues have been fascinated with this question for decades. Two quick and widely shared answers would be antinuclearism, or the pacifist and antinuclear views of large parts of Japanese society, on the one hand, and extended deterrence, or the nuclear umbrella provided by the United States, on the other.

The former viewpoint is based on the disastrous experience of Hiroshima and Nagasaki, as well as the *Lucky Dragon No. 5* (*Daigo Fukuryu-Maru*) incident of 1954, which led to the rise of a strong stance against nuclear weapons across Japanese society, a viewpoint often seen as part of a unique Japanese identity.[1] This basic idea, that Japan has always adopted an antinuclear stance, is often seen as the basis for a number of foreign policy decisions—for example, the confirmation of the three nonnuclear principles as national policy in 1971, the reversion of an explicitly nonnuclear Okinawa to Japan in 1972, and Japan's strong commitments to various nuclear disarmament and nonproliferation related treaties, such as the Nuclear Nonproliferation Treaty (NPT).[2] Hence this unique moral position cannot be ignored when we examine the history of Japan's nuclear policy.[3]

Japan has also cherished and held on to the U.S.-Japan alliance as the basis of its security policies.[4] Traditionally, from a realist point of view, it appears somewhat odd that Japan did not develop or seek to possess its own nuclear weapons in the context of an insecure regional environment in which three of its closest neighbors, Russia (formerly the Soviet Union), China, and North Korea, possess nuclear weapons. Nevertheless, Japan chose to rely on the U.S. nuclear umbrella as it secured a new strategic position within the region after World War II.

Previous works have tended to focus on one or more of the explanations above, but they have seldom discussed the relationship that may exist among these explanations. Thus how pacifist movements and the nuclear umbrella might have been related (or not) remains an area in need of further research. This is because while actors in civil society have generated antinuclearism, government policy makers have generated decisions about the nuclear umbrella. Far from maintaining a close relationship, these two groups of actors tend actively to alienate each other, and the divide is not only institutional but also political. Antinuclearism enjoys support from so-called leftists, while the nuclear umbrella is supported by conservatives.

A more fundamental yet simple question can also be asked: Did Japan ever really consider going nuclear? Here, one can use "Japan" to refer to both the Japanese decision-making community and the Japanese public. The focus, however, should clearly be on the decision-making community, namely, the politicians and bureaucrats, since ultimately the decision to go nuclear or not lay in the hands of those individuals. Previous studies have started from the viewpoint that Japan explicitly or implicitly had the *will* to go nuclear given the right conditions but eventually *decided* not to. Is this, however, truly the case?

This chapter will reexamine the nuclear policy of Japan in the 1950s and 1960s with a special focus on events leading up to China's nuclear test of 1964, looking into independent studies conducted by several government-related groups, together with the dynamics of the antinuclear movement that swept through Japan in the 1950s. The challenge is to reconsider existing discourses while reevaluating, rather than outright discarding, the importance of Japan's unique position as the only country to experience a nuclear attack.

The first section looks at the dynamics of the antinuclear movement that rose to prominence in Japan in 1954 and examines the rise and fall of the movement. It should not be surprising that the antinuclear movement and the atmosphere it created did not eventually obtain long-term and comprehensive support from both government officials and Japanese society as a whole. However, we should not conclude from this that it had no effect whatsoever. Although it may be impossible to trace *direct* effects on governmental decisions, the antinuclear movement appears to have exercised an *indirect* influence on

Japan's nuclear decisions. The three nonnuclear principles, which Prime Minister Satō Eisaku announced in 1968 and became national policy in 1971, serve as a perfect example. The important point here is that this announcement was a unilateral decision by the government to tie itself to the nonnuclear option. This action, of course, was a strategic bargaining chip that Japanese officials proposed in an attempt to preserve the U.S.-Japan alliance and nuclear deterrence. But had the government not taken the antinuclear movement seriously, whether directly or indirectly, the bargaining resulting in the three nonnuclear principles would not have been undertaken.

The second section examines the government's nuclear policy decisions, with a special focus on China's nuclear test of 1964 and the Japanese government's perception of the threat involved. Here, one should keep in mind that threat perceptions and actual threats are two different things. As the chapter will discuss further, parts of the decision-making community were, in fact, deeply worried about China's potential to become the fifth country to possess nuclear weapons. On the other hand, the actual threat was out of sync with the threat perceptions that dominated bureaucrats in the Ministry of Foreign Affairs. In many cases, they had other priorities that were considered more important than the nuclear option, including the possibility of better relations with China and securing the U.S.-Japan alliance.

The Rise and Fall of the Antinuclear Movement

Origin of the Movement: The Signature Campaign

After the dropping of the atomic bombs on Hiroshima and Nagasaki in 1945, there was a long period of press censorship during the Allied Occupation of Japan. When the U.S.-Japan Security Pact and the San Francisco Peace Treaty came into force in 1952, many press reports and publications began to make public information related to Hiroshima and Nagasaki, as well as images of the damage done by the bombs.

Thus when the Japanese fishing vessel *Lucky Dragon No. 5* was exposed to the fallout from an American hydrogen bomb test on March 1, 1954, members of the general public were beginning to realize how damaging atomic bombs were and how much damage they had caused to Hiroshima and Nagasaki. The scoop article by *Yomiuri shimbun* on March 6 shocked many Japanese citizens, and a huge wave of antinuclear emotion spread throughout the country.[5]

About a month later, on April 16, an appeal from a member of the Suginami Woman's Council (Suginami fujin dantai kyogikai) was followed by the drafting of the signature campaign, which led to the creation of the Suginami

Council on the Signature Campaign against Atomic and Hydrogen Bombs (Gensuibaku kinshi shomei undo suginami kyogikai), chaired by Yasui Kaoru. The campaign started on May 14, and more than thirty million signatures were collected by August 4.[6]

On August 8 the Japan Council on the Signature Campaign against Atomic and Hydrogen Bombs (Nihon gensuibaku kinshi shomei undo zenkoku kyogikai) was established for the purpose of garnering wider support for the campaign. The group hoped to "convey the consensus of the Japanese people indicated in the signatures in and around the country, and to build up worldwide public opinion against atomic and hydrogen bombs" in a nonpartisan manner.[7] The antinuclear movement garnered widespread interest and enthusiasm from local governments as well as from the Japanese government.

The Movement's Golden Age

On August 6, 1955, strong support from nearly a third of the population of Japan led the movement to hold the First World Conference against Atomic and Hydrogen Bombs. Approximately fifty delegations from eleven countries, and nearly five thousand domestic participants, gathered in Hiroshima and announced the "Hiroshima appeal," which stated that the movement against atomic and hydrogen bombs must "develop until utter peace is achieved," and that "today is the starting point" for this movement.[8]

To help achieve this goal, the Japan Council on the Signature Campaign and the Preparatory Meeting for the World Conference merged into the Japan Council against Atomic and Hydrogen Bombs (Gensuibaku kinshi Nihon kyogikai: Gensuikyo) in September. Two important purposes of this group were to promote the antinuclear movement and to support and initiate relief movements for the victims of the atomic bombs (*hibakusha*).[9]

In parallel with the rise of this civic group, atomic bomb victims themselves established independent organizations throughout the country. At the Second World Conference against Atomic and Hydrogen Bombs, the Japan Confederation of Victims of the Atomic and Hydrogen Bomb Organizations (Nihon gensuibaku higaisha dantai kyogikai: Hidankyo) was inaugurated. This took place in the context of a growing consensus around strong antinuclear sentiments and support for the victims of nuclear weapons.[10] As the "Message to the World" proclaimed at the first meeting of Hidankyo stated: "Humanity must never again inflict nor suffer the sacrifice and torture we have experienced. Atomic power, which has a tendency to follow the road to destruction and extermination, must absolutely be converted to a servant for the happiness and prosperity of humankind. This is the only desire we hold as long as we live."[11] The *hibakusha* were seen as a symbol of these movements, engaging in "saving humanity from its crisis through lessons learned" from their own experiences.[12]

The Third World Conference against Atomic and Hydrogen Bombs in August 1957 was another success, with strong domestic and international support, as approximately five thousand domestic delegates and ninety-four international delegates from twenty-two countries gathered in Tokyo.[13]

The First Cleavage

Unfortunately, the golden age did not last long. The antinuclear movement was soon affected by various external factors as the international environment changed dramatically. It also became more difficult to manage diverse viewpoints as a wide variety of people continued to join the movement. A clear fault line emerged between members who wanted to limit the movement strictly to antinuclear issues and those who emphasized the importance of bringing in as many people as possible to make sure their voices were heard.[14]

One of the most controversial issues was the revision of the U.S.-Japan Security Treaty. At the March 1 event commemorating the fifth anniversary of the *Lucky Dragon* incident, Gensuikyo adopted a declaration specifying that the movement would "appeal to [those] in and out of the country to work toward the immediate conclusion of a nuclear test ban treaty and opposition toward the revision of the U.S.-Japan Security Treaty."[15] Various people, including members of Gensuikyo, the Socialist Party, and the General Council of Trade Unions of Japan (Sohyo), came together to establish a group calling for opposition to treaty revisions, and Gensuikyo became one of the core corresponding groups. This action alarmed the Liberal Democratic Party (LDP) as it was a clear move against the party's current policy of reinforcing and expanding ties with the United States. The LDP criticized the decision as "a move under the pretext of antinuclear [sentiment for] what is clearly a political campaign."[16]

On July 9, 1959, the Hiroshima Prefectural Assembly decided to cut by 300,000 yen its subsidy to the Hiroshima Prefectural Council against Atomic and Hydrogen Bombs (Hiroshima-ken gensuikyo). The council had applied for 500,000 yen from the Prefectural Assembly on June 8, and, while the latter had already initially approved a budget of 300,000 yen, these funds were ultimately withdrawn owing to strong opposition from the LDP. This move quickly spread throughout the country, as local assemblies withdrew subsidies for local groups related to Gensuikyo. The biggest concern was that the antinuclear movement had become a political movement led by the Socialist and Communist Parties.

Gensuikyo tried to amend its policy to show that it was not necessarily committed to strong opposition to treaty revision, and words such as "objection toward revision" were not included in any of the appeals, declarations, or resolutions. Nevertheless, concerns about the possibility of Japan going nuclear, the revival of militarism, and the deployment of troops overseas were repeatedly mentioned. Although the "enemy of peace" argument was starting to become an issue, delegates at the Fifth World Conference against Atomic and Hydrogen Bombs in Hiroshima all agreed that "any peace movement does not affiliate with any politics, but it also cannot be detached from politics," and that peace movements are "meant to direct politics toward peace."[17] The Hiroshima-ken gensuikyo was repulsed by Gensuikyo's policies and issued a statement calling for the establishment of a new antinuclear movement group.

The Second Cleavage

The year 1960 began with serious debates over the direction of the Sixth World Conference against Atomic and Hydrogen Bombs. The Communist Party together with Sohyo argued for a further confrontation with the government to take the antinuclear movement a step forward. Gensuikyo decided at its board meeting to oppose the Japanese government's decision to reinforce its commitment to any military alliance, to promote the restoration of diplomatic ties with China, and to plan the Sixth World Conference under the theme "toward demilitarization."[18]

In the end, the Sixth World Conference became a "conference fighting against enemies of peace." The closing remarks stated that there was a need to unite against the "enemies of peace" who adhered to policies that promoted imperialism, aggressive military alliances, and the construction of military bases.[19] Here, the "enemies" were the United States and the Japanese government: the United States in the sense that it had been conducting policies under "imperialism and colonialism," and the Japanese government in the sense that it had followed the U.S. policy by reinforcing the alliance system and seeking to review the security treaty.[20] Such a hard-line stance was clearly the result of the Communist Party's influence on the antinuclear movement. This ideologically biased attitude brought about strong rebukes and led to the withdrawal of some groups, including the National Federation of Regional Women's Organizations (Zenkoku chiiki fujin dantai renrakukai: Chifuren) and the Japan Youth Council (Nihon seinendan kyogikai: Nisseikyo).

Members related to the Democratic Socialist Party, who had been critical of Gensuikyo's policies, decided on January 17, 1960, to establish a new antinuclear group, which led to the creation of the People's Conference on the

Abolition of Nuclear Weapons and Building Peace (Kakuheiki haizetsu heiwa kensetsu kokumin kaigi, or Kakkin) on November 15, 1961.[21]

Paralleling this move, Gensuikyo hosted the Seventh World Conference against Atomic and Hydrogen Bombs under the theme "a conference for solidarity." Despite this more hopeful theme, the conference unfolded in much the same way as the previous year's conference had, with the Communist Party ruling and the Socialist Party in opposition. The members who were working toward establishing Kakkin gathered in Tokyo to host their own antinuclear conference, with support from approximately ten thousand people from various groups, including Sohyo, the Democratic Socialist Party, and the National Women's Federation.[22]

The existing cleavage within Gensuikyo became even more serious with the Soviet Union's decision to recommence its nuclear tests on September 1, 1961.[23] Soviet resumption of nuclear testing threw the situation surrounding the antinuclear movement into confusion: people related to the Communist Party saw nuclear weapons owned by the Communist bloc as "good/necessary nuclear weapons," differentiating them from nuclear weapons owned by Western nations. The fundamental aim of the movement was to ban nuclear testing altogether, and the decision by the Communist bloc introduced yet another political wrinkle, complicating the situation and allowing many, even within the socialist community, to distance themselves from the movement.

The Third Cleavage

At the Eighth World Conference against Atomic and Hydrogen Bombs in August 1962, a deeper confrontation between the Communist Party groups and the Socialist Party groups became obvious, with the former arguing that the conference should call for an immediate withdrawal of American imperialism from Asia, while the latter argued that the conference should show resistance to any nation's nuclear tests, including those within the Communist bloc. The Socialist Party ideas lacked support and their backers exited the conference, leading to the failure to adopt a conference manifesto and hinting that the cleavage was perhaps irreparable.[24] Seven years after its founding, Gensuikyo was forced to suspend its activities for nearly six months.

Meanwhile, Kakkin hosted yet another conference in Hiroshima and emphasized that it was not a secondary organization but a separate peace movement group, differentiating itself from Gensuikyo. Hidankyo, which had been working side by side with Gensuikyo, temporarily wavered but ultimately decided to avoid a split with Gensuikyo.[25]

The Socialist Party and Sohyo, on the other hand, took matters more seriously and started to seek opportunities to establish yet another antinuclear group. The move quickly resulted in a meeting in Hiroshima with 1,500 participants from across the nation. The meeting touched on the importance of positive neutrality, which was the core policy of the Socialist Party.[26] The success of this meeting allowed Socialist Party backers eventually to establish their own antinuclear movement group.

Although Gensuikyo attempted to reunite the two sides, and although for a time there was some hope for success, the Communist Party groups showed a stubborn attitude, especially toward the idea that the movement should call for an end to all nuclear tests, even those conducted by the Communist bloc. Unrepaired, the cleavage only further persuaded the Socialist Party groups of the need for a new organization separating themselves from Gensuikyo. They decided not to participate in any conference ruled by the Communist Party groups, and although a World Conference was held, many groups decided to keep their distance from an antinuclear movement that seemed plagued by divisiveness. In contrast to West Germany's antinuclear movements that led to a broader peace movement, with various factions reinforcing, not conflicting with, one another, as discussed in Holger's Nehring's contribution to this volume (chapter 11), in Japan, the antinuclear movement quickly lost its unity, and this situation remained largely unchanged from 1964 onward.

The Three Nonnuclear Principles: A Strategic Conclusion Based on an Antinuclear Foundation

Although the antinuclear movement was an unprecedented event in Japanese history, it did not directly influence the government's viewpoint on nuclear weapons. The Japanese government focused instead on the changing international environment, paying special attention to the relationship with the United States and the pursuit of Japan's national interest. At times Japan even strongly considered the possibility of going nuclear, contrary to the wishes of the antinuclear movement of the 1960s.

On the other hand, although there was no direct link between the antinuclear movement and nuclear policy decisions made by the government, the antinuclear movement that rose and fell in the 1950s and 1960s nurtured the deep roots of nuclear antipathy that spread across Japanese culture. For example, following the *Lucky Dragon* incident, both the House of Representatives and the House of Councilors approved a resolution banning atomic weapons in April 1954. Several more bipartisan resolutions followed in 1956, 1957, and 1959, all signs of wide support among Japanese citizens for a ban on atomic and hydrogen bombs.

The level of antipathy toward nuclear weapons and their devastating power was indeed unique to Japan, and even though the government distanced itself from the antinuclear movement since the late 1950s, this was more a matter of political posture than it was a matter of disagreement about antinuclear principles.

The Intersecting Moment of the Nuclear Story: The Three Nonnuclear Principles

As Peter J. Katzenstein has pointed out, Japan's nonnuclear policy was "never complete nor attached to specific political issues."[27] In other words, antinuclear sentiment in the general public was unequivocal but vague, and this was the case within the decision-making community as well. While the movement had since 1954 clearly reinforced antinuclear sentiment, the government had not officially announced its stance toward a nonnuclear policy.[28] Thus the announcement of the idea of nonnuclear principles by Prime Minister Satō in December 1967 was an important turning point in Japanese politics regarding Japan's position on nuclear weapons.

Satō introduced the idea for the three nonnuclear principles at the fifty-seventh special session of the Diet in 1968. Replying to questions regarding the return of the Ogasawara islands, which were under U.S. Occupation along with Okinawa at the time, he chose to elaborate on Japan's nonnuclear policy. Restricted not by the constitution but rather by the Atomic Energy Basic Law, Japan could not, strictly speaking, develop or possess nuclear weapons, even for the purpose of self-defense. The remaining issue was that the Atomic Energy Basic Law did not prohibit the importation of nuclear weapons, and should the prime minister himself overtly support the three nonnuclear principles, it might have important consequences, especially regarding relations with the United States.

Acknowledging this fact, Satō touched on the topic of "how to live in the nuclear age" in his 1968 administrative policy speech.[29] Owing to the general public's strong desire to see the abolition of nuclear weapons, Japan would "not venture to possess" nuclear weapons. Satō explicitly mentioned that as "the only citizens victimized by the atomic bomb," Japanese must provide "critical suggestions" as well as become a "big indicator" in international politics, "preserve the right to speak," and "provide positive opinion to international society" in the field of nuclear energy.

Although Satō's speech garnered wide cross-party support, it did not result in a "nonnuclear resolution," nor did it result in the Diet resolution that the opposition parties soon started to demand. The biggest concern from the ruling parties and the government was that if the three nonnuclear principles were acknowledged in a Diet resolution, the diplomatic freedom that was essential for them to negotiate with the United States might be lost.[30] The top priority for the Satō administration at the time was the return of Okinawa, and a nonnuclear resolution would only have made matters more difficult.

Hence the four pillars of Japan's nuclear policy (*Nihon kaku no yonhon hashira*) were announced in January 1968 at a plenary session of the House of Representatives.[31] This was a strategic decision to moderate a firm nonnuclear status by putting forward three other nuclear policies that were also extremely important to Japan at the time: reliance on extended deterrence, promotion of nuclear disarmament, and promotion of the peaceful use of nuclear energy. The most important aspect of this announcement was that the three nonnuclear principles would be maintained only hand-in-hand with the other three policies, and that neither set of policies would stand alone.[32] Satō again tried to steer debate in the Diet away from the adoption of the principles in a resolution, hoping to avoid tensions that might influence the ongoing Okinawa negotiations. Although the three nonnuclear principles were clearly a priority for his government, Satō shelved the idea of enshrining them in an official resolution.

Three years later, however, at the extraordinary session of the Diet of 1971, the Satō administration's position had weakened. Faced with a number of issues in the realm of international politics, including the so-called Nixon Shock and the Sino-U.S. rapprochement, Satō was simultaneously experiencing serious domestic problems, which caused fissures between the ruling and opposition parties over the return of Okinawa.[33] At this point, reviving the issue of enshrining the three nonnuclear principles in a Diet resolution became a card that Satō could use to push for domestic support over Okinawa.

Thus the three nonnuclear principles, which have widely been accepted as symbols of Japan's strong antinuclearism, were not purely a result of this antinuclearism but were also born of a strategic decision that reflected the importance that Japan placed on its security alliance with the United States and the promotion of the peaceful use of nuclear energy.[34] Satō could have promoted the U.S.-Japan security alliance on its own but instead chose to tie the issue to Japan's nonnuclear policy, which eventually restricted the country's nuclear options and took a number of cards off the table for future negotiations.

This decision can be traced at least in part to the antinuclear movement of the late 1950s. Although there was no direct link to decisions made by the government concerning nuclear policies, the antinuclear movement had an indirect influence by establishing Japan's fundamental antipathy toward anything related to nuclear weapons.

Scholars have traditionally placed too much emphasis on the antinuclear characteristics of Japan's nuclear policy precisely because of their uniqueness. However, while the Japanese public did indeed tend to be sensitive about any nuclear issue, Japanese decision makers acted pragmatically in attempting to navigate international politics and bolster the U.S.-Japan security relationship.

It was the simultaneous rigidity and flexibility of Japan's nonnuclear policy that allowed the nuclear umbrella provided by the United States and the antinuclear stance to coexist. As Katzenstein pointed out, although there were regular doubts about "not permitting the introduction" of nuclear weapons, the third nonnuclear principle was repeatedly breached, and the public tolerated these breaches because the U.S.-Japan security alliance had implicitly become accepted as being in Japan's long-term interest.[35] As mentioned by Kurosaki Akira, Satō initially was not going to address this principle in his speech, yet several members of the government and LDP insisted on putting it in the packet so that the Japanese public and members of the opposition parties could relate to and show support for the principles.[36] As the three nonnuclear principles enjoyed widespread support, there were serious concerns that political chaos might result if the government chose to violate these norms.[37] In reality, however, the principles of "not possessing" and "not producing" nuclear weapons were far more rigid than the principle of "not permitting the introduction" of nuclear weapons, a condition that was clearly the result of Japan's reliance on the United States for its security policies.

China's Nuclear Test of 1964 and Japan's Threat Perception

While the grassroots movements were rising and falling, the Japanese government confronted international situations that forced it to reconsider and redefine Japan's future security policies. Here I focus on China's 1964 nuclear test in order to reexamine perceptions surrounding a threat that might have led Japan to consider building its own nuclear weapons.

China's Nuclear Test of 1964

China's nuclear buildup in the 1960s alarmed the Japanese government. After China detonated its first nuclear device in 1964, the United States became concerned that Japan might consider acquiring a nuclear arsenal in response. However, this concern proved unfounded. Why was this the case?

One way of tackling this question is to reexamine whether Japan was truly facing serious threats that could convince the country to move toward acquiring nuclear weapons. In other words, a reevaluation of the threat from China's nuclear activities as well as Japanese perceptions of that threat is necessary in order to understand the dynamics of Japan's nuclear policy decisions at that time. The simplest conclusion would be that China was not considered a real threat back in the 1960s, especially among the bureaucrats at the Ministry of Foreign Affairs. Why was this so?

First, decision makers at both the bureaucratic and the political levels shared the understanding that China was at an initial stage of nuclear development.[38] Even three years after the first detonation, the Ministry of Foreign Affairs concluded that there were still technical issues for China to overcome before it could make strategic use of its nuclear devices, and that it would "still take a long period of time" before these weapons became effective. China's capacity to deliver a nuclear device was viewed as similarly undeveloped. Although it was clear that the country was moving quickly toward building intercontinental ballistic missiles, it was still far behind other developed nations.[39]

Second, and more significant, decision makers placed a great deal of importance on relations with the United States, with a heavy reliance on the U.S.-Japan security alliance. As a result, although the United States was very concerned about the possibility of Japan going nuclear, according to Shigaki Minrō it continued to put faith in Japan, which created a certain sense of security.[40]

The reliance on the United States could be observed even among decision makers who were much more sensitive about China's nuclear test. For example, during the late 1960s governmental agencies in Japan conducted a series of studies on the possibility of developing a nuclear arsenal. They all concluded that Japan "could but would not" possess nuclear weapons, which was in some ways a provocative conclusion in the context of the relationship with the United States. However, decision makers held a basic and implicit understanding "not to go against the U.S. intentions" and therefore did not even consider that the results of these studies might alarm the United States. They were even comfortable with the results being shared with the United States, although, according to Shigaki, this never came to pass.[41]

In fact, in some ways Japan's reliance on the United States turned the Chinese nuclear test of 1964 into an opportunity for Japan to reinforce the U.S.-Japan security alliance. The Chinese threat appeared to be a compelling reason for Japan to reconfirm the necessity of the U.S. extended nuclear deterrence, and it might also prove to be the most effective way to claim to the general public that the security alliance was a valuable tool for Japan's security policy.

Finally, although China's military buildup was indeed a potential threat to Japan's security, the issue that gained most attention was the recognition of the PRC as "China," with the right to claim its seat at the United Nations. Since more and more nations were conveying such recognition, Japan considered it wise to adjust to this situation. The government sought an early restoration of diplomatic ties with China and avoided statements and postures that would irritate China in any way.[42] The Ministry of Foreign Affairs did not want to ignore the general public's desire "to have relations with mainland China and its people."[43]

This point was reinforced by the fact that the media, especially newspapers, focused less on the potential negative security consequences of China's nuclear test and more on potential economic ties with China, which created positive emotions among the general public. As Wakaizumi Kei pointed out, although some academics were well aware that China's nuclear test would have a large impact on Japan's security and would affect the relationship between the two countries, the nation as a whole did not take the test seriously.[44] As newspapers offered little information on the military aspects of the nuclear test, the general public remained largely ignorant of the Chinese nuclear threat.[45]

Governmental Studies regarding Japan's Nuclear Options

Although the threat perception regarding China's nuclear buildup and 1964 nuclear test was far more muted than many scholars have argued, this does not mean that the potential threat to Japan's security went entirely unnoticed. In the latter half of the 1960s, during the Satō administration, three ministries (or related study groups) undertook studies on Japan's nuclear policy: the defense community (but not the Defense Agency itself), the Ministry of Foreign Affairs, and the Cabinet Secretariat (which requested studies from groups of academics). Although these studies were done independently and without the three groups consulting one another, they clearly show that Japan was at a crossroads regarding security policy. The conclusions were unanimous: it would not be beneficial for Japan to build or possess nuclear weapons.

The Defense Community

The first study was prepared by a group named the Security Research Commission (Anzenhosho chosa-kai), which completed four reports between 1966 and 1969. One report, entitled "Japan's Security-Outlook for 1970" (*Nihon no anzenhosho-1970nen eno tenbo*), focused on threat perceptions and mentioned a number of analyses of Japan's nuclear options. This report was written in the context of more active discussions about security during the late 1960s.[46] Although this group was not directly under the direction of the Defense Agency, many executives and junior executives from the agency, the National Institute for Defense Studies, and related ministry sections involved in national security were called in; thus it can be assumed that the outcome would have been highly influential and likely incorporated the viewpoints of the defense community at the time.[47]

The first report, issued in 1966, included a section entitled "Measures against Communist China's Nuclear Test," which noted that, although Japan could not independently confirm the test without proper detection tools, future tests would have a direct impact on Japan, a serious concern for policy makers. Moreover, it touched on Japan's nuclear option but concluded that "Japan possesses a certain kind of religious purity which is the foundation of its national policy," and that Japan should rely on the nuclear weapons of the United States as the "sole and only deterrent" option. However, the report also mentioned that some skeptics of the deterrence ability of the United States felt that it was necessary for Japan to go nuclear.[48]

The second report, in 1967, included a section that dealt with Japan's nuclearization more explicitly. This section, entitled "Future Perspective: Possibility of Japan's Nuclearization," mentioned that although Japan cherished the idea of "self-reliant defense," if a foreign nation chose to take aggressive action, including launching "nuclear attacks," a defenseless Japan would have to rely on "protection from the United States."[49] It would not be rational to discard the option of going nuclear, given that there might come a time when Japan would no longer be able to rely on the United States.

Although technical barriers and specific time frames were not directly mentioned in the 1967 report, the 1968 report touched on the ability to produce both nuclear warheads and delivery devices. At the same time, however, it also mentioned that this know-how did not directly link Japan to the development of nuclear weapons: "from conservatives to revolutionists, there is little understanding that Japan, in the future, will go nuclear, nor should go nuclear."[50]

In short, the reports point to the conclusion that Japan did not have the national will to develop or possess nuclear weapons, and even if it had, the decision to go nuclear would have incited deep fears in neighboring nations, with the result that the regional security environment would further deteriorate. Thus, at the time, relying on the nuclear deterrence of the United States was the best option when it came to Japan's security policy.

The Diplomatic Community

The diplomatic community was also looking closely at security issues, especially after China's first nuclear test. A report by the Foreign Policy Planning Committee (Gaiko seisaku kikaku iinkai) entitled "Japan's Foreign Policy Guideline" (*Waga kuni no seisaku taiko*), put together in September 1969, indicates Japan's official position at the time.[51] The committee dealt with broad issues surrounding Japan's national interest, and although it did not include a section specifically dedicated to nuclear issues, it did touch on such issues when dealing with policies toward China and security in general.

On security issues, the committee considered the alliance with the United States to be indispensable because Japan was unable to provide sufficient security on its own (particularly in scenarios involving a nuclear attack). The report emphasized that, aside from the United States, "no other country would be able to provide effective cooperation."[52] Although Japan considered itself uniquely equipped to serve as a leader on issues of disarmament, it was cautious about taking any action that might undermine the U.S.-Soviet security balance and jeopardize U.S. protection. It was also conscious of the fact that attitudes toward China required discretion.[53]

In such circumstances, the nuclear option "would not be realistic in the near future, with or without Japan being a part of the NPT," but, at the same time, Japan "needs to maintain economic and technical potentials for the development of nuclear weapons."[54] Furthermore, educating and enlightening the general public that "policies regarding nuclear weapons in general are the results of cost and benefit calculations" was highly recommended so that unnecessary confusion would not occur "should situations in which tactical nuclear weapons might be brought into" the country arise.[55]

While the committee's report represented a relatively broad perspective on Japan's security policy in the 1960s, a more detailed argument regarding Japan's nuclearization can be seen in the 1966 internal memo written by the Disarmament Section (Gunshuku-kyoku) of the Ministry of Foreign Affairs. According to this memo, entitled "Japan's Nuclearization and the Nuclear Nonproliferation Treaty (unfinished manuscript)" (*Waga-kuni no kaku buso to kaku kakusan boshi jyoyaku [miteikou]*), since Japan's national policy was "not to possess nuclear weapons" and Japan's security was to be "secured under the U.S.-Japan Security Treaty," the Ministry of Foreign Affairs reconfirmed internally that "as long as it continued its basic policies," Japan was unlikely to face serious consequences.[56] The security provided by the U.S.-Japan security alliance was a question "of vital interest" for Japan.[57]

This did not mean, however, that Japan immediately rejected the option of developing its own nuclear weapons. According to the memo, a realistic scenario for Japan to consider its nuclear option would be if China possessed the ability to launch a nuclear attack on the United States that would weaken the U.S. nuclear deterrence.

The memo also touched on the fact that "setting stages" was necessary when proceeding toward the acquisition of a nuclear arsenal, which meant that Japan needed a clear understanding of China's level of nuclear development; Japan's nuclear buildup was considered "possessing deterrence capability against Communist China's nuclear attacks." The first stage (labeled the "previous stage" [*mae dankai*]) represented a scenario in which China did in fact possess a robust offensive nuclear capability (including delivery systems) vis-à-vis Japan but had only a negligible capability to attack the United States. In this case, U.S. deterrence would have full effect against China, and Japan could secure itself by relying on the United States. At the same time, maintaining this deterrence required that Japan reaffirm the U.S. commitment by, for example, rewriting the words of Article 5 of the U.S.-Japan Security Treaty, which require the United States to come to the defense of Japan in the event of an attack.[58]

The second stage (labeled the "after stage" [*ato dankai*]) described a scenario in which China possessed an offensive nuclear arsenal that was capable of a substantial attack on the United States. In such a scenario, deterring threats and attacks against Japan might not be effective, requiring that Japan "seriously consider going nuclear or not."[59] These descriptions indicate that Japan's nuclearization was deeply linked to the development of China's nuclear capability and the threat that it might hold for Japan's security situation.

Of course, certain standards also needed to be met. First of all, Japan, with its limited territory, would struggle to store the nuclear weapons necessary for a strategic deterrent; securing sites for nuclear tests would also be difficult. Second, the number of nuclear weapons necessary to execute an effective strategic nuclear deterrence needed to be calculated, and the issue of finance would become crucial. And third, the rising consensus toward the creation of the NPT at that moment would presumably trigger a huge debate, not just within Japan but throughout the international community, should Japan go nuclear.

Cabinet Secretariat Community

As is clear, there was little consensus among the general public and politicians about the threat posed by China's nuclear test and nuclear buildup. Part of the bureaucratic community became frustrated and concerned about this lack of consensus. The Cabinet Secretariat, which was one of these concerned bureaucratic sectors, launched a number of studies inviting opinions from various scholars and professionals regarding Japan's security policy vis-à-vis China's nuclear test and buildup.

Two well-known internal reports entitled "Basic Study on Japan's Nuclear Policy" (*Nihon no kaku seisaku ni kansuru kisoteki kenkyu*), issued in 1968 and

1970, represented the aggregation of the Cabinet Secretariat's related studies on nuclear issues.[60] These reports had their origins in a 1964 report on China's nuclear test and Japan's security written by Wakaizumi Kei.[61]

As Wakaizumi mentioned in his report, Japan regarded the 1964 nuclear test as an important opportunity to "seriously consider its security policies." The impact of the Chinese nuclear test for Japan was "mentally and politically of exceeding significance," but, at the same time, the military significance should not be overestimated, and "the situation should be put to practical use" as an opportunity to raise awareness among the Japanese public on how "important national security and defense" are to the country.[62]

Wakaizumi's report looks at three options that Japan might take: unarmed neutrality, nuclearization, and policies based on the U.S.-Japan security alliance. The first option, the report concluded, would be "totally impossible to materialize" as well as an "irresponsible abstract opinion." It would therefore be necessary to provide the Japanese general public with a realistic and critical notion of China's circumstances and intentions. The second option, if Japan were to go forward with it, would be carried out in the context of the rivalry with China and the Soviet Union. In other words, Japan would need to engage in and complete a "large-scale, effective, and invulnerable independent nuclearization." This, however, was thought to be unrealistic from a financial perspective. In short, the only remaining option for Japan would be to reinforce its national policies based on the U.S.-Japan Security Treaty as well as to obtain concrete assurance from the United States that it would commit to nuclear retaliation should that become necessary.[63]

Two years later, in 1967, the Cabinet Secretariat gathered the best professionals in Japan at the time, from nuclear physics to international politics, to "examine 'the technical, organizational, and financial possibilities of establishing an independent nuclear force'" in parallel with "research on the status quo (and near future) of Japan's nuclear development ability."[64]

The two reports that came out in 1968 and 1970 as a result of these studies indicated that, should Japan go nuclear, it would almost certainly increase political uncertainty. However, this path would still be worth considering as a "political option" if it reinforced Japan's security situation. In other words, for Japan, there would be technical, strategic, diplomatic, and political strings attached to the idea of possessing nuclear weapons, and thus Japan would not be able to actually possess them entirely without constraint. However, the members of the study group did not consider this inability to be particularly harmful to Japan's security.[65]

The study had been kept internal owing to the fact that, since the initiation of the project, neither the Cabinet Secretariat nor the study group members were certain what its recommendation would be: if the conclusion had supported the creation of an independent Japanese nuclear force, it would have caused chaos among the media and the public at large.[66] Nuclear issues were still a taboo within Japanese society.[67]

Implications of the Bureaucracy-Related Studies

All the bureaucratic studies mentioned above point to the fact that any conclusion about an independent nuclear force required weighing not just technical, financial, and organizational conditions but also the strategic, national-psychological, political, and diplomatic aspects of the issue.[68] It was a common understanding among the bureaucratic community that, of these conditions, political will was the most important in any decision to launch a nuclear weapons program.

It remains unclear whether the prime minister at that time actually got hold of these reports directly or structured his policies based on their conclusions. We can only speculate on this point, but we are aware that about two hundred copies were distributed to high-ranking officials during the Satō administration, and, at the very least, it seems logical to assume that these officials would have read the reports and incorporated their views into concrete policy. Furthermore, given that the reports were found among the belongings of Satō's principal executive secretary, Kusuda Minoru, we can at least assume that he would have looked into their contents, as Satō himself was very much interested in nuclear issues at the time.[69] It has been pointed out that Satō had, on one occasion, reproved the head of the Cabinet Research Office by referring to the point where the report mentions that Japan had the technological ability to promptly develop nuclear weapons. He argued that the development of nuclear weapons would not be an easy matter.[70]

Moreover, although the reports concluded that Japan did not have a strategic interest in possessing nuclear weapons, this does not mean that decision makers adopted this view wholesale, if and when they read the report. However, these multiple reports and memos, all pointing in the same direction in the late 1960s, show that the bureaucratic community likely had an understanding that Japan's best option would be to remain a nonnuclear state while maintaining strong ties to the United States.

Conclusion

The traditional explanations for Japan's decision not to go nuclear point in contradictory directions. First, the antinuclear movement in Japan cannot be viewed as a strong restraint on the acquisition of nuclear weapons. True, the antinuclear movement that began in 1954 had a clear vision to ban any activities related to atomic and hydrogen bombs. The fear that radiation would pollute everyday life, originating from housewives, fishermen, and others at the grassroots, soon became a nationwide movement with bipartisan support. However, other issues quickly undermined the movement's unity, and irreparable cracks soon became visible. There was nothing strategic about the emotions generated by the events in Hiroshima, Nagasaki, and on Bikini Atoll; they were simply what the Japanese felt, then and today. But the three major fissures in the antinuclear movement weakened the movement and led certain political parties to distance themselves from the entire issue of nuclear weapons.

With the general public struggling with, keeping their distance from, or simply ignoring the antinuclear movement, decision makers contemplated the international environment from a steady, strategic viewpoint, even going so far as to put the nuclear option on the table if necessary. In this sense, although the antinuclear movement in Japan was an unprecedented development in the history of peace movements, it did little directly to influence policy makers as they decided whether Japan should go nuclear.

This, however, did not mean that Japan's unique status as the only victim of an atomic attack was discarded entirely. The three nonnuclear principles exemplify the fact that politicians were not able entirely to neglect the notion of antinuclearism. At the same time, they also showed that Japan could not abandon the U.S.-Japan alliance and the nuclear umbrella.

Second, China's nuclear buildup and nuclear test of 1964 did not create strong incentives for Japan to consider the acquisition of a nuclear arsenal since the threat was not perceived as serious enough to make the issue a priority. This, however, did not mean that there was no threat from China. Clearly, as the bureaucratic community showed in their respective reports and memos, Japanese policy makers recognized China's nuclear buildup and test as threatening actions. But we should be careful to separate the actual threats from the way they were perceived at the time. In Japan's case, one can argue that in the late 1960s the perceived threat was fairly small, making the nuclear option a low priority. This was reinforced by the notion that Japan had more important policies to pursue, such as maintaining a strong relationship with the United States in order to secure the deterrence that came with the U.S.-Japan security alliance. Politicians, bureaucrats, and the general public all tended to keep their distance from the idea of Japan as a nuclear-armed nation; nuclear weapons were not a high priority for anyone in Japan.

This low priority can relate to Etel Solingen's explanation of Japan's nuclear restraint: political leaders in Japan were opposed to the thought of developing nuclear weapons since they considered the economic costs too high and focused instead on spending money on the nation's comprehensive economic growth.[71] Developing nuclear weapons can be categorized as one of the many projects and policies that Japan could have pursued, but its priority was fairly low compared to that of economic reconstruction. An important understanding here is that the U.S.-Japan security alliance with its nuclear umbrella was a necessary condition to move forward with economic reconstruction. The same can be said regarding Japan's nonnuclear policy, and perhaps Japan's security policy in general: like it or not, the relationship with the United States has always had a massive influence on Japan's decision-making process.

Even if nuclear weapons were considered a low priority, however, this did not necessarily mean that the Japanese decision-making community had totally abandoned the idea of the country going nuclear. The complicated nuance here is that, leaving the idea on the table as a future option did not necessarily mean that Japan had the exact will in doing so, nor was it considering utilizing that option as a hedge against the rest of the world. Again, we should be cautious in using the term "hedge," since one cannot deny the fact that gaining access to sensitive nuclear technologies, such as enrichment and reprocessing, did provide Japan with the implicit opportunity to strategically imply that alternative, keeping in mind the international concern surrounding nuclear proliferation at that time. Having the potential technologies and the will to further develop them, albeit only for peaceful purposes, can send out a strong message to the rest of the world and can also act as a negotiation tool should Japan be in a worse situation. However, this implicit hedging did not suggest that Japan would actually go nuclear. In Japanese society, the issue of nuclear energy was in a sense cut off from the issue of nuclear weapons. (See also Shinsuke Tomotsugu's discussion in chapter 7 of this volume.) Indeed, the Japanese language specifically refers to nuclear energy and nuclear weapons as two separate terms, *genshiryoku* and *kakuheiki*, respectively, which implies that developing nuclear energy technology might not create the same level of public resentment in Japan and therefore was hardly considered as a hedging tool.

In short, the events discussed in this chapter encourage us to reconsider the idea that Japan "did not go nuclear." Members of the Japanese public were either against or ignorant of the possibility of the country obtaining nuclear capabilities. Government personnel, including bureaucrats and other parts of the decision-making community, believed that although it would not harm Japan to possess the technical capability to go nuclear one day, the contemporary strategic situation made this option a low priority. Hence, for Japan, becoming a nuclear-armed state was an unnecessary option: whatever the technological and strategic circumstances, the final will was obviously not there.

10

Nuclear Revolution and Hegemonic Hierarchies

HOW GLOBAL HIROSHIMA PLAYED
OUT IN SOUTH AMERICA

Matias Spektor

WHEN NEWS OF THE BOMBING of Hiroshima hit the press in South America, the public recoiled in horror at the images of nuclear devastation. But in scientific and political circles, the dominant attitude was fascination. Within a few years, governments in the two most powerful countries in the region—Argentina and Brazil—were actively seeking to purchase and indigenously develop dual-nuclear technologies, as well as train a generation of nuclear scientists to build up the foundations for national nuclear industrial complexes. In the eyes of governing elites in both countries, the onset of the nuclear revolution threatened the world with the prospect of destruction, but also with a new and palpable chasm: a clash over the institutions, rules, and norms that should govern global nuclear order between technology-savvy industrial states and backward, peripheral countries of the Third World. It is therefore unsurprising that when South Americans grappled with Hiroshima, they saw long-lasting economic, commercial, diplomatic, and security implications. From that moment onward, their quest for nuclear-related knowledge and capability was never conceived of exclusively—or even primarily—as a tool for national survival in an uncertain world. For them, deterrence was never a concern. Rather, in South America nuclear politics were from the outset intertwined with issues of hierarchy and hegemonic imposition in an unequal international system. In their eyes, the nuclear revolution became a new battlefield in the struggle for modernity, where issues of international political power and scientific knowledge came together to structure a novel form of global political rankings. Issues of technology assistance and denial, centrifuge design and construction, nuclear trade and "trigger lists" came to be see through the prism of national autonomy and standing in the global pecking order.

South American dynamics were not unique, as the most cursory glance at the record of "Global Hiroshima" across the developing world will show similar dynamics elsewhere. Perhaps the most notable one pertains to the case of Iran. In 2005, when he was chief nuclear negotiator for Iran, Hassan Rouhani told the audience at the Supreme Cultural Revolution Council: "If one day we are able to complete the fuel cycle and the world sees that it has no choice, that we do possess the technology, then the situation will be different. The world did not want Pakistan to have an atomic bomb or Brazil to have the fuel cycle, but Pakistan built its bomb and Brazil has its fuel cycle, and *the world started to work with them*. Our problem is that we have not achieved either one, but we are standing at the threshold."[1] Rouhani's statement is analogous to the utterances of several officials in both Argentina and Brazil across time. According to such a view, the global nuclear order is not (and never was) a neutral formation but one that has denied large developing states their rightful place among nations. There is a recurrent emphasis on the victim status of countries on the fringes of the Western world, and a call for action to claim a full and proper standing in the international system. In such a conception, nuclear technology serves purposes that go well beyond military power, the ability to deter enemies, or the capacity to project influence abroad. Instead, nuclear technology—although not necessarily nuclear weapons—is conceived of as a tool to redress the perceived imbalance that results from a history of exclusion, alienation, and submission to the imperial imprint of the major powers, and in particular of the United States.

The reception of Hiroshima in the South American experience is tightly linked to perceptions of the United States in the postwar order as a revolutionary power. Whereas most scholarly commentary and policy practice in the West assumes that the United States should be seen as a status quo power in the nuclear realm—perhaps a durable legacy from the days of nuclear monopoly (1945–1949)—South American decision makers always saw U.S. practice in the nuclear arena as revisionist. From the carefree attitude of Atoms for Peace in the 1950s to the militant nonproliferation policies of the late 1970s, from lashing out against the nuclear ambitions of India before the 2000s to the embrace of India as a de facto nuclear-armed state afterward, the United States was and is seen as constantly changing the rules of the game to skew it in its own favor.

On the face of it, there should be no surprises there: "The strong do what they can and the weak suffer what they must," reads the Melian dialogue. But seeing global nuclear order through the eyes of those sitting in Buenos Aires or Rio de Janeiro opens up potentially profitable avenues for an inquiry into the conditions for stable nuclear governance in global politics moving forward. It also helps explain why 122 nations at the United Nations voted in 2017 to adopt a treaty imposing a total ban on nuclear weapons, to the consternation of the nuclear weapons states. If we as a community of scholars and practitioners can open up to the possibility that at key moments in nuclear history the United States behaved as an "irresponsible stakeholder," we might then be in a better position to make sense of the backlash against U.S. conceptions of nuclear order that has recurred across the developing world.

This chapter presents an account of South America's encounter with the nuclear revolution that seeks to address two questions: First, how did the use of nuclear weapons in 1945 affect South American visions of global nuclear order? Second, how did Brazil and Argentina seek to operate within that order?

Nuclear Order as United States–Dominated

South America as a regional system in the twentieth century was never properly bipolar. Not only was the region a direct zone of influence of U.S. hegemony, but challengers to that hegemony were rare and unsuccessful. Joseph Stalin never tried to export the revolution to South America, and, when prompted by local communist movements, he turned them down in full knowledge of the enormous cost that would ensue. In turn, Adolf Hitler briefly tried but then failed to ensure that sympathetic leaders in South America would be in a position to follow him and honor their commitment to keep trade ties untouched during the Second World War in the face of U.S. opposition. It is no wonder, then, that the onset of nuclear ordering in South America in the aftermath of Hiroshima should also be the story of American hegemony in this particular part of the world. Against that background, the bombing of Hiroshima and Nagasaki by the United States set in motion two interconnected dynamics that ended up having long-lasting effects in Argentina, Brazil, and South America more widely: nuclear anticolonial nationalism and intra-regional technological competition.

Brazil moved fast to nationalize its own reserves of uranium, rare earths, and thorium—three sensitive commodities that it had exported to the United States on the basis of exclusive, secret agreements since the onset of the Second World War—on the understanding that the military uses of nuclear power would create a brutally skewed market for such materials. In particular in the case of uranium, domestic debates about property rights echoed those that were beginning to emerge with regard to oil (Brazilian authorities would eventually nationalize oil fields in 1952). Leaders in both nations expected the global nuclear order to become rife with disputes over the commerce of such commodities and thought it wise to avoid the preferential trade arrangements of the 1940s and 1950s with the United States that they came to see as "unequal treaties." At a time when nationalization of natural resources and infrastructure was spreading across the Third World, the minerals involved in the nuclear enterprise took center stage. This is the primary reason why the outset of the nuclear era in South America was seen less as an issue of international security than as one of international justice dividing North and South.[2]

Yet the emphasis on the North/South divide conceals an underlying dynamic that is best seen in the Brazilian case: as decision makers in the capital city set out to mine and mill uranium in the backward mines of Minas Gerais and Bahia, they reproduced a pattern of nuclear governance that was undoubtedly racialized. In the process of extracting uranium from the soil, Brazilian authorities committed a vast range of crimes against the indigenous, nonwhite populations on whose lands exploration took place and whose workforce was employed in conditions that resemble the well-known horror stories of uranium mining in Africa.[3] If we are to examine the nuclear orders that Hiroshima helped establish worldwide from a non-Western perspective, then we need to come to grips with the fact that racial violence is a core element of national stories too. This should be seen as an addition to the existing works on the global racialized nuclear dynamics that Sean Malloy explores in detail in chapter 4 in this volume. When we look at South American encounters with nuclear technology from the perspective of race, what emerges is not only a narrative of global colonial relations but also one that highlights the connections between race and *nuclearity* in national state-building.

It was at this juncture that the aspiration took root in Argentina and Brazil to secure "autonomy" in nuclear technological development. By the late 1940s the acquisition of nuclear-related know-how came to be seen as part and parcel of a broader developmental enterprise that went well beyond nuclear power itself: nuclear power became a proxy for modernity in a postcolonial world. As such, nuclear politics became intertwined with issues of standing and independence in international affairs, and negotiations over the terms of global nuclear governance ended up being couched in Argentina and Brazil in a language of equality, distribution, and fairness. Twenty years later, when the Nuclear Suppliers Group began to take shape, Argentina and Brazil were convinced that the critical divide in nuclear global governance was not between the "haves" and the "have nots" but between major industrial states that dominated some or all of the major civilian uses of nuclear energy and those countries whose access to such technologies was blocked. Their focus was not on the possession of nuclear weapons but on the acquisition of dual technologies for purposes beyond deterrence. In their eyes, industrial nuclear powers barred the dissemination of technology not so much because proliferation would have destabilizing effects in the security realm but because it would disturb the lucrative business of an exclusive club of states in the Global North.[4]

From the 1940s onward, then, Argentina and Brazil set out to build large developmental states bent on acquiring and developing nuclear technologies. They also put plans in place to train a generation of nuclear scientists. Their universities set up new academic departments in fields like chemistry, physics, mathematics, and engineering with a view to generate the human capital that would be necessary to sustain indigenous nuclear industries. If the nuclear revolution was bound to produce a global political cleavage between those nations that mastered nuclear technologies and those that did not, possession of the nuclear fuel-cycle—rather than possession of nuclear weapon—would soon become the dividing line between the two camps.[5]

To be sure, this view was informed by these countries' prior experience with neocolonialism under the Spanish, the Portuguese, the British, and the Americans. Imbibing the nationalist philosophies that were born in the Third World, Argentines and Brazilians conceived of technological autonomy as a crucial tool in the kit. By the mid-1950s the nuclear estate in both countries was a sprawling complex of institutions, with their own National Nuclear Energy Commissions running programs and dishing out funds to create indigenous nuclear industries. Key individuals within those institutions saw themselves as members of the burgeoning global network of scientists, officials, and diplomats circulating around major laboratories and international institutions like the International Atomic Energy Agency (IAEA).

It is therefore unsurprising that Brazil and Argentina should have taken up U.S. offers of nuclear civilian cooperation under Atoms for Peace.[6] President Eisenhower's program to promote the dissemination of scientific information on most aspects of the civil nuclear fuel cycle (except uranium enrichment) helped Argentina and Brazil consider alternative technologies in developing the nuclear fuel cycle, like the reprocessing of spent fuel. They also rolled out the program's emphasis on government subsidies to establish national civilian nuclear industries.[7] Moreover, the United States provided these countries with information, training, and aid in acquiring equipment and materials, including nuclear research reactors (for which Washington offered a financial subsidy of $350,000 each).[8] More specifically, under Atoms for Peace the United States supplied Brazil with three research reactors, which were installed in São Paulo (1957), Belo Horizonte (1960), and Rio de Janeiro (1965). In the case of Argentina, the program included plans for a research reactor built at the Centro Atómico Constituyentes in 1958. To keep these reactors running, Argentina and Brazil bought highly enriched uranium fuel from the United States.[9]

In Latin America, Atoms for Peace also paved the way for the creation of the Inter-American Nuclear Energy Commission within the Organization of American States and conferences on peaceful nuclear applications in Argentina (1959), Brazil (1960), Mexico (1962), and Chile (1964).[10] This was done with the support and financing of the United States, whose arsenal under President Eisenhower alone grew from 1,200 warheads in 1952 to some 18,700 in 1960.[11] In an international system that was still permissive about the trade of nuclear know-how, Argentina and Brazil negotiated nuclear cooperation agreements elsewhere, including Western Europe and the Soviet Union.[12]

There was an important difference between the evolution of nuclear policy in Argentina and Brazil, however. From inception, the nuclear community emerging in Brazil was divided over purpose and policy. Private lobbies and state companies wanted the program to generate cheap electricity to quell the energy demands of a fast-growing industrializing economy: their preference was for the fast acquisition of ready-made technologies and turn-key reactors abroad. By contrast, the armed forces and the scientific community preferred to focus on propping up indigenous nuclear fuel-cycle technologies. They estimated that global nuclear trade would divide the industrial North as a technological oligopoly from a technologically backward, dependent South, so they preferred investment in bottom-up technological development. These clashes were not settled until the late 1970s, when the world refused to sell Brazil sensitive technologies and authorities had little option but to develop their own. Through the 1950s and 1960s, then, nuclear policy in Brazil remained prey to division, fragmentation, and conflict. By contrast, Argentine officials coalesced around notions of nuclear autonomy from the outset and focused their energies on in-house technological development. At least until the 1980s, Argentina seemed to be ahead of Brazil in its ability to produce scientific and technological breakthroughs in the nuclear field.[13]

Regional Competition

The military use of nuclear power in 1945 also awakened Argentines and Brazilians to the prospects of heightened mutual competition in the atomic age. As authorities in each state pursued nuclear fuel-cycle technologies, they also became aware that emerging capabilities could trigger security-dilemma dynamics with revolutionary effects on regional stability. After all, they had been rivals since time immemorial. Now Atoms for Peace added yet another competitive dimension to the Argentine-Brazilian bilateral relationship. Unsurprisingly, national and international media and foreign nonproliferation analysts soon came to see the evolution of dual-technology capabilities in South America through the prism of regional geopolitical competition. These concerns filtered through the national security communities of each country, with the military in particular interpreting technological developments on the other side of the border from a national security perspective. Such dynamics never turned into anything resembling a military race for reasons that we shall see below, but they guaranteed an enduring source of competition and a fair amount of suspicion in the Argentine-Brazilian relationship.[14]

That mutual suspicions of an intent to acquire nuclear weapons never became dominant in either Brazil or Argentina is a function of how little appeal such weapons had in South America. The voices that argued for the active pursuit of nuclear weapons were in the minority and never secured the necessary traction with their political masters. Arguments in favor of the bomb appeared in the public statements of some military officials in both countries and the writings of scholars in academic journals more often than in the secret correspondence within each government that is now declassified and open for historical research. And yet the quest in both countries for technological acquisition—in particular uranium enrichment—soon became mixed up with and often confused for the search for nuclear weapons. As the nuclear era progressed and Argentina and Brazil came to actively pursue enrichment technologies, international observers and commentators believed they were seriously moving toward a weapon capability.[15] We now know that such assessments at the time were widely overstated or simply mistaken, a fact that has been lately confirmed by the declassification of primary sources from the U.S. intelligence agencies.[16]

But the force of anticolonial nationalism in the face of a U.S.-led nuclear global order was stronger than the competitive dynamics between the two regional neighbors. For all the rivalry that was typical of Argentine-Brazilian relations, the beginnings of the nuclear age actually contributed to drawing these two countries closer together in opposition to U.S. conceptions of nuclear order.

The reason for this was joint opposition to the evolution of U.S. nonproliferation policy and the emergence of a global nonproliferation regime. As officials in South America bent on acquiring dual technologies bumped up against resistance in Washington from the 1950s onward, a powerful glue sealed bilateral nuclear cooperation ever since. Rivalry between the two did not preclude them from building a common shield against what they saw as an unjust global order and a hostile United States. The Argentine-Brazilian entente to cope with the global nuclear order was powerful enough to make each side support the other's decision to acquire or develop fuel-cycle capabilities. Mutual sympathy rather than fear set the tone of the bilateral relationship in the nuclear age.[17]

Consider, for instance, the Argentine-Brazilian attitude toward the Cuban Missile Crisis in October 1962. Alongside Mexico, the two South American states worked toward the creation of a nuclear-weapons-free zone in Latin America.[18] The push toward a region free from these weapons came from a generation of politicians and career diplomats who self-identified as progressives at home and neutralists abroad. Throughout the 1960s they set out to turn Argentina and Brazil into champions of global nuclear disarmament. They had already opposed the Soviet nuclear test of September 1961, and, at the Eighteen-Nation Disarmament Committee meetings in March 1962, the Brazilians had argued for the cessation of all nuclear testing. Activism in global nuclear proliferation debates, they thought, would help them polish their credentials as modernizing frontiersmen in the emerging Third World movement. Now the Cuban Missile Crisis further strengthened this development but highlighted the urgency of such principles. By denouncing both the United States and the Soviet Union as the "nuclear irresponsibles," Argentine and Brazilian diplomats were rolling out a new brand of "independent foreign policy" that was more autonomous and more defiant of the United States. Their nuclear diplomacy posture allowed them to side with the Non-Aligned Movement and keep open channels with Fidel Castro in Havana. Denouncing the superpowers for their nuclear behavior became a common staple in the Brazilian administrations of Jânio Quadros (1961) and João Goulart (1961–1964) and in the Argentine administrations of Arturo Frondizi (1958–1962), José Maria Guido (1962–1963), and Arturo Illia (1963–1966).[19]

A countermovement to challenge the nuclear progressives of the early 1960s in Brazil developed among military officers, diplomats, and politicians on the center right and the anticommunist far right who rejected any overtures to Cuba and socialist movements in the postcolonial world. In the eyes of these officials, any commitments to denuclearization would unnecessarily close off future options for Brazil. In this they had the support of Marcelo Damy Souza Santos. Damy, as he was known, was the top Brazilian nuclear official after founding and directing the Institute of Research on Nuclear Energy (1956–1961) and then heading the National Nuclear Energy Commission (1961–1964). Damy advocated for Brazil to build its own nuclear device sometime in the future and argued it would be irresponsible preemptively to close off that option by signing on to restrictive nonproliferation international agreements like a nuclear-weapons-free zone in the region.[20]

According to the U.S. Embassy in Brazil, Damy "aspired to be the Brazilian Bhabha." None of his intentions ever materialized, however. "Brazil has a small but reasonable scientific base upon which it could erect a nuclear device program if the political decisions to do so were made and the government were prepared to and capable of following through with the necessary funds and sustained effort," the embassy reported. Yet "small staff resources and large technological gaps" would make the cost and effort considerably larger than in the cases of Canada, Israel, and India. "The Brazilian technological base would not seem sufficient to support a production reactor program of reasonable size in anything like the near future, especially if such a program were to be domestically based and hence 'safeguards-free.'" The U.S. Embassy also doubted that Brazil had the acumen in the foreseeable future to build "domestically modified centrifuges sufficient for a cascade capable of producing weapons-grade enriched uranium in significant quantities."[21]

They were correct, and all evidence points to the fact that Argentina made a similar assessment. By the mid-1960s Brazil and Argentina were fast becoming staunch, overt defenders of the legality and legitimacy of "peaceful nuclear explosions" (PNEs).[22] By the time U.S. officials realized that their original promotion of nuclear energy under Atoms for Peace could propagate dual technologies in ways they could not control, the indigenous rush to develop atomic energy in South America had been in motion for a while. Officials in Argentina and Brazil had already embraced the idea that U.S. laboratories had promoted in the 1950s that PNEs could perform major economic functions in big public works like dredging ports, digging canals, opening pathways through rocks and mountains, or extracting natural resources underground.

With negotiations over the Nuclear Nonproliferation Treaty raging in Europe, Brazil and Argentina were firmly committed to resisting any major commitments to nonproliferation. As the world transitioned from the 1950s to the 1960s, Argentina and Brazil knew full well they were soon going to become targets of incipient U.S. nonproliferation policies.

Joint opposition to the NPT—and support for the legality and legitimacy of PNEs—provided the glue to an emerging South American nuclear order where the two major states both agreed to defend one another's right to full mastery of the nuclear cycle. Such an operation, however, was not without cost.

Taming U.S. Power while Avoiding a Regional Security Dilemma

Even before negotiations began in earnest for the NPT, Brazil and Argentina shared a common view of the international nonproliferation regime as intrusive, discriminatory, and detrimental to their own quest for technology acquisition. The connection between the two was strong enough that since 1962 they sent alternate ambassadors to the IAEA's Board of Governors, one side speaking on behalf of the other. From the outset of the process that eventually led to the signing of the NPT, Argentines denounced the attempt by the superpowers to "further disarm the disarmed," while Brazilians critiqued superpower attempts at "freezing world power" by denying sensitive technologies to developing countries. The two also acted in tandem during negotiations of the Tlatelolco Treaty, which would eventually turn Latin America into a nuclear-weapons-free zone.

In these negotiations, Buenos Aires and Brasília formed a coalition in defense of the legality of PNEs at the expense of the Mexican delegates, who feared potential weaponization activity. This brand of anti-major-power cooperation was not exceptional in the nuclear field. Since the late 1950s it had become a normal feature across policy realms, as the foreign policies of the two states became more staunchly nationalist and, as officials put it at the time, "independent" (mostly from the United States, but also from the East-West divide typical of the Cold War).[23] As the global nonproliferation regime—and U.S. nonproliferation policy—became tighter in the 1970s, Argentina and Brazil coalesced even further in defending each other's pursuit of the fuel cycle.

The more their own relations with the global nonproliferation regime and with Washington deteriorated, the more both countries found common ground for mutual nuclear policy reinforcement. Both nations, for instance, resented the creation of the Nuclear Suppliers Group, first organized in secret by Henry Kissinger in London in 1974. The group proceeded to restrict nuclear exports by nuclear states to nonnuclear ones. By the late 1970s both Brazil and Argentina were energetically trying to secure a seat for themselves in the group or, alternatively, to weaken its ability to "lay down the law" to them. In the process, they exchanged information and built common positions on the core exports issue—a process that socialized the diplomats, military men, scientists, and politicians of both sides to one another. Bilateral nuclear cooperation was to a large extent a way to avoid pressures from U.S. nonproliferation policy and from the nonproliferation regime itself.[24]

In 1974 West Germany and Brazil negotiated the terms of a broad nuclear cooperation agreement that involved long-term training, capacity building, and technology transfers. The issue of self-sufficiency in the production of nuclear fuel for future reactors had become a dominant theme in Brazilian policy circles because in the aftermath of the 1973 energy crisis the United States was refusing to guarantee future contracts for fuel purchases from Brazil. This cast a shadow of uncertainty as to the future of Brazil's nuclear electricity generation program and irked Brazilian officials. When negotiations between Bonn and Brasília came to a draft text, this was the largest technology transfer agreement ever signed between an industrialized country and an industrializing one. According to the agreement, Brazil would import eight reactors and receive technologies to develop the nuclear fuel cycle at home: uranium prospecting and mining; uranium enrichment; manufacturing fuel rods; and reprocessing spent fuel rods. At an anticipated value of 10 billion marks (roughly $4 billion), this was the largest single export order in German history.[25] At the time, Argentina was actively searching for technological breakthroughs in the field of uranium enrichment. Within a few years, it would disclose to the world that a secret facility in Pilcaniyeu had been set up for that purpose.

By the late 1970s both countries had begun their pursuit of uranium-enrichment technology, reinforcing fears in the U.S. intelligence community of the emergence of a security dilemma with serious geopolitical ramifications. The belief was widespread that both countries were trying to develop nuclear weapons programs of their own with a view to either equalizing or surpassing each other's technological capabilities—the kind of dynamic that could spiral out of control.[26]

Yet Argentine-Brazilian cooperation in the face of a hostile external environment gained additional traction in the aftermath of the election of President Jimmy Carter in 1976. Carter had since the campaign trail criticized his predecessor's and Henry Kissinger's policy as too tolerant of the nuclear ambitions of Argentina and Brazil. Now in office, Carter was adamant to curtail the access of these countries to dual technologies, while also targeting them for their use of torture against domestic opponents and other blatant violations of human rights. The scientific communities in both countries worried that the United States and Western Europe would continue to deny technology transfers, and both saw closer Argentine-Brazilian cooperation as a tool to transcend an ever more restrictive global regime. These fears were proven well-founded in 1977, when Carter convinced West Germany to deny uranium reprocessing and enrichment technologies to Brazil. These developments spurred Argentine-Brazilian nuclear cooperation as Argentina, too, was involved in a heated dispute with the United States over the right to buy a third power reactor and heavy water production facility without accepting full-scope safeguards.[27]

It is not surprising that in January 1977 the governments of Argentina and Brazil should have issued a joint communiqué stressing the need for bilateral cooperation in the nuclear field and systematic exchanges of nuclear technology. The technical exchanges were central to bilateral nuclear rapprochement, as the respective nuclear energy commission officials built up personal relationships with their national counterparts.

The military regimes governing Argentina and Brazil realized that bilateral nuclear cooperation could operate as a common defensive shield against an intrusive international nonproliferation regime. To bring this off, they first had to resolve their energy and water disputes in the Parana River region, which had fueled a great deal of mutual resentment throughout the 1970s. In May 1980 they negotiated an agreement for the exchange of technical information, material, and products on all aspects of the nuclear fuel cycle, leading to the first visit by a Brazilian president to Argentina in more than four decades.

The return to civilian rule in both countries in the 1980s was important in facilitating the nuclear rapprochement that had begun before. President Raul Alfonsín of Argentina sought cooperation with Brazil soon after taking office in late 1983 in the belief that layers of international commitments in the field of nonproliferation would help him reassert authority at home, tame an unruly military complex, and build up an image of statesmanship that was bound to be instrumental in the domestic struggles to come. For his part, Brazilian general João Figueiredo was interested in moving toward cooperation with Argentina as a way of signaling to his military colleagues that Brazil was indeed to transition to civilian rule from 1985 onward. Opening up internationally would then feed back into the political liberalization at home. Argentina also hoped to end the diplomatic and economic isolation it endured in the wake of the Falklands War (1982).

By the early 1980s Argentina and Brazil were also rethinking their national security doctrines, coordinating their nuclear foreign policies, imposing new restraints on their own national nuclear programs, and, to everyone's surprise, cosponsoring a formal mechanism for mutual inspection of nuclear-related facilities. Observers twenty years earlier would have considered such an outcome unthinkable. In turn, this transformation fostered an incipient security community in the wider South American region that moved toward becoming a zone of international peace, democratic governance, and market economies, where there was little or no incentive for major investments in nuclear weapons technologies. This path toward a stable peace happened while Argentina and Brazil were still under military rule. Political reconciliation did not follow social integration and economic interdependence, but the other way around.

Presidential diplomacy was critical to the process of Argentine-Brazilian rapprochement. In July 1987 President Sarney of Brazil visited the Pilcaniyeu nuclear facility near Bariloche, Argentina. Argentina had never before made that facility accessible to the public, which rendered the nature of the visit even more historic. The Viedma Joint Statement on Nuclear Policy signed on that occasion signaled a joint commitment to end the secrecy surrounding the countries' nuclear programs and to deepen bilateral cooperation in the nuclear field. In April 1988 Sarney reciprocally invited Alfonsín to visit Brazil's hitherto secret nuclear installation in São Paulo, after which the Ipero Joint Statement on Nuclear Policy was issued announcing the decision to set up a permanent commission on nuclear cooperation. Again, in November 1988 Sarney visited Argentina's Ezeiza facility near Buenos Aires, where Sarney and Alfonsín issued the Ezeiza Joint Statement on Nuclear Policy reaffirming their earlier commitments. These presidential statements served to restore civilian control over the two national nuclear programs and signal this decision to the international community.

Both Alfonsín and Sarney took unilateral steps to bring about a nuclear rapprochement. On the eve of announcing Argentina's capacity to enrich uranium in 1983, the government there made it a point to give early warning to Brazil. Four years later, when Brazilian authorities were about to announce their own enrichment capability, they too repeated the gesture vis-à-vis their neighbors.

The United States played a galvanizing role in Argentine-Brazilian nuclear cooperation. From the late 1970s onward, Washington officials introduced the idea in informal conversations with decision makers in Buenos Aires and Brasília to the effect that a system of mutual inspections might provide the basis for stability and confidence building. Although turning such an idea into policy would end up taking more than twenty years (in 1991 the two countries moved toward such a system for mutual nuclear inspections), it is remarkable that American policy makers never sought credit for the idea and never pushed these countries to adopt it overtly, a move that might have backfired. Perhaps more remarkable is the fact that the dominant attitude by the 1980s in the United States was one of accommodation of Argentine-Brazilian nuclear policies. By the 1990s South America's nuclear order was solidly built around Argentine-Brazilian mutual inspections, easing the path for their signing of the NPT and acceptance of a range of international nonproliferation norms and commitments.

The position of Argentina and Brazil within the global nuclear order since then has been far from obvious. Although the two countries have long relinquished their defense of PNEs and both have tied themselves up in a range of international nonproliferation commitments, they both remain critical of the way nuclear weapons states have behaved. They are particularly opposed to what they see as the ever more intrusive set of rules pertaining to transparency and accountability, such as the national Additional Protocols to the NPT that have become common currency worldwide, in exchange for little or no progress in disarmament. Both took part in negotiations for a treaty to make nuclear weapons illegal (which Brazil eventually signed, though Argentina did not), and both have raised their voices to come out in defense of Iran's "inalienable right" to enrich uranium. In the process, they have contested the evolution of U.S. nuclear policy as deterrence comes back to the top of the international agenda, and they promise to continue to do so in the near future.

Crucially, the issue of nuclear latency is currently being relegitimized in both countries. In the case of Brazil, it has become a core tenet of the national security policy that the country should build a nuclear-propeled submarine. Work at the shipyard has begun already, and current plans envisage commissioning around 2030. If Brazil does indeed make its nuclear submarine operational in the near future, then it is plausible to believe that a series of unpredictable feedback effects are likely to ripple through South America. In its turn, Argentina has doubled down on nuclear energy production with the building of new energy reactors, and officials have privately suggested naval nuclear propulsion might be in the cards at some point in the future. This speaks to the broader issue of the nuclear taboo that Nina Tannenwald tackles in chapter 16 in this volume. To be sure, one of the recurring themes of global nuclear politics today is the return of nuclear weapons as core components of national security strategies across various nuclear weapons states, and the widening gap between those states and the vast majority of countries who voted for a treaty banning nuclear weapons. But the issue of nuclear latency confounds and complicates any attempt at neatly dividing possessors and nonpossessors. Argentina and Brazil illustrate the point: these are states that are happy to condemn the nuclear powers for not disarming and can go as far as negotiating the terms of a ban treaty. But they also, simultaneously, insist on the utility of dual technologies and organize their national priorities accordingly. In watching the evolution of the taboo that has applied to the use of nuclear weapons, we should not lose sight of the far less visible, informal understandings countries have developed over time as to the desirability of nuclear power in the twenty-first century.

Conclusion

The evolution of nuclear politics in South America has three main implications for our understanding of global nuclear order. First, the image of a stable core order around the major powers and their allies that progressively expanded to incorporate latecomers from the non-Western world needs to give way to a messier picture where the rules of the game are contested in a setting of vast asymmetry. Hiroshima triggered new alignments and unsettled the existing hierarchy in South America's regional order, with key states in there perceiving the United States as an unpredictable and often hostile revisionist hegemonic power. Second, one of the major legacies of Hiroshima in South

America was to create a global order in which South American policy makers and national leaders could legitimately opt to double down on their quest for national autonomy through the building of powerful developmentalist states bent on conquering nuclear science and building up nuclear infrastructure. Possessing nuclear technology and its industrial applications—although not necessarily nuclear weapons—came to be seen as an integral part of what it meant to be a modern sovereign polity in the South American postwar order.

Third, there is a powerful case for making the study of nuclear politics truly global. One might expect the study of nuclear politics to be global by its nature. It is not just that the nuclear world we inhabit is the result of the transnational circulation of scientists, natural uranium and yellow-cake, centrifuge designs, nuclear weapons, and the political economy of nuclear energy production, but also the fact that the rules, norms, and institutions that make up the nuclear order today are the product of intense political exchanges and disputes among nations. And yet the global dimensions of the nuclear era are rarely apparent in theories and histories that remain stubbornly national or largely derived from the experience of a small collection of states.

In this chapter I have offered an account of how we might appreciate the "Age of Hiroshima" from the standpoint of South America. If the dropping of the first atomic bomb opened a new chapter in human history, that chapter was about far more than the intersection of technologies of destruction in great-power politics or the story of the proliferation of nuclear weapons capabilities in a dozen or so states across the globe. I have argued that in order to understand the impacts of Hiroshima around the world, we ought to focus on the way old global hierarchies came to filter new ordering dynamics coming from nuclear weapons and the world they created. Orthodox accounts of the impacts of Hiroshima are inadequate because their analysis is too narrowly focused on great-power politics.

The mid-twentieth century—the historical time when the bomb over Hiroshima inaugurated the nuclear age—coincides with the global wave of independence movements in Africa and Asia, the rise of nationalist reassertion in the Middle East and Latin America, and what some came to call the "revolt against the West." An appreciation of how the nuclear ordering born in Hiroshima mingled with that embodied by geopolitical developments across the developing world will help us better grasp the tension and contradictions that we experience in the field of global nuclear politics today.

11

Remembering War, Forgetting Hiroshima

"EUROSHIMA" AND THE WEST GERMAN
ANTI-NUCLEAR WEAPONS
MOVEMENTS IN THE COLD WAR

Holger Nehring

IN JANUARY 1959, at a student conference against nuclear weapons at the Free University in West Berlin, the existentialist German-Jewish philosopher Günther Anders, Hannah Arendt's first husband and a disciple of Martin Heidegger, developed twenty-two "Theses for the Atomic Age." Anders's first thesis addressed "Hiroshima as a World Condition." The first-ever use of a nuclear bomb on the Japanese city had, Anders argued, signaled the arrival of a "New Age." "At any given moment," he wrote, "we have the power to transform any given place on our planet, and even our planet itself, into a Hiroshima." Hiroshima was, Anders, implied, more than a concrete geographical location. It was fundamentally a signifier for the existential helplessness of human beings in the face of a new technology that endowed them with unprecedented power, but also made them completely powerless: "everybody is in reach of everybody else," even across generations: "Hiroshima is everywhere."[1]

The history of the emergence of "Hiroshima" as a synonym for the power of technology and the possibility of global destruction as well as a political trope has been well rehearsed.[2] This interpretation has characterized the historical and contemporary discourse of the Japanese population as victims that Kiichi Fujiwara analyzes as the "Hiroshima discourse" in chapter 12 of this volume. Through Andrew Rotter's interpretation in *Hiroshima: The World's Bomb*, this global framework has now entered the historiography on the specific decision making and legacies of the American nuclear weapons that were used during the bombing of Hiroshima and Nagasaki. This has come with its own problematic consequence of eliding the question of specific U.S. responsibilities, as the chapters by Campbell Craig, Alex Wellerstein, and Sean Malloy in this volume emphasize.[3] The turn to the global has obscured the ways in which the emergence of a "global Hiroshima" has developed through specific local political, social, and cultural contexts.

Like Wakana Mukai's and Fujiwara's chapters on Japan, this chapter seeks to reveal these contexts. It considers the ways in which "Hiroshima" emerged as a political argument within the context of the West German debates about nuclear weapons and traces its transformation. It follows the ways in which West German campaigners for peace and against nuclear weapons appropriated "Hiroshima" from the 1950s into the 1980s, and how "Hiroshima" became "Euroshima," with Germany as its main victim. In particular, this chapter highlights how West German evocations of Hiroshima in the second half of the twentieth century were sutured to experiences and memories of mass death and genocide before 1945.[4] Specifically, it argues that "Hiroshima" offered West German activists a shorthand for discussing the bombing raids of the Second World War as well as the Holocaust. In that sense, West German discussions were similar to the developments Fujiwara outlines for Japan: speaking about Hiroshima has fundamentally been a way to speak about the Second World War. They were not simply reflections of popular emotions nor geostrategic considerations, as Mukai demonstrates for Japanese discussions about nuclear weapons from the 1950s into the late 1960s.

For the West German activists, expressing experiences and memories of Hiroshima, in conjunction with experiences and memories of the bombing of German cities, was not just about representing a historical reality. Following innovative work by Alon Confino and Peter Fritzsche, this chapter is interested in investigating "how memory *forms* social relations" in social movements.[5] This methodology requires an approach to sources that considers not only traditional movement sources, such as pamphlets, flyers, and participants' recollections, memoirs, and diaries. It considers newspaper sources as well as visual representations to understand the ways in which the West German movements against nuclear weapons framed the issues.[6]

West Germany is an especially pertinent case study for the interrelationship between local appropriation and global factors with regard to "Hiroshima." West Germany and Japan share a number of similar features: the nuclear weapons dropped on Japan were initially developed for use on Germany; both Germany and Japan were totally defeated in the Second World War, and some of their main cities lay in ruins; both sought to overcome the legacy of war through programs of economic modernization; and both societies witnessed the emergence of interpretations of victimhood that pushed war crimes to one side of official discourse as they became members of the ideological alliance of liberal democracies in the Cold War.[7]

Recent research has already highlighted the importance of these memories for West German society and political culture.[8] It has thus challenged and refuted W. G. Sebald's claim that the destruction of German cities by Allied bombers "seems to have scarcely left a trace of pain behind in the collective consciousness" and that the memory was itself "obliterated."[9] While this strand of research has provided useful analyses of the role of memories of the bombing campaign in arguments of the West German peace movements at the local level, we still lack a systematic interpretation of the role of Hiroshima in these discussions.[10]

Providing such an interpretation is not simply about filling some empirical and interpretative gaps. This chapter argues that an engagement with these discussions leads to a more precise understanding of the nature of the Cold War and the nuclear age—it brings out the nature of the Cold War as a frozen conflict that became real for people through the experiences and memories of real wars. In a landmark study, Jeffrey Herf has provided us with powerful analysis, controversially debated at the time, of the problems of West German memory politics in the context of the peace movement: he argues that notions of victimhood, nationalism, and anti-Americanism—and the use of "Auschwitz" and "Hiroshima" as political arguments in the West German peace movement—were a fundamental challenge to the Cold War democratic consensus and therefore also the political stability of the Federal Republic.[11]

Interpretations such as Herf's have remained primarily focused on the ideological level and regard evocations of past memories primarily in terms of their political functions. They are also rather vague about the relationship between local and national identities and global developments.[12] Ran Zwigenberg has recently highlighted Hiroshima's role "in the making of global memory culture" and elucidated how Hiroshima and the emergence of an American memory culture focused on the Holocaust were connected.[13] But his study concentrates on the U.S.-Japanese relationship as a shorthand for "global" and thus has difficulty in highlighting the latent meanings and tacit understandings that undergirded Hiroshima beyond this bilateral relationship.[14]

Mirroring Fujiwara's essay on competing Japanese discourses about the Second World War in chapter 12, this chapter seeks to connect this transformation of the public memories of war and Holocaust to the emergence of

"Hiroshima" as a site of commemoration in the West German protests against nuclear weapons. It does this by linking these literatures around a global memory culture with more recent approaches that have emphasized a postwar perspective for German and European history in order to give them more contextual depth.[15] It emphasizes the fundamental status of war experiences and memories for the ways in which "Hiroshima" was appropriated—or not—by West German protesters.

Daniel Levy and Natan Sznaider have developed a compelling argument about how the emergence of the Holocaust as a symbol of barbarism occurred as part of a process of decontextualization. They have also highlighted how this process of universalization was accompanied by a "renationalization" of memories. In a dialectic development in which "universalisation [was a] precondition for re-nationalisation" the global memory of the Holocaust became self-reflective and self-referential.[16] Thus by the end of the Cold War, West German discussions saw a "persistent rhetorical amplification that has made 'Auschwitz' or 'Hiroshima' signifiers for all genocide or mass technological destruction."[17]

Building a Secure Germany: Hiroshima and Memories of Mass Violence in the 1950s and 1960s

From August 2 to 6, 1958, some 3,500 citizens of the southwestern German city of Stuttgart signed a book that commemorated the victims of Hiroshima, as they watched a pacifist vigil on the city's central market square. As they did so, they probably considered the bombing of their own community during the Second World War. Stuttgart was one of the cities most heavily affected by the Allied bombing campaign.[18] The vigil was part of the Campaign against Atomic Death, which the West German Social Democratic Party (SPD) and a number of trade unions organized. The purpose of the campaign was to prevent the stationing of a new generation of tactical nuclear weapons in the Federal Republic. The contributions to the campaign's opening congress in the Frankfurt Paulskirche in late March 1958 already contained frequent references to the fate of Hiroshima and Nagasaki, including a graphic report by the popular science writer Robert Jungk on his recent visit to Japan.[19] Many of the campaign's demonstrations and marches carried banners asking passers-by to "remember Hiroshima."[20] The campaign mobilized hundreds of thousands of Germans over a couple of years and led to the creation of an independent anti–nuclear weapons movement, the Easter Marches of Atomic Weapons Opponents, which remained the main peace movement in German politics into the 1980s.[21]

For these movements, arguments about the relevance of Hiroshima, together with the evocation of experiences and memories of the Second World War, played a fundamental role in forging a community of protesters by creating a master frame around the lessons to be learned from the Second World War. The main pamphlet of the Campaign against Atomic Death showed a picture of bombed-out ruins underneath a red-yellow sky, while its chairman Walter Menzel exhorted readers to "learn from Hiroshima and Nagasaki."[22] The experiences and memories of violence, suppressed in mainstream political culture—and the anticipation of an all-engulfing war in the near future—led to the formation of a new community of activists.[23]

Activists not only regarded themselves as the undeserving victims of the past war; they also imagined themselves as the certain victims of a future nuclear war, mirroring the focus on the future that characterized both governmental and popular debates about nuclear weapons in Japan.[24] The destruction at Hiroshima and Nagasaki was the yardstick for what might be expected in such a situation. Without saying or perhaps even realizing it, they saw what Edith Wyschogrod called the "man-made mass death" at Hiroshima and Nagasaki through the lens of their own German experiences, specifically the at least tacit knowledge that "mass annihilation" was possible.[25] As one contemporary commentator put it, the "Japanese victim cities of Hiroshima and Nagasaki" had become the "devil's modern Golgatha": the "devastation of life is—with regard to its quantity, the suffering involved, and its abomination—without comparison in human history so far."[26]

By pointing to past violence in far-away Japan, Germans imagined themselves as victims of past and future wars—and bypassed a discussion of the violence meted out by Germans during the Second World War and the Holocaust. Nonetheless, movement activists derived a special responsibility from their imagined victimhood and their own history, now that the nuclear weapons posed anew the question of the "life and survival" of the German people, when Berlin could be turned overnight into an "atomic cemetery."[27] Germany could be turned into "multiple Hiroshimas."[28] Through references to their personal war experiences—and aerial warfare in the context of the National Socialist regime in particular—activists argued for a specific political and moral obligation to the present. They pointed out that past German guilt, rendered entirely in the abstract, could not be left by one side—which meant that they constantly wondered how to avoid becoming guilty.[29]

West German activists drew a direct line from the past destruction of German cities in the Second World War to imagining the future of their cities as German Hiroshimas, painting an arc of destruction that had started with the death camps of Auschwitz, that continued with the first test of hydrogen bombs in 1954, and that meant that human beings were now able to destroy life on Earth as such. The seemingly peaceful present was no longer peaceful, as the permanent threat of war loomed over the world—and as the victims of Hiroshima and Nagasaki still bore the burdens of the last war.[30] Typical for such an argument was a pamphlet issued by a student conscientious objectors' association in Munich in 1959. The pamphlet showed two entries from the *Brockhaus Encyclopedia*—one on Hiroshima, the other detailing the heavy damage to Munich during the Second World War. The entry on Munich included an empty space, with an arrow pointing toward it: "left empty for amendment." The caption read: "It is up to you that this terrible amendment . . . will never occur. We have come together in order to prevent that a 6 August 1945 will happen with us."[31]

Such evocations of Hiroshima and Nagasaki were commonly used to reference Germans' own experiences of aerial bombardment and "became . . . opportunities to explore the horrors of man-made mass death, past, present, and future."[32] As around 150,000 protesters gathered at the Hamburg Rathausmarkt on April 17, 1958, to campaign against the stationing of nuclear weapons in the Federal Republic, there were frequent direct references to the World War II aerial bombing campaign and the infamous firestorm.[33] A pamphlet wondered: "1943 Hamburg—1945 Hiroshima—tomorrow the whole world?"[34] The poster advertisement for the screening of the documentary *Hiroshima*, shown as part of the protests, depicted a ruined cityscape, a mushroom cloud in the background, and Hiroshima written horizontally and vertically to form a cross.[35]

Similarly, in the North-Rhine Westphalian city of Hagen and in the Franconian cities of Würzburg and Nuremberg, as well as in Kassel in Hesse, protesters portrayed the "city as victim of Nazism and war"[36] and showed only bombed-out ruins, not the civilian dead—in stark contrast to the heroic memories of German soldiers at the time.[37] Other towns and cities, such as the southwest German city of Pforzheim, which was among those communities most heavily bombed, used a comparison with Guernica.[38] Campaign organizers frequently expressed concerns that the images shown not be too graphic. At one point, the campaign office rejected the suggestion of using images and survivors from Hiroshima for marketing purposes: they would not have a "mass effect" as they were "too gruesome."[39] Behind this hesitation to confront the cruelty of death and dying directly were the immediate experiences of the bombing campaign that provided the dark foundation for West Germany's "economic miracle" and the emergence of consumerism.[40] Often, atomic destruction and images of the ruins and survivors of Hiroshima were juxtaposed with the awesome powers of the peaceful uses of nuclear energy.[41]

The Cold War as a System: Victimhood and Technological Modernity

By the beginning of the 1960s, such arguments about Germany as a potential battlefield of the Cold War took on a different twist. Activists now began to analyze the Cold War less in direct relationship to the experiences and memories of the Second World War. Instead, they began to understand the Cold War as a system of its own and to investigate the system's operation. The first voice for such an interpretation was Günther Anders. Anders saw the geopolitical and ideological differences in the Cold War as mere epiphenomena. Rather than focus on them, he instead chose to zoom in on the existential condition of the "atomic age." For him, the "atomic age" meant that there was a "growing gap" between "our *action* and our *imagination*," that is, "of the fact that we are unable to conceive what we can construct, to mentally reproduce what we can produce." In particular, the effects of the bombings of Hiroshima and Nagasaki "surpass[ed] all imagination."[42] The real political threat did not therefore stem from this or that political ideology. Rather, it came from the system of deterrence that undergirded Cold War geopolitics. That threat was "totalitarian": it "transforms our globe into one vast concentration camp from which there is no way out."[43]

Anders, however, remained a marginal figure in the West German protests of the late 1950s and early 1960s. Apart from his appearance at the Berlin Student Conference against Nuclear Weapons in early 1959, he spoke rarely, and his work was not fully discussed among mainstream protesters at the time. It was not until the general West German public—and activists in particular—had a clearer sense of the bureaucratic and technological understanding of the Holocaust that ideas similar to Anders's achieved broader currency.[44] The first public intellectual to make this connection powerfully was Hans Magnus Enzensberger, who had been close to the anti–nuclear weapons protests. In an essay entitled "Reflections before a Glass Cage," which appeared as a commentary on the trial of Adolf Eichmann trial in 1962, he discussed the moral and political equivalences that resulted from the destructive potential of bureaucratic and technocratic modernity, in which human beings were "technically capable of everything." Similar to Anders, he pointed out that traditional political language and concepts were no longer appropriate to capture the political challenges of the day: "What happened in the 1940s does not age; instead of becoming more remote, it inches up on us and forces us to revise all human forms of thinking and relating to each other."[45]

Enzensberger's essay culminated in a polemical comparison of Eichmann, the Auschwitz commander, and the futurist and military strategist Herman Kahn. Both, he argued, developed "game plans"—and he found that the "power of sovereignty" in the nuclear age had become the power to "depose of nuclear weapons": "this implement is the present and future of Auschwitz."[46] As "posterity attempt[ed] to judge those responsible for Hitler's 'Final Solution,' . . . it [busied] itself with the preparation of its own."[47]

Enzensberger had drawn on such analogies before, for example, when he campaigned against the Algerian War: "Algeria is everywhere, it is here, too, like Auschwitz, Hiroshima and Budapest."[48] But now his thinking percolated more deeply into the West German movement against nuclear weapons. This movement was now no longer part of the campaign by the SPD but had transformed itself into an independent social movement, calling itself "Easter Marches" and ultimately becoming part of the broader "extraparliamentary opposition" in West Germany over the course of the 1960s.[49] In 1961 one activist still wrote: "The terms Auschwitz and Hiroshima are connected with horror and shame in our people. But they do not yet mobilize human courage and rational hope everywhere."[50] A poster by the West German Trade Union Federation relating to a May 1 rally in 1962 was one of the first to blend the imagery of concentration camps—with their barbed wire—with the iconic mushroom cloud: "No atomic weapons, no genocide!"[51] Increasingly, the commemoration of the dropping of the first nuclear bomb on Hiroshima on August 6, 1945, became a fixed feature of the Easter March campaigns at the local level and helped to change these perceptions—together with an increased awareness of Nazi crimes and the Holocaust.[52] The Easter March campaign already counted events in seventeen cities in 1961—a number that grew in subsequent years.[53]

This transformation was accompanied by a shift of focus in interpretations of the National Socialist German past, from an emphasis on specific individuals and their continued influence in the Federal Republic to an emphasis on a specific system of rule, linked to modern capitalism. This engagement with the National Socialist past had been "at best incomplete and at worst flawed": a deeper understanding of the Holocaust in its context was marginal, as activists primarily discussed the nature of fascism as a systematic product of capitalism.[54]

Such interpretations were close to the official views of the bombing war that had developed there since the 1950s, an interpretation that "divested allied bombing of its original context of World War II and recontextualized the campaign as the first act of imperialist aggression in the Cold War."[55] Activists began to interpret the Vietnam War as genocide, as the "Auschwitz of our generation," with violence meted out by U.S. troops and supported by an all-too-willing West German government under Chancellor Ludwig Erhard.[56] They initially followed the example of the radical American anti–Vietnam War movement by calling acts of war "murder": "Erhard and the Bonn parties support MURDER," a poster produced by the West German Socialist German Student Federation (SDS) screamed, "Murder by napalm bombs! Murder by poisonous gas! Murder by atom bombs!"[57] West German protesters specifically highlighted the fears that the Vietnam War might turn nuclear: as Germans had already experienced "total bombing war," they claimed to have a specific understanding of Vietnamese victims.[58]

Vietnam now appeared to activists as a "world war of a new type."[59] It was a war that seemed to be dominated by advanced technology, new chemical weapons, and bombing simultaneously, while also betraying the U.S. commitment to human rights and human values.[60] For Ulrike Meinhof, a prominent activist and New Left journalist at the time, the Vietnam War stood in a direct line traced by the development of technologies of death.

This meant that German and international history now appeared differently: "Auschwitz's gas apparatuses have found their technical perfection in the atomic bomb," Meinhof argued in an essay on the twentieth anniversary of the July 1944 plot to assassinate Hitler: "playing with atomic bombs [was to] . . . play with a crime of Hitlerist proportions."[61] Meinhof's views brought Anders's and Enzensberger's initial analyses into the activist mainstream. Against this backdrop, the area bombing of German cities appeared in a different light. In a review of David Irving's book on the Dresden bombings, Meinhof called them an "act of barbarism and inhumanity, for which there is no justification."[62] Like activists in the 1950s and early 1960s, the peace campaigners of the 1960s drew direct conclusions from their analysis of the German past for their own actions. But rather than regarding their own activism as acts of individual and collective resistance, they now developed a more abstract and systematic understanding of the problem: "democracy" and nuclear weapons were incompatible: "Nuclear armaments and dissolution of democracy condition each other, means of mass annihilation and terror belong together, technically, organizationally, and factually."[63] Such arguments related to the broader debates in West German society at the time about *Sachzwänge*—the power of bureaucracy and technology to frame decisions— and about the essentially political nature of technology.[64] In line with the framework, images of the bombing war disappeared from the visual politics of the West German peace campaigns. Instead, we can observe the emergence of a visual discourse that focused, on the one hand, on the stylized representation of activists breaking the chains of power and bureaucracy, often through the image of the classic revolutionary; on the other hand, we see the emergence of a humanitarian frame that zooms in on the suffering of the victims of war in foreign lands.[65]

From Experiences to Memories: "Hiroshima" as "Condition of the World" and the Critique of Deterrence

The denouement of the student movements around 1968 also brought an end to peace campaigning: with détente, the issue of nuclear weapons lost its salience as debates in domestic politics started to focus on the Chancellor Willy Brandt's Social Democratic–Liberal coalition government and its program of ambitious social and political reforms, as environmental and identity issues around sex and gender grew in prominence, and as the debates about the left-wing terrorism of the Red Army Faction, the June 2 Movement, and their alleged left-wing sympathizers consumed most of the domestic political attention.[66]

Discussions about nuclear weapons regained traction only when plans by the U.S. government to deploy a new type of weapon, the "neutron bomb," were leaked.[67] A public debate started around the commemorations of the thirty-second anniversary of the Hiroshima and Nagasaki bombings in August 1977, when the grassroots Catholic peace group Pax Christi used the arrival of the new weapons to argue that the danger of nuclear war was greater than ever before. It also argued the new weapons symbolized a degeneration of human values, as they would leave buildings intact but kill everyone in and around them.[68] Later that year the SPD politician Egon Bahr called the bombs a "symbol of the perversion of thought."[69]

The debates about the neutron bomb prefigured a number of themes that characterized the framing of nuclear weapons and the memory and legacy of Hiroshima and Nagasaki in the 1980s: the increased use of memories of the bombing campaign and of "Auschwitz" and "Hiroshima," less as direct historical experiences and socially contextualized memories and more as political arguments, where the "Third Reich," as well as Hiroshima, had become a "quarry for all parties";[70] the emphasis on the environmental and radiation effects of the weapons with reference to specific scientific findings; the increased focus on actual weapons and weapons systems; and, not least, the significant increase in the volume and significance of visual representations relating to the debates.

Unlike in the late 1950s and early 1960s, Günther Anders was now, in the 1980s, one of the main public intellectuals arguing on behalf of the peace activists. In a best-selling book on the renewed relevance of the Sermon on the Mount for creating peace and understanding, the Catholic journalist Franz Alt paraphrased Anders's insights from the 1950s as if they were new: "for the first time ever, humans have the ability to end their history," he wrote. And like Anders three decades before him, Alt combined the two symbolic markers of twentieth-century mass death: an "atomic holocaust would annihilate 4.5 billion human beings worldwide and would make billions of future lives impossible."[71] Such attacks, many feared, could be triggered through computers, as waging war had become part of a process of all-encompassing automation.[72] Alt cited Japanese survivors to illustrate the consequences in graphic detail and endow his argument with an air of authenticity: "nothingness" and "deathly silence" would follow after a nuclear attack.[73] As Anders put it succinctly in a reader that was highly popular among peace activists at the time: "Hiroshima" had become "the condition of the world."[74]

While the protests about the neutron bomb remained small, a broader movement developed that campaigned against NATO's dual-track decision and turned into the largest protest movement of the Federal Republic. This decision, developed and supported by West German chancellor Helmut Schmidt (SPD), envisaged the deployment of a new generation of intermediate-range ballistic missiles (Pershing II) in Western Europe (and especially West Germany) if the Soviet Union did not withdraw its SS20 missiles from Eastern bloc countries.[75] The coalition of activists that campaigned against the deployment was much broader than in the 1950s and early 1960s. It encompassed a political spectrum ranging from communist groups and groupuscules across social democrats and left-wing liberals as well as the growing environmental movement and traditional pacifist groups and encompassing both Protestants and Catholics.[76] Unlike in the 1950s and early 1960s, activists now regarded themselves not as members of an anti–nuclear weapons campaign but as peace campaigners: they not only focused on the weapons themselves but used the debates to develop broader ideas about political and social transformation, regarding themselves as the main agents in that transformation and their movement as the prefiguration of the kind of society they wished to create.[77]

Now, the main frame through which activists interpreted nuclear weapons was one in which the Cold War appeared as a system bent on its own destruction, in which the importance of the differences between Eastern and Western ideologies paled against the threat of mutual annihilation: "there are no differences between the systems that justify to threaten each other with a genocide without example."[78] This contemporary diagnosis of "exterminism," an interpretation West German activists saw strengthened by the powerful interventions of their British colleague E. P. Thompson, meant that "responsible political action [was] no longer possible."[79]

This called for new forms of political mobilization, but it also meant that, until new political actors had asserted themselves, the "1980s [were] increasingly the most dangerous decade in the history of humanity."[80] For the Green politician Otto Schily, nuclear weapons had reached the "destructive potential" of "one million times Hiroshima."[81] Campaigners linked to the fellow-traveling Deutsche Friedens-Union (DFU) stated that, for the first time since 1945, "atomic war limited to Europe has become possible" and that Germany's "national and [each citizen's] individual existence" were at stake.[82] Structurally, this argument resembled those Japanese protesters in the 1950s and early 1960s who, in Wakana Mukai's account in this volume, protested against the U.S.-Japan Security Treaty by questioning the close ties that treaty meant between U.S. and Japanese defense and security policies and the significant dangers it seemed to unilaterally impose on Japan.

Much more graphically than before, West German activists in the 1980s relied on descriptions from Hiroshima survivors to underline their case. They embedded these perceptions in a diffuse mixture of general fears about environmental degradation, for which the American science writer Jonathan Schell's best-selling *The Fate of the Earth*, published in West Germany in 1982, is a good example: not hundreds of thousands, like in Hiroshima and Nagasaki, would die in the case of a nuclear war, Schell argued, but millions upon millions—and the book included graphic and gory descriptions of the suffering in Hiroshima and Nagasaki to show the consequences of a nuclear attack.[83]

The activists' development of a functional understanding of the memory of bomb survivors and of the memory of war to make specific arguments about the workings of the Cold War was accompanied by a similar shift with regard to interpretations of the Nazi past and the Holocaust.[84] In a controversial interview, the Green politicians Joschka Fischer and Otto Schily, who had close ties to the peace movement, drew direct comparisons between the Holocaust, Hiroshima, and Nagasaki and current U.S. war planning. Amplifying arguments made by Anders, Enzensberger, and others before them, Fischer stated: "I find it morally abhorrent that it is obviously not taboo, within the systemic logic of modernity even after Auschwitz, to continue preparing mass annihilation—this time not along racial lines, but along the lines of the East West Conflict."[85]

Schily subsequently justified this response in a special section of a parliamentary debate on this issue arguing that there "were in the end state of affairs when one was unable to decide politically but had to abdicate in favor of military necessities."[86] The Protestant professor of rhetoric Walter Jens, one of the most powerful public supporters of the peace movements of the 1980s, regarded this kind of logic as the "entrance to hell," as the "kind of rationality and logic, how they existed on this end of the gas chambers at the ramp of Auschwitz."[87] Often, such arguments had gendered dimensions: feminist activists referred to the "crazy male power" behind such developments and linked their emergence and use specifically to American "cowboys" who had created a new technology that resembled a "death factory," a characterization made by Dorothee Sölle.[88] Anton-Andreas Guha seems to have been the first popular writer to have used the term "atomic holocaust" in this context to great effect when calling the deployment of new nuclear weapons "Europe's Holocaust."[89] The social-democratic politician Erhard Eppler explicitly blamed "American planners" for preparing such an inferno—given their history, "Germans must not [be complicit with] it."[90]

As in Japan in the 1980s, discussions occurred as part of the transformation of the ways in which movement activists interpreted the Cold War in light of the experiences and memories of the Second World War.[91] Warnings of a potential "atomic holocaust" that would lead to a "Euroshima" relate directly to this changed perception among protesters.[92] Although their resonance and meaning were specifically German, similar arguments were made by other anti–nuclear weapons campaigns around the world, including Japanese campaigners.[93] The term "atomic Auschwitz" seems to have come to West Germany from the context of the U.S. peace movement—the peace activist Petra Kelly claimed that it was coined by Archbishop Hunthausen at a speech at a navy base in Seattle, Washington.[94]

One key element of such visions was that they imagined Europe, and particularly Germany, as the site of a future world war.[95] Peace activists turned the scenarios developed by the U.S. war gamers against them and accused them of toying with the destruction of an entire continent, thus fundamentally questioning the meaning of NATO.[96] This argument became especially widespread from 1982 onward when the details of the Air Land Battle strategy and Field Manual 100–5, which envisioned Germany as an "extended battlefield" in a nuclear war, became public knowledge.[97] This scenario was discussed in great detail when, following a U.S. documentary, it emerged that the small Hessian village of Hattenbach would be "ground zero" in a potential future nuclear war, and that a weapon "17 times the strength of Hiroshima's bomb" would be detonated there.[98] Such discussions increasingly imagined "Europe," and Germany at the center of it, as the victims of a future nuclear conflagration caused by external powers, and specifically the United States. This is evident from the poster by GDR artist Wolfgang Kenkel (fig. 11.1), whose visual language was specific to both East and West.[99]

Accordingly, the German Green Party staged a reenactment of the Nuremberg War Crimes Tribunal, this time "against first-strike and mass annihilation weapons in East and West" in February 1983 that referred directly to such scenarios.[100] In late November 1983 Otto Schily cited a "shocking" letter to the editor of the *New York Times*, whose writer had argued that Germans should be prepared to make a sacrifice, given that they were liberated from National Socialism, just like the people of Hiroshima had made, many of them still alive.[101]

FIGURE 11.1. Wolfgang Kenkel, poster, 1982: "Euroshima?" Deutsches Historisches Museum, DHM, P90/1140. https://www.dhm.de/archiv/magazine/plakate/schluss_damit/frieden_bilder_gross/euroshima.htm.

Activists imagined Germany not only as the site of a future nuclear war but also as the location of armaments and war preparation. A number of books and pamphlets sought to make this militarization visible through maps in order to highlight the "phony peace" (*fauler Friede*) that had existed in Cold War West Germany since 1945.[102] Dorothee Sölle argued that "the bombs are falling now," bringing together poverty, world hunger and nuclear weapons in an apocalyptic scenario about the militarization of life and everyday violence.[103]

Although Sölle had direct war experiences herself, interventions like hers, which began to interpret "war" metaphorically, indicate a shift in thinking about the character of the Cold War and the role of nuclear weapons within it. Activists began to interpret these dynamics no longer as part of a real war but as part of an imaginary one. Whereas "aerial bombardment" was a "technically perfect 'strategy from above,' " and the view from planes allowed for perfect aerial views of cities in their totality, those without that view, and especially those on "atomic submarines and rocket silos," had to turn to fiction to make sense of the Cold War: "they fantasize about an opponent, who is only familiar to me through the movies and propaganda films."[104]

From this perspective, West German peace activists began to highlight "psychological militarization,"[105] in particular, alongside the traditional anti-militarist arguments about the cost of armaments as a driver of world poverty and a humanitarian frame that highlighted the plight of the victims of war. This shift led to a recalibration of what activists understood about violence and how it was wielded.[106] They conceptualized violence no longer directly as the physical injury of human bodies but as a structural condition that prevented human beings from reaching a state of self-fulfillment indirectly and mainly through psychological means.[107] Accordingly, they saw war planners in the U.S. administration also through this psychological prism: "Reagan's planning staff" suffered from a "necrophiliac illusion" and contemplated "suicide as a result of a sick security delusion."[108]

Conversely, peace activists now also stressed the problematic psychological consequences of the Cold War system of deterrence. They argued that the system of deterrence had pushed the important regulatory function of fear to the sidelines—fear therefore had to be brought back into the public domain, since "fear can teach us to defend ourselves" (*Die Angst kann lehren, sich zu wehren*).[109] In making these arguments, activists engaged directly with prominent public intellectuals with backgrounds in psychoanalysis.

In West Germany, Horst Eberhard Richter was perhaps the most prominent among these. Richter and others relied directly on the findings of American psychologists such as Robert J. Lifton in their work on atomic bomb survivors in Japan. They emphasized the role of trauma and called, on that basis, for a deeper "knowledge . . . of the horror of the past and the unspeakable and horrible possibilities of the future."[110] Lifton in particular highlighted the issue of "psychic numbing" among survivors, and Richter followed him, referring not only to the nuclear age but also to Second World War experiences.[111] This frame of interpretation penetrated deeply into the more political campaign literature, for example, when the SPD politician Oskar Lafontaine discussed the "psychological crippling" caused by "the mass murder apparatuses" (*Massenmordgeräte*), or when Petra Kelly included in a best-selling peace movement reader a letter from her grandmother relating the trauma of her experiences in the Second World War to her fears of a Third World War.[112]

This led activists to discuss the parameters of politics in the nuclear age more broadly, specifically with regard to the question of how political resistance to government could be justified under the conditions of the nuclear age.[113] At a rally near the Pershing II base at Mutlangen, a small village around thirty miles to the east of Stuttgart in southwestern Germany, a group of senior citizens carried banners at a demonstrations stating "Pershing makes us free" (*Pershing macht frei*), a reference to the inscription at the Auschwitz gate: "Work makes us free" (*Arbeit macht frei*).[114]

Another feature of this turn to the past as a political argument was the direct link between the war experiences of their own community, Hiroshima, and the scenario for a future nuclear war that activists sought to establish. Theirs was, activists argued through texts and images, a society thoroughly shaped by war, although it appeared peaceful. Scenarios and images therefore came to play a key role in evoking the dangers stemming from nuclear weapons in their observations, their actions, and their visual representations.[115] Accordingly, Gertrud Gumlich, chair of the Berlin Initiative of Physicians against Atomic Energy and Atomic Weapons and the final speaker at a peace rally in 1982, noted the continued (infrastructural) relevance of the Second World War for Berlin's cityscape in order to emphasize the militarization of everyday life in the early 1980s: "every glance at city map, public transport map, ID card" shows the importance of World War II.[116] Younger activists, by contrast, began to see the nuclear age in its own terms. Activist Thomas mentioned that he had seen a documentary on Hiroshima and been shocked by it: "There I have seen things that I have never seen before. And if I now think that, in two or three weeks' time, the radiation is coming towards me . . . then I get frightened."[117]

The West German peace campaigns of the 1980s often operated with direct references to the damage caused by nuclear radiation among survivors. Under the motto "The survivors will envy the dead," the German section of the International Physicians for the Prevention of Nuclear War (IPPNW) showed a "Nagasaki child," which was based on a real photograph from the Japanese city in 1945.[118] Other posters just listed the number of deaths and amount of radiation damage to be expected in case of a nuclear attack on a respective city and gave the emergency numbers of the police and fire departments.[119]

In drawing up these scenarios, West German peace activists based their assessment on U.S. studies, specifically one that had simulated a nuclear attack on Washington, DC, and on research by Steven Fetter and Kosta Tsipis at MIT that tested the impact of different types of nuclear incidents, from a reactor explosion to a nuclear bomb falling onto a nuclear reactor, which would produce, as the West German journalist put it, a "radioactive holocaust" that would completely destroy Germany for a hundred years.[120] Increasingly, activists and their supporters chose to highlight specific images of human suffering, such as deformities and specific symptoms of radiation damage, rather than merely discuss these abstractly or focus solely on damage to physical infrastructure as activists had done in the early 1950s and 1960s.[121] Accordingly, a poster produced in 1981 by the citizens' initiative Düsseldorf Citizens against Atomic Weapons graphically depicts both what the activists sought to protect—a cheerful group of playing children—and the gruesome consequences of a nuclear attack, in the form of charred body, probably from Hiroshima.[122]

This shift in focus also meant that the air war in the Second World War was no longer the main or only yardstick but now appeared as a past reference point, "as prologue of the apocalypse" in the future.[123] In this vein, Antje Huber, an SPD MP from the Ruhr city of Essen, argued in the key parliamentary debate about the stationing of missiles that 75 percent of her own city had been destroyed in the Second World War: "But we did not live in Hiroshima, this desert of deathly radiation and unimaginable victims. Hiroshima was the rehearsal for the new technological possibilities."[124] With hindsight, activists now began to interpret mass death in the Second World War as the birth pangs of the atomic age. Activists also staged "die-ins," "demonstrative mass dying," to highlight the fact that they already lived in wartime.[125] Such actions had already been tested during some Hiroshima commemoration events before as well as during the Vietnam War protests, to highlight the urgency of the threat that the nuclear arms race posed.[126] Also during the early 1980s, crosses for every community (*Gemeinde*) in the state of Baden-Württemberg were displayed on a field in front of the Pershing II missile depot in Mutlangen as a warning of nuclear war.[127]

Activists not only outlined the threat of violence from a "global Hiroshima" at the local level but also highlighted the importance of local communities for preventing an impending apocalypse where they lived.[128] Thus the peace movement organizer Klaus Vack predicted in August 1983 that, because of the importance of impending decisions about the deployment of missiles and the strength of the movement in the small town near the Mutlangen Pershing II base, "Gmünd will become a world city in the next few days."¹²⁹ In line with this local focus of peace activism, a key theme that undergirded the fears about destruction was the importance of protecting the *Heimat*, the local and national homeland.¹³⁰ A prominent Green Party election poster from 1983 showed the traditional German houses that were to be protected from nuclear war in what looked like an idyllic small-town setting.¹³¹ By showing the houses that were to be protected, the poster makes an argument that is, in its general thrust, remarkably reminiscent of earlier renderings of political and social threats.¹³²

Increasingly, the peace demonstrations and peace camps themselves emerged as the prefigurations of the peace the activists wished to create.¹³³ Against what Robert Jungk described as the cold and anonymous technology, structural violence, and profound lack of democracy of the "atomic state," peace camps and protest marches offered the warmth of direct interpersonal relations.¹³⁴ This theme even became part of a transnational visual discourse among peace activists, as in the American Len Munnik's design for a button that was worn widely in West German peace movement circles.¹³⁵ Another motif that was frequently used was that of a bonsai tree growing out of an army helmet that was turned upside down, with three children sitting in the tree that, from farther away, was even reminiscent of the shape of a mushroom cloud (fig. 11.2).

As the literary scholar Klaus Scherpe has argued, discussions were at once "dramatized" and "de-dramatized."¹³⁶ As a consequence, "Auschwitz" and "Hiroshima" became free-floating "ciphers" or metaphors to encapsulate broader and more complex issues and problems.¹³⁷ They stood in for the larger complex of technological modernity and key developments in twentieth-century politics and society. As the peace campaigner Volkmar Deile put it: "Auschwitz is a lasting ability of human beings to deal with human beings."¹³⁸ By inference, many activists believed that the same was true for Hiroshima and Nagasaki, so that nuclear weapons became "nothing more than the final sign in the game of simulation."¹³⁹

Conclusions

Similar arguments and discourses continued into the post–Cold War period: they framed German debates about the bombing of cities in the former Yugoslavia and then again about the terrorist attacks on the World Trade Center on September 11, 2001. As in Japan, the Cold War systems of thought the peace activists had developed in the 1980s did not simply disappear with the fall of the Berlin Wall in November 1989 and German reunification in 1990, although the geopolitical landscape had fundamentally changed.¹⁴⁰ When commenting

FIGURE 11.2. Lithograph by Friedenswerkstatt Sindelfingen, 1980. Deutsches Historisches Museum, DHM, PK 2014/901. http://www.dhm.de/datenbank/dhm.php?seite=5&fld_0=ZD030226.

on an exhibition on Hamburg's "Firestorm" in 2003, Theo Sommer, former editor of the liberal German weekly *Die Zeit*, called the Hamburg bombing in 1943 a "nonatomic Hiroshima," referencing the apocalypse of St. John.[141]

W. G. Sebald's diagnosis, in the early twenty-first century, of amnesia surrounding the bombing campaign responded directly to the late–Cold War linkage of the bombing campaigns, Hiroshima, and Auschwitz. In his *New Yorker* article, Sebald cites Elias Canetti's account of a Hiroshima survivor, comparing its function to Hans Erich Nossack's account of the Hamburg "firestorm." But with the ideological and geopolitical framework of the Cold War gone, "Hiroshima" and "Auschwitz," in conjunction with "Hamburg," "Dresden," "Cologne," and the other German cities that were bombed, were mere words without direct experiences attached to them, free-floating memory icons without broader meaning, calling for a history more deeply anchored in nature.[142]

Jörg Friedrich's best-selling *The Fire (Der Brand)* sought to provide such a "natural history of destruction" and claimed to fill this gap in national memory for the first time. Friedrich, a journalist with close links to peace activism in the 1980s, used emotional language when describing the bombing of German cities. It reminded many readers of descriptions of the Holocaust and the death camps, while his language and citations reproduced directly the language of National Socialist propaganda without proper contextualization, implying that the Allies had committed genocidal acts by bombing Germans.[143] Not unlike Japan, where this pattern had been evident from the 1950s onward, post–Cold War Germany thus saw the emergence of arguments about the bombing campaign that bridged the divide between the left and the nationalist right, in which the United States appears as the main villain of the Second World War as well as the Cold War, and in which Germany becomes its abiding victim.

Right-wing liberals, such as the Anglo-German journalist Alan Posener, deeply anchored in the Western ideological consensus of the Cold War, call out the anti-Americanism of such arguments. Assuming that the hegemony of the Cold War consensus was still intact, they diagnosed the "uncanny silence" of Germans with regard to the seventieth anniversary of the dropping of the atomic bombs on Hiroshima and Nagasaki, wondering whether the fear of bombs had disappeared with communism and arguing that talk of a Third World War had been a displacement activity of those who had not experienced the Second.[144]

This chapter has provided a historical interpretation of these contemporary voices in German politics and has also sought to unveil how West Germans thought about nuclear weapons within the context of the Cold War. From the end of the war, Germans had an "uncanny knowledge of what total annihilation was."[145] Their discussions and arguments about nuclear weapons were a form of expressing this knowledge without directly referring to it. Throughout the Cold War, they interpreted nuclear weapons—their stationing on German soil and their potential use—as related to the fundamental question of death and survival, of the world, the German nation, the cities and individuals within it. They told the story of the Cold War as a story of their and their country's potential future deaths.

This story follows the pattern that Dirk Moses has shown to be the fundamental characteristic of the status of the past in post-1945 West Germany: the emphasis on distance and a new collectivity distinct from past crimes, or efforts to "make the national past bearable through a variety of displacement strategies."[146] Michael Geyer has captured this more specifically as a "stigma of violence," which has permeated not just Germany's political and popular culture but also its historiography: "Silence about violence as an intrinsic element of German modernity was the most immediate and direct result. This entailed forgetting the violent origins of society and the desperate effort to disguise its present appearance in foreign images."[147]

The discussions about "Hiroshima," "Auschwitz," and the bombing of German cities are one form in which we can find this "stigma of violence." They highlight how this trope intersected with the *threat* of mass violence and destruction that the Cold War signified in Europe. In the debates of the 1950s and 1960s, the experiences and memories of violence were still real and close—the reference points for the potential future death through nuclear weapons were the sites of specific German deaths in the immediate past: Hamburg, Dresden, Cologne. Hiroshima played only an indirect role.

By the early 1960s the discussions about the legacies of National Socialism, memories of the bombing war, and the Cold War became entwined. As the first broader insights about the National Socialist genocide were more widely discussed and more direct experiences of German destruction faded away, the "stigma of violence" began its work: West German student protesters began to link the cause of violence in the Cold War specifically to American actions. Pointing to the U.S. bombing campaign in the Southeast Asia, protesters made the U.S. Air Force into the embodiment of the dialectics of modernity, which entailed both enlightenment and knowledge and their potential for violent destruction.

Within the arguments developed by the West German peace movements, and structurally similar to the assumptions in the "Hiroshima discourse" that Fujiwara analyzes for Japan, Germans appeared as the unwitting victims of the violent force of modernity, as represented by the United States—the violence now began to be portrayed in "foreign images," with a warning that the German future in the Cold War could soon look like Vietnam. It was against this backdrop that "Hiroshima" joined "Auschwitz" in the debates about nuclear weapons in West Germany in the mid-1970s: it became a general signifier for the destructiveness of technological modernity that was both foreign and real. As direct experiences of German destruction and German violence were less readily available, memories and commemorations took their place; analogies were used to develop lessons and arguments for the present.[148]

These shifts had direct repercussions for how the West German peace activists and their supporters interpreted the Cold War. In the 1950s and early 1960s, referencing German ruins, they developed an understanding of the Cold War that focused on what Michael Geyer has called "German Angst." The Cold War would mean a Third World War with Germany as its main victim, resulting in the country's total annihilation. This understanding was born of a deep but tacit understanding of the power of the state to kill.[149]

By the middle of the 1960s, and especially over the course of the 1970s and 1980s, "the fascination with fright [*Schrecken*] . . . [was] overtaken to a degree by a fascination with deterrence [*Abschreckung*, literally being frightened away]."[150] For the West German peace protesters, deterrence as the core of the Cold War system of geopolitics was now the main problem that had to be resolved: for them, deterrence was a fiction that, through technological problems, human mistakes, or the escalation of ideologies through cycles of "militarization," could lead to the destruction of the world, with Germany as the main battlefield. "Hiroshima," together with "Auschwitz" and the destroyed German cities, provided powerful textual and visual analogies that allowed West Germans to think through the implications of their own past in the context of the global Cold War.

Ironically, the West German protesters began to protest against Cold War structures and Cold War ways of thinking and to adopt a systems-theoretical optic of the Cold War precisely at a time when this system was beginning to wither away, just as 1980s West Germans waved good-bye to their understanding of the Bonn Republic as a provisional state at a time when its foundations began to falter.[151] The appropriation of "Hiroshima" by local memory culture began when it could no longer be anchored in real experiences of war and aerial bombing—it was a device in a by-and-large self-reflective debate.

At that point in the 1980s, Hiroshima still appeared as the synonym for the "world condition" that Günther Anders had diagnosed, ahead of his time, in the late 1950s. But it now joined the many other pressing global problems as one among equals. From that perspective, the story of Hiroshima's (non)appropriation in Cold War West Germany offers some clues for global understandings of our own time as fundamentally shaped by the nuclear age—a foundation that is now, in mainstream political culture, more or less forgotten.

12

Hiroshima, Nanjing, and Yasukuni

CONTENDING DISCOURSES ON THE
SECOND WORLD WAR IN JAPAN

Kiichi Fujiwara

FOLLOWING PREVIOUS CHAPTERS on the movements and politics that have revolved around nuclear weapons, this chapter examines the politics of war memories in Japan. There is little doubt that Hiroshima has been remembered in Japan; if it remains a vibrant cultural symbol on a worldwide scale, as discussed in chapter 1 of this volume, it should come to no surprise that the symbolic significance of Hiroshima is even greater in Japan today. The centrality of Hiroshima in Japanese war memories, however, leads to yet another question: Where do the memories of Hiroshima stand in relation to other memories of war? In this chapter I will discuss Japanese memories of World War II, comparing three major sets of discourses: the Hiroshima discourse, the Nanjing discourse, and the Yasukuni discourse. Let me first lay out the gist of my argument.

Historical discourse here is a shorthand expression that may be loosely defined as a set of linguistic and symbolic expression that attaches meaning to past experiences of a certain community. This expression cannot be a collection of individual experiences, for the actual experiences of individuals are diverse by definition. The meaning attached to the supposedly shared experience will also be of an extremely arbitrary nature, for the implicit nuance that goes with individual experiences will be lost in the translation to a more abstract representation of a shared sense of the past. The construction of historical discourse in a public sphere, therefore, is a highly selective process where some events or experiences are elevated to the public sphere while others are not.

There is no doubt that the bombings of Hiroshima and Nagasaki have been elevated to the center of various memories of the Second World War in Japan. The Japanese public shared this attention not only because of the massive civilian deaths caused by the attacks but also from an anxiety that another nuclear attack might happen amid the confrontation between the Soviet Union and the United States. Here the memories of the past war were combined with fear of yet another one: the rallying cry was not just about remembering Hiroshima but also about avoiding another nuclear holocaust in the future. A narrative with the victims of the nuclear bombings at the core, the *Hiroshima discourse* has dominated public memories of the war in Japan.[1]

As a call to avoid thermonuclear wars in the future, the Hiroshima discourse carried a universal legitimacy and significance that extended beyond national boundaries. The victims who appeared in the Hiroshima discourse, however, were almost exclusively limited to Japanese civilians, with little attention paid to others. The Hiroshima narrative, therefore, at once aspired for a universal appeal and yet was quite selective in the choice of victimhood.

This selection of victimhood was a serious and unacceptable omission for the people who suffered from the Japanese invasion and the ensuing atrocities, where the most important aspect of the war was the death not of Japanese but of non-Japanese civilians. Here we find a different narrative of the war that focuses on non-Japanese victims, a narrative I will call the *Nanjing discourse*.

And then there were the memories of the Japanese soldiers who were mobilized in the war. Their experiences could not be covered by either the Hiroshima or the Nanjing discourse. For the Hiroshima narrative, the soldiers were the ones who had brought the nation to war and victimized Japanese civilians; for the Nanjing discourse, the Japanese soldiers were the perpetrators of wartime atrocities. The soldiers, however, were drafted mainly against their will and sought recognition of their sacrifice to the Japanese nation. This is what I will call the *Yasukuni discourse*.

During most of the three-quarters of a century following the end of the war, the Hiroshima discourse has continued to enjoy an almost exclusive attention in Japan, while the Nanjing and Yasukuni discourses were left in obscurity. The centrality of the Hiroshima discourse, however, was based on the likely possibility of nuclear war between the United States and the Soviet Union, a possibility that was somewhat reduced with the end of the Cold War and the collapse of the Soviet Union. The rise of conservative politics in Japan, moreover, promoted the Yasukuni discourse in public debates, which then stimulated the Nanjing discourse, for the contrast between the German and Japanese approaches to history was conspicuous.

The centrality of the Hiroshima discourse in Japan, therefore, came under increasing challenge in the midst of the contention between the Nanjing and

Yasukuni discourses. I will argue, however, that the Hiroshima discourse remains the dominant narrative of the war. To understand this, we must go back to the process through which public memories of war were constructed.

Remembrance and Oblivion

What is to be written? The choice of subject matter in history may not be up to historians or scholars, for who and what should be written into history are subjects that emanate from and bite into our views of ourselves: where we come from and where we are. To the extent that we historians do not have a monopoly on defining ourselves, such thorny issues cannot remain within the academic terrain.

Imagine a historian who believes that the choice of historical subjects should only follow his or her interest and curiosity, where professional training grants the privilege of choosing what is history and what is not. That historian runs the peril of populist indignation against his or her arrogance. Who gave the historian the right to talk about *us*? The choice of subject matter, therefore, is very much a political matter, and neither the choice of historical subjects nor the confusion and controversies over those choices can be determined by academic concerns alone.

To put this another way, the choice (and neglect) of historical subjects in a certain community may reveal what the community or society thinks of itself. What is recorded and what is remembered are not necessarily the consequences of a historian's whim but are reflections of what is taken to be the *legitimate representation* of that community's past. Serious gaps or mutual conflicts within that representation, in this context, may point to a controversial agenda that cannot be easily articulated in that society.

Here the question is not what is to be written but what has been written and what not; the focus lies not on the historian's choice but on the collective, communal choice. The choice will be changed by time; a longitudinal research of historical representation will illustrate changes in the ideals and conventional wisdom of that community. This archaeology of memory, to follow Maurice Halbwachs, can also be applied to the present, for the communal choice of the subject should not necessarily be confined to the past; thus the archeologist may also work as an anthropologist of memory.[2]

Among the wide range of historical subjects, the choice of the dead ranks among the most controversial. Some deaths not only are remembered but are celebrated by local or national communities in religious or pseudo-religious rituals that bind the immortal spirits to the mortals of the present. Here, the veneration of heroes and martyrs, to follow Kenneth Foote, adds to the sustaining or strengthening of communal or national identities.[3]

Other deaths, however, are not as cerebral. Most deaths are devoid of heroic lessons; friends or kin remember the dead more often than other members of a community do. Memories of their deaths thus remain in the private sphere and are seldom articulated in the political space.

Moreover, memories of acts of violence can be upsetting, leading the victims of incidents to suppress their memories rather than openly share their experiences. Mass murders committed by psychopaths or ugly mass hysteria such as witch-hunts in Salem are seldom remembered in open public space. Legacies of ugly violence, in those cases, are erased from memory, along with the mark of shame, to quote Foote again, that may associate oneself to such violence.

This combination of remembering and forgetting should lead to a better understanding of the highly arbitrary selection of victims in the politics of commemoration. We can expect the heroes and martyrs to form the core of commemorative rituals, while the legacies of criminal acts that may be related to those still alive would be suppressed, unless the victims of such crimes take an upper hand in the dictation of events. A study of commemoration, in turn, should illustrate both these senses of pride and shame—what that community is proud of and what makes it feel ashamed.

A quick glance over Japanese writings about World War II will show that the majority do not glorify or praise the war; it is simply wrong to argue that the Japanese have kept on whitewashing war crimes. The actors, however, are almost exclusively limited to ethnic Japanese, and it is rare to find non-Japanese perspectives on the war. Major war museums in Japan exhibit only civilian Japanese as the victims of war, with the Yushukan Museum located at the Yasukuni Shrine as virtually the sole exception. One seldom sees Japanese soldiers commemorated as national heroes; neither does one see Chinese or Indonesian victims of Japanese aggression remembered in Japan.

Here, then, is the puzzle. Why are both non-Japanese victims and Japanese soldiers excluded from war memories? Why only Japanese? Why only women and children? The answer to this puzzle, I believe, is much more complicated than a simple Japanese "amnesia" over the past, for the agenda here is not amnesia but a collective and intentional selection of what to remember and what to forget, revealing how the Japanese have thought themselves to be.

A Victimized Nation

Simone Weil, in her fascinating discussion on the effect of the French Revolution on the sense of belonging, noted a significant twist of state-society relations within French discourse on patriotism:

When the illusion of national sovereignty showed itself to be manifestly an illusion, it could no longer serve as an object of patriotism; on the other hand, kingship was like one of those severed plants one does not plant again. Patriotism had to change its meaning and turn itself towards the State. But thereby it straightaway ceased to be popular. For the State was not something brought into being in 1789; it dated from the beginning of the seventeenth century, and shared some of the hatred nursed by the people against the monarchy.[4]

It may sound like a stretch to compare Japan after World War II to France after the revolution: if the merger of the state and society in Japan was based on coercive mobilization dictated by the state, the French Revolution, for all its horror and violence, took place at the social level. Nevertheless, we may still observe a divorce between the state and society in both postrevolutionary France and postwar Japan. For losing the war was a turning point of nationalism in Japan, from a nationalism that binds the state and the society into an organic whole to one that separates the state and society.

During World War II the people and the state were bound together by the myth of Japan as a divine nation, where an individual was deemed to be meaningless unless incorporated into an organic whole. Such a historicist merger of the state and society, akin to German Romanticism, left little room for liberal constraints on state power or civil society.

The deconstruction of national symbolism and remorse over the dead not only crushed the basis of wartime nationalism but added an important twist. After defeat, ordinary people came to see themselves as having been duped by leaders who started a war that could not be won. Here the state was the "they" who brutalized "us" in society; the enemy here was neither the Japanese nor the Americans but the Japanese state. Before the war, political leaders symbolized the unity of the nation; after the war, the leaders had become "them," as opposed to "us," a nation that had been victimized by a handful of irresponsible militarists.

Thus emerged a narrative of a victimized nation, where only the Japanese appeared as the victims of war. Public discourse on the war was more commonly told from the viewpoint of Japanese noncombatants. It was the story of rationed food, forced labor, air raids, and children running around cities in flames. Lacking in those images were the Japanese soldiers abroad, along with their adversaries and their victims.[5]

This was not necessarily self-deception or hypocrisy. After all, most Japanese had no experience of the battlefields. For the majority of Japanese citizens who stayed in mainland Japan, the war certainly was a hard life under a regimented society and constant fear of aerial bombings. If the Japanese cared little about their victims abroad, they certainly cared about their own dead. That was sufficient to lead them to a total denunciation of war as a tool of foreign policy.

The emphasis on noncombatants made it easy for the Japanese to develop a victim mentality. In the case of Japanese soldiers, there is little chance of escaping the charges of war crimes, for they were the obvious killers in the overseas theaters. A focus on the soldiers would have made it more difficult to talk of a united "we," since that "we" would have included the victims at home as well as the killers abroad. As far as the average noncombatant Japanese at home were concerned, on the other hand, very few would question their war responsibility.

This sense of victimization became fused with a civic nationalism, one that unites a society against the irresponsible political leaders who had brought the misery of defeat. As contradictory as it may sound, this nationalism was not directed against the Americans as the adversary, for postwar Japanese society embraced the Occupation forces. The new constitution, essentially drafted by the Americans and aimed at effectively disarming the Japanese, was widely endorsed, or even embraced, by the public. Only the very few political elites of the wartime days took this as a betrayal of their nation.

The public took issue, however, with the Cold War policy of the United States, which was thought to bring Japan to the edge of war, leading to public pressure on the Japanese government to avoid developing nuclear weapons, as discussed by Wakana Mukai in chapter 9 of this volume. A cruel twist here was that the public took the new constitution, with its Article 9 ruling out possession of arms by Japan, as a political weapon against the Americans, under whose occupation that constitution was drafted. A born-again pacifist nation that used to be united under the emperor was now directing liberal and pacifist political ideals; the Pygmalion who had tutored a roughneck that brutalized the world to develop into a democratic nation in the postwar liberal international order had, by then, become more interested in making an arsenal out of Japan than in promoting democracy and demilitarization. A new civic nationalism thus came to be articulated against its own mentor.

The Rise of the Hiroshima Discourse

Among the many tragedies of civilian annihilation, the bombings of Hiroshima and Nagasaki stood out, especially after the test explosions of thermonuclear weapons at Bikini Atoll. The fear of future wars connected revived public attention to the two cities. The suffering of *hibakusha*, the victims of the bombings of Hiroshima and Nagasaki, was no longer a mere memory of past tragedies but came to carry an ominous message: that we all may suffer like the *hibakusha* in the next world war. *Hibakusha*, therefore, played the role of a Cassandra who warned of total annihilation in the future.[6]

But it took time for Hiroshima to be remembered. The first reason for this involved censorship. Owing to both military intelligence concerns about the new weapon and management of public relations regarding a possibly hostile nation, the Allied Occupation took great care to conceal media coverage of the bombings of Hiroshima and Nagasaki.[7] For example, two short stories on the bombings, both written in 1945, were shelved for nearly three years. When the two stories, Hara Tamiki's "Natsu no hana" (Summer flower) and Ohta Hiroko's "Shikabane no machi" (City of corpses) did come out, many lines were blacked out. The Americans themselves undertook a thorough opinion survey of 3,135 Hiroshima survivors, but the results were made public only in 1974.

The other reason was the lack of attention toward nuclear nightmares in the future. This may be hard to swallow for contemporary observers, but it took a full decade after Hiroshima for a shared vision of nuclear doomsday to emerge in public opinion. By 1949 the bombing of Hiroshima and Nagasaki had become common knowledge, but that experience was still buried among other wartime atrocities, such as the air raids over Tokyo and Osaka. Even during the Korean War, which placed Japan in a critical geopolitical position, there was a conspicuous lack of fear over a possible nuclear nightmare.

The test explosions of thermonuclear weapons at Bikini Atoll in 1954 changed the whole picture. The Soviets had already disclosed their possession of nuclear armaments in 1953; U.S. secretary of state John Foster Dulles had announced the strategy of mass retaliation in January 1954. The paradox here is that war scare escalated *after* the truce in Korea. When the Bikini tests affected a Japanese fishing vessel, *Daigo Fukuryu-Maru* (*Lucky Dragon No. 5*), causing radioactivity-related diseases in its crew, something like a panic broke out in Japan.

The fear of possible nuclear annihilation was certainly not limited to the peace activists who gathered for antinuclear conventions. For example, the fictional beast in *Godzilla*, the hit movie of 1954, was supposed to have emerged out of nuclear tests in the South Pacific, an obvious allusion to the Bikini tests that added a touch of reality to a very unreal monster.[8]

The war metaphor is plain to see. Godzilla raids the city of Tokyo in a succession of waves from the Tokyo Bay, just like the B-29 bombers attacking Tokyo during the war. In the film there is a miniature of a Western-style building in the center of a devastated Tokyo that looks identical to Hiroshima's Genbaku Dome, a structure known for its destruction by the bomb. *Godzilla*, certainly not a film intended for political propaganda, nevertheless captured the audience with an allegory of nuclear nightmares, a harbinger of tradition in Japanese mass culture.[9]

In such a milieu of war scares, Hiroshima arose from the past and indicated a future—or a lack of future, to be exact—for the Japanese. Tales of the Hiroshima survivors, some of which had been published since 1949, suddenly hit the best-seller list. Trade unions formed study groups and began pilgrimages to Hiroshima, which then extended to junior and senior high school students. In 1955 the first International Anti-Nuclear Convention took place in Hiroshima.

The city of Hiroshima had been involved in public atonement and memorials since 1949, issuing public denouncements of nuclear armaments. Such activities, which had garnered little public attention, suddenly appeared in the limelight. The annual Hiroshima Day memorial became a national event; the Peace Museum opened with financial support from the government. Hiroshima was no longer a forgotten episode of the war but part of a "national" and public memory.

Cutting across a wide political spectrum, Hiroshima became a shared symbol of the past that should not be repeated in the future. Exactly who or what was to blame remained ambiguous. Should the Japanese, the ones who started the war, assume responsibility? Or should the Americans, who used these weapons of mass destruction on civilian targets, be blamed? Or was it mankind in general, as the Buddhist monks would say, that should atone for its sins and weakness? The responsibility issue was never resolved, but the conviction that nuclear weapons should never be put to use again was shared by a surprisingly large population. It was a national form of pacifism.

Hiroshima could foster the core of a nationalist pacifism because it corresponded to the perception that Japanese civilians were the main victims of World War II, a perception widely shared in Japan. *Barefoot Gen*, a comic based on the author Kenji Nakazawa's own experience of the bombing of Hiroshima, is a case in point. Nakazawa's story of the victims of war was widely read and shared in Japan, possibly because the work was expressed in the form of a comic, or *manga*. In *Barefoot Gen*, World War II was a war started by the Japanese military, and the victims were Japanese civilians.[10] Readers observe the protagonist Gen's resentment against the military not because it invaded other nations and victimized non-Japanese civilians but because it started a war that brought suffering to the Japanese. As Akiko Hashimoto points out, we see little connection between the bombing of Hiroshima and the Japanese aggression that preceded the blast.[11]

Here I must point out the difference in political discourse between Hiroshima and Nagasaki, the second city to suffer from the use of atomic weapons. Nagasaki is a city with a large Christian population, many of whom had kept their belief throughout the Tokugawa Shogunate, which brutally suppressed Christendom in Japan. That faith led some of the A-bomb survivors to believe the bombing was a punishment for the sins committed by the Japanese. For example, at the joint memorial meeting for atonement held on November 23, 1945, Nagai Takashi, himself an A-bomb victim who wrote the first report of the aid activities for A-bomb victims after the bombing of Nagasaki, stated that the atomic bomb was a punishment by the Lord for our sins (*Tenbatsu*) that took the lives of families and burnt down the church.[12] This was one of the earliest cases in which the narrative of suffering was combined with the sense of political responsibility for the Japanese aggression and violence. Such recognition of Japan as an aggressor, however, was seldom exhibited in the case of Hiroshima.

Hiroshima Discourse during the Cold War

In Japan, the policy implications of Hiroshima were not focused on political responsibility for starting an aggressive war in the past but on the future direction of national security policy, especially concerning the role of nuclear weapons. The Hiroshima discourse was almost always accompanied by a call for the abolition of nuclear weapons, as an imperative step required to prevent the suffering of A-bomb victims in the future. After the Occupation the Japanese government, on the other hand, had formed an alliance with the United States so that U.S. forces might provide national security. As the United States was the nation with the largest nuclear arsenal on Earth, the alliance implied extended deterrence, and one provided by nuclear arms at that.

This led to a political confrontation that defined Japanese party politics. On one side was the left, mainly composed of the Socialist Party and the Communist Party, who not only called for nuclear disarmament but also challenged the political leadership that accepted nuclear deterrence. On the other side, the ruling Liberal Democratic Party (LDP) was in support of the U.S.-Japan alliance, U.S. military bases on Japanese soil, as well as the extended deterrence based on U.S. nuclear capabilities. The call for the abolition of nuclear weapons therefore enhanced political division between the left and right.

The political division here should not be overstated. For one thing, the political priority of the LDP was economic development, and spending a large chunk of the budget for defense would be a fiscal burden on achieving that objective. It was therefore quite convenient for conservative politicians to have "peaceniks" at home: Prime Minister Yoshida Shigeru and his successors kept referring to the pacifists in order to sabotage Washington's requests for a larger Japanese military. The political left offered the government a useful tool for avoiding the defense burden and thus free riding on the U.S.-Japan alliance. Even Prime Minister Sato Eisaku, possibly the most pro-U.S. premier in Japanese history, stubbornly stuck to the nonnuclear principles, which were adopted in an exceptional bipartisan resolution, using them against U.S. demands to retain nuclear warheads in Iwakuni and Okinawa.

Moreover, public endorsement of the antinuclear message remained remarkably strong, cutting across political preferences. If the left wanted Japan out of the alliance and the right supported the nuclear umbrella, the Japanese public supported both the alliance and the abolition of nuclear weapons. Hiroshima was more "national" and politically acceptable than other peace symbols or agendas, many of which were too leftist for the mainstream. Throughout the 1960s, a period in which public protest toward the U.S.-Japan Security Treaty and U.S. military bases had waned in general (with Okinawa an important exception), the case of Hiroshima remained unchallenged.

It was always a given political fact in Japan that the core of nationalist pacifists came from the left. Adherents to the World Peace Council, one of the earliest examples of an antinuclear organization, openly stated that Soviet nuclear armament served "peaceful objectives." Most supporters of antinuclear movements came either from trade unions that supported the Socialist Party or from mass organizations closely associated with the Communist Party of Japan.

That the peace movement tended to be leftist was not much of a problem until serious divisions within the Socialist camp led to fragmentation within the movement. The Sino-Soviet dispute, Chinese nuclear armament, and the debates over the Nuclear Nonproliferation Treaty had split the Japanese peace movements into two major organizations, Gensuikin (Socialist Party–oriented) and Gensuikyo (Communist Party–oriented). The bitter partisan debate that ensued led to disillusionment among supporters.[13]

The political consumption of the antinuclear agenda was already evident in the 1960s, but the fear of nuclear annihilation was somehow sufficient to gather public support for peace movements in and outside of Hiroshima. The Reagan administration in the United States, with renewed confrontation against the Soviet Union and the proposed deployment of intermediate nuclear weapons, caused alarm about a possible nuclear doomsday, leading to massive demonstrations against the arms race from 1982 to 1983, along with waves of protests in Britain and other nations in Europe.[14]

Hiroshima Discourse after the End of the Cold War

The antinuclear campaigns of 1982 to 1983 proved to be the last peace movement accompanied by mass mobilization. Soviet-American tension was significantly reduced after 1988, followed by the fall of the Berlin Wall and the collapse of the Soviet Union. In terms of nuclear weapons, after a few diplomatic overtures, the START arms reduction process began to take shape in the 1990s. Though a far cry from the ban on nuclear weapons, and though powers other than the United States and Russia were reluctant to reduce their nuclear arsenals, the possibility of nuclear annihilation was greatly reduced.

Decreasing tensions between the United States and Russia took away a sense of urgency from the antinuclear agenda. Since the nuclear tests at Bikini Atoll, the memories of Hiroshima and Nagasaki had been continuously revived because of the very real dangers that accompanied the nuclear arms race. With less likelihood of a Russo-American nuclear war, the nexus between war memories of the past and a dystopian future was significantly weakened.

In East Asia, geopolitical confrontation obstinately persisted after the end of the Soviet-American Cold War, with North Korea, mainland China, and the three Indochinese nations placed under the rule of Communist Parties. Lacking the dramatic regime changes that took place in both the Soviet Union and its East European satellites, ideological cleavages between communist and capitalist democracies imposed a limit on the extent of cooperation that might develop between individual governments.

Geopolitical concerns, moreover, outlived ideologies. Mainland China significantly moved away from the ideological influence of Marxist-Leninism, but that change did not reduce its military buildup; in terms of military capability, China became more of a geopolitical challenge than during the Cold War period. The case of North Korea was even more disturbing, with the testing of Scud missiles in 1984 and 1988 and a Rodong missile in 1990. East Asia emerged as a region of geopolitical instability, in diametrical opposition to Europe after the end of the Cold War.

The end of the Cold War, moreover, led to the demise of the political left in Japanese politics. In 1993 the Liberal Democratic Party stepped down from political power for the first time in forty-eight years. This gave an opportunity for the Japan Socialist Party (JSP) to join a coalition government, but only after withdrawing from an ideological pacifist position and accepting the alliance with the United States, as a beneficiary of extended deterrence provided by the U.S. nuclear capability. With the socialists shifting toward pragmatism, the Hiroshima discourse lost its most active political advocate.

The Nanjing Discourse

The Hiroshima discourse was based on the view that Japanese civilians were the victims of war. Although it was true that Japanese civilians suffered during the war, this victim mentality was a subject of debate, as it was obvious that the Japanese were also, and in fact predominantly, the aggressors in the war. Even during the Cold War years, both journalists and scholars finally began to unravel the atrocities committed by Japanese troops abroad, mainly in China. And almost immediately after such unraveling, dismissal of those war crimes burst out.

Probably the best known of all cases is that of Honda Katsuichi, an *Asahi* reporter, and his coverage in 1971 of the Nanjing massacre. Honda's series of articles, later edited into his *Chugoku no tabi* (Journey to China), ignited violent reactions from the conservative media, which labeled Honda as a traitor who gave in to Chinese propaganda at the price of the nation's honor. And unlike the unanimous support for the Hiroshima case, the Japanese public was deeply divided over Nanjing, and the moral judgment about Japanese aggression in general. Although only a handful favored the conservatives, the number of those who supported Honda's investigative journalism was also remarkably limited.[15]

The Nanjing massacres, after initial international media coverage and also after the Tokyo trials, were long buried among the many wartime atrocities committed by Japanese troops in China. Neither did it help that Nanjing was under Kuomintang rule, which did not fare well in the Chinese Communist Party's reading of its history at the time. But even before Nanjing became the cornerstone of Chinese war memories, it had become a symbol of fake memories among Japanese conservatives, who believed that it fabricated the actual war record. Thus conservative revisionists found a national project to confront the mainline "liberal" media.[16]

Liberal pacifists, on the other hand, faced a dilemma. Here was a case that could break the national unity of Japanese pacifism. Reactions from established peace movements were meek at best. A common argument was that confronting nuclear nightmares in the future should take priority over fact-finding about past atrocities. The more progressive and radical members of the peace movements were astonished to find that only a handful were willing to denounce Japanese war crimes.

The new focus on Japan as the aggressor, in fact, directly challenged the basis of nationalist pacifism, which acted as if all Japanese were noncombatant victims of the war. Some people, including many Japanese historians, proceeded to examine the process of Japanese aggression; others simply shelved the issue as too political and divisive.

Here we find a remarkable difference in the reactions of survivors of Hiroshima and those of Nagasaki. Survivors of the Hiroshima bombing were extremely reluctant to include references to the Japanese as aggressors; it was only after 1994 that the Hiroshima Peace Museum agreed to exhibit evidence of Japanese war crimes, arguing that such a focus would divert attention from the more important message, that is, the elimination of nuclear weapons. Survivors of the Nagasaki bombing, on the other hand, were eager to integrate studies of Japanese aggression into their messages. Peace activists used to point to Hiroshima's fury and Nagasaki's prayers; activists in Nagasaki did not find the references to the Japanese atrocities as challenging as those in Hiroshima did.

Another challenge to nationalist unity was the non-Japanese victims of the bombings of the two cities. Both cities historically had non-Japanese populations of considerable size. Many Koreans and Chinese, moreover, were forced into labor camps, especially in the case of Hiroshima. If the Japanese victims demanded medical treatment from the government, why should the non-Japanese victims be left out? Was pacifism for Japanese nationals only?

Again, Hiroshima and Nagasaki showed different responses. Nagasaki, an international port since the Tokugawa Shogunate, was far more cosmopolitan than Hiroshima. Dutch, Brazilian, and Taiwanese victims started to receive intensive medical treatment in the late 1970s; such attention began in Hiroshima only in the early 1980s. Hiroshima, like Nagasaki, had prospered from weapons manufacturing, sometime relying on non-Japanese forced labor. Seen from the nationalist-pacifist discourse, this was dirty linen that was considered best forgotten.

The limits and the narrowness of the "national" and the "victim" character of nationalist pacifism were increasingly obvious after the end of the Cold War. In the early 1990s the Chinese political leadership shifted their source of political legitimacy from Marxist-Leninism to nationalism, and a massive political campaign drummed the image of the Chinese Communist Party as the savior of national independence against the Japanese invasion. The Nanjing discourse, therefore, became an international issue, the Chinese accusing the Japanese of amnesia concerning wartime atrocities.

Facing such challenges, the Hiroshima survivors stuck to their classical position, that is, the immediate danger of a nuclear holocaust. The danger, however, was not felt to be as immediate as it had seemed during the Cold War era, and exclusive attention to Japanese victimhood made it difficult to accommodate the image of the Japanese as the aggressors of the war. Hiroshima, once again, retreated from the limelight.

Yasukuni's Return

Another challenge to the Hiroshima discourse emerged from the opposite end of the political spectrum: Japanese soldiers as heroes. If victims and veterans composed the core of public war memories, such memories in Japan were quite exceptional in that the experiences of Japanese troops were hidden in the background, with no war heroes publicly extolled. This was of course due to the fact that the troops were the protagonists who brought violence and injustice to those both abroad and at home. Moreover, commemorating soldiers would raise the issue of political responsibility for the war, an issue somehow conveniently avoided in the Hiroshima discourse.

It was not that the soldiers were silent: they did speak out, but mostly as victims of an irresponsible political leadership just like their counterparts at home. Initial movements tried to favorably compare soldiers drafted against their will to civilian victims at home. A typical case was that of the Wadatsumi-kai, a group of Tokyo University students who were drafted and sent to the Chinese theater of war. Those who survived compiled and published private letters of their friends; the result, *Kike Wadatsumino koe*, ranks among the most eloquent statements against the war in Japan, although a non-Japanese observer may be perplexed to find that the group talked only about their own miseries and not about the calamities that they themselves, as soldiers, had inflicted on the Chinese.[17]

For civilian Japanese, Wadatsumi-kai could be tolerated because it denounced the war, but for some veterans, it did a disservice to the dead by neglecting a just cause. For these hard-liners, representation of Japanese soldiers would be complete only when public recognition of the *legitimacy* of the war accompanied proper representation of the soldiers. The focus of this route of recognition was the Yasukuni Shrine.[18]

The shrine opened in 1869 on the orders of Emperor Meiji. Its initial objective was to atone for those who died during the civil war (Boshin Senso), but the shrine quickly developed into a meeting place of sorts for the spirits of all soldiers who died in battle. It was a place that would bring the mortal spirits together and elevate them as the immortal legacy of the Japanese nation. The kamikaze bombers or banzai attackers would commit collective suicide only after shouting "See you in Yasukuni." One's spirit after death would gain meaning and significance by being written into the record of Yasukuni.

But the postwar Yasukuni had become a private religious institution, along with the separation of Shintoism and the state. Veterans, arguing on behalf of the floating spirits, demanded that the Japanese government subsidize Yasukuni. The ruling Liberal Democratic Party, for well over a decade after 1969, had drafted bills that would put the shrine under national control. This in turn ignited strong reactions from Christians and Buddhists, for a state subsidy of Yasukuni was reminiscent of the state Shintoism that had suppressed all other religions. The opposition parties trashed virtually all the Yasukuni bills; the first Yasukuni debate was therefore a domestic political issue that focused on the secularism of the Japanese state.

In October 1978 Grade A war criminals were incorporated into the immortal spirits remembered at the shrine. Although few recognized the significance of this move and both the Chinese and Korean governments were quiet at the time, this in effect connected the representation of dead soldiers with the legitimation of World War II. From then on, Yasukuni was not only a case of state subsidy; it had become a symbol of both representation and legitimacy.

When Prime Minister Nakasone Yasuhiro visited Yasukuni in August 1983, Beijing reacted fiercely, arguing that Tokyo was about to whitewash its past. The debate continued until 1985, when a task force under Minister Fujinami concluded that an official visit by the prime minister to Yasukuni did not violate the constitution. The recognition of constitutionality, however, did not lead to another Nakasone visit.

After Nakasone, a long list of prime ministers juggled this issue. Miyazawa Kiichi, an outspoken liberal, visited Yasukuni after making sure that there was no press coverage; Hashimoto Ryutaro insisted that his visit to the shrine in July 1996 was for the occasion of his own birthday. And finally, Koizumi Junichiro, after assuming office in May 2001, declared of his intention to visit Yasukuni. Koizumi's successors, including Abe Shinzō, at first avoided the shrine, possibly out of concern that such visit would lead to a major diplomatic crisis, most obviously with Beijing but also with the world in general. In November 2012, however, during his second administration, Abe did visit Yasukuni, leading to shattered relations with China for two full years, until 2014.

Yasukuni can be observed as a barometer of the shifts in Japanese nationalism, from a civic nationalism based on the separation of state and society to more classical organic statist nationalism, where society and the state form an inseparable unity in the name of the nation. It is not the case that supporters of Yasukuni wish to start a war; for all its belligerent choice of words, the Yasukuni discourse is more of a symbolic process. By reclaiming that inseparable unity, and by reconnecting the present to the past, the new nationalists wish to defend their nation's glory to themselves as well as to the Americans, Chinese, and Koreans, who, according to them, deprived them of their national pride. The Yasukuni discourse was a mirror image of the Nanjing discourse, and in the midst of intense confrontation between these two images of the past, a discourse that centers on the bombings of Hiroshima and Nagasaki slipped from the core of Japanese war memories.

The Resilience of the Hiroshima Discourse

Both the Nanjing and Yasukuni discourses cracked open the Hiroshima discourse, an almost exclusive attention given to the Japanese civilians as the victims of war. This crack, which had been there from the beginning but had remained beneath open public discourse, came to be exposed by two contending discourses that chose different victims as the key protagonists of the war.

Can we say, then, that the life and times of the Hiroshima discourse have experienced a demise?

There is much to be said for this argument. In 1989, some 560,000 students visited the Hiroshima Peace Museum; ten years later, the number of visitors decreased to 350,000. Meanwhile, student visitors to the war memorials in Okinawa, which numbered only 80,000 ten years ago, now number 300,000. If peace discourse in the 1950s and the 1960s was dominated by Hiroshima, that of the 1980s and beyond has focused on Nanjing, Okinawa, and Yasukuni. The most heated debate on war memories is no longer about Japanese victimization but about the atrocities overseas, especially after the Japanese textbook debate of 1982. Nanjing and Okinawa, both of which do not fit the "national" form of pacifism, have challenged the historical role that Hiroshima had played in the past. Challenges to the "victim" and "national" character of Hiroshima symbols had reduced the efficacy of the Hiroshima discourse. The end of the Cold War added salt to the wound.

We also must not neglect the increasing military tensions in East Asia. The expansion of the Chinese Navy and its activities in the South China Sea have resulted in anxieties over China's geopolitical intentions, while North Korea, now a nuclear power, has accelerated the number of its missile and nuclear tests. Extended nuclear deterrence may seem not to be a problem but a solution in face of military threats from neighboring nations. After all, Abe Shinzō, the current prime minister of Japan, most certainly belongs to the right of the political spectrum, as a member of the revisionist Nippon Kaigi and a regular visitor to the Yasukuni Shrine before becoming prime minister. That Abe is now leading the most stable administration since Koizumi's may lead one to expect political discourse concerning war memories to be dominated by the Yasukuni discourse.

That does not seem to be the case, however. Despite the rise of geopolitical risk and anxiety in face of China and North Korea, and despite the shift in political leadership toward a classical narrative of national glory, the Hiroshima discourse remains as the most commonly accepted memory of the war. The numbers show the resilience of this discourse. Visitors to the Hiroshima Peace Museum are now increasing: 1,739,000 people visited in 2016, almost three times as many as in 1989.[19] President Barack Obama's visit to Hiroshima in May 2016, possibly the reason for this jump in visitors, was enthusiastically greeted by the Japanese public, with even the rightist-oriented *Sankei* reporting 98 percent of the population in support.[20] Another public opinion poll conducted by Asahi TV in December 2017 show 57 percent of the public in support of the Nuclear Weapon Ban Treaty, a treaty that Tokyo refused to sign. This is a perplexing figure if we consider that the Abe administration is supported by 43.7 percent and the ruling party LDP by 42.3 percent.[21]

One explanation for the resilience of the Hiroshima discourse may be the depoliticization of Hiroshima. By the turn of the century, the left had become a negligible force in Japanese politics, but the paradoxical effect of this was the liberation of the Hiroshima discourse from the left-right dichotomy. A new generation emerged in Japan that embraced the Hiroshima discourse without engaging in, or even being aware of, the sharp political divisions that had accompanied it in the past. Hiroshima was no longer a symbol of the left but had become a truly national symbol.

New attempts have been made, furthermore, to bridge the gap between antinuclear movements and government policy. Governor Yuzaki Hidehiko of Hiroshima Prefecture has taken leadership in organizing a series of meetings titled the Hiroshima Roundtable, where both scholars and policy practitioners from nine nations discuss policy options for deescalation and nuclear disarmament.[22] Hiroshima is no longer a symbol tied only to peace movements but one that carries implications for policy makers as well.

Conclusion

The Hiroshima discourse has rested on the unsustainable proposition that the Japanese were the victims of World War II, a rather convenient view that avoided discussion of the non-Japanese victims of the war and overlooked the political responsibility for engaging in brutal atrocities overseas. The resilience of the Hiroshima discourse, then, does not do justice to the war crimes committed in the past.

It was Ian Buruma who focused on the fallacy of this proposition and dubbed Hiroshima as the exclusive site of Japanese victimhood. To Buruma, Hiroshima was only an attempt to forget Japanese war crimes by presenting Japanese as victims. Although I disagree with Buruma's choice of strong words, I can only agree with him that Hiroshima did actually play such a role in Japanese minds.[23]

There is something very touching, however, in the way in which the Japanese are horrified by the memories of Hiroshima. For the discussion on Hiroshima entailed the passionate force of a vision of dusk and death, a view that an age is about to come to an end, and that humankind will be foolish enough to eliminate itself from the planet by man-made weapons. If this dark vision seems too bizarre, substitute "Japanese" for "humankind" and one can see what the war meant to the Japanese public. The war put an end to everything. The bombing of Hiroshima literally wiped out a whole city. Aside from any political propaganda, this vision of total destruction was what Hiroshima meant to most Japanese.

Most probably, few Japanese paid little attention to the atrocities committed by their soldiers overseas. At the same time, many did care about the Japanese victims, and about the grotesque violence their militarist government brought upon them. Hiroshima signified the ugliest dimension of all. Those who argued for Hiroshima were not necessarily making apologies for the Soviets or exhibiting antiAmerican nationalism; Hiroshima, to many Japanese, simply showed what one gets when one starts a destructive war.

Moreover, underneath such pacifism lay a fatalistic vision that another war would take place anyway. By this I do not mean only the intellectual argument advanced by the Sengo Keimo, or postwar Enlightenment. The strange aspect in postwar Japanese mass culture is the prevalence of a vision of doomsday, of the total annihilation that will ensue after another world war. One finds such gloomy visions not only in the like of *Akira*, the Japanese dystopian anime, but also in *Doraemon*, a popular TV cartoon series that caters to middleclass children.

I believe Buruma is wrong in attributing simple hypocrisies to Hiroshima. The Hiroshima discourse has offered a lesson to remember the future instead of imagining one, based on a selective choice of war victimhood that allowed for a sense of national solidarity. With all the false consciousness that accompanies collective identity, such discourse will maintain its resilience, however challenged by the Nanjing or Yasukuni discourses.

PART III
Revolutions and Transformations

13

The End of the Beginning

CHINA AND THE CONSOLIDATION OF
THE NUCLEAR REVOLUTION

Avery Goldstein

IN THE BEGINNING, there was Hiroshima. At the time, it was not clear that this first use of nuclear explosives as a weapon of war would transform international politics. Although some immediately grasped key strategic implications of what would be the most genuine revolution in military affairs in modern times, it would be several decades before many of the essential features of the nuclear age were more fully understood. Indeed, the thirty years following Hiroshima can be viewed as a period of strategic learning and discovery. By the mid-1970s, experience had begun to clarify the meaning of this revolution, though experts continued to debate the right lessons to be learned. These decades coincided with the period when new technologies consolidating the nuclear revolution (especially hydrogen bombs and ballistic missiles) were also developed and deployed, rendering persistent conventionalized thinking about the possible uses of nuclear weapons difficult if not obsolete.[1]

In this brief discussion, I highlight some of the most significant ways in which China's experience between 1955 and 1974 helps clarify and refine our understanding of the nuclear revolution.[2] I do this by focusing on eight respects in which China's history either challenged or cast in a different light early beliefs about the new nuclear age. For each of the eight, I offer a general introduction and then draw on the Chinese case to illustrate key points.

The discussion is based on China's experience as it moved beyond its immediate reactions to the Hiroshima bombing. China's leaders initially joined others, especially its Soviet ally, in asserting that the results of the bombing demonstrated that these new weapons were not revolutionary, that people and politics mattered more than weapons in determining the outcomes of wars, and that the United States was exaggerating the destructive power of atomic bombs to frighten and coerce adversaries that it could not defeat militarily.[3] Beijing argued that Japan had been defeated by conventional warfare, China's resistance struggle, and the Soviet intervention in August 1945, not by atomic bombing. China's public stance adhered to this interpretation of Hiroshima even as its Soviet ally abandoned it after Stalin's death. (See David Holloway's essay in chapter 5 of this volume.) But China's actions belied its rhetoric. By the mid-1950s the threat from the United States prompted Beijing to decide that nuclear weapons were essential for its own security. Over the following decades, China shifted course as it accepted the distinctiveness of these new weapons and the strategic importance of the nuclear revolution.

In another respect, however, China's view about the Hiroshima bombing never changed. Beijing continues to criticize accounts of the bombing that cast Japan as a victim.[4] Instead, China emphasizes the devastating harm that Japan's military aggression inflicted on others (especially the Chinese people), and thus Japan's own responsibility for the consequences it suffered. Beijing's position was reasserted in 2015 in discussions of a draft statement at the Nuclear Nonproliferation Treaty review conference. China's representative, Fu Cong, rejected attempts to link the review to the experiences of Hiroshima and Nagasaki, arguing that Japan was "trying to portray Japan as a victim of the Second World War, rather than a victimizer."[5] (See also chapter 12 for Kiichi Fujiwara's discussion about the roles of aggressor and victim in Japan's Hiroshima discourse.)

Before I turn to the chapter's substantive discussion, a final comment on the alleged usefulness of lessons from China's experience is in order. Such lessons cannot resolve enduring disagreements about the implications of nuclear weapons for international politics and security. Those disagreements endure in part because, thankfully, since August 9, 1945, nuclear weapons have been used only as force held in reserve to back up threats—what the political science literature has dubbed "coercive diplomacy."[6] But the significance of those disagreements has grown in recent years as competing ideas about nuclear strategy that had been vetted during the Cold War are once more in play. Are these old arguments reappearing in the contemporary policy debate because dramatic changes in technology or international politics justify revisiting their claims? Or do they reflect "zombie ideas" whose fatal flaws will again be revealed as analysts rediscover shortcomings identified decades ago, but whose relevance has been forgotten?

Perhaps forgetfulness is understandable. During the first two decades of the post–Cold War era, attention pivoted from the dangers of nuclear war to other pressing security challenges, especially the threat from nonstate actors embracing terrorism and insurgency. But even if there was a period of "nuclear amnesia," surely it had ended by the second decade of the twenty-first century when a renaissance in nuclear security studies among diplomatic historians (with growing access to declassified documents) and political scientists (applying more sophisticated methods) had begun.[7] Thus at this point the resurrection of old nuclear ideas likely reflects something more than mere forgetfulness. It may be that there are now sound reasons to revive previously discarded ideas about the role of nuclear weapons as a tool of statecraft. But it is also possible that their newfound appeal reflects a misreading of the lessons of nuclear history. To guard against the latter possibility, renewed efforts to reach a consensus on what we know about the past can contribute to today's debates about nuclear policy. Revisiting China's nuclear experience as it unfolded in the decades after World War II is, in this sense, fruitful even if not decisive.

Proliferation

This club is exclusive; it should, can, and will remain exclusive.

From the earliest years after World War II, the United States championed the idea that the possession of nuclear weapons should be and could be effectively restricted. Once it was clear that the brief flirtation with the idea of placing nuclear weapons under international control would fail, the second-best solution was to try to limit membership in the nuclear club to a small number of advanced industrial states who could be trusted to manage these massively destructive devices responsibly.[8] This goal seemed realistic because it was believed that the barriers to entry were so steep that states other than the most advanced would be unable to clear them absent assistance from current members of the club. The preference to keep the club as exclusive as possible inspired practical measures that are now collectively referred to under the term *counterproliferation*.[9]

Nevertheless, China, the first of what would be a second wave of nuclear weapons states, exploded any illusions about the feasibility of keeping the nuclear club as exclusive as initially hoped.[10] As a weak, poor, developing state, China pioneered a path that others would later follow and demonstrated the profound challenges facing any attempt to prevent the nuclear club from growing.[11] China's nuclear weapons program showed that the technological and economic hurdles for states in the developing world would not remain insuperable barriers for long. There would be no need for states to mount a Manhattan Project–scale effort. Globalization of an international scientific community, even with the unevenness imposed by Cold War limitations that slowed cross-bloc exchanges, was accelerating in the postwar years. The result was the spread of the knowledge (theoretical science and engineering) necessary to develop nuclear weapons. China was the first, but not the last, to show that by relying on a combination of domestic and foreign-trained experts, as well as civilian nuclear assistance from willing donors, developing states determined to undertake a large but not unreasonably burdensome investment could eventually succeed in joining the once exclusive club.

However, to say that China showed it was *possible* for a developing state to enter the club does not mean that China showed that it was *inevitable* that all would want to make the concerted effort required. For developing countries, the decision to mount a nuclear weapons program is especially tough since the poorer they are, the greater the opportunity costs these states confront.[12] Their governments have less to work with and less margin for error. They need to weigh especially carefully the tradeoffs not just between "guns and butter" but also between "guns and guns." Of all the limits on the size of the nuclear club, the decision by many of the states that could develop nuclear weapons that the price is not worth paying may be the most important. Under Mao Zedong's leadership, China decided that the investment in a nuclear weapons program was worth the diversion of resources from other daunting development challenges, and that the investment would yield security dividends that exceeded alternative types of military spending. The latter is crucial, since developing states already shoulder the burden of fielding nonnuclear forces—in China's case a combination of regular conventional forces geared toward traditional offensive and defensive operations, and "irregular" conventional forces to be used in the deterrent and compellent strategies of popular resistance known as "people's war."

International events can be important catalysts that convince leaders the costly pursuit of nuclear weapons is the correct choice, as was the case for China. U.S. nuclear coercion during confrontations in the Taiwan Strait led Mao and his colleagues to believe that Washington would have a free hand to "blackmail" China unless Beijing had its own atomic bombs.[13] But if external threats often tip the balance, domestic enthusiasts may also play an important role in persuading top leaders about the urgency and viability of the nuclear project and in ensuring its progress.[14] Scientists, civilian analysts, or military advisers to the top leadership in this sense can become members of a nuclear coalition of the eager. General Nie Rongzhen ("father of China's atomic bomb"), the brilliant American-trained scientist Qian Xuesen ("father of China's ballistic missile program"), and Foreign Minister Chen Yi were influential advocates in Beijing who worked hard to reinforce the regime's (and Mao's) determination that China should and could do whatever it took to develop its own nuclear arsenal.

China's experience also revealed the complex challenges facing efforts to discourage entry to the nuclear club. Often the challenges reflect the familiar difficulties of collective action that complicate attempts to coordinate policy among large groups of states and of eliminating uncertainty about reliably enforcing restrictions or sanctions that the group may agree to impose on nuclear aspirants who defy them. China's experience, however, illuminates the challenges faced even when the counterproliferation effort is undertaken unilaterally by a powerful and strategically essential ally who should have all the advantages of leverage that a credible threat to withhold economic and security benefits confers.[15]

The Soviet Union was China's ally when Beijing made its key decisions to pursue a nuclear capability in the 1950s. The Soviet Union was not just China's ally; it was China's only ally. The Soviets were also China's only source of significant economic assistance as it began an arduous recovery from decades of domestic and international conflict and impoverishment, its only source of military assistance as it initiated the modernization of its backward conventional military, and its only strategic counterweight to the serious threat posed by a nuclear-armed American superpower. And yet when the Soviets decided that it was essential to prevent China from going nuclear after initially providing nonmilitary nuclear assistance, neither Moscow's carrots nor its sticks were effective.[16] Indeed, for reasons that are at least partly a result of the idiosyncrasies of Mao Zedong, these efforts if anything strengthened China's determination that it must pursue its nuclear project regardless of the heavy sacrifices that would entail.[17]

Finally, China's experience also illustrated the difficulty of frustrating a state's nuclear ambitions by relying on the most obvious alternative to political pressure from either the international community or an ally: military action. China was the first, but again would not be the last, in a string of developing states whose nuclear programs elicited thoughts of preventive strikes. And while Israel's attacks against the reactor complexes in Iraq (1981) and Syria (2007) showed what can be accomplished, they remain exceptions that underscore two reasons why such preventive attacks have not been attempted more frequently. First, the Israeli strikes occurred very early in the adversary's development effort, before they could be justified as eliminating an imminent nuclear threat. Preventive attacks, in contrast with preemptive attacks that can be justified as self-defense, are a diplomatically unpalatable option.[18] Second, and probably more important, the strikes were launched without fear of a response from either the victim of the attacks or an ally. In the case of China, the latter fear loomed large.

There was little doubt by late summer 1964 that China was nearing the nuclear threshold, finally realizing a goal it had openly proclaimed. A preventive strike to at least delay the arrival of China as a nuclear weapons state was militarily feasible and politically attractive to the U.S. government. Washington was gravely concerned about the possible cascade effect among East Asian neighbors who might want their own nuclear arsenals if China's program succeeded and about the prospect of nuclear weapons emboldening Mao to spread revolution in the region and perhaps beyond. Moreover, there were sound reasons for the U.S. government to believe that the Soviet Union, having tried and failed to stop China's nuclear weapons program in the late 1950s, might be amenable to letting Washington do the dirty work that, for political reasons, the leader of the socialist bloc, embroiled in an ideological rivalry with Beijing, could not. Yet the U.S. government hesitated. Prudence required it to ponder what could go wrong—a consideration that looms especially large when nuclear weapons are in play. What if the Soviets did not sit idly by? What if, however unlikely in light of the rancorous Sino-Soviet ideological dispute, Moscow concluded that its failure to respond to an unprovoked military attack against its treaty ally would severely damage its reputation for resolve in the bipolar global rivalry with the United States, a context that encouraged zero-sum perceptions about the international contest for power? In other words, however little the Soviets might object to the setback to China's nuclear program, they might feel their self-interest required a response of some sort, a response that escalated the potential risks of a U.S. preventive strike on China.[19] Thus the Johnson administration concluded in September 1964 that before deciding whether to exercise its preventive military option, it would be best to sound out the Soviets.[20] The full story about the contact made and the response received is not yet known, but the surprising decision to consult the Soviets is documented. It indicates, at a minimum, the concern about an unpredictable response from China's nuclear-armed ally and suggests that this consideration played a role in the U.S. decision to refrain from a preventive strike. This also suggests that what is generally referred to as extended deterrence prevailed and did so in a case where its credibility seemed doubtful. The case of China helped clarify the logic and practice of extended deterrence in other ways as well.

Extended Deterrence

Nice umbrella, but let me hold it!

Extended deterrence, pledges to inflict unacceptable punishment on an adversary that challenges the vital interests of one's allies, has been thoroughly explored in the literature and has played a central role in policy debates since the 1950s. Often it has been part of a strategy of inhibition, to use Frank Gavin's term, designed to reassure states who would otherwise be motivated to ensure their security by developing their own nuclear arsenals. (See also Wakana Mukai's discussion in chapter 9 about the way the logic of extended deterrence and pacifist public opinion interacted in shaping Japanese nuclear policy in the 1950s and 1960s.) The difficulty in invoking extended deterrence as a reason why an ally can forgo self-reliance is not, as in the conventional era, that the patron offering protection might be hard pressed to deploy enough capabilities to protect itself and its ally. Instead, the difficulty is doubt about the willingness to use a nuclear capability (which can easily be large enough for both national and extended deterrent roles) on behalf of an ally if doing so means running grave risks of catastrophic conflict with a nuclear-armed adversary. To address this concern, strategists suggested seemingly sensible ways to make extended deterrent promises more credible. Their focus was typically on figuring out how to reassure an ally who feared the nightmare of abandonment in its hour of need.[21] But the unenforceability of contracts in the anarchic international realm limited the credibility of extended deterrent promises. The best a nuclear guarantor could do was to *increase* its credibility by setting up physical tripwires (forward deployment of its troops and their civilian dependents), or issuing public statements (creating the specter of damage to its leader's domestic or international reputation) as more convincing signs of commitment. Such steps, however, do not completely eliminate the possibility of abandonment or alter the reality that it would probably be irrational for the powerful patron to follow through on its promise if extended deterrence failed, since doing so entails risking a large nuclear exchange over another state's interests. This harsh reality has motivated some states to pursue their own deterrent as a hedge against the possibility that their patron's promised nuclear umbrella will prove unreliable.

Yet this familiar focus on doubts about the credibility of extended deterrence has obscured just how easily it seems to have been made effective in the nuclear age, *despite* the apparent irrationality of fulfilling the pledge on which it rests. If it has been effective (and that judgment requires demonstrating the causes of nonevents—that actors were motivated to challenge the status quo but did not because they feared retaliatory punishment), it is because nuclear weapons fundamentally alter thinking about low-probability events. Even if the adversary believes it is highly unlikely that a nuclear patron would fulfill the promise to its ally, highly unlikely is not very reassuring when it actually means "unlikely but possible" and when that unlikely possibility entails absorbing a nuclear strike.[22] In short, when the specter of nuclear weapons looms, uncertainty generates *both* the doubt that makes an ally nervous about the possibility of abandonment *and* the doubt that makes the adversary nervous that the extended deterrent threat might be carried out.

China's experience in the 1950s manifests the challenges of extended deterrence. It also illuminates how attempts to cope with its inherent complications can inadvertently increase the motivation of a nonnuclear ally to seek its own arsenal. As noted above, in 1957 Moscow had second thoughts about technical assistance it was providing to Beijing that was paving the way for an independent Chinese nuclear capability. This prompted the Soviets to try two approaches to minimize the risks they foresaw. First, the Soviets tried to convince the Chinese that there was no pressing need to rush their weapons program because the Sino-Soviet alliance meant that Moscow had China's back. Second, the Soviets tried to persuade the Chinese that the extended deterrent would be even more effective, and the alliance of which both were a part would be stronger, if the relevant military forces and command and control in China were more tightly integrated with that of the Soviet Union (especially by setting up joint radar installations and communications networks). When it was clear that these approaches were not curbing Beijing's nuclear appetite and in fact were angrily rejected out of hand by Mao, Moscow concluded that the danger of facilitating a fully independent nuclear capability in the hands of this kind of ally was unacceptable and decided to terminate its nuclear assistance to China.[23]

Moreover, the Soviet attempt to harness its ally's nuclear ambitions didn't just fail; it backfired. Regardless of Moscow's original intentions—and there is little reason to think that Nikita Khrushchev was interested in anything more than ensuring the alliance had a safely managed nuclear deterrent force, one reliably providing for China's security—Mao interpreted Khrushchev's approach to bolstering extended deterrence as evidence of Soviet interest in controlling China by limiting its sovereign independence on the most vital questions of national security.[24] It is unclear whether Mao actually believed this charge or seized on it as a politically useful rallying cry to promote a Chinese nuclear project to which he had become fully committed. Clearly, however, he understood the resonance his claims would have among Communist Party leaders who had dedicated their lives to overcoming the legacy of China's century of humiliation and subjugation at the hands of foreigners.

The irony is that the mutually reinforcing fears of entrapment and abandonment that drove the Soviets to want greater control and the Chinese to want greater independence both reflected exaggerated worries about the difficulty of extending a deterrent umbrella over a state with closely (even if not perfectly) aligned security interests. The Sino-Soviet alliance was not a mere scrap of paper. It manifested the Soviet Union's self-interest in cooperating with China against a powerful common adversary, the United States. Early in the Cold War, any serious American challenge to China would unavoidably have been interpreted as a challenge to Soviet interests as well, regardless of treaty language or the unenforceability of contracts in the anarchic international system. As noted above, Soviet self-interest would provide an incentive for leaders in Moscow to respond, if only to preserve their own reputation in American eyes.[25]

Nevertheless, because the sheltered ally cannot be certain that its patron will fulfill its pledge, it is motivated to hedge against catastrophic abandonment. And because a true test of extended deterrence is so unlikely, lesser events have big effects on perceptions of the nuclear patron's credibility and intentions. On three matters, Mao adopted worst-case interpretations of Soviet behavior to highlight alleged reasons for China to worry about the Soviet nuclear guarantee of China's security. First, Beijing was understandably concerned about the apparently limited usefulness of the alliance for coping with American threats against China during the tensest moments of the crises in the Taiwan Strait in 1954–1955 and 1958. But Mao exaggerated the importance of the Soviet reluctance to more actively back China. After all, Mao himself remained confident that he was carefully managing the crises to reduce the risk that the United States would carry out its vague nuclear threats against China.[26] Second, Beijing predictably balked at the Soviet proposals for integrating the alliance's deterrent under Moscow's leadership (America's British and French allies also bridled at such proposals). But Mao's likening these plans to the old unequal treaties imperialists had imposed on China amounted to willful misrepresentation of Soviet suggestions that were not extraordinary in the context of a modern military alliance. And third, Beijing had reason to worry that the Soviet Union's deployment of ICBMs would reduce Moscow's need for security partners (since the Soviet Union could be self-reliantly secure once it could target the U.S. homeland). But the conclusion that Khrushchev's related shift to a grand strategy of peaceful coexistence in an era of mutual deterrence and arms control presaged the end of support for allies like China required a worst-case interpretation of Soviet thinking that Mao encouraged his colleagues to embrace.

Requirements of Nuclear Deterrence

That's not a nuclear deterrent ... this is a nuclear deterrent.

The two superpowers often insisted that other states, surely developing countries, would not be able to meet the requirements of a true deterrent force, even if they could master the technology to test a nuclear warhead. This claim rested on the belief that nuclear deterrence is costly and complicated, requiring a relatively large and assuredly survivable retaliatory capability under a sophisticated national command authority that can preserve negative and positive control.[27] Such requirements allegedly put a genuine nuclear deterrent beyond either the technical or financial reach of any but the wealthy, advanced industrial states. China, however, showed that many other states would be capable of fielding a nuclear deterrent that satisfied their security needs. China, in a sense, was the first to claim a new nuclear identity—developing states that believe they can practice effective deterrence at a discount, with nuclear weapons serving as weapons of the weak.

The superpowers viewed less capable states' nuclear aspirations as dangerous vanity projects that would only undermine security by contributing to crisis instability.[28] In a crisis, insufficiently robust deterrents would allegedly increase first-strike incentives by presenting the strong with tempting targets for preemption and by increasing the pressure on the weak to "use 'em or lose 'em." First-strike incentives would also encourage smaller nuclear powers to keep their vulnerable forces on a very high level of readiness, reducing the margin for error in the event of ambiguous warning about an imminent attack, a problem exacerbated by the allegedly fragile command and control that such states would be able to put in place.

However, despite their claims about the infeasibility of nuclear deterrence of the strong by the weak, the superpowers' actions seemed to belie their rhetoric. Even questionably viable nuclear arsenals have more than once dissuaded big nuclear powers from embracing the option of preventive strikes before small states have fully deployed their capability. Such hesitation reflects the very high bar of supreme confidence in success that must be cleared before a state undertakes a first strike when the target of the attack may have nuclear weapons. Contrary to claims about the daunting hurdles to deploying a credible retaliatory force, with nuclear weapons deterrence is easy and first strikes are hard. Because the consequences of imperfection may well be catastrophic, an attacker must consider all the things that can go wrong, as well as the possibility that some flaws in the plan may not even be recognized—the Rumsfeldian unknown unknowns—until horrifying retaliatory punishment is on its way.

After China's weapons test in 1964, concern about the possibility that China could use some of its crude arsenal to inflict devastating punishment quickly took root. This concern provided a basis for effective deterrence despite the fact that in the early years of deployment, when the Soviet Union had become China's principal adversary, it is not at all clear that China really had much of an ability to deliver retaliatory punishment against any but the closest targets in Asia. The most credible nuclear threat China posed after the mid-1960s was to the huge numbers of Soviet military forces put in place along the Chinese border and perhaps to the port of Vladivostok. Until China deployed longer-range nuclear capable ballistic missiles (the DF-4 IRBM in 1975), the key countervalue targets—cities west of the Urals, especially Moscow—were probably safe. China's only option for delivering nuclear punishment against Moscow was the unlikely approach of relying on nuclear-capable bombers which could, in theory, reach Moscow if they flew one-way missions. Carrying conventional munitions, such a scenario would be a pointless waste of valuable aircraft and crews, especially since China's planes would have only a small chance of evading Soviet antiaircraft defenses long enough to reach their target. With bombers carrying nuclear munitions, however, such a scenario becomes a strategically significant, if suboptimal, long shot. The sacrifice of the craft and crew (with only a slight hope to eject and fend for themselves after dropping their ordnance) could be baked into the planning. In what would probably be a suicide mission, the specially selected crew could pilot the craft with reckless abandon, increasing the chances of penetrating Soviet air defenses.[29] Moreover, unlike the accuracy required of conventional bombing runs, the use of thermonuclear bombs meant that the mission's success would require only that a few aircraft get close to the designated targets. However farfetched this scenario, once China was known to possess deliverable warheads it was a possibility that prudent planners in Moscow could not simply ignore.

Whether it was the prospect of nuclear strikes in the Soviet Far East or the outside chance of nuclear-armed bombers reaching Moscow, during the 1969 Sino-Soviet border crisis when the Soviets entertained the possibility of undertaking preventive strikes against China, they refrained from putting the plan into action. Instead, they sought a path to defuse tensions with the Chinese, a climb-down that was cemented with the meeting between Alexei Kosygin and Zhou Enlai at the Beijing airport in September 1969.[30] The potentially catastrophic consequences of an imperfect attack when the victim had nuclear weapons was a strong argument for caution, not a temptation to action, especially while there was a chance to avoid conflict altogether.

In retrospect, the surprising deterrent effect of China's dubious nuclear capability in the 1960s and early 1970s is similar to what has been seen with other late-developing nuclear weapons states. The Indian and Pakistani nuclear programs, even before open testing in 1998, appear to have introduced caution in their militarized disputes because each worried that the other might well be capable of quickly assembling a nuclear force in the heat of major conflict.[31] Perhaps more telling, uncertainty about North Korea's actual nuclear capability, both before and after its testing series, has been enough to render the American option of a preventive strike unattractive, an option repeatedly left on the table where U.S. presidents have insisted all options were being kept.[32] In sum, China's experience (and that of other developing world nuclear states and aspirants) suggests that nuclear deterrence is much easier than asserted by those who insist on the importance of a certainly survivable, massive retaliatory capability. A *potentially* survivable and deliverable small nuclear force suffices to instill the fear that deters even the mightiest adversary from challenging a state's vital interests. A secure second-strike force that can inflict assured destruction of the sort that was associated with the superpowers during the Cold War might be desirable to strengthen deterrence. But it is not necessary.

The Challenges of Nuclear Deterrence

Not so fast! Nuclear deterrence is not as easy as small nuclear states hope.

The relatively small size of nuclear weapons makes them easy to conceal and hard for an adversary to count with precision, frustrating its ability to be confident that it knows the full target set to be destroyed in a preemptive or preventive strike; unsure that it can target all the nuclear weapons, it cannot rule out some kind of retaliatory strike. But while the adversary worries that its attack might fail, the prospective victim of such a strike worries that it might succeed. Thus it has an incentive to increase the reliability of the threat that it will be able to deliver an unacceptably punishing retaliatory blow.

For China prior to the 1980s, and for other smaller and poorer nuclear weapons states, acting on this incentive is challenging.[33] Scarce resources have to be invested not just in warheads but also in delivery systems appropriate to the adversary to be deterred. The goal for states facing tight resource constraints is not, as noted above, a fully secure second-strike capability that assures the levels of destruction within reach of superpowers. Instead, the goal is a capability (including a national command authority) that has a chance of surviving counterforce first-strikes, penetrating the adversary's defenses, and delivering nuclear warheads against a set of targets whose destruction the adversary cannot bear.

If a state (like China) hopes to dissuade an adversary whose most valuable targets are very far away, developing an adequate delivery capability can be an especially daunting challenge. Fielding bombers is hard enough, though they have the advantage of easily being loaded with relatively large and heavy crude nuclear bombs for delivery close to the intended target. Fielding ballistic missiles tipped with nuclear warheads is at once more desirable (because missiles can be deployed in sheltered ways that reduce their vulnerability and because of their superior ability to penetrate defenses) and much more difficult. In addition to developing reliable missiles, fashioning nuclear warheads (especially thermonuclear warheads) that are light enough for a missile to lift and can survive the heat and stress of reentry and ensuring that the missile-warhead combination provides for even the modest accuracy necessary with nuclear weapons pose tough engineering challenges.[34]

Early during the first two decades of China's nuclear weapons program, Beijing recognized the importance of investing in ballistic missiles, the most promising solution to its problem of a more credible delivery system to target its distant adversary's heartland. Although China's bombers were the readily available means of delivery after the test in 1964, Beijing was already determined to field nuclear-capable ballistic missiles. The goal was a delivery system that held the adversary's most valuable targets at risk. But that meant China needed intercontinental-range missiles to reach the American homeland when the rocket program began, and at least intermediate-range missiles to strike cities in the western reaches of the Soviet Union when the strategic nuclear arsenal came online. Even with an early start in the 1950s, initial assistance from Soviet programs until the end of the 1950s, and heavy investment in the missile program, it took China twenty years to test and deploy its IRBM and thirty years for its ICBM—this despite the fact that rocketry was one of the stronger aspects of China's military technology.[35]

Nuclear Entitlement

We're different; we need 'em and we deserve 'em!

In justifying their pursuit of a nuclear capability, states often point to their extraordinary security challenges that require that they avail themselves of this option. But some states, like China, also draw explicit or implicit distinctions between the reasons they need to deploy a nuclear arsenal and the reasons others claim they have deployed them. From the moment of its first nuclear weapon test in October 1964, China insisted that it was a different kind of nuclear weapon state. It would never be the first to use these weapons, fielded a nuclear arsenal as a force for peace, and remained committed to the abolition of this necessary evil. For decades, Chinese officials and analysts even refused to accept that China practiced nuclear deterrence, since this was allegedly a strategy resting on threats and coercion, behaviors Beijing associated with arrogant hegemons.[36]

Beyond making its case to the international community about the special security requirements that justify deployment of a nuclear arsenal, a state may offer a rationale geared to its domestic audience—the claim that nuclear weapons, the coin of the realm for military power in the contemporary era, are a capability to which a country "like ours" is entitled. The self-perception that a state is heir to a historically great civilization, is engaged in reviving itself as a once-great power, or is the specially designated champion of a grand international or transnational cause can establish the normative belief that the country does not just need these weapons; its status means that it *should* have these weapons.

The belief that the PRC is the modern political heir to Chinese civilization's long and glorious history and that it must set its sights on regaining the stature of being one of the world's leading countries reflects a sense of exceptionalism that runs deep in China.[37] In addition, during the decades when China was developing and first deploying its nuclear arsenal, its leaders also claimed a special new identity as champions of the Third World, spreading the kind of revolutionary changes that the superpowers opposed. Thus when China proudly celebrated realizing its national nuclear ambition, it also proclaimed that breaking the nuclear monopoly of the superpowers was a triumph not just for China but for true revolutionaries around the globe.[38]

Arguments invoking a sense of pride can also be helpful in rallying political support for the initial decision to pursue a nuclear deterrent and then for seeing the effort through as a national mission when it proves a tough slog, especially for a developing country. When Mao called on his colleagues to seek a nuclear capability in the mid-1950s as a response to American bullying, he was able to tap into his colleagues' (and his people's) sensitivity about foreign powers humiliating China over the preceding century. And in the late 1950s, when he lost confidence in continued nuclear assistance from the Soviet Union, Mao made a more self-reliant Chinese security strategy (for which a nuclear arsenal would be essential) part of his call to mobilize the Chinese people in the Great Leap Forward.[39]

The emotional rallying behind the nuclear program was reflected in other ways as well. At the elite level, the challenges of pressing on despite the cutoff of Soviet nuclear assistance led not to despair but to prideful calls for resolve and sacrifice. This determination was evident in Nie Rongzhen's statement cited above. It was also manifest in the lament from China's foreign minister, Chen Yi, that he could not stand tall in international forums unless China had a nuclear weapon. He stressed the need for China to make huge sacrifices to get nuclear weapons after the Soviet cutoff even while the country was mired in the depression and famine the Great Leap had produced. As Chen famously put it, he would "pawn his own trousers" if that's what was needed to press ahead with China's nuclear program.[40]

Rogues and Nuclear Restraint

They're different; they're dangerous.

The concern that regimes, or the leaders of regimes, in some new nuclear weapons states, especially those in the developing world, will not be reliably guided by the same rational calculus as the leaders of responsible or "normal" nuclear states is by now a familiar refrain. China, as Francis Gavin's work reminds us, was considered a "rogue" before the label rogue was in vogue. Its experience, however, revealed a pattern that would be repeated in other cases—widespread international alarm or outrage about its new nuclear capability followed by gradual acceptance that, like others, it would be constrained by the obviously self-defeating consequences of nuclear recklessness.[41]

Rogue leaders commanding only conventional military forces are free to dabble in adventurism when they are confident they will have time to manage the costs if their military gambits fail.[42] But when rogue leaders command nuclear arsenals, or even are suspected of having them, they find themselves in the cross-hairs of other nuclear states who fear their arsenal and who have a clear capability to respond by promptly inflicting devastating punishment. Rogue leaders indulging fantasies of nuclear use may not have time to rethink the wisdom of their actions. More important, as Kenneth Waltz among others has emphasized, rogue leaders are leaders as well as rogues and have an abiding self-interest in preserving a viable realm over which to continue exercising their roguish style of leadership.[43]

China with nuclear weapons was a frightening thought for the United States and the Soviet Union. Both the Americans and the Soviets worried that a nuclear China would somehow be able to harness its newfound capability to an agenda of spreading its radical brand of revolutionary socialism in Asia. American and Soviet leaders were also troubled by the prospect that China's nuclear weapons would be at the disposal of a leader, Mao, who had a track record of impetuous behavior. He had blithely cast aside accepted economic wisdom and arguably common sense in forcing the Chinese people to endure the Great Leap Forward and its devastating aftermath. But perhaps most important, Mao seemed oblivious to the extreme dangers his actions courted when he had knowingly confronted the overwhelming military might of the United States, deciding to enter the Korean War in 1950 and twice triggering crises in the Taiwan Strait. And when others breathed a sigh of relief once the United States and the Soviet Union avoided World War III during the Cuban Missile Crisis, Mao had instead taunted the Soviets as "capitulationist" because they decided to step back from the nuclear brink.

There was little doubt that Mao was a highly risk-acceptant leader. But then, that is the point. There is a difference between being risk-acceptant and being irrational. Even a leader as risk-acceptant as Mao was aware of the exceptional risks that nuclear weapons created. Cheap talk aside (including outrageous claims that China did not fear nuclear war and could ride out and rebound from the loss of hundreds of millions of Chinese lives if nuclear war came), Mao's actions were those of a leader who pulled back whenever the risks jeopardized regime survival. In every instance, Mao and China quickly followed provocation with risk management and ultimately compromise. The consequences for the survival of the People's Republic of China if it actually triggered a nuclear war were easy enough to understand. And making decisions with an eye to ensuring regime survival is the kind of rationality that suffices to make nuclear rogue states behave more like normal regimes than they might otherwise prefer.[44]

Military Conflict among Nuclear Weapons States

The sturdy child of terror? A nuclear peace, if you can keep it.

Although the nuclear peace is sturdy because of the extreme caution that the fear of quickly suffering unacceptable damage induces, sturdy is not the same as indestructible.[45] Even a tight constraint is not a foolproof guarantee. Nuclear weapons do not eliminate the underlying causes of interstate conflict—the permissive condition of anarchy and the proximate causes of particular wars that reflect the interests and attributes of states and their leaders. Military conflict not only remains possible when nuclear states are unable to resolve their disagreements through diplomacy but has occurred. These conflicts have erupted when states are sufficiently motivated to fight, despite the specter of nuclear devastation. The Korean War, the Vietnam War, the Sino-Soviet border skirmishes in 1969, the India-Pakistan Kashmir crisis of 1990, and their Kargil conflict in 1999 all are instances where states fought—in some cases fought a lot and over a long period of time—despite varying degrees of concern about nuclear escalation.[46] In each instance, however, the nuclear Sword of Damocles constrained states to fight with one eye on that risk of escalation, shaping the course of fighting and ultimately forestalling a full-scale war, let alone a nuclear war. Unless one embraces the arbitrary and formalistic definition of war adopted by the Correlates of War project (any interstate conflict that results in more than a thousand battle deaths), all the events mentioned above are noteworthy for what they did *not* become—general or total wars. Instead they remained either bloody skirmishes or clearly limited wars, even though some (like Korea and Vietnam) resulted in significant fighting and massive casualties.

The recurrence of such fighting without escalation to total war in the nuclear context in part reflects what Glenn Snyder labeled the "stability-instability paradox."[47] The paradox captures the inhibiting fear of escalation that has kept military conflict between nuclear states limited, even as it nurtures a belief that the unattractiveness of total nuclear war permits (and may even tempt) states to fight conventional wars of various sorts. But that fear is effective only if escalation remains possible—in other words, if nuclear weapons do not make it completely safe to fight conventional wars. On the contrary, nuclear weapons make it dangerous for nuclear weapons states to fight conventional wars with each other. It is precisely the danger that leads them to be fought within constraints that did not exist prior to the nuclear age. Robert Jervis, at the height of the Cold War, dissected this logic and exposed the many flaws in claims about the importance of "escalation dominance" and the existence of discrete, sequenced rungs on the "ladder of escalation." Contrary to "conventionalized thinking" about the decisiveness of relative capabilities, Jervis drew attention back to the unavoidable reality of the contemporary era—the availability of an absolute capability to inflict unacceptable punishment shapes behavior in any militarized confrontation between nuclear weapons states.[48]

China's experience is again illustrative. After it tested its nuclear weapon, China was involved in several armed conflicts where it had to face the risk of nuclear escalation. The first was the series of Sino-Soviet skirmishes in 1969, the largest and most dangerous of which occurred in March at Zhenbao (or Damansk) Island along the disputed border of the Ussuri River. With only limited documentation available, analysts have long debated the immediate trigger for the fighting, though most now seem to agree that Chinese troops attacked first and then faced a ferocious Soviet counterassault.[49] The fighting itself was intense but was quickly reined in by both sides, who understood where it could all lead. In part because China had nuclear weapons that could dramatically increase the prompt damage the Soviets might face (a concern compounded when the United States indicated it would not permit the Soviets a free hand in dealing with China), Moscow considered, but eschewed, further escalation, including preventive strikes against China's small nuclear capabilities.[50] And because China was no match for the conventional military forces the Soviets could bring to bear, Beijing's most effective—perhaps only effective—option if the conflict expanded would have been to quickly introduce nuclear threats. That reality encouraged the Chinese, even the risk-acceptant Mao, to instead opt for escalating only their rhetoric, while quietly negotiating a deescalation with their loathed Soviet counterparts (as well as to nurture and consolidate the helpful leverage against Soviet threats that American warnings had suggested the United States could provide).[51]

While the 1969 border clashes offer the most dramatic example of the kind of constrained military conflict that can occur between nuclear weapons states, there are other instances where China's caution may have reflected concerns about the new dangers of total war. Not wanting to reprise the Korean War experience, in Vietnam the Americans and the newly nuclear Chinese tried to better signal each other about their restraint. As U.S. bombing runs inched ever northward, the Americans were careful to avoid the kind of provocation that had occurred when General MacArthur led UN troops towards the Yalu River in October 1950. And when China became increasingly involved in supporting North Vietnam, it took great care to disguise its assistance as nonmilitary, providing a modicum of plausible deniability that reduced the chance that American bombing runs killing Chinese "engineers" on the ground, or that Chinese-manned antiaircraft fire killing American pilots, would draw the two nuclear weapons states into a larger, direct conflict like the one they fought in Korea.[52]

Thus conventional military conflict still occurs in the presence of nuclear weapons, though within limits set by the constraining fear of escalation. The caution that fear induces, however, depends on a genuine possibility of escalation. But that also means that each side may be tempted to manipulate that fear and engage in brinkmanship—a dynamic that Thomas Schelling famously described as a competition in risk taking where each side seeks leverage by conveying threats that leave something to chance. Such brinkmanship is inherently frightening, akin to a struggle between entangled adversaries near the edge of a cliff shrouded in dense fog where a misstep could be disastrous for both. Fortunately, nuclear weapons provide powerful incentives for adversaries to pause well before they get very close to the brink of the precipice, a pattern evident in Cold War nuclear crises. As the risk of losing control becomes more serious, peacetime proclamations about hypothetical conflicts, declaratory doctrine about the use of nuclear weapons, and even operational doctrine that guides deployments and training give way to "doctrine in practice" with political leaders focusing on catastrophe prevention (i.e., crisis and conflict management) rather than narrowly focusing on a push for advantage and victory.[53]

Still, the Sino-Soviet border conflict in 1969 could have turned out differently. Because the risk that encouraged caution was a real risk of disaster, the parties might have somehow stumbled into a nuclear exchange. Even if logic suggests this counterfactual was unlikely, it was a possibility and could have had devastating consequences for wide areas of the region.[54] But it is also important to recognize that, absent nuclear weapons along the heavily armed and intensely disputed border, it is plausible that the Soviet leaders would have been tempted to solve their deepening China problem through major military operations intended to discredit Mao and produce a more pliable leadership in Beijing as the CCP was being rebuilt after the chaos of the Cultural Revolution. Absent nuclear weapons, the risk of failure for the Soviets would have been defeat and withdrawal, an embarrassment but not a catastrophe. With nuclear weapons in play, the risk they would face in such a campaign against China was prompt, devastating destruction inflicted by a regime sensing its end days and a catastrophic outcome arriving before the operation could be called off. That risk would almost certainly eclipse the temptation to produce regime change in Beijing.

The Limits of Nuclear Deterrence

Pretty, pretty good—but not good enough.

Nuclear weapons constrain states to avoid all-out war, and the fear of escalation provides even smaller nuclear states with the ability to confront much more powerful adversaries whose capabilities they cannot hope to match, with danger they dare not court. Yet the scope of this payoff from a nuclear arsenal is neither automatic nor unlimited.

First, the usefulness of nuclear weapons is limited to contingencies where a state is prepared to run grave risks because the stakes are important enough that nuclear escalation is not entirely implausible. Nuclear weapons can be used to secure clearly vital interests because such interests are the most important basis on which the adversary assesses whether an actor has the resolve needed to court the extraordinary danger inherent in a confrontation between nuclear-armed states. On peripheral matters or in distant places, establishing the importance of one's interests at stake can be difficult. Where it is not possible, an adversary is unlikely to be dissuaded by the fear of escalation. Consequently, if a state has interests that it views as important enough to warrant spending its blood and treasure through military action, but that fall short of vital interests, it will have to supplement its nuclear capabilities with conventional forces better suited to the mission. Such contingencies are the ones where the implications of the stability-instability paradox are most evident—not because nuclear weapons somehow cancel each other out, but because the issues at stake render nuclear escalation so implausible.

Second, even in situations where vital interests are at stake, the usefulness of nuclear weapons is limited to situations where the adversary can be forced to face the risk of escalation. If an adversary can achieve its goals and infringe on the targeted state's vital interests before the latter can respond with threats of escalation, it may believe that it can safely take action and present the victim with a fait accompli. Scenarios involving such faits accomplis are not likely to involve full-scale invasion and conquest where the risks of escalation are hard to avoid. But a military operation that seeks limited gains against a rival's vital interests is conceivable. To head that off, a nuclear-armed state requires military forces that make quick success for the adversary difficult. What is needed are conventional forces that convince the adversary it will simply not be able to achieve its limited objectives without raising the risk of nuclear escalation.[55]

In China's experience before 1974, the first sort of limitation was of minor relevance because, unlike for the superpowers, its security concerns were narrowly focused on protection of the homeland. One could suggest perhaps that China's nuclear capability proved useless in its broader goal of promoting international revolution, or in its rivalry with the Soviet Union to win the allegiance of competing revolutionaries in the developing world. But it is not clear that China truly saw these missions as important enough to warrant a serious military effort. Still, to support its interests in Africa and elsewhere, China's conventional military assistance, rather than its nuclear capabilities, was what counted.

The second sort of limitation, however, was more interesting and relevant to China's experience. In the years when China lacked a nuclear deterrent, and even for many years after its initial deployment, Beijing touted the primacy and effectiveness of "people's war" as the self-reliant approach to guarantee the country's national security. The prospect of a punishing popular resistance movement facing any occupier was touted as a deterrent against any aggressors who might invade China. But dissuading the United States and later the Soviet Union from invading and occupying China by relying on the threat to mount a people's war addressed only one scenario, arguably the least likely one, in which a powerful adversary could harm China's vital interests. Militarily superior adversaries could attempt to coerce China by using airpower against valuable targets on the mainland or, even more worrisome once the Soviets were the principal adversary after 1968, ground power to carry out an armored strike seizing valuable chunks of Chinese territory within reach of a Soviet blitzkrieg attack.[56]

Without adequate conventional military capabilities to counter air and ground power, China could well have been presented with a fait accompli if the Soviets sensed that they could achieve their objective before China brought nuclear threats to bear, or before it was able to solicit backing from the United States. Until China had conventional capabilities that could slow down and frustrate a Soviet assault so that there would be time for trepidation about nuclear escalation to kick in (most likely as China visibly increased the readiness of its nuclear arsenal), Beijing faced the possibility that the Soviets might seize a swath of the industrial base in Manchuria or the geographic buffer of the Mongolian steppe northwest of Beijing. What then?

At that point, China could have issued nuclear threats to compel the Soviets to give up their gains. But compellence, especially nuclear compellence, is typically more difficult than deterrence because it puts the onus of taking the first dangerous step on the side demanding a change in the status quo.[57] Moreover, the insights of prospect theory suggest that compellence would be an especially difficult approach for reversing the faits accomplis described.

Prospect theory argues that actors value what they hold more than what they covet, indicating that the balance of resolve is likely to favor the side trying to preserve its position. In the scenarios above, Soviet actions would transform the situation on the ground into one in which the Chinese were operating in the domain of gains (we want to regain our territory you now hold) and in which the Soviets, having decided it was important enough to use military force to violate another sovereign state's territorial integrity, were operating in the domain of losses (we won't give up this valuable asset we now control).[58]

The point is not that such faits accomplis are ever easy or without risk when undertaken against a nuclear-armed rival, but instead that such possibilities mean that even relatively resource-poor states will view their nuclear weapons as a necessary but never sufficient solution to ensuring their vital interests. Unsurprisingly, then, the need to remedy the deficiencies in China's conventional capabilities—the donut hole between nuclear retaliation and people's war—was the first item on Beijing's agenda for military modernization once the ideological blinders imposed by Mao Zedong were set aside following his death.[59]

Conclusion

The lessons of Hiroshima would emerge only gradually as analysts pondered the implications of this massively destructive technology for international politics, and as Cold War experience began to provide evidence about its strategic significance. By the 1970s most of the key ideas about the distinctiveness of the nuclear age had been vetted, if not universally accepted. In this sense, the 1970s marked the end of the beginning of a new era that would ultimately transcend the Cold War and that continues in the twenty-first century. Although much of the literature about this era understandably focused on the two superpowers, examining China's experience from 1955 until the 1970s usefully enriches our understanding of the nuclear revolution.

But how relevant is that understanding to today's world? After all, even during the Cold War some analysts and policy makers had rejected claims about the revolutionary strategic implications of nuclear weapons for international politics. And when the Cold War ended, concerns about conflict among nuclear-armed great powers became an afterthought. Strategists, policy makers, and the public turned their attention to regional wars and to coping with the challenges of nonstate actors engaged in terrorism. To the extent nuclear weapons were discussed, it was mainly in debates about how deeply the existing nuclear weapons states should cut the size of their arsenals and how best to deal with continued proliferation. In the second decade of the twenty-first century, however, old debates about the meaning of the nuclear revolution have resurfaced.

Some, pointing to advanced technology that may make offensive counterforce strikes and defensive ballistic missile defenses more effective, are proffering nuclear warfighting strategies that represent a revival of what was once disparaged as "conventionalized thinking."[60] Is such thinking now warranted? This is a question of overriding importance inasmuch as accepting and acting on claims about a new kind of nuclear era could entail massive resource commitments and, more important, could increase the risk of instability during a future crisis by encouraging the use of force that could lead to nuclear escalation. However confident today's nuclear innovators may be in the warrant for their claims, it is worth recalling that the atomic bombing of Hiroshima demonstrated that when wars start, one can never be sure where and how they will end. It is therefore only prudent to determine whether assertions about what is newly feasible and desirable are in fact well founded. Have the undeniably impressive advances in technology in recent decades fundamentally altered the reality reflected in the nuclear history of China described in this chapter? China's experience underscores the revolutionary strategic consequences that resulted from the availability of weapons whose destructive power shapes the decisions of states as long their leaders cannot be fully confident they can eliminate the danger of catastrophic retaliation. If new technologies do not alter *that* harsh reality, then the nuclear revolution endures.

14

Data, Discourse, and Disruption

RADIATION EFFECTS AND NUCLEAR ORDERS

Sonja D. Schmid

AFTER HIROSHIMA AND NAGASAKI, scientists from both the nation that dropped the bombs and the nation the bombs had been dropped on first started to observe, measure, and document the medical consequences of radiation exposure.[1] The knowledge thus produced was detailed, systematic, and—however narrowly it was initially shared—extensive. It allowed for a narrative to emerge that condemned nuclear weapons for their harmful consequences on the environment and human health and forged a parallel narrative about the "peaceful" uses of nuclear energy.[2] (For a thoughtful discussion of the definition of "nuclear harm," see also chapter 15 by Shampa Biswas in this volume.) The production of knowledge about the effects of radiation on the human body and its natural (and built) environment, then, went hand in hand with the production of a social order that condemned the use of nuclear weapons but approved the operation of nuclear power reactors. Hence even Japan, victim of nuclear weapons, could justify developing a robust commercial nuclear power reactor fleet.

Fast forward to Chernobyl: this catastrophe threatened a social order based on the separation of nuclear weapons and nuclear power. As a consequence, the Soviet Union's government minimized the production of knowledge about the disaster's effects.[3] There was scant monitoring and limited surveying, and even where scientists and medical doctors did record data, they were often instructed to falsify, suppress, or lose reports. To this day, the most basic scientific information about where the soil was contaminated, by what isotopes, and to what levels; what dose individuals were exposed to; and how this had been determined is incomplete, contradictory, or unsystematically documented. And yet, in the end, Chernobyl did not upset the global nuclear order that had emerged in the wake of Hiroshima, despite the fact that it became a hugely important argument in European (and especially German) antinuclear discourse (not dissimilar to what Holger Nehring notes in chapter 11 about uniquely German ways of imbuing "Hiroshima" with meaning). Instead, Chernobyl was ultimately integrated into a discourse of overcoming crisis, of coming out stronger on the other side, and in the end confirmed the idea that disasters were not supposed to happen, and therefore were not going to happen again, in the civilian nuclear sphere. It took twenty-five years and the Fukushima nuclear accident to shake this discourse and, perhaps more important, to prompt some institutional changes, however uneven in individual nations, to reimagine the connection between the civilian nuclear industry and nuclear weapons.[4]

Using Hiroshima and Chernobyl as two critical touchstones of the nuclear age, I argue in this chapter that scientific knowledge about the effects of ionizing radiation—the data that were collected and the data that were not, along with the particular interpretations of these data—produced a specific social order that situated military and civilian uses of nuclear energy in a certain way (one was unacceptable but unavoidable, the other a benign vehicle for human progress), and that this social order, in turn, determined what kind of scientific knowledge about the effects of radiation and nuclear energy was permitted to be produced. This argument does not preclude the possibility of alternative orders in the future; in fact, it is my hope that discourses and institutions will change to address the new (and old) challenges of our nuclear world. I also hasten to add that, as in any social order, there are of course pockets of resistance and deviation in our current nuclear order, with significant implications for the production of alternative knowledge about radiation effects.[5]

The Argument

This chapter is inspired by the interpretative framework of "co-production": "shorthand for the proposition that the ways in which we know and represent the world (both nature and society) are inseparable from the ways in which we choose to live in it. Knowledge and its material embodiments are at once products of social work and constitutive of forms of social life; society cannot function without knowledge any more than knowledge can exist without appropriate social support."[6] Following Sheila Jasanoff and the authors in *States of Knowledge*, I assume that the particular account I offer here only comes "into distinct view through the lens of co-production," as an answer to questions that arise "when we explicitly inquire into the social arrangements that prop up particular natural orders, or, in reverse, the epistemologies that help to sustain particular social orders." By focusing primarily on the "ordering instruments" of *discourse* and *institutions*, I try to illuminate not only "how cognitive understandings of the world we live in are tied at many points to social means of intervening in or coping with that world," but also how the social means of organizing (or ordering) our world suggest, shape, and at times outright determine how we understand the world through the collection of data.[7]

For students of nuclear history, the separation of expertise on nuclear weapons, on the one hand, and on civilian (or "peaceful") uses of nuclear power, on the other, is nothing new. What I argue here is that these areas are typically connected in one and only one way—nuclear weapons have tremendous destructive potential, which makes them ideal instruments of deterrence, while nuclear power reactors (and to some extent other nonmilitary applications of ionizing radiation) are instruments of peace and prosperity. Experts and expertise in these two nuclear spheres tend to have clearly defined territories whose boundaries are rarely transgressed. These different epistemic communities rely on separate journals, focus on separate concerns, and emphasize the importance of different, distinct orders: the diplomatic order of international relations and national security versus the regulatory order of industrial energy generation, isotope management, and safety policy. And, in a typical act of organizational self-preservation, these communities appear to have little interest in building bridges but are instead driven by maintaining exclusive access to their own areas of expertise and influence.[8]

Let us explore this separation in a little more detail. According to the pattern I suggest, nuclear things today are twofold. On the one hand, we have nuclear weapons, terrifying and devastating crown jewels of national weapons arsenals that have been tested by eight (arguably nine) nations, either to demonstrate that a particular ruler or nation has them (and thus ought to belong to the "nuclear club") or to make sure they work (not a foregone conclusion in an era of comprehensive bans on nuclear explosions) and that they will work in ever varying configurations, yields, and conditions.[9] These weapons are loaded onto various delivery vehicles and—according to the dominant strand of international relations theory—are used to "deter" other nations from using theirs. The questionable nature of the deterrence doctrine aside, the idea essentially is *not* to use these weapons in actual armed conflicts. Nuclear weapons have the diplomatic power ascribed to them precisely because of the apocalyptic nature of their consequences, and this puts, as Nina Tannenwald argues, a "taboo" on their use (see her essay in chapter 16 of this volume).[10] Hiroshima and Nagasaki serve as canonical reminders of what happens when a nuclear device (even a small one by today's standards) is detonated in an urban area. Nobody questions the deadly nature of a nuclear blast, and, in fact, it is the undeniably catastrophic consequences of a nuclear detonation, its devastating impacts on the environment and human health, that maintain the narrative of nuclear war as the ultimately terrifying, undesirable outcome of an international confrontation gone awry.[11]

On the other hand, nuclear energy has been touted as a beneficent panacea for progress, not only in terms of electricity generation but also in terms of medical, agricultural, industrial, transportation, and other applications. This "peaceful" narrative emerged at around the same time the weapons narrative solidified in the contours I've outlined above (apocalypse, deterrence, and nuclear winter). Whether it was redemption for having developed nuclear weapons or the quest for a scientifically exciting, socially beneficial application of a technology that had escaped the control of scientists, the seemingly endless possibilities provided by "peaceful uses of atomic energy" occupied some of the brightest minds of the 1950s and 1960s.[12]

One of the most popular enterprises was the generation of electricity by nuclear power reactors.[13] We are familiar with the slogans "too cheap to meter" and similar optimistic prognoses for this particular application of nuclear energy.[14] The literature on the early period of nuclear industries in the United States, as well as in other nations, shows clearly and convincingly the powerful role of the nation-state in developing nuclear industries, even in countries where these industries were nominally built by private corporations (as in the United States).[15]

Although nuclear weapons and nuclear power reactors relied on the same materials, processes, and machines; were typically administered, managed, and regulated by the same organizations, at least initially; and drew on the same pool of scientists and engineers, the accompanying narratives that emerged were radically different. Gradually established over the first few decades of the atomic age, this separation has since been maintained, reinforced, and re-created with every nuclear weapon tested, every nuclear reactor started up, and every commercial and diplomatic treaty on nuclear matters signed. So far, every incident that had the potential to shake this separation has ultimately served only to solidify the line between military and civilian applications, between terrifying and beneficent nuclear applications.

This line and its remarkable resilience over time—the fact that its normative power has not budged much, despite the fact that it is clearly porous, blurry, and ambiguous—are what my argument tries to capture.[16] Technologies come and go, military to civilian technology transfer appears to be ubiquitous, and yet in the nuclear realm we have a strange consistency that begs the question of the associated social order (and who benefits from maintaining it).[17] This question remains salient even if we add opponents of nuclear power into the picture. Antinuclear groups oppose nuclear energy because of the undesirable risks it entails, and they refer to nuclear weapons to illustrate the point that nothing good will come from anything nuclear. But it is precisely the underlying assumption that "peaceful" applications of nuclear energy would be acceptable if and as long as they can be operated safely (that is, risk- and accident-free) that ultimately supports a clear separation of military and civilian applications. It is severe accidents at "peaceful" nuclear facilities—Three Mile Island, Chernobyl, Fukushima—that threaten to disrupt a clear narrative that assigns "catastrophe" to nuclear weapons and "social benefit" to (safely operated) nuclear power plants. As a consequence, nuclear industry proponents and political leaders to date have managed to reframe every one of these accidents as a narrative of conquering crisis and making nuclear power operations safer in the end.

Having separated the essence of military and peaceful applications in this way is a historical achievement, and this division now serves to sustain a specific kind of social order, a "nuclear order" of sorts that surpasses the deterrence-based military order (which relies on nuclear exceptionalism) and supports what Gabrielle Hecht has referred to as nuclear banality: the nuclear industry is like any other; of course there are risks, as in any other industrial enterprise; nuclear power plants do what any other power plant does too (boiling water and so forth).[18] Severe accidents (not the kind of everyday incidents that every industrial system invariably experiences) involving civilian nuclear applications, and here mostly powerful industrial-scale reactors, pose a threat to this nuclear order, and that cannot be. The way this boundary is enforced, and military and civilian nuclear applications are being kept rhetorically, administratively, and imaginatively distinct, starts and ends with knowledge: the data that are collected (or not), the sense that is made of those data (how we interpret them), and the consequences these data suggest (and whether we act on them).

Nuclear power and nuclear weapons still rely on some of the same materials and technological processes: most important, both utilize uranium, enriched to various degrees, and produce or use specific isotopes of plutonium. Entire formations of centrifuges (so-called cascades) accomplish uranium enrichment, and the plutonium used in nuclear warheads originates in the very fission processes that nuclear reactors use to heat water, to produce steam, to drive turbines, and to generate electricity. And yet in one instance—the weapons case—these materials and processes are made out to be special, in need of careful accounting, monitoring, and often international control; in the other, they are portrayed as mundane, barely more dangerous than a banana or a transatlantic flight.[19] In the former case, nuclear is dangerous, ready to inflict apocalypse on the world, affecting human health and the environment for generations to come, and therefore the ultimate instrument of deterrence. In the latter case, nuclear is benign, "too cheap to meter," and a carbon-friendly alternative to fossil fuels that threaten to collapse the planet's climate.

This distinction between dangerous nuclear weapons and beneficent nuclear power stations is a process of world making that a curious alliance of scientists, journalists, and government leaders have carved out as the official discourse since the 1940s and 1950s.[20] This discourse has since then solidified around the world and has been cast into international treaty language and organizational statutes. The distinction has also congealed in institutions and their organizational arrangements: today in almost all countries, different agencies, ministries, and other entities are responsible for weapons, on the one hand, and research and power-related nuclear applications, on the other.[21] This organizational bifurcation goes so far as to be embodied in think tanks that devote their activities either to nuclear weapons control and disarmament efforts or to nuclear safety, best practices, and emergency preparedness and response. They rely on different human capital pipelines, train their staff differently, talk to different decision makers, and operate under a fundamentally different set of priorities. In case these priorities are in conflict, these groups find it increasingly difficult to communicate and to negotiate solutions.[22]

Data Point 1: The ABCC and the Rise of Japan's Nuclear Power Program

Japan's is a unique story with regard to collecting data to support a specific kind of nuclear order. Its story condemns nuclear weapons as harmful and barbaric while at the same time promoting "peaceful" applications—research and power generation—as beneficent, the solution to a resource-scarce economy, and even identity-conferring for generations of peace-loving Japanese who turn available reactor designs into seismically resilient, sophisticated engineering achievements.

Following the dropping of the atomic bombs on Hiroshima and Nagasaki, Japanese scientists and medical doctors immediately started collecting data to document the effects of radiation.[23] The lead scientist, Masao Tsuzuki, head of the Japan's National Research Council, oversaw the collection of critical clinical data until the end of the Occupation in 1952.[24] The first studies based on these data were being published in Japanese medical journals starting in fall 1945. Various sections of the Supreme Commander for the Allied Powers (SCAP), however, prevented some of these invaluable early reports from getting published or rigorously censored them, apparently on the presumption that they might "disturb public tranquility."[25]

Within a couple of months, the Japanese scientists were joined by teams from the U.S. Army and Navy and the Manhattan District, and in October 1945 they merged to form the Joint Commission for the Investigation of the Effects of the Atomic Bombs. The reports produced by this commission ended up being classified and were published only decades later. In May 1946 representatives of the Joint Commission recommended establishing a permanent organization to study the long-term effects of the bomb. On November 26 President Truman issued a directive that established this group, which, according to anecdotes, "called itself the 'Atomic Bomb Casualty Commission' for lack of an official title."[26] The ABCC was a scientific endeavor funded jointly by the Japanese government and the United States. Its staff grew rapidly, and by 1951 it employed over 140 Allied and over 900 Japanese personnel.[27] While collecting data, the ABCC never offered care for the survivors it meticulously monitored over the years—an ongoing point of contention.[28] And despite the fact that the ABCC's credibility in Japan may have been impaired, the data it assembled served as the basis for setting international standards on radiation effects and allowed authoritative conclusions about the devastating effects of nuclear weapons on human health.[29]

The point I want to emphasize here is that although technically the results of the ABCC research were used broadly to understand radiation effects on the human body, *as an ordering discourse*, they were interpreted as documenting the effects of nuclear *weapons* only. This allowed scientists, politicians, and others to condemn nuclear weapons, mobilized people around the world for nuclear disarmament, and served as the justification for the Japanese government to forgo its own weapons program (and instead arrange for nuclear protection by the very nation that had inflicted the harm on its cities and citizens in the first place). The research was not deemed relevant for discussions about potential risks involved in the development of a domestic nuclear power industry.[30] Instead, technology transfer and seismic engineering questions dominated the Japanese civilian program, which associated nuclear power with "a triumph of Science over Mother Nature and a symbol of Japan's miraculous recovery" after World War II.[31] By 2011 Japan had built more than fifty power reactors that provided some 30 percent of the country's electricity needs.

Data Point 2: The Soviet Nuclear Program between Secret Sites and "Nuclear Boilers"

Within Soviet official discourse on nuclear energy, Hiroshima became the symbol that marked the beginning of a clear separation between military uses of nuclear energy, on the one hand (associated with the United States and its allies), and "peaceful" applications, on the other, with the latter firmly associated with the Soviet Union.[32] In the mid-1960s this process eventually resulted in attempts to realign the organizational landscape governing nuclear energy according to this distinction, with certain institutions appointed to develop systems and produce materials for the defense of the homeland and others designated to exploit the "peaceful atom" for the benefit of humankind.

In the immediate aftermath of Hiroshima, the Soviet mass media were careful in their portrayal of the events of August 1945.[33] Images of the devastation and the mushroom cloud were not widely publicized for over a decade, while the propaganda masterminds figured out exactly how to fit Hiroshima into the grand Soviet narrative. It was not until the mid-1950s that party ideologues found a recipe that portrayed "peaceful nuclear applications" as the antidote to nuclear annihilation, however utopian and futuristic they remained at that point.[34] Soviet official discourse rhetorically tied peaceful nuclear applications to Soviet disarmament proposals *and* the might of Soviet science and technology, which would inescapably further social progress as well.

The first United Nations Conference on Peaceful Uses of Atomic Energy, which took place in 1955 in Geneva, Switzerland, fit into the emerging dualism of military aggression (epitomized by the mushroom cloud) and peaceful developments in the realm of nuclear energy.[35] Eventually, toward the early 1960s, a coherent story line emerged that consistently portrayed the Soviet Union as a peace-loving world power that was developing and testing nuclear weapons solely to defend itself against Anglo-American aggressors, who not only had killed thousands of innocent civilians in 1945 but also were clearly preparing to inflict the same harm on Soviet people.

Soviet journalists, in tandem with scientists and party ideologues, eventually accomplished a clear-cut discursive separation of military versus civilian: on the one hand, the aggressive military arms buildup in the United States (with the Soviet nuclear weapons program merely a defensive reaction), and, on the other hand, the ambitious development of a civilian nuclear power program in the USSR that was intended to alleviate environmental pollution and promote scientific advancement and technological progress, along with tangible social improvements. The scientists, eager to justify their involvement in the nuclear weapons program, came up with the famous slogan "May the atom be a worker, not a soldier," which managed to condense the Soviet way of doing things nuclear.[36]

Perhaps more sharply than in other contexts, Soviet civilian nuclear power occupied a precarious position at the boundary of a secret nuclear weapons program, on the one hand, and the prestigious, bombastic, ever expanding electric power industry with its megalomaniac dam projects, high voltage transmission lines, and fossil fuel plants of every imaginable type, on the other. Civilian nuclear reactors promised to deliver on the promise of extending the 1920s State Electrification Plan (GOELRO) by continuing to electrify the country, including households, transportation, and industry. Nuclear power plants fit seamlessly within the narrative of Lenin's "electrification of the entire country" as a necessary part of communism and of the unstoppable progress of Soviet technological sophistication and scientific prowess. But at the same time, the stuff these new plants were to operate on was being guarded jealously by those in charge of delivering nuclear weapons to the Soviet state.

Despite the material proximity, the discursive separation of military and civilian purposes succeeded and laid the groundwork for an organizational separation. In 1966 the Central Committee and the Council of Ministers issued a joint decree that put all new nuclear power plants (and those already under construction) under the authority of the Ministry of Energy and Electrification (Minenergo), while the design of reactors, fuel delivery, and reprocessing—in short, all the sensitive nuclear parts of the plant—remained under the aegis of the secret Ministry of Medium Machine Building (Sredmash).[37]

While this division of labor to some extent provided "tried-and-true repertoires of problem-solving," these institutional arrangement also produced new problems almost immediately.[38] Responsibilities overlapped and led to ongoing confrontations among agencies; the vague prose of the 1966 transfer decree made additional negotiations necessary; and, over the years, a series of "exceptions" impaired effective ways of transferring relevant knowledge.[39] To make matters worse, randomly invoked rules of secrecy prevented tacit knowledge and valuable experience, especially about mishaps, to be passed on to everyone involved with nuclear technologies.[40]

On the other hand, an increasing clarity about organizational responsibilities provided new opportunities for scientific research and knowledge production. One of the fascinating details about Kate Brown's *Plutopia*, a comparative study of plutonium production facilities and their associated settlements in Hanford and Chelyabinsk, is the astonishing amount of information she surfaced that documents Soviet scientific research on contamination, both of the environment and of the human body, as well as evacuation and resettlement policies that were a direct result of that research (even if they were only partially implemented).[41]

Brown shows that state-sanctioned Soviet scientists, unrestricted by public scrutiny, special interest groups, and apparently even party doctrine, meticulously documented the effects of radionuclides on local communities' health. Their data were used to determine which villages ought to be resettled and what decontamination measures should be selected. The threat of whistleblowers or counterexperts who would challenge either the data or the conclusions drawn did not exist: the social order of the Soviet state, which did not tolerate alternative explanations, allowed scientists to study and evaluate a natural world that was in many ways scarier, because it was more detailed, than its American counterpart. By contrast, Brown recounts Hanford's history as one of obfuscation, denial, and deliberate ignorance. Soviet scientists studied environmental contamination and health effects among downstream residents in ways that Hanford "downwinders" could never hope for, simply because the data were considered "safe" in one context and a threat to the legitimacy of the state in the other.[42] In other words, in a closed society without public scrutiny, data collection proceeded without inhibition, as opposed to the refusal to collect potentially incriminating data in the first place, as in the case of a free society.

This methodical data collection, however, did not extend to the Soviet civilian program (at least prior to Chernobyl). Data on contamination and its health effects were collected only where they concerned Soviet facilities associated with the military nuclear program.[43] Soviet scientists were never tasked with, nor did they decide to study, the potential effects of radioactive contamination from civilian facilities (research reactors, power plants, and various medical, agricultural, and industrial uses of radioactive isotopes).[44] Nonmilitary nuclear applications were part of the "peaceful," safe nuclear order and thus did not need scientific examination.

The narrative and the organizational setup that had established military nuclear facilities as fundamentally different from civilian ones, then, resulted in different ways of studying them as risky or safe. Civilian nuclear facilities were supposed to represent the controlled, mastered version of the military facilities, which were objects of study. The weapons program had been understood to be dangerous to the health of people involved, directly or inadvertently, but its relevance could not be questioned; the civilian program was much more contested and faced repeated challenges as to its economic viability and its necessity given the availability of vast natural resources. But it was never envisioned as anywhere near as hazardous as the military program. Perhaps this explains (at least in part) why nuclear safety regulation in the Soviet Union lagged behind its international counterparts by decades, and why the first attempts at articulating a regulatory framework for nuclear safety were directly inspired by norms and frameworks presented at international scientific conferences and experienced firsthand during the Soviet construction of the first Finnish nuclear reactors.[45] The Three Mile Island accident in 1979 imparted a new urgency on Soviet policy makers to create a systematic regulatory framework for civilian nuclear applications.[46]

Disruptions

A severe accident at a *civilian* nuclear site challenges the established separation and threatens to collapse a carefully maintained boundary. It blurs the boundary between military and peaceful uses of nuclear energy and connects data that were collected after incidents at military facilities to the effects of a civilian disaster. If a "peaceful" nuclear reactor can explode and contaminate large areas for centuries to come, how different is this from what had been envisioned as the consequences of a nuclear weapon's detonation? Finally, how did the imaginary that supported a bifurcated nuclear world allow for, or prevent, data collection to connect the military use of nuclear weapons and the havoc wreaked by severe accidents at civilian nuclear sites? While focusing on Chernobyl, I also want to reflect on the effects of Fukushima on the discursive and institutional bifurcation of our nuclear order.

Chernobyl

The catastrophic accident at the Chernobyl nuclear power plant on April 26, 1986, overturned the seemingly clear-cut distinction between military and peaceful applications. The Soviet Union reacted to the disaster first by making organizational changes within its nuclear industry, and only then by reviewing personnel policies and implementing technical modifications. Nuclear power plants were separated out from under Minenergo and put under a separate "nuclear power ministry," a move that acknowledged anew the volatile position that civilian nuclear plants occupied at the boundary of the nuclear weapons program and the civilian power sector. Creating an *independent* ministry also signaled that the civilian nuclear sector was still considered fundamentally separate from the weapons program. Over the three years following the accident, Soviet public discourse, encouraged in its newly found critical voice by Gorbachev's policy of *glasnost*, increasingly wove together apocalyptic stories from Hiroshima and Chernobyl and ultimately eroded the remaining organizational separation.[47]

Much was at stake in drawing Chernobyl and Hiroshima together: Soviet discourse had meticulously constructed Hiroshima's relevance not only for public perception of nuclear energy but also for justifying the Soviet civilian nuclear program (namely, as the "other" to military nuclear programs). Deconstructing the established discourse was consequential also in that it jeopardized carefully formed social institutions. Combined with the economic and political calamities of the early 1990s, Soviet nuclear organizations threatened to disintegrate. The nuclear power ministry created in 1986 faltered only three years into its existence. It turned out that the ministry was unable to provide support to the country's nuclear sector without intimate access to the infrastructure of both ministerial motherships (Sredmash and Minenergo). As a consequence, the Soviet government merged all things nuclear back under one organizational roof, tacitly acknowledging that, mushroom cloud or not, nuclear things were best kept from exploding.[48] In essence, then, the Chernobyl catastrophe exposed the artificiality of the distinction between military and peaceful applications that had taken decades to set up and had come to appear as natural.

The Soviet media's defiant comparison of what ought not to be compared also explains the heated debate over classifying the explosion at Chernobyl as thermal or nuclear. Advocates of the thermal explosion classification, typically nuclear scientists and engineers from around the world, were quick to dismiss the latter claim as symptomatic of ignorance or, worse, a result of "radiophobia." After all, they argued, at Chernobyl there had been no mushroom cloud. Those who claimed the reactor had been destroyed by a nuclear explosion insisted that while a power reactor and a nuclear warhead were clearly designed very differently, the same prompt critical nuclear reaction that a nuclear weapon exploits to maximize destructive power had occurred inside Chernobyl's reactor number 4 and produced a nuclear disaster of unprecedented proportions.

Why did this question about the nature of the explosion matter, and why was it debated so persistently, with so much passion? I argue that neither physics nor nuclear engineering could provide a final answer: much more was at stake. Depending on the answer, Chernobyl was either an unfortunate but ultimately normal industrial accident that could be managed by civilian authorities (a thermal explosion) or proof that nuclear reactors were potentially just as dangerous as nuclear weapons and therefore needed the oversight, discipline, and control commonly associated with military authorities (a nuclear explosion). In other words, the question could be reframed as whether Chernobyl was *like Hiroshima*, and the answer had fundamental implications for the organization of the Soviet nuclear sector. The established narrative could withstand a "thermal" explosion but not a "nuclear" one.

Ultimately, though, Chernobyl did not shatter the universally accepted boundary between military and civilian nuclear uses. Despite its potential to become a state-breaking device, it ended up serving a state-making discourse, in at least two of the successor states of the Soviet Union (Russia and

Ukraine).[49] The narrative strategy that allowed the boundary to stay put elsewhere in the world was to dismiss Chernobyl as something uniquely Soviet, something that "could never happen here"—wherever the "here" was. By associating Chernobyl with a crumbling state, its manifestly backward industrial capacity, and its corrupt elites, rather than with the civilian nuclear project in general, the existing division could remain intact. This strategy proved useful for many nations operating nuclear power plants and only prompted an outcry in Germany (and Austria), a curious pocket of nuclear resistance in central Europe.

Among the former Soviet Republics that took the brunt of Chernobyl's fallout (Russia, Ukraine, and Belarus), the Soviet successor state of Belarus was by far worst off in terms of the total area affected, the percentage of national territory contaminated, and the severity of the contamination. Maps of contaminated territory were first published three years after the accident, and by 2001, fifteen years later, they still showed over 20 percent of the newly independent nation's territory contaminated with Cesium-137.[50] In contrast to Ukraine, where Chernobyl became a "national tragedy" and was embedded in the new constitution to an extent that eventually allowed roughly 7 percent of its population to claim eligibility for benefits as a Chernobyl victim, Belarus went a very different route.[51]

As Olga Kuchinskaya has documented in *The Politics of Invisibility*, the initial data collection that led to the establishment of "zones" that were subject to either mandatory, delayed, or voluntary evacuation was soon discouraged, defunded, and eventually outright sabotaged by a government that neither could afford to follow the letter of the law nor wanted to allow Chernobyl and its inconveniently lingering consequences to upset its friendly ties with Russia. Scientists were encouraged to abandon research on health effects from Chernobyl and instead to move into different fields; research laboratories were consolidated in remote locations without access to contaminated areas, all effectively pulling the rug from under a community that had successfully contended with international agencies (WHO, IAEA) over establishing a causal link between Chernobyl and thyroid cancer in children—an effect now widely accepted as directly traceable to Chernobyl.[52] This community's success is even more remarkable when we take into account that they fought not only for the interpretation of their data but for the collection of data in the first place. Kuchinskaya argues that "the lack of recognition from the IAEA does affect Belarusian state policies," including "radiation protection measures, Chernobyl-related benefits and compensation, and state support for research institutes and the directions of scientific research in Belarus."[53] In effect, the Belarusian government used the UN agencies' reluctance to support the interpretation of Chernobyl data to justify cutting off data collection altogether: data that might jeopardize its preferred strategy of downplaying the effects of the disaster.

Fukushima

Just as the world was getting ready to commemorate the twenty-fifth anniversary of the Chernobyl disaster, Fukushima hit. After a massive earthquake off the eastern coast of Japan, a huge tsunami disabled the emergency systems at the Fukushima-Daiichi nuclear power plant. Three reactors melted down, and explosions destroyed the reactor buildings. Almost eighty thousand people evacuated, and the disaster continues to this day, as the plant releases radioactive water into the Pacific Ocean.

Unlike Chernobyl, which was easily blamed on a bad design, incompetent workers, and a corrupt system, Japan was a high-tech giant with the world's leading experts in earthquake-resistant engineering, a legendarily disciplined workforce, and an industrial system emulated by nations around the globe. Fukushima shattered the discourse of safe, peaceful nuclear applications. The nuclear order was upset, as the interpretations of the accident's causes filled accident investigation report after investigation report.[54] Were the American reactor designs used at Fukushima different in significant ways? Were they "tainted," and could the design therefore be blamed after all? Were the workers too eager to obey orders instead of prioritizing the plant's safety, supposedly a reflection of Japanese national or corporate culture? Were the ties between the nuclear industry and the nuclear regulators too close to allow for effective industry oversight? International nuclear experts were grasping at straws.

As a direct reaction to the disaster, the Japanese government ordered all nuclear power plants shut down, only to be restarted after a thorough review and restructuring of the entire nuclear industry's management and regulatory regime. And while debates rage over adequate accident compensation, while grassroots groups organize around do-it-yourself radiation meters, and while crowd-sourced contamination maps challenge official narratives, we learn about dilapidated radiation monitoring stations around nuclear plants: clearly, collecting radiation data around a civilian facility had not been a priority.[55] Whoever put measuring posts there never bothered to maintain them. We are assured that food grown in areas affected by the radioactive releases is "safe to eat" while fishing communities along the plant's shoreline are struggling to conserve some sense of identity, and farmers in the path of the Fukushima plume find it impossible to sell their—now diligently monitored and measurably clean—produce.[56] The nuclear order is in disarray: today, discourses once reserved for the effects of nuclear weapons scare residents of nuclear power communities, and medical attention turns to direct and intergenerational consequences of low-dose exposure.

Data collection, once again, is at the heart of this now volatile nuclear order: who is collecting what, from whom, and to what ends? As the social order that used to neatly bifurcate the nuclear world keeps eroding, it is no longer clear what we know, how we know it, and why we would want to know.

Conclusion

Collecting data, then, is critical to the social order that can be maintained, challenged, or newly produced. What we know, how we know it, and why we care to know originate in the way we perceive the nuclear order and at the same time have the capacity to reshape that order. The jury is still out on whether Fukushima will end up being framed as yet another "conquered accident," a regrettable misstep that has ultimately made the nuclear industry safer and the peaceful prospects of clean nuclear energy more reliable, or whether it has dealt the final blow to an already troubled sector that will perhaps survive as a boutique industry, not entirely removable from view until and unless nuclear weapons disappear as well.[57]

What we knew about Hiroshima and *how* we knew about it (that is, data collected, and data interpreted) shaped the way we have ordered our nuclear industries. By reconnecting Hiroshima with Chernobyl (and Fukushima), a long-promoted discourse believed to be stable and secure unraveled. What Chernobyl did for the management overhaul of the Soviet nuclear industry, Fukushima may accomplish for the world, albeit in surprising diversity: Russia seems to have confidently found its path in offering commercial, politics- and accident-free reactors for sale, turn-key ready and (if so desired) built, owned, and operated by the Russian nuclear state corporation Rosatom; France has quietly devised rapid response forces capable to deploy to any French nuclear plant in distress; Britain is embarking on an unprecedented experiment with China (whose financial investment in the Hinkley Point C plant keeps growing) and without the rest of Europe; Germany and Switzerland have committed to a complete nuclear phase-out; and former Soviet satellites in Central and Eastern European emphatically support existing and pursue future nuclear power ambitions, as do China, India, and (at least until very recently) South Korea.

There may be factors involved here that distinguish states with nuclear weapons from those without them in how they order their nuclear world, thereby complicating the boundary discussed here. But curiously enough, at least in the past, there did not have to be an indigenous nuclear weapons program in place to make the "peaceful" discourse operate properly according to the discursive logic I have outlined above. Perhaps it was the mere idea of nuclear weapons and their apocalyptic potential that served as a powerful placeholder in these instances, where the collection of data on harm to human health and the environment was limited to weapons exploding, or weapons facilities spewing poisonous byproducts. Perhaps it was a gradual realization that a nuclear weapons program did not have to be the logical extension of any type of nuclear program.[58] There are also nuances associated with postcolonial history (see chapter 15 in this volume) in many parts of the world that refract a trajectory that I have sketched out here in simple strokes for the purpose of clarity.

But unless and until scientists are allowed to be interested (i.e., receive funding) in collecting data on benign nuclear applications, as they were allowed to study the effects of Hiroshima and Nagasaki, we may have to make do with nuclear imaginaries made in Hollywood.

15

Nuclear Harms and Global Disarmament

Shampa Biswas

There are two ways to lose oneself: walled segregation in the particular or dilution in the "universal." ... My conception of the universal is a universal enriched by all that is particular, a universal enriched by every particular; the deepening and coexistence of all particulars.

—AIME CÉSAIRE, 1956

From States to the Global

Much of the scholarship in international relations more broadly, and security studies more specifically, has been premised on the Westphalian state as the primary unit of world politics, even in the nuclear age. Yet early political realists like Hans Morgenthau and Reinhold Niebuhr understood the profound challenge that the nuclear revolution posed to the state-centricity of the discipline of international relations.[1] If the legitimacy of the state's monopoly on violence rests on its capacity to serve as the guarantor of the kind of security that makes civilized life possible, then the development of thermonuclear weapons that can "mutually assure (absolute) destruction" makes the state's guarantee of national security considerably more precarious.[2] The doctrine of deterrence was one statist effort to respond to this challenge.[3] Making the argument that states are able to control and hold at bay the enormously destructive potential of such weapons through sensible strategy and mutual understanding, deterrence offered a way for states to relegitimize their own authority as wielders of these most potent instruments of death, which, if unleashed, could annihilate their own populations. But it has become increasingly clear even to its most ardent advocates that deterrence is a temporary and imperfect resolution of the dilemma posed by the nuclear revolution, generating a balance that works only as long as there is rationality and predictability in relations among states. This is precisely why concerns about proliferation to states (and nonstate actors) with leaders deemed irrational and unpredictable have reanimated anxieties about the capacity of states to deliver on the security that is the very basis of their legitimacy as states. In other words, the status of the state as the primary vehicle for delivering security in an anarchy replete with thermonuclear weapons remains very much a question with which international relations theorists need to grapple.

Many approaches to nuclear disarmament stall in the face of this persistent hold of the state. The literature on nuclear acquisition (or abstinence) has documented the wide variety of reasons for the pursuit of nuclear weapons by states—security in an anarchic world, national prestige on the world stage, powerful profiting interests within the state—all of which generate deep investments in the continued possession of weapons with such enormous lethal and affective currency.[4] Approaches to nuclear disarmament that rely on the state to take graduated steps toward nuclear zero—reducing arsenals, dealerting weapons, declaring no first-use policies, and so on—are certainly valuable in tamping down the potential for nuclear conflict but fail to dislodge the state's deep investments in the continued possession of weapons that bestow considerable power and prestige. When states derive their interests exclusively from within the logic of stateness—that is, what kinds of decisions make the state (or dominant groups within it) more secure and more powerful at the expense of other states *from which they remain ontologically separate* (and in an always potentially adversarial relationship)—arguments for nuclear disarmament seem to unravel. Can one escape the logic of state centricity by articulating arguments for nuclear disarmament in more globalist terms? What kind of global ethic can inform an approach to nuclear disarmament that does not pit state against state in a competitive cycle that appears impossible to break? How can we rethink the question of "state interests" in a nuclear world?

Using postcolonial theory, this chapter interrogates the conception of "the global" that underlies some of the approaches to nuclear disarmament. I will argue that these approaches to "the global" of global disarmament are either too parochial, generalizing from a particular perspective (generally that of the powerful nuclear states of the world), or tend toward the overly abstract by erasing difference and hierarchy among states and communities. I am interested in asking: How can we develop a conception of the global that can respect the historical specificities of different nuclearizations while developing some notion of a shared universality of nuclear experience? Using postcolonial theorist Edward Said's notion of contrapuntality, I suggest developing a formulation of global nuclear connections that might help enunciate a global disarmament ethic from the perspective of the varied victims of nuclear power. This requires developing a complex conception of "nuclear harms" that broadens the category to include the effects of direct bomb blasts (both atomic bombs and depleted uranium munitions), but also of radioactive fallout, nuclear tests, reactor accidents, work in nuclear mills and factories and uranium mines, and waste storage and disposal. In sum, I make the case for a nuclear disarmament position that rejects speaking in broad universals in favor of developing a relational ethic out of context-specific materialities attentive to power and difference.

I begin by analyzing and critiquing two prominent approaches to global nuclear disarmament—the position articulated by "the gang of four" and the abolitionist perspective informed by Jonathan Schell's writings. I then flesh out the concept of contrapuntality and discuss the conception of "the global" in Edward's Said's writings before using the subsequent section to theorize a global conception of real-time nuclear harms that join the peripheries of the nuclear world. In the following section, I undertake a sympathetic critique of the Humanitarian Consequences Initiative's conception of global nuclear harms. I conclude with a meditation on nuclear harms as forms of slow and unequal violence.

Interrogating "the Global" of Global Disarmament

A central challenge in articulating a global ethic of disarmament is the conceptualization of what constitutes "the global." The global is often articulated in the form of some "universal" experience, value, or concept. Postcolonial theory helps us identify two kinds of problems faced by many such attempts to craft global universalisms. On the one hand are accounts of the global that are simply the generalization of some parochial perspective. These versions draw from the experiences of a particular place to posit a universal public good. This is what we usually characterize as Eurocentricity[5] or what Julian Go refers to as "metrocentricity"—"the generalized analytic practice of Eurocentric universality ... the practice of false universalism: taking a specific parochial or particular experience and assuming it is universal."[6] On the other hand is the tendency for the global to lapse into an abstract universalism, erasing both historical specificity and cultural difference. These accounts posit a singular, unifying value that is presumed to be shared across social groups and cultures. Some formulations of universal human rights or humanitarian principles take this form. Although not necessarily the case, closer interrogation might reveal such abstractions themselves to be more parochial than they might at first appear. Both these forms of globalism are at work in the nuclear politics literature and reveal themselves in different nuclear disarmament positions.

Metrocentricity is quite prevalent in the field of nuclear security. Most of our inherited histories, theories, and perceptions of the bomb have been crafted from the perspective of the "great powers," so that comprehending Third World or non-Western nuclear pursuits poses certain challenges. For instance, despite whatever disagreements there might be among the signatories of the Nuclear Nonproliferation Treaty (NPT) as to the significance of Article 6 in the grand bargain of that treaty,[7] there is no question that the NPT has now conferred a certain degree of legitimacy to the nuclear weapons possessions of the five states that are officially recognized as "Nuclear Weapons States" (NWS) in the treaty.[8] As a result, nuclear pursuits by less powerful states are generally seen as a form of unfortunate mimicry and a profound threat to an otherwise stable international order. This means that arguments for nuclear pursuits by weak states that feel embattled or marginal within the existing international order are rarely accorded legitimacy or even taken seriously on their own terms.[9] Similarly, much of our thinking and imagination on the utility of the bomb comes from theorizations in metropolitan contexts. For instance, much of what we know about if, how, and when deterrence works or about the workings of the stability-instability paradox comes from analyses that pertain to the relationships among the recognized nuclear states, the Cold War superpowers in particular. Thus it is no surprise that proliferation to states that seem (culturally and politically) different and hence appear inscrutable generates enormous anxieties that rarely attach to the nuclear pursuits of the permanent members of the United Nations Security Council (P5).

Some of the new positions on universal nuclear disarmament are premised on this Eurocentric form of globalism. This, for instance, is the position on universal disarmament proffered by the "gang of four," sometimes referred to as "the four horsemen"—two former secretaries of state (George Shultz and Henry Kissinger), one former secretary of defense (William J. Perry), and one former chairman of the Senate Armed Services Committee (Sam Nunn). These well-known cold warriors in the United States, who have together mounted a fairly visible public relations campaign to persuade current leaders and policy makers of the wisdom of moving to global nuclear zero,[10] were at one time fierce defenders of nuclear weapons for the "nuclear club" and many of them architects of nuclear deterrence doctrines that justified the possession of those weapons. The fears that drive their urgent call for disarmament now emerge from the perils of proliferation outside the club—the slow horizontal spread of nuclear weapons to nonnuclear states (as well as its possible diagonal spread to nonstate actors)—agents who, they believe, can no longer be counted on to behave with the requisite rationality necessary for deterrence to function. In other words, the argument of this group is essentially that we need to get to nuclear zero because a deterrence doctrine that worked during the Cold War will obviously fail in the "second nuclear age," when untrustworthy and less rational actors possess or may possess nuclear weapons. The position of the gang of four is certainly much more globalist in its calls for universal disarmament than those who respond to the anxieties of the second nuclear age by explicitly rejecting abolition in favor of arguments for U.S. nuclear primacy.[11] But its universalism nevertheless offers a parochial globalism that rests on certain Eurocentric or Orientalist presuppositions about the dangers of nuclear proliferation to non-European actors.[12] It should be no surprise that in an updated op-ed in the *Wall Street Journal* a couple of years later, these recently converted abolitionists clarified that, despite their commitment to long-term universal disarmament, as long as nuclear weapons existed, the United States needed to "retain a safe, secure and reliable nuclear stockpile primarily to deter a nuclear attack and to reassure our allies through extended deterrence."[13] In other words, in this form of parochial global ethic, the goal of disarmament always recedes in the face of proliferation concerns, in the end becoming largely an abstract goal.

But there is a different kind of abstraction in the positions on nuclear disarmament that articulate the horrors of an absolute weapon that must be abolished for humankind (in the singular) to survive. For instance, Jonathan Schell's powerful and eloquent case for nuclear abolition rests on articulating the horrors of nuclear war, not just for particular states but for humanity as a whole, or indeed, as he titled his best-known work, for "the fate of the earth." Schell describes in excruciating detail the immediate and long-terms effects on humans, society, and the ecosphere of the use of nuclear weapons, weapons that he unflinchingly describes as "radical[ly] evil" instruments of "genocide," "annihilation," and "extinction." The nuclear peril, in Schell's conceptualization, is a global problem that requires global solutions, which, in turn, requires transcending the state-centricity of world politics—or what he calls "the system of sovereignty." This, Schell recognizes, is because the state is inadequate as the problem-solving unit in a nuclear world. In fact, Schell mounts a scathing critique of the state, and, in particular, the formulation of deterrence as a form of "national interest" that risks the annihilation of the Earth and the human species for parochial, narrow needs.[14]

There is no question that Schell is a globalist invested in articulating a global disarmament ethic.[15] He articulates nuclear abolition as an obligation that emerges from both spatial (affecting the entire world) and temporal (affecting unborn generations, while destroying a trust from our ancestors) concerns. Yet a position like his risks slipping into a mode of abstract universalism about which postcolonial theory also teaches us to be cautious. What is missing from Schell's account is both contextual specificity and attentiveness to power. His arguments are bold and expansive in their reach, but his mode of inclusion invites us to imagine a global condition where the differences among different groups pursuing, or affected by, nuclear weapons programs matters little. In doing so, Schell's account erases the very particular uses for nuclear weapons (and power) in particular historical moments, the different desires that motivate nuclear pursuits for different states that are positioned very differently (and unequally) in the world, and the different effects of nuclear weapons production and use as experienced by communities and peoples in different times and places.[16] Perhaps unwittingly in his quest to raise awareness of the urgent global perils of nuclear weapons, Schell's account ends up suggesting that the distribution of vulnerabilities in a nuclear world is democratic, which, as I will argue in a later section, is far from the case. In addition, both the gang of four's and Schell's forms of universalism end up fetishizing nuclear weapons as absolute weapons—as evil incarnate whose powers of destruction are utterly different from any other kinds of weapons—and can inadvertently drive the desire for nuclear weapons.[17]

Contrapuntal Globalism

In place of an abstracted or parochial globalism, I would like to draw from Edward Said to make the case for a different kind of globalism that involves a concrete and sympathetic awareness of the multiple experiences of a cohabited nuclear world. As intellectuals, we all carry, says Said, some "working understanding or sketch of the global system," but it is our "direct encounters with it in one or another specific geography, configuration, or problematic" that shape our political commitments.[18] So, in a sense, we are all formed parochially, but instead of generalizing from that one experience or abstracting away from it, we need to connect that experience, suggests Said, with other distinct but overlapping experiences and worlds and account for the multiple histories that are also distinct but intertwined.

In an interview with Jennifer Wicke and Michael Sprinker, Said rejects the indiscriminate use of the word "internationalism," reiterating the deep roots of processes in a local or national situation despite their location in varied and larger contexts.[19] Similarly, he criticizes the rampant use of the word "human" in much of the universalist discourses on "humanitarian intervention," which, as he points out, is conducted largely by visiting violence on distant humans.[20] While much of Said's work critiques the imperial underpinnings of universalizing claims to power and authority, what he offers in their stead are locally sensitive and context-informed universals. It is important to reiterate here that

Said is not arguing for a reification of the local. As Aamir Mufti points out with respect to Said's work, while the whole can be comprehended only contingently "from one possible location within it or a trajectory through it," "the genuine alternative to [the] universalism of contemporary Eurocentric thought is not a retreat into the local, into so many localities, but rather a *general* account of the play of the particular in the universalizing processes of capitalist-imperial modernity."[21]

The method that Said offers for developing this notion of a universal is "contrapuntality." Contrapuntal readings, Said suggests, are an "attempt at a globalized (not total) description," readings that offer a method for cultivating a "sense of multiple worlds and complex interacting traditions" in order to craft less parochial understandings of global politics.[22] Borrowing from music theory, Said conceptualizes contrapuntal readings as forms of analysis that attempt to arrive at a global understanding by accounting for various unique, distinct, yet interconnected histories and geographies—composing, as it were, not so much a symphony but an "atonal ensemble."[23] Such readings account for the specificity and individuality of multiple experiences: "We must be able to think through and interpret together experiences that are discrepant, each with its particular agenda and pace of development, its own internal formations, its internal coherence and system of external relationships," while remembering that they are all "co-existing and interacting with others."[24] Said is insistent that these histories and experiences are distinct and that none are to be privileged; his plea, however, is not to simply valorize plurality but to theorize a "wholeness" out of them while remaining attentive to power and hierarchy.[25]

If a "postimperial intellectual attitude" that is attentive to global power and hierarchy requires looking at different experiences contrapuntally,[26] this would mean rereading the cultural archive "with a simultaneous awareness both of the metropolitan history that is narrated and of those other histories against which (and together with which) the dominating discourse acts."[27] What would it mean to read the histories of the nuclear bomb much more contrapuntally than we have so far? Since the bomb is so nationalized—revered as a national monument and built through restricted, secretive, state deliberations—many of our existing nuclear histories are primarily in the form of national stories, a large number of which are engaged in the task of figuring out what was going on within the black box of the state in the decision making on whether to acquire, use, or forsake the bomb.[28] While yielding considerable important context-specific information on state decision-making processes, many of these accounts treat the national unit as distinct and largely autonomous. Go argues that contrapuntality helps overcome this problem of "analytic bifurcation" so common in the social sciences—"the ontological and methodological treatment of spaces, places, peoples, and entities as separate rather than related"—often manifesting in disciplines like IR as "methodological nationalism" where the nation-state is both prioritized and separated from its outside.[29] It does so by replacing such epistemic divisions "with a methodological law of connection: sustained examinations of mutual connection across expansive social space."[30]

So, for instance, rejecting a univocal reading that understands the decision to bomb Hiroshima and Nagasaki entirely from the metropolitan perspective of the United States, a contrapuntal reading urges us to not reject that history but read it with and against the other histories of World War II. This would include, most important, histories from the perspective of the Japanese victims of the atomic bombs, as well as histories of Japanese involvement and actions in that war.[31] But it would also include histories from the perspective of the Allies like the British and the French who would go on to mimic U.S. nuclear might as compensation for their own losses as colonial powers.[32] This in turn is related to the history of those colonial subjects who were recruited into that war for or against the Japanese through their own complicated relationships with the Allies, of which some, like India, would go on to build their own nuclear programs as an attempt to recover their dignity in a new postwar world that had demonstrated the awesome force of the atom.[33] Of course, all these histories are in part national stories. But as Vilashini Coopan points out, contrapuntality does not entail the rejection of the national to get to the global. Rather, it conceptualizes the relationship of the national to the global as neither chronological nor entirely oppositional and instead understands their mutual and simultaneous imbrication in ways that can help reconceptualize the national in less bounded, more global forms.[34] I think that this sort of contrapuntal reading begins to offer us a much more complex and global history of complicity in the legacy of nuclear arms proliferation, while remaining attentive to the concrete circumstances of choices and decisions to pursue or forsake the bomb or keep open the paths toward it. In addition, it helps reconfigure and unbound the tightly bounded concept of "national interests" prevalent in dominant accounts of state security. Said asks us to look for these sorts of what he calls "counterpoints" to dominant narratives, to recover "what has been left out" of dominant historical accounts and to do so in a manner that "will not allow conscience to look away or fall asleep."[35] What kinds of nuclear counterpoints might yield a conceptualization of "the global" that is neither abstract nor parochial, while remaining attentive to power and difference in the world? How can we craft a global disarmament ethic that acknowledges the specificities of a coinhabited nuclear world?

A Contrapuntal Reading of Global Nuclear Harms

I would like to suggest that a more useful counterpoint to the metrocentric, state-oriented narratives of nuclear power would be to start from the margins of the nuclear world. This, I believe, would yield a much fuller and more accurate conception of "nuclear harms" that would inform a more robust global disarmament ethic. This is not because narratives from the center are less important or less consequential than experiences from the peripheries, but because, despite the fact that all views are partial, the margins offer us a view that arguably provides a fuller conception of nuclear harms. "Between a modern master and the non-modern slave, one must choose the slave," says postcolonial theorist Ashis Nandy, not because the slave's suffering is superior or the slave is oppressed, but because the slave "represents a higher-order cognition which perforce includes the master as a human, whereas the master's cognition has to exclude the slave except as a 'thing.'"[36] It is from the margins, suggests Said, that a more expansive view of the global is available, "from which to rethink and remake universalist (ethical, political, cultural) claims, thus displacing its assignation as the site of the local."[37] What Said is offering us here, then, is a felt commitment to the concrete and the situated, especially via the lived experiences of those most marginalized by contemporary global politics. What, indeed, would it mean in the nuclear world to "represent all those people and issues that are routinely forgotten or swept under the rug"[38]—to build the global less from state-centric institutions of world politics and more from the spaces where the bodies least protected by state pursuits of nuclear power reside? In other words, where are the margins of the nuclear world? In what kinds of peripheral places can we find the reach of nuclear power and perspectives on that power that help augment the narratives from the center? What kind of universals can we build from those narratives?

Any conception of nuclear harms must, necessarily, begin with the devastation of the atomic bombings of Hiroshima and Nagasaki. The 13-kiloton uranium bomb that the United States dropped on Hiroshima on August 6, 1945, is believed to have killed between 90,000 and 166,000 people in the first four months after the explosion. The U.S. Department of Energy estimated around 200,000 or more dead after five years, while the city of Hiroshima estimated that 237,000 people died directly or indirectly by burns, radiation sickness, and cancer. On August 9, 1945, a 21-kiloton plutonium bomb was dropped on Nagasaki, which is estimated to have killed between 40,000 and 75,000 people immediately after the explosion, that figure rising to 80,000 by the end of 1945.[39] In addition, to grasp the enormity of the damage, one must include the severe injuries caused by the blast and resulting fires, radiation-related sicknesses that developed over the long term, diseases passed on to future generations, psychological effects of the bombing, destruction of both cities and their infrastructure, and the long-term effects on the environment.

The devastation visited on Hiroshima and Nagasaki was immense and profound, so it is entirely appropriate that when we think of nuclear harms, our imaginations are often captured by the spectacular dangers of the use of a nuclear bomb. However, to the extent that the doctrine of deterrence appeared to allay concerns about the use of nuclear weapons, that danger became too distant and too abstract—often depicted as the "unthinkable" horrors of nuclear weapons with fantastical powers whose use should and could be prevented. But if we broadened our reach to think of nuclear weapons not as a fetish commodity with internally generated magical powers but as an "object" that emerges out of a production process[40] and whose institutionalization as an absolute weapon has required a series of human decisions to ensure its potency, we begin to see an entire gamut of insufficiently accounted-for nuclear harms that are not reducible to "nuclear use" as conventionally understood. For example, our focus on the enormous brutality of Hiroshima and Nagasaki as the only historical moment in the "use" of nuclear weapons makes it possible to divert attention away from the 2,056 other nuclear "test" explosions that might well be considered to be "used minibombs."[41] The United States conducted 1,054 of these tests, making it, arguably, the most nuclear-bombed country in the world.[42] From this perspective, the first use of an atomic bomb was the testing of a plutonium device at Trinity, New Mexico, on July 16, 1945, whose contaminated future was contrapuntally conjoined to Nagasaki, where a tested plutonium bomb was dropped less than a month later.[43]

The history of nuclear testing forces us away from a metrocentric formulation of nuclear harms, reminding us of the colonial peripheries on which established nuclear weapons states conducted much of their explosive testing. On April 24, 2014, the Republic of the Marshall Islands filed lawsuits against the nine nuclear-armed states for failing to comply with their obligations under international law to pursue negotiations for universal nuclear disarmament. The attentiveness of the Marshall Islands to the usually ignored Article 6 of the Nuclear Nonproliferation Treaty is, of course, not accidental.[44] From 1946 to 1958 the United States conducted sixty-seven nuclear tests in the Marshall Islands. If their combined explosive power was divided equally over that twelve-year period, it would equal 1.6 Hiroshima-size explosions per day.[45] The point here is not to diminish the scale of destruction wrought in Hiroshima and Nagasaki but to draw attention to the longer history of damage caused by nuclear weapons if one were not to isolate two instances of wartime weapons use.[46]

Similarly, we could expand our category of nuclear harms if we considered the long-term radiological effects of "depleted uranium" munitions—with a radioactive half-life of 4.51 billion years—but that do not quite make it into our category of nuclear weapons. Nina Tannenwald's work has helped popularize the term "nuclear taboo"—the unwillingness of states to use nuclear weapons—which she sees as evidence of successful global norms diffusion.[47] (See also Tannenwald's essay in chapter 16 of this volume.) But the nuclear taboo has not operated to curtail the use of depleted uranium munitions by the United States in Afghanistan, Bosnia, Kosovo, Kuwait, Serbia, Somalia, and Chechnya and in unprecedented quantities during the Iraq War of 2003, whose unfolding effects we continue to witness.[48] Unusually high sickness rates in Vieques, Puerto Rico, brought attention to the use of depleted uranium in military training exercises on the peripheries of U.S. territory.[49] A contrapuntal reading of the history of depleted uranium munitions reveals their origins in the over one billion pounds of nuclear waste generated from U.S. nuclear weapons and nuclear power production—a lingering global effect of the superpower arms race on which metrocentric nuclear histories focus. Depleted uranium munitions are relatively cheap ways for the U.S. Department of Defense and U.S. Department of Energy to hand over some of this waste to arms manufacturers to make weapons that are not taboo to use. They are, in effect, a form of waste management—or rather a way to export nuclear waste, continuing a long history of the disposal of toxic waste in poor countries—albeit in this case through much more directly deadly explosive forms.[50]

If we unravel the nuclear production process more fully, we begin to see harms that begin even earlier and continue into the indefinite future—from uranium mining, to milling, processing, enriching, reprocessing, and separating, and all the way to storing and disposing of nuclear waste—harms that are borne disproportionately by workers who handle nuclear materials, communities that house nuclear sites, and future generations who must live with nuclear waste.[51] Gabrielle Hecht has shown how the shifting designation of "nuclearity," especially to aspects of the nuclear production process furthest removed from actual weapons production, has had profound consequences for what kinds of nuclear effects become legible, what kinds of regulatory apparatuses can be created, and who can claim protections from harms. Starting at the beginning of this production chain, Hecht shows that it can be extremely difficult for workers and communities to both recognize and articulate the particular occupational hazards of uranium mining and seek and receive recognition and redress for its health hazards.[52] The "radioactive colonialism" of Navajo lands and lives for the U.S. nuclear program has now been somewhat well documented and has received some public attention.

After a long period of resistance to acknowledging the health effects of radiation exposure, a standard for acceptable radiation exposure was finally established in 1971, and the Radiation Exposure Compensation Act (RECA) passed in 1990, targeting those suffering from the health effects associated with atmospheric nuclear testing and uranium mining in the United States.[53] But much less is known about the colonial conditions of uranium mining in Africa that helped inaugurate the nuclear age, and it has continued to be difficult for uranium miners in Africa who are not even recognized as nuclear workers, even when they are recognized as fully human, to be legible as nuclear victims.[54] It bears reminding here that the uranium for the U.S. bombs dropped on both Hiroshima and Nagasaki came from Belgian Congo, connecting three continents in a shared toxic history. Shiloh Krupar shows how difficult it is still for workers in decommissioned plutonium-producing factories, where we know a lot more about the medical effects of chronic toxic exposure, to register their claims, including in the United States where there is now a compensatory regime in place.[55] That regime, ironically and contrapuntally, created its compensatory metrics from data on radioactivity exposure studies of Japanese atomic bomb survivors who were victims of the bombs these workers helped create. (See Sonja Schmid's essay in chapter 14 of this volume for a discussion of how the data generated by the Atomic Bomb Casualty Commission, jointly funded by Japan and the United States, helped develop the current international standards for radiation safety and the effects of radioactive exposure.)

The situation at the end of the production chain looks equally grim. Given the enormous challenge the United States has faced in securing appropriate waste disposal sites, a plutonium-production site like Hanford, Washington, is now strewn with levels of nuclear waste that have made it the most contaminated place in North America.[56] Juxtaposing Hanford's history to the history of the plutonium production site Ozersk in Russia, Kate Brown offers a contrapuntal analysis of atomic cities that were connected through their adversarial relations during the Cold War and now share the experience of the human and environmental harms of nuclear contamination.[57] A different kind of contrapuntal analysis links Hanford, where the plutonium for "Fat Man" was produced, to Nagasaki, where that bomb was dropped—two cities linked by their common fates of nuclear harms, albeit in quite different ways.

As Krupar has so brilliantly enumerated, nuclear waste not only lives in leaky barrels and open fuel tanks but also accumulates in soil, water, and the air, in "the crawl spaces of downwind homes," and especially within the bodies of workers.[58] Workers and communities most adversely affected by uranium mining, reactor sitings, nuclear testing, and waste storage are among the poorest, often indigenous, historically colonized populations of the world, revealing something that postcolonial IR scholars have been belaboring for a while—that the so-called long peace of the Cold War, presumably maintained through the Mutual Assured Destruction that nuclear weapons provided—was neither particularly peaceful nor cold from the perspective of these victims of nuclear pursuits. The Cold War was "hot," not just for the victims of many of the superpower proxy wars around the world but also within the territorial boundaries of those superpowers, contaminating large swathes of lands and proliferating countless diseased and broken bodies who are also victims of superpower nuclear might. In other words, a contrapuntal analysis of nuclear harms reveals that the margins of the nuclear world cross-cut the boundaries of states and more traditional North-South geopolitics, to form connections, common interests, and shared perspectives that might inform a more robust disarmament ethic. For example, Sean Malloy in chapter 4 of this volume offers an account of how racially marginalized groups within the U.S. had a much more acute understanding of the colonial racism driving nuclear policy and, by extension, the connections they shared with those harmed by nuclear weapons (and a longer history of colonial violence) overseas.

In a world in which far too many nuclear weapons remain on hair-trigger alert and in a context in which nuclear use remains part of the strategic doctrine of many countries, one should certainly not minimize the dangers of nuclear use. Yet the less visible but much more widespread nuclear harms that I have discussed in this section are a reminder that nuclear weapons are dangerous not just in any possible future use as that "absolute weapon" that nuclear abolitionists rightly frighten us about but also in their *possession*, generating harms in real time. Unraveling the production chain of nuclear objects is also a reminder that the pursuit of nuclear energy, long considered to be benign and sharply distinguished from nuclear weapons in treaties like the NPT, produces its own share of harms, and not just in the spectacular form of reactor accidents such as at Three Mile Island, Chernobyl, and Fukushima that do occasionally catch the world's attention.[59] A contrapuntal analysis allows us to account for these sorts of spatially and temporally intersecting connections between victims of direct bomb blasts (atomic bombs or depleted uranium munitions), victims of fallout, victims of nuclear tests, victims of reactor accidents, nuclear workers, nuclear downwinders, and uranium miners, thus generating a relational global ethic focused on context-specific concrete harms. Without conflating quite distinct experiences, transnational alliances built around such shared nuclear harms can hold accountable nuclear weapons-possessing states and a massive global nuclear industry composed of mining companies, reactor producers, weapons manufacturers, clean-up contractors, and powerful lobbies.

The Humanitarian Consequences Initiative and Global Nuclear Harms

The Humanitarian Consequences Initiative (HCI) is a relatively recent formulation of a global disarmament approach that has gained some traction. HCI approaches its primary goal of nuclear abolition through three related means—shifting from a state-centered, deterrence-focused discourse to consideration of the severe humanitarian consequences of nuclear weapons; framing nuclear weapons as fundamentally inhumane and unlawful; and advocating for a nuclear ban treaty instead of a traditional step-by-step arms control approach.[60] As a result of the work of several activist organizations advocating this approach,[61] on July 7, 2017, roughly two-thirds of the countries at the United Nations adopted the text of "The Treaty on the Prohibition of Nuclear Weapons"—the much sought-after nuclear ban treaty prohibiting all signatories from the possession, production, testing, use, threat of use, transfer, or overseas stationing of nuclear weapons. While none of the nuclear weapons states participated in the deliberations, this ban treaty was, still, a significant accomplishment and demonstration of a bold and unambiguous moral stand against nuclear weapons. The treaty prefaces its approach to nuclear disarmament on "the catastrophic humanitarian consequences that would result from any use of nuclear weapons."[62] In addition to making the case that nuclear weapons violate international law, various publications issued by these organizations elaborate in great detail the enormous material harms that the use of nuclear weapons would inflict on people, societies, and the environment—the direct health effects from the blast, nuclear fallout, heat, and electromagnetic pulse; the impact on the environment from global cooling, ozone depletion, and radioactive waste; and the impact on the economy, agriculture, and development more broadly.[63]

Drawing lessons from previously successful efforts to ban antipersonnel landmines and cluster munitions, HCI is intent on enacting a discursive and normative shift that devalorizes and stigmatizes nuclear weapons.[64] Their attempt at "ideational reframing" of nuclear weapons discourse rejects the dry, technical language of arms control initiatives in favor of mobilizing affect that can generate compassion, shame, and outrage.[65] It does so by articulating a victim-centered global discourse that is focused on nuclear harms that would affect communities across the world. In other words, the HCI's approach to nuclear disarmament takes the broader conception of nuclear harms for which I have argued in this chapter. Yet despite its laudable work in documenting the concrete effects of nuclear weapons use, even the HCI's formulation of "the global" tends toward the abstract in at least two different ways. First, the focus of HCI remains "nuclear use," conventionally understood, even though it understands the harms of that use much more broadly and extensively. Decades after Jonathan Schell's writings, the destructive capacities of nuclear weapons, now in the hands of more states, remain enormous, and this work of reminding the world of their large-scale and long-lasting consequences remains as urgent as ever. But the focus of the HCI, as with Schell, on the future dangers of currently (precariously) restrained weapons diverts attention from the ways that nuclear possession itself has continued to damage communities and people around the world. Second, despite HCI's occasional acknowledgment that poorer states and communities are more vulnerable to nuclear harm and its laudable attempts to highlight the voices of survivors, women, and states from the Global South, the initiative often speaks in too broad strokes about a "global community" in the singular. Laura Considine points out how HCI ends up repeating some of the same clichés that underlie the deterrence discourse from which it wants to distinguish itself—"existential threat, urgent and unprecedented danger, catastrophic and unthinkable consequences"— dangers too profound, too large, and ultimately too abstract in their conceptualizations. Moreover, in centering "humanity" as the object of security, the humanitarian approach makes nuclear weapons appear as "an external affliction imposed on humanity," so that the goal of disarmament becomes to protect a "global us" from a future of nuclear weapons use.[66] Ultimately, formulations of a global we or us are inadequately attentive to power and difference and, in conjuring a global community with pregiven interests in nuclear disarmament, depoliticize what is a profoundly political problem.

I have argued in favor of an approach to global disarmament that centers the context-specific real-time harms of nuclear weapons possession and use and remains focused on the unequal sharing of the burdens of that possession. I have suggested that conceptualizing such harms contrapuntally is a way to generate shared interests in nuclear disarmament, without privileging one particular experience or ignoring relations of power. For instance, the story of Fat Man connects communities in as disparate locations as the mining towns of Congo; areas around Hanford, Washington, and Trinity, New Mexico, in the United States; the testing grounds at Bikini Atoll; and the people of Nagasaki, Japan—each location with its specific history of nuclearization and different experiences of nuclear harm, but arguably providing perspectives on their own nuclear legacies that could be mobilized into shared interests in disarmament. These interests exceed national boundaries, reminding us of the state's incapacity to protect its own citizens from the pursuit of nuclear weapons whose targets are the citizens of a different state from whom they appear ontologically separated. Rather than emphasizing the apocalyptic nature of a nuclear future, which in itself bolsters arguments for retaining weapons with such potent powers for the purposes of deterrence, Harrington argues that arguments for nuclear abolition should be based on the "real-time costs of maintaining a nuclear arsenal" that highlight the threats of nuclear weapons to a state's own land and people and paint an image of nuclear weapons as "dirty, poisonous, and difficult to maintain."[67] The challenge for a global disarmament movement is to go a step further to generate shared interests out of what may appear to be disparate real-time costs of a state's own nuclear possessions—in effect, replacing "filiation" with "affiliation." Said offers us this form of contrapuntal "worlding" as a way to reimagine geography through accounting for the complex connections between imperial and colonial societies.[68] I have tried to show how the margins of both powerful nuclear weapons possessors and their less powerful victims of production, testing, and use are connected through all kinds of nuclear harms, many of which are much more mundane and much less visible than the immediate harms of nuclear weapons use. Assigning responsibility to and demanding accountability from states and corporations invested in nuclear weapons production requires transnational alliances between such marginal groups.

Conclusion: The Slow and Unequal Violence of Nuclear Pursuits

"Slow violence" is the term that Rob Nixon uses to describe "a violence that is dispersed across time and space, an attritional violence that is typically not viewed as violence at all . . . a violence that is neither spectacular nor instantaneous, but rather incremental and accretive, its calamitous repercussions playing out across a range of temporal scales." The distinctiveness of nuclear weapons has usually and rightly been described in spatial terms, in terms of the *scale* of its destructive power. This scale expands outward toward enormous areas of devastation, and inward into cellular mutations within the human body that exposure to radiotoxins causes, overwhelming any state's capacity to contain the damage.[69] But to that scalar distinctiveness of nuclear weapons, one should add the *temporal distinctiveness* of nuclear power, as a form of power whose toxicity plays out across such a vast stretch of time that it even further overwhelms all our existent institutions of accountability.[70] This kind of violence does not register as violence both because it lacks the spectacularity of bomb use and because its effects are borne mostly by the marginal, dispossessed, disposable populations of the world whose legibility as victims of nuclear violence is much harder to establish. But such harms—concrete, particular, material—are real, affecting and connecting vulnerable populations across territorial boundaries.

A grounded universalism, of the sort that Said suggests, is best crafted from the perspective of the marginalized because it is a reminder that while "we" all are vulnerable in a world with nuclear weapons (and we all really are vulnerable despite whatever the states that protect us tell us about the effectiveness of nuclear weapons), the distribution of that vulnerability is not democratic—so that some of "us" have already been harmed by the pursuit of the security promised to all of us, some of "us" with less access to the means of civil defense will be rendered more insecure if the security promised to us via nuclear weapons fails, and some of "us" are already dead or dying so that others can enjoy cheaper and "cleaner" electricity and richer lifestyles. A couple of years back, citing the dangers posed to humanity by global climate change and the continued existence of enormous arsenals of nuclear weapons, the *Bulletin of the Atomic Scientists* moved the hands of the Doomsday Clock two minutes closer to midnight, and then another thirty seconds to account for the election of a U.S. president with little regard for scientific expertise and prone to reckless talk, so that it now stands at 2.5 minutes to midnight. This move implicitly recognizes that while the rush toward nuclear energy reliance may have appeared to stall post-Fukushima, this hesitance cannot be expected to last in a world in which nuclear energy is offered as the panacea for Green development. This is true even more so for countries in the Global South on whom the pressure to "catch up" to the standards of Global North consumerism while minding their carbon footprints is immense.

A heart-wrenching opinion piece in the *New York Times* connected the threat of planetary annihilation posed by *both* nuclear weapons and global climate change—risks that face us all, exposing us all to our death as a species, risks that teach us, says the author, that perhaps the task that looms before us in a futureless world is to learn how to die. But, the author also reminds us, those risks are not distributed evenly, and so while it may be that we should all prepare to die, the ethical demand in learning how to die as a species is for each of us to learn to live in a way that does not ask others to let go of more of their lives, or live with more fear of imminent death. The author recognizes the powerful idiom of the Doomsday Clock but also its built-in problem of universalism—"It puts us all at the same place on the same timepiece. We know, of course, that in the ticking-clock drama of planet Earth, some of us are closer than others to the zero hour. And some have reached it already."[71] What I have urged in this chapter is the need to craft a form of universalism that can account for our common vulnerability in a nuclear world, while remaining attentive to the multiple, disparate, yet interconnected nuclear experiences of that world and, especially, in solidarity with those who have suffered the most from its excesses. Our survival as a species depends on taking stock of these global connections.

16

The Legacy of the Nuclear Taboo in the Twenty-First Century

Nina Tannenwald

SINCE AUGUST 1945, when the United States dropped two nuclear bombs on Japan in the closing days of World War II, no nation has employed nuclear weapons during war. Instead, a more than seventy-year tradition of nonuse of nuclear weapons has arisen. As the introductory chapter noted, nuclear weapons have military, political, economic, and environmental effects and can therefore be "used" in different ways. In this chapter I focus on the military detonation of nuclear weapons during war, or, more precisely, the striking absence of such military use since 1945. Scholars have debated the explanation for this surprising tradition of nonuse, including deterrence, fear of escalation, the lack of military utility of nuclear weapons, the reputational concerns of using such destructive weapons, moral concerns, and sheer luck.[1] These factors have all played a role.

Nevertheless, it is impossible to fully understand the pattern of restraint across more than seventy years without taking into account the rise of a powerful taboo against the first use of nuclear weapons that has developed in the global system. Although this taboo is not a fully robust prohibition, it has stigmatized nuclear weapons as unacceptable weapons of mass destruction. World leaders have recognized its significance. In an important summit statement in November 2010, U.S. president Barack Obama and Indian prime minister Manmohan Singh stated that they "support strengthening the six-decade-old international norm of non-use of nuclear weapons."[2] Without the emergence of this normative stigma since 1945, there might have been more "use."

Today, however, the taboo appears under challenge. Nuclear weapons are being relegitimized in states' security policies. Increased regional tensions in

Europe and Asia are leading to new technological arms races in both nuclear and nonnuclear systems, and security doctrines that renew the salience of nuclear weapons. This chapter evaluates the legacy of the taboo for contemporary world politics and its status particularly in the past fifteen years.[3] How do we assess the historical legacy of efforts to stigmatize nuclear weapons—the sources of such efforts, their consequences, and the future of the nuclear taboo? This is a way of asking about the changing normative status of nuclear weapons.

The Nuclear Taboo

The phrase "nuclear taboo" has come to mean several different things in international politics. First, it may mean a normative prohibition on the first use of nuclear weapons. Second, it may represent a more general antinuclearism, as in the case of Japan, where the phrase is often used to refer to a sort of national allergy to acquiring nuclear weapons. Third, in the Israeli context it refers to Israel's long-standing policy against acknowledging the existence of its nuclear arsenal.[4] Finally, the phrase is sometimes used to refer to a deep-seated opposition to civilian nuclear power in some countries. In this chapter I use nuclear taboo in the first sense: a widespread inhibition on the use of nuclear weapons, stemming from a powerful sense of revulsion associated with such destructive weapons. It is a taboo on use, not on possession, although it increasingly has spillover effects for possession.

The taboo is the *belief about the behavior*, not the behavior (of nonuse) itself. Leaders and publics have come to view avoidance of nuclear use not simply as a rule of prudence but as a taboo, with an explicitly normative aspect—a sense of obligation—attached to it. There is thus an important intersubjective aspect to the nuclear taboo: it is a taboo because people *believe it to be such*. Political and military leaders themselves began to use the term to refer to this normative perception starting in the early 1950s, well before it made any sense to speak of a "tradition" of nonuse. In a meeting in March 1953, for example—only eight years after Hiroshima and Nagasaki—President Dwight D. Eisenhower, concerned about the constraints posed by negative public opinion on the U.S. freedom to use nuclear weapons, urged that "somehow or other the tabu [sic] which surrounds the use of atomic weapons would have to be destroyed."[5] Thus the term taboo captures an important normative and perceptual element that goes beyond simply the notion of tradition.

Nevertheless, the nuclear taboo departs in some ways from the anthropological conception of taboo. It does not totally prohibit the taboo objects: under the terms of the 1968 Nuclear Nonproliferation Treaty (NPT), the five declared nuclear powers (the United States, Russia, France, Britain, and

China) are allowed to possess nuclear weapons temporarily pending complete nuclear disarmament. They also continue to prepare military plans for using nuclear weapons. Thus the taboo is not fully robust, is not an absolute constraint, and can vary with broader international political circumstances.

Until recently, the taboo was only an informal or de facto prohibition. There was no specific international legal ban on the use of nuclear weapons such as exists for, say, chemical and biological weapons. Rather, over time the legitimacy of the use of nuclear weapons declined and the realm of legality was increasingly circumscribed by various arms control agreements (such as nuclear-weapons-free zones).

Nevertheless, in an important development in July 2017, the United Nations adopted for the first time a legal prohibition on nuclear weapons, over the objections of the nuclear powers. As discussed further below, one of the explicit goals of the ban treaty was to codify and strengthen the taboo. The new ban seeks to deepen and extend the international norms against use and possession of nuclear weapons, including for the nuclear powers, thereby making the taboo more "complete." Whether the ban has this hoped-for effect will remain to be seen.

Assessing the strength or status of a norm at any given moment is difficult. More feasible is to look at the direction of trends over time—is the taboo strengthening or weakening relative to some earlier period? To assess or "measure" strengthening or weakening, it is useful to look at discourse, the nuclear policies of states, and the degree of institutionalization of the taboo. The most obvious evidence lies in discourse, that is, the way people talk about nuclear weapons and how this has changed since 1945. Today virtually no one refers to nuclear weapons as "just another weapon." There has been a significant shift in attitudes toward nuclear weapons since 1954 when President Eisenhower declared at a press conference that nuclear weapons should be "used just exactly as you would use a bullet or anything else."[6] No one thinks this way today, when nuclear weapons are widely viewed only as a weapon of last resort. Should world leaders begin to talk as if they think nuclear weapons are usable, that would represent a weakening of the taboo.

A second source of evidence for the taboo lies in the degree to which states downgrade the role of nuclear weapons in their security policy (for example, how heavily they rely on nuclear weapons, their policies about nuclear use, the size of their arsenals, and the buildup of conventional alternatives). Finally, a third source of evidence is the degree to which the taboo is institutionalized, that is, embedded in international law and agreements that restrict freedom of action with respect to nuclear weapons, such as arms control agreements or the new nuclear prohibition treaty. Norms that are codified and institutionalized generally have more staying power than those that are not.

While we still lack a full picture of how the nuclear taboo operates in key countries, over the past decade a growing body of research has investigated the role of the taboo in, among other countries, the United States, Japan, Israel, Russia, Britain, France, and Pakistan.[7]

The Rise of the Nuclear Taboo

No taboo existed in July 1945 when the United States dropped two atomic bombs on Hiroshima and Nagasaki. Although some U.S. officials and atomic scientists privately expressed moral hesitations about using the bomb, for the U.S. military the atomic bomb was simply a bigger blast and a logical continuation of the strategic firebombing with conventional weapons that by spring 1945 had devastated many Japanese cities.[8]

That a taboo emerged was not inevitable. Rather, it emerged as a result of both strategic interests and moral concerns. Its origins lie in policy precedents established in the immediate postwar period, both domestically in the United States and internationally at the United Nations, that marked out atomic weapons as different from conventional weapons. A key development was the UN definition in 1948 of a class of "weapons of mass destruction." This formally linked atomic weapons to previously banned chemical and biological weapons and established a category in which the taboo took root.[9] In addition, gradually increasing knowledge about the consequences of the Japan bombings, including radiation effects, contributed to growing public fear of, and revulsion toward, nuclear weapons. John Hersey's widely disseminated essay on Hiroshima in the *New Yorker* in August 1946, a year after the bombings, contributed to a turning point in American public perceptions of atomic weapons.

Beginning in the 1950s, the taboo was promoted by the efforts of a global grassroots antinuclear weapons movement to stigmatize nuclear weapons and mobilize public opinion in favor of nuclear restraint. As Wakana Mukai's essay in chapter 9 of this volume shows in the case of Japan, the antinuclear movement that swept that country in the 1950s played an indirect but crucial role in influencing the Japanese government's view of nuclear weapons and its ultimate decision to tie the country to nonnuclear policies. Similar movements arose in Europe and the United States to lobby both their governments and at the United Nations. Disarmament diplomacy at the UN also played a role, as did Cold War power politics, as Soviet propaganda efforts sought to sow fears about U.S. atomic weapons. Starting in the 1960s the taboo began to become implicitly institutionalized in multilateral and U.S.-Soviet bilateral and arms control treaties and institutions, including the SALT agreements, the Anti-Ballistic Missile Treaty (1972), and other superpower arms control agreements. This development was driven significantly by U.S. and Soviet leaders' increasing recognition of their shared interest in nonuse in an era of mutual assured destruction.[10] The rise of the taboo may also be associated with the U.S. democratic identity and the general reconstruction of humanitarian norms after 1945.

This brief history points to several key mechanisms behind the rise of the taboo: active efforts by nonnuclear states and civil society to stigmatize nuclear weapons, the role of public opinion, the moral concerns of individual leaders, the iterated behavior of nonuse by nuclear states over time, and the acceptance of the taboo by successive national leaders.

The Legacy of Hiroshima for the Nuclear Taboo

What role did the atomic bombings themselves play in fostering a taboo? There were those—among them Albert Einstein and Robert Oppenheimer—who thought that any use of atomic bombs would be followed by more use.[11] Others, including many atomic scientists such as James Conant, Edward Teller, and Vannevar Bush, as well as Secretary of War Henry Stimson, argued that using the bomb was essential to shocking the world into nonuse and discouraging major war and future use of nuclear weapons. Skeptics might argue that the latter view was merely rationalization after the fact, a desperate effort to salvage some moral and practical benefit from this horrendous event. Alternatively, perhaps the effects of shock and horror might have been achieved with a demonstration shot, as some atomic scientists proposed in 1945, which would have displayed the destructive power of the bomb without killing any civilians. Indeed, even if the bomb had never been used in 1945, because nations engaged in nuclear testing in subsequent years, atmospheric nuclear test explosions might also have demonstrated the power of the bomb. Since nuclear testing and its fallout were major stimuli of the grassroots movement against nuclear weapons that began in the mid-1950s, perhaps the tradition of nonuse could have been achieved without use of the bomb in anger.

It does appear from the historical record, however, that the "demonstration effect" of the use of the bomb on Japan did contribute to the shock, horror, and sense of revulsion that later emerged among the public, as well as to the rise of a taboo and subsequent efforts to control the bomb. One of the major factors that prevented U.S. leaders from resorting to the use of atomic bombs after 1945 was their repeatedly stated concern about the terrible consequences that would arise if they used the bomb again on Asians.[12] A State Department assessment in November 1950 predicted negative consequences of the use of atomic weapons in the Korean War: "A repetition of Hiroshima and Nagasaki [i.e., use on Asian cities] would produce the most damaging reaction."[13] This inhibition would not have existed without a first use on Japan.

The Legacy of the Nuclear Taboo

The rise of a nuclear taboo has had three main effects. First, as noted earlier, the taboo has made it impossible to view nuclear weapons as "just another weapon." This shift in discourse is the single most important legacy of the global movement against nuclear weapons. In chapter 11 of this volume, Holger Nehring illuminates how the antinuclear movement in West Germany contributed to this stigmatization of nuclear weapons. In this case, from the 1960s onward, peace activists—in a country that had been totally destroyed by World War II—drew on the collective memory of both "Hiroshima" and the Holocaust as symbols of massive technological destruction to problematize and oppose Cold War nuclear deployments in Germany. The normative branding of nuclear weapons as "unacceptable" and "inhumane" weapons is strong today and has been actively reinforced in recent years by the campaign of nonnuclear states and civil society to highlight the devastating humanitarian consequences of any use of nuclear weapons. I argue elsewhere that this normative stigma helped to constrain U.S. leaders' resort to use of nuclear weapons in crises during the Cold War and after.[14]

Second, the taboo has reinforced mutual deterrence between nuclear powers; that is, it has helped to undergird and reinforce stable nuclear deterrence. This is especially evident in the history of the U.S.-Soviet nuclear arms control relationship. By embedding deterrence doctrine and practice in a set of regulative and constitutive norms (for example, in various arms control agreements, such as SALT, the Anti-Ballistic Missile Treaty, and the Nuclear Nonproliferation Treaty), it has helped to stabilize the practice of nonuse and legitimized "deterrence" rather than "use" as the appropriate role for the bomb.

Third, at the same time, and more speculatively, the taboo has undermined deterrence between nuclear and nonnuclear states. General Chuck Horner, U.S. commander of the air war in the Gulf War of 1991, said in an interview after the war that the threat to use nuclear weapons against a nonnuclear state was no longer credible.[15] There is significant evidence that this view is widespread today. The fact that nonnuclear states have not been deterred from fighting nuclear-armed states (for example, Vietnam versus the United States, Iraq versus the United States, Afghanistan versus the Soviet Union, and Argentina versus Britain) suggests some empirical support.[16] Indeed, former national security adviser Brent Scowcroft stated in his memoirs that U.S. leaders privately ruled out use of nuclear weapons in response to Iraqi use of chemical weapons during the 1991 Gulf War and that U.S. nuclear threats during that war were bluffs.[17]

However, we lack a complete understanding of the decision making on the nonnuclear side in these cases. New evidence that Iraqi leader Saddam

Hussein believed that a first use of nuclear weapons by the United States was a real possibility in the Gulf War paints a more complex picture.[18] However, his thinking is hard to figure out. He seemed to suffer from every source of misperception in the book, including living in a reality-challenged bubble about how well Iraq was doing in the war. As a brutal leader whose entire career was based on ruthless violence, it is clear he was personally unrestrained by *any* norms—domestic or international—against the use of force or violence. It seems unlikely that someone who was unconstrained by norms himself would believe that a norm of nonuse would operate for others.

Finally, the taboo helps explain additional puzzles: why the legitimacy of making nuclear threats has declined, why even small ("tactical") nuclear weapons are regarded as immoral (the taboo is a prohibition on a whole class of weapons), and why there has been less nuclear proliferation than expected (a taboo reduces the value of nuclear arms).

Nevertheless, the delegitimization of nuclear weapons is incomplete. Although widespread support exists for further stigmatizing such weapons, as the achievement of the ban treaty shows, the general opprobrium is far from universal or complete. The nuclear powers themselves continue to believe firmly in the benefits of retaining their nuclear capabilities. Wider alliance systems such as NATO continue to tout the great value of deterrence and first use as the basis for security, a position that has been revalorized today by Russia's intervention in Ukraine. When President Obama contemplated declaring a no-first-use policy in summer 2016, Japan and other allies under the U.S. nuclear "umbrella" pushed back in alarm.[19] The commitment to the taboo among some of the "new" nuclear powers, such as Pakistan, may be tenuous. Further, thanks to Vladimir Putin, Kim Jong Un, and Donald Trump, nuclear weapons are once again being celebrated as symbols of national power. The continued role of nuclear weapons as a symbol, and even conferrer, of great-power status imposes limits to a fully robust taboo and inhibits the complete delegitimization of nuclear weapons.[20] For the older nuclear powers, nuclear weapons have become a matter of both national identity and habit.

Beyond constraining use and reinforcing deterrence, the taboo also possesses implications for disarmament and the nuclear nonproliferation regime.

The Nuclear Taboo and Disarmament

The spread, strengthening, and internalization of the taboo are widely seen as a step on the route to disarmament, as the campaign for the recent ban treaty suggests. Nevertheless, Western powers have sought to associate the taboo with being a "responsible" nuclear power. The taboo could also become an obstacle to disarmament if the nuclear powers maintain that acceptance of the taboo preserves stable deterrence and therefore justifies their (responsible) possession of nuclear weapons in perpetuity.

In practice, as an ideational phenomenon, the taboo points toward normative, rather than material, strategies for nuclear disarmament. The history of nuclear disarmament efforts suggests that it is politically easier to ban the use of nuclear weapons than to eliminate the weapons themselves. Debates over nuclear disarmament have traditionally bogged down in concerns about "breakout" by one or more states, the technical challenges of verifying disarmament, and stability at low numbers. The negotiations on nuclear disarmament that began under the auspices of the United Nations in the 1950s have proven to be far more effective in contributing to the normative opprobrium against nuclear weapons than in reducing their numbers. The biggest reductions have actually come through unilateral moves by the United States and Russia, not through negotiations (President George H. W. Bush's pledge in September 1991 that the United States would unilaterally reduce its tactical nuclear arsenal spurred a reciprocal response by Soviet leader Mikhail Gorbachev).[21] The UN negotiations to adopt a nuclear weapons ban that concluded in July 2017 are the first multilateral negotiations on nuclear weapons since those over the comprehensive test ban in 1994–1996. However, even the organizers of this recent effort saw the primary impact of the new treaty as further stigmatizing nuclear weapons and strengthening norms against their use and possession, not immediately reducing their numbers.

The Taboo and the Nuclear Nonproliferation Regime

Historically, the nuclear taboo and the nonproliferation norm have been mutually reinforcing. Initially, the difficulty of mastering nuclear technology helped prevent nuclear weapons from spreading quickly in the immediate post–World War II period. This, in turn, bought time for the normative opprobrium regarding nuclear weapons to take hold. The fact that nuclear weapons remained in the hands of a very small number of states in the 1940s and 1950s, combined with an emerging taboo, helped to prevent the normalization of nuclear arms. The stigmatization of nuclear weapons, in turn, facilitated creation of the nonproliferation norm by the mid-1960s. Once created, the 1968 NPT further inhibited the spread of such weapons through normative, legal, and institutional barriers and thus reduced the chances that nuclear weapons might be used. In sum, if nuclear weapons had spread quickly early on, it is much less likely that a taboo on their use would have emerged.

Today the taboo—the sense that nuclear weapons are illegitimate—is fundamental to the future of the nonproliferation regime. A prohibition regime cannot be sustained over the long haul by sheer force, coercion, or physical denial; it requires an internalized belief among its participants that the prohibited item is illegitimate and abhorrent. Further, the NPT's long-term sustainability requires that the prohibition apply equally to all states.

Conversely, a robust nonproliferation norm helps sustain the taboo. If the norm against possession erodes, this may put pressure on the taboo. For example, North Korea's acquisition of nuclear and ballistic missile capabilities over the last fifteen years, partly in violation of the NPT, have enabled a highly risky policy of nuclear threats and brinkmanship that provoked fears of nuclear war on the Korean peninsula. Further, as William Potter has pointed out, "the NPT is not as explicit as one might like in prohibiting the use of nuclear weapons, or even the threat of their use against non-nuclear states."[22] This has led to repeated calls by nonnuclear states for legally binding "negative" security assurances from nuclear weapons states or for a legal ban on nuclear weapons and threatening their use.

Status of the Taboo in the Contemporary Period

Today the taboo appears under challenge, although the picture is mixed. On one hand, as a norm of the international community, the belief that nuclear weapons should not be used remains widely shared. Efforts continue by civil society and nonnuclear states to further delegitimize the weapons. At the same time, growing regional tensions and new technological arms races are once again increasing the salience of nuclear weapons in security policies. Not just the nuclear taboo but the larger nuclear normative order is fraying.

On the positive side, continued, if slow, reductions in numbers of nuclear weapons have reduced the world's arsenals to about 13,890 nuclear warheads, down from about 70,000 at the height of the Cold War in the 1980s. Deployed weapons in Europe have been reduced by more than 97 percent since their peak in the 1970s.[23] The George W. Bush presidency (2001–2009) was a low point for the taboo in recent years, as the administration repudiated key arms control restraints by withdrawing from the 1972 Anti-Ballistic Missile Treaty, proposed development of new "bunker-buster" nuclear weapons, and expanded the circumstances under which nuclear arms could be used. The United States would rely on nuclear weapons to deter or respond to nonnuclear threats, including use of chemical or biological weapons, even against countries that adhered to the NPT.[24] Russian and Indian nuclear doctrine closely paralleled this evolution of U.S. thinking.

After President Barack Obama took office in January 2009, by contrast, U.S. nuclear policies were more supportive of the taboo. Obama elevated disarmament to a moral commitment. In his important speech in Prague in April 2009, he outlined his vision of a nuclear-free world, stating, "As the only nuclear power to have used a nuclear weapon, the United States has a moral responsibility to act [to pursue disarmament]." This was followed shortly by the New START Treaty, under which the United States and Russia agreed to reduce their strategic-warhead deployments by nearly a third and their launchers by half.

Perhaps even more important for the taboo than the reductions in numbers were the shifts in thinking about nuclear use. The Obama administration's nuclear posture review (NPR), released in April 2010, substantially narrowed the conditions under which the United States would use nuclear weapons. It ruled out their use against nonnuclear countries that adhere to the NPT or in response to chemical and biological attacks. While maintaining a first-use option, it limited the role of U.S. nuclear weapons to deterring "nuclear attack on the United States, our allies and our partners." For the first time ever, the nuclear posture review explicitly addressed the value of the taboo, declaring that "it is in the US interest and that of all other nations that the nearly 65-year record of nuclear non-use be extended forever."[25] In an interview, Obama described his policy as part of a broader effort to edge the world toward making nuclear weapons obsolete and to create incentives for countries to give up any nuclear ambitions.[26]

The Obama administration also increased the practice of public "taboo talk"—explicit reference to the tradition or norm of nonuse and the obligation to uphold it. U.S. officials began to regularly use the phrase about extending the record of nonuse "forever" in their speeches.[27] In May 2016 Defense Secretary Ash Carter pushed back publicly against Russian president Vladimir Putin's nuclear saber rattling, saying that it "raises troubling questions about Russia's leaders' commitment to strategic stability, their respect for norms against the use of nuclear weapons, and whether they respect the profound caution that nuclear-age leaders showed with regard to brandishing nuclear weapons."[28] These statements serve as valuable public affirmations of the importance of nonuse. Likewise, the historic visits to Hiroshima by Secretary of State John Kerry and President Obama in spring 2016 were important symbolic pilgrimages to remind the world of the catastrophic destructive power of nuclear weapons and the need to do everything possible to ensure that they are never used again.[29]

In contrast, there is little evidence that President Donald J. Trump shares this kind of commitment to the taboo. During his campaign for the White House in 2016, Trump suggested that Japan and South Korea might need nuclear weapons, before reversing himself in the face of criticism from across the political spectrum.[30] Once in the White House in January 2017, Trump stated he wanted to vastly increase the U.S. nuclear arsenal, which he described during the campaign as in "terrible shape."[31] Reflecting Trump's grandiose desire to have the biggest "nuclear button," the Trump administration's *Nuclear Posture Review*, released in February 2018, represented a giant leap backward for the taboo.[32] It embraced the outdated view that nuclear superiority matters. It betrayed a deep skepticism that North Korean or Russian leaders are rational enough to be deterred by the 6,550 weapons of the still-massive U.S. nuclear arsenal that could catapult both countries back to the Stone Age. The report called for maintaining a robust nuclear stockpile and for expanding the "flexibility and range" of U.S. nuclear weapons at the cost of over $1 trillion. This includes the development of new "low-yield" nuclear weapons and acceptance of more ways to use them, including widening the rules on using them first. This could include responding to large-scale cyberattacks with nuclear weapons, an option previous U.S. presidents rejected. U.S. pursuit of smaller, more discriminate warheads that are less destructive may reduce inhibitions on using them.

Nevertheless, Trump's most direct effect on the taboo was to dramatically change the discourse surrounding nuclear weapons. Trump's exchange of bellicose nuclear rhetoric with North Korean leader Kim Jong Un risked dangerously normalizing the possibility of a nuclear first strike. In August and September 2017 his impulsive and reckless wielding of threats to rain down "fire and fury like the world has never seen" and to "totally destroy" North Korea significantly escalated tensions on the Korean peninsula, raising the risk of miscalculation and inadvertent nuclear war.[33] Trump's hints of preventive nuclear war against the North Korean regime undermined decades of shared understandings about both mutual nuclear deterrence and the taboo.

Equally troubling, some opinion surveys in the United States suggest that the taboo is weakening among the American public. Recent survey experiments have found that a significant portion of the American public would support a nuclear strike against an enemy that attacked the United States with conventional weapons or to save the lives of U.S. troops. In one finding, 60 percent of Americans would support a nuclear attack on Iran that would kill two million civilians, if it prevented an invasion that might kill twenty thousand American soldiers.[34] This suggests that American opinion today would not pose a significant constraint should U.S. leaders desire to use nuclear weapons. While these findings are incomplete, they are disturbing nonetheless.[35] They are independent of the Trump effect, since this research was conducted before his administration. If the American public's antipathy to nuclear use is indeed waning today, this eliminates what has been, historically, an important source of restraint.

Beyond the United States

Trump's seeming indifference to existing norms of nonuse, nonproliferation, and disarmament contributes to a broader fraying of the nuclear normative order, in which the taboo appears to be weakening. Today nuclear weapons are being relegitimized in states' security policies. Especially troubling is the renewed salience of nuclear weapons in the NATO-Russia confrontation along with a frightening new rhetoric of nuclear use. Russia, aware of its conventional military inferiority vis-à-vis NATO, has talked openly about putting nuclear weapons on alert during the Crimea operation, has deployed nuclear-capable missiles to Kaliningrad, and has even made nuclear threats against NATO member states.[36] NATO is responding by strengthening its deterrent and promoting its plans for ballistic missile defenses, which only continues the cycle.[37] Igor Ivanov, a former Russian foreign minister who now runs a Russian government think tank, said in March 2016 that "the risk of confrontation with the use of nuclear weapons in Europe is higher than in the 1980s."[38] Former U.S. secretary of defense William J. Perry has been airing similar concerns.[39]

The lowered threshold for use is also reflected in some of the nuclear-armed states' nuclear doctrines. Doctrines are the set of ideas about how nuclear weapons would be used to achieve outcomes. The doctrines of several countries today increase the salience of nuclear weapons in security policy, blur the line between nuclear and conventional weapons, and emphasize "early" use. For example, analysts debate whether Russia plans to rely on a so-called "escalate to de-escalate" strategy—a limited nuclear strike involving a few low-yield nuclear weapons in response to large-scale aggression with conventional weapons by NATO. The goal would be to frighten the United States into ending the conflict on terms favorable to Moscow. (Russia, for its part, believes that it is the United States that has lowered the bar for nuclear use.)[40] China, in contrast, has maintained a no-first-use policy since it exploded its first nuclear bomb in 1964. It has repeatedly reaffirmed that it would not use nuclear weapons against nonnuclear states or in nuclear-weapons-free zones.[41] China maintains a nuclear retaliatory capability based on a relatively small force and a second-strike posture.[42] It continues to modernize its nuclear arsenal while maintaining that it is primarily for defensive purposes.

Whether the taboo operates in the "new" nuclear states may be the most pressing question. If one factor strengthening the taboo in a state is a long period of nonuse, then the taboo will be inherently less powerful for the new nuclear states. India, after shocking the world with its nuclear weapons tests in May 1998, announced in August 1999 that it was adopting a no-first-use policy and pledged it would never use nuclear weapons against nonnuclear states. In

2003, however, India modified its doctrine to allow use of nuclear weapons to respond to chemical and biological attacks, thus emulating a policy that had been adopted by the United States.[43] Like China, India has resisted concepts of deterrence that rely on nuclear war-fighting capabilities and counterforce targeting. Yet if it moves toward multiple-warhead missiles, then this strategic restraint will disappear.[44] Indeed, India already appears to be in a state of doctrinal drift away from its "credible minimum deterrent" posture, and some analysts suggest that it may move away from its no-first-use doctrine.[45] Most recently, India joined the other nuclear powers in skipping the nuclear ban negotiations while insisting that it supports a verifiable disarmament convention negotiated in the consensus-based Conference on Disarmament.[46]

In contrast, Pakistan's highly risky posture of "asymmetric escalation" threatens early use of battlefield nuclear weapons if hostilities erupt in Kashmir.[47] Pakistan's military strategy relies on nuclear weapons to offset India's conventional superiority. In recent years Pakistan, irritated by the 2008 U.S.-India deal on civil nuclear cooperation, has been steadily expanding its nuclear arsenal, increasing the number of warheads, stockpiling weapons-grade nuclear material, and expanding plutonium production facilities.[48] Not surprisingly, Pakistan rejected India's proposal to sign a bilateral no-first-use agreement after conducting its own nuclear tests in 1998. Pakistan's development and testing of nuclear-capable short-range missiles is widely viewed as a destabilizing and potentially dangerous development—and a striking reversal of trends since the end of the Cold War of phasing out tactical or battlefield nuclear weapons. Since such weapons are regarded as more "usable," it suggests that Pakistan would seriously contemplate use on the battlefield in the event of a military invasion by India. Pakistan has pledged no-first-use against non-nuclear states but has not ruled out first use against a nuclear-armed aggressor, such as India.[49]

Both India and Pakistan are examples of "new" nuclear states with doctrines and postures that increase the risk of destabilizing dynamics and arms racing in the region. Their doctrines either are "ambiguous about how to address crucial deterrence related issues" or demonstrate "a clear mismatch between the security challenges faced by [the] state and the kind of role it assigns to nuclear weapons."[50] Because of unresolved tensions over Kashmir between these two nuclear-armed states, the risk of nuclear use is increasing in South Asia.

North Korea appears to be an intriguing case for the taboo. On one hand, North Korean leaders' penchant for threatening preemptive strikes suggests that they think nuclear weapons are usable. North Korean leader Kim Jong Un has accelerated the nuclear weapons program with a torrent of bomb and ballistic missile tests, threatening South Korea and the United States with a "nuclear sword of justice."[51] Along with Russia and Pakistan, North Korea likely believes that nuclear weapons are a legitimate means to deter and counter a conventional threat, a retreat from the view that nuclear weapons should be used only to deter other nuclear weapons.

On the other hand, it has become increasingly clear that North Korea's goal is to become accepted—like India—as a "normal" nuclear power. This means embracing the ostensible norms of "responsible" nuclear powers, including nonproliferation, disarmament and the nuclear taboo. In a statement released on April 20, 2018, in the run-up to a first-ever meeting with South Korean president Moon Jae-in, Kim Jong Un stated, "We will never use nuclear weapons unless there is a nuclear threat or nuclear provocation to our country." He added that North Korea would not transfer nuclear weapons or nuclear technology, and that "the suspension of nuclear testing is an important process for global disarmament."[52] While it is unclear how serious these statements are, they are nevertheless a striking demonstration of North Korea's effort to normalize its nuclear status by publicly embracing key norms of the global nuclear order. Still, the penchant for erratic behavior on the part of both Trump and Kim makes for a worrisome combination in the event of increasing tension over North Korea's nuclear program.

Finally, Iran presents a different kind of case. Although Iran is not a nuclear power, its prior pursuit of nuclear weapons and its vitriolic rhetoric against Israel certainly raise concerns about whether Iranian leaders hold the taboo. Yet they have stated at various times that nuclear weapons are "un-Islamic."[53] The country's supreme leader, Ayatollah Ali Khamenei, issued a fatwa in 2004 describing the use of nuclear weapons as immoral. In a subsequent sermon, he declared that "developing, producing or stockpiling nuclear weapons is forbidden under Islam."[54] In 2008 he repeated this after a meeting with the head of the International Atomic Energy Agency, Mohammed El Baradei.[55]

We need not take the Iranians' words at face value, of course. But as Fareed Zakaria has pointed out, "it seems odd for a regime that derives its legitimacy from its fidelity to Islam to declare constantly that these weapons are un-Islamic" if it intends to acquire or use them.[56] As a strategy of disarmament diplomacy and domestic norm internalization, the West might hold Iranian leaders to these statements. It is worth noting that no other head of state ever declared publicly that nuclear weapons are, say, "un-Christian," "un-Jewish," or "un-Hindu."

From Nonuse to Nonpossession: The Humanitarian Consequences Campaign and the New Nuclear Ban Treaty

In the middle of this normative fraying comes the latest effort to strengthen the taboo. On July 7, 2017, the United Nations adopted the first-ever treaty imposing a total ban on nuclear weapons. This Nuclear Prohibition Treaty outlaws all aspects of nuclear weapons, including their use and threat of use, testing, development, possession, sharing and stationing in a different country. It provides a pathway for countries with nuclear weapons to join and destroy their nuclear arsenals. One hundred twenty-two nations—all nonnuclear—voted to adopt the treaty. Only the Netherlands voted against, and Singapore abstained. It will enter into force when fifty states have ratified it. As of this writing, twenty-six have.

The ban campaign continued the historical pattern of nuclear stigmatization in which nonnuclear states and activists, often aided by the United Nations, push forward the nuclear taboo. The ban effort was largely boycotted by the nuclear-armed states and their allies, who correctly perceived it as an effort to delegitimize nuclear deterrence.[57] The Obama administration lobbied its allies against it. U.S. officials warned of dire consequences if it were adopted, arguing that it would undermine existing nonproliferation and arms-control efforts and that it "aims to delegitimize the concept of nuclear deterrence upon which many US allies and partners depend."[58] The Trump administration has largely continued the Obama administration's policy of opposition to the treaty, although it expresses more hostility to the ban activists themselves.

The ban treaty was the outcome of a seven-year campaign on the part of nonnuclear states and civil society to further delegitimize nuclear weapons.[59] By now, many reports, commissions, and studies have called for the delegitimization or devaluing of nuclear weapons.[60] It is not a new idea. The nuclear powers themselves endorsed it in the 2010 Action Plan of the NPT, where they committed in principle to devalue nuclear weapons, framed as steps to "further diminish the role and significance of nuclear weapons in all military and security concepts, doctrines and politics."[61] The United States made slight changes in doctrine in this direction but, on balance, the nuclear powers have taken few steps to implement this in practice.

Frustrated by this situation and by the overall slow pace of disarmament, at the NPT review conference in 2010 key states with strong support of civil society launched a new campaign to push the delegitimization project forward by highlighting the devastating humanitarian consequences of nuclear use. Led eventually by Austria, Brazil, Ireland, Mexico, South Africa, and New Zealand, the campaign built on the humanitarian concerns of the grassroots antinuclear movements of the 1950s but made a more explicit effort to link antinuclear activism to the framework of international humanitarian law. (Interestingly, both Brazil and South Africa at one point had active nuclear weapons programs.) Campaigners warned how using even a small number of nuclear weapons could kill millions of people in nonnuclear countries through radioactive fallout, drops in temperature, and large-scale crop failures leading to famine. In highlighting the devastating medical, environmental, and economic effects of nuclear war, the campaign challenged the identities of the nuclear-armed countries as "civilized."

Drawing on the playbook of earlier efforts to ban landmines and cluster bombs, the campaign sought to reframe the debate around nuclear weapons by shifting it from a security to a humanitarian framing.[62] It sought to create a tension, especially for the three democracies of the United States, Britain, and France, between the values they assign to nuclear weapons and their self-identity as upholders of international law and humanitarian values.[63] The more radical elements moved the focus of the campaign to a ban treaty. At conferences in Oslo in 2013 and in Mexico and Vienna in 2014, and through the Open-Ended Working Group (OEWG) at the United Nations in 2016, the campaign successfully mobilized support of a majority of states for a legal ban on nuclear weapons. In December 2016, the General Assembly voted 113–35 in favor of holding treaty negotiations, despite objections from the United States, Russia, Britain, and France.[64] All NATO allies except for the Netherlands opposed negotiations (the Dutch parliament voted to require the government to participate in the negotiations).[65] China, India, Pakistan, Japan, and South Korea abstained.

The goal of the ban treaty was to declare nuclear weapons illegal, just as chemical and biological weapons are, and thereby strengthen the international norms against use and possession of nuclear weapons. The participation of the nuclear powers was not needed for this. Indeed, the strategy was explicitly to leave them out, so that they could not hold up action as on ratification of the Comprehensive Test Ban Treaty, which has yet to come into force. (A voluntary testing moratorium has been in place since 1996, contributing to the creation of a widely shared de facto norm against nuclear explosive testing; North Korea had flouted this but has shown recent interest in supporting the no-testing norm.) The nuclear-armed states are certainly needed in order to physically eliminate nuclear weapons, and to negotiate a detailed nuclear weapons convention that might follow, but they are not needed in order to take the initial step of declaring nuclear weapons illegal. As one advocate put it, "You cannot wait for the smokers to institute a smoking ban."[66]

For activists, the ban campaign is an explicit effort "to codify under international law the 'nuclear taboo' or moral imperative not to use nuclear weapons" and to eliminate the legal asymmetry of the NPT.[67] If nuclear weapons are declared illegal, they "become a collective international liability rather than an individual national asset."[68] The hope is that this will foster a domestic political debate about nuclear weapons, especially in the democratic nuclear weapons states.

The United States and other nuclear powers immediately announced that they are not bound by any treaty they did not join; therefore, by retaining nuclear weapons, they are not outside the law.[69] Even so, a legal ban introduces new political challenges for the United States and other nuclear-armed nations. The treaty's prohibition on threats of nuclear weapons use directly challenges deterrence policies. It will likely complicate policy options for U.S. allies under the U.S. nuclear umbrella, who are accountable to their parliaments and civil societies. It may also have implications for where the United States can base its overseas nuclear weapons, and where its nuclear-armed ships and submarines can navigate. Admittedly, it is less clear what effect the ban treaty will have on Russia and China. Notably, no members of Russian or Chinese civil society attended the ban negotiations.

The ban treaty may not result in the physical destruction of nuclear weapons any time soon, but it forces a renewed discourse of nonuse and nonpossession and puts the nuclear powers on the defensive about the humanitarian consequences of their nuclear weapons.

Looking to the Future

The nuclear taboo, while widely supported, has also always been incomplete. The United States, as the leading democracy, the most powerful nuclear-armed state, and the only country to have ever used nuclear weapons in war, has played a leading role in the creation of the taboo. At the same time, U.S. leaders have also firmly resisted turning the taboo into a legally binding commitment, because it would undermine deterrence. They prefer the de facto norm. The contested nature of the ban treaty captures this tension and also the current limits to strengthening the taboo. The United States remains central to the future of the taboo. Today, renewed major power rivalry, bellicose nuclear rhetoric, fading memories of Hiroshima, and increasing reliance on nuclear weapons in nuclear states' military doctrines are weakening the taboo. The possessors of nuclear weapons are themselves the ones whose policies are most eroding the taboo.

Nevertheless, despite downward pressure on the taboo, the belief that nuclear weapons should not be used continues to be widely shared. Most of the rest of the world was alarmed by President Trump's nuclear brinkmanship. The key drivers of nuclear stigmatization remain the coalition of nonnuclear states and antinuclear movements. For more than seven decades they have castigated nuclear weapons as inhumane, while using the United Nations and other forums to call for disarmament and strengthened legal restraints on use of nuclear weapons. Yet the absence of a widespread grassroots antinuclear movement today (as existed in the 1950s or 1980s), combined with a possibly waning public antipathy to nuclear weapons, eliminates an important source of restraint historically. Today the taboo may be an increasingly elite phenomenon—that is, held primarily by elites in government and the military, and perhaps in some segments of society. Reasons for this are unclear and warrant further research, but they may be connected to the general downward pressure on norms of restraint exerted by the perceived need to fight the global "war on terror."

Most difficult to know is how robust the taboo is in the face of strategic pressures. Unfortunately, the current political climate of heightened nuclear tensions makes this question all too timely. The Trump era has increased awareness that the restraints on nuclear use by a U.S. president are less robust than previously thought. The revival of nuclear brinkmanship makes clear that the nonuse of nuclear weapons continues to depend disproportionately on the steadiness of individual leaders who are guided by both norms and rationality.[70]

In the face of increasing geopolitical tensions and technological challenges, for the taboo to be sustained, leaders need to undertake active measures to reaffirm it. Beyond measures to deal with the underlying strategic tensions, this would include strong public statements from world leaders about the value of the taboo ("taboo talk"), ratification of the Comprehensive Test Ban Treaty, reduction of the role of nuclear weapons in security policies, and education to enhance public knowledge about the effects of nuclear weapons. Finally, efforts to institutionalize the taboo should be supported. Rather than castigating the ban treaty, the nuclear powers must find a way to engage with its goals even if they do not intend to join any time soon. One important measure would be for the other nuclear powers to join China and India in adopting "no first use" policies.[71] As a first step in this direction, leaders should establish a dialogue about the conditions under which a first use of nuclear weapons would be morally acceptable.[72]

The nuclear taboo has survived for more than seventy years. We should do everything possible to make sure it survives forever.

17

History and the Unanswered Questions of the Nuclear Age

REFLECTIONS ON ASSUMPTIONS, UNCERTAINTY, AND METHOD IN NUCLEAR STUDIES

Francis J. Gavin

HOW MUCH DO WE KNOW about nuclear weapons, foreign policy, and international relations? We have been living with the bomb for eight decades and have expended an extraordinary amount of intellectual and institutional capital in an effort to understand why states do or do not seek nuclear weapons, how they deploy these weapons to achieve their aims in the world, and how and in what ways the weapons influence state decisions about war and peace. This chapter will contend that our scholarly legacy is mixed. While much has been learned, there remain deep and often bitter divides, not only over the answers to key questions but over the assumptions and methods that frame our work.

Furthermore, these issues are not simply a concern of the academy. Nuclear studies are an area where policy makers and scholars have long been intertwined, sometimes enthusiastically, at other times warily, but often with great consequence. Acknowledging this relationship is especially important today, as new nuclear crises emerge and international consensus on the nuclear order dissolves. The United States, the prime driver of nuclear dynamics since 1945, currently finds itself at an important crossroads, pulled in two different, mutually exclusive directions, between disarmament and deterrence. Nuclear studies can and should play a role in these debates, though only after we acknowledge our own struggles to make sense of the bomb and its consequences.

This chapter will revisit the core questions that have animated nuclear studies from the beginning, while laying out the challenges that have prevented us from achieving consensus. One overarching issue, however, hangs over all our research on nuclear weapons. The core question driving all our work, whether we recognize it or not, is why nuclear weapons have not been used since 1945. In essence, we've been trying to write a history of something that never happened.[1] This question, which is the taproot of all our other queries, is hard, if not impossible, to answer with full confidence. To an extent we rarely acknowledge, the very nature of the nuclear revolution makes certainty elusive. Acknowledging this epistemological challenge, however, may help provide the humility and perspective necessary to generate insight and craft better policies.

What have been the intellectual contributions of the nuclear studies community? On the one hand, we are fortunate to be in the midst of what has been called a renaissance in nuclear studies, within both political science and international history.[2] The passage of time, the opening of new archives, and the deployment of new methods have all contributed greatly to our understanding.[3] Let me provide three important examples. First, in the past decade, scholars from around the world have exploited new sources to help us understand nuclear decision making in a wide variety of states. The list of new national nuclear histories includes Brazil, Japan, Israel, Romania, West Germany, Sweden, Italy, Iran, South Korea, and Pakistan, among others.[4] This has led to a second crucial development—a deeper, more nuanced understanding of "nuclear proliferation." In the past, states were coded as either nuclear or nonnuclear in a binary way. This new scholarship, however, has called into question whether this is simply an either/or question. Terms like "recessed deterrent," "threshold state," "nuclear reversal," "latency," "hedging," and "opacity" reveal what might be thought of as a spectrum of nuclear outcomes that are historically and politically short of a full-blown survivable nuclear deterrent.[5] The notion of who is "nuclear" and what that means is more complex than we had understood. Finally, we have a greater sense of the lengths the United States has gone to, with both foe and friend, in order to slow, halt, and reverse the rise of new independent weapons states.[6] This work has gone far in undermining the so-called grand bargain conventional wisdom surrounding the nuclear nonproliferation regime, by highlighting the willingness of two bitter Cold War enemies to collude in preventing proliferation.[7]

Work on these and other subjects has been impressive, and more is being produced all the time. Yet I sometimes fear we have achieved less than we might have hoped and, in some senses, are spinning our wheels. I see two reasons for this less than ideal outcome. The first has to do with what questions scholars are asking. Much of the research assumes the most important questions—the core issues on which our assumptions rest and on which we build out work—have already been answered, when in fact they have not.[8] Second, steep, but often unrecognized, methodological challenges prevent us from getting good answers. This includes not only the disciplinary gaps between both history and political science and theoretical, qualitative, formal, and quantitative divides within the international relations subfield; more important, as I will explain, it also includes challenges in the very nature of how we study and think about nuclear weapons.[9]

As a scholar who interacts with both the history and international relations fields, I want to use this opportunity for reflection. Frustratingly, I will not offer answers, but only more questions. My goal is not to offer anything new but to suggest that we might gain much by revisiting old questions, challenging the unstated assumptions that undergird our research and scholarship, and thinking more deeply about how we, in the broader nuclear studies community, do our work.

Writing the History That Never (Thank God) Happened

There is a tension between historical work and the demands of both international relations theory and policy.[10] Most people study nuclear questions for the understandable reason that they want to know what makes for good policy, and what lessons the past can provide for the present and the future. Good historians, however, embrace uncertainty, context, and the nongeneralizable. This is, understandably, a deeply disappointing and unsatisfying answer for policy makers and many social scientists. Why study the past if we can't learn direct lessons that can be applied to current, vexing policy situations? This frustration is especially acute on military issues and the grave matter of war and peace. Mistakes in this realm have the most terrible human consequences, and we are eager to have all the knowledge and wisdom possible to avoid disaster.

Perhaps even more frustrating is that historians traffic in ironies. War and military competition are rife with dilemmas and puzzles. For example, we obviously understand that modern conflict is horrific. Of course, we also understand that war can be a necessary evil. And in a terrible irony, war and military competition have played a large role in the extraordinary economic, political, social, and technological progress the so-called Western world has achieved in the past few centuries. There is hardly a political practice, a beloved technology, or an improved norm—from the rise of finance capitalism and greater wealth, to the navigation and transportation revolution, to modern medicine, to representative democracy and efficient bureaucracy, to civil rights for African Americans and women—that cannot be traced to, if not war, then military and international political competition. This helps explain why historians are often humble, crusty, and ironic (in both their scholarship and their demeanor). We hate war. But we understand that what the distinguished scholar William McNeill called "the pursuit of power" has created a remarkable, lasting legacy.[11]

The ironies and uncertainties with regards to nuclear weapons are, if anything, far greater than in other areas of conflict and military competition. Thermonuclear weapons are especially monstrous, potentially civilization-ending weapons. Yet we intuit that it is the very destructiveness of the weapons that has prevented the recurrence of great power war since 1945. Great power land wars had been the scourge of Eurasia, killing tens of millions on the battlefield and tens of millions more through disease and political upheaval, for thirty-one years before the United States dropped atomic weapons on Hiroshima and Nagasaki. Seventy plus years ago, most responsible people expected a third world war to follow the first and second, with consequences far worse than those. We are all around today because that war never came, and, to misuse a title from a famous Paul Fussell essay, it has led many people to proclaim, "Thank God for the atom bomb."[12]

Did nuclear weapons prevent World War III, and do these weapons have the intended effect of stabilizing world politics by making great power war unthinkable? This potent notion is the foundation of what we have come to call nuclear deterrence, and much of our thinking about nuclear weapons is centered on the concept. A large part of U.S. national security strategy has been driven for well over a half century by the idea that an attack on the United States or its allies might elicit a nuclear response, even if our adversary did not use nuclear weapons first. We have so come to take this posture for granted that we have long since forgotten, in the context of American history, how novel it was or what the United States had to do to implement it.

Think about it for a moment—from its founding until 1950, the United States entered no permanent peacetime alliances, was almost completely demobilized during peacetime, and pursued strategies that allowed it to be hit first and mobilize slowly and massively to win wars of attrition. This strategy allowed for powerful civilian control over the military and strong legislative oversight over the executive branch in matters of war and peace, while remaining relatively isolated from world affairs.[13] The thermonuclear revolution, and the strategies the United States adopted to deal with it, demanded permanent alliances, forward military deployments, and an often preemptive military strategy that left enormous discretion in the hands of battlefield commanders, permanently shifting the power to make war away from Congress to the president.[14] Do we fully understand this story, this extraordinary break from our past?

Again, this strategy is premised on the idea that deterrence—the promise of awful retribution if we are attacked—kept the United States relatively safe and the world relatively stable for decades. Most important, it is widely believed that it prevented thermonuclear war.[15] But do we know this to be true? How can we be sure that thermonuclear weapons, and the deterrence that flowed from them, maintained peace and stability?

The problem is that we are trying to understand something that, thank God, never happened, and we hope will never happen—a thermonuclear war. We have an almost impossible time understanding the causes for things that did happen—as many unresolved arguments over what caused the First World War demonstrate.[16] Trying to understand why something did not happen is a methodological nightmare: a situation that eludes a definitive answer from even our most powerful and sophisticated social science methods. While the idea of nuclear deterrence is intuitively compelling, one can imagine other explanations for the relative peace and stability of world affairs after 1945. As I discuss later in this chapter, there are compelling alternative explanations, because deterrence involves explaining something that did not occur.

Why does this epistemological point matter, especially to those interested in the hard realities of nuclear policy? There are two crucial trends shaping the nuclear world, pulling in different directions. The first is the disarmament movement, which is animated by the idea that the world should move toward eliminating nuclear weapons altogether. This aspiration was officially endorsed by no less than President Barack Obama in his Prague speech in 2009, though presidents ranging from Harry Truman to Ronald Reagan also at times shared this goal. On the other hand, nuclear weapons are playing an increasing role in world politics. We all know about the tense negotiations over Iran's nuclear ambitions and the challenges generated by North Korea's burgeoning weapons program. Less well-known is the significant expansion and modernization of the nuclear programs of Russia, China, and Pakistan. The United States is also committed to a $350 billion nuclear modernization program over the next decade.

One strand moves the world toward delegitimizing and eventually eliminating nuclear weapons; the other strand pulls in the opposite direction, highlighting the importance to states of nuclear weapons for achieving national security and foreign policy objectives. Which is correct? These worldviews, and the policies that flow from them, center around if and how nuclear deterrence works and whether it is responsible for the absence of great power war since 1945. These questions, of course, are hard, if not impossible, to answer with certainty and must be explored with both rigor and humility.

And, of course, the right approach to the disarmament versus deterrence debate also turns on a number of other important questions from our past, questions where answers are as elusive as they are consequential. There are a number of puzzles I wrestle with as a historian of the nuclear age, but I want to focus on four of them. Debating and thinking about them are not only important in and of themselves but also help us assess contemporary and future nuclear dilemmas and choices. They cut to the fundamental questions surrounding nuclear weapons, deterrence, peace, and stability.

Revisiting the Core Questions

Many would protest that revisiting the core questions would be a waste of time. Wouldn't it be more profitable to spend time on new issues? Think of the recent quantitative work on nuclear crisis dynamics, leadership experiences, or the forward deployment of nuclear and nonnuclear forces and their influence on extended deterrence and proliferation.[17] Other profitable areas of research are opening up all the time. For example, we are witnessing large global investments in civilian nuclear energy around the globe.[18] Will this lead to more weaponization? I am sure we can all think of good, medium-range questions worth asking. These new questions and issues, it might be argued, are where we should focus our scholarly efforts.

The problem is that many of the small and medium issues build on these larger questions that we believe, quite wrongly, are settled. This goes beyond the question of whether we know whether and how nuclear deterrence works and whether the nuclear revolution prevented great power war. We take for granted other core concepts and phenomena that are, in fact, highly contestable upon further examination. Some of the foundational concepts that are less solid but that we assume include the following:

- that there is a universally shared definition of strategic stability (there were wide variations in how it was understood) and that the superpowers sought it (they did not);
- that there is a meaningful and easy distinction between deterrence and compellence (the historical record reveals there is not);
- that arms control always leads to political stability and is about the weapons, not underlying political questions (the ABM/SALT decision led to deep political problems in the United States, the Soviet Union, and Western Europe that *increased* political tensions);
- that security dilemma dynamics drove the arms race; and
- that the decision to go nuclear lies largely in the hands of the potential proliferator (U.S. nuclear nonproliferation efforts have been a, if not *the*, key variable).

This is not to say these concepts, theories, and arguments are wrong or cannot provide great insight into nuclear dynamics; they can and do. We just should force ourselves to revisit and challenge such claims.

There are four big questions in particular that I am interested in and believe there is great benefit to wrestling with. How dangerous have nuclear weapons made world politics? How does nuclear deterrence work, and can nuclear weapons be used to achieve other political goals? What determines whether a state decides to pursue nuclear weapons? Once it possesses these weapons, what is the ideal number to have, and what are the best strategies to employ them? There are no doubt other core questions, and I do not have certain answers for any of them. I do think it is of great benefit, however, to revisit them in an honest and thorough way.

How Close Did We Come to a Thermonuclear Conflict during the Cold War?

Did nuclear weapons create the so-called long peace between otherwise bitter adversaries, the Soviet Union and the United States, during the Cold War? The belief that they did is widely held and informs much of our understanding of nuclear deterrence. And if nuclear weapons prevented a war that would have occurred otherwise, can we infer that nuclear deterrence can likewise prevent wars at other times, in other regions, and in other circumstances? Once again, we are trying to explain a "nonevent," yet many of our theories rely implicitly on calculations and probabilities about how close we came to nuclear war.

There are at least three ways to look at this: First, through the course of the whole Cold War, did nuclear weapons and the strategies the superpowers employed make great power war and a nuclear exchange more or less likely? Second, how did nuclear weapons, and the risk of nuclear war, affect state behavior during sharp political crises? Did nuclear weapons make it easier or harder to exit crises without a risk of war? And third, how high were the risks of an unintentional nuclear launch or a nuclear accident?

On this last question, nuclear weapons clearly had contradictory effects. Writ large, the fear and horrors of thermonuclear war no doubt gave both Soviet and American leaders pause, both during stable times and in crises. That said, one could not read this history without some feeling of terror. Eric Schlosser's *Command and Control* joins the works of scholars such as Scott Sagan and others in highlighting the mistakes, accidents, and near misses that plagued nuclear management.[19] It is frightening to read documents on both sides of the Cold War during the Berlin crises from 1958 to 1961, the Cuban Missile Crisis in 1962, or the set of challenges during 1983 and NATO's Able Archer exercise.

Perhaps more important, the most significant and dangerous crises of the Cold War were generated by the very existence of nuclear weapons. In other words, if one tried the counterfactual of a world without nuclear weapons, the

Cuban Missile Crisis makes no sense. Even the crises over West Berlin are nuclear to their core, if they were, as we now believe, initiated by the Soviet Union to express its anger over the United States moving to arm the West German *Bundeswehr* with nuclear weapons. It is hard to create the counterfactual where the crises over Euromissiles in the late 1970s and the Soviet fear of a NATO nuclear first strike occur in a nonnuclear world. Could it be that in a nonnuclear Cold War, the United States and the Soviet Union, and NATO and the Warsaw Pact, balance each other perfectly, grudgingly accept each other's sphere of influence, and avoid major crises? Who knows? But it is a scenario worth thinking about.

What this means is that the simple notion laid out by John Lewis Gaddis, Kenneth Waltz, Robert Jervis, and John Mearsheimer—that nuclear weapons generated stability between the superpowers—is certainly open to question. On the other hand, the bitter ideological and geopolitical rivalry did not lead to nuclear or even conventional war between the superpowers. What role did nuclear weapons play in either making the world safer, more dangerous, or both? Given that this historical experience forms the foundation for our thinking on deterrence, it would be well worth encouraging younger scholars to revisit the role of nuclear weapons during the Cold War.

Nuclear Weapons: What Are They Good For?

Many argue that nuclear weapons are good for only one thing: deterrence, or preventing states from challenging the global status quo. In theory, this allows nuclear weapons to keep the peace.

The historical record reveals, however, that one person's deterrence may be another's compellence. In other words, nuclear-armed states have issued deterrent threats that most likely appeared aggressively *coercive* to their target. During the dangerous crises between 1958 and 1961, was Khrushchev trying to compel the Western powers to leave West Berlin or deter the United States from supporting West Germany's nuclearization? Or both? Did the U.S. threat to use its superior nuclear strength to protect West Berlin, an isolated and conventionally indefensible outpost deep within enemy territory, constitute a reasonable definition of deterrence? The distinction between deterrence, which is stabilizing, and compellence, which is not, was often in the eye of the beholder.

Nuclear deterrence is not always peace inducing. Some believe strategic nuclear deterrence allows and even encourages military conflict at lower levels. Furthermore, since the use of nuclear weapons is *incredible* in almost any circumstance, a reckless leader can take advantage of a more responsible nuclear state to make gains through nuclear threats. Furthermore, states do not always view deterrence as an unalloyed good. One imagines that China deeply resents a status quo, buttressed by American nuclear deterrence, that prevents it from exercising what it believes is its legitimate claims to Taiwan (claims it likely would have long since exercised in a nonnuclear world). One reason the United States goes to such great lengths to limit nuclear proliferation is that it does not like being deterred by others. As a state with overwhelming conventional military, economic, and soft-power advantages, it has shown that it will do whatever it can to prevent its freedom of action from being limited by the nuclear deterrent efforts of others.

On the other side of the coin, if the use of nuclear weapons becomes increasingly unthinkable, is even their role as a deterrent undermined? After the Cuban Missile Crisis, one senses that few leaders in the Soviet Union or the United States could imagine *any* political circumstance where they would use nuclear weapons, even as both developed military strategies predicated on increasing the credibility of the threat to use them. Since the Cold War, this skepticism has only increased. While it may not rise to the level of a taboo, it is hard to dispute that there is a powerful norm against their use.[20]

Why Do States Pursue Nuclear Weapons, and Why Do So Few States Possess Them?

Our world is far less nuclearized than was predicted fifty years ago. If nuclear deterrence is so powerful, if nuclear weapons guarantee a state's sovereignty and security, it seems puzzling that there are currently fewer than ten nuclear-armed states.

We have many powerful explanations for this lower than expected number.[21] There are arguments about capacity and technology—building a weapons program was beyond the technological or organizational capabilities of the states that most wanted them, especially in an age where sanctions and export controls were becoming more prevalent and the global supply of nuclear materials less easily accessed. There are ideational and normative arguments—nuclear weapons were increasingly seen as ineffective or immoral or both, even in the rough-and-tumble world of international politics. Related are institutional arguments, as the Nuclear Nonproliferation Treaty added other arrangements like the London Suppliers Group and strengthened organizations like the International Atomic Energy Agency to become an increasingly effective regime. There are arguments about a state's political system, orientation, and leadership types that were more prone to acquire nuclear weapons, as well as how a state positioned itself in the global economic order. Finally, there are the traditional security arguments. Some argued that, in many cases, nuclear weapons were not needed to generate state security, whereas others argued that the vigorous nonproliferation efforts of others, especially the United States, kept the number of nuclear weapons states lower than expected. Perhaps, one might respond, the lower numbers are not a puzzle at all, and nuclear weapons are less appealing, provide fewer benefits and expose more vulnerabilities, or are more difficult to develop and deploy than some of our theories expect.

In certain circles in Washington, Geneva, Vienna, and elsewhere, there is no puzzle. A slower than anticipated rate of nuclear proliferation has simply been a function of the effectiveness of the NPT. As such, all efforts should be focused on strengthening and reinforcing the regime, and implementing the so-called grand bargain whereby the nuclear powers move more quickly toward their promise of disarmament.

There are several issues with that interpretation. The first is that many policy makers and analysts were skeptical the NPT could work. Even beyond the obvious (and, many thought, unsustainable) hypocrisy that allowed a few states to possess nuclear weapons when others could not, when in the past had any treaty prevented the spread of powerful military technologies? Nuclear weapons possessed qualities that were bound to be appealing to a government: their powerful deterrent effects practically guaranteed, for the first time in history, that a state could maintain its sovereignty, independence, and freedom from conquest. Regardless of any treaty, how reasonable was it to expect states to eschew a technology that accorded protection, power, and prestige?

There were further reasons to question the durability of the NPT. The Nixon administration was notably unenthusiastic about a treaty negotiated by the Johnson administration and did little to encourage states to sign and ratify it.[22] Furthermore, the sense that the bipolar international system was giving way to a more multipolar system led observers to anticipate that middle powers (countries like Italy, Japan, Sweden, and Yugoslavia) would acquire the bomb. Finally, the acute energy crisis, marked by dramatically rising oil prices, increased the appeal of civilian nuclear energy programs. The NPT, which recognized the right of states to build a robust civilian nuclear architecture, was woefully inadequate to regulate those who used this path to pursue nuclear weapons. Much of the 1970s saw efforts by international organizations like the London Suppliers Group and domestic policies in the United States to close the gaping loopholes between civilian and military programs left by the NPT.[23]

And, in fact, there were more nuclear proliferation pressures than we once thought. Australia, Italy, and Japan, it appears, may have used signing the treaty (but not ratifying it) as an opportunity to reconsider the weapons option.[24] Other countries, from Argentina and Brazil to South Korea and

Taiwan, explored nuclear weapons. An intense nuclear rivalry commenced in South Asia.

Still, if you told someone in 1968 that over fifty years later the number of nuclear weapons states would remain in the single digits, they would have been both surprised and grateful. Why—especially given the rough circumstances in the decade following the NPT—did so few states acquire and deploy nuclear weapons?

Again, we don't fully know the answers, and we have many opinions that demand consideration. There is one interesting surprise in the historical record, however. The United States has expended as much effort to keep its friends and allies—countries ranging from West Germany to Japan, South Korea, Australia, Sweden, Italy, and Taiwan—nonnuclear as it has to keep its adversaries nonnuclear. And it was quite willing to work against its friends and with its major adversary, the Soviet Union, to achieve this end.

How Much Is Enough?

In other words, what are the force and strategy requirements for nuclear deterrence? Are they different from the requirements for (re)assuring allies? Can a state achieve meaningful nuclear superiority, and, if so, what are the supposed benefits of achieving such primacy?

This is a complex question, but during the Cold War there were two leading views within the United States. Many of the academic and think-tank analysts—renowned thinkers like Bernard Brodie, Robert Jervis, and Kenneth Waltz—believed that once a state possessed survivable forces—in other words, enough nuclear weapons that even after an attack on them they could inflict unacceptable damage on the enemy—there was really no point building more forces.[25] Strategic stability was achieved, and building a larger or more accurate strategic nuclear force, or spending money on missile defenses, was a waste.

Many American decision makers did not seem to accept this logic. From the beginning of the atomic age and accelerating from the early 1950s to the mid-1960s, the United States actively pursued nuclear supremacy. We once thought that by the late 1960s, U.S. decision makers had abandoned what many strategists saw as either a pointless or a destabilizing pursuit and accepted mutual vulnerability and strategic stability. These views appeared to be enshrined in the ABM and SALT treaties of 1972 and the SALT II treaty of 1979. Even here, however, there is a puzzle. Concurrent with signing these treaties limiting the *number* of strategic nuclear weapons, the United States undertook massive investments in strategic nuclear weapons and associated programs that sought (and appeared to achieve) massive *qualitative* superiority over the Soviet Union. Instead of seeking more and larger bombs, the United States invested in faster, more accurate, stealthier nuclear forces, a posture that likely looked quite menacing and flew in the face of strategic stability. The United States developed and deployed multibillion-dollar programs—the Trident D-5, the Peacekeeper, the B-1 and B-2, cruise missiles and the Pershing II, upgrades to C3-I, missile defense, and massive investments in antisubmarine warfare and sub silencing—in what appeared to be an effort to (re)achieve nuclear superiority. What did American decision makers think they were getting for this massive investment, for these counterforce systems that arguably *undermined* strategic stability, and did they get what they sought?

There is, by the way, limited, but revealing, evidence that the Soviet side understood that the Americans were trying to acquire *meaningful* superiority in the 1970s and 1980s, based on capabilities that the Soviet Union possessed neither the technology nor the economic resources to match, and it worried them. It is an interesting contrast to what appears to be a much different attitude in China today, where despite an increasingly vigorous foreign policy based on an impressive economic and technological base, leaders seem relatively sanguine about being on the short end of the nuclear balance with the United States.

This whole story is in many ways puzzling. On the one hand, both superpowers sought to limit quantitative arms races, while also acknowledging the increasing incredibility of any use of nuclear weapons. On the other, they pursued weapons that undermined stability and acted or reacted as if one could obtain meaningful political benefit from nuclear superiority far short of a first strike. What was going on here? Were the superpowers simply hedging? Were they purposively pursuing a form of arms racing, similar to Andrew Marshall's notion of competitive strategies, to expose the adversary's weaknesses and force them to put scarce resources into expensive weapons systems?[26] And how much of this experience "travels," given that, at least to this point, China does not seem to have pursued similar policies? There is much we don't know, and this is an area scholars should be encouraged to explore.

How Do We Answer These Questions?

There are obviously many other big questions we can revisit with profit, and other ways of framing them. Yet we are limited not only by what questions we ask: I have become convinced we face barriers—often unrecognized—to developing better insight into nuclear dynamics. I count at least four: identifying the appropriate method; properly accounting for chronology, perspective, and belief; recognizing the interconnectedness between nuclear dynamics and larger political questions; and morality and judgment.

Challenge One: Method

The reason we are interested in a variety of questions surrounding nuclear dynamics—especially why states do or not acquire nuclear weapons and what factors influence that decision—emerge from one great concern: How do we ensure nuclear weapons are never detonated again? A conclusive answer, however, has eluded us. As I have suggested, it is obviously challenging to come up with causal explanations for something that did not happen. That said, there are at least three competing hypotheses.

First is the well-known concept of nuclear deterrence. The argument here is simple, familiar, and powerful: nuclear weapons are horrific, and launching them, intentionally or otherwise, would be catastrophic. That very characteristic of the weapon, however, makes their use unlikely. There is no political goal worth the cost of a nuclear war. Most realists and many American strategists embrace this view and believe this explains why there have been no nuclear wars since 1945.

Second, there are those who argue that we have avoided nuclear use through sheer luck, which we would be foolish to count on lasting. These analysts point to the dangerous crises, the near misses, the accidents, and even the Schellingesque competitions in risk taking that almost led to nuclear use in the past and are bound to lead to disaster at some point in the future. Nuclear weapons can even create dangers where none existed before: it is hard to imagine the dangers of a third world war over Soviet forces in Cuba or the jurisdictional status of West Berlin in a nonnuclear world. Some observers with this viewpoint challenge whether deterrence was ever as robust as advocates claim (and, even if it was robust, point out that it has to work 100 percent of the time forever if we are to put our confidence in it). Others see nuclear deterrence as uniquely associated with the Cold War rivalry between the Soviet Union and the United States, and not as relevant to the post–Cold War world of regional conflicts, middle-sized powers, so-called rogue states, and nonstate actors. Furthermore, many fear that the faith in the overwhelming power of in nuclear deterrence lulls policy makers into false and dangerous overconfidence that makes war more, not less, likely.

Third, there are those who think factors that have nothing to do with nuclear weapons explain the absence of world war since 1945. Shifting demographic patterns, globalization, and the changing nature of power have made conquest far less appealing than in the past. Land is no longer a source of power—states aim to be Singapore, not Kazakhstan—and ethnic and national differences make occupation far costlier now than during the imperial age. Others see norms against war and violence as playing a key role. While the nuclear revolution may have given states pause in the first few decades of the

Cold War, since at least the 1970s, nuclear weapons have been largely irrelevant to explaining what matters in international politics.

What does this mean for how we study these questions? Which framework is best? How we think about specific issues—our attitudes toward disarmament, for example, or proliferation writ large, or specific cases, like Iran's nuclear program—emerges directly from these largely unprovable hypotheses about the influence of nuclear weapons on world politics. I am on record as challenging how helpful some of the most cutting-edge social science methods, like statistics, can be when the n is nine, two, or zero. When there is a large n, the data sets are, to put it mildly, horrifying to a historian. How one defines (codes), for example, nuclear crises or deals with the selection effects inherent in any question surrounding nuclear deterrence are formidable challenges that have not been handled impressively in the international relations literature. Formal models can illuminate tradeoffs and highlight strategic calculations under ideal conditions, but they forgo most context and interconnectedness.

That said, it is not clear that qualitative methods offer much more than theory and interpretations that are hard, if not impossible, to test against the empirical record. Nuclear policy is shrouded in secrecy and evidence is hard to come by. Even when evidence exists, there is often a gap between what policy makers say and do, which is especially perplexing when studying nonoccurrences. (See, for example, Alex Wellerstein's excellent analysis in chapter 3 of this volume highlighting President Harry S. Truman's confusing and even contradictory statements about nuclear weapons, their uses, and his decision to authorize the attacks on Hiroshima and Nagasaki.) There is an even deeper issue: if the nuclear revolution did have a transformative effect on world politics, presumably there are few appropriate lessons or models from pre-1945 history that can help us make sense of nuclear dynamics. In other words, unless one is careful, reasoning from historical analogies may impede rather than explain what is driving the issues we care about.

Challenge Two: Chronology, Perspectives, and Beliefs

Certain periods are marked by clear beginnings and endings. The First World War began weeks after the assassination of Austria-Hungary's archduke, Franz Ferdinand, by state-supported Serbian terrorists and ended a little over four years later when Germany surrendered to the Entente powers in November 1918. For other events, the beginning and the end are open to debate: Did the Cold War begin in 1949, 1946, or even as early as 1917? Did it end when Mikhail Gorbachev took power, after the surprising Reykjavik conference in 1986, or when the Soviet Union collapsed?

It is far easier to assess and analyze an event or phenomenon that exists within explicit temporal bounds. We know when the nuclear age began, but we have no idea when, if ever, it will end, so we don't know where we are in the story or how it will turn out. We must guard against outcome bias—things are much clearer in the rear-view mirror of history than in the rainstorm in the night that is the future through the front windshield. (See Srinath Raghavan's excellent insights on this issue regarding the history of India's nuclear weapons program in chapter 8.)

Periodization is different depending on the actor. The Cold War and nuclear dynamics were interconnected in the nuclear relationship between the Soviet Union and the United States; less so for France and Great Britain. For other actors, the Cold War was of far less or even no significance, even if their nuclear decision making took place during the Cold War. There is a move within international history to look at the 1970s, and even the 1960s, as being distinct from the Cold War, with global forces outside of the bipolar conflict driving important issues (even, according to Daniel Sargent's book, between the superpowers).[27]

Furthermore, it is likely that the influence of nuclear weapons on international relations evolves and changes over time, similar to the systems effects process so well described by Robert Jervis.[28] Pardon the pun, but we are studying a moving target: attitudes and policies about nuclear weapons have changed quite a bit over the past seventy years and will continue to shift, and these changes will interact within both national and international political processes and culture to produce an ever-changing set of realities.

Finally, much of what has evolved over time are ideas and beliefs about nuclear weapons. This makes our task even harder: ideational and normative factors are far more elusive than material or structural factors. How does one identify an idea, how it is generated and circulated, and when and how it matters? Ideas diverge among different groups, both within a society and between states. Epistemic communities—especially in the field of arms control—often hold ideas across national borders. How do we assess their influence, especially as they evolve over time?

The so-called wizards of Armageddon, the RAND strategists of the early nuclear age, had powerful and important ideas about how policy makers should think about nuclear weapons. Bruce Kuklick suggests that these ideas had far less influence on policy—on what actually happened—than we once thought.[29] Even if they did matter, they emerged from a certain time and place. Thomas Schelling developed many of his ideas about nuclear dynamics during the crises over Berlin and Cuba from 1958 to 1962. In retrospect, many aspects of the history of this period were bizarre and sui generis. Should that influence how we assess the theories that emerged from this experience—something David Holloway has termed "frozen theories"?[30]

Challenge Three: Interconnectedness of Issues

Nuclear studies often suffers from a certain narrowness, as if nuclear weapons can be studied as a thing alone, separate from the other great forces in politics and history. There is little doubt these weapons profoundly altered international affairs. But nuclear weapons are still tools of statecraft and must be understood within particular national and international contexts, related to a state's goals and the realities of international relations.

Let me give you an example. In the early and mid-1950s NATO embraced a military strategy—pushed by the Eisenhower administration—that called for the early and massive use of nuclear weapons. It was clearly a preemptive strategy, seeking to blunt the adversary's ability to use its nuclear weapons before a conflict began, and, as is often the case with preemptive, counterforce strategies, produced both huge target lists and a great deal of predelegated authority to use nuclear weapons. This was what David Rosenberg labeled the "origins of overkill," and it has often been interpreted as the (especially U.S.) military's love of weapons and offensive strategies.[31] In other words, this massive buildup of nuclear weapons, combined with hair-raising plans to use them early and massively, was seen as a terrifying mix of bureaucratic and organizational politics combined with ideology.

But does that really tell the full story? It turns out that in the early and middle 1950s, NATO and especially the United States were wrestling with the incredibly complicated issue of defending Western Europe while dealing with the politics of the German question. Western Europe could not really be defended without a meaningful economic and military contribution from the nascent Federal Republic of Germany. Yet rearming Germans so soon after the horrors of the Second World War was, to say the least, deeply problematic. The West Germans, for their part, had to be given something in order to sign on to the Western Alliance—powerful neutral instincts and incentives existed within the German political system. The ideal outcome—a West Germany that was fully aligned with the West, contributing its ample economic and conventional military capabilities to the defense of Europe, but not possessing its own nuclear weapons (an outcome that neither the Soviets nor the Western European allies would allow) presented a difficult challenge. For their part, the West Germans would (understandably) not sign on to a military strategy that saw NATO thrown back to France after a Soviet invasion, turning its territory into a nuclear battlefield. West Germany had to be defended in Eastern Europe and the Soviet Union if it was to sign on to contributing conventional forces but eschewing its own nuclear weapons. In other words, the political realities of the German question—and not strictly military preferences—demanded a preemptive nuclear strategy, which in order to work required predelegation.[32] As an aside, to get the French to go along with all this, the United States found itself reluctantly underwriting France's disastrous policies in Southeast Asia. The political logic driving the military strategy is often overlooked.

The point is that it makes no sense to look at NATO nuclear strategy, or proliferation dynamics, or whatever question we are interested in, in a vacuum. Nuclear weapons matter quite a bit, and they may push international politics to new limits. But they don't make politics irrelevant or secondary.

Challenge Four: Morality and Judgment

Scholarship, especially in the social sciences, seeks objectivity. We tell ourselves we want to know why things happened in the past and what will happen in the future, without interjecting our own prejudices and hoped-for outcomes in our analysis. This is a noble but typically unreachable objective when studying war and peace, and especially when exploring nuclear dynamics. At some level, we study nuclear dynamics because there is an outcome we all desperately want to avoid. This tends to make us, as a community, passionate about our views. Passion can be a good thing, but it can also hinder our efforts to be as objective as we might be. Nuclear studies often drifts into an area closer to advocacy than scholarship.

Think about how many within nuclear studies simply assume arms control is always and everywhere a good thing. An unimpeachable belief in the strategy and arms-control community is that SALT and SALT II were unalloyed goods, the cornerstone of strategic stability. There is an alternative view. Negative reactions within the United States poisoned foreign policy debates and gave rise to neoconservatism.[33] The Soviet military was furious as well, which may have led to the deployment of SS-20 missiles.[34] The SALT agreements inspired great mistrust and unhappiness among many of America's European allies, and the deployment of the SS-20s generated a crisis in NATO.[35] These efforts to establish strategic stability, it could be argued, perversely helped undermine détente by the late 1970s.[36] Might the enormous political capital expended on the SALT negotiations between the Russians and Americans have been more productively spent on other issues? Long-held moral judgments prevent this kind of counterintuitive insight.

More broadly, consider the deterrence versus disarmament debate. Advocates on both sides share a similar hope of avoiding thermonuclear war. Each side tends to belittle the views of the other. Neither side—for reasons mentioned above—can prove its argument is right, yet neither tends to acknowledge its own uncertainty or demonstrate the humility that is usually the product of trying to understand difficult questions. We have seen this in the recent debate within the United States over the nuclear deal with Iran, where, with a few exceptions, opponents have laid out the issues in the most stark, binary terms, neither side acknowledging that the other may have a point or two. Both sides want the same thing, share the same moral vision—a world without nuclear war—but have strongly held, opposing views on how to get there. There are important and thoughtful efforts to balance between the moral horrors of nuclear use and the potential benefits of nuclear deterrence.[37] This balance, however, eludes most of our debates and discussion.

Conclusion

I have no answer to any of these challenges, or the others that burden our efforts. Some are inherent to intellectual inquiry, especially historical work, while others are unique to nuclear studies. I can fully understand why the plea for epistemological modesty on such critical questions would be vexing to social scientists and policy makers alike. But I do think we should confront these challenges and assumptions explicitly, undertake a rigorous stock taking and comparison of the hypotheses we have generated, and work together to find more effective methods to produce more definitive insights into these extraordinarily consequential issues.

Why is this necessary? If for no other reason than that the important policy choices faced in Washington and abroad emerge from beliefs—often implicit and uninterrogated—about these questions. Given the broad range of paths that policy makers confront—from eliminating nuclear weapons or recognizing their centrality to world politics and American national security policy—the ideas driving these options matter. There is no more important, more consequential issue facing U.S. policy makers. Generating answers to the scholarly questions I posed would go a long way toward helping us navigate the nuclear choices we have in front of us.

NOTES

Chapter 1. Introduction: Hiroshima's Legacies

1. Gar Alperovitz, *The Decision to Use the Atomic Bomb and the Architecture of an American Myth* (New York: Knopf, 1995); Robert Jay Lifton and Greg Mitchell, *Hiroshima in America: Fifty Years of Denial* (New York: Putnam's, 1995); Ronald Takaki, *Hiroshima: Why America Dropped the Atomic Bomb* (Boston: Little, Brown, 1995); Robert P. Newman, *Truman and the Hiroshima Cult* (East Lansing: Michigan State University Press, 1995); Kai Bird and Lawrence Lifschultz, eds., *Hiroshima's Shadow* (Stony Creek, CT: Pamphleteer's, 1998); Michael J. Hogan, ed., *Hiroshima in History and Memory* (Cambridge: Cambridge University Press, 1996). There are, of course, dozens if not hundreds more titles one could reference.

2. See Martin Harwit, *An Exhibit Denied: Lobbying the History of Enola Gay* (New York: Copernicus, 1996); and Philip Nobile, ed., *Judgment at the Smithsonian* (New York: Marlowe, 1995).

3. See especially Richard B. Frank, *Downfall: The End of the Imperial Japanese Empire* (New York: Random House, 1999).

4. Robert Jervis, *The Meaning of the Nuclear Revolution* (Ithaca, NY: Cornell University Press, 1990) remains the seminal work mapping out a whole research agenda. See also Michael Mandelbaum, *The Nuclear Revolution: International Politics before and after Hiroshima* (Cambridge: Cambridge University Press, 1981); and Lawrence Freedman, *The Evolution of Nuclear Strategy*, 2nd ed. (New York: St. Martin's Press, 1989). On the downscale effects of the nuclear revolution on the production of knowledge, see Paul Erickson, Judy L. Klein, Lorraine Daston, Rebecca Lemov, Thomas Sturm, and Michael D. Gordin, *How Reason Almost Lost Its Mind: The Strange Career of Cold War Rationality* (Chicago: University of Chicago Press, 2013).

5. See, as a very incomplete list, George Perkovich, *India's Nuclear Bomb: The Impact on Global Proliferation* (Berkeley: University of California Press, 1999); Feroz Hassan Khan, *Eating Grass: The Making of the Pakistani Bomb* (Stanford, CA: Stanford University Press, 2012); Avner Cohen, *Israel and the Bomb* (New York: Columbia University Press, 1998); and Nic von Wielligh and Lydia von Wielligh-Steyn, *The Bomb: South Africa's Nuclear Weapons Programme*, trans. Sandra Mills (Pretoria: Litera, 2015).

6. See Michael D. Gordin, "Nuclear Mythology and Nuclear Uselessness," *Nonproliferation Review* 20, no. 2 (2013): 375–80.

7. See especially Gabrielle Hecht, *Being Nuclear: Africans and the Global Uranium Trade* (Cambridge, MA: MIT Press, 2012); Itty Abraham, "The Ambivalence of Nuclear Histories," *Osiris* 21 (2006): 49–65; and Scott D. Sagan, "Why Do States Build Nuclear Weapons: Three Models in Search of a Bomb," *International Security* 21, no. 3 (Winter 1996–1997): 54–86.

8. M. Susan Lindee, *Suffering Made Real: American Science and the Survivors of Hiroshima* (Chicago: University of Chicago Press, 1994).

9. Mandelbaum, *The Nuclear Revolution*, 1.

10. Jeffrey Lewis, *The 2020 Commission Report on the North Korean Nuclear Attacks against the United States: A Speculative Novel* (New York: Mariner Books, 2018).

11. Robert Jervis, "A Horrifying and Believable Path to Nuclear War with North Korea," *War on the Rocks*, September 4, 2018.

Chapter 2. The Atom Bomb as Policy Maker: FDR and the Road Not Taken

1. The best survey of the literature is J. Samuel Walker, *Prompt and Utter Destruction: Truman and the Use of Atomic Bombs against Japan*, 3rd ed. (Chapel Hill, NC: University of North Carolina Press, 2016).

2. On the American policy debates during the summer of 1945, see Martin Sherwin, *A World Destroyed: Hiroshima and Its Legacies*, 3rd ed. (Stanford, CA: Stanford University Press, 2003); Barton Bernstein's response in Gar Alperovitz, Robert L. Messer, and Barton J. Bernstein, "Marshall, Truman, and the Decision to Drop the Bomb," *International Security* 16, no. 3 (Winter 1991–1992): 204–21; Barton Bernstein, "The Atomic Bombings Reconsidered," *Foreign Affairs* 74 (January/February 1995): 135–52; and Richard Rhodes, *The Making of the Atomic Bomb* (New York: Simon and Schuster, 1986).

3. For representative arguments, see, for example, Alonso Hamby, *Man of the People: Life of Harry S. Truman* (New York: Oxford University Press, 1995); Wilson Miscamble, *The Most Controversial Decision: Truman, the Atomic Bombs, and the Defeat of Japan* (Cambridge: Cambridge University Press, 2011); and Paul Fussell, *Thank God for the Atom Bomb and Other Essays* (New York: Summit Books, 1988).

4. Michael Dobbs sees casualty avoidance as dominant in the priorities of both FDR and Truman. See Dobbs, *Six Months in 1945: Stalin, Churchill and Truman—from World War to Cold War* (New York: Knopf, 2012).

5. See Tsuyoshi Hasegawa, *Racing the Enemy: Stalin, Truman, and the Surrender of Japan* (Cambridge, MA: Harvard University Press, 2005); Arnold Offner, *Another Such Victory: President Truman and the Cold War* (Stanford, CA: Stanford University Press, 2002); Gar Alperovitz, *The Decision to Use the Atomic Bomb and the Architecture of an American Myth* (New York: Knopf, 1995); and Robert Messer, *The End of an Alliance: James F. Byrnes, Roosevelt, Truman, and the Origins of the Cold War* (Chapel Hill: University of North Carolina Press, 1982).

6. For example, Alperovitz, *Decision*. In an eight-hundred-page book, Alperovitz discusses FDR in only one chapter and tangentially elsewhere.

7. On this point, see Alperovitz, *Decision*, 662–63.

8. The USSR had not yet declared war on Japan, which provided an ostensible reason for its exclusion from the declaration. But, as Hasegawa shows (and Byrnes acknowledges in his memoirs), Truman and his secretary of state wanted to exclude the Soviet Union in any event, rather than take the simple step of asking Stalin to sign it irrespective of formal Soviet belligerence, a step that would indisputably have intensified the effect of the declaration on Japan, if securing

its surrender before using the bomb was actually the aim. Hasegawa thus points out that the Soviet absence from the declaration emboldened the Japanese leadership, who perceived this as a sign of division among their adversaries and enhanced their hopes that the Soviet Union might act as a mediator. See Tsuyoshi Hasegawa, "Soviet Policy toward Japan during World War II," *Cahiers du Monde Russe* 52 (2011): esp. 8–11.

9. See Bernstein, "Atomic Bombings Reconsidered."

10. See Warren Kimball, *The Juggler: Franklin Roosevelt as Wartime Statesman* (Princeton, NJ: Princeton University Press, 1991); Mark Stoler, "A Half-Century of Conflict: Interpretations of US World War Two Diplomacy," *Diplomatic History* 18 (Summer 1994): 375–403; and Richard Rhodes, *The Making of the Atomic Bomb* (New York: Simon and Schuster, 1986). On the importance of FDR's concern not to rely on the bomb while it remained only prospective, see Warren Kimball, *Forged in War: Roosevelt, Churchill, and the Second World War* (Chicago: Ivan Dee, 1997), 281.

11. Kimball, *Forged in War*, 329.

12. Bernard Brodie, "The Atom Bomb as Policy Maker," *Foreign Affairs* 4 (October 1948): 24–25.

13. The novel consequences of atomic warfare that Brodie describes presage, but are not the same as, those of the nuclear revolution. With thermonuclear warheads and intercontinental missiles, the two sides were able to wage decisive intercontinental war but had to reckon with the fact that each side could also retaliate with second-strike attacks for which there was no defense, attacks that threatened the complete destruction not only of the states involved but of the human race. See Robert Jervis, *The Illogic of American Nuclear Strategy* (Ithaca, NY: Cornell University Press, 1984); Robert Jervis, *The Meaning of the Nuclear Revolution* (Ithaca, NY: Cornell University Press, 1989); Daniel Deudney, "Nuclear Weapons and the Waning of the Real-State," *Daedalus* 124 (Spring 1995): 209–31; and Campbell Craig, *Glimmer of a New Leviathan: Total War in the Realism of Niebuhr, Morgenthau and Waltz* (New York: Columbia University Press, 2003).

14. On free security, see C. Vann Woodward, "The Age of Reinterpretation," *American Historical Review* 66 (October 1960): 1–19; Campbell Craig, "The Not-So-Strange Career of Charles Beard," *Diplomatic History* 45 (Spring 2001): 251–74; Campbell Craig and Fredrik Logevall, *America's Cold War: The Politics of Insecurity* (Cambridge, MA: Harvard University Press, 2012); and Andrew Preston, "Monsters Everywhere: A Genealogy of National Security," *Diplomatic History* 38 (June 2014): 477–500.

15. Brodie, "Policy Maker," 26.

16. Brodie goes on to suggest that the United States should take advantage of this superiority.

17. A general war fought with atomic bombs and airplanes would not threaten human survival in the way a thermonuclear missile war would. But it could have threatened the social survival of the warring states in a way that even the destruction of the Second World War did not. See Daniel Deudney, *Bounding Power: Republican Security Theory from the Polis to the Global Village* (Princeton, NJ: Princeton University Press, 2007).

18. See Paul Boyer, *By the Bomb's Early Light: American Thought and Culture at the Dawn of the Atomic Age* (New York: Pantheon, 1985).

19. Daniel Deudney, in *Bounding Power*, argues that the size of viable states is defined by the destructive scope of extant military technology: with the advent of nuclear weapons, this size becomes planetary.

20. See Rhodes, *Making of the Atomic Bomb*.

21. Michael Gordin, *Five Days in August: How World War II Became a Nuclear War* (Princeton, NJ: Princeton University Press, 2007), 40.

22. On FDR's determination to avoid Wilson's mistakes, see John Lewis Gaddis, *The United States and the Origins of the Cold War* (New York: Columbia University Press, 1972); and Kimball, *Forged in War*, 332–33.

23. Mark Stoler, *Allies in War: Britain and America against the Axis Powers, 1940–45* (London: Hodder Arnold, 2005).

24. On FDR's vision, see Kimball, *The Juggler*; and Lloyd C. Gardner, *Spheres of Influence: The Great Powers Partition Europe, from Munich to Yalta* (Chicago: Ivan Dee, 1993). For a recent treatment sympathetic to Roosevelt, Susan Butler, *Roosevelt and Stalin, Portrait of a Partnership* (New York: Vintage, 2015), especially chap. 10.

25. On the veto, see Craig and Radchenko, *The Atomic Bomb*; and Butler, *Roosevelt and Stalin*, 296–97.

26. See Kimball, *The Juggler*, 100–101.

27. See Mary E. Glantz, *FDR and the Soviet Union: The President's Battles over Foreign Policy* (Lawrence: University Press of Kansas, 2005); and Wilson Miscamble, *From Roosevelt to Truman: Potsdam, Hiroshima, and the Cold War* (Cambridge: Cambridge University Press, 2007), esp. chap. 2.

28. For an overview of FDR foreign policy historiography, see Stoler, "Half-Century of Conflict."

29. Glantz, *FDR and the Soviet Union*.

30. On this point, see Gaddis, *Origins of the Cold War*.

31. Craig and Radchenko, *The Atomic Bomb*, esp. chaps. 4 and 6.

32. On the Hyde Park memorandum, see Sherwin, *World Destroyed*; Rhodes, *Making of the Atomic Bomb*; and Craig and Radchenko, *The Atomic Bomb*. Butler, *Roosevelt and Stalin*, 314–15, argues that FDR agreed to reject international control simply as a result of being bullied by Churchill. This is an odd interpretation, as FDR had little reason to accede to any of Churchill's demands at this point, hosted the secret conference at his home, told none of his advisers about the decision, and adhered to the agreement until his death.

33. See Kimball, *The Juggler*; and Butler, *Roosevelt and Stalin*, 318.

34. See Rhodes *Making of the Atomic Bomb*; Craig and Radchenko *The Atomic Bomb*; and Miscamble, *Roosevelt to Truman*.

35. On Anglo-American conflict over the atomic question in 1943, see Stoler, *Allies in War*; and Craig and Radchenko, *The Atomic Bomb*.

36. Quotation from Craig and Radchenko, *The Atomic Bomb*, 23.

37. See Kimball, *Forged in War*, 328.

38. The literature on Yalta is vast. For a recent argument highly critical of FDR, see Miscamble, *Roosevelt to Truman*.

39. As Alexander George puts it, Poland threatened to jeopardize "his postwar plans right from the beginning." Quoted in Miscamble, *Roosevelt to Truman*, 60.

40. See Sean Malloy, *Atomic Tragedy: Henry Stimson and the Decision to Use the Bomb against Japan* (Ithaca, NY: Cornell University Press, 2008), esp. chap. 4; and Craig and Radchenko, *The Atomic Bomb*, 113–15.

41. See Gordin, *Five Days in August*, esp. chap. 3.

Chapter 3. The Kyoto Misconception: What Truman Knew, and Didn't Know, about Hiroshima

For their comments and discussions as this article evolved over time, I would like to thank in particular Ellen Bales, Barton J. Bernstein, William Burr, Michael D. Gordin, Tsuyoshi Hasegawa, John Horgan, G. John Ikenberry, Sean Malloy, Patrick McCray, Robert S. Norris, Benoît Pelopidas, Nina Tannenwald, J. Samuel Walker, Nasser Zakariya, and the participants of the conferences in Princeton and Hiroshima that led to this volume.

1. For brevity, I will simply point to two excellent historiographical essays by J. Samuel Walker that survey the literature quite well: J. Samuel Walker, "The Decision to Use the Bomb: A Historiographical Update," *Diplomatic History* 14, no. 1 (January 1990): 97–114; and J. Samuel Walker, "Recent Literature on the Atomic Bomb: A Search for a Middle Ground," *Diplomatic History* 29, no. 2 (April 2005): 311–34. Some of the questions and topics in this chapter were initially explored by the late Stanley Goldberg. Barton J. Bernstein deservedly critiqued Goldberg's conclusions, sources, and methods in a series of papers. Here, I have approached these questions from a somewhat different and, I hope, more careful perspective. For Goldberg's approach, see Stanley Goldberg, "What Did Truman Know and When Did He Know It?," *Bulletin of the Atomic Scientists* (May/June 1998): 18–19. For Bernstein's critique, see Barton Bernstein, "Reconsidering the 'Atomic General': Leslie R. Groves," *Journal of Military History* 67, no. 3 (July 2003): 889–920, esp. 884–86.

2. "Notes by Harry S. Truman on the Potsdam Conference," July 25, 1945 (hereafter cited as "Truman journal"), Harry S. Truman Library and Museum. https://www.trumanlibrary.org/whistlestop/study_collections/bomb/large/documents/pdfs/63.pdf.

3. Bernstein, "Reconsidering the 'Atomic General,'" 904–5.

4. "Log of the President's Trip to the Berlin Conference, 6 July to 7 August 1945," 50, copy in the Harry S. Truman Library and Museum (hereafter cited as HST), https://www.trumanlibrary.org/calendar/travel_log/documents/index.php?pagenumber=96&documentid=17&documentdate=1945-08-06&studycollectionid=TL&nav=ok.

5. Henry A. Wallace diary entry of August 10, 1945, in Henry A. Wallace, *The Diary of Henry Agard Wallace, January 18, 1935–September 19, 1946* (Glen Rock, NJ: Microfilming Corp. of America, 1977), 162.

6. Harry S. Truman, "Draft of the Gridiron Dinner Speech," December 15, 1945, HST, https://catalog.archives.gov/id/201508.

7. Quoted in Barton Bernstein, "Truman and the A-Bomb: Targeting Noncombatants, Using the Bomb, and His Defending 'the Decision,'" *Journal of Military History* 62, no. 3 (July 1998): 562.

8. For an evenhanded discussion of Truman's role in the bombing, see especially J. Samuel Walker, *Prompt and Utter Destruction: Truman and the Use of the Atomic Bombs against Japan* (Chapel Hill: University of North Carolina Press, 2004).

9. Barton Bernstein, "Eclipsed by Hiroshima and Nagasaki: Early Thinking about Tactical Nuclear Weapons," *International Security* 15, no. 4 (Spring 1991): 159–60.

10. Sean L. Malloy, "'The Rules of Civilized Warfare': Scientists, Soldiers, Civilians, and American Nuclear Targeting, 1940–1945," *Journal of Strategic Studies* 30, no. 3 (2007): 501–5.

11. Gar Alperovitz, *The Decision to Use the Atomic Bomb and the Architecture of an American Myth* (New York: Knopf, 1995), 527.

12. Nina Tannenwald, *The Nuclear Taboo: The United States and the Non-Use of Nuclear Weapons since 1945* (Cambridge: Cambridge University Press, 2007), 67. I prefer Tannenwald's sense of the taboo as an emotional/moral response, as opposed to a merely calculating "tradition of nonuse," but either one can work for my interpretation. On the tradition of nonuse, see T. V. Paul, *The Tradition of Non-Use of Nuclear Weapons* (Stanford, CA: Stanford University Press, 2009).

13. Examples of what I label as epistemological approaches to the history of the atomic bomb include Michael D. Gordin, *Five Days in August: How World War II Became a Nuclear War* (Princeton, NJ: Princeton University Press, 2007); Michael D. Gordin, *Red Cloud at Dawn: Truman, Stalin, and the End of the Atomic Monopoly* (New York: Farrar, Straus and Giroux, 2009); Sean Malloy, "'A Very Pleasant Way To Die': Radiation Effects and the Decision to Use the Atomic Bomb against Japan," *Diplomatic History* 36, no. 3 (June 2012): 515–45; and Rebecca Press Schwartz, "The Making of the History of the Atomic Bomb: Henry DeWolf Smyth and the Historiography of the Manhattan Project" (PhD diss., Princeton University, September 2008). One might also include Barton J. Bernstein, "Reconsidering Truman's Claim of 'Half a Million American Lives' Saved by the Atomic Bomb: The Construction and Deconstruction of a Myth," *Journal of Strategic Studies* 22, no. 1 (1995): 54–95.

14. See, for example, the discussion by Walker, *Prompt and Utter Destruction*, 1–6. On the development of the "decision" narrative and its political implications, see especially Alperovitz, *The Decision to Use the Atomic Bomb*. Alperovitz's overall argument about the motivations behind the use of the atomic bombs remains controversial; his final chapters, which are focused on how the "orthodox" narrative about the justifications for the atomic bombings were developed and disseminated in the postwar, hold up much better, and merit attention even from historians who do not accept his arguments about the motivations for the use of the bombs.

15. See Barton J. Bernstein, "Understanding the Atomic Bomb and the Japanese Surrender: Missed Opportunities, Little-Known Near Disasters, and Modern Memory," *Diplomatic History* 19, no. 2 (Spring 1995): 227–73; and Bernstein, "Reconsidering Truman's Claim."

16. See especially Gordin, *Five Days in August*, for discussions about this methodological difficulty.

17. Bernstein, "Truman and the A-Bomb," 549–50.

18. Malloy, "The Rules of Civilized Warfare," contains an excellent survey and interpretation of the targeting discussion.

19. Indeed, it was Stimson (via Marshall), and not Truman, who formally approved the specific order to use the first nuclear weapons. See George Marshall to Thomas Handy, TERMINAL cable VICTORY 281 [CM-IN-24908], July 25, 1945, in *Correspondence ("Top Secret") of the Manhattan Engineer District, 1942–1946*, microfilm publication M1109 (Washington, DC: National Archives and Records Administration, 1980) (hereafter cited as *CTS*), Roll 1, Target 6, Folder 5E, "TERMINAL Cables."

20. See Bernstein, "Truman and the A-Bomb"; and R. Gordon Arneson, "Notes of the Interim Committee Meeting, Thursday, 31 May 1945," copy in *Harrison-Bundy Files Relating to the Development of the Atomic Bomb, 1942–1946*, microfilm publication M1108 (Washington, DC: National Archives and Records Administration, 1980) (hereafter cited as *H-B*), Roll 8, Target 14, Folder 100, "Interim Committee—Minutes of Meetings."

21. "Notes on the Initial Meeting of the Target Committee [held on 27 April 1945]," May 2, 1945, and Maj. John A. Derry and Norman F. Ramsey to Leslie R. Groves, "Summary of Target Committee Meetings on 10 and 11 May 1945," and "Minutes of Third Target Committee Meeting" (May 28, 1945), all in *CTS*, Roll 1, Target 6, Folder 5D, "Selection of Targets."

22. Malloy, "The Rules of Civilized Warfare."

23. Henry L. Stimson diary, June 1, 1945, in *The Henry Lewis Stimson Diaries*, microfilm edition retrieved from the Center for Research Libraries, original from Manuscripts and Archives, Yale University Library, New Haven, CT (hereafter cited as "Stimson diary").

24. "Minutes of meeting held at the White House on Monday, 18 June," June 20, 1945, HST, https://www.trumanlibrary.org/whistlestop/study_collections/bomb/large/documents/pdfs/21.pdf.

25. Leslie Groves, *Now It Can Be Told: The Story of the Manhattan Project* (New York: Harper, 1962), 265.

26. Derry and Ramsey to Groves, "Summary of Target Committee Meetings on 10 and 11 May 1945."

27. "Reserved Areas," June 27, 1945, *CTS*, Roll 3, Target 8, Folder 25, "Documents Removed from Groves' Locked Box." Why Niigata replaced Kokura in the initial list is not clear, and neither is why Yokohama was not placed on this list. Yokohama was subjected to an incendiary raid by over 450 B-29s on May 29, which removed it from further consideration. Kit C. Carter and Robert Mueller, *U.S. Army Air Forces in World War II: Combat Chronology 1941–1945* (Washington, DC: Center for Air Force History, 1991).

28. According to Carter and Mueller, *U.S. Army Air Forces in World War II*, Nagasaki itself was conventionally bombed at least four times prior to the atomic bombing, the last involving fifty B-24s attacking the dock and harbor area on August 1, 1945.

29. On Stimson's role, see Otis Cary, "The Sparing of Kyoto—Mr. Stimson's Pet City," *Japan Quarterly* 22 (October–December 1975): 337–47; on interpreting the morality question, see Bernstein, "Truman and the A-Bomb." See also Jason M. Kelly, "Why Did Henry Stimson Spare Kyoto from the Bomb?: Confusion in Postwar Historiography," *Journal of American-East Asian Relations* 19 (2012): 183–203; and Robert S. Norris, *Racing for the Bomb: General Leslie R. Groves, the Manhattan Project's Indispensable Man* (South Royalton, VT: Steerforth Press, 2002), 386–88.

30. Stimson diary, March 3, 1929.

31. See also Sean Malloy, *Atomic Tragedy: Henry L. Stimson and the Decision to Use the Bomb against Japan* (Ithaca, NY: Cornell University Press, 2008), 105–109; and Cary, "Atomic Bomb Targeting." There does not seem to be much evidence behind the oft-told story that Stimson had spent his honeymoon in Kyoto; Cary's article goes perhaps as far as one might want to in exploring the possibilities of Stimson's motivation, attributing Stimson's fascination with the place as being rooted, potentially, in the interest of a young ward of his, Henry Loomis. In a letter from 1950, Stimson commented that "I have had the pleasure of visiting many cities in

Japan, but the city of Kyoto was always my favorite. I knew its beauties, and that it was the center of Japanese art and culture. I, therefore, intervened and prevented the bombing of the city." Henry L. Stimson to Gyokujo Masuda, May 11, 1950, in *The Papers of Henry Lewis Stimson*, microfilm edition retrieved from the Center for Research Libraries, original from Manuscripts and Archives, Yale University Library, New Haven, Connecticut (hereafter cited as "Stimson papers"), Reel 123, Series 1.

32. Groves, *Now It Can Be Told*, 273. See also Malloy, *Atomic Tragedy*, 107–8.

33. Interview of Leslie R. Groves by Stephane Groueff, part 9, January 7, 1965, transcribed at Atomic Heritage Foundation, *Voices of the Manhattan Project*, http://www.manhattanproject voices.org/oral-histories/general-leslie-grovess-interview-part-9.

34. On the evolution of the firebombing strategy, see Thomas R. Searle, "'It Made a Lot of Sense to Kill Workers': The Firebombing of Tokyo in March 1945," *Journal of Military History* 66, no. 1 (January 2002): 103–33.

35. Stimson diary, June 1, 1945.

36. LeMay stated: "We have destroyed all the target area we set out to burn.... You cannot go in with a few tons and expect an entire city to burn.... I now promise they will have nothing more to look forward to than complete destruction of their cities." John Beaufort, "Air over Japan," *Christian Science Monitor*, May 31, 1945.

37. Stimson diary, June 1, 1945.

38. Stimson diary, May 16, 1945, with attached memo from Stimson to Truman, May 16, 1945. If Stimson had these feelings when the incendiary tactics started in March 1945, the death of Roosevelt in April and the overall difficulties of the transition to a new president may have delayed him until May.

39. Stimson diary, June 6, 1945.

40. "Pictures," June 15, 1945, *CTS*, Roll 3, Target 8, Folder 25, "Documents Removed from Groves' Locked Box." The folder contains maps and photographs of Kyoto, Kokura, and Niigata. The Kyoto roundhouse still exists—it is the Umekoji Steam Locomotive Museum. At this time, scientists did not know the exact power of the Fat Man design (and would not until Trinity) and estimated it would be much smaller, on the order of 5 kilotons, *if* the implosion lenses were successful. Fifteen kilotons was still considered a likely maximum value for the Little Boy design—evidence, if any were needed, that they intended to bomb Kyoto *first* with what they were still considering the "big" bomb.

41. "Kyoto," July 2, 1945, *CTS*, Roll 1, Target 6, Folder 5D, "Selection of Targets."

42. Derry and Ramsey to Groves, "Summary of Target Committee Meetings on 10 and 11 May 1945."

43. George Harrison to Henry Stimson [WAR 35987], July 21, 1945, *CTS*, Roll 1, Target 6, Folder 5E, "TERMINAL Cables."

44. Henry Stimson to George Harrison [VICTORY 189], July 21, 1945, *CTS*, Roll 1, Target 6, Folder 5E, "TERMINAL Cables"; Stimson diary, July 21, 1945.

45. Stimson diary, July 19, 1945.

46. Stimson diary, July 22, 1945.

47. Stimson diary, July 23, 1945.

48. Henry Stimson to George Harrison [VICTORY 218], July 23, 1945, *CTS*, Roll 1, Target 6, Folder 5E: "TERMINAL Cables."

49. George Harrison to Henry Stimson, TERMINAL cable WAR 36791, July 23, 1945, CTS, Roll 1, Target 6, Folder 5E: "TERMINAL Cables."

50. Stimson diary, July 24, 1945.

51. For comparison, see Barton J. Bernstein, "The Atomic Bombings Reconsidered," *Foreign Affairs* 74, no. 1 (January/February 1995): 135–52, esp. 144.

52. See, for example, Tsuyoshi Hasegawa, *Racing the Enemy: Stalin, Truman, and the Surrender of Japan* (Cambridge, MA: Harvard University Press, 2005), 61, 130; Walker, *Prompt and Utter Destruction*, 7–10; John J. McCloy diary entry, July 20, 1945, from John J. McCloy Papers, Box DY1, folders 16–19, Archives and Special Collections, Amherst College Library, https://www.amherst.edu/media/view/390254/original/McCloy_diary_1945.pdf.

53. Truman journal, July 25, 1945. We might also look at a postwar but pre-*Memoirs* Truman statement on this meeting, which came in a letter to Stimson sent on December 31, 1946, urging Stimson to write an article setting forth the deliberations about the bomb in the face of criticism. In it, Truman admitted he had forgotten a lot of the details but noted: "If you will remember our conversation in Potsdam, we came to the conclusion that the bomb should be dropped on a town which was engaged almost exclusively in war work. Hiroshima was the town picked out and then Nagasaki was the second one." The unreliability of this is clear from the inclusion of Nagasaki, which was only added to the target list that day. Harry Truman to Henry Stimson, December 31, 1946, Stimson papers, Reel 116, Series 1.

54. In an early draft of his *Harper's* piece, Stimson described Kyoto as a "predominantly non-military target," and he was criticized by at least one person he consulted for editorial views. The final version of the article described Kyoto as "a target of considerable military importance." Henry L. Stimson, "The Decision to Use the Atomic Bomb," *Harper's Magazine* 194, no. 1161 (February 1947): 105. See also the late draft in H-B, Reel 4, Target 2, File 56, "Winant-Stimson Correspondence." For the criticism, see Rudolf A. Winnacker to McGeorge Bundy, December 13, 1946, Stimson papers, Reel 116, Series 1. Winnacker, who worked for the Office of Strategic Services during World War II, objected to the original characterization that "a Mitsubishi factory for aircraft engine valves was in a suburb, and with dispersion of Japanese industry starting in the fall of 1944 much work important to the Japanese war effort, was moved to Kyoto to take advantage of the skilled labor in this city."

55. John N. Stone to Henry H. Arnold, July 24, 1945, copy in the Nuclear Testing Archive, Las Vegas, NV (hereafter cited as NTA), accession number NV01379877. Copy also available in William Burr, "The Atomic Bomb and the end of World War II," *National Security Archive Electronic Briefing Book No. 162*, August 4, 2014, http://nsarchive.gwu.edu/NSAEBB/NSAEBB162.

56. Col. Frank McCarthy (personal aide to Marshall) to Scott and Col. Hansell M. Pasco, TERMINAL cable VICTORY 350 [CM-IN-26711], July 26, 1945, H-B, Roll 4, Target 10, Folder 64, "Interim Committee—Potsdam Cables."

57. Col. Hansell M. Pasco to Leslie R. Groves, July 27, 1945, CTS, Roll 1, Target 6, Folder 5, "Events Preceding and Following the Dropping of the First Atomic Bombs at Hiroshima and Nagasaki," Subfile 5B, "Directives, Memorandums, etc., to and from the Chief of Staff, Secretary of War, etc." In Truman's *Memoirs*, he claimed that "before the selected targets [Hiroshima, Kokura, Niigata, and Nagasaki] were approved as proper for military purposes, I personally went over them in detail with Stimson, Marshall, and Arnold, and we discussed the matter of timing and the final choice of the first target." Harry S. Truman, *Memoirs*, vol. 1, *Year of Decisions*

(New York: Doubleday, 1955), 463. Yet the Stone memo, which as far as the record indicates was the only information that was transmitted about these targets, was not available at Potsdam until after Stimson had left, and after the target order had been issued. It is easy to reconstruct that Stimson, Marshall, and Arnold each discussed targeting questions—what is harder to substantiate is that they discussed them with Truman. On Stimson and Arnold, for example, see John W. Huston, ed., *American Airpower Comes of Age: General Henry H. "Hap" Arnold's World War II Diaries*, vol. 2 (Maxwell Air Force Base, AL: Air University Press, January 2002), entries for 1945, especially July 22 ("Secretary of War had me for hour before lunch on Super bombing, where, why and what effects. I told him I would get up a recommendation. Am sending Stone back to US to see Spaatz and Groves to prepare recommendation"), July 23 ("conference with Secretary of War re ultra bombing effort") on p. 379, and July 24 ("Secretary of War came to see me re ultra Super Bombing; I told him to wait until I heard from Spaatz") on p. 380. On July 25 (pp. 380–81), Arnold describes a series of meetings, including one with Stimson and Marshall in the morning, and then later one with Marshall and other generals. He also mentions Marshall meeting with Truman but does not indicate if he himself met with Truman that morning. Stimson's diary for July 25, 1945, does not indicate any meetings with Truman or Arnold; it is largely concerned with a meeting Stimson had with Stalin and his preparations to leave Potsdam. The July 25, 1945, cable that approved the bombing order is timestamped 6:45 a.m. (UTC), which is to say, 10:45 a.m. Berlin time (CEMT), which puts serious limitations on how much discussion could have taken place *prior* to the order being approved. George Marshall to Thomas Handy, TERMINAL cable VICTORY 281 [CM-IN-24908], July 25, 1945, CTS, Roll 1, Target 6, Folder 5E, "TERMINAL Cables."

58. Lt. William M. Rigdon, *Log of the President's Trip to the Berlin Conference (6 July to 7 August 1945)*, HST, https://www.trumanlibrary.org/calendar/travel_log/key1947/berlintrip_toc.htm.

59. As Truman wrote after the fact in a note dated August 10 (which matches the "offered to surrender" piece) but clearly corresponds with Truman's schedule of August 9: "While all this has been going on, I've been trying to get ready a radio address to the nation on the Berlin conference. Made the first draft on the ship coming back. Discussed it with Byrnes, Rosenman, Ben Cohen, Leahy and Charlie Ross. Rewrote it four times and then the Japs offered to surrender and it had to be done again." Longhand note of Harry S. Truman, August 9 or 10, 1945, transcript and copy available in HST, https://www.trumanlibrary.org/whistlestop/study_collections/trumanpapers/psf/longhand/index.php?documentid=hst-psf_naid 735229-01&documentYear=1945&documentVersion=both&pagenumber=1. Truman's schedule can be compared on another page on the Truman Library website: https://www.trumanlibrary.org/calendar/main.php?currYear=1945&currMonth=8&currDay=9.

60. Harry S. Truman, "Radio Report to the American People on the Potsdam Conference," August 9, 1945, HST, https://www.trumanlibrary.org/publicpapers/?pid=104.

61. The only line referencing it is, "Since then they have seen what our atomic bomb can do. They can foresee what it will do." "Draft of a Speech by President Truman on Berlin Conference" (n.d., first draft), Papers of Samuel I. Rosenman, HST, "Report to the Nation (Potsdam)." (This collection is hereafter cited as SR.)

62. "Draft of a Speech by President Truman on Berlin Conference" (n.d., second draft), SR.

63. "Memorandum of Conference with the President," August 8, 1945, attached to Stimson diary, August 8, 1945.

64. Representative coverage from the Associated Press is "Atom Bomb Destroyed 60% of Hiroshima; Pictures Show 4 Square Miles of City Gone; B-29 Dropped New Explosive by Parachute," *New York Herald Tribune*, August 8, 1945.

65. "200,000 Believed Dead in Inferno That Vaporized City of Hiroshima," *Boston Globe*, August 9, 1945. This number is considerably higher than most Hiroshima fatality estimates, which generally range from 60,000 to 100,000, and appears to be a rough application of the figure of 60 percent (the *area* of the city damaged) with the listed prewar population of Hiroshima.

66. Paul M. A. Linebarger, "Memorandum for Colonel Buttles: Identification of atomic bomb targets as being military in character," August 9, 1945, Paul M. A. Linebarger Papers Prepared during World War II, vol. 5, Hoover Institution Archives on War, Peace and Revolution, Stanford, CA. I am grateful to Sean Malloy for providing me with a copy of this document. In General Groves's office diary, at 1:35 p.m. on August 8, it is noted that Buttles, who was part of Propaganda G-2, was trying to make an appointment with Stimson and other members of the Office of War Information, and Harrison thought that Groves would want to be included. This gives some hint of how "high" the authorities likely were. Office diary of Leslie R. Groves, August 11–14, 1945, National Archives and Records Administration, RG 200, Papers of Leslie Richard Groves, Entry 7530G, Boxes 1–4, courtesy of Robert S. Norris.

67. Arthur H. Compton, *Atomic Quest: A Personal Narrative* (New York: Oxford University Press, 1956), 236–37, and 237n.7. Oppenheimer himself appeared to consider the difference in magnitude important in his later security clearance hearing. "Q. You knew, did you not, that the dropping of that atomic bomb on the target you had selected will [*sic*] kill or injure thousands of civilians, is that correct? A. Not as many as turned out. Q. How many were killed or injured? A. 70,000. Q. Did you have moral scruples about that? A. Terrible ones." Testimony of J. Robert Oppenheimer, *In the Matter of J. Robert Oppenheimer* (Washington, DC: U.S. Government Printing Office, 1954), 235.

68. Archibald MacLeish to Samuel I. Rosenman, August 8, 1945, SR.

69. "Draft of a Speech by President Truman on Berlin Conference" (n.d., fifth draft), SR. The third draft made minor changes to the second draft (for example, "first bombs" was changed to "first bomb"), and there were no relevant differences between the third and fourth drafts.

70. Richard B. Russell to Harry S. Truman, August 7, 1945, HST, https://www.trumanlibrary.org/whistlestop/study_collections/bomb/large/documents/index.php?documentid=8&pagenumber=1.

71. Harry S. Truman to Richard B. Russell, August 9, 1945, HST, https://www.trumanlibrary.org/whistlestop/study_collections/bomb/large/documents/index.php?documentdate=1945-08-09&documentid=9&pagenumber=1.

72. A point Barton Bernstein noted. Bernstein, "Perils and Politics of Surrender," 15n.55; and Bernstein, "Truman and the A-bomb," 577.

73. The Russell telegram is time-stamped as received by the White House at 9:05 p.m. Truman returned to the White House at 10:45 p.m. on August 7 and had no scheduled meetings on August 8 until 10:15 a.m. He met with Stimson about the effects of the bomb at 10:45 a.m. and

had a busy schedule (he signed the United Nations Charter, among other things) until his 1:00 p.m. lunch. Nothing else was on his schedule until 3:00 p.m., when he announced Soviet entry into the war. This suggests that he drafted the response to Russell on the morning of August 8. On his schedule, see the Harry S. Truman Library website, https://www.trumanlibrary.org/calendar/main.php?currYear=1945&currMonth=8&currDay=8.

74. At Potsdam, Truman inquired about the schedule of the bombings. Stimson apparently gave him a telegram that described only the schedule of the "tested-type" (implosion design) that suggested a bomb would be ready around August 6 and another around August 24. If Truman did not internalize that there were two types of bombs, he may not have realized two would be ready at the beginning of August. George Harrison to Henry Stimson, TERMINAL cable WAR 37350, July 24, 1945, *CTS*, Roll 1, Target 6, Folder 5E, "TERMINAL Cables."

75. Norman F. Ramsey, "History of Project A," September 27, 1945, copy in Coster-Mullen, *Atom Bombs*, "Documents."

76. Groves, on the other hand, *was* given forewarning and appears to have passed it on in a limited fashion. On August 8 he sent a note to General Brehon B. Somervelle that "our second attempt is on. The first Fat Boy [*sic*] is on the way and by morning I hope he has done his job." In the same letter, he indicated that he had also informed Lt. General LeRoy Lutes, Somervelle's planner. There are no indications that he informed anyone else; Stimson's diary makes it clear that he learned of the attack after the fact. Leslie R. Groves to Brehon B. Somervelle (August 8, 1945), *CTS*, Roll 1, Target 6, Folder 5B, "Directives, Memorandums, etc., to and from the Chief of Staff, Secretary of War, etc."

77. The original target for the second strike, the Kokura Arsenal, was more in line with the Target Committee ethos of targeting a military facility surrounded by civilian houses, but clouds, or smoke, over the target had necessitated the choice of Nagasaki as the fallback target.

78. Stimson diary, August 10, 1945, captures the feeling of the day well.

79. Leslie R. Groves to George Marshall, August 10, 1945, copy in Burr, "The Atomic Bomb and the End of World War II."

80. Henry A. Wallace diary entry of August 10, 1945, in Henry A. Wallace, *The Diary of Henry Agard Wallace, January 18, 1935-September 19, 1946* (Glen Rock, NJ: Microfilming Corp. of America, 1977), 162.

81. James Forrestal diary entry for August 10, 1945, in *Diaries of James V. Forrestal, 1944–1949 Secretary of the Navy, 1944–1947, and First Secretary of Defense, 1947–1949: Complete and Unexpurgated Diaries from the Seeley G. Mudd Manuscript Library, Princeton University*, microfilm collection (Marlborough, UK: Adam Matthew, 2001). The United States did conduct several bombing raids in the interim; it should be noted, however, that no firebombing raids, even the most deadly ones, had mortality rates as high as the atomic bombs. The Tokyo raids, being unexpected, novel, and launched against one of the most populous cities in the world, were still less deadly per square mile destroyed than the atomic bombs by a significant factor. For a speculative exercise on the counterfactual question of what would have been the casualties had Tokyo been atomic bombed in March 1945, instead of firebombed, see Alex Wellerstein, "Tokyo vs. Hiroshima," *Restricted Data: The Nuclear Secrecy Blog*, September 22, 2014, http://blog.nuclearsecrecy.com/2014/09/22/tokyo-hiroshima/.

82. John Balfour to Foreign Office, August 14, 1945, FO800/461, Public Record Office, Kew, United Kingdom, http://discovery.nationalarchives.gov.uk/details/r/C4267560.

83. There are reasons to think that, if the war had continued, that there would have been considerable pressure on Truman to authorize further strikes. General Groves's office diary of August 11–14, 1945, makes it clear that many of those whom Groves spoke with thought that atomic bombings might soon resume. George Harrison, Stimson's assistant, told Groves on August 13 that Stimson "approved Gen Marshall's order on stoppage but today he walked with McCloy and thinks shipments [of bomb cores] should start again, and Harrison thought Groves might want to take it up with Marshall." Office diary of Leslie R. Groves, August 11–14, 1945, National Archives and Records Administration, RG 200, Papers of Leslie Richard Groves, Entry 7530G, Boxes 1–4, courtesy of Robert S. Norris.

84. This fits well with the *hypercontrol*—an impulsive decisiveness exhibited under duress—described in Robert Jay Lifton and Greg Mitchell, *Hiroshima in America: A Half Century of Denial* (New York: Avon Books, 1995), 126. Lifton and Mitchell argue that many of Truman's apparent stress-related symptoms (he also told Wallace, at the same meeting on August 10, that he was suffering from headaches, both physical and figurative) were because of his internalizing the use decision.

85. Harry S. Truman to Samuel M. Calvert, August 11, 1945, HST, http://www.trumanlibrary.org/whistlestop/study_collections/bomb/large/documents/index.php?documentdate=1945-08-11&documentid=11&studycollectionid=abomb&pagenumber=1.

86. Truman, "Draft of the Gridiron Dinner Speech"; Bernstein, "Truman and the A-Bomb." Per tradition, Gridiron speeches are not recorded, so we do not know exactly what he delivered.

87. See, for example, Alperovitz, *The Decision to Use the Atomic Bomb*, book 2.

88. One of the few exceptions to this is that Truman authorized the invasion of Kyushu only in June 1945 and took a wait-and-see approach to the invasion of Honshu. This gives perhaps some sense of scale that was necessary to require presidential intervention. "Minutes of meeting held at the White House on Monday, 18 June," June 20, 1945, HST, https://www.trumanlibrary.org/whistlestop/study_collections/bomb/large/documents/pdfs/21.pdf.

89. On the various forms of intellectual "work" that went into the construction of the atomic bomb as "special" and different from conventional bombing, see Gordin, *Five Days in August*. Gordin argues that the "specialness" of the bomb was not conclusive until after the surrender of Japan, but there were those who advocated for its special nature throughout the process of its development. Truman's amazement at the Trinity test appears to highlight this.

90. See, for example, Richard G. Hewlett and Oscar E. Anderson, Jr., *The New World, 1939–1946* (University Park: Pennsylvania State University Press, 1962); and Richard G. Hewlett and Francis Duncan, *Atomic Shield, 1947–1952* (Washington, DC: U.S. Atomic Energy Commission, 1969).

91. National Security Council, "United States Policy on Atomic Warfare (NSC-30)," in *Foreign Relations of the United States, 1948*, vol. 1, part 2 (Washington, DC: United States Government Printing Office, 1976), 624–31. It is clear from other correspondence that this issue was very much undecided at the time, and that there were alternative proposals being discussed (such as having the Joint Chiefs of Staff be more heavily involved in such a decision, or having

the use of nuclear weapons be "automatic" in the event of general war), which the presidential-authority scheme was seen as opposing. For context, see Kenneth C. Royall, "United States Policy on Atomic Warfare" (May 19, 1948); and undated notes from the State Department on Kenneth C. Royall's "United States Policy on Atomic Warfare" (May 19, 1948), both in the same *FRUS* volume, 570–73.

92. On the "custody dispute," see especially L. Wainstein et al., "The Evolution of U.S. Strategic Command and Control and Warning, 1945–1972," Institute for Defense Analysis Study S-467 (June 1975), part 1, chap. 3 ("Custody of the Atomic Bombs and the Authority to Use Them"), http://www.dtic.mil/dtic/tr/fulltext/u2/a331702.pdf; Office of the Assistant to the Secretary of Defense (Atomic Energy), "History of the Custody and Deployment of Nuclear Weapons, July 1945 through September 1977," February 1978, http://www.dod.mil/pubs/foi/Reading_Room/NCB/306.pdf.

93. Lilienthal diary, July 21, 1948, in David E. Lilienthal, *Journals of David E. Lilienthal*, vol. 2: *The Atomic Energy Years, 1945–1950* (New York: Harper & Row, 1964), 390–91.

94. Of course, nuclear weapons have arguably been "used" in peacetime and wartime many times since 1945, if "used" does not merely mean "dropped on enemies." Nuclear testing, nuclear deterrence, nuclear blackmail, and so on all are forms of "use." See Gordin and Ikenberry's introduction to this volume in chapter 1.

95. Tannenwald, *Nuclear Taboo*, 67.

96. On this point, I find Lifton and Mitchell, *Hiroshima in America*, persuasive.

Chapter 4. "When You Have to Deal with a Beast": Race, Ideology, and the Decision to Use the Atomic Bomb

1. Huey P. Newton, "Statement by Minister of Defense to the Black World," *Black Panther*, May 15, 1967.

2. The best single-volume history of the party is Joseph Bloom and Waldo E. Martin, Jr., *Black against Empire: The History and Politics of the Black Panther Party* (Berkeley: University of California Press, 2013). On the party's international connections, see Sean L. Malloy, *Out of Oakland: Black Panther Party Internationalism during the Cold War* (Ithaca, NY: Cornell University Press, 2017).

3. Quoted in Matthew Jones, *After Hiroshima: The United States, Race and Nuclear Weapons in Asia, 1945–1965* (Cambridge: Cambridge University Press, 2010), 19.

4. Vincent J. Intondi, *African Americans against the Bomb: Nuclear Weapons, Colonialism, and the Black Freedom Movement* (Stanford, CA: Stanford University Press, 2015), 14–18; Jones, *After Hiroshima*, 37.

5. On the black left and the bomb, see Intondi, *African Americans against the Bomb*, 21–28. The best study of the black left, anticolonialism, and the CPUSA is Penny M. Von Eschen, *Race against Empire: Black Americans and Anticolonialism, 1937–1957* (Ithaca, NY: Cornell University Press, 1997).

6. Laura Hein and Mark Selden, "Commemoration and Silence: Fifty Years of Remembering the Bomb in America and Japan," in *Living with the Bomb: American and Japanese Cultural Conflicts in the Nuclear Age*, ed. Laura Hein and Mark Selden (London: Routledge, 1997), 7; Sado Asada, "The Mushroom Cloud and National Psyches: Japanese and American Perceptions

of the Atomic-Bomb Decision, 1945–1995," in Hein and Selden, *Living with the Bomb*, 175, 187. Also see Ian Buruma, *The Wages of Guilt: Memories of War in Germany and Japan* (New York: New York Review of Books, 1994), 98.

7. Barton J. Bernstein, "Seizing the Contested Terrain of Early Nuclear History: Stimson, Conant, and Their Allies Explain the Decision to Use the Atomic Bomb," *Diplomatic History* 17, no. 1 (January 1993): 35–72.

8. John Dower, *Cultures of War: Pearl Harbor/Hiroshima/9-11/Iraq* (New York: Norton, 2010), 225, 241.

9. Ronald Takaki, *Hiroshima: Why America Dropped the Atomic Bomb* (Boston: Little, Brown, 1995), 146.

10. Gar Alperovitz, *The Decision to Use the Atomic Bomb* (New York: Knopf, 1995), 655.

11. Robert P. Newman, "Hiroshima and the Trashing of Henry Stimson," *New England Quarterly* 71, no. 1 (March 1998): 31.

12. Michael Kort, *The Columbia Guide to Hiroshima and the Bomb* (New York: Columbia University Press, 2007), xv. Also see Stephen E. Ambrose and Brian Loring Villa, "Racism, the Atomic Bomb, and the Transformation of Japanese-American Relations," in *The Pacific War Revisited*, ed. Günter Bischof and Robert L. Dupont (Baton Rouge: Louisiana State University Press, 1997), 181.

13. Dower, *Cultures of War*, 276.

14. Richard B. Frank, *Downfall: The End of the Imperial Japanese Empire* (New York: Random House, 1999), 336. For similar sentiments, see Jones, *After Hiroshima*, 8, 22–23; and Dower, *Cultures of War*, 156, 161, 166.

15. Dower, *Cultures of War*, 156.

16. Leslie R. Groves, "Policy Meeting," May 5, 1943, Correspondence ("Top Secret") of the Manhattan Engineer District, 1942, microfilm publication M1109, file 23, National Archives (hereafter cited as Groves Papers). For a good summary of U.S. intelligence about the state of other nations' progress toward the bomb, see Robert S. Norris, *Racing for the Bomb: General Leslie R. Groves, the Manhattan Project's Indispensable Man* (South Royalton, VT: Steerforth Press, 2002), 281–311.

17. Jack Derry, "Summary of Target Committee Meetings on 10 and 11 May 1945," Groves Papers, file 5D.

18. Takaki, *Hiroshima*, 94.

19. Harry S. Truman to Samuel McCrea Cavert, August 11, 1945, Harry S. Truman Papers, Official File, 692-A: Manhattan Project.

20. See, for example, Newman, "Hiroshima and the Trashing of Henry Stimson," *New England Quarterly* 71, no. 1 (March 1998): 5–32. My own work on Stimson concluded that race was not an important factor in Stimson's decision making about the bomb, a conclusion that I no longer believe to be correct. Sean L. Malloy, *Atomic Tragedy: Henry L. Stimson and the Decision to Use the Bomb Against Japan* (Ithaca, NY: Cornell University Press, 2008), 169.

21. United Nations Educational, Scientific, and Cultural Organization (UNESCO), *Four Statements on the Race Question* (Paris: UNESCO, 1969), 32.

22. Office of Policy Planning and Research, United States Department of Labor, *The Negro Family: The Case for National Action* (Washington, DC: U.S. Government Printing Office, 1965);

Osmah F. Kahlil, *America's Dream Palace: Middle East Expertise and the Rise of the National Security State* (Cambridge, MA: Harvard University Press, 2016), 182–84.

23. Robert Vitalis, *White World Order, Black Power Politics: The Birth of American International Relations* (Ithaca, NY: Cornell University Press, 2015), 4.

24. Takaki, *Hiroshima*, 146.

25. Jones, *After Hiroshima*, 276; Christina Klein, *Cold War Orientalism: Asia in the Middlebrow Imagination, 1945–1961* (Berkeley: University of California Press, 2003), 14–15.

26. Jones, *After Hiroshima*, 2. Emphasis added.

27. Richard Rothstein, *The Color of Law: A Forgotten History of How Our Government Segregated America* (New York: Liveright, 2017).

28. Barbara J. Fields, "Slavery, Race, and Ideology in the United States of America," in *Racecraft: The Soul of Inequality in America Life*, ed. Karen E. Fields and Barbara J. Fields (London: Verso, 2012), 121.

29. Fields, "Slavery, Race, and Ideology," 120.

30. See, for example, Michael Hunt, *Ideology and U.S. Foreign Policy* (New Haven, CT: Yale University Press, 1987), 69–77.

31. Vitalis, *White World Order, Black Power Politics*, 178.

32. Micha Zenko and Jennifer Wilson, "How Many Bombs Did the United States Drop in 2016?," Council on Foreign Relations blog, https://www.cfr.org/blog-post/how-many-bombs-did-united-states-drop-2016.

33. Sean L. Malloy, "Civilians in the Combat Zone: Anglo-American Strategic Bombing," in *A Companion to World War II*, vol. 1, ed. Thomas W. Zeiler and Daniel M. DuBois (Oxford: Blackwell, 2013), 551–58.

34. A similar argument about the use of the machine gun as a tool of mass killing that began its life in European colonial wars can be found in John Ellis, *The Social History of the Machine Gun* (Baltimore: Johns Hopkins University Press, 1975), 79–148. For similar arguments about the evolution of aerial bombing in the context of Anglo-American colonialism, see Sven Lindqvist, *A History of Bombing*, trans. Linda Haverty Rugg (New York: New Press, 2003); and Sean L. Malloy, "Liberal Democracy and the Lure of Bombing in the Interwar United States," in *Making the American Century: Essays on the Political Culture of Twentieth Century America*, ed. Bruce J. Schulman (New York: Oxford University Press, 2014), 111.

35. M. Susan Lindee, *Suffering Made Real: American Science and the Survivors at Hiroshima* (Chicago: University of Chicago Press, 1997).

36. Gabrielle Hecht, *Being Nuclear: Africans and the Global Uranium Trade* (Cambridge, MA: MIT Press, 2014).

37. Shane J. Maddock, *Nuclear Apartheid: The Quest for American Atomic Supremacy from World War II to the Present* (Chapel Hill: University of North Carolina Press, 2010), ix.

38. Doug Brugge and Rob Goble, "The History of Uranium Mining and the Navajo People," *American Journal of Public Health* 92, no. 9 (2002): 1410–19.

39. Jean Allman, "Nuclear Imperialism and the Pan-African Struggle for Peace and Freedom: Ghana, 1959–1962," *Souls* 10, no. 2 (2008); Intondi, *African Americans against the Bomb*, 82–83.

40. Jones, *After Hiroshima*, 407, 429, 435; Maddock, *Nuclear Apartheid*, 242.

41. Vitalis, *White World Order, Black Power Politics*.

Chapter 5. Racing toward Armageddon? Soviet Views of Strategic Nuclear War, 1955–1972

1. David Holloway, *Stalin and the Bomb* (New Haven, CT: Yale University Press, 1994), chaps. 1–3.

2. I. A. Andriushin, A. K. Chernyshev, and Iu. A. Iudin, *Ukroshchenie iadra: Stranitsy istorii iadernogo oruzhiia i iadernoi infrastruktury SSSR* (Sarov: Krasnyi Oktiabr', 2003), 50–54; David Holloway, "Barbarossa and the Bomb," in *Intelligence in the European State System*, ed. Jonathan Haslam and Karina Urbach (Stanford, CA: Stanford University Press, 2014), 37–80.

3. See especially the series of volumes in *Atomnyi proekt SSSR: Dokumenty i materialy* (hereafter cited as *AP SSSR*), published by various publishers under the general editorship of L. D. Riabev between 1998 and 2010.

4. Svetlana Alliluyeva, *20 Letters to a Friend* (Harmondsworth, UK: Penguin Books, 1967) 164.

5. David Holloway, "Jockeying for Position in the Postwar World: Soviet Entry into the War against Japan in August 1945," in *The End of the Pacific War*, ed. Tsuyoshi Hasegawa (Stanford, CA: Stanford University Press, 2007), 145–88.

6. Robert Pickens Meiklejohn, *World War II Diary*, vol. 2, Library of Congress, Harriman Papers, Box 211, 721.

7. W. Averell Harriman and Elie Abel, *Special Envoy to Churchill and Stalin 1941–1946* (New York: Random House, 1975), 491.

8. "Postanovlenie GOKO No. 9887ss/op," in *AP SSSR Tom II Atomnaia bomba 1945–1954 Kniga 1*, 11–13. The Special Committee was at first attached to [*pri*] the State Defense Committee, then to the Council of People's Commissars, and later to the Council of Ministers after the State Defense Committee was abolished in September 1945.

9. See, for example, "Postanovlenie SNK SSSR No. 3117–937ss," in *AP SSSR Tom II Atomnaia bomba 1945–1954 Kniga 2* (Moscow: Nauka, VNIIEF, 2002).

10. Holloway, *Stalin and the Bomb*, 226.

11. Holloway, *Stalin and the Bomb*, 128.

12. A. A. Gromyko, *Pamiatnoe*, vol. 1, 2nd ed. (Moscow: Politizdat, 1990), 276.

13. Anatolii Gromyko, *Andrei Gromyko. V labirintakh Kremlia* (Moscow: Avtor, 1997), 65.

14. Douglas Birch, "Putin: Vietnam Worse than Stalin Purges," *Associated Press*, June 21, 2007.

15. "Putin Highlights Dark Side of America's History in TV Interview," *Wall Street Journal*, June 11, 2013.

16. The story of Bohr's activities is well told by Margaret Gowing, *Britain and Atomic Energy* (London: Macmillan, 1964), 346–66; and Abraham Pais, *Niels Bohr's Times, in Physics, Philosophy, and Polity* (Oxford: Clarendon Press, 1991), 473–508.

17. Andriushin et al., *Ukroshchenie iadra*, 131.

18. Dwight D. Eisenhower, "Radio and Television Address to the American People on the Geneva Conference," July 25, 1955, available via Gerhard Peters and John T. Woolley, *The American Presidency Project*, http://www.presidency.ucsb.edu/ws/?pid=10316.

19. Peter Caterall, ed., *The Macmillan Diaries: The Cabinet Years, 1950–1957* (London: Macmillan 2003), 458–59.

20. N. S. Khrushchev, "Memuary Nikity Sergevicha Khrushcheva," *Voprosy istorii*, 1992, 8–9, 75.

21. "Telegram from the Embassy in the United Kingdom to the Department of State," April 25, 1956, *Foreign Relations of the United States, 1955–1957*, vol. 20: *Regulation of Armaments; Atomic Energy* (Washington, DC: U.S. Government Printing Office, 1990), 380.

22. NSC 162/2 "Basic National Security Policy," *Foreign Relations of the United States, 1952–1954*, vol. 2: *National Security Policy* (Washington, DC: U.S. Government Printing Office, 1984), 582. On peaceful coexistence, see Holloway, *Stalin and the Bomb*, 335–37.

23. NSC 5501, "Basic National Security Policy," January 7, 1955, *Foreign Relations of the United States 1955–1957*, vol. 19: *National Security* (Washington, DC: U.S. Government Printing Office, 1990), 32, 33.

24. For Stalin's speech, see I. V. Stalin, "Rech' na predvybornom sobranii izbiratelei Stalinskogo izbiratel'nogo okruga goroda Moskvy," February 9, 1946, in *I. V. Stalin, Works*, vol. 3: *1946–1953*, ed. Robert H. McNeal (Stanford, CA: Hoover Institution Press, 1967), 2. For Khrushchev's speech, see *XX s"ezd KPSS* (Moscow: Politizdat, 1956), 36–38.

25. V. N. Iakovlev, ed., *Raketnyi shchit otechestva* (Moscow: TsIPK, RVSN, 1999), 68.

26. See National Intelligence Estimate, 11–8/1–61, "Strength and Deployment of Soviet Long-Range Ballistic Missile Forces," September 21, 1961, in *CORONA: America's First Satellite Program*, ed. Kevin C. Ruffner (Washington, DC: Central Intelligence Agency, 1995), 150.

27. V. D. Sokolovskii, *Sovremennaia voina* (Moscow: Izdatel'stvo Voennoi Akademii General'nogo Shtaba, 1960). This book is not to be confused with the volume on military strategy edited by Sokolovskii, which was published openly in 1962 (*Voennaia strategiia* [Moscow: Voenizdat, 1962]). The latter work has much less to say about nuclear war and is much less explicit about military operations.

28. Sokolovskii, *Sovremennaia voina*, 48, 42, 50, 76.

29. V. A. Zolotarev, ed., *Istoriia voennoi strategii Rossii* (Moscow: Kuchkovo pole, 2000), 442. This is an important study. Col. Gen. A. A. Danilevich, who served as assistant for doctrine and strategy to the chief of the General Staff from 1984 to 1990, headed the authors' collective.

30. David Alan Rosenberg, "The Origins of Overkill: Nuclear Weapons and American Strategy, 1945–1960," *International Security* 7, no. 4 (Spring 1983): 36.

31. Zolotarev, *Istoriia voennoi strategii*, 441.

32. *Die Strategie des Kernwaffenkrieges*, 39. This book was apparently published in Moscow in late 1964. It does not appear to have been published in a declassified form. The version used here is *Die Strategie des Kernwaffenkrieges*, Unter den Redaktion von Marschall der Sowjetunion R. J. Malinowski, Arbeitsübersetzung, Herausgegeben im Auftrage des Ministers für National Verteidigung von der Abteilung Militärwissenschaft des MfNV, 1964. BA-MA DVL/3/29942.

33. *Die Strategie des Kernwaffenkrieges*, 86.

34. Zolotarev, *Istoriia voennoi strategii*, 406.

35. "Nepravlenaia stenogramma doklada N.S. Khrushcheva na soveshchanii v TsK KPSS komanduiushchikh, nachal'nikov shtabov i chlenov Voennykh Sovetov okrugov o sokrashchenii Vooruzhennykh Sil SSSR," December 18, 1959, in *Zadacha osoboi gosudarstvennoi vazhnosti: Iz istorii sozdaniia raketno-iadernogo oruzhiia i Raketnykh voisk strategicheskogo naznacheniia (1945–1959)*, ed. V. I. Ivkin and G. A. Sukhina (Moscow: ROSSPEN, 2010), 894, 895.

36. "Nepravlenaia stenogramma," 901–2.

37. Bernard Brodie, *Strategy in the Missile Age* (Princeton, NJ: Princeton University Press, 1965 [1959]), 408–9, 269.

38. Matthew Evangelista, *Unarmed Forces: The Transnational Movement to End the Cold War* (Ithaca, NY: Cornell University Press, 1999). For a different emphasis, see Steven Zaloga, *The Kremlin's Nuclear Sword: The Rise and Fall of Russia's Strategic Nuclear Forces* (Washington, DC: Smithsonian Institution Press, 2002).

39. Alain C. Enthoven and K. Wayne Smith, *How Much Is Enough? Shaping the Defense Program, 1961–1969* (New York: Harper and Row, 1971), 170–74.

40. "Draft Memorandum from Secretary of Defense McNamara to President Johnson," December 6, 1963, *Foreign Relations of the United States, 1961–1963*, vol. 8: *National Security Policy* (Washington, DC: U.S. Government Printing Office, 1996), 549.

41. Vladimir Dvorkin and Aleksei Prokudin, *Povest' o 4 TsNII MO i iadernom sderzhivanii* (Iubileinii: izdatel'stvo PSTM, 2009), 38.

42. Both institutes had been set up after World War II to work on rocket development, and in the 1960s they both became engaged in systems analysis of strategic arms. The first came under the Ministry of Machine Building (the missile production ministry) from 1965, and the second was attached to the Strategic Rocket Forces when they were formed in 1959.

43. Yu. A. Mozzhorin, *Tak eto bylo* (Moscow: ZAO "Mezhdunarodnaia programma obrazovaniia," 2000), 145–49.

44. Mozzhorin, *Tak eto bylo*, 148.

45. Among the main sources are Mozzhorin, *Tak eto bylo*, 144–74; and S. N. Koniukhov, ed., *Prizvany vremenem. Ot protivostoianiia k mezhdunarodnomu sotrudnichestvu* (Dnepropetrovsk: ART-PRESS, 2004), 198–209.

46. Mozzhorin, *Tak eto bylo*, 160–61.

47. There are two detailed accounts by participants in the meeting: Mozzhorin, *Tak eto bylo*, 165–74; and M. A. Onishchenko, an engineer who accompanied the missile designer M. K. Yangel to the meeting. His account is to be found in Lev Andreev and Stanislav Koniukhov, *Iangel': Uroki i nasledie* (Dnepropetrovsk: ART-PRESS, 2001), 527–65.

48. Dvorkin and Prokudin, *Povest' o 4 TsNII*, 49.

49. See Holloway, "Barbarossa and the Bomb," 38–41.

50. James Cameron, *The Double Bluff: The Demise of America's First Missile Defense System and the Rise of Strategic Arms Limitation* (New York: Oxford University Press, 2018), 72–85, On the budget request, see William Beecher, "Johnson Wants Stand-by Fund for Nike-X System," *New York Times*, January 25, 1967.

51. Mikhail Pervov, *Sistemy raketno-kosmicheskoi oborony Rossii sozdavalis' tak*, 2nd ed. (Moscow: Aviarus-XXI, 2004), 469.

52. *Pravda*, October 25, 1961.

53. Pervov, *Sistemy raketno-kosmicheskoi oborony*, 203–4.

54. For a discussion of what Kosygin said, see Raymond L. Garthoff, "BMD and East-West Relations," in *Ballistic Missile Defense*, ed. Ashton B. Carter and David N. Schwartz (Washington, DC: Brookings Institution, 1984), 295–97.

55. Pervov, *Sistemy raketno-kosmicheskoi oborony*, 203–8; Iu.V. Votintsev, "Neizvestnye voiska ischeznuvshei sverkhderzhavy," *Voenno-istoricheskii zhurnal*, no. 9 (1993): 35–36.

56. "Remarks by Secretary of Defense Robert S. McNamara, September 18, 1967," *Bulletin of the Atomic Scientists*, December 1967, 26–31.

57. Pervov, *Sistemy raketno-kosmicheskoi oborony*, 259.

58. *Mech i Shchit Rossii: Raketno-iadernoe oruzhie i sistemy protivoraketnoi oborony* (Kaluga: Kaluga-press, 2007), 341; Grigorii Kisun'ko, *Sekretnaia zona: Ispoved' general'nogo konstruktora* (Moscow: Sovremmenik, 1996), 474.

59. Pervov, *Sistemy raketno-kosmicheskoi oborony*, 262; Aleksandr G. Savelyev and Nikolai N. Detinov, *The Big Five: Arms Control Decision-Making in the Soviet Union* (Westport, CT: Praeger, 1995), 22.

60. Pervov, *Sistemy raketno-kosmicheskoi oborony*, 227–30.

61. Wladimir S. Semjonow, *Von Stalin bis Gorbatschow: Ein halbes Jahrhundert in diplomatischer Mission 1939–1991* (Berlin: Nicolai, 1995), 348–49.

62. B. Ye. Chertok, *Rakety i liudi*, vol. 3 (Moscow: izdatel'stvo "RTSoft," 2007), 144.

63. Savelyev and Detinov, *The Big Five*, 22–23.

64. Evangelista, *Unarmed Forces*, 231; Lev Andreev and Stanislav Koniukhov, *Iangel': Uroki i nasledie* (Dnepropetrovsk: ART-PRESS, 2001), 553; Savelyev and Detinov, *The Big Five*, 18.

65. Zolotarev, ed., *Istoriia voennoi strategii Rossii*, 410.

66. Zolotarev, ed., *Istoriia voennoi strategii Rossii*, 379.

67. Zolotarev, ed., *Istoriia voennoi strategii Rossii*, 410; V. F. Utkin and Iu.A. Mozzhorin, "Raketnoe i kosmicheskoe oruzhie," in *Sovetskaia voennaia moshch'*, ed. A. V. Minaev (Moscow: "Voennyi parad," 1999), 186. See also Raymond L. Garthoff, *Deterrence and the Revoluion in Soviet Military Doctrine* (Washington, DC: Brookings Institution, 1990), 83. Garthoff argues that there was a Central Committee instruction to the military to make its plans and preparations on the basis that it would not be the first to use nuclear weapons, but he dates it from 1973 to 1975, not 1969.

68. Doklad A. A. Grechko, in *Materialy razbora operativno-strategicheskoi voennoi igry "zapad," provedennoi v oktiabre 1969g* (Moscow: Ministerstvo Oborony, 1969), 33. Accessed at Parallel History Program website, http://www.php.isn.ethz.ch/lory1.ethz.ch/index.html.

69. "O mezhdunarodnon polozhenii," Doklad tov. L. I. Brezhneva na Plenume TsK KPSS, May 19, 1972. RGANI f. 2, op. 3, d.265, l. 50.

70. David Alan Rosenberg, "Constraining Overkill: Contending Approaches to Nuclear Strategy, 1955–1965," 1, http://www.history.navy.mil/colloquia/cch9b.html.

71. Daniel Ellsberg, *The Doomsday Machine. Confessions of a Nuclear War Planner* (New York: Bloomsbury, 2017), 3.

72. Andrei Sakharov, *Vospominaniia* (New York: izd. Antona Chekhova, 1990), 353.

Chapter 6. The Evolution of Japanese Politics and Diplomacy under the Long Shadows of Hiroshima and Nagasaki, 1974–1991

1. On the Yoshida Doctrine, see Kōsaka Masataka, *Saishō Yoshida Shigeru* [Prime Minister Shigeru Yoshida] (Tokyo: Chuō Kōron, 1968); Nagai Yōnosuke, *Gendai to senryaku* [Modernity and strategy] (Tokyo: Bungei Shunjū, 1985); Michael J. Green, *Japan's Reluctant Realism: Foreign Policy in an Era of Uncertain Power* (New York: Palgrave, 2001), 11–17 ; Andrew L. Oros, *Normalizing Japan: Politics, Identity, and the Evolution of Security Practice* (Stanford, CA: Stanford Uni-

versity Press, 2008), 52–70; Richard J. Samuels, *Securing Japan: Tokyo's Grand Strategy and the Future of East Asia* (Ithaca, NY: Cornell University Press, 2007), 29–37.

2. Tadashi Aruga, "Japan and the United States: A Half-Century of Partnership," in *Japan and the United States: Fifty Years of Partnership*, ed. Chihiro Hosoya and A50 Editorial Committee (Tokyo: Japan Times, 2001), 1–29. On the Yoshida School, see Takuya Sasaki and Hiroshi Nakanishi, "The 1950s: Pax Americana and Japan's Postwar Resurgence," in *The History of US-Japan Relations: From Perry to the Present*, ed. Makoto Iokibe and Tosh Minohara (London: Palgrave, 2017), 159; John W. Dower, *Empire and Aftermath: Yoshida Shigeru and the Japanese Experience, 1878–1954* (Cambridge, MA: Harvard University Press, 1979), 315–16, 338.

3. Kishi's turbulent public life is exhaustively and critically examined in Hara Yoshihisa, *Kishi Nobusuke: Kensei no seijika* [Nobusuke Kishi: A politician of power and influence] (Tokyo: Iwanami, 1995). See also Hara's extensive interview with Kishi in Hara Yoshihisa, ed., *Kishi Nobusuke shōgenroku* [The testimony record of Kishi Nobusuke] (Tokyo: Mainichi Shimbun, 2003); and Kishi's own recollection in Kishi Nobusuke, *Kishi Nobusuke kaikoroku: Hoshu gōdō to anpokaitei* [The memoirs of Kishi Nobusuke: The conservative consolidation and the revision of the security treaty] (Tokyo: Kōsaidō, 1983). Of numerous books and articles published on the revision of the security pact, the most comprehensive study is Sakamoto Kazuya, *Nichibei dōmei no kizuna: Anpo jōyaku to sōgosei no mosaku* [The bond of alliance: The security treaty and search for mutuality] (Tokyo: Yūhikaku, 2000).

4. Yoshida's speech on June 12, 1962, at the American-Japan Society in Tokyo, in *Mō hitotsuno nichibei kankeishi: Nichibei kyokai siryo de yomu 20 seiki* [Another history of Japan-U.S. interaction: The 20th century through reading the documents of the American-Japan Society], ed. Nichibei kyokai (Tokyo: Chuō Kōron, 2012), 212. Ikeda's comment is cited in Itō Masaya, *Ikeda Hayato to sono jidai* [Ikeda Hayato and his times] (Tokyo: Asahi Shimbun, 1985), 234. Satō's remarks are in Edwin Reischauer to Dean Rusk, December 29, 1964, *Foreign Relations of the United States, 1964–1968*, vol. 13 (Washington, DC: U.S. Government Printing Office, 2001), 56; and in Tōgō Fumihiko's memorandum of conversation with Prime Minister Satō, October 7, 1969, http://www.mofa.go.jp/mofaj/gaiko/mitsuyaku/pdfs/k_1972kaku2.pdf; Bōei Chō, *Nihon no boei: Boei hakusho* [The defense of Japan: The white paper on defense] (Tokyo: Gyōsei, 1970), 36.

5. On Japan's ratification of the NPT, consult Kurosaki Akira's award-winning *Kakuheiki to nichibei kankei* [Nuclear weapons and Japanese-American relations] (Tokyo: Yūshisha, 2006). The Japanese diplomat was Murata Ryōhei, former undersecretary at the Foreign Ministry. Murata Ryōhei, *Kaisōroku: Tatakai ni yabureshi kuni ni tsukaete (jo kan)* [Memoirs of Murata Ryōhei: Having served a nation that lost a war, vol. 1] (Kyoto: Minerva Shobō, 2008), 212. Ushiba Nobuhiko, a prominent career diplomat at the Foreign Ministry, concurred with Murata, stating that "it is absolutely intolerable for Japan to be ranked as a second-rate nation permanently in international society as a result of Japan's entry into the NPT." Asami Tamotsu, *Hensetsu to aikoku: Gaikōkan Ushiba Nobuhiko no shōgai* [Defection and patriotism: The life of diplomat Ushiba Nobuhiko] (Tokyo: Bungei Shunjū, 2017), 169–70.

6. On Nixon's surprise announcement regarding China and its complicated repercussions in Asia, including Japan, see Masuda Hiroshi, ed., *Nikuson hōchū to reisen kōzō no henyō: Beichū sekkin no shōgeki to shūhen shokoku* [Nixon's visit to China and transformation of the Cold War structure: The impact of U.S.-Sino rapprochement on the peripheral nations]

(Tokyo: Keio University Press, 2006). See also John Pomfret, *The Beautiful Country and the Middle Kingdom: America and China, 1776 to the Present* (New York: Henry Holt, 2016), 452–61.

7. Kurosaki, *Kakuheiki to Nichibei Kankei*, 239; James Mann, *About Face: A History of America's Curious Relationship with China, from Nixon to Clinton* (New York: Vintage Books, 1998), 43; Michael Schaller, *Altered States: The United States and Japan since the Occupation* (New York: Oxford University Press, 1997), 230; Ishii Osamu, *Haken no kageri* [The sign of hegemonic decline] (Tokyo: Kashiwa Shobō, 2015), 149. Kissinger's remark to the Australian ambassador in August 1974 was reported in *Sankei shimbun*, April 15, 2004.

8. Matsunaga memorandums, October 7, 11, and 21, 1974, http://www.mofa.go.jp/mofaj/gaiko/mitsuyaku/pdfs/k_1960kaku3.pdf; memorandum of conversation between Tōgō and Hodgson, November 15, 1974, http://www.mofa.go.jp/mofaj/gaiko/mitsuyaku/pdfs/k_1960kaku4.pdf; Kurihara Takakazu memorandum, June 22, 1981, ibid.; George R. Packard, *Edwin O. Reischauer and the American Discovery of Japan* (New York: Columbia University Press, 2010), 243–44; *Asahi shimbun*, July 20, 1985. Kurihara, director of the Treaties Bureau, later recalled that his superiors who had read his memorandum told him that "your proposal is quite understandable. Still we cannot do anything regarding this whole matter." Kurihara Takakazu, *Gaikō shōgenroku* [The testimony record of diplomacy] (Tokyo: Iwanami, 2010), 255–56.

9. *Public Papers of the Presidents: Gerald Ford, 1975*, vol. 2 (Washington, DC: U.S. Government Printing Office, 1976), 1112–17, 1950–55. On the strategic importance of the Miki-Ford joint statement, see also Kurosaki, *Kakuheiki to nichibei kankei*, 258–59.

10. On South Korea's nuclear program, see Etel Solingen, *Nuclear Logics: Contrasting Paths in East Asia and the Middle East* (Princeton, NJ: Princeton University Press, 2007), chap. 4.

11. On the evolution of Japanese defense policy under the Miki administration, see Tanaka Akihiko, *Anzen hoshō* [National security] (Tokyo: Yomiuri Shimbun, 1997), 253–64; Yoshihide Soeya and Robert D. Eldridge, "The 1970s: Stresses on the Relationship," in Makoto and Minohara, *The History of US-Japan Relations*, 183. On Japan's participation in the NSG, see William Burr, "A Scheme of 'Control': The United States and the Origins of the Nuclear Suppliers' Group, 1974–1976," *International Historical Review* 36 (2014): 254–55.

12. Yoshida Shingo, *Nichibei dōmei no seidoka* [The institutionalization of the Japan-U.S. alliance] (Nagoya: Nagoya University Press, 2012), 252–56. Kubo's memorandum is cited in Sasaki Yoshitaka, "Kakusenryaku no nakano Nihon" [Japan in the nuclear strategy], in *Kaku to taiketsusuru nijjuseiki* [Confronting nuclearism: The twentieth-century world in crisis], ed. Sakomoto Yoshikazu (Tokyo: Iwanami, 1999), 264–65. On the evolution of Japanese foreign policy in the late 1970s, see Nakanishi Hiroshi, "Jiritsuteki kyōchō no mosaku [The search for autonomous cooperation], in *Sengo Nihon gaikōshi* [The diplomatic history of postwar Japan], ed. Iokibe Makoto (Tokyo: Yūhikaku, 2014), 169–86.

13. Robert A. Wampler, "Reversals of Fortune?: Shifting U.S. Images of Japan as Number One, 1979–2000," in *Partnership: The United States and Japan 1951–2001*, ed. Akira Iriye and Robert A. Wampler (Tokyo: Kodansha International, 2001), 249.

14. On the Fukuda administration's foreign and defense policy, see Soeya and Eldridge, "The 1970s," 186–88; Green, *Japan's Reluctant Realism*, 80, 170–71. On Brzezinski's visit to Tokyo and his conversation with Fukuda, see Zbigniew Brzezinski, *Power and Principle: Memoirs of Na-*

tional Security Adviser, 1977–1981, rev. ed. (New York: Farrar, Straus and Giroux, 1985), 218. PD 8, approved on March 24, 1977, is in *Foreign Relations of the United States, 1977–1980*, vol. 26 (Washington, DC: U.S. Government Printing Office, 2015), https://history.state.gov/historicaldocuments/frus1977-80v26/d330 (italics in original). See also Don Oberdofer, *Senator Mansfield: The Extraordinary Life of a Great American Statesman and Diplomat* (Washington, DC: Smithsonian Books, 2009), 461–66.

15. The Kōsaka report is in Tanaka, *Anzen hoshō*, 278.

16. On the Ōhira administration's foreign and defense policy, see Soeya and Eldridge, "The 1970s," 188–90; Mōri Kazuko, *Nichū kankei* [Japan-China relations] (Tokyo: Iwanami, 2006), 106–16; Takeda Yū, *Keizai taikoku Nihon no taibei kyōchō* [Major economic power Japan's cooperative diplomacy toward the United States] (Tokyo: Minerva Shobō, 2015). Satisfied with his meeting with Ōhira on May 2, 1979, President Carter wrote in his diary that it "was one of the most productive diplomatic sessions of our administration." Jimmy Carter, *White House Diary* (New York: Farrar, Straus and Giroux, 2010), 317. According to George Packard, who published an excellent biography of Edwin Reischauer, Reischauer's "favorite Japanese politician was Ōhira Masayoshi." He quoted Reischauer as saying, "Ōhira is a real intellectual as well as a statesman, and a man of character and principle. He is also a very good politician. I think that we can expect great things of him." Packard, *Edwin Reischauer and the American Discovery of Japan*, 177.

17. Shimizu Ikutarō, *Nihon yo kokka tare: Kaku no sentaku* [Japan! Be a sovereign nation: A nuclear option] (Tokyo: Bungei Shunjū, 1980). See also Ōtake Hideo, *Nihon no boei to kokunai seiji: Detanto kara gunkaku he* [Japan's defense and domestic politics: From détente to military enlargement] (Tokyo: San-ichi Shobō, 1983), which provides a critical overview of the political situation of Japan in the 1970s.

18. Nakasone recalls his eventful political career in Nakasone Yasuhiro, *Tenchi yūjo* [The sentience of heaven and earth] (Tokyo: Bungei Shunjū, 1996); see 120–21, 210–11 for Nakasone's scathing comment on Yoshida and his recollection of Ikeda's remarks. On Nakasone's secret order regarding the possible development of nuclear weapons, see Nakasone Yakuhiro, *Jiseiroku: Rekish hotei no hikoku toshite* [The record of self-reflection: As a defendant in the court of history] (Tokyo: Shinchōsha, 2004), 224–25.

19. Nakasone's National Press Club speech and his conversation with Laird are in Sasaki, "Kaku senryaku no nakano nihon," 292; and Hattori Ryuji, *Nakasone Yasuhiro: Daitoryōteki shushō no kiseki* [Yasuhiro Nakasone: The trajectory of a presidential prime minister] (Tokyo: Chuō Kōron Shinsha, 2015), 121.

20. William R. Nester, *Power across the Pacific: A Diplomatic History of American Relations with Japan* (London: Macmillan, 1996), 347–50; Nakasone, *Tenchi Yūjo*, 430; George P. Shultz, *Turmoil and Triumph: My Years as Secretary of State* (New York: Scribner's, 1993), 185–86.

21. Peter Katzenstein, *Cultural Norms and National Security: Police and Military in Postwar Japan* (Ithaca, NY: Cornell University Press, 1996), 128; Thomas U. Berger, *Cultures of Antimilitarism: National Security in Germany and Japan* (Baltimore: Johns Hopkins University Press, 1998), 135–37.

22. Amy L. Catalinac, "Why New Zealand Took Itself out of ANZUS: Observing 'Oppositions for Autonomy' in Asymmetric Alliances," *Foreign Policy Analysis* 6 (2010): 319; Hans Kris-

tensen, "Section 4: The 'Secret' Agreement," in *Japan under the US Nuclear Umbrella*, http://www.nautilus.org/archives/library/security/papers/Nuclear-Umbrella-4.html.

23. For Nakasone's response to this affair, see articles in the *Asahi shimbun* from January 20, 26, and 27, and February 5, 9, 17, and 20, 1985.

24. Matsunaga Nobuo, *Aru gaikōkan no kaisō* [A diplomat's recollections] (Tokyo: Nihon Keizai Shimbun, 2002), 111; Schaller, *Altered States*, 254–60; Walter LaFeber, *The Clash: U.S.-Japanese Relations throughout History* (New York: Norton, 1997), 379–89. Senator Tsongas's remark is cited in Michael Schallar and George Rising, *The Republican Ascendancy: American Politics, 1968–2001* (Wheeling, IL: Harlan Davidson, 2001), 115. On Trump's advertisement, see, for example, *New York Times*, September 2, 1987. On the increasingly acrimonious bilateral relationship in the late 1980s and early 1990s, see Ishii Osamu, "Pāru Hābā no zanzō: Nichibei no keizai shakai bunka masatsu, 1982–92nen" [The afterimage of Pearl Harbor: The economic, social and cultural friction between Japan and the U.S., 1982–92], in *Kioku toshiteno Pāru Hābā* [Pearl Harbor as memory], ed. Hosoya Chihiro, Iriye Akira, and Ōshiba Ryo (Kyoto: Minerva Shobō, 2004), 52–70.

25. Ishi Osamu, "Pāru Hābā no zanzō," 57–66; Martin Harwit, *An Exhibit Denied: Lobbying the History of Enola Gay* (New York: Copernicus, 1996). Japanese media gave Ambassador Armacost the nickname "Mr. Gaiatsu" ("Mr. External Pressure") owing to his forceful manner of dealing with the Japanese negotiators over trade and defense. See Michael H. Armacost, *Friends or Rivals?: The Insider's Account of U.S.-Japan Relations* (New York: Columbia University Press, 1996), 68–72.

26. *Washington Post*, March 27, 1990; Report of the Bush Administration on the Strategic Framework for the Asian Pacific Rim, April 19, 1990 (Washington, DC: U.S. Government Printing Office, 1990).

27. George H. W. Bush address, September 27, 1991, http://www.presidency.ucsb.edu/ws/index.php?pid=20035. See also George Bush and Brent Scowcroft, *A World Transformed* (New York: Knopf, 1998), 544.

28. The 1992 law stipulated that before Japan's SDF may be dispatched, five conditions need to be met: (1) a cease-fire must be in place; (2) the parties to the conflict must consent to the peacekeeping operation; (3) the operation must maintain strict impartiality; (4) Japan's participation may be terminated if any of the above conditions fails to be satisfied; and (5) SDF's use of force must be limited to a minimum and only in self-defense. The Miyazawa comment is cited in Yoshida Fumihiko, *Shōgen: Kaku yokushi no seiki* [Testimony: The century of nuclear deterrence] (Tokyo: Iwanami, 2000), 317–18. On the complicated issue of memories of the Asia-Pacific War that continued to affect the Asia-Pacific region, see Kiichi Fujiwara's essay in chapter 12 of this volume and *Sensō o kiokusuru* [Remembering war] (Tokyo: Kodansha, 2001); Marc Gallicchio, ed., *The Unpredictability of the Past: Memories of the Asia-Pacific War in U.S.-East Asian Relations* (Durham, NC: Duke University Press, 2007). That Ozawa's book was immediately translated into English and published as *Blueprint for a New Japan: The Rethinking of a Nation* (New York: Kodansha International, 1994), with an introduction by Senator Jay Rockefeller, is an indication of Ozawa's powerful political and international influence in the 1990s. It should be noted that Ozawa does not argue for a nuclear Japan in the book; rather, he emphasizes the importance of nuclear disarmament under Japan's initiative.

Chapter 7. The Bandung Conference and the Origins of Japan's Atoms for Peace Aid Program for Asian Countries

The research for this chapter was partially supported by the Ministry of Education, Science, Sports and Culture, Grant-in-Aid for Scientific Research (C), 2016–2018 (16K03519, Shinsuke Tomotsugu), as well as 2019–2021 (19K01501, Shinsuke Tomotsugu).

1. As far as I know, Mara Drogan was the first scholar to point out the importance of the nexus between the Bandung Conference and the U.S. Atoms for Peace campaign overseas. Mara Drogan, "Nuclearism and the Bandung Conference of 1955," Conference Paper for Society for Historians of American Foreign Relations Annual Meeting, Lexington, Kentucky June 19, 2013. This chapter will focus not on this nexus but on the related issue of the origins of Japan's nuclear aid program.

2. On February 8, 1955, Vyacheslav Mikhailovich Molotov called on the United States to compete with the USSR in nuclear energy rather than nuclear weapons.

3. There were two A-bomb development projects in Japan during World War II: the Ni-Project, sponsored by the Imperial Japanese Army, and the F-Project, sponsored by navy. Nishina took command of the Ni-Project team at the Institute of Physical and Chemical Research (RIKEN), while Arakatsu Bunsaku, physicist and professor at Kyoto Imperial University, conducted the F-Project. See John W. Dower, "Science, Society, and the Japanese Atomic Bomb Project during WWII," *Bulletin of Concerned Asian Scholars* 10, no. 2 (April–June 1978): 41–54.

4. Hiroshige Tetsu, *Sengo Nihon no kagaku undo* (Tokyo: Chuo Koron, 1960), 206–7.

5. Yamamoto Akihiro, *Kaku to Nihonjin: Hiroshima, Gozilla, Fukushima* (Tokyo: Chuo Koronshinsha, 2015), 18.

6. The JSP split into the Right Socialist Party and the Left Socialist Party in 1951; however, they were reunited in October 1955. Whether it was right or left, the JSP in the 1950s supported nuclear energy for peaceful purposes while opposing nuclear weapons. On the party's pronuclear energy stance, see Tetsuro Kato, *Nihon no Syakaisyugi: Genbaku hantai, Genpatsu Suishinnno ronri* (Tokyo: Iwanami Shoten, 2013). See also Sumitomo Akifumi, "Genshiryoku Kaihatsu to 55 nen taisei," in *Kaku no Seiki: Nihon Genshiryoku Kaihatsu shi*, ed. Kojita Yasunao, Okada Tomohiro, Sumitomo Akifumi, and Tanaka Kiyo (Tokyo: Tokyodo Shuppan, 2016), 168–92.

7. Carolien Stolte, "Social and Political Movements: Experiments in Anti-imperialist Mobilization," in *Explorations in History and Globalization*, ed. Cátia Antunes and Karwan Fatah-Black (Abingdon, UK: Routledge, 2016), 105–6.

8. Asia Shokoku Kaigi Nihon Junbi Iinkai, *14 okuninno koe: Asia shokoku Kaigi no kiroku* (Tokyo: Orizon, 1955), 207–33.

9. Asia Shokoku Kaigi Nihon Junbi Iinkai, *14 okuninno koe*, 111–13.

10. Tominaga Gorō, "Asia shokoku no kagaku rentai" [Solidarity of Asian countries in science], *Shizen* 10, no. 9 (1955): 38–45.

11. Matthew Jones, *After Hiroshima: The United States, Race and Nuclear Weapons in Asia, 1945–1965* (Cambridge: Cambridge University Press. 2010), esp. chap. 7.

12. "Memorandum from the Acting Chief of the Reports and Operations Staff (Gilman) to the Secretary of the State," February 8, 1955, *Foreign Relations of the United States, 1961–1963*, vol. 21: *Africa* (Washington, DC: Government Printing Office, 1995), 30.

13. Yuka Tsuchiya, "Reisen no media toshiteno USIS eiga," in *Denpa denei denshi*, ed. Mamie Misawa, Makoto Kawashima, and Takumi Sato (Tokyo: Seikyusya, 2012), 363.

14. "Takasaki daihyou no ippan enzetsu," Asia Africa Kaigi Ikken B'-0049, Diplomatic Archives of the Ministry of Foreign Affairs of Japan (hereafter cited as DAMOFA).

15. According to historian Taizō Miyagi, two lines of thoughts existed within MOFA on how to behave at the conference. One group attached more importance to ties with the Western bloc, while the other group regarded friendship with other countries, communist or capitalist, as more important. Taizō Miyagi, *Bandonkaigi to Nihon no Ajia Fukki: Amerika to Ajia no Hazamade* (Tokyo: Soshisha, 2001), 85.

16. Gaimu Sho Kokusai kyoroku kyoku Daisan Ka, "A.A. Kaigi Kanren Shiryo Dai 2–3: Genshiryoku Heiwatekiriyo no mondai ni kansuru wagakuni no taido-dainiji an," April 12, 1955, B'5. 1.0. J/U9, in *Nichibeikan Genshiryoku no Higunjitekiriyo ni kansuru Kyouryoku Kyouteikankei*, vol.1, DAMOFA. To this memorandum MOFA, "with deliberation with Science Council," attached a different one titled "Comments on the Effects of Radioactive Damages," although this was not declassified. MOFA argued that the latter "could be used as official comments of the Japanese representative." This indicates the frequent contact between scientists and the diplomats.

17. See Akira Kurosaki, "Japan's Nuclear Disarmament and Non-proliferation Diplomacy during the Cold War: The Myth and Reality of a Nuclear Bombed Country," in *Joining the Non-Proliferation Treaty Deterrence, Non-Proliferation and the American Alliance*, ed. John Baylis and Yoko Iwama (Abingdon, UK: Routledge, 2018).

18. Gaimu Sho Kokusai kyoroku kyoku Daisan Ka, "A.A. Kaigi Kanren Shiryo Dai 2–3."

19. Gaimu Sho Kokusai kyoroku kyoku Daisan Ka, "Genshiryoku heiwa riyo ni kansuru A.A. chiiki nai ni okeru Kakkoku Kannno kyoryoku no kanousei," April 12, 1955, B'5. 1.0. J/U9, in *Nichibeikan Genshiryoku no Higunjitekiriyo ni kansuru Kyouryoku Kyouteikankei*, vol. 1, DAMOFA.

20. Kokkai dai 22 Shoko Iinkai, *Shugi In Kaigiroku Joho*, http://kokkai.ndl.go.jp/SENTAKU/syugiin/022/0216/02205130216011c.html.

21. Keisoshobo ed. Taketani Mitsuo senshu (anthologies), "Kaisetsu," in *Kaku Jidai: Shokoku Shugi to Taikoku Shugi* (Tokyo: Keisoshobo, 1974), 361. According to the editor, Taketani's argument originally appeared in the journal *Sekaihyoron* in 1957. These editions of *Sekaihyoron* have been lost, however. Masayuki Karasudani noted Taketani's argument for the first time in his article "Futatsu no Kaku Gensetsu to Kaku Arerugi," *Hogaku kenkyu*, no. 2 (2016): 189–211.

22. Regarding the details of the internal dispute and policy-making process within the Eisenhower administration about the Asian Nuclear Center, see Tomotsugu Shinsuke, "Ajia Genshiryoku Center Kōso to Sono Zasetsu" [The initiative and setback of the "Asian Nuclear Center": An aspect of the Eisenhower administration's East Asian diplomacy], *Kokusai seiji* [International relations], no. 163 (2011): 14–27.

23. Li Qianyu, "America no Asia Africa kaigi ni kansuru shiron" [A study of the U.S. policy toward the Asian-African conference], *Shakai shisutem kenkyu* 32 (2016).

24. Onward Saving Telegram from Bangkok to Foreign Office: Addressed to Foreign Office telegram No. 10 Saving of February 25, 1955, FO 371/116923, Discussions and Meetings of the Manila Treaty, United Kingdom National Archive (hereafter cited as UKNA).

25. NSC, Progress Report on NSC5405, December 21,1955; and NSC, Progress Report on

NSC5405 and Portions of NSC5429/5, July 11, 1956, George Washington University, National Security Archive.

26. Memorandum, A. A.Wells (director, Division of International Affairs, United States Atomic Energy Commission) to Philip J. Farley, Department of the State, "McKinney Review—Draft History of the Proposal for an Asian Nuclear Center," February 10, 1960, RG59, Special Assistant to the Secretary of Energy and Outer Space, Records relating to Atomic Energy Matters 1955–63, Box 352, National Archives at College Park (hereafter cited as NACP).

27. John W McDonald, Brookhaven Team, Draft Working Paper, RG59, Special Assistant to the Secretary of Energy and Outer Space, Records relating to Atomic Energy Matters 1944–63; Study for A Colombo Plan Nuclear Center, Preliminary Edition, August 15, 1956, Prepared for the International Cooperation Administration by Brookhaven National Laboratory Associated Universities Inc., Box 351, NACP.

28. Memorandum of Conversation, Participants, Mr. Robertson FE, Sir Hubert Graves, John Roper British Embassy, Gerald Smith S/AE, "Asian Nuclear Center," October 19, 1955, RG59, Box 352, NACP.

29. Memorandum, Gerald Smith to Herbert Prochnow, "Asian Nuclear Center—Your Memorandum of November 23, 1955," November 25, 1955, RG59, Box 352, NACP.

30. Nakasone Yasuhiro, "Ajia Genshiryoku Center ni kansuru Shitumon [nitsuite]" [On the Inquiry about the Asian Nuclear Center], December 3, 2009. This two-page typed letter was sent as a reply to an inquiry I made when I wrote my dissertation. In it, Nakasone argues that "the governmental initiative to invite the atomic center you inquired about was [as a result of] what I took action [on] in consultation with Mr. Tomabechi Gizo."

31. Memorandum of Conversation, Participants, The Undersecretary, Sadao Iguchi Ambassador of Japan, FE-William Sebald, "Regional Research and Training Center for Nuclear Energy in Asia," December 13, 1955, RG59, Box 352, NACP.

32. Department Telegram 1222, Embassy Telegram 1339, Ambassador John Allison to the Secretary of State John F. Dulles, December 13, 1955, RG59, Box 352, NACP.

33. Shingo Tanaka, "Nichibei genshiryoku Kyotei eno dotei-beikoku ni okeru Kakuheiki shiyo no kioku 1951–1955" [The U.S.-Japan Agreement for "Peaceful Use" of Nuclear Energy 1951–1955: The memory of the usage of nuclear weapons and Cold War strategy], *Doshisha America kenkyu*, no. 52 (2016): 1–17.

34. Memorandum, R. L. Sneider to G. A. Morgan, "Japanese Participation in the Asian Nuclear Center," June 12, 1955, RG59, Box 352, NACP.

35. Special Committee for the Promotion of Science and Technology, Minutes, May 11, 1956, http://kokkai.ndl.go.jp/SENTAKU/syugiin/024/0068/02405110068021.pdf.

36. Special Committee for the Promotion of Science and Technology, Minutes, February 13, 1956, http://kokkai.ndl.go.jp/SENTAKU/syugiin/024/0068/02402130068002.pdf.

37. Minutes, Second Meeting of Special Committee of Atomic Energy under the Science Council of Japan, June 2, 1956, Nukiyama Heiichi Record, Tohoku University Archive.

38. Minutes, Committee on the Atomic Energy Problem under the Science Council of Japan, October 24, 1956, Sakata Archival Library, Department of Physics, Nagoya University.

39. Minutes, Atomic Nucleus Special Commission under the Science Council of Japan, June 14, 1956, Sakata Archival Library, Department of Physics, Nagoya University.

40. Special Committee for the Promotion of Science and Technology, Minutes, November 20, 1956, http://kokkai.ndl.go.jp/SENTAKU/syugiin/025/0068/02511120068002.pdf.

41. Christopher J. Lee argues Gamal Abdel Nasser, concerned about the UK's lingering influence and the Baghdad Pact, used the Bandung Conference to have closer ties with and obtain mentorship from Nehru. See Christopher J. Lee, "The Rise of Third World Diplomacy Success and Its Meanings at the 1955 Asian-African Conference in Bandung, Indonesia," in *Foreign Policy Breakthroughs: Cases in Successful Diplomacy*, ed. Robert Hutchings and Jeremi Suri (Oxford: Oxford University Press, 2015), 47–71.

42. Lee, "The Rise of Third World Diplomacy Success."

43. Special Committee for the Promotion of Science and Technology, Minutes, March 12, 1957, http://kokkai.ndl.go.jp/SENTAKU/syugiin/026/0068/02603120068013.pdf. According to a telegram from the British Embassy in Rangoon, Burma, to the Canadian Department of External Affairs on January 2, 1956, the United Kingdom conducted a geographical survey at the request of Burma. The Burmese government was advised at the Geneva Conference on the Use of Atomic Energy (held in August 8–20, 1955) that Burma would be a very promising country in which to find radioactive material. File No. 14003-B-12-1-40 from RG25, vol. 7881, Interim box no. 375. Library and Archives Canada (LAC).

44. Sagane was a nuclear physicist who joined Nishina Yoshio's team during World War II to develop a Japanese atomic bomb. In 1953 Nakasone Yasuhiro met with Sagane, who worked at the Lawrence Laboratory in Berkeley at the time, at the Japanese Consulate-General in San Francisco. Sagane explained to Nakasone the importance of establishing an unwavering national nuclear policy, drawing up related legislation and a budget, and gathering preeminent scholars for the purpose. Nakasone Yasuhiro, "Genshiryoku no shinwa jidai" [The mythical age of atomic energy], keynote lecture at Tokyo Institute of Technology, October 31, 2006, *Nihon Genshiryoku Gakkaishi* [Journal of Atomic Energy Society of Japan] 49, no. 2 (2007): 38–42.

45. Nihon Gakujutsu Kaigi, Gakujutsu Ka, "Ajia Genshiryoku Center Uchiawasekai (I)" [The Consultation on the Asian Nuclear Center (I)], June 7, 1957, Asia Nuclear Center File, Science Council of Japan Library (hereafter cited as SCJL).

46. Nihon Gakujutsu Kaigi, Gakujutsu Ka, "Ajia Genshiryoku Center Uchiawasekai-shusseki hokoku (II)" [Consultation on Asian Nuclear Center—attendance report (II)], June 11, 1957, Asia Nuclear Center File, SCJL.

47. Nihon Gakujutsu Kaigi, Genshiryoku Mondai Iinkai, "Ajia Genshiryoku Center ni kansuru Iken" [Opinion on the Asian Nuclear Center] (handwritten manuscript), June 19, 1957. Asia Nuclear Center File, SCJL.

48. Ajia genshiryoku Kyoryoku taisei no kakuritu ni kansuru Ketsugi, November 18, 1957, National Archives of Japan.

49. Instead of an "Asia Radio Isotope Center," originally planned to provide training with Southeast Asian countries, JAERI established the "Radioisotopes School."

50. Angela N. H. Creager, *Life Atomic: A History of Radioisotopes in Science and Medicine* (Chicago: University of Chicago Press, 2013), 107–42.

51. Nuclear White Paper, 1962, http://www.aec.go.jp/jicst/NC/about/hakusho/wp1962/index.htm. There were also trainees from Burma (6), Czechoslovakia (1), Hong Kong (1), Iran (3), Iraq (1), Italy (1), Mexico (1), the Philippines (6), Ceylon (3), United Arab Republic (1), and South Vietnam (2). The numbers listed here probably indicate the number of students at the school at the time the report was published.

52. Special Committee for the Promotion of Science and Technology, Minutes, March 8, 1962, http://kokkai.ndl.go.jp/SENTAKU/syugiin/040/0068/04003080068012.pdf.

53. H. B. Shepheard at Whitehall "Cairo Radioisotope Nuclear Centre," July 1, 1960, EG1/522 Establishment of a regional radioisotope centre in Cairo, UKNA.

54. International Atomic Energy Agency, Board of Governors, Gov. Or. 283, April 24, 1962, *Official Record of the Two Hundred and Eighty-third Meeting Held at the Neue Hofburg, Vienna, on Friday 2 March 1962, at 10:55 am*, EG1/522 Establishment of a regional radioisotope centre in Cairo, UKNA.

55. Memorandum from the Deputy Under Secretary of State for Political Affairs (Murphy) to the Under Secretary of State (Hoover), *Foreign Relations of the United States, 1955–1957*, vol. 15: *Arab-Israeli Dispute, January 1–July 26, 1956*.

56. "Agreement on Providing Radioisotopes Training Courses by the IAEA," *Genshiryoku iinkai geppo* [Atomic power monthly] 9, no. 5 (May 1964), http://www.aec.go.jp/jicst/NC/about/ugoki/geppou/V09/N05/196407V09N05.HTML.

57. IAEA, "Japan and Atomic Co-operation," *IAEA Bulletin* 7–3 (September 1965): 11–18, https://www.iaea.org/sites/default/files/publications/magazines/bulletin/bull7-3/07304701118.pdf.

58. *Asahi shimbun*, March 14, 1963.

59. In 1960 Japan and fourteen other countries, including the United States, the United Kingdom, and Canada, had jointly proposed international safeguards at the IAEA.

Chapter 8. India in the Early Nuclear Age

1. Bharat Karnad, *Nuclear Weapons and Indian Security: The Realist Foundations of Strategy* (New Delhi: Macmillan, 2002).

2. George Perkovich, *India's Nuclear Bomb: The Impact of Global Proliferation* (Berkeley: University of California Press, 2001), 14–15, 20.

3. The concept of "nuclear ambivalence" is a major theme of the pioneering work of Itty Abraham. Among his many publications, see "The Ambivalence of Nuclear Histories," *Osiris* 21, no. 1 (2006): 49–65; and *The Making of the Indian Atomic Bomb: Science, Secrecy and the Postcolonial State* (London: Zed Books, 1998).

4. Srinath Raghavan, *India's War: The Second World War and Modern South Asia* (New York: Basic Books, 2016), 88–94.

5. Raghavan, *India's War*, 327–28.

6. Raghabendra Chattopadhyaya, "The Idea of Planning in India, 1930–1951" (PhD diss., Australian National University, 1985); Benjamin Zachariah, *Developing India: An Intellectual and Social History c. 1930–1950* (New Delhi: Oxford University Press, 2005).

7. Medha Kudaisya, "'The Promise of Partnership': Indian Business, the State and the Bombay Plan of 1944," *Business History Review* 88 (2014): 97–131.

8. Jagdish N. Sinha, *Science, War and Imperialism: India in the Second World War* (Leiden: Brill, 2008).

9. Cited in Jahnavi Phalkey, *Atomic State: Big Science in Twentieth-Century India* (New Delhi: Permanent Black, 2013), 66–72. The quotation appears on page 67.

10. For Nehru's stand on these running debates, see Jawaharlal Nehru, *The Discovery of India* (Calcutta: Signet Press, 1946), passim.

11. Note of September 5, 1946, *Selected Works of Jawaharlal Nehru, Second Series*, vol. 1 (New Delhi: Distributed by Oxford University Press, 1984–) (hereafter cited as *SWJN-SS*).

12. Interview with press, April 5, 1946, *Selected Works of Jawaharlal Nehru, First Series* (New Delhi: Orient Longman, 1972–), 121.

13. Editorial by Nehru in *National Herald*, July 2, 1946, *SWJN-SS*, 1:543–44.

14. Letter to Peston Grover, October 26, 1945, in *Collected Works of Mahatma Gandhi* (New Delhi: Publications Division, Ministry of Information and Broadcasting, Government of India, 1958) (hereafter cited as *CWMG*), 88:450.

15. "Atom Bomb and Ahimsa," *Harijan*, July 7, 1946, *CWMG*, 91:276.

16. Robert S. Anderson, *Nucleus and Nation: Scientists, International Networks, and Power in India* (Chicago: University of Chicago Press, 2010), 127–28, 186.

17. Cited in Phalkey, *Atomic State*, 119, 125–26.

18. Cited in Anderson, *Nucleus and Nation*, 187.

19. Speech, January 4, 1947, *SWJN-SS*, 1:377–78.

20. Nehru to Baldev Singh, *SWJN-SS*, 5:420.

21. Cited in Phalkey, *Atomic State*, 243.

22. Cited in Perkovich, *India's Nuclear Bomb*, 19–20.

23. Anderson, *Nucleus and Nation*, 199–200.

24. Resolution of AEC, August 20, 1948, Jawaharlal Nehru Papers, Nehru Memorial Museum & Library.

25. Minutes of a Special Meeting of the Indian Atomic Energy Commission, January 16, 1950, Bibliothèque Nationale de France (BnF), Institut Curie Archives, Paris, Carton F-86, CEA: Relations avec l'Inde (1948–50), Papers of Frédéric Joliot-Curie, accessed at Nuclear Proliferation International History Project, Woodrow Wilson Center, Washington, DC.

26. Robert J. McMahon, *The Cold War on the Periphery: The United States, India and Pakistan* (New York: Columbia University Press, 1994).

27. Cited in Perkovich, *India's Nuclear Bomb*, 24.

28. Cited in Anderson, *Nucleus and Nation*, 187.

29. Jayita Sarkar, "'Wean Them Away from French Tutelage': Franco-Indian Nuclear Relations and Anglo-American Anxieties during the Early Cold War, 1948–1952," *Cold War History* 15, no. 3 (2015): 374–94.

30. Press conference, October 4, 1952, *SWJN-SS*, 19:139.

31. Statement in Parliament, May 10, 1954, *SWJN-SS*, 25:124–26.

32. Statement in Parliament, April 2, 1954, *SWJN-SS*, 25:445–48.

33. Nehru to Churchill, April 4, 1954, *SWJN-SS*, 25:449.

34. *Hindu*, October 11, 1957.

35. Perkovich, *India's Nuclear Bomb*, 28–29.

Chapter 9. The Unnecessary Option to Go Nuclear: Japan's Nonnuclear Policy in an Era of Uncertainty, 1950s–1960s

1. On Japan's antinuclear movement, see Maruhama Eriko, *Gensuikin shomei undo no tanjyo: Tokyo, Suginami no jyumin pawaa no suimyaku* [The origin of the signature campaign against atomic and hydrogen bombs: The stream of powers of the Suginami, Tokyo citizens]

(Gaifusha: Tokyo, 2011); Araki Keiko, "Hibakukoku no gyakusetsu: 1957nen kara 1963nen no hankaku undo no seisui" [The paradox of Japan, the victim of nuclear attacks: A history of the nuclear disarmament movement in Japan, 1957–1963], *Hitotsubashi Journal of Law and International Studies* 7, no. 2 (July 2008); Lawrence S. Wittner, *Resisting the Bomb: A History of the World Nuclear Disarmament Movement* (Stanford, CA: Stanford University Press, 1997), 8–10, 241–46.

2. It should be noted, however, that committing to nuclear disarmament and nonproliferation policies and signing or ratifying the actual treaties are two different things. For example, Japan had a hard time ratifying the NPT in 1976 despite having signed the treaty in 1970. Antinuclear sentiments may have been used in making a final political push for ratification, but contemporary strategic situation was also important. For more, see Mitchell Reiss, *Without the Bomb: The Politics of Nuclear Nonproliferation* (New York: Columbia University Press, 1988), 123–27; Maria Rost Rublee, *Nonproliferation Norms: Why States Choose Nuclear Restraints* (Athens: University of Georgia Press, 2009), 66–68; Mark Fitzpatrick, *Asia's Latent Nuclear Powers: Japan, South Korea and Taiwan* (London: Routledge, 2016), 73–77.

3. Etel Solingen, *Nuclear Logics: Contrasting Paths in East Asia & the Middle East* (Princeton, NJ: Princeton University Press, 2007), 66–69; Rublee, *Nonproliferation Norms*, 55–57; Fitzpatrick, *Asia's Latent Nuclear Powers*, 112–13.

4. For example, see Kurosaki Akira, *Kakuheiki to nichibei kankei: America no kakufukakusan gaiko to nihon no sentaku 1960–1976* [Nuclear weapons and U.S.-Japan relations: U.S. nonproliferation diplomacy and Japan's decision 1960–1976] (Tokyo: Yushisha, 2006); Kurt M. Campbell and Tsuyoshi Sunohara, "Japan: Thinking the Unthinkable," in *The Nuclear Tipping Point: Why States Reconsider Their Nuclear Choices*, ed. Kurt M. Campbell, Robert J. Einhorn, and Mitchell B. Reiss (Washington, DC: Brookings Institution, 2004), 219; Llewelyn Hughes, "Why Japan Will Not Go Nuclear (Yet)," *International Security* 31, no. 4 (Spring 2007): 75–80; Canberra Commission on the Elimination of Nuclear Weapons, "Report of the Canberra Commission on the Elimination of Nuclear Weapons," August 1996, 35, http://dfat.gov.au/about-us/publications/international-relations/Documents/the-canberra-commission-on-the-elimination-of-nuclear-weapons.pdf; Sugita Hiroki, *Kensho hikaku no sentaku: Kaku no genba wo ou* [Examining the nonnuclear decision: Tracing the nuclear scene] (Tokyo: Iwanami Shoten, 2005), 89; and Fitzpatrick, *Asia's Latent Nuclear Powers*, 104–9. For literature on the U.S.-Japan security alliance in general, see, for example, Michael J. Green and Patrick M. Cronin eds., *The U.S.-Japan Alliance: Past, Present, and Future* (Washington, DC: Council on Foreign Relations Press, 1999); and Takashi Inoguchi, G. John Ikenberry, and Yoichiro Sato, *The U.S.-Japan Security Alliance: Regional Multilateralism* (New York: Palgrave Macmillan, 2011).

5. Maruhama, *Gensuikin shomei undo no tanjyo*, 207–10.

6. Maruhama, *Gensuikin shomei undo no tanjyo*, 320.

7. "Gensuikin shomei undo zenkoku kyogikai kessei saru" [The Japan Council on the Signature Campaign against Atomic and Hydrogen Bombs established], *Asahi shimbun*, August 9, 1954.

8. Hiroshima Heiwa Bunka Tosho Kankokai, ed., *Hiroshima no shogen: Heiwa wo kangaeru* [Hiroshima's testimony: Thinking about peace] (Tokyo: Nihon Hyoron-sha, 1969), 367–68.

9. Ubuki Satoru, *Hiroshima sengo-shi: Hibaku taiken wa dou uketomeraretekitaka* [Postwar history of Hiroshima: How Hiroshima dealt with the experience of the dropping of the atomic

bomb] (Tokyo: Iwanami Shoten, 2014); Hiroshima Heiwa Bunka Tosho Kankokai, *Hiroshima no shogen*, 368.

10. Hiroshima Heiwa Bunka Tosho Kankokai, *Hiroshima no shogen*, 369.

11. "Message to the World," Nihon Hidankyo, http://www.ne.jp/asahi/hidankyo/nihon /english/about/about1-02.html.

12. "50 nen no ayumi" [50 years of history], Nihon Hidankyo, http://www.ne.jp/asahi /hidankyo/nihon/about/about2-02.html.

13. "Hiroshima no kiroku, 1957 8gatsu" [Chronicle of Hiroshima, August 1957], Hiroshima Peace Media Center (hereafter cited as HPMC), *Chugoku shimbun*, http://www.hiroshimapeacemedia.jp/?p=26291.

14. Muto Ichiyo, "Heiwa undo no naizaiteki ronri: 'Undo no tenki' to gensuibaku kinsi undo" [The immanent logic of the peace movement: "Turning point of the movement" and the movement against atomic and hydrogen bombs], *Shiso*, no. 418 (April 1959): 65; Kobayashi Yoshie, "Nihon ni okeru hankaku undo ni taisuru ichikosatsu" [Antinuclear movement and legacies of the Cold War], *Bulletin of Gumma Prefectural Women's College* 7, no. 2 (February 2013): 118; Araki, "Hibakukoku no gyakusetsu," 620.

15. "Hiroshima no kiroku, 1959 3gatsu" [Chronicle of Hiroshima, March 1959], HPMC, http://www.hiroshimapeacemedia.jp/?p=26262.

16. "Hiroshima no kiroku, 1959 7gatsu" [Chronicle of Hiroshima, July 1959], HPMC, http://www.hiroshimapeacemedia.jp/?p=26266.

17. Hiroshima Heiwa Bunka Tosho Kankokai, *Hiroshima no shogen*, 388.

18. "Hiroshima no kiroku, 1960 7gatsu" [Chronicle of Hiroshima, July 1960], HPMC, http://www.hiroshimapeacemedia.jp/?p=26254.

19. "Hiroshima no kiroku, 1960 8gatsu" [Chronicle of Hiroshima, August 1960], HPMC, http://www.hiroshimapeacemedia.jp/?p=26255.

20. "Dai-rokkai gensuibaku kinshi sekai taikai wo kaerimite" [Regarding the Sixth World Conference against Atomic and Hydrogen Bombs], *Naikaku kanbo chosa geppo* 5, no. 12 (December 1960): 6.

21. Kakkin does not have an official English translation of its organization name. For more information, see its website at http://www.kakkin.jp/.

22. "Hiroshima no kiroku, 1961 8gatsu" [Chronicle of Hiroshima, August 1961], HPMC, http://www.hiroshimapeacemedia.jp/?p=26243.

23. The Soviet Union conducted a series of atmospheric tests throughout the 1950s, with the final one held in November 1958. It then voluntarily suspended testing for nearly three years as part of the process of establishing a partial nuclear test ban agreement with the United States and Britain. The Soviet Union called for a test moratorium by all three countries while unilaterally announcing its own ban. However, owing to heavy pressure from the military, Nikita Khrushchev decided to resume testing in September 1961. For more, see, for example, William Burr and Hector L. Montford, "The Making of the Limited Test Ban Treaty, 1958–1963," August 8, 2003, *National Security Archive*, https://nsarchive2.gwu.edu/NSAEBB/NSAEBB94/.

24. "Hiroshima no kiroku, 1962 8gatsu" [Chronicle of Hiroshima, August 1962], HPMC, http://www.hiroshimapeacemedia.jp/?p=26231.

25. "Hiroshima no kiroku, 1962 9gatsu" [Chronicle of Hiroshima, September 1962], HPMC, http://www.hiroshimapeacemedia.jp/?p=262321.

26. "Hiroshima no kiroku, 1962 12gatsu" [Chronicle of Hiroshima, December 1962], HPMC, http://www.hiroshimapeacemedia.jp/?p=26235.

27. Peter J. Katzenstein, *Cultural Norms and National Security: Police and Military in Postwar Japan* (Ithaca, NY: Cornell University Press, 1996), 180.

28. Previous prime ministers as well as politicians, however, have repeatedly mentioned that Japan maintains a nonnuclear status in various ways. One such politician was Kishi Nobusuke, who regularly asserted that Japan would retain its nonnuclear status. On the other hand, Kishi also often noted that the "Nonnuclear Declaration" that the Socialist Party called for in 1959 failed to garner support from the LDP or Kishi himself, because of concerns about its effects on national security.

29. Speech by Satō on his administrative policy at the 58th Diet, January 27, 1968.

30. Kusuda Minoru, *Shuseki hishokan: Satō souri tono 10nen-kan* [Chief secretary: Ten years with Prime Minister Satō] (Tokyo: Bungei-shunjyu, 1975), 168–70; Wakaizumi Kei, *Tasaku nakarishi wo sinzem to hossu: Kaku mitsuyaku no shinjitsu (shinso-ban)* [The best course available: A personal account of the secret U.S.-Japan Okinawa reversion negotiations (new edition)] (Tokyo: Bungei-shunjyu, 2009), 140–41.

31. Prime Minister Satō's statements at the plenary session of the 58th Diet, House of Representatives. For more, see "Dai 58kai Kokkai shugiin kaigiroku dai 3gou" [Minute of the plenary session of the 58th Diet, House of Representatives, no. 3] (Tokyo: Ministry of Finance Printing Bureau, 1968); Wakaizumi, *Tasaku nakarishi wo sinzem to hossu*.

32. Wakaizumi, *Tasaku nakarishi wo sinzem to hossu*, 141.

33. See, for example, Wakaizumi, *Tasaku nakarishi wo sinzem to hossu*. For further information on the return of Okinawa, see, for example, Nakajimma Takuma, *Okinawa henkan to nichibei anpotaisei* [Reversion of Okinawa and the Japan-U.S. security arrangements] (Tokyo: Yuhikaku, 2012); Gabe Masaaki, *Sengo nichibeikankei to anzenhosho* [Postwar Japan-U.S. relations and security] (Tokyo: Yoshikawa Kobunkan, 2007), 151–211.

34. Yomiuri Shimbun-sha Seiji-bu, ed., *Kiroku kokkai anpo tousou 1: Sokkiroku to toten kaisetsu* [Records of the campaign against the U.S.-Japan Security Treaty 1: Stenographic records and explanations] (Tokyo: Yomiuri Shimbun-sha, 1968), 149–51.

35. Katzenstein, *Cultural Norms and National Security*, 146–48; Fitzpatrick, *Asia's Latent Nuclear Powers*, 66–67.

36. Kurosaki Akira, "Nichibeianpo kaku wo meguru nihon no kokunaiseiji to 'kakunokasa' izonseisaku no keisei, 1964–1968" [Domestic politics regarding U.S-Japan security alliance and nuclear issues, and the creation of a 'nuclear umbrella' reliant policy, 1964–1968], in *Amerika no kaku gabanansu* (U.S. nuclear governance), ed. Kan Hideki and Hatsuse Ryuhei (Tokyo: Koyoshobo, 2017), 130–31.

37. Akaha Tsuneo, "Japan's Three Nonnuclear Principles: A Coming Demise?," *Peace and Change* 11, no. 1 (Spring 1985): 75.

38. Ministry of Foreign Affairs, "Chukyo no genbaku ni kansuru Indo kokkai giin danwa no touchi houdou buri no ken" [Reports on Indian statesmen's remarks on Communist China's atomic bomb test], Hong Kong no. 262, March 9, 1960; Ministry of Foreign Affairs, "Chukyo no genbaku jikken ni kansuru houdou no ken" [Regarding reports on Communist China's atomic bomb test], Thailand no. 231, March 10, 1960; Ministry of Foreign Affairs, "Chukyo no kakubakuhatsu jikken ni kansuru hankyo no ken" [Regarding reactions on Communist China's

nuclear explosive test], no. 79, March 11, 1960; Ministry of Foreign Affairs, "Chukyo no kakujikken ni kansuru ken" [Regarding Communist China's nuclear test], India no. 145, March 11, 1960. Furthermore, Koizumi Jyunya addressed the view of the Defense Agency at the Budget Committee in October 1964 that China needed more time to develop its transportation capacity and therefore would presumably take about ten years to actually deploy nuclear weapons. For more, see "Sangiin yosaniin-kaigiroku (Dai 46kai kokkai heikai-go)" [Minute of the Budget Committee, after the 46th Diet, House of Councilors] (Tokyo: Ministry of Finance Printing Bureau, October 30, 1964), 4.

39. Ministry of Foreign Affairs, Asia Bureau, China Division, "Chukyo no Suibaku Jikken" [Communist China's hydrogen bomb test], June 19, 1967, 2–3.

40. Interview with Shigaki Minrō, December 20, 2012. Shigaki was a core figure in the creation of reports written by scholars such as Nagai Yonosuke, Kakihana Hidetake, and Royama Michio at the request of the Cabinet Secretariat in the late 1960s. It was Shigaki who consulted with Nagai, one of the key members, to create the study committee, resulting in the two reports discussed below.

41. Interview with Shigaki Minrō, December 20, 2012.

42. "Chugoku kakujikken no kokusai-teki hamon honsha kisha zadankai" [International interest regarding China's nuclear test, round-table discussion by *Asahi shimbun* reporters], *Asahi shimbun*, evening edition (Tokyo: Asahi Shimbun-sha, October 17, 1964).

43. Ministry of Foreign Affairs, "Chukyo no sho-zentei to kanou na taisaku" [Prerequisites regarding issues on Communist China and possible countermeasures], March 15, 1961, 10.

44. "Tokushu: Chukyo no kakubuso to Nihon no anzen wa mizukara no te de (zadankai)" [Feature article: Communist China's nuclearization and Japan (roundtable discussion)], *Jiyu* 7–3 (March 1965): 70.

45. Interview with Shigaki Minrō, December 20, 2012. Also, as Tanaka Akihiko points out, although the 1960s witnessed a number of security-related issues, including China's nuclear tests, the Vietnam War, and the Cultural Revolution, these were not necessarily considered direct crises in Japan. For more, see Tanaka Akihiko, *Anzen hosho: Sengo 50nen no mosaku* [Security—a search for 50 years after the war] (Tokyo: Yomiuri Shimbun-sha, 1997), 219.

46. Anzenhosho Chosa-kai [Security Research Commission], *Nihon no anzenhosho—1970nen eno tenbo—1966nen ban* [Japan's security—outlooks toward 1970—1966 edition], 1966.

47. One of the most important participants was Kaihara Osamu, director of the Cabinet National Defense Council [Naikaku kokubo jimukyoku]. For more, see Sugita, *Kensho hikaku no sentaku*, 67–70.

48. Sugita, *Kensho hikaku no sentaku*, 67, 79–80.

49. Anzenhosho Chosa-kai, *Nihon no anzenhosho—1970nen eno tenbo— 1967nen ban* [Japan's security—outlooks toward 1970—1967 edition], 1967, 109–19.

50. Anzenhosho Chosa-kai, *Nihon no anzenhosho—1970nen eno tenbo— 1967nen ban*, 114–15; *Nihon no Anzenhosho—1970nen eno tenbo—1968nen ban* [Japan's security—outlooks toward 1970—1968 edition) (Tokyo: Asagumo Shimbun-sha, 1968), 293.

51. Gaiko seisaku kikaku iinkai [Foreign Policy Planning Committee], "Waga kuni no seisaku taiko" [Japan's foreign policy guideline], September 25, 1969. This report compiles studies and discussions between May and September 1969. Since the discussions took place within a small community of people, the report does not necessarily reflect the general views of the

Ministry of Foreign Affairs nor of the administration at the time; indeed, this is explicitly pointed out on the first page of the document.

52. Gaiko seisaku kikaku iinkai, "Waga kuni no seisaku taiko," 62–64. On a different note, the report points out that with the possibility that the U.S. image may deteriorate in the future, Japan should in principle rely on nuclear deterrence as well as large-scale, quick-response air-sea offensive power and supply ability and aim for self-reliance regarding other matters.

53. Gaiko seisaku kikaku iinkai, "Waga kuni no seisaku taiko," 71.

54. Gaiko seisaku kikaku iinkai, "Waga kuni no seisaku taiko," 67–68; "Kono kuni no zahyo: Hikaku–bei senryaku no kage (8)" [The coordinates of this country: Nonnuclear—the shadow of U.S. strategy (8)], *Kanagawa shimbun*, August 30, 2005.

55. Gaiko seisaku kikaku iinkai, "Waga kuni," 67–68.

56. Ministry of Foreign Affairs, Disarmament Section, "Waga-kuni no kaku buso to kaku kakusan boshi jyoyaku (miteikou)" [Japan's nuclearization and the Nuclear Nonproliferation Treaty (unfinished manuscript)], May 6, 1966, 10–11; Ministry of Foreign Affairs, "Kakuheiki no fukakusan ni kansuru jyoyaku eno wagakuni no kamei ni yoru rigai tokushitsu" [Merits and demerits of Japan joining the Nuclear Nonproliferation Treaty], August 1969, 1–2.

57. Ministry of Foreign Affairs, Disarmament Section, "Waga-kuni no kaku no seisaku taiko kakusan boshi jyoyaku," 11.

58. Ministry of Foreign Affairs, Disarmament Section, "Waga-kuni no kaku kakusan boshi jyoyaku," 1–3.

59. Ministry of Foreign Affairs, Disarmament Section, "Waga-kuni no kaku kakusan boshi jyoyaku," 1–3.

60. For studies on these reports, see, for example, Kase Yuri, "The Cost and Benefits of Japan's Nuclearization: An Insight into the 1968/1970 Internal Report," *Nonproliferation Review* 8, no. 2 (Summer 2001): 55–68.

61. Interview with Shigaki Minrō, February 26, 2013; Kokusai jyosei kenkyukai, "Chukyo no kakujikken to Nihon no anzen hosho: Wagakuni no toru beki kihon seisaku no houkou ni tsuite (toshin dai 49-gou)" [Communist China's nuclear test and Japan's security: Directions of basic policies for Japan to take (report no. 49)], December 2, 1964. Shigaki, who was in charge of studies by the Cabinet Secretariat, noted that after the success of China's nuclear test, the first person he consulted was Wakaizumi Kei, who went on to write this report. The report was distributed within the Cabinet Research Office, and Wakaizumi later also gave a lecture based on it.

62. Kokusai jyosei kenkyukai, "Chukyo no kakujikken to Nihon no anzen hosho," 1, 2–3.

63. Kokusai jyosei kenkyukai, "Chukyo no kakujikken to Nihon no anzen hosho," 12–13, 15–16.

64. "Nihon no kaku seisaku ni kansuru kiso kenkyu (sono ichi)—Dokuritsu kaku senryoku no gijyutsuteki, soshikiteki, aaiseiteki kanousei" [Basic studies on Japan's nuclear policy, part 1—technological, organizational, financial possibility for an independent nuclear force], September 1968, introduction (2).

65. "Nihon no kaku seisaku ni kansuru kiso kenkyu," 1968, 28.

66. Royama Michio, "'Nihon no kaku seisaku ni kansuru kiso kenkyu' ni tsuite no fuki" [Remarks on 'Basic studies on Japan's nuclear policy'] (n.d., presumably 2006), 3–4 (paper provided to the author by Royama); interview with Shigaki Minrō, December 20, 2012.

67. Interview with Shigaki Minrō, December 20, 2012.

68. "Nihon no kaku seisaku ni kansuru kiso kenkyu," 1968, 62.

69. Interview with Shigaki Minrō, December 20, 2012; NHK Special Report Team, *"Kaku" wo motometa Nihon: Hibakukoku no shirarezaru shinjitsu* [Japan, a country that wished for "nuclear": The unknown truth of a country that suffered from the dropping of the atomic bomb] (Tokyo: Kobunsha, 2010), 86–87.

70. "Kaku no kyoi dai san-bu Nihon no yokushiryoku (1) Bei no kasa honto ni yuko ka" [Nuclear threat part 3: Japan's deterrent ability (1) Is the U.S. umbrella really effective?], *Yomiuri shimbun*, March 20, 2007.

71. Solingen, *Nuclear Logics*, 57–81.

Chapter 10. Nuclear Revolution and Hegemonic Hierarchies: How Global Hiroshima Played Out in South America

1. Text of speech by Hassan Rouhani, Supreme National Security Council secretary, to the Supreme Cultural Revolution Council: "Beyond the Challenges Facing Iran and the IAEA Concerning the Nuclear Dossier," *Rahbord*, September 30, 2005, 7–38 (emphasis added).

2. Emanuel Adler, *The Power of Ideology: The Quest for Technological Autonomy in Argentina and Brazil* (Berkeley: University of California Press, 1987); Carlo Patti, "Brazil in Global Nuclear Order" (PhD diss., University of Florence, 2012; Diego Hurtado de Mendoza, *El sueño de la Argentina atómica: política, tecnología nuclear y desarollo nacional (1945–2006)* (Buenos Aires: Edhasa, 2014).

3. Gabrielle Hecht, *Being Nuclear: Africans and the Uranium Global Trade* (Boston: MIT Press, 2012).

4. Michael Anthony Barletta, "Ambiguity, Autonomy, and the Atom: Emergence of the Argentine-Brazilian Nuclear Regime" (PhD diss., University of Wisconsin-Madison, 2000); Rodrigo Mallea, "La cuestión nuclear en la relación argentino-brasileña (1968–1984)" (MA thesis, IESP-UERJ, 2012).

5. Adler, *The Power of Ideology*.

6. Lawrence Scheinman, *The International Atomic Energy Agency and World Nuclear Order* (Baltimore: Johns Hopkins University Press, 1987); Klaus B. Stadie, "The Nuclear Weapons Legacy: Closing the Circle on the Splitting of the Atom and Estimating the Cold War Mortgage," *Environment: Science and Policy for Sustainable Development* 38, no. 1 (1996); G. Bunn, "Does the Non-Proliferation Treaty (NPT) Require Its Non-Nuclear-Weapon Members to Permit Inspection by the International Atomic Energy Agency (IAEA) of Nuclear Activities That Have Not Been Reported to the IAEA?," unpublished report, Center for International Security and Arms Control, Stanford University, 2012.

7. Stadie, "Nuclear Weapons Legacy," 24; Norman Gall, "Atoms for Brazil, Dangers for All," *Bulletin of the Atomic Scientists* 32, no. 6 (1976): 4–9; Barletta, "Ambiguity, Autonomy, and the Atom."

8. Scheinman, *International Atomic Energy Agency*; Martin J. Medhurst, "Atoms for Peace and Nuclear Hegemony: The Rhetorical Structure of a Cold War Campaign," *Armed Forces & Society* 23, no. 4 (1997): 571–93, quoted in Barletta, "Ambiguity, Autonomy, and the Atom."

9. W. Grabendorff, "La política nuclear y de no-proliferación de Brasil," *Estudios internacio-*

nales 20, no. 80, (1987): 520–68; Carlos Castro Madero and Esteban A. Takacs, *Política Nuclear Argentina: Avance o Retroceso?* (Buenos Aires: Editorial El Ateneo, 1991); Barletta, "Ambiguity, Autonomy, and the Atom."

10. Barletta, "Ambiguity, Autonomy, and the Atom."

11. David Fischer, *History of the International Atomic Energy Agency: The First Forty Years* (Vienna: International Atomic Energy Agency, 1997), 11.

12. Carlo Patti, "The Origins of the Brazilian Nuclear Program, 1951–1955," *Cold War History* 15, no. 3 (July 3, 2015): 353–73. For a useful collection of primary sources on this period, see Arquivo Álvaro Alberto, University of São Paulo; Elisabeth Roehrlich, "The Cold War, the Developing World, and the Creation of the International Atomic Energy Agency," *Cold War History* 16, no. 2 (2016): 195–212.

13. Adler, *Power of Ideology*; Steven Flank, "Exploding the Black Box: The Historical Sociology of Nuclear Proliferation," *Security Studies* 3, no. 2 (1993): 259–94; Maria Regina Soares de Lima, *The Political Economy of Brazilian Foreign Policy: Nuclear Energy, Trade and Itaipu* (Brasília: Fundação Alexandre de Gusmão, 2013).

14. Barletta, "Ambiguity, Autonomy, and the Atom"; Rodrigo Mallea, Matias Spektor, and Nicholas J. Wheeler, eds., *Origins of Nuclear Cooperation: A Critical Oral History between Argentina and Brazil* (Washington, DC: Woodrow Wilson International Center for Scholars and FGV, 2015).

15. For an early assessment, see Leonard Spector, *Nuclear Proliferation Today* (New York: Vintage Books, 1984). More contemporary works include Matthew Fuhrmann and Benjamin Tacks, "Almost Nuclear: Introducing the Nuclear Latency Dataset," *Conflict Management and Peace Science* 32 (2015): 443–61; Paul Nelson and Christopher Spreecher, "Are Sensitive Technologies Enablers of Civil Nuclear Power? An Empirical Study," *Atoms for Peace: an International Journal* 3 (2010); Dong-Joon Jo and Erik Gartzke, "Determinants of Nuclear Weapons Proliferation," *Journal of Conflict Resolution* 5 (2007): 167–94; Matthew Kroenig, "Importing the Bomb: Sensitive Nuclear Assistance and Nuclear Proliferation," *Journal of Conflict Resolution* 53 (April 1, 2009): 161–80; Mitchell Reiss, *Bridled Ambition: Why Countries Constrain Their Nuclear Capabilities* (Washington, DC: Woodrow Wilson Center Press, 1995); Sarah E. Kreps and Matthew Fuhrmann, "Attacking the Atom: Does Bombing Nuclear Facilities Affect Proliferation?" *Journal of Strategic Studies* 34 (2011): 161–87.

16. Jacques E. C. Hymans, "Of Gauchos and Gringos: Why Argentina Never Wanted the Bomb, and Why the United States Thought It Did," *Security Studies* 10, no. 3 (Spring 2001): 153–85; Mallea, "La cuestión nuclear en la relación argentino-brasileña"; Matias Spektor, "The Evolution of Brazil's Nuclear Intentions," *Nonproliferation Review* 23, no. 5–6 (2016): 635–52; John Redick, *Nuclear Illusions: Argentina and Brazil* (Washington, DC: Henry L. Stimson Center, 1995); Julio C. Carasales, "The Argentine-Brazilian Nuclear Rapprochement," *Nonproliferation Review* 2 (Spring–Summer 1995): 39–48; Barletta, "Ambiguity, Autonomy, and the Atom"; Togzhan Kassenova, *Brazil's Nuclear Kaleidoscope: An Evolving Identity* (Washington, DC: Carnegie Endowment for International Peace, 2014); Sara Z. Kutchesfahani, "The Role of an Epistemic Community in Argentina and Brazil's Creation of a Joint Safeguards Agreement," in *International Cooperation on WMD Nonproliferation*, ed. Jeffrey W. Knopf (Athens: University of Georgia Press, 2015); Mallea, Spektor, and Wheeler, eds., *The Origins of Nuclear Cooperation*. See also Jacques E. C. Hymans, *Achieving Nuclear Ambitions: Scientists, Politicians, and Prolifera-*

tion (Cambridge: Cambridge University Press, 2012); Alexander H. Montgomery and Adam Mount, "Misestimation: Explaining US Failures to Predict Nuclear Weapons Programs," *Intelligence and National Security* 29 (May 4, 2014): 357–86.

17. John R. Redick, Julio C. Carasales, and Paulo S. Wrobel, "Nuclear Rapprochement: Argentina, Brazil, and the Nonproliferation Regime," *Washington Quarterly* 18, no. 1 (March 1, 1995): 107–22; Adler, *Power of Ideology*; Mallea, Spektor, Wheeler, eds., *The Origins of Nuclear Cooperation*.

18. James G. Hershberg, "The United States, Brazil, and the Cuban Missile Crisis, 1962 (Part 1)," *Journal of Cold War Studies* 6, no. 2 (April 1, 2004): 3–20; James G. Hershberg, "The United States, Brazil, and the Cuban Missile Crisis, 1962 (Part 2)," *Journal of Cold War Studies* 6, no. 3 (July 1, 2004): 5–67; Ryan Musto, "The Watchdog without a Bite: Argentina, Brazil, OPANAL, and Nuclear Nonproliferation in Latin America 1973–1990" (MA thesis, Columbia University and London School of Economics and Political Science, 2011); Carlo Patti and Rodrigo Mallea, "American Seeds of ABACC? Findley's Proposal to Create a Mutual Nuclear Inspections System between Brazil and Argentina," *International History Review* (2018).

19. K. L. Storrs, "Brazil's Independent Foreign Policy, 1961–1964; Background, Tenets, Linkage to Domestic Politics, and Aftermath" (PhD diss., Cornell University, 1974); Lima, *Political Economy*; Patti, "Global Nuclear Order"; San Tiago Dantas, *Política Externa Independente*, updated ed. (Brasilia: FUNAG, 2011). For a curated collection of key documents from Brazil's experience with "Política Externa Independente," see Álvaro Costa Franco, *Documentos da Política Externa Independente*, vol. 1 (Brasília: FUNAG, 2007); Felipe Pereira Loureiro, "The Alliance for Progress and President João Goulart's Three-Year Plan: The Deterioration of U.S.-Brazilian Relations in Cold War Brazil (1962)," *Cold War History* 17, no. 1 (January 2, 2017): 61–79.

20. Exposições de Motivos, November 29, 1962, and May 10, 1963, CNEN; Information, August, 12 1963, Gabinete Militar. Both documents are quoted in Joaquim Augusto Whitaker Salles, "Brasil e Tlatelolco. Uma Apreciação Crítica Sobre a Relevância do Tratado Para a Proscrição de Armas Nucleares na América Latina para a Política Externa do Brasil" (thesis, Curso de Altos Estudos, Instituto Rio Branco, 1988), 36–38.

21. AmEmbassy Rio de Janeiro to Department of State, Secret Airgram 792, May 23, 1968, RG 59, Subject-Numeric Files 1967–1969, Box 2895, AE 1 Brazil, NARA, in William Burr, Nuclear Intelligence via Three Martinis blog, May 30, 2017, wilsoncenter.org/blog-post/nuclear-intelligence-three-martinis.

22. Ryan Musto, "'Keep the Nuclear Beast in a Cage': Brazil, the United States, and Peaceful Nuclear Explosions under the Treaty of Tlatelolco, 1964–1967," paper presented at SHAFR Annual Meeting, Arlington, VA, June 23, 2017.

23. Musto, "Nuclear Beast."

24. Mallea, "La cuestión nuclear."

25. William Glenn Gray, "Commercial Liberties and Nuclear Anxieties: The US-German Feud over Brazil," *International History Review* 34, no. 3 (2012): 449–74. For a curated collection of key documents, see Dani K. Nedal and Tatiana Coutto, "Brazil's 1975 Nuclear Agreement with West Germany," Nuclear Proliferation International History Project, August 13, 2013, https://www.wilsoncenter.org/publication/brazils-1975-nuclear-agreement-west-germany.

26. Joao Resende-Santos, "The Origins of Security Cooperation in the Southern

Cone," *Latin American Politics and Society* 44, no. 4 (2002): 89; Charles A. Kupchan, *How Enemies Become Friends: The Sources of Stable Peace*, reprint ed. (Princeton, NJ: Princeton University Press, 2010); James Doyle, *Nuclear Safeguards, Security and Nonproliferation: Achieving Security with Technology and Policy* (Boston: Butterworth-Heinemann, 2008); Redick, "Nuclear Rapprochement"; Mitchell Reiss, *Bridled Ambition: Why Countries Constrain Their Nuclear Capabilities* (Washington, DC: Woodrow Wilson Center Press, 1995); and Paulo Wrobel, "Counterproliferation: A View from South America," in *International Perspectives on Counterproliferation*, ed. Mitchell Reiss and Harald Muller (Washington, DC: Woodrow Wilson International Center for Scholars, 1995), 122–45.

27. Carlo Patti and Matias Spektor, "'We Are Not a Non-proliferation Agency': Henry Kissinger's Policy of Accommodation towards Nuclear Brazil (1974–1977)," *Journal of Cold War Studies*, forthcoming.

Chapter 11. Remembering War, Forgetting Hiroshima: "Euroshima" and the West German Anti–Nuclear Weapons Movements in the Cold War

1. Günther Anders, "Theses on the Atomic Age," *Massachusetts Review*, no. 3 (1962): 493, 495; Günther Anders, *Hiroshima ist überall* (Munich: Beck, 1982). On the background, see Jason Dawsey, "After Hiroshima: Günther Anders and the History of Anti-Nuclear Critique," in *Understanding the Imaginary War: Culture, Thought and Nuclear Conflict, 1945–90*, ed. Matthew Grant and Benjamin Ziemann (Manchester: Manchester University Press, 2016), 140–64.

2. Susan Neimann, "Forgetting Hiroshima, Remembering Auschwitz: Tales of Two Exhibits," *Thesis Eleven* 129 (2015): 7–26.

3. Andrew J. Rotter, *Hiroshima: The World's Bomb* (Oxford: Oxford University Press, 2008).

4. Michael Geyer, "Cold War Angst: The Case of West-German Opposition to Rearmament and Nuclear Weapons," in *The Miracle Years: A Cultural History of West Germany*, ed. Hanna Schissler (Princeton, NJ: Princeton University Press, 2001), 376–408; Holger Nehring, *Politics of Security: The British and West German Protests against Nuclear Weapons and the Early Cold War, 1945–c. 1970* (Oxford: Oxford University Press, 2013).

5. Alon Confino and Peter Fritzsche, "Introduction: Noises of the Past," in *The Work of Memory: New Directions in the Study of German Society and Culture*, ed. Alon Confino and Peter Fritzsche (Urbana: University of Illinois Press, 2002), 5. Cf. also Alon Confino, "Collective Memory and Cultural History Problems of Method," *American Historical Review* 102, no. 5 (1997): 1386–1403.

6. One of many pioneers for the use of visual sources was Benjamin Ziemann, "The Code of Protest: Images of Peace in the West German Peace Movements, 1945–1990," *Contemporary European History* 17, no. 2 (2008): 237–61. On framing, see Robert D. Benford and David A. Snow, "Framing Processes and Social Movements: An Overview and Assessment," *Annual Review of Sociology* 26 (2000): 611–39.

7. Cf. Robert G. Moeller, *War Stories: The Search for a Usable Past in the Federal Republic of Germany* (Berkeley: University of California Press, 2001); Franziska Seraphim, *War Memory and Social Politics in Japan, 1945–2005* (Cambridge, MA: Harvard University Press, 2006); Ann Sherif, *Japan's Cold War: Media, Literature and the Law* (New York: Columbia University Press,

2016); Sebastian Conrad, *The Quest for the Lost Nation: Writing History in Germany and Japan in the American Century* (Berkeley: University of California Press, 2010).

8. The key works here are Dietmar Süß's magisterial *Tod aus der Luft: Kriegsgesellschaft und Luftkrieg in Deutschland und England* (Munich: Siedler, 2011), translated into English by Lesley Sharpe and Jeremy Noakes as *Death from the Skies: How the British and the Germans Survived Bombing World War II* (Oxford: Oxford University Press, 2014); Jörg Arnold's case study of Kassel and Magdeburg, *The Allied Air War and Urban Memory: The Legacy of Strategic Bombing in Germany* (Cambridge: Cambridge University Press, 2011); and Malte Thießen's case study of Hamburg, *Eingebrannt ins Gedächtnis: Hamburgs Gedenken an Luftkrieg und Kriegsende 1943 bis 2005* (Munich: Dölling und Galitz, 2007). For excellent summaries of the state of the field, see Jörg Arnold, Dietmar Süß, and Malte Thießen, eds., *Luftkrieg: Erinnerungen in Deutschland und Europa* (Göttingen: Wallstein, 2009); David F. Crew, *Bodies and Ruins: Imagining the Bombing of Germany 1945 to the Present* (Ann Arbor: University of Michigan Press, 2017).

9. W. G. Sebald, "A Natural History of Destruction," *New Yorker*, November 4, 2002, 67. Sebald has been shown to be mistaken even for the field of literature. See Volker Hage, *Zeugen der Zerstörung: Die Literaten und der Luftkrieg* (Frankfurt/Main: Fischer, 2003). For a good summary of this historiographical debate, see Mary Nolan, "Air Wars, Memory Wars," *Central European History* 38, no. 1 (March 2005): 7–40.

10. In addition to the works cited in note 8 above, cf. Jörg Arnold, "'Kassel 1943 mahnt....' Zur Genealogie der Angst im Kalten Krieg," in *Angst im Kalten Krieg*, ed. Bernd Greiner, Christian Th. Müller, and Dierk Walter (Hamburg: Hamburger Edition, 2009), 464–94; Susanne Schregel, *Der Atomkrieg vor der Wohnungstür: Eine Politikgeschichte der neuen Friedensbewegung in der Bundesrepublik 1970–1985* (Frankfurt/Main: Campus, 2011).

11. Jeffrey Herf, *War by Other Means: Soviet Power, West German Resistance and the Battle of the Euromissiles* (New York: Free Press, 1991). See also the more diffuse collection edited by Benjamin Ziemann, *Peace Movements in Western Europe, Japan and the USA during the Cold War* (Essen: Klartext, 2007).

12. For comparison, see the thought-provoking essay by Daniel Levy and Natan Sznaider, *Erinnerunng im globalen Zeitalter: Der Holocaust* (Frankfurt/Main: Suhrkamp, 2007), 9. See also the important case study by Andrew Oppenheimer, "Air Wars and Empire: Gandhi and the Search for a Usable Past in Postwar Germany," *Central European History* 45 (2012): 669–96. For an overview of global Holocaust memories, see *Holocaust Memory in a Globalizing World*, ed. Jacob S. Eder, Philipp Gassert, and Alan E. Steinweis (Göttingen: Wallstein, 2017).

13. Ran Zwigenberg, *Hiroshima: The Origins of Global Memory Culture* (Cambridge: Cambridge University Press 2014), 3, 12.

14. On this conceptualization of latency, see Hans Ulrich Gumbrecht, *After 1945: Latency as the Origins of the Present* (Stanford, CA: Stanford University Press, 2013).

15. Robert G. Moeller, "Germans as Victims? Thoughts on a Post-Cold War History of World War II's Legacies," *History and Memory* 17 (2005): 147–94; Nolan, "Air Wars, Memory Wars"; Alon Confino, "Remembering the Second World War, 1945–1965: Narratives of Victimhood and Genocide," *Cultural Analysis* 4 (2005): 46–75. On conceptualizing postwar history, see Richard Bessel and Dirk Schumann, eds., *Life after Death: Approaches to a Cultural and Social History of Europe during the 1940s and 1950s* (Cambridge: Cambridge University Press, 2003); Frank Biess and Robert G. Moeller, eds., *Histories of the Aftermath: The Legacies of the Second World War in Europe* (New York: Berghahn, 2010).

16. Levy and Sznaider, *Erinnerung*, 12, 16, 75.

17. Anson Rabinbach, *In the Shadow of Catastrophe: German Intellectuals between Apocalypse and Enlightenment* (Berkeley: University of California Press, 1997), 12. For an in-depth discussion about German views of American interpretations of the Holocaust, see Eder, *Holocaust Angst*.

18. Günter Fritz to Alexander Maass, June 27, 1959, Archiv der sozialen Demokratie, Friedrich Ebert Foundation, Bonn (hereafter cited as AdsD), 2/PVAM000014.

19. Kampf dem Atomtod (Frankfurt am Main), March 23, 1958: "Das Leben retten—den Frieden sichern. Der Frankfurter Kongreß ruft alle zum Kampf gegen den Atomtod," AdsD, 2/PVAM00005.

20. Photo of a protest march against nuclear weapons by the Friends of Nature youth organization in Hesse, September 1959, AdsD, 2/PVAM000018. Cf. also Walter Menzel to Klaus Vack, October 8, 1959, AdsD, ASAF000177: extracts from minutes about the incidents around the Atomic Vigil of the Berlin Working Group against Atomic Death, Schöneberg District, at Lauterplatz, September 12, 1958.

21. On this history, see Alice Holmes Cooper, *Paradoxes of Peace: German Peace Movements since 1945* (Ann Arbor: University of Michigan Press, 1996); Nehring, *Politics of Security*.

22. Broschüre Kampf dem Atomtod, March 1958, 4, Federal Archives, Koblenz (hereafter cited as BAK), ZSg 1-E70. Cf. also the poster by the fellow-traveling Action Community Bavaria against Atomic Death: Deutsches Historisches Museum (hereafter cited as DHM), DG60/1030, http://www.dhm.de/datenbank/dhm.php?seite=5&fld_0=D2Z35954.

23. Eva Kramm, "Eine 'empfindsame Reise' nach Hiroshima. Zum Hiroshima-Tagebuch von Günther Anders," *Das Argument. Blätter der Westberliner Studentengruppen gegen Atomrüstung*, November 27, 1959 (Nr. 11), 2, AdsD, 2/PVAM000034.

24. See chapter 9 by Wakana Mukai and chapter 12 by Kiichi Fujiwara in this volume.

25. Oppenheimer, "Air War," 682; e.g., Eugen Kogon, "Der teilbare Frieden und der unteilbare Krieg," *Frankfurter Hefte* 14, no. 2 (1959): 85–88; "Daten zum Stand der kalkulierten Massenvernichtung," *Frankfurter Hefte* 20, no. 2 (1965): 89–92. For comparison on these references and the broader context, see Daniel Gerster, *Friedensdialoge im Kalten Krieg: Eine Geschichte der Katholiken in der Bundesrepublik 1957–1983* (Frankfurt/Main: Campus, 2012), 65–66.

26. Alexander Maass to Prof. Dr. Ing. Gerloff (Bielefeld), November 6, 1958, enclosure: pamphlet "Angst oder Gewissen?" von Professor Dr. Ing Helmuth Gerloff (Bielefeld), c. 1958, 2, AdsD, 2/PVAM000014.

27. Resolution by the Schleswig-Holstein Committee against Atomic Death, May 16, 1958, AdsD, 2/PVAM000022.

28. Draft for a Berlin Program (Political Manifesto of Atomic Weapons Opponents), n.d., 5, Archiv Berliner Akademie der Künste, Hans Werner Richter papers (hereafter cited as HWR), 72.86.512.

29. Cf., for example, Andreas Buro, *Gewaltlos gegen den Krieg: Lebenserinnerungen eines streitbaren Pazifisten* (Frankfurt/Main: Brandes und Apsel, 2011), esp. 13–15; Komitee für Grundrechte und Demokratie, ed., *"Tradition heißt nicht, Asche aufheben, sondern die Flamme am Brennen erhalten!": Für und über Klaus Vack* (Sensbachtal: Komitee für Grundrechte und Demokratie, 1985), 153, 175; Ekkehart Krippendorff, *Lebensfäden: Zehn autobiographische Versuche* (Heidelberg: Graswurzelrevolution, 2012), 19–70. On this idea of the past as permanent

exhortation more generally, see A. Dirk Moses, *German Intellectuals and the Nazi Past* (Cambridge: Cambridge University Press, 2007), 70.

30. *Was Niemöller sagt—wogegen Strauß klagt. Niemöllers Kasseler Rede vom 25.1.1959 im vollen Wortlaut* (Darmstadt: Stimme-Verlag 1959), 10, Archives of the Hamburger Institut für Sozialforschung (hereafter cited as HIS), SBe 540. Cf. also Helmut Walther (Schwäbisch-Hall/Backnang) to Campaign against Atomic Death, December 29, 1958, including an article on a lecture by Niemöller at the Station Hotel Backnang, AdsD, 2/PVAM000021.

31. Horst W. Blome, Internationaler Studentischer Arbeitskreis der Kriegsdienstgegner (IAK), Bundesgeschäftsstelle, München to Campaign against Atomic Death, January 13, 1959, enclosure, AdsD, 2/PVAM000016.

32. Oppenheimer, "Air Wars," 694.

33. Thießen, *Eingebrannt ins Gedächtnis*, 215–17.

34. Oppenheimer, "Air Wars," 694. Cf. also, with a similar reference to Frankfurt, Hans-Konrad Tempel to Christel Küpper, March 4, 1961, Institut für Zeitgeschichte, Munich, Christel Küpper papers (hereafter cited as IfZ), ED702–1.

35. *"Kampf dem Atomtod!": Die Protestbewegung 1957/58 in zeithistorischer und gegenwärtiger Perspektive*, ed. Forschungsstelle für Zeitgeschichte in Hamburg (Hamburg: Dölling und Galitz, 2009), 23. Cf. also Heinz Gärtner to Alexander Maass, December 15, 1958, AdsD, 2/PVAM 000025, for a detailed report on the activities at Hamburg University, including an exhibition with images of nuclear bomb survivors.

36. Neil Gregor, "Trauer und städtische Identitätspolitik. Erinnerungen an die Bombardierung Nürnbergs," in *Luftkrieg: Erinnerungen in Deutschland und Europa*, ed. Jörg Arnold, Dietmar Süß, and Malte Thießen (Göttingen: Wallstein, 2009), 131–45.

37. Ralf Blank, "Zerstört und vergessen? Hagen, das Ruhrgebiet und das Gedächtnis des Krieges," in *Luftkrieg: Erinnerungen in Deutschland und Europa*, ed. Jörg Arnold, Dietmar Süß, and Malte Thießen (Göttingen: Wallstein, 2009), 178; Gregor, "Trauer," 140, which is also useful on the comparison with soldiers; Georg Seiderer, "Würzburg, 16. März 1945. Vom 'kollektiven Trauma' zur lokalen Sinnstiftung," in *Luftkrieg: Erinnerungen in Deutschland und Europa*, ed. Jörg Arnold, Dietmar Süß, and Malte Thießen (Göttingen: Wallstein, 2009), 158; Arnold, "'Kassel mahnt.'" On soldiers, cf. Frank Biess, *Homecomings: Returning POWs and the Legacies of Defeat in Postwar Germany* (Princeton, NJ: Princeton University Press, 2009); and Jörg Echternkamp, *Soldaten im Nachkrieg: Historische Deutungskonflikte und westdeutsche Demokratisierung 1945–1955* (Munich: Oldenbourg, 2014).

38. Christian Groh, "'Was Pforzheim angetan wurde!' Erinnerungsorte und Denkmäler zum Luftkrieg," in *Luftkrieg: Erinnerungen in Deutschland und Europa*, ed. Jörg Arnold, Dietmar Süß, and Malte Thießen (Göttingen: Wallstein, 2009), 184–88.

39. Alexander Maass to Hartmut Schaefer, cand. phil. (Göttingen), July 13, 1959, AdSD, 2/PVAM000020. Cf. also the letter of the Japan Council against A- and H-Bombs to Schaefer offering the images, AdSD, 2/PVAM000020.

40. This connection is explicitly made in Ria and Carl-Christian Kaiser (Frankfurt/Main) to Walther Menzel, March 26, 1958, AdsD, 2/PVAM000027. On this relationship more generally, see Paul Betts and Greg Eghigian, eds., *Pain and Prosperity: Reconsidering Twentieth-Century German History* (Stanford, CA: Stanford University Press, 2002); and, for the discussion of war and nuclear weapons, the brilliant essay by Geyer, "German Angst."

41. Hessen Campaign against Atomic Death, Exhibition Prospectus, "The Atom—Curse or Blessing?," Frankfurt Römerhallen, AdsD, 2/PVAM000027. On the general pattern, see Holger Nehring, "Cold War, Apocalypse and Peaceful Atoms: Interpretations of Nuclear Energy in the British and West German Protests against Nuclear Weapons," *Historical Social Research* 29, no. 3 (2004): 150–70.

42. Günther Anders, "Commandments in the Atomic Age [1957]," in *Burning Conscience*, by Claude Eatherly (New York: Monthly Review Press, 1961), 12, 16. On the background, see Dawsey, "After Hiroshima." On perceptions among West German Protestants in the 1960s and 1970s, see Michael Schüring, *"Bekennen gegen den Atomstaat": Die evangelischen Kirchen in der Bundesrepublik Deutschland und die Konflikte um die Atomenergie 1970–1990* (Göttingen: Wallstein, 2015), 41–67.

43. Anders, "Theses," 495.

44. On Anders and his reception, see Günther Bischof, Jason Dawsey and Bernhard Fetz, eds., *The Life and Work of Gunther Anders: Emigre, Iconoclast, Philosopher, Man of Letters*, (Innsbruck: Studien-Verlag, 2015), especially the chapter by Dawsey.

45. Hans Magnus Enzensberger, "Reflections before a Glass Cage," in *Critical Essays*, ed. Reinhold Grimm and Bruce Armstrong (New York: Continuum, 1982), 101, 113, 101.

46. On game plans, see Enzensberger, "Reflections before a Glass Cage," 102, 105.

47. Enzensberger, "Reflections before a Glass Cage," 114.

48. Cited in Wilfried Mausbach, "Von der 'zweiten Front' in die friedliche Etappe? Internationale Solidaritätsbewegungen in der Bundesrepublik 1968–1983," in *Das Alternative Milieu: Antibürgerlicher Lebensstil und linke Politik in der Bundesrepublik Deutschland und Europa 1968–1983*, ed. Sven Reichardt and Detlef Siegfried (Göttingen: Wallstein, 2010), 426.

49. Karl A. Otto, *Vom Ostermarsch zur APO* (Frankfurt/Main: Campus, 1977).

50. Letter by Arno Klönne, n.d. [c. summer 1961], enclosure 2: article by Christian Geissler in a special edition of the *Westdeutsches Tageblatt*, July 1, 1961, AdsD, 2/PVAM000017. Geissler was the editor of the *Catholic Werkhefte katholischer Laien*.

51. AdsD 6/PLKA006622: cited in Ziemann, "Code of Protest," 244 n. 25.

52. On Nazi crimes and Holocaust awareness, see Harold Marcuse, "The Revival of Holocaust Awareness in West Germany, Israel and the United States," in *1968: The World Transformed*, ed. Carole Fink, Philipp Gassert, and Detlef Junker (Cambridge: Cambridge University Press, 1998), 421–38.

53. Ostermarsch der Atomwaffengegner, minutes of Central Committee meeting, Kassel, October 14/15, 1961; minutes of Central Committee meeting, Kassel, September 7/8, 1963, IfZ, ED702-4. On pamphlets and slogans, see minutes of Central Committee meeting, Kassel, ED702-3: Kampagne für Abrüstung, OM der Atomwaffengegner, Central Committee, c. 1964; Pamphlet Ostermarsch der Atomwaffengegner/Kampagne für Abrüstung, Easter March 1963, AdsD, 2/PVAM000033.

54. Hans Kundnani, *Utopia or Auschwitz: Germany's 1968 Generation and the Holocaust* (London: Hurst, 2009), 19, 181; Volker Paulmann, "Die Studentenbewegung und die NS-Vergangenheit in der Bundesrepublik," in *Erfolgsgeschichte Bundesrepublik? Die Nachkriegsgesellschaft im langen Schatten des Nationalsozialismus*, ed. Stephan Alexander Glienke, Volker Paulmann, and Joachim Perels (Göttingen: Wallstein, 2008), 185–215, esp. 195, 197, and 205–7.

55. Arnold, *Allied Air War*, 123.

56. Kundnani, *Utopia or Auschwitz*, 31.

57. Cited in Ingrid Gilcher-Holtey, "Transformation by Subversion? The New Left and the Question of Violence," in *Changing the World, Changing Oneself. Political Protest: Political Protest and Collective Identities in West Germany and the U.S. in the 1960s and 1970s*, ed. Belinda Davis, Martin Klimke, Wilfried Mausbach, and Carla MacDougall (New York: Berghahn, 2010), 160.

58. Gerster, *Friedensdialoge*, 164. On this theme more generally, see Wilfried Mausbach, "America's Vietnam in Germany, Germany in America's Vietnam: On the Relocation of Spaces and the Appropriation of History," in *Changing the World, Changing Oneself. Political Protest: Political Protest and Collective Identities in West Germany and the U.S. in the 1960s and 1970s*, ed. Belinda Davis, Martin Klimke, Wilfried Mausbach, and Carla MacDougall (New York: Berghahn, 2010), 41–64.

59. Ulrike Meinhof, "Vietnam und die Deutschen [1967]," in *Die Würde des Menschen ist antastbar: Aufsätze und Polemiken* (Berlin: Wagenbach, 1980), 108.

60. Herbert Marcuse, "Vietnam—Analyse eines Exempels," *Neue Kritik* 7, nos. 36/37 (July/August 1966): 30–40, reprinted in *Frankfurter Schule und Studentenbewegung: Von der Flaschenpost zum Molotowcocktail 1946–1995*, ed. Wolfgang Kraushaar, vol. 2 (Hamburg: Hamburger Edition, 1998), 205–9. For an example of the reappropriation of this motif during the 1980s, see the poster by Terres des Hommes Berlin about the victims of Agent Orange in 1983, printed in *Flugblätter und Dokumente der Westberliner Friedensbewegung 1980–1985*, ed. Fritz Teppich (West Berlin: Verlag Das europäische Buch, 1985), 172.

61. Ulrike Meinhof, "Zum 20. Juli [1964]," in *Die Würde des Menschen ist antastbar: Aufsätze und Polemiken* (Berlin: Wagenbach, 1980), 50–51.

62. Ulrike Meinhof, "Dresden [1965]," in *Die Würde des Menschen ist antastbar*, 64.

63. Ulrike Meinhof, "Die Würde des Menschen [1962]," in *Die Würde des Menschen ist antastbar*, 29.

64. For comparison, by way of background, see Christian Dries, *Die Welt als Vernichtungslager: Eine kritische Theorie der Moderne im Anschluss an Günther Anders, Hannah Arendt und Hans Jonas* (Bielefeld: transkript, 2012); Christian Dries, *Günther Anders* (Munich: Fink, 2009); Adelheid Voskuhl, "Emancipation in the Industrial Age: Technology, Rationality, and the Cold War in Habermas's Early Epistemology and Social Theory," *Modern Intellectual History* 13 (2016): 479–505.

65. On these general developments, see Ziemann, "Code of Protest," 253–54.

66. For general overviews, see Bernd Faulenbach, *Das sozialdemokratische Jahrzehnt: Von der Reformeuphorie zur neuen Unübersichtlichkeit. Die SPD 1969–1982* (Bonn: Dietz, 2011); and Karrin Hanshew, *Terror and Democracy in Germany* (Cambridge: Cambridge University Press, 2014). For the protest milieu, see Sven Reichardt, *Authentizität und Gemeinschaft: Linksalternatives Leben in den siebziger und frühen achtziger Jahren* (Berlin: Suhrkamp, 2014).

67. On the background, see Kristina Spohr Readman, "Germany and the Politics of the Neutron Bomb, 1975–1979," *Diplomacy & Statecraft* 21, no. 2 (2010): 259–85.

68. Jan-Ole Wiechmann, *Sicherheit neu denken: Die christliche Friedensbewegung in der Nachrüstungsdebatte 1977–1984* (Baden-Baden: Nomos, 2017), 171; Gerster, *Friedensdialoge*, 225.

69. "Neutronenbombe. Neue Kraftprobe," *Der Spiegel*, December 5, 1977, 30.

70. Helmut Dubiel, *Niemand ist frei von der Geschichte: Die nationalsozialistische Herrschaft in den Debatten des Deutschen Bundestages* (Hamburg: Hanser, 1999), 193.

71. Franz Alt, *Frieden ist möglich: Die Politik der Bergpredigt* (Munich: Piper, 1983), 30. On the broader context, see Jan-Ole Wiechmann, "Der Streit um die Bergpredigt: Säkulare Vernunft und religiöser Glaube in der christlichen Friedensbewegung der Bundesrepublik Deutschland (1977–1984)," *Archiv für Sozialgeschichte* 51 (2011): 343–74.

72. Alt, *Frieden*, 45; Oskar Lafontaine, *Angst vor den Freunden: Die Atomwaffen-Strategie der Supermächte zerstört die Bündnisse* (Reinbek: Rowohlt, 1983), 15–20.

73. Alt, *Frieden*, 58–59.

74. Günther Anders, "Hiroshima als Weltzustand," in *Lasst uns die Kraniche suchen: Analysen, Berichte, Gedanken*, ed. Petra K. Kelly (Munich: Werkhaus, 1983), 54–61.

75. On the history of the decision, see Leopoldo Nuti, "The Origins of the 1979 Dual Track Decision—a Survey," in *The Crisis of Détente in Europe: From Helsinki to Gorbachev, 1975–1985*, ed. Leopoldo Nuti (London: Routledge, 2009), 54–71; Kristina Spohr Readman, "Conflict and Cooperation in Intra-Alliance Nuclear Politics: Western Europe, the United States, and the Genesis of NATO's Dual-Track Decision, 1977–1979," *Journal of Cold War Studies* 13, no. 2 (Spring 2011): 39–89.

76. For an overview, see Christoph Becker-Schaum, Philipp Gassert, Wilfried Mausbach, Martin Klimke, and Marianne Zepp, eds., *The Nuclear Crisis: The Arms Race, Cold War Anxiety, and the German Peace Movement of the 1980s* (New York: Berghahn, 2016).

77. Ziemann, "Code of Protest," 254–56.

78. Horst-Eberhard Richter, "Die Angst kann lehren, sich zu wehren," in *In letzter Stunde: Ein Aufruf zum Frieden*, ed. Walter Jens et al. (Munich: Kindler, 1982), 131.

79. Lafontaine, *Angst*, 77. On the broader context, with particular reference to Green Party politics, see Silke Mende, *"Nicht rechts, nicht links, sondern vorn." Eine Geschichte der Gründungsgrünen* (Munich: Oldenbourg, 2011), 372–82. On discussions about exterminism, see Andrea Humphreys, "'Ein atomares Auschwitz': Die Lehren der Geschichte und der Streit um die Nachrüstung," *Grünes Gedächtnis* (2008): 40; Ziemann, "Code of Protest," 250. See also E. P. Thompson, "Notes on Exterminism, the Last Stage of Civilization," *New Left Review*, no. 121 (1980): 3–31.

80. "Krieg dem Krieg!" Materialien zur Anti-Kriegs-Demo am 10. Oktober 1981 in Bonn, Aktionsgemeinschaft ArfA Uni Bonn, HIS, SBe544, Box 02.

81. Deutscher Bundestag, Stenographische Berichte, 10. Wahlperiode (hereafter cited as BT debates), November 21, 1983, 2364A. See for comparison also Vogt (Greens), June 15, 1983, 782A: "1.6 times Hiroshima."

82. "Der Atomtod bedroht uns alle—Ein Aufruf zum Gespräch von Professor Dr. Helmut Ridder (Gießen), Gösta von Uexküll (Hamburg) und Josef Weber (Köln)," DFU, 1980, http://www.dearchiv.de/php/dok.php?archiv=bla&brett=B80_10&fn=ATOMTOD.A80&menu=b1980.

83. Jonathan Schell, *Das Schicksal der Erde: Gefahr und Folgen eines Atomkriegs* (Munich: Piper, 1982), 60–65. On this change toward more graphic depictions, cf. Ziemann, "Code of Protest," 246–47, 254, emphasizing a shift toward an emphasis on activism.

84. See the important article by Humphreys, "'Atomares Auschwitz.'"

85. "'Wir sind ein schöner Unkrautgarten': Die grünen Abgeordneten Joschka Fischer und Otto Schily über die Auseinandersetzungen in ihrer Partie," *Der Spiegel*, June 13, 1983, 26.

86. Otto Schily, BT debates, June 15, 1983, 787D. Cf. also Gert Bastian, "Die Lebenden werden die Toten beneiden" Rede auf dem Hamburger Ärztekongreß gegen die Atomkriegs-

gefahr am 19. September 1981," in *Atomtod oder europäische Sicherheitsgemeinschaft* (Cologne: Pahl Rugenstein, 1985), 108–16.

87. Walter Jens, in Walter Jens et al., *In letzter Stunde* (Munich: Kindler, 1982), 15.

88. Belinda Davis, "The Gender of War and Peace: Rhetoric in the West German Peace Movement of the Early 1980s," *Mitteilungsblatt des Instituts für soziale Bewegungen* 32 (2004): 123, 128–29. See also Anne Bieschke, *Die unerhörte Friedensbewegung. Frauen, Krieg und Frieden in der Nuklearkrise 1979–1983* (Essen: Klartext, 2018).

89. Anton Andrea Guha, *Die Nachrüstung: Der Holocaust Europas* (Freiburg: Dreisam, 1981). On the use of the word, see Herf, *War*, 133; Humphreys, "'Atomares Auschwitz,'" 59. For more references to this theme, cf. Herf, *War*, 155, 171.

90. Eppler, *Tödliche Utopie*, 92.

91. See Fujiwara's chapter 12 in this volume.

92. Dorothee Sölle, "Paul Tibbett, Euroshima und der Widerstand," in *Lasst uns die Kraniche suchen: Analysen, Berichte, Gedanken*, ed. Petra K. Kelly (Munich: Werkhaus, 1983), 48–50. Cf. also the panel discussion on the U.S. Grenada invasion and Hiroshima, December 1983, Alternative Liste, in Teppich, *Flugblätter*, 254. On general debate in the context of the "politics of the past" in 1980s' West Germany, see Humphreys, "'Ein atomares Auschwitz,'" and the almost identical discussion in English in Kundnani, *Utopia or Auschwitz*, 167–91, as well as, more broadly anchored in primary sources, Eckart Conze, "Geschichte als Argument: Nationalsozialismus, Zweiter Weltkrieg und Holocaust in der Auseinandersetzung um nukleare Rüstung um 1980," in *Teilungen überwinden: Europäische und internationale Geschichte im 19. und 20. Jahrhundert. Festschrift für Wilfried Loth*, ed. Michaela Bachem-Rehm, Claudia Hiepel, and Henning Türk (Munich: Oldenbourg, 2014), 33–47; and Conze, "Modernitätsskepsis und die Utopie der Sicherheit NATO-Nachrüstung und Friedensbewegung in der Geschichte der Bundesrepublik," *Zeithistorische Forschungen* 7 (2010): 220–39.

93. See Ran Zwigenberg, "Never Again: Hiroshima, Auschwitz and the Politics of Commemoration," *Asia-Pacific Journal—Japan Focus* 13, no. 3 (2015): 1–22.

94. Petra Kelly in BT debates, June 15, 1983, 756B-C. On this connection, see Humphreys, "'Ein atomares Auschwitz.'"

95. For this and the following, see Schregel, *Atomkrieg*, 164–77; and the account by Benjamin Ziemann, "German Angst? Debating Cold War Anxieties in West Germany, 1945–1990," in *Understanding the Imaginary War: Culture, Thought and Nuclear Conflict, 1945–90*, ed. Matthew Grant and Benjamin Ziemann (Manchester: Manchester University Press, 2016), 116–39.

96. Alfred Mechtersheimer, *Zeitbombe NATO* (Cologne: Diederichs, 1984), 15. Cf. also the translation by Nigel Calder, *Atomares Schlachtfeld Europa?* (Hamburg: Hoffmann und Campe, 1980).

97. Mechtersheimer, *Zeitbombe*, 36–42. On the background, see Wiechmann, *Sicherheit neu denken*, 178; Herf, *War*, 129, 136.

98. "Warum ausgerechnet Hessen?," 1983, 5, HIS, SBe544, Box 02. On this debate and this interpretation, see Schregel, *Atomkrieg*, 164–77.

99. For an interpretation of this image and comparison, see Gerhard Paul, "'Mushroom Clouds': Entstehung, Struktur und Funktion einer Medienikone im interkulturellen Vergleich," in *Visual History: Ein Studienbuch* (Göttingen: Vandenhoeck und Ruprecht, 2006), 257–58.

100. Humphreys, "'Ein atomares Auschwitz,'" 41, 50.

101. BT debates, November 21, 1983, 2366D.

102. Wolfgang Prosinger, *Laßt uns in Frieden. Porträt einer Bewegung* (Reinbek: Rowohlt, 1982), 98–107, esp. 98–99; Burkhard Luber, *Bedrohungsatlas Bundesrepublik Deutschland* (Wuppertal: Jugenddienst-Verlag, 1982); Schregel, *Atomkrieg*, 107, 114.

103. Dorothee Sölle, "'Die Bomben fallen jetzt,'" in *Begegnungen: Texte zu Frieden und Versöhnung*, ed. Wolfgang Brinkel (Berlin: Aktion Sühnezeichen/ Friedensdienste, 1985), 129.

104. Oskar Negt and Alexander Kluge, *Geschichte und Eigensinn* (Frankfurt/Main: Zweitausendeins, 1981), 810–11. I owe this reference to Klaus Scherpe, "Dramatization and De-Dramatization of 'The End': The Apocalyptic Consciousness of Modernity and Post-Modernity," *Cultural Critique*, no. 5 (Winter 1985/6): 121.

105. Richter, "Angst," 133.

106. Claudia Kemper, *Medizin gegen den Kalten Krieg: Ärzte in der anti-atomaren Friedensbewegung der 1980er Jahre* (Göttingen: Wallstein, 2016), 90. Cf. also, for example, "Das geplante Inferno: Horst Eberhard Richter über die Ursachen des 3. Weltkriegs und das Ende der Menschheit," *Der Spiegel*, September 21, 1981, 113–21.

107. See, for example, Dorothee Sölle, "Einseitig für das Leben," in *Bonn 10.10.1981. Friedensdemonstration für Abrüstung und Entspannung in Europa. Reden, Fotos . . .* , ed. Aktion Sühnezeichen/ Friedensdienste Aktionsgemeinschaft Dienst für den Frieden (Bornheim: Lamuv, 1982), 74–76. The locus classicus for this is Johan Galtung, "Violence, Peace, and Peace Research," *Journal of Peace Research* 6, no. 3 (1969): 167–91.

108. Erhard Eppler, *Die tödliche Utopie der Sicherheit* (Reinbek: Rowohlt, 1983), 207, 30. Cf. also the Green Party documents: Die Grünen, "Das Bundesprogramm," Bonn 1980, 19, https://www.boell.de/sites/default/files/assets/boell.de/images/download_de/publikationen/1980_001_Grundsatzprogramm_Die_Gruenen.pdf; Die Grünen, "Diesmal die Grünen. Warum? Ein Wahlaufruf zur Bundestagswahl 1983," Bonn 1983, 4, https://www.boell.de/sites/default/files/assets/boell.de/images/download_de/publikationen/1983_Wahlaufruf_Bundestagswahl.pdf.

109. Richter, "Angst." On the general background of these debates, see Kemper, *Medizin*, 94; Judith Michel, "'Die Angst kann lehren, sich zu wehren'—Der Angstdiskurs der westdeutschen Friedensbewegung in den 1980er Jahren," *Tel Aviver Jahrbuch für deutsche Geschichte* 38 (2010): 246–69.

110. Zwigenberg, *Global Hiroshima*, 145; on Lifton, cf. 144–75.

111. Kemper, *Medizin*, 100–104.

112. Lafontaine, *Angst*, 116; Kunigunde Birle, "Brief an mein totes Enkelkind Grace Patricia Kelly," in Kelly, *Lasst und die Kraniche suchen*, 126–27. Cf. also Ute Dombrowski and Helmut Walter, "'. . . daß ich nach einer Inszenierung suchte, die mir das Leben ermöglichte, solange es eben von außen noch möglich war,'" in *Friedensbewegung—Persönliches und Politisches*, ed. Klaus Horn and Eva Senghaas-Knobloch (Frankfurt/Main: Fischer, 1983), 246–65, esp. 249–50. On these and more examples, see Humphreys, "'Ein atomares Auschwitz,'" 50; Saskia Richter, *Die Aktivistin: Das Leben der Petra Kelly* (Munich: DVA, 2010), 156–62, 251–52.

113. "Wir sind ein schöner Unkrautgarten," 26. Cf. also the debate about how to commemorate the fortieth anniversary of the end of the Second World War in *Die Grünen im Bundestag: Sitzungsprotokolle*, vol. 2, ed. Josef Boyer and Helge Heidemeyer with Tim B. Peters (Düsseldorf: Droste, 2008), January 29/30, 1985, 701–3.

114. "Senioren- und Manöverblockade 1987," *Pressehütte*, http://www.pressehuette.de/buch

.php?ID=74. Cf. also Ina Deter's 1981 song "Vierzig Jahre Danach" [40 Years Later], http://lyrics.wikia.com/wiki/Ina_Deter:40_Jahre_Danach.

115. The most iconic mushroom cloud image at the time was perhaps Klaus Staeck's poster "Topic: Security. The next world war is certainly the last" (1981), https://www.pinterest.de/pin/341429215487926002/?lp=true. On the background, see Paul, "'Mushroom Clouds,'" 257; Ziemann, "Code of Protest," 250.

116. Gertrud Gumlich, "Eine Widerstandsbewegung gegen die Resignation. Friedensmarsch '82," in *Frauen für den Frieden: Analysen, Dokumente und Aktionen aus der Frauenfriedensbewegung*, ed. Eva Quistorp (Frankfurt/Main: päd extra, 1982), 57.

117. Prosinger, *Laßt und in Frieden*, 141.

118. Kemper, *Medizin*, 343. Cf. also Sabrina Müller, "'Frieden Schaffen ohne Waffen': Der gewaltlose Widerstand gegen die Nachrüstung," in *Zerreißprobe Frieden: Baden-Württemberg und der NATO-Doppelbeschluss*, ed. Haus der Geschichte Baden-Württemberg (Stuttgart: Haus der Geschichte Baden-Württemberg, 2004), 22.

119. Teppich, *Flugblätter*, 97; cf. also 121. On Hamburg, see Thießen, *Eingebrannt ins Gedächtnis*, 277–97, 298–99; on Berlin, see the image in Ziemann, "Code of Protest," 251.

120. Kemper, *Medizin*, 253; Horst Rademacher, "Eine Bombe genügt," *Die Zeit*, June 5, 1981, htp://www.zeit.de/1981/24/eine-bombe-genuegt/komplettansicht.

121. Thiessen, *Eingebrannt ins Gedächtnis*, 304.

122. "Düsseldorf—Zielscheibe in einem Atomkrieg?," 1981: DHM, DG83/163, http://www.dhm.de/datenbank/dhm.php?seite=5&fld_0=D2Z34211. For a similar poster, see "Nein zur Raketenrepublik Deutschland," Klaus Staeck, 1983, in Müller, "'Frieden Schaffen ohne Waffen,'" 21. On this pattern of argumentation, cf. Ziemann, "Code of Protest," 255–56. On similar, though less graphic, arguments for Karlsruhe and Würzburg, see Sabrina Müller, "Volksversammlung als Symbol und Appell: Die Menschenkette von Stuttgart nach Neu-Ulm am 22. Oktober 1983," in *Aufbruch, Protest und Provokation: Die bewegten 70er- und 80er-Jahre in Baden-Württemberg*, ed. Reinhold Weber (Stuttgart: Theiss, 2013), 124; *Nachdenken statt Nachrüsten: Karlsruher Wissenschaftler für den Frieden* (Karlsruhe: Von Loeper, 1984), 15–21. On Würzburg (1983), see DHM, DO2 2000/806, http://www.dhm.de/datenbank/img.php?img=20001677&format=1.

123. Süß, *Tod aus der Luft*, 543.

124. Antje Huber, BT debates, November 21, 1983, 2412A-B. See also similar arguments in the leaflets published in Teppich, *Flugblätter*, 15; and "Aufruf zum 8. Mai 1985," in Teppich, *Flugblätter*, 361. For similar arguments in other German cities, see Thießen, *Eingebrannt ins Gedächtnis*, 310. For Kassel, cf. the overview by Jörg Arnold, "'Kassel 1943 mahnt . . . ,'" 488–93.

125. "Krieg dem Krieg!" Materialien zur Anti-Kriegs-Demo am 10. Oktober 1981 in Bonn, Aktionsgemeinschaft ArfA Uni Bonn, HIS, SBe544, Box 02.

126. Schregel, *Atomkrieg*, 51, 235–42. On the background to this symbolic politics, see Wilfried von Bredow and Rudolf H. Brocke, *Krise und Protest: Ursprünge und Elemente der Friedensbewegungen in Westeuropa* (Opladen: Westdeutscher Verlag, 1987), 157–58.

127. Manfred Laduch, Heino Schütte, and Reinhard Wagenblast, *Mutlanger Heide: Ein Ort macht Geschichte* (Schwäbisch Gmünd: Remsdruckerei, 1990), 123.

128. On the general context of this debate, cf. Schregel, *Atomkrieg*, 149–50.

129. Laduch et al., *Mutlanger Heide*, 115.

130. On the context, see Axel Schildt and Detlef Siegfried, *Deutsche Kulturgeschichte: Die Bundesrepublik von 1945 bis zur Gegenwart* (Munich: Hanser, 2009), 427–35.

131. Landesarchiv Baden-Württemberg, Plakatsammlung, J153 Nr. 498, https://www.archivportal-d.de/item/652UJ4S45EBDLCDRQ4MCYLSI2VKK5SY5?rows=20&sort=random_341214042427553890&offset=5700&facetValues%5B%5D=context%3DTESFVY5OM625ODRSQXLHYP7P5KSFMUQB&viewType=list&hitNumber=5705; for this interpretation, see Ziemann, "Code of Protest," 252.

132. Cf. also the Munich SPD's election poster from 1920: DHM P 61/1481, https://www.dhm.de/lemo/bestand/objekt/spd-poster-for-the-parliamentary-elections-1920.html.

133. Ziemann, "Code of Protest," 256.

134. Schüring, *Atomstaat*, 239–40; Ziemann, "Code of Protest," 257–58. More generally, see Sven Reichardt, "'Wärme' als Modus sozialen Verhaltens?: Vorüberlegungen zu einer Kulturgeschichte des linksalternativen Milieus vom Ende der sechziger bis Anfang der achtziger Jahre," *Vorgänge* 44 (2005): 175–87.

135. Len Munnik, peace movement button, 1980/1985, DHM A90/3166, http://www.dhm.de/datenbank/dhm.php?seite=5&fld_0=XX007143. On the general background, see Kathrin Fahlenbrach, "Die Grünen: Neue Farbenlehre der Politik"; Fabio Crivellari, "Blockade: Friedensbewegung zwischen Melancholie und Ironie," in *Das Jahrhundert der Bilder: 1949 bis heute*, ed. Gerhard Paul (Göttingen: Vandenhoeck und Ruprecht, 2008), 474–81, 482–89.

136. Scherpe, "Dramatization and De-dramatization."

137. On the conceptualization of this, see Susanne Vees-Gulani following Matthias Neutzner, "'Phantomschmerzen': Durs Grünbeins *Porzellan* und neue Wege in der Literatur über den Luftkrieg," in *Luftkrieg: Erinnerungen in Deutschland und Europa*, ed. Jörg Arnold, Dietmar Süß, and Malte Thießen (Göttingen: Wallstein, 2009), 280.

138. Volkmar Deile, "Die Lehre aus Holocaust: Schluss mit Apologetik und Verdrängung," in *Begegnungen: Texte zu Frieden und Versöhnung*, ed. Wolfgang Brinkel (Berlin: Aktion Sühnezeichen/ Friedensdienste, 1985), 33.

139. Scherpe, "Dramatization and De-dramatization," 97. Problematically, this contemporary assessment is now beginning to make inroads into the historiography of the Cold War, without appropriate reflection on its historicity. See, for example, Matthew Grant and Benjamin Ziemann, eds., *Understanding the Imaginary War: Culture, Thought and Nuclear Conflict, 1945–90* (Manchester: Manchester University Press, 2016).

140. Andreas Huyssen, "Air War Legacies: From Dresden to Baghdad," in *Germans as Victims: Remembering the Past in Contemporary Germany*, ed. Bill Niven (Basingstoke: Palgrave, 2006), 181–93. On the continuation of Cold War ways of thinking, cf. Michael Geyer, "Der kriegerische Blick: Rückblick auf einen noch zu beendenden Krieg," *Sozialwissenschaftliche Informationen* 19, no. 2 (1990): 111–17.

141. Theo Sommer, "Das Hamburger Inferno," *Die Zeit*, July 24, 2003, http://www.zeit.de/2003/31/A-Gomorrha/komplettansicht. For comparison on the broader context with reference to this article, see Thiessen, *Eingebrannt ins Gedächtnis*, 420–25.

142. Hans Erich Nossack, *Hamburg 1943: The End*, trans. Joel Agee (Chicago: University of Chicago Press, 2004); Sebald, "Natural History," 75–76.

143. See Jörg Friedrich, *Der Brand: Deutschland im Bombenkrieg* (Munich: Propyläen, 2002); and the volume of official photographs of the bomb damage, *Brandstätten: Der Anblick des*

Bombenkrieges (Munich: Propyläen, 2003), in English translation by Allison Brown, *The Fire: The Bombing of Germany 1940–1945* (New York: Columbia University Press, 2006). On the debate, see Lothar Kettenacker, ed., *Ein Volk von Opfern? Die neue Debatte um den Bombenkrieg* (Berlin: Rowohlt, 2003).

144. See, for example, Alan Posener, "Die unheimliche Stille der Deutschen zum Jahrestag," August 3, 2015, https://www.welt.de/kultur/literarischewelt/article144759672/Die-unheimliche-Stille-der-Deutschen-zum-Jahrestag.html. On the background of such debates on the left, see Kundnani, *Utopia or Auschwitz*, 193–212, 235–58.

145. Geyer, "Cold War Angst," 398.

146. Moses, *German Intellectuals*, 5.

147. Michael Geyer, "The Stigma of Violence, Nationalism, and War in Twentieth-Century Germany," *German Studies Review* 15 (1992): 102.

148. On the relationship between experiences and commemoration, see Thießen, *Eingebrannt ins Gedächtnis*, 391–93.

149. Conceptually, see Geyer, "German Angst," as well as the new landmark study by Frank Biess, *Republik der Angst. Eine andere Geschichte der Bundesrepublik* (Berlin: Rowohlt, 2019).

150. Scherpe, "Dramatization and De-dramatization," 128.

151. Andreas Wirsching, *Abschied vom Provisorium: Geschichte der Bundesrepublik Deutschland 1982–1990* (Munich: DVA, 2006).

Chapter 12. Hiroshima, Nanjing, and Yasukuni: Contending Discourses on the Second World War in Japan

1. Lisa Yoneyama's work still stands out in addressing the politics of war memories *within* what I have called the Hiroshima discourse. Lisa Yoneyama, *Hiroshima Traces: Time, Space, and the Dialectics of Memory* (Berkeley: University of California Press, 1999).

2. Maurice Halbwachs, *The Collective Memory*, trans. Francis J. Ditter, Jr., and Vida Yazdi Ditter (New York: Harper & Row, 1980). See also Paul Connerton, *How Societies Remember* (Cambridge: Cambridge University Press, 1989); and Patrick Hutton, *History as an Art of Memory* (Hanover, NH: University Press of New England, 1993).

3. Kenneth E. Foote, *Shadowed Ground: America's Landscapes of Violence and Tragedy* (Austin: University of Texas Press, 1997).

4. Simone Weil, *The Need for Roots: Prelude to a Declaration of Duties towards Mankind* (London: Routledge, 2001), 111.

5. John Dower has been the leading scholar on Japanese war memories. See his "'An Aptitude for Being Unloved': War and Memory in Japan" and "The Bombed: Hiroshima and Nagasakis in Japanese Memory," in *Ways of Forgetting, Ways of Remembering* (New York: New Press, 2012), 105–35, 136–60.

6. Many survivors' tales of the atomic bombings are available online, as in the *Asahi shimbun* website Messages of Hiroshima and Nagasaki, available in both Japanese and English. See http://www.asahi.com/hibakusha/english/ for the English translation. See also Gaynor Sekimori, trans., *Hibakusha: Survivors of Hiroshima and Nagasaki* (Tokyo: Kosei, 1989).

7. Glenn D. Hook, "Censorship and Reportage of Atomic Damage and Casualties in Hiroshima and Nagasaki," *Bulletin of Concerned Asian Scholars* 23 (January–March 1991): 13–25.

8. Kerry Brougher, "Art and Nuclear Culture," *Bulletin of the Atomic Scientists* 69, no. 6 (November 2013): 11–18.

9. Kiichi Fujiwara, *Senso wo kiokusuru* [Remembering the war] (Tokyo: Kodansha, 2001), 128–29; Kiichi Fujiwara, "Imagining the Past, Remembering the Future," *Social Science Japan*, no. 3 (1995).

10. Kenji Nakazawa, *Barefoot Gen*, vols. 1–10 (San Francisco: Last Gasp, 2004–2010). The Japanese edition was published as *Hadashi no Gen* (Tokyo: Chobunsha, 1983–1987); original publication 1975.

11. Akiko Hashimoto, *The Long Defeat: Cultural Trauma, Memory, and Identity in Japan* (New York: Oxford University Press, 2015), 11–12.

12. Hiroko Okuda, *Hibakusha ha naze matenai ka: Kaku/genshiryoku no sengoshi* [Why hibakusha cannot wait: Postwar history of nuclear/atomic power] (Tokyo: Iwanami Shoten, 2015), 174–77.

13. The most comprehensive study on antinuclear peace movements is Ubuki Satoru, *Hiroshima sengoshi: Hibaku taiken wa do uketomeraretaka* [Postwar history of Hiroshima: How the bombing experience was faced] (Tokyo: Iwanami Shoten, 2014).

14. Ohnishi Hitoshi, "Nihonno hankaku undo—1982nen Zenhannno SSDII Kokumin Undo Suishin Renraku Kaigi no Undo wo Chusshinni [Antinuclear movements in Japan: Coordinating Office for SSDII National Movement in early 1982], *Hogaku* (Tohoku University) 49, nos. 2, 3 (1985).

15. Honda Katsuichi, *Chugoku no tabi* [Journey to China] (Tokyo: Asahi Shimbunsha, 1972); Honda Katsuichi, *Nankin no Nihongun* [Japanese military in China] (Tokyo: Asahi Shimbunsha, 1986); Fujiwara, *Senso wo kiokusuru*, 132.

16. Debates on the Nanjing Massacre present a methodological issue on historical facts and truth, as discussed by Daqing Yang, "The Challenges of the Nanjing Massacre: Reflections on Historical Inquiry," in *The Nanjing Massacre in History and Historiography*, ed. Joshua A. Fogel (Berkeley: University of California Press, 2000), 133–44.

17. Nihon Senbotsu Gakusei Kinen-kai, ed., *Listen to the Voices from the Sea (Kike Wadatsumi no koe): Writings of the Fallen Japanese Students*, trans. Midori Yamanouchi and Joseph L. Quinn (Tonawada, NY: distributed by University of Toronto Press, 2000). Original Japanese version first published by the University of Tokyo Coop Publishing, 1949.

18. On the Yasukuni Shrine, see Akiko Takenaka, *Yasukuni Shrine: History, Memory, and Japan's Unending Postwar* (Honolulu: University of Hawaii Press, 2015); and Franziska Seraphim, *War Memory and Social Politics in Japan, 1945–2005* (Cambridge, MA: Harvard University Press, 2006), 226–57.

19. Hiroshima City, http://www.city.hiroshima.lg.jp/www/contents/1491263589626/files/01.pdf.

20. *Sankei*, http://www.sankei.com/politics/news/160530/plt1605300002-n1.html.

21. Asahi TV, http://www.tv-asahi.co.jp/hst/poll/201712/index.html.

22. The Hiroshima Roundtable has been held since 2012, with the chairman's statement issued at the end of the meeting. For the 2017 meeting, see Hiroshima Prefecture, https://www.pref.hiroshima.lg.jp/kouhou/weekly-topic-detail.html?d=20170804&n=1.

23. Ian Buruma, *The Wages of Guilt: Memories of War in Germany and Japan* (New York: Farrar Straus Giroux, 1994), 96.

Chapter 13. The End of the Beginning: China and the Consolidation of the Nuclear Revolution

1. Robert Jervis, *The Meaning of the Nuclear Revolution: Statecraft and the Prospect of Armageddon* (Ithaca, NY: Cornell University Press, 1989); Michael Mandelbaum, *The Nuclear Revolution: International Politics before and after Hiroshima* (New York: Cambridge University Press, 1981). For summaries of the sharp disagreements about how revolutionary these weapons were, see Lawrence Freedman, *The Evolution of Nuclear Strategy* (New York: Palgrave Macmillan, 2003); Fred Kaplan, *The Wizards of Armageddon* (New York: Simon and Schuster, 1983); Gregg Herken, *Counsels of War* (New York: Knopf, 1985); John E. Mueller, *Retreat from Doomsday: The Obsolescence of Major War* (New York: Basic Books, 1989).

2. The classic account of this history remains John W. Lewis and Xue Litai, *China Builds the Bomb* (Stanford, CA: Stanford University Press, 1988). See also Robert S. Norris, *British, French, and Chinese Nuclear Weapons* (Boulder: Westview Press, 1994); Avery Goldstein, *Deterrence and Security in the 21st Century: China, Britain, France and the Enduring Legacy of the Nuclear Revolution* (Stanford, CA: Stanford University Press, 2000).

3. See Mark A. Ryan, "Early Chinese Attitudes toward Civil Defence against Nuclear Attack," *Australian Journal of Chinese Affairs*, no. 21 (January 1989): 81–109; also M. Taylor Fravel and Evan S. Medeiros, "China's Search for Assured Retaliation: The Evolution of Chinese Nuclear Strategy and Force Structure," *International Security* 35, no. 2 (Fall 2010): 61–62; Henrietta Harrison, "Popular Responses to the Atomic Bomb in China 1945–1955," *Past & Present* 218, suppl. 8 (April 2013): 98–116.

4. China's view is similar to that of critics of the proposed *Enola Gay* exhibition at the Smithsonian in 1994, discussed by Michael Gordin and John Ikenberry in chapter 1 of this volume.

5. Shannon Tiezzi, "Chinese Diplomat: Hiroshima and Nagasaki Were Bombed for a Reason," *Diplomat*, May 13, 2015, https://thediplomat.com/2015/05/chinese-diplomat-hiroshima-and-nagasaki-were-bombed-for-a-reason/.

6. Especially the seminal works by Thomas Schelling and Alexander George. See Thomas C. Schelling, *Arms and Influence* (New Haven, CT: Yale University Press, 1966); Alexander L. George, *The Limits of Coercive Diplomacy; Laos, Cuba, Vietnam* (Boston: Little, Brown, 1971); Alexander L. George, *Forceful Persuasion: Coercive Diplomacy as an Alternative to War* (Washington, DC: United States Institute of Peace Press, 1991). On additional reasons for the inconclusiveness of the debate about the nuclear revolution, see chapter 17 in this volume by Frank Gavin.

7. See Stephen M. Walt, "A Renaissance in Nuclear Security Studies?," *Foreign Policy*, January 21, 2010, http://foreignpolicy.com/2010/01/21/a-renaissance-in-nuclear-security-studies/; Scott D. Sagan, "Two Renaissances in Nuclear Security Studies," H-Diplo/ISSF Forum on "What We Talk about When We Talk about Nuclear Weapons," 2014, http://issforum.org/ISSF/PDF/ISSF-Forum-2.pdf.

8. On the early efforts to preclude nation-based nuclear arsenals, see "The Acheson-Lilienthal & Baruch Plans, 1946," *Milestones in the History of U.S. Foreign Relations*, May 9, 2017, https://history.state.gov/milestones/1945-1952/baruch-plans. For discussion of the way such concerns shaped Roosevelt's and then Truman's thinking about sharing information about the bomb and its uses, see Campbell Craig's discussion in chapter 2.

9. The United States sharply limited its nuclear sharing with allies who had participated in the Manhattan Project and adopted an array of policies to reduce the chances that nonmembers would join the club. These included policies to restrict nuclear sharing to the peaceful, civilian uses of this new technology, with the expectation that recipients of such assistance would not exploit it to develop nuclear weapons. The McMahon Act and the Atoms for Peace project were key elements in this effort. Francis Gavin has even argued that U.S. attempts to inhibit the spread of nuclear weapons were an underappreciated central element of U.S. grand strategy during the Cold War. Francis J. Gavin, "Strategies of Inhibition: U.S. Grand Strategy, the Nuclear Revolution, and Nonproliferation," *International Security* 40, no. 1 (Summer 2015): 9–46.

10. Unlike Paul Bracken, I see continuity in the motivation and behavior of those who have more recently followed in China's nuclear footsteps. A true "second nuclear age," to use Bracken's phrase, would emerge if nonstate actors were ever able to command nuclear forces, since this would challenge key assumptions on which current reasoning about nuclear strategy and behavior rest. Paul Bracken, *Fire in the East: The Rise of Asian Military Power and the Second Nuclear Age* (New York: HarperCollins, 1999).

11. Efforts to restrict the transfer of materials and equipment to states who might master the requisite knowledge were effective at slowing rather than preventing determined states from realizing their nuclear ambitions. On related issues, see Vipin Narang, "Strategies of Nuclear Proliferation: How States Pursue the Bomb," *International Security* 41, no. 3 (Winter 2017): 110–50.

12. Aside from the material constraints facing developing states, political pressures (domestic and international) may also discourage proliferation even in states where the effort could be made, as in the case of Japan discussed by Takuya Sasaki in chapter 6. Public pressure will be less significant where secrecy about the nuclear project prevails—as in the United States during the wartime Manhattan Project and in Mao Zedong's China.

13. See Goldstein, *Deterrence and Security in the 21st Century*, 111.

14. For broader consideration of the interaction between domestic and international influences in states contemplating nuclear weapons programs, see Etel Solingen, *Nuclear Logics: Contrasting Paths in East Asia and the Middle East*, Princeton Studies in International History and Politics (Princeton, NJ: Princeton University Press, 2007); Målfrid Braut-Hegghammer, "Revisiting Osirak: Preventive Attacks and Nuclear Proliferation Risks," *International Security* 36, no. 1 (Summer 2011): 101–32; Jacques E. C. Hymans, *Achieving Nuclear Ambitions: Scientists, Politicians and Proliferation* (New York: Cambridge University Press, 2012).

15. For a careful review of this leverage, see Nuno P. Monteiro and Alexandre Debs, "The Strategic Logic of Nuclear Proliferation," *International Security* 39, no. 2 (Fall 2014): 7–51.

16. The Soviets did not begin their assistance intending to foster a Chinese nuclear weapons program. In 1956–1957, however, Nikita Khrushchev apparently decided to eliminate many of what we would today label "safeguards" on this assistance and made a preliminary decision to help China develop a weapon. There is some uncertainty about the conditions under which Khrushchev was prepared to follow through, but he quickly decided that he would not provide the promised assistance, likely reneging on a clear commitment. See discussion in Nicola Horsburgh, *China and Global Nuclear Order: From Estrangement to Active Engagement* (Oxford: Oxford University Press, 2015), 44.

17. See Gavin, "Strategies of Inhibition," 34. In his July 3, 1960, memo to Mao, Nie Rongzhen

wrote, "The Soviet side's stranglehold on us on the crucial issue of key technology is really infuriating. But indignation is useless. We are just going to have to show them. Maybe this kind of pressure will instead become the impetus for developing our science and technology so we strive even more resolutely for independence and autonomy and self-reliance in science and technology, rather than counting on foreign assistance": "Report by Nie Rongzhen to Mao Zedong Regarding Science and Technology (Abridged)," http://digitalarchive.wilsoncenter.org/document/114348. Resentment at what was perceived as a powerful ally's selfishness when it came to nuclear sharing has also been evident in other cases. But China's reaction to Soviet attempts to rein in an ally differed in one important respect from, for example, the reaction of American allies after the late 1950s when Washington tried to use its leverage to convince them to forgo or abandon their nuclear aspirations: China did not attempt to hide its intentions. By contrast, the programs of most U.S. partners after 1960 typically remained secretive—part of a new pattern of opaque proliferation—as they hoped to avoid incurring Washington's wrath for defying its nonproliferation preference while continuing to enjoy the economic or security benefits the United States provided. In some cases, American pressure was effective because of the draconian penalties the United States was prepared to impose (for example, Republic of Korea, Republic of China). See also Gene Gerzhoy, "Alliance Cohesion and Nuclear Restraint: How the United States Thwarted West Germany's Nuclear Ambitions," *International Security* 39, no. 4 (Spring 2015): 91–129. In other cases, American pressure was not effective, though even in those cases states opted for surreptitious development and deployment. See Avner Cohen and Benjamin Frankel, "Opaque Nuclear Proliferation," *Journal of Strategic Studies* 13, no. 3 (September 1990): 14–44; Devin T. Hagerty, *The Consequences of Nuclear Proliferation: Lessons from South Asia* (Cambridge, MA: MIT Press, 1998). See also Monteiro and Debs, "The Strategic Logic of Nuclear Proliferation."

18. For some relevant considerations that are pertinent to preventive strikes against possible nuclear aspirants, see Alexandre Debs and Nuno P. Monteiro, "Known Unknowns: Power Shifts, Uncertainty, and War," *International Organization* 68, no. 1 (January 2014): 1–31.

19. The uncertainty about how the Soviet Union would respond to preventive strikes led the United States to refrain from acting on this option, which was discussed more than once in the Kennedy administration. See discussion and citations to relevant declassified documents in Goldstein, *Deterrence and Security in the 21st Century*, 101–9.

20. See William Burr and Jeffrey T. Richelson, "Whether to 'Strangle the Baby in the Cradle': The United States and the Chinese Nuclear Program, 1960–64," *International Security* 25, no. 3 (Winter 2000/2001): 54–99; see also Goldstein, *Deterrence and Security in the 21st Century*, 105–6; "Memorandum of Conversation with Ambassador Dobrynin," September 25, 1964, Document no. 54, in *Foreign Relations of the United States, 1964–1968*, vol. 30: *China* (Washington, DC: U.S. Government Printing Office, 1998).

21. Glenn Snyder noted the resulting tension with the nuclear patron's interest in avoiding entrapment in confrontations by a partner who might be emboldened to challenge the common foe if given an airtight pledge of support. Glenn H. Snyder, "The Security Dilemma in Alliance Politics," *World Politics* 36, no. 4 (July 1984): 461–95.

22. Kenneth Waltz famously captured the transformed nature of uncertainty about warfighting in such situations: "In a conventional world, one is uncertain about winning or losing. In a nuclear world, one is uncertain about surviving or being annihilated." Kenneth N. Waltz, "The

Spread of Nuclear Weapons: More May Be Better: Introduction," *Adelphi Papers* 21, no. 171 (1981): 7.

23. Khrushchev may also have worried that facilitating a Chinese nuclear weapons program would provide the United States with a pretext to share nuclear weapons with its West German ally, something that chronically concerned the Soviets and was not entirely unfounded. See Marc Trachtenberg, *A Constructed Peace: The Making of the European Settlement, 1945–1963* (Princeton, NJ: Princeton University Press, 1999), esp. chaps. 6 and 7. On questions about effective U.S. control over American nuclear weapons in Germany, see Richard K. Betts, *Nuclear Blackmail and Nuclear Balance* (Washington, DC: Brookings Institution, 1987), 84.

24. See Thomas J. Christensen, *Useful Adversaries: Grand Strategy, Domestic Mobilization, and Sino-American Conflict, 1947–1958* (Princeton, NJ: Princeton University Press, 1996), 209–11.

25. For debates about the importance of reputation, see Jonathan Mercer, *Reputation and International Politics* (Ithaca, NY: Cornell University Press, 1996); Daryl Grayson Press, *Calculating Credibility: How Leaders Evaluate Military Threats*, Cornell Studies in Security Affairs (Ithaca, NY: Cornell University Press, 2005); Alex Weisiger and Keren Yarhi-Milo, "Revisiting Reputation: How Past Actions Matter in International Politics," *International Organization* 69, no. 2 (Spring 2015): 473–95.

26. See Goldstein, *Deterrence and Security in the 21st Century*, 82–84.

27. Negative control is the ability to prevent unauthorized use of military forces (so that a nuclear-armed state can avoid accidental or inadvertent use); positive control is the ability to ensure that authorized orders to use military force are executed (so that a nuclear-armed state's threatened use is credible).

28. U.S. defense secretary Robert McNamara, in his famous line, condemned small nuclear forces—even those of advanced industrial allies Britain and France—as "dangerous, expensive, prone to obsolescence and lacking in credibility as a deterrent." Peter Malone, *The British Nuclear Deterrent* (New York: St. Martin's Press, 1984), 156.

29. The ability of an actor unconcerned about survival to take the initiative and innovate as it encounters resistance is a strategic advantage that has made suicide bombing an attractive strategy for some contemporary extremist groups. See Robert A. Pape, "The Strategic Logic of Suicide Terrorism," *American Political Science Review* 97, no. 3 (August 2003): 343–61; Michael C. Horowitz, "Nonstate Actors and the Diffusion of Innovations: The Case of Suicide Terrorism," *International Organization* 64, no. 1 (Winter 2010): 33–64.

30. See Richard Wich, *Sino-Soviet Crisis Politics* (Cambridge, MA: Harvard University Press, 1980), chaps. 9 and 10; James H. Mann, *About Face: A History of America's Curious Relationship with China, from Nixon to Clinton* (New York: Knopf, 1998), 20–23. China's proposals for reducing tensions that Premier Zhou Enlai presented to Kosygin (who stopped at the Beijing airport while returning to Moscow from Vietnam) called for separating ideological from interstate disputes, avoiding military clashes, and maintaining the status quo while negotiations proceeded on the border dispute. Zhou Enlai, *Zhou Enlai nianpu*, vol. 3 (Beijing: Zhongyang Wenxian Chubanshe, 1997), 320–21. On the application of military pressure and the range of options the Soviets considered to coerce the Chinese to agree to resume negotiations during the summer of 1969, see Christian F. Ostermann, "New Evidence on the Sino-Soviet Border Dispute, 1969–71," *Cold War International History Project Bulletin*, no. 6–7 (Winter 1995–96): 186–93. For

Mao's anticipation of Soviet preventive strikes against China's nuclear weapons facilities, see Mao Zedong, "Mao Zedong's Talk at a Meeting of the Central Cultural Revolution Group (Excerpt), 15 March 1969 [Document no. 4, trans. Chen Jian]," *Cold War International History Project Bulletin*, no. 11 (Winter 1998): 161–62.

31. See Hagerty, *The Consequences of Nuclear Proliferation*.

32. In the North Korean case, preventive (or preemptive) strikes against its nuclear arsenal would have to be accompanied by strikes that destroyed the thousands of artillery shells it has prepositioned for quickly devastating strikes against the residents (including hundreds of thousands of foreign civilians) and property in Seoul, South Korea. Despite North Korean denials, it remains possible that some of the artillery could be used to deliver chemical or biological weapons. This capability, then, constitutes a conventional threat that supplements the nuclear threat and augments the dissuasive effect of the North's deterrent strategy.

33. In subsequent years, a more prosperous China has certainly acted on this incentive. See M. Taylor Fravel and Evan S. Medeiros, "China's Search for Assured Retaliation: The Evolution of Chinese Nuclear Strategy and Force Structure," *International Security* 35, no. 2 (Fall 2010): 48–87.

34. The arduous challenge has been on full display in the difficulties that North Korea encountered in its warhead and missile tests beginning in 1998, with progress punctuated by spectacular failures.

35. The classic account of China's ballistic missile development program is John Wilson Lewis and Hua Di, "China's Ballistic Missile Programs: Technologies, Strategies, Goals," *International Security* 17, no. 2 (Fall 1992): 5–40. Lewis and Hua assert the absence of an "overarching strategic doctrine" guiding the program, though their history makes clear the strategic incentives to target China's two superpower adversaries that established the goals for China's scientist and engineers.

36. For an elaboration that emphasizes the continuing distinctiveness of China's understanding of deterrence, see Li Bin, "Chinese Thinking on Nuclear Weapons," *Arms Control Today*, December 2015, http://www.armscontrol.org/ACT/2015_12/Features/Chinese-Thinking-On-Nuclear-Weapons. China's proclamation of its benign, defensive intentions was, of course, self-serving since it aimed to deny neighbors (Japan, South Korea, Taiwan, and India) the pretext of a threatening nuclear China to pursue their own arsenals, while also providing a rationale for Chinese nuclear assistance to Pakistan, once it could invoke China's own logic in pointing to the challenge it faced from India.

37. More recently manifest in Chinese President Xi Jinping's emphasis on the Chinese dream of rejuvenation. See Zheng Wang, "Not Rising, but Rejuvenating: The 'Chinese Dream,'" *Diplomat*, February 5, 2013, http://thediplomat.com/2013/02/chinese-dream-draft/; "China's Peaceful Rise: A Road Chosen for Rejuvenation of a Great Nation," *Xinhuanet*, February 19, 2017, http://news.xinhuanet.com/english/2004-02/19/content_1321769.htm.

38. See "Statement of the Government of the People's Republic of China," October 16, 1964, in Lewis and Xue, *China Builds the Bomb*, 241–43.

39. See Christensen, *Useful Adversaries*. With the callous disregard for human welfare and recklessness characteristic of the Great Leap Forward, Mao's mobilized masses played an important role as labor that gathered and began to process the uranium for China's nuclear program, an effort chronicled by Lewis and Xue in *China Builds the Bomb*.

40. See Lewis and Xue, *China Builds the Bomb*, 130; "China's Atomic Weapon Story Told," *New York Times*, May 5, 1985, http://www.nytimes.com/1985/05/05/us/china-s-atomic-weapon-story-told.html. The bitter reaction to the perceived arrogance of the Soviets and their alleged attempts to control China (which also fed China's nuclear resolve) was reflected in the decision to name China's first atomic bomb "596," the year and month of the letter from Khrushchev that terminated nuclear assistance to China.

41. The expectation of a strong nuclear constraint on recklessness in such states was a central tenet of Kenneth Waltz's nuclear optimism. See Waltz, "The Spread of Nuclear Weapons"; Scott D. Sagan and Kenneth N. Waltz, "The Great Debate," *National Interest*, no. 109 (2010): 88–96; Kenneth N. Waltz, "Why Iran Should Get the Bomb," *Foreign Affairs* 91, no. 4 (July/August 2012): 2–5.

42. Rogue leaders can also indulge in grotesquely cruel and arbitrary behavior toward their own citizens who are unable to effectively resist or retaliate.

43. Despite their disagreements about the optimal responses to North Korea's nuclear weapons program, Victor Cha and David Kang share a belief that the DPRK's leaders are fundamentally rational when regime survival is on the line. See Victor Cha and David C. Kang, "Think Again: North Korea," *Foreign Policy*, March 25, 2013, http://foreignpolicy.com/2013/03/25/think-again-north-korea/.

44. Even in domestic politics, where rogues can more safely let their passions prevail, Mao abandoned his revolutionary fantasies and compromised his principles when the fate of CCP rule hung in the balance—in 1961 as the Great Leap Forward produced a regime-rattling economic collapse, and in 1967 as the Cultural Revolution, which had decimated party ranks, schools, and factories, threatened to tear apart the last pillar of central control, the Chinese military.

45. "Safety will be the sturdy child of terror, and survival the twin brother of annihilation," Winston Churchill's characterization of the Cold War's nuclear order in 1955. Winston Churchill, "Never Despair," speech to the House of Commons, London, March 1, 1955, http://www.winstonchurchill.org/resources/speeches/1946-1963-elder-statesman/never-despair.

46. On the India-Pakistan conflicts and the role of nuclear weapons, see Hagerty, *The Consequences of Nuclear Proliferation*; Vipin Narang, "Posturing for Peace? Pakistan's Nuclear Postures and South Asian Stability," *International Security* 34, no. 3 (Winter 2009): 38–78. Ashley J. Tellis, C. Christine Fair, and Jamison Jo Medby, *Limited Conflicts under the Nuclear Umbrella: Indian and Pakistani Lessons from the Kargil Crisis* (Santa Monica, CA: Rand, 2001); Scott Sagan and Kenneth Waltz. *The Spread of Nuclear Weapons: A Debate Renewed*, 2nd ed. (New York: Norton, 2003); Sumit Ganguly and Devin T. Hagerty, *Fearful Symmetry: India-Pakistan Crises in the Shadow of Nuclear Weapons* (Seattle: University of Washington Press, 2005); Paul S. Kapur, *Dangerous Deterrent: Nuclear Weapons Proliferation and Conflict in South Asia, Studies in Asian Security* (Stanford, CA: Stanford University Press, 2007); Peter R. Lavoy, *Asymmetric Warfare in South Asia: The Causes and Consequences of the Kargil Conflict* (Cambridge: Cambridge University Press, 2009).

47. Glenn Snyder, "The Balance of Power and the Balance of Terror," in *The Balance of Power*, ed. Paul Seabury (San Francisco: Chandler, 1965), 184–201.

48. Robert Jervis, *The Illogic of American Nuclear Strategy* (Ithaca, NY: Cornell University Press, 1986), esp. 56–63.

49. Some analysts have suggested that the factional rivalries of China in the wake of the Cultural Revolution upheaval motivated Lin Biao, Chairman Mao's "chief comrade in arms and designated successor," to order the attack as a way to demonstrate his antirevisionist bona fides and perhaps to consolidate his position by raising the need for military preparedness against an ever more dangerous Soviet socialist imperialist threat. It is also possible that the clashes were simply a predictable result of troops massed in close proximity along a disputed border that had been heavily militarized on both sides after 1965. For a useful survey, see Lyle J. Goldstein, "Return to Zhenbao Island: Who Started Shooting and Why It Matters," *China Quarterly*, no. 168 (December 2001): 985–97.

50. For extensive discussion of the delicate management of the crisis, see Michael S. Gerson, *The Sino-Soviet Border Conflict: Deterrence, Escalation, and the Threat of Nuclear War in 1969* (Arlington, VA: CNA, 2010), https://www.cna.org/CNA_files/PDF/D0022974.A2.pdf. See also Lyle Goldstein, *Preventive Attack and Weapons of Mass Destruction: A Comparative Historical Analysis* (Stanford, CA: Stanford University Press, 2006).

51. On the motivation for Mao to seek a strategic opening to the United States, see the crucial "Report by Four Chinese Marshals—Chen Yi, Ye Jianying, Xu Xiangqian, and Nie Rongzhen,—to the Central Committee, 'A Preliminary Evaluation of the War Situation' (Excerpt), 11 July 1969 [Document no. 9, trans. Chen Jian and Li Di]," *Cold War International History Project Bulletin* (Winter 1998), http://cwihp.si.edu/pdf.htm; "Report by Four Chinese Marshals—Chen Yi, Ye Jianying, Nie Rongzhen, and Xu Xiangqian—to the CCP Central Committee, 'Our Views about the Current Situation' (Excerpt), 17 September 1969 [Document no. 11, trans. Chen Jian and Li Di]," *Cold War International History Project Bulletin* (Winter 1998), http://cwihp.si.edu/pdf.htm.

52. See Allen S. Whiting, *China Crosses the Yalu: The Decision the Enter the Korean War* (Stanford, CA: Stanford University Press, 1960); Allen S. Whiting, *The Chinese Calculus of Deterrence: India and Indochina*, Michigan Classics in Chinese Studies, no. 4 (Ann Arbor: Center for Chinese Studies Publications, 2001); Zhai Qiang. *China and the Vietnam Wars, 1950–1975: The New Cold War History* (Chapel Hill: University of North Carolina Press, 2000). Soviet involvement was also carefully circumscribed as it, too, supplied and backed the North Vietnamese in their war with the United States.

53. The decisions taken during the second and third Berlin crises and the Cuban Missile Crisis manifested this cautiousness that belied declaratory doctrine and the options each side had developed, thinking they could be used to gain an advantage in such tense confrontations. Avery Goldstein, "First Things First: The Pressing Danger of Crisis Instability in U.S.-China Relations," *International Security* 37, no. 4 (Spring 2013): 81–82.

54. The most likely paths to nuclear disaster, if one occurs, are familiar, and some of the most worrisome ones have been identified in Scott Sagan's work that considers the inevitable error-proneness of large-scale complex organizations that possess, command, and control nuclear arsenals. See Scott D. Sagan, *The Limits of Safety: Organizations, Accidents, and Nuclear Weapons* (Princeton, NJ: Princeton University Press, 1993); also Scott D. Sagan, "The Perils of Proliferation: Organization Theory, Deterrence Theory, and the Spread of Nuclear Weapons," *International Security* 18, no. 3 (Spring 1994): 66–107. For a response by a skeptic, see Kenneth Waltz's exchange with Sagan in Scott Sagan and Kenneth Waltz, *The Spread of Nuclear Weapons: A Debate Renewed*, 2nd ed. (New York: Norton, 2003).

55. On the significance of such conventional forces in the nuclear context, see Robert Powell, "Nuclear Brinkmanship, Limited War, and Military Power," *International Organization* 69, no. 3 (Summer 2015): 589–626.

56. See Goldstein, *Deterrence and Security in the 21st Century*, 95–96.

57. See Thomas C. Schelling, *The Strategy of Conflict* (New York: Oxford University Press, 1960); Thomas C. Schelling, *Arms and Influence* (New Haven, CT: Yale University Press, 1966); Goldstein, *Deterrence and Security in the 21st Century*, 280; Todd S. Sechser and Matthew Fuhrmann, *Nuclear Weapons and Coercive Diplomacy* (Cambridge: Cambridge University Press, 2017).

58. The difficulty of devising an effective response to reverse Russia's seizure of Crimea is a contemporary manifestation of this problem. I thank Michael Gordin for pointing this out.

59. Paul H. B. Godwin, "The Chinese Defense Establishment in Transition: The Passing of a Revolutionary Army?" in *Modernizing China*, ed. A. Doak Barnett and Ralph N. Clough (Boulder, CO: Westview Press, 1986).

60. For examples of this second-wave literature revisiting ideas about the effectiveness of counterforce strikes, the feasibility of nuclear warfighting, and the requirements for and the robustness of deterrence, see Keir A. Lieber and Daryl G. Press, "The End of Mad? The Nuclear Dimension of U.S. Primacy," *International Security* 30, no. 4 (2006): 7–44; Keir A. Lieber and Daryl G. Press, "The New Era of Counterforce Technological Change and the Future of Nuclear Deterrence," *International Security* 41, no. 4 (Spring 2017): 9–49; Brendan R. Green and Austin Long, "The MAD Who Wasn't There: Soviet Reactions to the Late Cold War Nuclear Balance," *Security Studies* 26, no. 4 (2017): 606–41; Austin Long and Brendan Rittenhouse Green, "Stalking the Secure Second Strike: Intelligence, Counterforce, and Nuclear Strategy," *Journal of Strategic Studies* 38 (2015): 38–73; Matthew Kroenig, "How to Approach Nuclear Modernization?: A US Response," *Bulletin of the Atomic Scientists* 71, no. 3 (2015): 16–18; Matthew Kroenig, Miriam Krieger, and Hans Noel, "Monkey Cage: Why Nuclear Superiority Matters for Compellence," *Washington Post*, December 3, 2014, https://www.washingtonpost.com/news/monkey-cage/wp/2014/12/03/why-nuclear-superiority-matters-for-compellence/?utm_term=.75507ed8d1be.

Chapter 14. Data, Discourse, and Disruption: Radiation Effects and Nuclear Orders

1. Many thanks to Michael Gordin, John Ikenberry, and the participants of the 2017 workshop on "Global Hiroshima" for invaluable feedback. I'd also like to acknowledge helpful comments by Kathleen Vogel and by the participants of the 2017 "Science and Democracy Network" meeting at Harvard University, where I presented an earlier version of this chapter. All remaining errors are mine.

2. The details of how this narrative emerged are beyond the scope of this chapter; suffice it to point out here that critics of the ongoing nuclear weapons tests (perhaps inadvertently) enabled this narrative's initial formation, which received support from, among others, advocates of indigenous groups who anticipated or measured the detrimental consequences of nuclear fallout, as well as from the influential Atoms for Peace initiative that President Eisenhower's 1953 speech helped start (transcripts of the speech are widely available, e.g., at IAEA, https://

www.iaea.org/about/history/atoms-for-peace-speech. See M. Susan Lindee, *Suffering Made Real: American Science and the Survivors at Hiroshima* (Chicago: University of Chicago Press, 1994); Mary X. Mitchell, "Screening out Controversy: Human Genetics, Emerging Techniques of Diagnosis, and the Origins of the Social Issues Committee of the American Society of Human Genetics, 1964–1973," *Journal of the History of Biology* (2017); Mitchell, "Test Cases: Reconfiguring American Law, Technoscience, and Democracy in the Nuclear Pacific" (PhD diss., University of Pennsylvania, 2016).

3. Olga Kuchinskaya, *The Politics of Invisibility: Public Knowledge about Radiation Health Effects after Chernobyl* (Cambridge, MA: MIT Press, 2014); Alla Yaroshinskaya, *Chernobyl: The Forbidden Truth*, trans. Michèle Kahn and Julia Sallabank (Lincoln: University of Nebraska Press, 1995).

4. Reactions to Fukushima have varied greatly across the world. While they were predictable in the United States, the Japanese and European nuclear industries began subjecting their regulatory frameworks to fundamental review and restructuring. See, for example, Elena Shadrina, "Fukushima Fallout: Gauging the Change in Japanese Nuclear Energy Policy," *International Journal of Disaster Risk Science* 3, no. 2 (2012): 69–83; Vlado Vivoda and Geordan Graetz, "Nuclear Policy and Regulation in Japan after Fukushima: Navigating the Crisis," *Journal of Contemporary Asia* 45, no. 3 (2015): 490–509; Vlado Vivoda, "Japan's Energy Security Predicament post-Fukushima," *Energy Policy* 46 (2012): 135–43; European Nuclear Safety Regulators Group, "EU Stress Tests and Follow-up," http://www.ensreg.eu/EU-Stress-Tests.

5. I don't have the space here to elaborate on these, but suffice it to mention the Princeton Program on Science and Global Security, which, while primarily focused on nuclear weapons, also creates powerful arguments cautioning against other uses of fissile materials (see Harold Feiveson et al., *Unmaking the Bomb: A Fissile Material Approach to Nuclear Disarmament and Nonproliferation* [Cambridge, MA: MIT Press, 2014]), and the international expansion of the direct action group Greenpeace, an organization that—at least in parts of Europe—has become almost synonymous with protest against all things nuclear. See Michael Brown, *Greenpeace Story* (London: Dorling Kindersley, 1989); Frank Zelko, "Making Greenpeace: The Development of Direct Action Environmentalism in British Columbia," *BC Studies* 142/143 (Summer 2004): 197–239; Rex Weyler, *Greenpeace: How a Group of Ecologists, Journalists, and Visionaries Changed the World* (Vancouver: Raincoast Books, 2004).

6. Sheila Jasanoff, ed., *States of Knowledge: The Co-Production of Science and Social Order* (New York: Routledge, 2004), 2–3.

7. Jasanoff, *States of Knowledge*, 278, 274.

8. This remains true despite rhetorical efforts by reactor designers to portray new reactor types as "proliferation resistant," but also, I would argue, despite efforts by the security community to equip facilities with "built-in" safeguards from the outset: existing "bridges" between these communities still reaffirm their underlying division. For a recent assessment of the proliferation resistance of small modular reactors, see Jonas Siegel, Elisabeth A. Gilmore, Nancy Gallagher, and Steve Fetter, "An Expert Elicitation of the Proliferation Resistance of Using Small Modular Reactors (SMR) for the Expansion of Civilian Nuclear Systems," *Risk Analysis* (2017).

9. On the challenges of safeguarding the arsenal and testing what cannot be tested quite as before, see, for example, Hugh Gusteron, *Nuclear Rites: A Weapons Laboratory at the End of the*

Cold War (Berkeley: University of California Press, 1996); Donald Mackenzie, *Inventing Accuracy: A Historical Sociology of Nuclear Missile Guidance* (Cambridge, MA: MIT Press, 1990).

10. See also Nina Tannenwald, *The Nuclear Taboo: The United States and the Non-Use of Nuclear Weapons since 1945* (Cambridge: Cambridge University Press, 2007). I am going to set aside nonstate actors here for the moment: the concern that such "rogue elements" might get their hands on an actual nuclear weapon appears far-fetched for various reasons and need not involve us here. On nuclear weapons as "currency of power," see in particular Anne Harrington de Santana, "Nuclear Weapons as the Currency of Power: Deconstructing the Fetish of Force," *Nonproliferation Review* 16, no. 3 (2009): 325–45.

11. In their apocalyptic essence, then, nuclear weapons can support both a deterrence strategy (we avoid war by pointing many of them at each other), *and* a nuclear weapons ban initiative (note the Nobel committee's decision to award the International Campaign to Abolish Nuclear Weapons [ICAN] the 2017 Peace Prize). See, for example, Lynn Eden, *Whole World on Fire: Organizations, Knowledges, and Nuclear Weapons Devastation* (Ithaca, NY: Cornell University Press, 2004); and Judith Reppy and Catherine M. Kelleher, eds., *Getting to Zero: The Path to Nuclear Disarmament* (Stanford, CA: Stanford University Press, 2011).

12. Angela N. H. Creager, *Life Atomic: A History of Radioisotopes in Science and Medicine* (Chicago: University of Chicago Press, 2013); Stephen L. Del Sesto, "Wasn't the Future of Nuclear Energy Wonderful?" in *Imagining Tomorrow: History, Technology, and the American Future*, ed. Joseph J. Corn (Cambridge, MA: MIT Press, 1986), 58–76.

13. It was also arguably one of the riskier ones: I am unaware of severe accidents caused by industrial detection instruments using ionizing radiation or even by medical devices and procedures—although obviously there were some unspeakably horrifying experiments conducted and crimes committed that involved nuclear isotopes and human subjects, and some instances of "lost" sources that happened to be "found" by unsuspecting civilians, with dreadful consequences. See, for example, International Atomic Energy Agency, *The Radiological Accident in Goiânia* (Vienna: International Atomic Energy Agency, 1988); William Moss and Roger Eckhardt, "The Human Plutonium Injection Experiments," *Los Alamos Science* 23 (1995): 177–233; U.S. Department of Energy, *Human Radiation Experiments Associated with the U.S. Department of Energy and Its Predecessors* (Washington, DC: Department of Energy, 1995).

14. For some early utopian visions associated with nuclear energy, see, for example, Del Sesto, "Wasn't the Future of Nuclear Energy Wonderful?"

15. Brian Balogh, *Chain Reaction: Expert Debate and Public Participation in American Commercial Nuclear Power, 1945–1975* (Cambridge: Cambridge University Press, 1991); J. Samuel Walker, *Permissible Dose: A History of Radiation Protection in the Twentieth Century* (Berkeley: University of California Press, 2000); and J. Samuel Walker, *A Short History of Nuclear Regulation, 1946–1990* (Washington, DC: U.S. Nuclear Regulatory Commission, 1993).

16. The vast literature on proliferation, hedging, breakout, and nuclear latency illustrates just how precarious this line is: nuclear energy programs can be and have been used to produce nuclear weapons. By the same token, nuclear warheads have powered many a civilian reactor, and the threat of nuclear terrorism introduces an entirely new challenge to this division. For a recent "transgression," see the report below on the alleged national security dimension of the U.S. commercial nuclear industry. Former secretary of energy Ernest Moniz's new think tank (Energy Futures Initiative) published a report in which the authors not only reverse the

direction of the well-known personnel pipeline (from the nuclear navy to the commercial industry) but also emphasize the *material* needs of the weapons complex: the commercial sector, according to the report, ought to produce tritium, an isotope essential to maintain the readiness of the nuclear weapons stockpile, as a service to the nation's security. Energy Futures Initiative, *The U.S. Nuclear Energy Enterprise: A Key National Security Enabler* (Washington, DC: Energy Futures Initiative, 2017).

17. Obviously there are parallels to other dual-use technologies such as chemical, biological, and nano that challenge nuclear exceptionalism; I won't explore these here.

18. Gabrielle Hecht, *Being Nuclear: Africans and the Global Uranium Trade* (Cambridge, MA: MIT Press, 2012), and *The Radiance of France: Nuclear Power and National Identity after World War II* (Cambridge, MA: MIT Press, 1998).

19. For an argument pushing back on "nuclear fear," see, for example, Spencer R. Weart, *Nuclear Fear: A History of Images* (Cambridge, MA: Harvard University Press, 1988).

20. It is beyond the scope of this chapter to detail this process, but for a transnational comparison, see Dick van Lente, ed., *The Nuclear Age in Popular Media: A Transnational History, 1945–1965* (New York: Palgrave McMillan, 2012); Laura Fermi, *Atoms for the World: United States Participation in the Conference on the Peaceful Uses of Atomic Energy* (Chicago: University of Chicago Press, 1957).

21. On the face of it, the IAEA appears to be a curious exception: the agency is tasked with both preventing the spread of nuclear weapons *and* with promoting nuclear power and other "peaceful" applications (the so-called technical assistance track). This dual mandate is sometimes framed as a conflict of interest but was part and parcel of this international organization's formation. See Elisabeth Roehrlich, "The Cold War, the Developing World, and the Creation of the International Atomic Energy Agency (IAEA), 1953–1957," *Cold War History* 16, no. 2 (2016): 195–221. On the "utopian" nature of IAEA safety standards, see Sebastien Travadel, Franck Guarnieri, and Aurélien Portelli, "Industrial Safety and Utopia: Insights from the Fukushima Daiichi Accident," *Risk Analysis* (2017).

22. One example is manifest conflicts in attempting to increase safety vs. security at nuclear facilities, where, for example, a larger security perimeter with increased obstacles may deter intruders but will also hamper emergency response operations. Nathan E. Busch and James R. Holmes, "Russia's Nuclear Security Culture," in *Combating Weapons of Mass Destruction: The Future of International Nonproliferation Policy*, ed. Nathan E. Busch and Daniel H. Joyner (Athens: University of Georgia Press, 2009), 325–42.

23. George D. Kerr, Tadashi Hashizume, and Charles W. Edington, "Historical Review," in *U.S.-Japan Joint Reassessment of Atomic Bomb Radiation Dosimetry in Hiroshima and Nagasaki: Final Report*, vol. 1: *DS86 Dosimetry System 1986*, ed. William C. Roesch (Hiroshima: RERF, 1987), 1; Sey Nishimura, "Censorship of the Atomic Bomb Casualty Reports in Occupied Japan: A Complete Ban vs. Temporary Delay," *Journal of the American Medical Association* 274, no. 7 (1995): 520–22.

24. Frank W. Putnam, "The Atomic Bomb Casualty Commission in Retrospect," *Proceedings of the National Academy of Sciences of the United States of America* 95, no. 10 (1998): 5426–31; Nishimura, "Censorship," 520.

25. Nishimura, "Censorship," 520; Hiroko Takahashi, "The Reality of Nuclear War Concealed by U.S. And the A-Bomb Disease Certification Class-Action Lawsuits," in *Lest We Forget:*

Hiroshima Day, ed. Helena Corbin (Just World News blog, 2008), http://justworldnews.org/2008/08/lest-we-forget-hiroshima-day/.

26. Putnam, "Atomic Bomb Casualty Commission."

27. Lindee, *Suffering Made Real*, 99.

28. While the ABCC was not tasked to provide medical care, the practice raised grave ethical concerns among the Japanese.

29. After financial and political calamities, the ABCC became the Radiation Effects Research Foundation (RERF), founded in 1975 and in existence today. Lindee *Suffering Made Real*, 241–45. Note that the definition of "nuclear harm" the ABCC crafted is much narrower than that of Biswas's careful analysis in this volume.

30. In Japan, even movements against nuclear power rarely made this connection. See, for example, Koichi Hasegawa, "A Comparative Study of Social Movements in the Post-Nuclear Energy Era in Japan and the United States," *International Journal of Japanese Sociology* 4, no.1 (1995): 21–36; Kohta Juraku, Tatsujiro Suzuki, and Osamu Sakura, "Social Decision-making Processes in Local Contexts: An STS Case Study on Nuclear Power Plant Siting in Japan," *East Asian Science, Technology and Society: an International Journal* 1, no. 1 (2007): 53–75.

31. Maxime Polleri, "Tracking Radioactive Contamination after Fukushima," *Anthropology Now* 8, no. 2 (2016): 90–103, quotation on 90–91. See also Scott V. Valentine and Benjamin K. Sovacool, "The Socio-Political Economy of Nuclear Power Development in Japan and South Korea," *Energy Policy* 38, no. 12 (2010): 7971–79; Peter Dauvergne, "Nuclear Power Development in Japan: 'Outside Forces' and the Politics of Reciprocal Consent," *Asian Survey* 33, no. 6 (1993), 576–91; Richard J. Samuels, *The Business of the Japanese State: Energy Markets in Comparative and Historical Perspective* (Ithaca, NY: Cornell University Press, 1987); Tatsujiro Suzuki, "Japan's Nuclear Dilemma," *Technology Review* 94 (October 1991): 47–48; Jinzaburo Takagi, "Nuclear Power's Credibility Crunch," *Japan Quarterly* 35 (October–December 1988): 406.

32. Sonja D. Schmid, "Shaping the Soviet Experience of the Atomic Age: Nuclear Topics in Ogonyok, 1945–1965," in *The Nuclear Age in Popular Media: A Transnational History, 1945–1965*, ed. Dick van Lente (New York: Palgrave McMillan, 2012), 19–52.

33. Schmid, "Shaping the Soviet Experience of the Atomic Age."

34. In addition to early medical, agricultural, and industrial applications of radioactive isotopes, the most prominent "peaceful nuclear application" at that time was the 5MW reactor at Obninsk, which was touted as "the world's first nuclear power plant." Sonja D. Schmid, "Celebrating Tomorrow Today: The Peaceful Atom on Display in the Soviet Union," *Social Studies of Science* 36, no. 3 (2006): 331–65.

35. Fermi, *Atoms for the World*.

36. Sonja D. Schmid, *Producing Power: The Pre-Chernobyl History of the Soviet Nuclear Industry* (Cambridge, MA: MIT Press, 2015).

37. Schmid, *Producing Power*.

38. Jasanoff, *States of Knowledge*, 40.

39. These exceptions involved the first graphite-moderated boiling water reactors (RBMK) near Leningrad, the fast breeder reactor in Shevchenko, and the Lithuanian reactors, which Sredmash kept entirely under its control. At the same time, the ministry allowed other prototype reactors, for example at Beloiarsk and Bilibino, to be managed by Minenergo. For details, see Schmid, *Producing Power*.

40. Schmid, *Producing Power*. The problems alluded to here were almost exactly replicated in the relationship between the USSR and its Central and East European allies when setting up nuclear cooperation agreements in the 1950s and 1960s; in the mid-2000s, the Global Nuclear Energy Partnership (GNEP) proposal again reproduced a similar, highly problematic division of labor.

41. Kate Brown, *Plutopia: Nuclear Families, Atomic Cities, and the Great Soviet and American Plutonium Disasters* (Oxford: Oxford University Press, 2013).

42. On Hanford downwinders, see Bryan C. Taylor, et al., eds., *Nuclear Legacies: Communication, Controversy, and the U.S. Nuclear Weapons Complex* (Lanham, MD: Lexington, 2007). The U.S. government would not discuss contamination issues with local communities; it preferred to shut down data collection rather than discuss its findings with "outsiders."

43. Experience with military installations to some extent shaped occupational health regulation for civilian nuclear facilities, but critical public investigations of radiation effects from civilian nuclear operations did not gain traction in the USSR until after Chernobyl. Glenys A. Babcock, "The Role of Public Interest Groups in Democratization. Soviet Environmental Groups and Energy Policy-Making, 1985–1991" (PhD diss., RAND Graduate School, 1997); Douglas R. Weiner, *A Little Corner of Freedom: Russian Nature Protection from Stalin to Gorbachëv* (Berkeley: University of California Press, 1999); Jane I. Dawson, *Eco-Nationalism. Anti-Nuclear Activism and National Identity in Russia, Lithuania, and Ukraine* (Durham, NC: Duke University Press, 1996). To some extent, this may also be connected to the privileged status technical specialists enjoyed during the Soviet period. See, for example, Michael D. Gordin, Karl Hall, and Alexei Kojevnikov, eds., "Intelligentsia Science: The Russian Century, 1860–1960," special issue, *Osiris* 23, no. 1 (2008).

44. Quite to the contrary, even though there was clearly some appreciation that even such arcane scientific instruments as particle accelerators presented risks to their operators (famously documented in the movie *Deviat' dnei odnogo goda* [Nine days of one year]), these operators were still portrayed as heroes, with their sacrifices benefitting the progress of science and technology. In the aftermath of Chernobyl, the chairman of the Soviet state committee on peaceful uses of atomic energy, Andranik Petrosiants, famously blurted out at a press event that "science requires sacrifices/victims" (*nauka trebuet zhertv*). Chernobyl—a severe accident involving a civilian facility—marks the point when a statement like this went from expressing the attitude of the time to something that outraged Soviet people.

45. John Krige, "Atoms for Peace, Scientific Internationalism, and Scientific Intelligence," *Osiris* 21 (2006): 161–81; Viktor P. Tatarnikov, "Atomnaia elektroenergetika (s VVER i drugimi reaktorami," in *Istoriia atomnoi energetiki Sovetskogo Soiuza i Rossii. Istoriia VVER*, vol. 2, ed. Viktor A. Sidorenko (Moscow: IzdAt, 2002), 303–99.

46. The nuclear industry did anticipate certain risks from peaceful applications, although nothing as catastrophic as the scenarios generated by Hollywood and popular conspiracy theories. This adds some nuance to my argument and points to the importance of state-owned versus privately owned nuclear utilities: where the private sector was getting involved, business leaders wanted guarantees that their investments would succeed, and the government, in an effort to get industry onto the bandwagon, provided them with generous incentives, including waste disposal responsibilities (which was understood to be the new industry's Achilles' heel). In the Soviet context, by contrast, the state owned and ran both the military and the civilian

program and allocated responsibilities (such as quality control, operational safety, and monitoring) to different ministries. Differences like these allow us to see more clearly different strategies to organize, manage, and discursively hold apart the two nuclear worlds.

47. A memorial sculpture in the town of Chernobyl features reactor fuel assemblies and Hiroshima origami cranes.

48. As a consequence of Chernobyl, Minenergo was relieved of all responsibilities for nuclear power plants in 1986. That did not change even after the failure of the Ministry of Atomic Power in 1989 and its reintegration into the ministry formerly known as Sredmash. For details, see Schmid, *Producing Power*.

49. Adriana Petryna, *Life Exposed: Biological Citizens after Chernobyl* (Princeton, NJ: Princeton University Press, 2003); Sonja D. Schmid, "Transformation Discourse: Nuclear Risk as a Strategic Tool in Late Soviet Politics of Expertise," *Science, Technology & Human Values* 29, no. 3 (2004): 353–76; Babcock, *Role of Public Interest Groups*.

50. Kuchinskaya, *The Politics of Invisibility*, 96. Kuchinskaya is careful to point out the contingency of these maps: not only do they ignore soil type, which determines the transfer rate into the food chain, but also, while making radiation visible, these maps seek to settle "definitional struggles over the scale, degree, and urgency of risks." Ulrich Beck, *Risk Society: Towards a New Modernity*, trans. Mark Ritter (London: Sage, 1992), 46. As an "inscription device," they necessarily obscure whose numbers they are based on, the purpose for which they are created, and what data were left out or selected for inclusion.

51. Across all three affected post-Soviet states, the number most often cited is seven million Chernobyl victims entitled to state benefits. Petryna uses 3.5 million for Ukraine, which amounts to 5–7 percent of Ukraine's government spending and continues to be subject to debate. Petryna, *Life Exposed*, 5. In Ukraine, the idea that a civilian facility could cause a large area to be condemned indefinitely has recently sparked debate over real estate projects encroaching on the "exclusion zone" around the shut-down plant.

52. Kuchinskaya revealed in her interviews that "even the dramatic increase of radiation-induced thyroid cancer in children, now widely acknowledged, was for several years dismissed by international experts" before it was eventually recognized. Kuchinskaya *Politics of Invisibility*, 115. Mikhail V. Malko, "Chernobyl Accident: The Crisis of the International Radiation Community," in *Research about the Radiological Consequences of the Chernobyl NPS Accident and Social Activities to Assist the Sufferers by the Accident, Kurri-Kr-21*, ed. Tetsuji Imanaka (Kyoto: Kyoto University Research Reactor Institute, 1998), 14. Kuchinskaya talked to one scientist in particular, Tamara Belookaya, who lamented the international resistance to their research on Chernobyl-induced health effects, such as reproductive problems, brain tumors, and cardiovascular system pathologies.

53. Kuchinskaya, *Politics of Invisibility*, 135.

54. Kohta Juraku, "'Made in Japan' Fukushima Nuclear Accident: A Critical Review for Accident Investigation Activities in Japan," conference paper, Inaugural Meeting of the STS Forum on the 2011 Fukushima/East Japan Disaster, University of California Berkeley, 2013; National Diet of Japan Fukushima Nuclear Accident Independent Investigation Commission, *Executive Summary of the Official Report of Fukushima Nuclear Accident Independent Investigation Commission*, 5 July 2012 (Tokyo: National Diet of Japan, 2012); U.S. Nuclear Regulatory Commission, *Recommendations for Enhancing Reactor Safety in the 21st Century: The Near-Term Task*

Force Review of Insights from the Fukushima Dai-Ichi Accident (Washington, DC: U.S. Nuclear Regulatory Commission, 2011); International Atomic Energy Agency, *Mission Report: IAEA International Peer Review Mission on Mid- and Long-Term Roadmap Towards the Decommissioning of TEPCO's Fukushima Daiichi Nuclear Power Stations Units 1–4, Tokyo and Fukushima Prefecture, Japan, 15–22 April 2013* (Vienna: International Atomic Energy Agency, 2013).

55. Yasuhito Abe, "Safecast or the Production of Collective Intelligence on Radiation Risks after 3.11," *Asia-Pacific Journal* 12 (7), no. 5 (2014): 1–11.

56. Stefan Merz, Katsumi Shozugawa, and Georg Steinhauser, "Analysis of Japanese Radionuclide Monitoring Data of Food before and after the Fukushima Nuclear Accident," *Environmental Science and Technology* 49, no. 5 (2015): 2875–85; Peter Bossew, Gerald Kirchner, Marc De Cort, Gerhard de Vries, Aleksey Nishev, and Luca de Felice, "Radioactivity from Fukushima Dai-ichi in Air over Europe, Part 1: Spatio-Temporal Analysis," *Journal of Environmental Radioactivity* 114, no. 12 (2012): 22–34; Gerald Kirchner, Peter Bossew, and Marc De Cort, "Radioactivity from Fukushima Dai-ichi in Air over Europe, Part 2: What Can It Tell Us about the Accident?" *Journal of Environmental Radioactivity* 114, no. 12 (2012): 35–40.

57. At the time of this writing, Japanese utilities are gradually restarting reactors that had been shut down after the Fukushima disaster. Among the many media reports are Ken Silverstein, "Japan Circling Back to Nuclear Power after Fukushima Disaster," *Forbes.org*, September 8, 2017; Osamu Tsukimori and Aaron Sheldrick, "Japan Regulator Grants Safety Approval to TEPCO's First Reactor Restart since Fukushima," *Reuters online*, October 3, 2017.

58. Itty Abraham, "The Ambivalence of Nuclear Histories," *Osiris* 21 (2006): 49–65.

Chapter 15. Nuclear Harms and Global Disarmament

1. Campbell Craig, *Glimmer of a New Leviathan: Total War in the Realism of Neibuhr, Morgenthau and Waltz* (New York: Columbia University Press, 2003).

2. Daniel Deudney, "Nuclear Weapons and the Waning of the Real-State," *Daedalus* 124, no. 2 (Spring 1995): 209–31.

3. Bernard Brodie, *Strategy in the Missile Age* (Princeton, NJ: Princeton University Press, 1965).

4. See Tanya Ogilvie-White, "Is There a Theory of Nuclear Proliferation? An Analysis of the Contemporary Debate," *Nonproliferation Review* (Fall 1996): 43–60; and Scott D. Sagan, "The Causes of Nuclear Weapons Proliferation," *Annual Review of Political Science* 17 (March 2011): 225–46, for reviews of the literature on why states proliferate.

5. Aamir Mufti articulates Eurocentrism "as an epistemological problem"—"the social and cultural force of [the] idea of Europe in intellectual life, as in the phenomenal world of global power relations." Aamir Mufti, "Global Comparativism," in *Edward Said: Continuing the Conversation*, ed. Homi Bhabha and W.J.T. Mitchell (Chicago: University of Chicago Press, 2005), 110–11.

6. Julian Go, *Postcolonial Thought and Social Theory* (New York: Oxford University Press, 2016), 144.

7. Article 6 commits the Nuclear Weapons States recognized by the NPT to work toward the cessation of the nuclear arms race and total nuclear disarmament.

8. To officially count as an NWS in the NPT, a state should have exploded a nuclear device

before the cut-off date of January 1, 1967, thus conferring the status on the United States, Russia, the United Kingdom, France, and China. These, of course, are also now the veto-wielding Permanent Five (P5) of the UN Security Council.

9. Shampa Biswas, "'Nuclear Apartheid': Race as a Postcolonial Resource?," *Alternatives* 26, no. 4 (October–December 2001): 485–522; Shampa Biswas. *Nuclear Desire: Power and the Postcolonial Nuclear Order* (Minneapolis: University of Minnesota Press, 2014.)

10. The now widely circulated *Wall Street Journal* op-ed column by this "gang of four" first appeared in January 2007: George P. Schultz, William J. Perry, Henry A. Kissinger, and Sam Nunn, "A World Free of Nuclear Weapons," *Wall Street Journal*, January 4, 2007. It was followed by a reiteration of its message a year later in another op-ed column: Schultz et al., "Toward a Nuclear-Free World, *Wall Street Journal*, January 15, 2008. The group works closely with the organization Nuclear Threat Initiative. For a heroic narrative of the political evolution of this gang of four, as well as the contributions of theoretical physicist Sidney Drell, who has worked closely with the group, see Philip Taubman, *The Partnership: Five Cold Warriors and Their Quest to Ban the Bomb* (New York: Harper Collins, 2012). A video titled *Nuclear Tipping Point* that is largely based on conversations with this group was reportedly shown to President Barack Obama in April 2010. Of the many emerging treatises elaborating a step-by-step approach to disarmament, for one inspired by the Schultz et al. piece, see David Cortright and Raimo Väyrynen, *Towards Nuclear Zero* (New York: Routledge, 2009), Adelphi Papers 49, no. 410. Another abolitionist project initiated by former government officials is the Global Zero movement led by nuclear security expert Bruce Blair, which also produced a well-circulated *Countdown to Zero* video. See Taubman, *The Partnership*, for an account of some of the tensions between these two campaigns.

11. Colin Gray, *The Second Nuclear Age* (Boulder, CO: Lynne Rienner, 1999); Collin Gray, *Modern Strategy* (New York: Oxford University Press, 1999); Keith B. Payne, *Deterrence in the Second Nuclear Age* (Lexington: University Press of Kentucky, 1996); Paul Bracken, *Fire in the East: The Rise of Asian Nuclear Power and The Second Nuclear Age* (New York: Harper Collins, 1999); and Paul Bracken, *The Second Nuclear Age: Strategy, Danger, and the New Power Politics* (New York: Times Books, 2012). See Fred Iklé, *Annihilation from Within: The Threat to Nations* (New York: Columbia University Press, 2006), for a particularly alarmist narrative of the threat of proliferation for the United States; and William Langewiesche, *The Atomic Bazaar: The Rise of the Nuclear Poor* (New York: Farrar, Straus & Giroux, 2007), for an apocalyptic narrative of the rise of what he calls the "nuclear poor."

12. Hugh Gusterson discusses the "nuclear orientalism" that casts an infantilized "third world" given to impulse, passion, and fanaticism as untrustworthy custodians of nuclear weapons within a Western geopolitical imaginary that positions the West as policing agent of any proliferation transgressions (cast as "crime" and "theft"): Hugh Gusterson, "Nuclear Weapons and the Other in the Western Imagination," *Cultural Anthropology* 14, no. 1 (1999): 111–43. In this imaginary, the perception of Third World irrationality remains deeply and widely held, and Western possession of nuclear weapons remains largely unremarkable, despite all the evidence of safety mishaps, close calls, and aggressive nuclear behavior among existing NWS.

13. George P. Schultz, William J. Perry, Henry A. Kissinger, and Sam Nunn, "Deterrence in the Age of Nuclear Proliferation," *Wall Street Journal*, March 7, 2011.

14. Jonathan Schell's *Fate of the Earth*, first published in 1982, has been credited with helping

launch the Nuclear Freeze movement in the United States in the 1980s. The first section of the book, "A Republic of Insects and Grass," describes in extensive detail the multiple effects of the use of nuclear weapons; the second section, "The Second Death," focuses on the threat of extinction that nuclear weapons use poses. It is only in the final section, "The Choice," that Schell launches his critique of the state and national interests. Schell also recognizes the dilemma posed by nuclear weapons for the state's ability to solve the problem of anarchy by monopolizing the means of violence (215–16) and suggests that the only viable path toward peace in a world in which the knowledge and ability to develop nuclear weapons exists requires global disarmament, both nuclear *and* conventional. In *The Abolition*, first published in 1984, Schell continued to make his full-throated case for nuclear abolition, recognizing again the radical challenges to politics that the invention of nuclear weapons posed, which made a simple nuclear ban within the existing international political structure an unviable proposition (see esp. 27–28). Yet he appeared to budge a little from his earlier position by offering the concept of "weaponless deterrence" that accepted the contemporary state-centric political structure of the world, as well as the need for nuclear defenses and some conventional arms, albeit as interim measures toward the radical political overhaul that he saw as the ultimate goal (see the last part of the section titled "A Deliberate Policy"). In the *Gift of Time* (1998), Schell suggested that the dissolution of the Soviet Union provided a unique opportunity to pursue nuclear disarmament, providing a "threshold" between the abolition of nuclear weapons and their full-scale normalization. Jonathan Schell, *The Fate of the Earth and The Abolition* (Stanford, CA: Stanford University Press, 2000); Jonathan Schell, *The Gift of Time: The Case for Abolishing Nuclear Weapons Now* (New York: Metropolitan Book, 1998).

15. But, along with his strong critique of the state, Schell was also critical of some of the proposals for a "world state" as the solution to the nuclear predicament.

16. Indeed, Schell ends up making a case for why his policy of "weaponless deterrence" will require freezing the current parameters of the status quo, even with its injustices, so that nuclear abolition can proceed to eventually yield a world where the peaceful resolution of political differences is a real possibility (105–112). Placing considerable optimism in the "universal power" unleashed by the splitting of the atom to check the rise to global dominance of any one state (142–150), Schell seems to underestimate how nuclear power itself helps maintain an unequal global order in which a large number of poorer states and communities find themselves much more vulnerable.

17. Anne Harrington de Santana, "Nuclear Weapons as the Currency of Power: Deconstructing the Fetishism of Force," *Nonproliferation Review* 16, no. 3 (November 2009); Biswas, *Nuclear Desire*.

18. Edward W. Said, *Humanism and Democratic Criticism* (New York: Columbia University Press, 2003), 138.

19. Gauri Viswanathan, "Criticism and the Art of Politics," in *Power, Politics, and Culture*, ed. Gauri Viswanathan (New York: First Vintage, 2001), 132.

20. Viswanathan, "Criticism and the Art of Politics," 7.

21. Aamir Mufti, "Auerbach in Istanbul: Edward Said, Secular Criticism, and the Question of Minority Culture," in *Edward Said and the Work of the Critic: Speaking Truth to Power*, ed. Paul A. Bové (Durham, NC: Duke University Press, 2000), 238; and Mufti, "Global Comparativism," 194; italics in original.

22. Edward W. Said, *Culture and Imperialism* (New York: First Vintage, 1994), 194; Said,

Democratic Criticism, 52–53, 76. Timothy Brennan makes the important point that Said devised contrapuntal criticism as an alternative to hybridity, "conjuring images more of independently directed harmonizations and contacts than of mixture and mutual complicity." Timothy Brennan, "Resolution," in *Edward Said: Continuing the Conversation*, ed. Homi Bhabha and W.J.T. Mitchell (Chicago: University of Chicago Press, 2005), 48. While hybridity has found a more hospitable home in critical IR, and much of Said's own analysis shows a clear sympathy with the concept, contrapuntality offers in my view a much clearer approach to understanding global interactions, exchanges, processes, and, most important, power.

23. Said, *Culture and Imperialism*, 318. Said's inspiration for the concept of contrapuntal readings was the work of renowned pianist Glenn Gould: Bill Ashcroft and Pal Ahluwalia, *Edward Said* (New York: Routledge, 2009); and Shehla Burney, *Pedagogy of the Other: Edward Said, Postcolonial Theory, and Strategies for Critique* (New York: Peter Lang, 2012). Discussing the analogical significance of music for the conceptual development of contrapuntality, W.J.T. Mitchell points to Said's contrapuntal readings of Israeli and Palestinian histories that he once compared to a "tragic symphony." W.J.T. Mitchell, "Secular Divination: Edward Said's Humanism" in *Edward Said: Continuing the Conversation*, ed. Homi Bhabha and W.J.T. Mitchell (Chicago: University of Chicago Press, 2005), 104–5.

24. Said, *Culture and Imperialism*, 32.

25. Geeta Chowdhry, "Edward Said and Contrapuntal Reading: Implications for Critical Interventions in International Relations," *Millennium: Journal of International Studies* 36, no. 1 (2007): 105. Said develops the concept of contrapuntality largely as a method for reading literary texts in ways that show the mutual imbrication of metropolitan and colonial conditions. See Sirène Harb's discussion of works that read the attacks in New York City on September, 11, 2001, and the massacres of Sabra and Shatila, as well as of Beirut during the war, contrapuntally, to link together mutually constituted but separate American and Arab tragedies at different times and across disparate geographical locations. But contrapuntal readings are not limited to texts. For a scholarly attempt to read the Israeli-Palestinian conflict (and the Afghanistan and Iraq wars) contrapuntally, see Derek Gregory, *The Colonial Present* (Malden, MA: Blackwell, 2004). Postcolonial IR theorists have used contrapuntal analysis to both expose the limitations of Eurocentric analyses and examine the usually neglected contributions of the third world in the constitution of some of the foundational institutions of modernity and concepts of IR, such as sovereignty, the Westphalian state, system stability, or the very notion of security: Sankaran Krishna. "Race, Amnesia, and the Education of International Relations," in *Alternatives* 26, no. 4 (October–December 2001): 401–24; Tarak Barkawi and Mark Laffey, "The Postcolonial Moment in Security Studies," *Review of International Studies* 32 (2006): 329–52; Siba N. Grovogui, *Beyond Eurocentrism and Anarchy: Memories of International Order and Institutions* (New York: Palgrave Macmillan, 2006).

26. Said, *Culture and Imperialism*, 18.

27. Said, *Culture and Imperialism*, 51.

28. For an account of the ways that international collaborative efforts in nuclear production get scripted into national nuclear stories, see Itty Abraham, "The Ambivalence of Nuclear Histories," *Osiris*, 21, no. 1 (2006), 49–65.

29. Go, *Postcolonial Thought*, 105–6. For a critique of the "inside/outside" problematic of IR, see R.B.J. Walker, *Inside/Outside: International Relations as Political Theory* (New York: Cambridge University Press, 1993). For a critique from a postcolonial perspective, see Naeem In-

ayatullah and David L. Blaney, *International Relations and the Problem of Difference* (New York: Routledge, 2004).

30. Go, *Postcolonial Thought*, 114.

31. Lisa Yoneyama, *Hiroshima Traces: Time, Space, and the Dialectics of Memory* (Berkeley: University of California Press, 1999).

32. Sagan, "Nuclear Weapons Proliferation"; Gabrielle Hecht, "Nuclear Ontologies," *Constellations* 13, no. 3 (2006): 320–31; and Gabrielle Hecht, *Being Nuclear: Africans in the Global Uranium Trade* (Cambridge, MA: MIT Press, 2012).

33. Abraham, *Indian Atomic Bomb*. The emphasis on nuclear energy as a vehicle of modernity and progress was also a key aspect of nuclear relations within Soviet bloc countries, and indeed, both helped sustain the dependence of non-Russian territories and Eastern European satellite states on the Soviet Union and allowed at least some Eastern European states to leverage the Soviet Union to develop their own nuclear expertise: Sonja D. Schmid, "Nuclear Colonization?: Soviet Technopolitics in the Second World," in *Entangled Geographies: Empire and Technopolitics in the Global Cold War*, ed. Gabrielle Hecht (Cambridge, MA: MIT Press, 2011).

34. Vilashini Coopan understands W.E.B. DuBois's formulation of "double consciousness" through the concept of contrapuntality: Vilashini Cooppan, "The Double Politics of Double Consciousness: Nationalism and Globalism in the Souls of Black Folk," *Public Culture* 17, no. 2 (2005): 299–318. Go, in *Postcolonial Thought*, points out that many in the first wave of anticolonial thinkers, such as DuBois, Aime Césaire, Frantz Fanon, and Amilcar Cabral, even as they fought for national independence, envisioned postimperial forms that transcended the opposition between the local or national and the global.

35. Said, *Democratic Criticism*, 142.

36. Ashis Nandy, *The Intimate Enemy: Loss and Recovery of Self under Colonialism* (Delhi: Oxford University Press, 1983), xv–xvi. Go calls this the "subaltern standpoint" approach but, unlike my argument, rejects the notion that such a standpoint yields any epistemic privilege, instead suggesting that such an approach merely enriches existing dominant accounts, providing what he calls "epistemic difference"—a way to recover subjugated knowledges that offer a different perspective: Go, *Postcolonial Thought*, 161–62. Go suggests that while both approaches push toward relationality, Said's contrapuntal approach is distinct from a subaltern standpoint approach in its starting level of analysis (see 188). I am, however, more interested in connecting the two. I do agree with Go that a subaltern or marginal standpoint is not about the identity of the observer or the analyst. Instead, in my analysis, it is a perspective that opens up new ways to view the problem of nuclearization, yielding new concerns that have been underemphasized in studies of nuclear security.

37. Mufti, "Global Comparativism," 244.

38. Edward W. Said, *Representations of the Intellectual* (New York: First Vintage, 1996), 11.

39. See Atomic Heritage Foundation, https://www.atomicheritage.org/about-us.

40. For Marxist conceptualizations of nuclear weapons as objects that become "commodities" through the acquisition of exchange values, see Harrington de Santana, "Nuclear Weapons"; and Biswas, *Nuclear Desire*.

41. See Isao Hashimoto's simple but poignant video on the stream of nuclear explosions since the Trinity tests in 1945, https://www.youtube.com/watch?v=LLCF7vPanrY.

42. Joseph Masco, *The Nuclear Borderlands: The Manhattan Project in Post–Cold War New Mexico* (Princeton, NJ: Princeton University Press, 2006).

43. Kyōko Hayashi, Kyoko Selden, Yumi Selden, and Miya Elise Mizuta, "From Trinity to Trinity," *Review of Japanese Culture and Society* 19 (2007): 149–74.

44. Article 6 reads: "Each of the Parties to the Treaty undertakes to pursue negotiations in good faith on effective measures relating to cessation of the nuclear arms race at an early date and to nuclear disarmament, and on a treaty on general and complete disarmament under strict and effective international control."

45. Dan Zak, "A Ground Zero Forgotten: Marshall Islands, Once a U.S. Nuclear Test Site, Face Oblivion Again," *Washington Post*, November 27, 2015.

46. For an account of a "networked U.S. empire" whose expansive geography incorporated a series of overseas island territories that effectively served as nuclear laboratories, see Ruth Oldenziel, "Islands: The United States as a Networked Empire," in *Entangled Geographies: Empire and Technopolitics in the Global Cold War*, ed. Gabrielle Hecht (Cambridge, MA: MIT Press, 2011).

47. Nina Tannenwald, *The Nuclear Taboo: The United States and the Non-Use of Nuclear Weapons since 1945* (New York: Cambridge University Press, 2007).

48. Rob Nixon, *Slow Violence and the Environmentalism of the Poor* (Cambridge, MA: Harvard University Press, 2011).

49. Valeria Pelet, "Puerto Rico's Invisible Health Crisis," *Atlantic*, September 3, 2016.

50. Nixon, *Slow Violence*, 212.

51. This is the approach taken by the Nobel Peace Prize–winning organization International Physicians for the Prevention of Nuclear War, which has produced three volumes documenting the environmental and health effects at various nuclear sites around the world: *Radioactive Heaven and Earth* documents the effects of nuclear testing, *Plutonium: Deadly Gold of the Nuclear Age* documents the hazards of plutonium production and nuclear waste storage, and *Nuclear Wastelands* documents the effects of uranium mining and milling, plutonium reprocessing, and weapons assembly. Anthony Robbins, Arjun Makhijani, and Katherine Yih, *Radioactive Heaven and Earth* (Report of the International Physicians for the Prevention of Nuclear War International Commission to Investigate the Health and Environmental Effects of Nuclear Weapons Production and the Institute for Energy and Environmental Research) (London: Apex Press, 1991); Howard Hu, Arjun Makhijani, and Katherine Yih, *Plutonium: Deadly Gold of the Nuclear Age* (Report by a Special Commission of International Physicians for the Prevention of Nuclear War and The Institute for Energy and Environmental Research) (Cambridge, MA: International Physicians Press, 1992); Arjun Makhijani, Howard Hu, and Katherine Yih, eds., *Nuclear Wastelands: A Global Guide to Nuclear Weapons Production and Its Health and Environmental Effects* (Report by a Special Commission of International Physicians for the Prevention of Nuclear War and The Institute for Energy and Environmental Research) (Cambridge, MA: MIT Press, 1995).

52. Hecht, "Nuclear Ontologies"; Hecht, *Being Nuclear*.

53. The term "radioactive colonialism" is generally attributed to Ward Churchill and Winona LaDuke, "Native North America: The Political Economy of Radioactive Colonialism," in *The State of Native America: Genocide, Colonization, and Resistance*, ed. M. Annette Jaimes (Boston: South End Press, 1992), 241–66; Ward Churchill, *Struggle for the Land; Indigenous Resistance to*

Genocide, Ecocide, and Expropriation in Contemporary North America (Monroe, ME: Common Courage, 1993). A series of investigative articles by Judy Pasternak in 2006 in the *Los Angeles Times* about illnesses developed by specific members of the Navajo community continued to draw attention to this issue relatively recently. See Judy Pasternak, *Yellow Dirt: An American Story of a Poisoned Land and a People Betrayed* (New York: Free Press, 2010); Doug Brugge and Rob Goble "The History of Uranium Mining and the Navajo People," *American Journal of Public Health* 92, no. 9 (September 2002): 1410–19; and Doug Brugge, Timothy Benally, and Esther Yazzie-Lewis, eds., *The Navajo People and Uranium Mining* (Albuquerque: University of New Mexico Press, 2006), for extensive documentation and discussion of the effects of uranium mining on Navajo Indians.

54. Hecht, *Being Nuclear*.

55. Shiloh R. Krupar, *Hot Spotter's Report: Military Fables of Toxic Waste* (Minneapolis: University of Minnesota Press, 2013).

56. For accounts of local communities in the United States affected by nuclear weapons production and testing, see Masco, *The Nuclear Borderlands*; Janice Harper, "Secrets Revealed, Revelations Concealed: A Secret City Confronts Its Environmental Legacy of Weapons Production," *Anthropological Quarterly* 80 (Winter 2007): 39–64; and A. Costandina Titus, *Bombs in the Backyard* (Reno: University of Nevada Press, 2001). For nuclear waste disposal (particular in the Yucca Mountain region), see Valerie L. Kuletz, *The Tainted Desert: Environmental Ruin in the American West* (New York: Routledge, 1998). For a sharp account of the ways that efforts to convert some of the highly contaminated decommissioned nuclear sites in the western United States into nature preserves obscure the costs of the ongoing hazards of exposure, see Krupar, *Hot Spotter's Report*.

57. Kate Brown, *Plutopia: Nuclear Families, Atomic Cities, and Great Soviet and American Plutonium Disasters* (New York: Oxford University Press, 2015).

58. Krupar, *Hot Spotter's Report*, 131.

59. Sonja Schmid shows in chapter 14 of this volume the role of (scientific) knowledge-production in the creation of a social order that demarcates so sharply between nuclear energy and nuclear weapons programs, despite the common materials, technologies, and processes that both share, and the porosity between the two often revealed in the actual operations of nuclear power.

60. Elizabeth Minor, "Changing the Discourse on Nuclear Weapons: The Humanitarian Initiative," *International Review of the Red Cross* 97, no. 899 (2015): 711–30; Alexander Kmentt, "The Development of the International Initiative on the Humanitarian Impact of Nuclear Weapons and its Effect on the Nuclear Weapons Debate," *International Review of the Red Cross* 97, no. 899 (2015): 681–709; Louis Maresca and Eleanor Mitchell, "The Human Costs and Legal Consequences under International Humanitarian Law," *International Review of the Red Cross* 97, no. 899 (2015): 621–45; Tom Sauer and Joelien Pretorius, "Nuclear Weapons and the Humanitarian Approach," *Global Change, Peace & Security* 26, no. 3 (2014): 233–50; Richard Slade, Robert Tickner, and Phoebe Wynn-Pope, "Protecting Humanity from the Catastrophic Humanitarian Consequences of Nuclear Weapons: Reframing the Debate towards the Humanitarian Impact," *International Review of the Red Cross* 97, no. 899 (2015): 731–52.

61. Chief among them is the International Campaign to Abolish Nuclear Weapons (ICAN), with support from the Red Cross and Red Crescent Movement, Physicians for Social Respon-

sibility and International Physicians for Prevention of Nuclear War, Reaching Critical Will (part of the Women's International League for Peace and Freedom), and the think tank Chatham House. These groups together pushed for an open-ended working group within the United Nations in 2013 to address nuclear disarmament through a humanitarian lens, eventually leading the UN General Assembly to pass a resolution in 2016 to negotiate a "legally binding instrument to prohibit nuclear weapons."

62. See United Nations Conference to Negotiate a Legally Binding Instrument to Prohibit Nuclear Weapons, Leading towards Their Total Elimination, https://www.un.org/disarmament/ptnw/index.html.

63. These include the following reports: ICAN and Reaching Critical, *Unspeakable Suffering: The Humanitarian Impact of Nuclear Weapons*, http://www.icanw.org/wp-content/uploads/2012/08/Unspeakable.pdf; ICAN, *Catastrophic Nuclear Harm*, http://www.icanw.org/wp-content/uploads/2012/08/catastrophicharm2012.pdf); Physicians for Social Responsibility, *Nuclear Famine: Two Billion People at Risk*, http://www.psr.org/assets/pdfs/two-billion-at-risk.pdf; and United Nations Institute for Disarmament Research, *Viewing Nuclear Weapons through a Humanitarian Lens*, http://www.unidir.org/files/publications/pdfs/viewing-nuclear-weapons-through-a-humanitarian-lens-en-601.pdf. For the case that HCI makes about the violation of international law (specifically, the rules of war with respect to distinction, proportionality, precaution, damage to the environment, unnecessary suffering), see J. M. Henckaerts and L. Doswald-Beck, "Customary Humanitarian International Law," in *International Committee of the Red Cross*, vol. 1 (Cambridge: Cambridge University Press, 2009).

64. Matthew Bolton and Elizabeth Minor, "The Discursive Turn Arrives in Turtle Bay: The International Campaign to Abolish Nuclear Weapons' Operationalization of Critical IR Theories," *Global Policy* 7, no. 3 (2016): 385–95; John Borrie, "Humanitarian Reframing of Nuclear Weapons and the Logic of a Ban," *International Affairs* 90, no. 3 (2014): 625–46; Nick Ritchie, "Waiting for Kant: Devaluing and Delegitimizing Nuclear Weapons," *International Affairs* 90, no. 3 (2014): 601–23.

65. Borrie, "Humanitarian Reframing"; Bolton and Minor, "Discursive Turn."

66. Laura Considine, "The Standardization of Catastrophe: Nuclear Disarmament, the Humanitarian Initiative and the Politics of the Unthinkable," *European Journal of International Relations* (2015): 11.

67. Anne I. Harrington, "Power, Violence, and Nuclear Weapons," *Critical Studies on Security* 4, no. 1 (2016): 107.

68. Ashcroft and Ahluwalia, *Edward Said*.

69. Nixon, *Slow Violence*, 2.

70. Anthony Burke, "Nuclear Time: Temporal Metaphors of the Nuclear Present," *Critical Studies on Security* 4, no. 1 (2016): 73–90.

71. Paul Saint-Amour, "Waiting for the Bomb to Drop," *New York Times*, August 3, 2015.

Chapter 16. The Legacy of the Nuclear Taboo in the Twenty-First Century

1. See, for example, Scott Sagan, "Realist Perspectives on Ethical Norms and Weapons of Mass Destruction," in *Ethics and Weapons of Mass Destruction: Religious and Secular Perspectives*, ed. Sohail Hashmi and Steven Lee (Cambridge: Cambridge University Press, 2004), 73–95;

T. V. Paul, *The Tradition of Non-Use of Nuclear Weapons* (Stanford, CA: Stanford University Press, 2009).

2. Office of the Press Secretary, "Joint Statement by President Obama and Prime Minister Singh of India," news release, November 8, 2010, http://www.whitehouse.gov/the-press-office/2010/11/08/joint-statement-president-obama-and-prime-minister-singh-india.

3. Portions of this essay draw on Nina Tannenwald, "The Status and Future of the Nuclear Taboo," in *Handbook of Nuclear Proliferation*, ed. Harsh V. Pant (New York: Routledge, 2012): 62–74; and Nina Tannenwald, "How Strong Is the Nuclear Taboo Today?" *Washington Quarterly* 43, no. 1 (2018): 89–109.

4. Avner Cohen, *The Worse-Kept Secret: Israel's Bargain with the Bomb* (New York: Columbia University Press, 2010); Merav Datan, "Relaxing the Taboo: Israel Debates Nuclear Weapons," *Disarmament Diplomacy*, no. 43 (January–February 2000).

5. Special NSC Meeting, March 31, 1953, *Foreign Relations of the United States, 1952–54, National Security Affairs*, vol. 2, pt. 1 (Washington, DC: U.S. Government Printing Office, 1984), 827. According to Google "ngrams," which tracks mention of a phrase in thousands of books, the use of the term nuclear taboo began to rise around 1965 and has been on a generally upward trajectory since then.

6. Dwight D. Eisenhower, press conference, March 16, 1955, in *Public Papers of the President of the United States* (Washington, DC: U.S. Government Printing Office, 1959), 56.

7. See Nina Tannenwald, *The Nuclear Taboo: The United States and the Non-Use of Nuclear Weapons since 1945* (Cambridge: Cambridge University Press, 2007); Paul, *The Tradition of Non-use*; Bastien Irondelle, "Does the Nuclear Taboo Matter? French Nuclear Strategy and the Prohibitionary Norm of Use" (unpublished manuscript, 2010); Mike M. Mochizuki, "Japan Tests the Nuclear Taboo," *Nonproliferation Review* 14, no. 2 (July 2007): 303–28; Avner Cohen, "Israel and the Nuclear Taboo" (unpublished manuscript, 1999); Rizwana Abbasi, *Pakistan and the New Nuclear Taboo: Regional Deterrence and the International Arms Control Regime* (Oxford: Peter Lang, 2012); Richard Hanania, "Tracing the Development of the Nuclear Taboo: The Eisenhower Administration and Four Cases in Asia," *Journal of Cold War Studies* 19, no. 2 (Spring 2017): 43–83.

8. Barton Bernstein, "The Atomic Bombings Reconsidered," *Foreign Affairs* 74, no. 1 (January 1995): 140.

9. United Nations, *The United Nations and Disarmament 1945–1970* (New York: United Nations, 1970), 28.

10. See Tannenwald, *The Nuclear Taboo*, esp. chap. 7.

11. Robert P. Newman, *Truman and the Hiroshima Cult* (East Lansing: Michigan State University Press, 1995), 191.

12. Memorandum by the Planning Advisor, Bureau of Far Eastern Affairs, to the Assistant Secretary of State for Far Eastern Affairs, November 8, 1950, *Foreign Relations of the United States, 1950*, vol. 8: *Korea* (Washington, DC: U.S. Government Printing Office 1976), 1100, 1098; "Sino-Soviet and Free World Reactions to the Use of Nuclear Weapons in Limited Wars in the Far East," Top Secret, Special National Intelligence Estimate, SNIE 100-7-58, July 22, 1958, US Nuclear History, National Security Archive, 2.

13. *Foreign Relations of the United States, 1950*, 8:1098.

14. Tannenwald, *The Nuclear Taboo*.

15. Chuck Horner, interview by *Frontline*, 1996, http://www.pbs.org/wgbh/pages/frontline/gulf/oral/horner/1.html.

16. Todd S. Sechser and Matthew Fuhrmann, *Nuclear Weapons and Coercive Diplomacy* (Cambridge: Cambridge University Press, 2017).

17. George Bush and Brent Scowcroft, *A World Transformed* (New York: Knopf, 1998), 463.

18. Paul Avey, "Who's Afraid of the Bomb? The Role of Nuclear Non-Use Norms in Confrontations between Nuclear and Non-Nuclear Opponents," *Security Studies* 24, no. 15 (2015): 593–94. See also David Palkki, "Calculated Ambiguity, Nuclear Weapons, and Saddam's Strategic Restraint" (unpublished manuscript, Texas A&M University, 2014); Kevin M. Woods, David D. Palkki and Mark E. Stout, eds., *The Saddam Tapes: The Inner Workings of a Tyrant's Regime, 1978–2001* (Cambridge: Cambridge University Press, 2011); and Avner Golov, "Deterrence in the Gulf War," *Nonproliferation Review* 20, no. 3 (2013): 453–72. The Iraqi leader's decision not to use his chemical weapons appears due in part to fears of nuclear retaliation by the United States or Israel. It may also have been due to reduction of Iraqi chemical weapons production capacity as a result of U.S. bombing at the start of the Gulf War.

19. David Sanger and William J. Broad, "Obama Unlikely to Vow No First Use of Nuclear Weapons," *New York Times*, September 5, 2016; Josh Rogin, "U.S. Allies Unite to Block Obama's Nuclear 'Legacy,'" *Washington Post*, August 4, 2016.

20. Anne Harrington de Santana, "Nuclear Weapons as the Currency of Power: Deconstructing the Fetishism of Force," *Nonproliferation Review* 16, no. 3 (November 2009): 327.

21. "The Presidential Nuclear Initiatives (PNIs) on Tactical Nuclear Weapons at a Glance," Arms Control Association, https://www.armscontrol.org/factsheets/pniglance.

22. William C. Potter, "In Search of the Nuclear Taboo: Past, Present, Future," *Proliferation Papers*, no. 31, Security Studies Center, Institut Français des Relations Internationales, Paris (Winter 2010), http://www.ifri.org.

23. James R. Schlesinger. *Report of the Secretary of Defense Task Force on DoD Nuclear Weapons Management, Phase II: Review of the DoD Nuclear Mission* (December 2008), 59

24. *Nuclear Posture Review 2002* (excerpts), http://imi-online.de/download/Nuclear_Posture_Review.pdf.

25. U.S. Department of Defense, Office of the Secretary of Defense, *Nuclear Posture Review Report*, April 2010, vii, https://www.defense.gov/Portals/1/features/defenseReviews/NPR/2010_Nuclear_Posture_Review_Report.pdf.

26. David E. Sanger and Peter Baker, "Obama Limits When US Would Use Nuclear Arms," *New York Times*, April 5, 2010.

27. Rose Gottemoeller, "Priorities for Arms Control Negotiations Post-New START," February 21, 2013, http://www.state.gov/t/us/205051.htm.

28. Secretary of Defense remarks at EUCOM Change of Command, Stuttgart, Germany, May 3, 2016, http://www.defense.gov/News/Speeches/Speech-View/Article/750946/remarks-at-eucom-change-of-command.

29. Felicia Schwartz, "John Kerry, in Hiroshima, Reaffirms Need to Curb Nuclear Weapons," *Wall Street Journal*, April 10, 2016.

30. Demetri Sevastopulo, "Donald Trump Open to Japan and South Korea Having Nuclear Weapons," *Financial Times*, March 26, 2016.

31. "Transcript: Donald Trump on NATO, Turkey's Coup Attempt and the World," *New York Times*, July 16, 2016.

32. Office of the Secretary of Defense, *Nuclear Posture Review* (February 2018), https:// media. defense.gov/2018/Feb/02/2001872886/-1/-1/1/2018-nuclear-posture-reviewfinal-report.pdf.

33. David Nakamura and Anne Gearan, "In UN Speech, Trump Threatens to 'Totally Destroy' North Korea and Calls Kim Jong Un 'Little Rocket Man,'" *Washington Post*, September 19, 2017.

34. Scott Sagan and Benjamin A. Valentino, "Revisiting Hiroshima in Iran: What Americans Really Think about Using Nuclear Weapons and Killing Noncombatants," *International Security* 42, no. 1 (Summer 2017): 41–79.

35. Scott D. Sagan, Benjamin A. Valentino, and Daryl Press, "Atomic Aversion: Experimental Evidence on Taboos, Traditions and the Non-use of Nuclear Weapons," *American Political Science Review* 107, no. 1 (February 2013): 188–206; Scott D. Sagan and Benjamin A. Valentino, "Would the U.S. Drop the Bomb Again?" *Wall Street Journal*, May 19, 2016.

36. J. E. Barnes, "NATO Accuses Russia of Loose Talk on Nuclear Weapons," *Wall Street Journal*, February 13, 2013; Andrew E. Kramer, "Russia Speaks of Nuclear War as US Opens Missile Defense System," *New York Times*, May 12, 2016.

37. Samuel Charap and Jeremy Shapiro, "U.S.-Russian Relations: The Middle Cannot Hold," *Bulletin of the Atomic Scientists* 72, no. 3 (2016): 150.

38. Alex Culbertson, "European Nuclear War Imminent as Russia Relations Break Down," *Express* (London), March 19, 2016.

39. Robert Scheer, "Former Defense Secretary William Perry on the Nuclear Threat," *Huffington Post*, September 3, 2017.

40. Anya Loukianova Fink, "The Evolving Russian Concept of Strategic Deterrence: Risks and Responses," *Arms Control Today* (July/August 2017); Kristin Ven Bruusgaard, "The Myth of Russia's Lowered Nuclear Threshhold," War on the Rocks blog, September 22, 2017.

41. Tong Zhao, "Strategic Warning and China's Nuclear Posture: What the 2015 White Paper Tells Us about China's Nuclear Policy," *Diplomat*, May 28, 2015.

42. Fiona S. Cunningham and M. Taylor Fravel, "Assuring Assured Retaliation: China's Nuclear Posture and U.S.-China Strategic Stability," *International Security* (2015).

43. Harsh V. Pant, "India's Nuclear Doctrine and Command Structure," *Comparative Strategy* 24, no. 3 (2005): 277–93.

44. Michael Krepon, Travis Wheeler, and Shane Mason, eds., *The Lure and Pitfalls of MIRVS: From the First to the Second Nuclear Age* (Washington, DC: Stimson Center, May 2016).

45. Alicia Sanders-Zakre and Kelsey Davenport, "Is India Shifting Nuclear Doctrine?" *Arms Control Today*, May 2017.

46. "Committed to Nuclear Disarmament but Can't Be Party to UN Treaty, Says India," *Hindustan Times*, July 18, 2017.

47. Timothy Hoyt, "Pakistan's Nuclear Posture: Thinking about the Unthinkable?," in *Strategy in the Second Nuclear Age: Power, Ambition, and the Ultimate Weapon*, ed. Toshi Yoshihara and James R. Holmes (Washington, DC: Georgetown University Press 2012), 181–200.

48. Sanjeev Miglani, "Analysis: Pakistan Builds Low-Yield Nuclear Capability, Concern Grows," *Reuters*, May 15, 2011.

49. Paul Kerr and Marybeth Nikitin, "Pakistan's Nuclear Weapons: Proliferation and Security Issues," Congressional Research Service, August 1, 2016.

50. Mahesh Shankar and T. V. Paul, "Nuclear Doctrines and Stable Strategic Relationships: The Case of South Asia," *International Affairs* 92, no. 2 (January 2016): 1.

51. Rick Gladstone, "Democrats Warn Trump against Preemptive Attack against North Korea," *New York Times*, May 23, 2017.

52. Jen Kirby, "North Korea Announces a Freeze on Nuclear and Missile Tests Starting in April," *Vox*, April 20, 2018.

53. "Iran's Supreme Leader: Using Nuclear Weapons is Un-Islamic," *Deutsche Welle*, April 6, 2006, http://www.dw-world.de/dw/article/0,,2043328,00.html.

54. Iran's Statement at IAEA Emergency Meeting," Mehr News Agency, August 20, 2005, http://fas.org/nuke/guide/iran/nuke/mehr088905.html.

55. Rolf Mowatt-Larssen, "Islam and the Bomb: Religious Justification for and Against Nuclear Weapons," Belfer Center for Science and International Affairs, Harvard University, January 2011.

56. Fareed Zakaria, "What You Know about Iran Is Wrong," *Newsweek*, May 23, 2009.

57. Joint Press Statement from the Permanent Representatives to the United Nations of the United States, United Kingdom, and France Following the Adoption of a Treaty Banning Nuclear Weapons, July 7, 2017, https://usun.state.gov/remarks/7892.

58. "United States Non-Paper: 'Defense Impacts of Potential United Nations General Assembly Nuclear Weapons Ban Treaty,'" AC/333-N(2016)0029(INV), October 17, 2016.

59. Rebecca Davis Gibbons, "The Nuclear Ban Treaty: How Did We Get Here? What Does It Mean for the United States?" War on the Rocks blog, July 14, 2017.

60. For example, see Ken Berry, Patricia Lewis, Benoit Pelopidas, Nikolai Sokov, and Ward Wilson, *Delegitimizing Nuclear Weapons: Examining the Validity of Nuclear Deterrence* (Monterey, CA: Monterey Institute for International Studies, May 2010).

61. Review Conference of the Parties to the Treaty on the Non-Proliferation of Nuclear Weapons, 2010, Final Document, vol. 1: Conclusions and Recommendations for Follow-on Actions, NPT/CONF.2010/50.

62. U.S. Mission to Geneva to SecState, "Hungarian CD Presidency Circulates Unofficial Program of Work," cable, January 29, 2013.

63. Nick Ritchie, "Waiting for Kant: Devaluing and Delegitimizing Nuclear Weapons," *International Affairs* 90, no. 3 (2014): 601–23.

64. "Taking Forward Multilateral Nuclear Disarmament Negotiations," GA Resolution A/RES/71/258, December 23, 2016.

65. Ekaterina Shirobokova, "Why the Netherlands Is Participating in the Negotiations to Ban Nuclear Weapons," Charged Affairs blog, May 1, 2017.

66. Leo Hoffmann-Axthelm, "Germany: In Defense of Nuclear Weapons?" Heinrich Boell Stiftung, August 24, 2016, https://www.boell.de/en/2016/08/24/germany-defense-nuclear-weapons.

67. Alberto Perez Vadillo, *Beyond the Ban: The Humanitarian Initiative of Nuclear Disarma-

ment and Advocacy of No First Use Nuclear Doctrines (London: British-American Security Information Council, May 2016), 3.

68. Nick Ritchie, "Pathways to Nuclear Disarmament: Delegitimizing Nuclear Violence," Working Paper, Open-Ended Working Group, May 11, 2016, 7.

69. Briefing on Nuclear Ban Treaty by U.S. National Security Council Senior Director Christopher Ford, Carnegie Endowment for International Peace, August 22, 2017.

70. Alex Wellerstein, "No One Can Stop President Trump from Using Nuclear Weapons. That's by Design," *Washington Post*, December 1, 2016.

71. Steve Fetter and Jon Wolfsthal, "No First Use and Credible Deterrence," *Journal for Peace and Nuclear Disarmament* 1, no. 1 (April 2018).

72. George Perkovich, *Do unto Others: Toward a Defensible Nuclear Doctrine* (Washington, DC: Carnegie Endowment for International Peace, 2013).

Chapter 17. History and the Unanswered Questions of the Nuclear Age: Reflections on Assumptions, Uncertainty, and Method in Nuclear Studies

1. Francis J. Gavin, "How Dangerous? History and Nuclear Alarmism," in *Dangerous World? Threat Perception and U.S. National Security*, ed. John Mueller and Christopher Preble (Washington, DC: Cato Institute, 2014).

2. "Two Renaissances in Nuclear Security Studies," introduction by Scott D. Sagan, Stanford University, H-Diplo/ISSF Forum on "What We Talk about When We Talk about Nuclear Weapons," June 15, 2014, https://networks.h-net.org/node/28443/discussions/31776/h-diploissf-forum-"what-we-talk-about-when-we-talk-about-nuclear#_ftn14.

3. For a summary of the work in political science, albeit reflecting the author's preferences, see Jacques E. C. Hymans, "No Cause for Panic: Key Lessons from the Political Science Literature on Nuclear Proliferation," *International Journal* 69, no. 1 (2014): 85–93, http://ijx.sagepub.com/content/69/1/85.full.pdf+html.

4. What follows is a small sample of the new research on national nuclear programs, much of it supported by the path-breaking Nuclear Proliferation International History Project, https://www.wilsoncenter.org/program/nuclear-proliferation-international-history-project. On Australia, see Christine M. Leah, *Australia and the Bomb* (New York: Palgrave MacMillan, 2014); on Brazil, see Carlo Patti, "Origins and Evolution of the Brazilian Nuclear Program (1947–2011)," November 15, 2012, https://www.wilsoncenter.org/publication/origins-and-evolution-the-brazilian-nuclear-program-1947-2011; on Israel, see Avner Cohen, *The Worst-Kept Secret: Israel's Bargain with the Bomb* (New York: Columbia University Press, 2013); on Italy, see Leopoldo Nuti, "Italy's Nuclear Choices," *UNISCI Discussion Papers*, no. 25 (January 2011), https://revistas.ucm.es/index.php/UNIS/article/viewFile/UNIS1111130167A/26876; on Japan, see Fintan Hoey Sato, *America and the Cold War: U.S.-Japanese Relations, 1964–72* (New York: Palgrave MacMillan, 2015); on Pakistan, see Feroz Khan, *Eating Grass: The Making of the Pakistani Bomb* (Stanford, CA: Stanford University Press, 2012); on Romania, see Eliza Gheorghe, "Atomic Maverick: Romania's Negotiations for Nuclear Technology, 1964–1970," *Cold War History* 13, no. 2 (2013); on South Korea, see Se Young Jang, "Dealing with Allies' Nuclear Ambitions: U.S. Nuclear Non-proliferation Policy towards South Korea and Taiwan, 1969–1981" (PhD diss., Graduate Institute of International and Development Studies, 2015); on

Sweden, see Thomas Jonter, "The Swedish Plans to Acquire Nuclear Weapons, 1945–1968: An Analysis of the Technical Preparations," *Science & Global Security* 18 (2010): 61–86, http://scienceandglobalsecurity.org/archive/sgs18jonter.pdf; on West Germany, see Andreas Lutsch, "The Persistent Legacy: Germany's Place in the Nuclear Order," NPIHP Working Paper #5, Nuclear Proliferation International History Project (NPIHP), Woodrow Wilson International Center for Scholars, May 19, 2015, http://www.wilsoncenter.org/publication/the-persistent-legacy.

5. On hedging and nuclear reversal, see Ariel E. Levite, "Never Say Never Again: Nuclear Reversal Revisited," *International Security* 27, no. 3 (Winter 2002); for recessed deterrence, see Ashley Tellis, *India's Emerging Nuclear Posture between Recessed Deterrent and Ready Arsenal* (Santa Monica, CA: RAND, 2001), https://www.rand.org/content/dam/rand/pubs/monograph_reports/2008/MR1127part1.pdf; on nuclear threshold states, see Maria Rost Rublee, "The Nuclear Threshold States Challenges and Opportunities Posed by Brazil and Japan," *Nonproliferation Review* 17, no. 1 (March 2010), http://cns.miis.edu/npr/pdfs/npr_17-1_rost_rublee.pdf; on opacity, see Avner Cohen and Marvin Miller, "Bringing Israel's Bomb Out of the Basement," *Foreign Affairs* 89 (2010): 31; on latency, see Scott Sagan, "Nuclear Latency and Nuclear Proliferation," in *Forecasting Nuclear Proliferation in the 21st Century*, ed. William C. Potter and Gaukhar Mukhatzhanova (Stanford, CA: Stanford University Press, 2010), http://cisac.fsi.stanford.edu/sites/default/files/Sagan_Latency_Potter_Volume.pdf.

6. Francis J. Gavin, "Strategies of Inhibition: U.S. Grand Strategy, the Nuclear Revolution, and Nonproliferation," *International Security* 40, no. 1 (Summer 2015): 9–46, http://www.mitpressjournals.org/doi/pdf/10.1162/ISEC_a_00205.

7. For earlier efforts at superpower collusion, see Elisabeth Roehrlich, "The Cold War, the Developing World, and the Creation of the International Atomic Energy Agency (IAEA), 1953–1957," *Cold War History* 16, no. 2 (2016): 195–212.

8. As Steve Walt said, one reason is that there hasn't been that much *new* to say about the subject; the essential features of deterrence theory are well established by now, and the infeasibility of any sort of "nuclear war" seems to be pretty well understood (at least let's hope so). Stephen M. Walt "A Renaissance in Nuclear Security Studies?," *Foreign Policy*, January 21, 2010, http://foreignpolicy.com/2010/01/21/a-renaissance-in-nuclear-security-studies/. This belief in the infeasibility of nuclear war has come into doubt in recent years, in part because of statements and policies of the Donald Trump administration. For a fascinating view into the questions surrounding an order to use nuclear weapons by an American president, see Alex Wellerstein and Avner Cohen, "If a President Wants to Use Nuclear Weapons, whether It's 'Legal' Won't Matter," *Washington Post*, November 22, 2017, https://www.washingtonpost.com/news/posteverything/wp/2017/11/22/if-trump-wants-to-use-nuclear-weapons-whether-its-legal-wont-matter/?noredirect=on&utm_term=.8014bf04fd4b.

9. For my take on the failings of the most widely read and influential work on nuclear proliferation and nonproliferation, the debate between Scott Sagan and Kenneth Waltz, see Francis J. Gavin, "Politics, History and the Ivory Tower-Policy Gap in the Nuclear Proliferation Debate," *Journal of Strategic Studies* (August 2012): 573–600, http://www.tandfonline.com/doi/abs/10.1080/01402390.2012.715736#preview. For my critique of quantitative work on nuclear studies, see Francis J. Gavin, "What We Talk about When We Talk about Nuclear Weapons: A Review Essay," H-Diplo/ISSF Forum on "What We Talk about When We Talk about Nuclear

Weapons," June 15, 2014, http://issforum.org/ISSF/PDF/ISSF-Forum-2.pdf; and Francis J. Gavin, "What We Do, and Why It Matters: A Response to FKS" (Response to ISSF Forum 2), http://issforum.org/ISSF/PDF/ISSF-Forum-2-Response.pdf.

10. For an effort to overcome these challenges and apply historical work to aid policy makers, especially on nuclear issues, see Francis J. Gavin and James B. Steinberg, "Mind the Gap: Why Policymakers and Scholars Ignore Each Other, and What Can Be Done about It?," *Carnegie Reporter* (Spring 2012), http://teaching-national-security-law.insct.org/wp-content/uploads/2012/07/Carnegie-Corporation-of-New-York%C2%A0Mind-the-Gap.pdf.

11. William H. McNeill, *The Pursuit of Power: Technology, Armed Force and Society since A.D. 1000* (Chicago: University of Chicago Press, 1982). See also Charles Tilly, *Coercion, Capital and European States: AD 990–1992* (Cambridge, MA: Wiley-Blackwell, 1992).

12. Paul Fussell, *Thank God for the Atom Bomb and Other Essays* (New York: Summit, 1990).

13. Russell F. Weigley, *The American Way of War: A History of United States Military Strategy and Policy* (Bloomington: Indiana University Press, 1960).

14. Gavin, "Strategies of Inhibition"; see also Marc Trachtenberg, "The Nuclearization of NATO and U.S.-West European Relations," in *History and Strategy*, ed. Marc Trachtenberg (Princeton, NJ: Princeton University Press, 1991), 153–68.

15. John Lewis Gaddis, "The Long Peace: Elements of Stability in the Postwar International System," *International Security* 10, no. 4 (Spring 1986): 99–142.

16. For a sample of works commemorating the hundredth anniversary of the July 1914 crisis, see Francis J. Gavin, "History, Security Studies, and the July Crisis," *Journal of Strategic Studies* 37, no. 2 (2014): 319–31. An excellent and comprehensive review essay is Samuel R. Williamson Jr and Ernest R. May, "An Identity of Opinion: Historians and July 1914," *Journal of Modern History* 79 (June 2007): 335–87.

17. For a good overview of some of this work, see Erik Gatzke and Matthew Kroenig, "Nukes with Numbers: Empirical Research on the Consequences of Nuclear Weapons for International Conflict," *Annual Review of Political Science* 19 (2016): 397–412.

18. Steven E. Miller and Scott D. Sagan, "Nuclear Power without Nuclear Proliferation?" *Daedalus* (Fall 2009), https://www.belfercenter.org/publication/nuclear-power-without-nuclear-proliferation.

19. Scott Sagan, *The Limits of Safety: Organizations, Accidents, and Nuclear Weapons* (Princeton, NJ: Princeton University Press, 1993); Eric Schlosser, *Command and Control: Nuclear Weapons, the Damascus Accident, and the Illusion of Safety* (New York: Penguin, 2013).

20. On the taboo, see the path-breaking work of Nina Tannenwald, *The Nuclear Taboo: The United States and the Non-Use of Nuclear Weapons since 1945* (Cambridge: Cambridge University Press, 2007). For pushback against the power of this norm, see Scott D. Sagan and Benjamin A. Valentino, "Revisiting Hiroshima in Iran: What Americans Really Think about Using Nuclear Weapons and Killing Noncombatants," *International Security* 42, no. 1 (2017): 41–79. For an overview of the declaratory policies of different nuclear weapons states, see Ankit Panda, "'No First Use' and Nuclear Weapons," *Backgrounder—Council on Foreign Relations*, July 17, 2018, https://www.cfr.org/backgrounder/no-first-use-and-nuclear-weapons.

21. See the work of Jacques Hymans, Jeffrey Knopf, Etel Solingen, Maria Rost Rublee, Scott Sagan, Nina Tannenwald, Kenneth Waltz, etc.

22. Gavin, *Nuclear Statecraft*.

23. William Burr, "A Scheme of 'Control': The United States and the Origins of the Nuclear Suppliers' Group, 1974–1976," *International History Review* 36, no. 2 (2014): 252–76.

24. See the articles in Roland Popp and Andreas Wenger, eds., "The Origins of the Nuclear Nonproliferation Regime," special issue, *International History Review* 36 (2014); also the articles in Leopoldo Nuti and Christian Ostermann, eds., "Extended Deterrence in Europe and East Asia during the Cold War—a Reappraisal," special issue, *Journal of Strategic Studies* 39 (2016).

25. Bernard Brodie, "The Development of Nuclear Strategy," *International Security* 2, no. 4 (1978): 65–83; Robert Jervis, *The Illogic of American Nuclear Strategy* (Ithaca, NY: Cornell University Press, 1984); Kenneth Waltz, "Nuclear Myths and Political Realities," *American Political Science Review* 84, no. 3 (1990): 731–45.

26. A. W. Marshall, *Long-Term Competition with the Soviets: A Framework for Strategic Analysis (U)*, report prepared for the United States Air Force Project Rand, R-862-PR, April 1972, https://www.rand.org/pubs/reports/R862.html.

27. Daniel J. Sargent, *A Superpower Transformed: The Remaking of American Foreign Relations in the 1970s* (New York: Oxford University Press, 2014).

28. Robert Jervis, *System Effects Complexity in Political and Social Life* (Princeton, NJ: Princeton University Press, 1999).

29. Bruce Kuklick, *Blind Oracles: Intellectuals and War from Kennan to Kissinger* (Princeton, NJ: Princeton University Press, 2006).

30. Holloway has made this important and eloquent point several times in presentations to graduate students in the Nuclear Proliferation International History Project's "boot camp," https://www.wilsoncenter.org/nuclear-history-boot-camp.

31. David Alan Rosenberg, "The Origins of Overkill: Nuclear Weapons and American Strategy, 1945–1960," *International Security* 7, no. 4 (Spring 1983): 3–71.

32. Francis J. Gavin, "NATO's Radical Response to the Nuclear Revolution," in *Charter of the North Atlantic Treaty Organization: Together with Scholarly Commentaries and Essential Historical Documents*, ed. Ian Shapiro and Adam Tooze (New Haven, CT: Yale University Press, 2018).

33. See especially Justin Vaisse, *Neoconservatism: The Biography of a Movement* (Cambridge, MA: Harvard University Press, 2010).

34. Odd Arne Westad, "The Fall of Détente and the Turning Tides of History," in *The Fall of Détente: Soviet-American Relations during the Carter Years*, ed. Odd Arne Westad (Oslo: Scandinavian University Press, 1997), 15. To see further details of the Soviet reaction, and the theory that Brezhnev may have allowed the SS-20 deployment to placate a Soviet military angry over SALT I and SALT II negotiations, see David Holloway, "The Dynamics of the Euromissile Crisis, 1977–1983" (unpublished manuscript).

35. See especially Leopoldo Nuti, ed., *The Crisis of Détente in Europe: From Helsinki to Gorbachev, 1975–1985* (New York: Routledge, 2009). On documents relating to the Euromissile crisis, see Timothy McDowell, ed., *The Euromissiles Crisis and the End of the Cold War: 1977–1987* (Washington, DC: Wilson Center, 2009), http://www.wilsoncenter.org/publication/the-euromissiles-crisis-reader.

36. For the idea that obscure debates over nuclear strategies and deployments masked deeper differences in geopolitical outlooks, particularly in the United States, see Francis J. Gavin, "Wrestling with Parity: The Nuclear Revolution Revisited," in *The Shock of the Global:*

The 1970s in Perspective, ed. Niall Ferguson, Charles S. Maier, Erez Manela, and Daniel J. Sargent (Cambridge, MA: Harvard University Press, 2010), 189–204.

37. One example was the Obama administration's effort to apply the principles of distinction and proportionality to nuclear targeting. See the thoughtful essay by Jeffrey G. Lewis and Scott D. Sagan, "The Nuclear Necessity Principle: Making U.S. Targeting Policy Conform with Ethics & the Laws of War," *Daedalus* 145, no. 4 (2016): 62–74.

LIST OF CONTRIBUTORS

SHAMPA BISWAS is the Paul Garrett Professor of Political Science and chair of the Division of Social Sciences at Whitman College. A specialist on postcolonial security studies and political theory, she is the author of *Nuclear Desire: Power and the Postcolonial Nuclear Order* (Minneapolis: University of Minnesota Press, 2014).

CAMPBELL CRAIG is professor of international relations in the School of Law and Politics at Cardiff University. He has written extensively on both intellectual history and the Cold War, including *The Atomic Bomb and the Origins of the Cold War* (New Haven, CT: Yale University Press, 2008) with Sergey Radchenko, *America's Cold War: The Politics of Insecurity* (Cambridge, MA: Belknap Press of Harvard University Press, 2009) with Fredrik Loegvall, and *Destroying the Village: Eisenhower and Thermonuclear War* (New York: Columbia University Press, 1998).

KIICHI FUJIWARA is professor of international politics at the University of Tokyo, where he specializes on the topics of international conflict, historical memory, and Japanese foreign policy. He is the author and editor of several volumes in Japanese and English, including *Patterns of Order and Changes in International Relations: Major Wars and Their Aftermath* (Abu Dhabi: Emirates Center for Strategic Studies and Research, 2002).

FRANCIS J. GAVIN is the Giovanni Agnelli Distinguished Professor and director of the Henry A. Kissinger Center for Global Affairs at the Johns Hopkins School of Advanced International Studies. His writings include *Nuclear Statecraft: History and Strategy in America's Atomic Age* (Ithaca, NY: Cornell University Press, 2012) and *Gold, Dollars, and Power: The Politics of International Monetary Relations, 1958–1971* (Chapel Hill: University of North Carolina Press, 2004).

AVERY GOLDSTEIN is the David M. Knott Professor of Global Politics and International Relations at the University of Pennsylvania. He has published numerous articles and several books, including *Rising to the Challenge: China's Grand Strategy and International Security* (Stanford, CA: Stanford

University Press, 2005) and *Deterrence and Security in the 21st Century: China, Britain, France, and the Enduring Legacy of the Nuclear Revolution* (Stanford, CA: Stanford University Press, 2000).

MICHAEL D. GORDIN is Rosengarten Professor of Modern and Contemporary History at Princeton University, where he focuses on the history of science. Among other publications, he has written two monographs on nuclear history: *Five Days in August: How World War II Became a Nuclear War* (Princeton, NJ: Princeton University Press, 2007) and *Red Cloud at Dawn: Truman, Stalin, and the End of the Atomic Monopoly* (New York: Farrar, Straus & Giroux, 2009).

DAVID HOLLOWAY is Raymond A. Spruance Professor in International History Emeritus at Stanford University, where he is affiliated with both the History Department and the Department of Political Science. A leading scholar of the Soviet nuclear weapons complex, he is the author of numerous studies on Soviet foreign relations, including *Stalin and the Bomb: The Soviet Union and Atomic Energy, 1939–1956* (New Haven, CT: Yale University Press, 1994) and *The Soviet Union and the Arms Race* (New Haven, CT: Yale University Press, 1984).

G. JOHN IKENBERRY is the Albert G. Milbank Professor of Politics and International Affairs at Princeton University in both the Department of Politics and the Woodrow Wilson School of Public and International Affairs. He is also a Global Eminence Scholar at Kyung Hee University. He has edited and coedited over a dozen volumes and is the author of seven monographs, including *Liberal Leviathan: The Origins, Crisis, and Transformation of the American World Order* (Princeton, NJ: Princeton University Press, 2011) and *After Victory: Institutions, Strategic Restraint, and the Rebuilding of Order after Major Wars* (Princeton, NJ: Princeton University Press, 2001).

SEAN L. MALLOY is professor of History and Critical Race and Ethnic Studies at the University of California, Merced. A historian of U.S. foreign relations, he concentrates on questions of morality, colonialism, and war. He has published two books in these areas: *Atomic Tragedy: Henry L. Stimson and the Decision to Use the Bomb against Japan* (Ithaca, NY: Cornell University Press, 2008) and *Out of Oakland: Black Panther Party Internationalism during the Cold War* (Ithaca, NY: Cornell University Press, 2017).

WAKANA MUKAI is assistant professor at the Faculty of International Relations at Asia University in Tokyo. She specializes in issues of nuclear disarmament and nonproliferation, and is the author of several articles both in Japanese and in English.

HOLGER NEHRING holds the chair in Contemporary European History at the University of Stirling, where he concentrates on the history of social movements, violence and peace, the Cold War, and environmental history. He has coedited several volumes on these topics and is the author of *Politics of Security: British and West German Protest Movements and the Early Cold War, 1945–1970* (Oxford: Oxford University Press, 2013).

SRINATH RAGHAVAN is Professor of International Relations & History at Ashoka University. He is the author of four books on the international history of modern South Asia: *Fierce Enigmas: A History of the United States in South Asia* (New York: Basic Books, 2018); *India's War: The Second World War and the Making of Modern South Asia, 1939–1945* (New York: Basic Books, 2016); *1971: A Global History of the Creation of Bangladesh* (Cambridge, Mass.: Harvard University Press, 2013); and *War and Peace in Modern India: A Strategic History of the Nehru Years* (London: Palgrave Macmillan, 2010).

TAKUYA SASAKI is professor in the Department of Politics at the College of Law and Politics at Rikkyo University. He is the author and editor of several books in Japanese, including *Reisen* [The Cold War] (Tokyo: Yūhikaku, 2011), as well as articles on U.S. diplomatic history, especially with respect to Japanese foreign relations.

SONJA D. SCHMID is associate professor in the Department of Science, Technology, and Society at Virginia Tech. A specialist in the history and sociology of nuclear power, nuclear accidents, and Soviet studies, she is the author of *Producing Power: The Pre-Chernobyl History of the Soviet Nuclear Industry* (Cambridge, MA: MIT Press, 2015).

MATIAS SPEKTOR is associate professor and associate dean of Fundação Getulio Vargas's School of International Relations. He is the author or editor of four books and numerous academic articles on foreign policy, international history, and international security in Latin America. He is currently working on a monograph on the prevalence of nuclear latency in rent-seeking societies.

NINA TANNENWALD a senior lecturer in the Political Science Department at Brown University. She has worked on issues of nuclear institutions, norms, and nonproliferation both in academia and at the U.S. State Department. She is the author of *The Nuclear Taboo: The United States and the Nonuse of Nuclear Weapons since 1945* (Cambridge: Cambridge University Press, 2007).

SHINSUKE TOMOTSUGU is associate professor at the Center for Peace at Hiroshima University. He has published several articles in Japanese and English ranging widely across nuclear policy in Japan, terrorism and counterterrorism, nonproliferation, and the history of international development.

ALEX WELLERSTEIN is assistant professor of science and technology studies at the Stevens Institute of Technology. He specializes in the history of nuclear weapons, and his first monograph, on the history of U.S. nuclear secrecy, is forthcoming from the University of Chicago Press.

INDEX

2020 Commission Report on the North Korean Nuclear Attacks against the United States, The (Lewis), 16
20 Letters to a Friend (Alliluyeva), 72–73

Abe Shinzō, 215–16
ABM systems, 82–84, 87
Abraham, Itty, 341n3
activism: African American, 57–58; Bandung Conference and, 113; disarmament and, 272; discourses and, 207, 213; Germany and, 11, 180, 182–200; idealism and, 16; nuclear taboo and, 281, 290–91; peace and, 2, 9, 180, 187–200, 207, 213, 281; race and, 57, 68–69; South America and, 171
Afghanistan, 98, 127, 269, 281
Africa, 9, 62, 67–70, 96, 110, 131, 167, 178, 240, 270, 290
African Americans, 61–62, 297, 326n5; Black Panthers and, 56–57, 67–69; communism and, 58; Du Bois and, 58, 69–70; Jim Crow era and, 70; Malcolm X and, 68; Moynihan Report and, 62; Newton and, 56–57, 67, 69; police brutality and, 56; Robeson and, 58; Seale and, 56
After Hiroshima: The United States, Race, and Nuclear Weapons in Asia, 1945–65 (Jones), 63, 66
Age of Hiroshima, 1–3, 10, 12, 14–16, 178
Aikichi Kuboyama, 110, 112
Akira Kurosaki, 116
Alfonsin, Raul, 175–76
Algeria, 56, 186
Ali Khamenei, Ayatollah, 289

Allied Occupation of Japan, 65, 90, 146, 207, 209
Alliluyeva, Svetlana, 72–73
Allison, John M., 119–20
Alperovitz, Gar, 58–59
Alt, Franz, 188
Ambrose, Stephen, 59
American Civil War, 62
American Occupation in Japan, 5
American Revolution, 62
Anders, Günther, 179, 185, 187–90, 200, 351n1, 355n42
Anderson, Robert, 137
Anti-Ballistic Missile (ABM) Treaty, 8, 72, 279–81, 284, 299, 304
antinuclear movements: Atomic Energy Basic Law and, 152; discourses and, 207, 210–11, 217, 244, 246, 363n13; Eighth World Conference against Atomic and Hydrogen Bombs and, 150; Fifth World Conference against Atomic and Hydrogen Bombs and, 149; First World Conference against Atomic and Hydrogen Bombs and, 147; Germany and, 11, 182, 185, 189, 191; golden age of, 147–48; ICAN and, 5, 384n61; Japan and, 10, 92, 100, 110, 112, 116, 144–54, 161–62, 182, 191, 210, 277, 279, 342n1, 343n2; Liberal Democratic Party (LDP) and, 148; newspapers and, 146; nuclear taboo and, 277, 279, 281, 290, 293; nuclear weapons and, 10–11, 16, 68, 92, 100, 110, 112, 116, 144–54, 161–62, 179, 182, 185, 189, 191, 207, 210–11, 217, 244, 246, 277, 279, 281, 290–92; race

399

antinuclear movements (*cont.*) and, 68; Seventh World Conference against Atomic and Hydrogen Bombs and, 150; Signature Campaign and, 146–47; Sixth World Conference against Atomic and Hydrogen Bombs and, 149; Suginami Woman's Council and, 146–47; Third World Conference against Atomic and Hydrogen Bombs and, 148; three nonnuclear principles and, 151–54

Arendt, Hannah, 179

Argentina, 10–11, 164; Alfonsin and, 175–76; Atoms for Peace and, 165, 168–69, 172; Carter and, 173–74; Eighteen-Nation Disarmament Committee and, 171; Falklands War and, 175; Frondizi and, 171; Guido and, 171; historical perspectives and, 303; Illia and, 171; Nuclear Nonproliferation Treaty (NPT) and, 172–73; nuclear order and, 166–69; nuclear taboo and, 281; nuclear-weapons-free zone and, 171; regional competition and, 169–72; security and, 172–77; taming U.S. power and, 172–77; uranium and, 166–77

Arita Kiichi, 119

Armacost, Michael, 102

Armageddon: Cuban Missile Crisis and, 4, 19, 71, 88, 171, 235, 300–302, 308; nuclear weapons and, 4, 8, 71–88, 308; Soviet Union and, 71–88

arms race: Cold War and, 9, 61, 74, 83–87, 134, 140–41, 195, 210–11, 269, 277, 284, 299, 305; disarmament and, 269; discourses and, 210–11; Germany and, 195; historical perspectives and, 299, 305; India and, 134, 140–41; nuclear taboo and, 277, 284; race and, 61; Soviet Union and, 74, 83–84; Stalin and, 74

Arnold, Henry "Hap," 40, 42, 44, 321n57

Asahi shimbun newspaper, 94, 212, 362n6

Asian Nuclear Center, 111, 118–25, 128

Asia Pacific Economic Cooperation (APEC), 97

Asia Radio Isotope Center, 124

ASIATOM, 125, 127

assured destruction, 79–81, 85, 232, 271, 280

assured retaliation, 82, 86

Atlantic Charter, 25

Atomic Bomb Casualty Commission (ABCC), 5, 67–68, 248–49, 270, 375n29

atomic bombs: Bandung Conference and, 110–11, 117–18; Brodie on, 22–24; casualties and, 5, 20–21, 30, 37, 43, 46, 48, 50–52, 67, 236, 249, 270; China and, 222, 224, 242; Cold War and, 2, 7–10, 15–16, 33, 61, 74, 112, 130, 139–40, 185, 191, 193, 196, 198, 270, 279; decisions to use, 37–39, 56–70; demonstration effect of, 280; destruction of, 1–3, 5, 10–11, 22–23, 45–46, 75, 80, 88, 130, 134, 141, 147, 164, 178–81, 184, 191, 198–99, 207, 279; disarmament and, 261, 266–71; discourses and, 12, 208–9, 248–49; Einstein and, 280; Fat Man and, 270; foreign policy and, 22–24; Germany and, 179, 182–87, 193, 195, 198; historical perspectives and, 297; Holocaust and, 188, 191; implosion and, 72; India and, 10, 130, 134–42, 382n33; Interim Committee and, 21, 31–32, 38, 47; international control and, 12, 15, 22, 24, 26–32, 52, 74, 141–42, 302; Japanese politics and, 89, 99, 103; Little Boy, 1–2; Manhattan Project and, 19–20, 22, 26, 28, 32, 37–39, 60, 72, 74, 135, 140, 223; newspaper headlines and, 46–47; nonnuclear policies and, 10, 146–52, 162; nuclear taboo and, 279–80; Oppenheimer and, 47, 280; Pakistan and, 165; as policy makers, 19–33; Potsdam Conference and, 20–21, 33–34, 39, 41–48, 51; psychological impact of, 38, 41, 50, 57, 268; race and, 7, 56–70, 103; reason for using, 19–22; Reserved Areas and, 39; Roosevelt and, 6–7, 19–24, 27–33; South America and, 165, 178; Soviet Union and, 72–74, 87; Trinity tests and, 20–21, 41; Truman and, 3, 6–7, 15, 19–22, 31–55, 59, 61–62, 65, 73, 249

Atomic Diplomacy (Alperovitz), 58
atomic energy: Bandung Conference and, 112–15, 118–27; Bohr and, 29, 31, 74; Bush and, 29, 31, 33, 280; civilians and, 9, 53, 94, 115, 184; Committee on the Atomic Energy Problem and, 122; Committee on the Use of Atomic Energy and, 115; Conant and, 29, 31, 33, 280; Conference of Countries in Asia and the Pacific for the Promotion of Peaceful Uses of Atomic Energy and, 126–27; Council on Scientific and Industrial Research (CSIR) and, 135–36; discourses and, 246, 250; economic issues and, 15; Eisenhower and, 118; Germany and, 194; historical perspectives and, 302; India and, 135–38, 141–42; international control of, 26, 52, 74, 94; Japan Atomic Energy Research Institute (JAERI) and, 124; Japanese politics and, 94; nonnuclear policies and, 152; nuclear taboo and, 289; Smith and, 119; South America and, 168, 172; Soviet Union and, 74; Truman and, 54; UN Conference on Peaceful Uses of Atomic Energy and, 250; U.S.-Japan Agreement Concerning Civil Uses of Atomic Energy and, 120
Atomic Energy Act, 54, 125, 136
Atomic Energy Agency, 142, 302
Atomic Energy Basic Act, 120
Atomic Energy Basic Law, 152
Atomic Energy Commission (AEC), 53, 112, 121, 137
Atomic Nucleus Special Commission, 122
Atomic Weapons Opponents, 182
Atoms for Peace, 9; Bandung Conference and, 110–11, 114, 118, 120–27; India and, 141; Inter-American Nuclear Energy Commission and, 169; origins of, 120–27; South America and, 165, 168–69, 172
Auschwitz: Eichmann and, 185; Enzensberger and, 185, 187, 190; symbolism of, 11, 181–91, 194–200
Australia, 93, 97, 101, 125, 127, 303–4

Austria, 255, 290, 307
Avrora system, 83

B-29 bombers, 2, 103, 207
balance of power, 63, 73–74, 87
ballistic missiles: ABM systems and, 82–84, 87; Anti-Ballistic Missile (ABM) Treaty and, 8, 72, 279–81, 284, 299, 304; China and, 221, 224, 230–33, 242, 368n35; Cuba and, 4, 19, 71, 88, 171, 235, 300–302, 308; future conflicts and, 3; Germany and, 189; ICBMs and, 76, 79–84, 229, 233; inability to recall, 3; India and, 130; IRBMs and, 76, 230, 233; Ministry of Medium Machine Building and, 251, 331n42; MIRVs and, 80–83; MRBMs and, 74, 83–84; Nike-X system and, 82; nonnuclear policies and, 155; nuclear taboo and, 279, 281, 284, 287–88; Peacekeeper and, 305; Pershing II and, 189, 194–96, 305; Sentinel and, 83; SLBMs and, 79–80; Soviet Union and, 3, 71–72, 76–77, 82–84; Spartan and, 82; Sprint and, 82; SS-20 and, 100, 189, 310; Strategic Rocket Forces and, 76, 80–81; Trident and, 305; warheads and, 3, 71, 76, 80–86, 157, 169, 210, 229–32, 247, 254, 284–88
Bandung Conference, 9; activism and, 113; as Asian-African Conference, 109; Asian Nuclear Center and, 111, 118–25, 128; atomic bombs and, 110–11, 117–18; atomic energy and, 112–15, 118–27; Atoms for Peace and, 110–11, 114, 118, 120–27; Brookhaven National Laboratory and, 118–23; bureaucrats and, 124–25; China and, 114, 125; civilians and, 110, 115–16, 127–28; Cold War and, 112; Colombo Plan and, 111, 118–19, 125; colonialism and, 109; communism and, 112, 114, 118–19, 127; diplomats and, 111, 120, 128; economic issues and, 109, 115–19, 122, 124; Eisenhower and, 111, 118, 120, 125, 338n22; ethics and, 112; France and, 127; Iran and, 127; Japan and, 109–28;

Bandung Conference (cont.)
    Liberal Democratic Party (LDP) and, 119–20, 123, 125; *Lucky Dragon* incident and, 109–10, 112; military and, 110–13, 116; MOFA and, 115–17, 124–28; Nagasaki and, 109–10, 124; North Korea and, 113; nuclear energy and, 109–28; nuclear weapons and, 109–17; Pakistan and, 121, 125, 127; peace and, 9–10, 109–27; politicians and, 109, 111, 113, 116, 119–28; postwar issues and, 9; race and, 109; radiation and, 110, 112; science and, 110, 112, 115, 120, 122–24, 128; Science and Technology Agency (STA) and, 115, 124, 126, 128; security and, 118; socialism and, 113, 117, 337n6; South Korea and, 114, 127; Soviet Union and, 110, 115, 118, 126, 128; strategy and, 118; superpowers and, 110; technology and, 110, 114–15, 119–23, 127–28; Truman and, 120; United Kingdom and, 110, 118, 120, 127; uranium and, 121; World War II and, 115–17
banzai attackers, 214
Barefoot Gen (comic), 208
Basic National Security Policy, 76, 79
Belarus, 255
Belgian Congo, 68, 270, 273
Beria, Lavrentii, 73
Berlin Crisis, 4, 53, 71, 88, 300–301, 306, 308
Berlin Initiative of Physicians against Atomic Energy and Atomic Weapons, 194
Berlin Wall, 196, 210
Bhabha, Homi, 135–36, 138, 142
Bhatnagar, Shanti Swarup, 132–36, 139
Big Five, The (Savelyev and Detinov), 85–86
Bikini Atoll, 110, 112, 141, 162, 206–7, 211, 273
biological weapons, 137, 278–79, 284–85, 288, 291, 374n17
Biryuzov, S. S., 77
Biswas, Shampa, 13, 57, 67–68, 243, 259–75, 395
Blackett, Patrick, 136
Black Panthers, 56–57, 67–69

Bohr, Niels, 29, 31, 74
Bomber Command, 67
bombers: B-1, 305; B-2, 305; B-29, 2, 103, 207; C3-I, 305; China and, 231–33; discourses and, 207; *Enola Gay*, 2, 103; firebombing and, 38–39, 51–52, 67, 279; future conflicts and, 3; Germany and, 181–82, 184, 187, 198; kamikaze, 214; long-range, 23, 76; Soviet Union and, 76–77, 80; Truman and, 50; United Kingdom and, 67
Bosnia, 269
Bracken, Paul, 365n10
Brandt, Willy, 188
Brazil, 9–11, 164, 290; Atoms for Peace and, 165, 168–69, 172; Carter and, 173–74; Damy de Souza Santos and, 171–72; discourses and, 213; Eighteen-Nation Disarmament Committee and, 171; Figueiredo and, 175; Germany and, 173–74; Goulart and, 171; historical perspectives and, 295, 303; Institute of Research on Nuclear Energy and, 171; nationalization of oil fields and, 166–67; National Nuclear Energy Commission and, 171; Nuclear Nonproliferation Treaty (NPT) and, 172; nuclear order and, 166–69; nuclear taboo and, 290; nuclear-weapons-free zone and, 171; Quadros and, 171; regional competition and, 169–72; Sarney and, 175–76; security and, 172–77; taming U.S. power and, 172–77; Tlatelolco Treaty and, 173; uranium and, 166–77
Brezhnev, Leonid, 72, 81, 84, 87
Brockhaus Encyclopedia, 184
Brodie, Bernard, 22–24, 31, 33, 78–79, 85, 304, 315n13
Brookhaven National Laboratory, 118–23
Brown, Kate, 251–52
Brzezinski, Zbigniew, 96
Buddhists, 208, 214
Bulletin of the Atomic Scientists, 275
bunker-buster nuclear weapons, 284
bureaucrats, 9; Bandung Conference and,

124–25; Germany and, 185; India and, 132–33; nonnuclear policies and, 145, 155, 159–63; psychology and, 161; *Sachzwänge* and, 187; Soviet Union and, 81
Burma, 113, 121, 123, 128, 131
Buruma, Ian, 217–18
Bush, George H. W., 103–4, 283
Bush, George W., 284
Bush, Vannevar, 29, 31, 33, 280
Byrnes, James, 20–21, 31–33, 43

Cabert, Samuel, 50
Cabinet Secretariat, 159–61
Calcutta University, 138
Campaign against Atomic Death, 182–83
Canada, 127, 133, 140, 172
cancer, 255, 267
Canetti, Elias, 198
capitalism, 25, 27, 63, 186, 211, 265, 296
Carter, Ash, 285
Carter, Jimmy, 96–98, 174
cascades, 172, 226, 247
Castro, Fidel, 171
casualties, 50, 236; Atomic Bomb Casualty Commission (ABCC) and, 5, 67–68, 248–49, 270; avoidance of, 20–21, 30; Interim Committee and, 47; land invasion estimates of, 20, 37; newspaper headlines and, 46–47; Oppenheimer and, 47; target lists and, 43, 46, 48, 51–52, 270; victimhood and, 11, 181, 183, 185–87, 202, 204–6, 213, 217–18, 222
Catholics, 188–89
Central Committee, 84, 87, 251
Césaire, Aime, 259
Cesium-137, 255
Ceylon, 113, 119, 121–23, 126–27
Chechnya, 269
chemical weapons, 137, 278–79, 284–85, 288, 291, 374n17
Chen Yi, 224
Chernobyl: cover-up of, 243–44, 252; discourses and, 243–44, 247, 252–57; disruption at, 253–56; radiation and, 13, 243–44, 247, 252–57, 271, 377n48, 377n51; Schmid and, 13; social benefits vs. catastrophe and, 247
Chertok, Boris, 85
Chile, 169
China: atomic bombs and, 222, 224, 242; ballistic missiles and, 221, 224, 230–33, 242, 368n35; Bandung Conference and, 114, 125; Black Panthers and, 56; bombers and, 231–33; Chen Yi and, 224; civilians and, 224, 227; Cold War and, 222–23, 228, 232, 237–38, 241; communism and, 228; counterproliferation and, 223–25; Deng Xiaoping and, 97; deterrence and, 226–33, 239–41; diplomats and, 223, 225; economic issues and, 223, 225, 235; entitlement and, 233–34; Hinkley Point C plant and, 257; ideologies and, 226, 241; international control and, 223; labor camps and, 212; Mao Zedong and, 224–29, 234–38, 241, 370n49; military and, 221–30, 233, 235–41; Nagasaki and, 222; Nanjing, 11, 201–3, 211–13, 215–18; Nie Rongzhen and, 224; Nixon and, 92, 333n6; North Korea and, 231; nuclear age and, 12, 221, 227–28, 237, 241; nuclear energy and, 257; Nuclear Nonproliferation Treaty (NPT) and, 222, 278; nuclear revolution and, 12, 16, 221–22, 241–42; nuclear taboo and, 288; nuclear test of 1964 and, 154–56; nuclear weapons and, 145, 154–59, 162, 221–42; peace and, 229, 233, 236, 238; postwar issues and, 224; proliferation and, 223–26; public opinion and, 227; Qian Xuesen and, 224; restraint and, 234–36; rogues and, 234–36; science and, 222, 224; security and, 222–30, 233–34, 240; Sino-U.S. rapprochement and, 153; socialism and, 226, 235; Soviet Union and, 210, 221–22, 225–41, 365n16, 365n17; Stalin and, 222; strategy and, 12, 221–27, 229, 231, 233–34, 241–42; superpowers and, 225, 229–34, 240–41; Taiwan and, 114, 125, 127, 213, 224, 229, 235, 302, 304; technology and, 12,

China (*cont.*)
221–23, 229, 233, 241–42; Treaty of Peace and Friendship and, 96; United Nations and, 155; World War II and, 222–23, 235; Xi Jinping and, 368n37; Zhenbao conflict and, 237

Chinese Exclusion Act, 59

Chugoku no tabi (Journey to China) (Honda), 212

Churchill, Winston, 28–30, 141

civilians: atomic energy and, 9, 53, 94, 115, 184; Bandung Conference and, 110, 115–16, 127–28; China and, 224, 227; discourses and, 202, 204, 206, 208, 211, 214–15, 244–56; genocide and, 11, 56–57, 70, 180, 182, 186, 189, 198–99, 263; Germany and, 184; Great Purge and, 74; Hiroshima and, 7, 13, 34, 42–46, 74, 184, 202, 206, 208, 211, 215, 244, 253–54; historical perspectives and, 299, 303; India and, 132; Japan and, 3, 9, 13, 34, 40, 42, 45–46, 49, 54, 58, 60, 66, 74, 94, 115–16, 127, 202, 204, 208, 211, 214–15, 227, 239, 277, 303; LeMay on, 40; military targets and, 39–45; noncombatants and, 35, 42, 50–51, 54, 205–6, 212; nuclear energy and, 13, 110, 115–16, 127–28, 167–68, 175–76, 184, 244–56, 277, 297, 299, 303; nuclear taboo and, 277, 280, 286; nuclear weapons and, 7, 9, 36, 52–55, 60, 67, 94, 110, 184, 202, 206, 208, 224, 227, 245–46, 250–54, 280, 286; occupational health regulations and, 376n43; race and, 58, 60, 66–67; Roosevelt and, 52; Russell and, 47–48; South America and, 167–68, 175–76; Soviet Union and, 74; Stimson and, 40, 42–43, 48, 280; strategic bombing and, 20, 23, 40, 60, 67, 89, 279; Truman and, 34–36, 39–55; victimhood and, 11, 181, 183, 185–87, 202, 204–6, 213, 217–18, 222

civil rights, 58, 69

Civil Rights Congress (CRC), 58

Clancy, Tom, 102

Clinton, Bill, 104

Cold War: Armageddon and, 4, 8, 71–88, 308; arms race and, 9, 61, 74, 83–87, 134, 140–41, 195, 210–11, 269, 277, 284, 299, 305; atomic bombs and, 2, 7–10, 15–16, 33, 61, 74, 112, 130, 139–40, 185, 191, 193, 196, 198, 270, 279; Bandung Conference and, 112; China and, 222–23, 228, 232, 237–38, 241; détente and, 4, 16; disarmament and, 262–63, 270–71; discourses and, 11, 202, 206, 209–11, 213, 216; economic issues and, 8, 10, 15, 90–91, 101–4, 130, 139–40, 181, 223; end of, 2, 4, 11, 101–4; geopolitics and, 139–43; Germany and, 11, 179, 181–82, 185–91, 193, 196, 198–200; Hiroshima and, 209–11; historical perspectives and, 295, 300–308; India and, 10, 130, 139–40, 142–43; Japanese politics and, 89–91, 96, 101–4; mutual assured destruction and, 271; nuclear taboo and, 279, 281, 284, 288; orthodox/revisionist debate and, 7; Plaza Accord and, 101; race and, 58; Roosevelt and, 7, 15, 33; South America and, 173; Soviet Union and, 74–75, 77, 85; strategy and, 8, 67, 77, 85, 103–4, 140, 193, 222, 241, 288, 300, 302; as system, 185–87; thermonuclear conflict and, 300–301; Truman and, 15; victimhood and, 185–87; VNIIEF and, 75; World War II era and, 2

Colombo Plan, 111, 118–19, 125, 141

colonialism: Bandung Conference and, 109; disarmament and, 260–61, 263, 266–71, 274; discourses and, 258; India and, 131; nonnuclear policies and, 149; race and, 8–9, 57–58, 62, 65–69; South America and, 166–71

Columbia Pictures, 102

Coming War with Japan, The (Friedman and Lebard), 102

Committee on the Atomic Energy Problem, 122

Committee on the Use of Atomic Energy, 115

communism: African Americans and, 58; Bandung Conference and, 112, 114, 118–

19, 127; China and, 228; discourses and, 209–13, 251; Germany and, 189, 198; Japanese politics and, 90–91, 94; nonnuclear policies and, 148–51, 157, 159; race and, 58, 63, 65; Roosevelt and, 25, 30; South America and, 166, 171; Soviet Union and, 25, 76, 90
Communist Party USA, 58
Comprehensive Test Ban Treaty, 291
Compton, Arthur, 47
Conant, James, 29, 31, 33, 280
concentration camps, 11, 181–91, 194, 196–200, 212
Conference for the Relaxation of International Tension, 113
Conference of Asian Countries, 109, 111–13, 127
Conference of Countries in Asia and the Pacific for the Promotion of Peaceful Uses of Atomic Energy, 126–27
Confino, Alon, 180
conscientious objectors, 184
Considine, Laura, 273
consumerism, 184, 275
contrapuntalism, 13, 57, 261, 264–74
Coopan, Vilashini, 266
Correlates of War project, 236
Council on Scientific and Industrial Research (CSIR), 132–33, 135–36
Craig, Campbell, 7, 19–33, 52, 180, 395
Creager, Angela N. H., 125
Crete, 131
Crichton, Michael, 102
Crimea, 81, 287
Crowe, William, 101
Cuba, 4, 19, 71, 88, 171, 235, 300–302, 306, 308, 370n53
Cultures of War (Dower), 58–60
cyberattacks, 286
Cyprus, 131

Damansk conflict, 237
Damy de Souza Santos, Marcelo, 171–72
Debt of Honor (Clancy), 102

Declaration of the Greater East Asia War, 114–15
Defense Agency White Paper, 92
Defense Council, 81–86
de Gaulle, Charles, 99
Deile, Volkmar, 196
Delegation to Investigate Nuclear Energy for Peaceful Purposes, 122–23
Democratic Socialist Party, 149–50
Democrats, 27
Deng Xiaoping, 97
détente, 4, 16, 188, 310
Detinov, Nikolai, 85–86
Deutsche Friedens-Union (DFU), 190
Diet, 90, 94, 98–99, 101, 104, 116–17, 123, 152–53
diplomats: Bandung Conference and, 111, 120, 128; China and, 223, 225; discourses and, 215, 245–46; historical perspectives and, 15; Japanese politics and, 92–97, 105; nonnuclear policies and, 149, 152, 156–57, 160–61; postwar issues and, 6, 9, 15, 68; race and, 57, 59–60, 63, 65, 68–69; South America and, 164, 168, 171, 173, 175; strategy and, 9
disarmament: activism and, 272; Anti-Ballistic Missile (ABM) Treaty and, 8, 72, 279–81, 284; arms race and, 269; atomic bombs and, 261, 266–71; Atoms for Peace campaign and, 9, 110–11, 114, 118, 120–27, 141, 165, 168–69, 172; Cold War and, 262–63, 270–71; colonialism and, 260–61, 263, 266–71, 274; contrapuntalism and, 13, 57, 261, 264–74; Eighteen-Nation Disarmament Committee and, 171; ethics and, 260–63, 266–67, 271, 275; Eurocentricity and, 261–63, 265; global, 259–65; Hiroshima and, 266–70; historical perspectives and, 298–99; Humanitarian Consequences Initiative (HCI) and, 261, 272–74; international relations and, 259–60; metrocentricity and, 261–62, 267–69; military and, 269; morals and, 272; Nagasaki and, 266–70, 273; newspapers and,

disarmament (*cont.*)
379n10; nuclear age and, 13, 67, 259, 263, 270; nuclear energy and, 271, 275; nuclear harms and, 13, 57, 67, 243, 261, 267–74; Nuclear Nonproliferation Treaty (NPT) and, 262, 268, 271, 277–78; nuclear revolution and, 259–60; nuclear taboo and, 269, 279, 282–83; nuclear weapons and, 259–75; peace and, 271; plutonium and, 267–70; postwar issues and, 266; Russia and, 270; science and, 266; security and, 259–62, 266, 274–75; strategy and, 259, 271; superpowers and, 262, 269, 271; Treaty on the Prohibition of Nuclear Weapons and, 5, 272; United Nations and, 283; United States and, 262–63, 266–70, 273; uranium and, 261, 267, 269–71; World War II and, 266

discourses: activism and, 207, 213; antinuclear movements and, 207, 210–11, 217, 244, 246, 363n13; arms race and, 210–11; atomic bombs and, 12, 208–9, 248–49; atomic energy and, 246, 250; atonement and, 208–9; attachment of meaning and, 201; bombers and, 207; Chernobyl and, 243–44, 247, 252–57; civilians and, 202, 204, 206, 208, 211, 214–15, 244–56; Cold War and, 11, 202, 206, 209–11, 213, 216; colonialism and, 258; communism and, 209–13, 251; co-production framework and, 244–45; diplomats and, 215, 245–46; disruptions and, 253–57; economic issues and, 209, 252, 254; foreign policy and, 206; France and, 205; Fukushima and, 244, 247, 253, 256–57; heroes and, 184, 203–4, 213; Hiroshima and, 201–3, 206–18, 243–45, 248–50, 253–54, 257–58; ideologies and, 211, 250; institutions and, 244–45, 248, 250–51, 253–54; international control and, 247; international relations and, 245; labor camps and, 212; legacies and, 217; legitimate representation and, 203; Liberal Democratic Party (LDP) and, 209, 214, 217; martyrs and, 203–4; military and, 207–11, 216, 244–54; morals and, 212; Nagasaki and, 202, 206–15, 243, 245, 248, 258; Nanjing and, 11, 201–3, 211–13, 215–18; North Korea and, 211, 216; nuclear age and, 210–11, 244, 259, 263, 270; nuclear energy and, 243–46, 249–50, 253, 257; Nuclear Nonproliferation Treaty (NPT) and, 210; nuclear order and, 12–13, 69, 244, 247–48, 252–53, 256–57; nuclear taboo and, 245; nuclear weapons and, 201, 206–12, 216, 243–58; pacifism and, 206–13, 216, 218; peace and, 207–13, 216–17, 243–57; plutonium and, 247, 261; politicians and, 209, 249; postwar issues and, 11–12, 205–6, 214, 218; public opinion and, 207, 216; radiation and, 243–45, 248–49, 255–56; revisionist debate and, 7, 19–22, 58–59, 65, 165, 177, 212, 216; Russia and, 211, 254–55, 257; science and, 249–50; security and, 209–10, 245; socialism and, 209–11; South Korea and, 257; Soviet Union and, 202, 207, 210–11, 218, 243, 249–57; strategy and, 207, 255–56; technology and, 246–51; Truman and, 249; United Kingdom and, 210, 257; uranium and, 247; victimhood and, 11, 202, 204–6, 213, 217–18; war museums and, 204, 212, 216; World War II and, 5, 201–18, 249; Yasukuni and, 11, 201–4, 213–18

Doomsday Clock, 275
Dower, John, 58–60
Drogan, Mara, 110, 337n1
Du Bois, W.E.B., 58, 69–70
Dulles, John Foster, 90–91, 118, 207
Düsseldorf Citizens against Atomic Weapons, 195

Easter Marches, 182, 186
ECAFE, 127
economic issues: APEC and, 97; atomic energy and, 15; Bandung Conference and, 109, 115–19, 122, 124; China and, 223, 225, 235; Cold War and, 8, 10, 15, 90–91,

101–4, 130, 139–40, 181, 223; discourses and, 209, 252, 254; Falklands War and, 175; Germany and, 181, 184; historical perspectives and, 296, 302, 305, 309; India and, 130, 132, 136–40; Japanese politics and, 90–91, 95–105; nonnuclear policies and, 156, 158, 162–63; nuclear energy and, 246–48; nuclear taboo and, 276; Omnibus Trade Bill and, 102; Plaza Accord and, 101; race and, 62, 66, 70; Roosevelt and, 24–27; security and, 8–9, 27, 66, 90–91, 97, 100–101, 104, 118, 139, 156, 163–64, 175, 225, 302; South America and, 164, 172, 175; Soviet Union and, 77
Economic Planning Agency, 115
Egypt, 123, 126
Eichmann, Adolf, 185–86
Eighteen-Nation Disarmament Committee, 171
Eighth World Conference against Atomic and Hydrogen Bombs, 150
Einstein, Albert, 280
Eisenhower, Dwight D.: Atoms for Peace and, 118, 120, 141, 168–69; Bandung Conference and, 111, 118, 120, 125, 338n22; historical perspectives and, 309; India and, 141; Japanese politics and, 91; nuclear taboo and, 54, 277–78; race suicide and, 75; South America and, 168–69; Soviet Union and, 75–76, 79
El Baradei, Mohammed, 289
Electric Power Development, 115
Ellsberg, Daniel, 87
Enola Gay (bomber), 2, 103
Enzensberger, Hans Magnus, 185, 187, 190
Eppler, Erhard, 191
Erhard, Ludwig, 186–87
espionage, 29, 72–73
ethics: Bandung Conference and, 112; disarmament and, 260–63, 266–67, 271, 275; Japanese politics and, 104; legacies and, 12–13; security and, 12–13; Tetsuro and, 112

eugenicists, 62
EURATOM, 125, 127
Eurocentricity, 261–63, 265
European Atomic Energy Commission, 94
European Council for Nuclear Research (CERN), 119
Euroshima, 180, 191, 192f

Falklands War, 175
Fallows, James, 102
FAO, 127
Farley, Phillip, 118
Fate of the Earth, The (Schell), 190
Fat Man, 270
Federal Council of the Churches of Christ in America, 50
feminism, 190
Fetter, Steven, 195
Fields, Barbara J., 64–66, 69
Fifth World Conference against Atomic and Hydrogen Bombs, 149
Figueiredo, João, 175
Final Solution, 186
Finland, 252
Fire, The (Der Brand) (Friedrich), 198
firebombing, 38–39, 51–52, 67, 279, 324n81
First World Conference against Atomic and Hydrogen Bombs, 147
Fischer, Joschka, 190
fission, 1, 3, 72, 135, 142, 247
Foote, Kenneth, 203
Ford, Gerald, 93–94
foreign policy: adventurism and, 87; atomic bombs and, 22–24; discourses and, 206; historical perspectives and, 294, 298, 305, 310; Japanese politics and, 89, 91, 96–101; nonnuclear policies and, 144, 157; race and, 8, 58, 61–64, 69–70; Roosevelt and, 6, 26, 31–32; South America and, 171; Truman and, 7
Foreign Policy Planning Committee, 157
foreign relations, 61–64
Four Freedoms speech, 25, 30
Fox, William T. R., 23

France: Bandung Conference and, 127; de Gaulle and, 99; discourses and, 205; historical perspectives and, 308–10; India and, 137–38, 140; invasion of, 29; Japanese politics and, 95; nuclear energy and, 257; Nuclear Nonproliferation Treaty (NPT) and, 277; nuclear taboo and, 277, 279, 291; nuclear weapons and, 3; postrevolutionary, 205; rapid response forces of, 257; United Nations and, 25; U.S. bases in, 78

Frank, Richard, 60

Free University, 179

French Revolution, 204–5

Friedman, George, 102

Friedrich, Jörg, 198

Fritzsche, Peter, 180

Frondizi, Arturo, 171

Fuchs, Klaus, 72

fuel cycles, 165, 168–70, 173–75

Fujiwara Kiichi, 11, 179–81, 201–18, 222, 395

Fukuda Takeo, 96, 334n14

Fukushima: discourses and, 244, 247, 253, 256–57; disruption at, 256–57; public opinion and, 372n4; radiation and, 13, 244, 247, 253, 256–57, 271, 275, 372n4; social benefits vs. catastrophe and, 247

Fushimi Kōji, 112, 120–21

G-7 countries, 95, 100

Gaddis, John Lewis, 301

Gandhi, Indira, 129

Gandhi, M. K., 131, 133–35

Gavin, Francis J., 13–14, 37, 226–27, 234, 294–311, 395

Geiger counters, 2

Genbaku Dome, 207

General Council of Trade Unions of Japan (Sohyo), 148–50

Geneva conferences, 75, 113, 250, 303

genocide, 11, 56–57, 70, 180, 182, 186, 189, 198–99, 263

George, Alexander, 364n6

Germany: activism and, 11, 180–200; Anders and, 179, 185, 187–90, 200; antinuclear movements and, 11, 182, 185, 189, 191; arms race and, 195; atomic bombs and, 179, 182–87, 193, 195, 198; atomic energy and, 194; Auschwitz and, 11, 181–91, 194–200; ballistic missiles and, 189; Berlin Crisis and, 4, 53, 71, 88, 300–301, 306, 308; Berlin Wall and, 196, 210; Black Panthers and, 56; bombers and, 181–82, 184, 187, 198; Brazil and, 173–74; bureaucrats and, 185; Campaign against Atomic Death and, 182–83; Carter and, 173–74; civilians and, 184; Cold War and, 11, 179, 181–82, 185–91, 193, 196, 198–200; communism and, 189, 198; critique of deterrence and, 188–96; destruction in, 180–82; economic issues and, 181, 184; Euroshima and, 180, 191, 192f; Free University and, 179; historical perspectives and, 301, 309–10; Hitler and, 40–41, 166, 186–87; Holocaust and, 8, 61, 180–86, 190, 198, 281, 355n52; ideologies and, 181, 185, 189, 198, 200; mass violence and, 182–84, 199; military and, 185, 190; morals and, 183, 185, 190; Nagasaki and, 180–85, 188, 190, 194, 196, 198; Nazis and, 60, 63, 87, 184–86, 190, 198–99, 355n52; nuclear age and, 181, 186, 194, 200; nuclear energy and, 184; nuclear weapons and, 179–200; Nuremberg War Crimes Tribunal and, 191; pacifism and, 182, 189; peace and, 180–84, 187–96, 199–200; politicians and, 188–91, 194; postwar issues and, 11, 182; psychology and, 193; race and, 56–57, 60; radiation and, 244; reunification and, 196; science and, 182, 190; security and, 182–84, 190, 193; Social Democratic Party (SPD) and, 182, 186, 188–89, 191, 194–95; socialism and, 183, 186–87, 191, 198–99; Soviet Union and, 189; strategy and, 180, 185, 191, 193, 199; student movements and, 179, 184–85, 187–88, 199; technology and, 179, 182, 185, 187, 190, 195–96, 200; U.S. bases in, 78; victimhood and, 181, 183, 185–87; World War II and, 11, 180–86, 191, 194–95, 198; Yalta Conference and, 26–32

Geyer, Michael, 199–200
Go, Julian, 261, 265–66, 382n36
Godzilla (film), 207
Goldstein, Avery, 12, 221–42, 395–96
Gorbachev, Mikhail, 283, 307
Gordin, Michael D., 1–16, 396
Gotōda Masaharu, 100
Goulart, João, 171
Grant, Madison, 62
Greater East Asian Assembly, 114–15
Greater East Asian Co-Prosperity Sphere, 97, 114–15
Great Purge, 74
Grechko, A. A., 86–87
Greece, 126, 131
Green politics, 189, 196, 275, 357n79
Gridiron Dinner speech, 51
Gromyko, Andrei, 74
Groves, Leslie R., 39–42, 44, 49, 324n76, 325n83, 327n16
Guha, Anton-Andreas, 191
Guido, José Maria, 171
Gulf War, 103, 105, 281–82
Gumlich, Gertrud, 194

Hall, Theodore, 72
Hanford, Washington, 251–52, 270, 273
Hara Tamiki, 207
Harriman, Averell, 73
Harrison, George, 325n83
Hashimoto Ryutaro, 215
Hatoyama Ichiro, 113–14
Hecht, Gabrielle, 247
Heidegger, Martin, 179
Herf, Jeffrey, 181, 352n11
heroes, 184, 203–4, 213
Hill, Archibald V., 133
Hindus, 289
Hinkley Point C plant, 257
Hirano Gitaro, 113
Hiroshima: Age of, 1–3, 10, 12, 14–16, 178; as metonym for nuclear destruction, 1; Brodie on, 22–24; civilians of, 7, 13, 34, 42–46, 74, 184, 202, 206, 208, 211, 215, 244, 253–54; as condition of world, 179, 188–96; deaths from, 267, 323n65; demonstration effect of, 280; destruction of, 1, 3, 5, 8, 10–11, 16, 22, 45–46, 71, 73, 88–89, 109–10, 130, 134, 164, 178–79, 182–84, 189, 191, 200, 207–8, 218, 222, 241–42, 267–68, 281, 285, 297; disarmament and, 266–70; discourses and, 201–3, 206–18, 243–45, 248–50, 253–54, 257–58; *Enola Gay* and, 2, 103; fiftieth anniversary of bombing of, 2; Genbaku Dome and, 207; genocide and, 11, 56, 180, 182, 186; Germany and, 179–200; global, 165, 180, 195, 371n2; historical perspectives and, 297, 307; intended victims of, 34; international order and, 9; Japanese Army headquarters and, 34; Japanese politics and, 89, 92, 95, 103; legacy of, 1–16, 55, 71, 87, 104–5, 165, 177, 180, 188, 266, 280–81; Little Boy and, 1–2; military targeting of, 39–48; newspaper headlines and, 46–47; nuclear revolution and, 3; nuclear taboo and, 277–81, 285, 292; Obama's visit to, 5; orthodox/revisionist debate over, 7, 19–22, 58–59, 65, 177; radiation at, 13, 88, 162, 188, 194–95, 244, 248, 267, 270, 279; reason for bombing, 19–22; as religious punishment, 208–9; as Reserved Area, 39; scholarship on, 19; seventy-fifth anniversary of bombing of, 5; South America and, 164–67, 177–78; Stalin and, 7, 15, 20, 72–75, 166, 222; Truman's level of knowledge of, 34–36, 39–55
"Hiroshima as a World Condition" (Anders), 179
Hiroshima Peace Memorial, 5–6
Hiroshima Peace Museum, 212, 216
Hiroshima Roundtable, 217, 363n22
Hiroshima: The World's Bomb (Rotter), 179
Hiroshima: Why America Dropped the Atomic Bomb (Takaki), 58–59
historical perspectives: arms race and, 299, 305; atomic bombs and, 297; atomic energy and, 302; civilians and, 299, 303; Cold War and, 295, 300–308; diplomats

historical perspectives (*cont.*)
and, 15; disarmament and, 298–99; discourses and, 201–3 (*see also* discourses); economic issues and, 296, 302, 305, 309; Eisenhower and, 309; foreign policy and, 294, 298, 305, 310; France and, 308–10; Germany and, 309–10; Hiroshima and, 297, 307; ideologies and, 301, 309; international relations and, 15, 294, 296, 307–9; Iran and, 295, 298, 307, 311; military and, 296–97, 301–3, 309–10; morals and, 302, 305, 310–11; Nagasaki and, 297, 307; North Korea and, 298; nuclear age and, 13–14, 294–311; nuclear energy and, 299, 303; Nuclear Nonproliferation Treaty (NPT) and, 302–4; nuclear order and, 294; nuclear revolution and, 14, 295, 297, 299, 306–7; nuclear weapons and, 294–311; Obama and, 298; Pakistan and, 295, 298; peace and, 294–301, 305, 310; Reagan and, 298; revisionist, 7, 20–22, 58–59, 65, 165, 177, 212, 216; Russia and, 77–78, 86, 298–310; science and, 295–96, 298, 307, 310; security and, 297–302, 311; South Korea and, 295, 303–4; strategy and, 297–310; superpowers and, 300–301, 305, 308; technology and, 296, 302–3, 305; Truman and, 54–55, 298, 307; unanswered questions and, 293–300, 304–11; United Kingdom and, 308; United States and, 294–311; writing history that never happened and, 396–99; World War II and, 14–15, 103, 297, 309
Hitler, Adolf, 40–41, 166, 186–87
Hollister, John B., 119
Holloway, David, 8, 71–88, 222, 393n30, 396
Holocaust, 8, 61, 180–86, 190, 198, 281, 355n52
Honda Katsuichi, 212
Hong Kong, 131
Hoover, Herbert, 39, 119–20
Hosokawa Morihiro, 105
Huber, Antje, 195
Humanitarian Consequences Initiative (HCI), 261, 272–74, 289–92
human rights, 88, 174, 187, 261
Hungary, 307
Huntington, Samuel P., 62
Hussein, Saddam, 281–82, 387n18
hydrogen bombs, 3, 100, 140–41, 146–51, 162, 183–84, 221
hypercontrol, 325n84

idealism, 16, 25
ideologies: atomic bombs and, 56–70; China and, 226, 241; discourses and, 211, 250; foreign policy and, 61–64; Germany and, 181, 185, 189, 198, 200; historical perspectives and, 301, 309; nonnuclear policies and, 149; postwar issues and, 11, 66; race and, 61–70; religious, 157, 203, 214; U.S. foreign relations and, 61–64
Iguchi Sadao, 120
Ikeda Hayato, 91–92, 99, 116
Ikeda Masanosuke, 113
Ikenberry, G. John, 1–16, 396
Illia, Arturo, 171
ILO, 127
imperialism, 62, 76, 149–50, 186, 229
incendiary raids, 39
India: arms race and, 134, 140–41; atomic bombs and, 10, 130, 134–42, 382n33; atomic energy and, 135–38, 141–42; ballistic missiles and, 130; Board of Scientific and Industrial Research and, 132; British Raj and, 131–32; bureaucrats and, 132–33; civilians and, 132; Cold War and, 10, 130, 139–40, 142–43; colonialism and, 131; Council on Scientific and Industrial Research (CSIR) and, 132–33, 135–36; economic issues and, 130, 132, 136–40; Eisenhower and, 141; France and, 137–38, 140; geopolitical position of, 134, 139–43; as Great Power, 134; Industrial Planning Organization and, 132; international control and, 141–42; international relations and, 130; Iran and, 131; Kargil conflict and, 236; Kashmir and, 236, 288; Manhattan Project and, 135, 140; military and,

130–31, 136–39, 142; morals and, 129, 135; Nagasaki and, 130, 134; National Chemical Laboratory and, 132–33; National Institute of Sciences of India and, 133; National Physical Laboratory and, 132–33; National Planning Commission and, 132; Nehru and, 10, 113, 121, 129–30, 133–42; New Delhi conference and, 109, 111–14, 127; nuclear age and, 10, 129–43; nuclear energy and, 135–39, 257; Nuclear Nonproliferation Treaty (NPT) and, 129, 142; nuclear order and, 140; nuclear revolution and, 10; nuclear taboo and, 288; nuclear weapons and, 129–30, 134–35, 138, 141, 143; Pakistan and, 139, 142, 236; peace and, 129, 133–34, 137, 140–42; plutonium and, 142; politicians and, 132, 135, 139; postwar issues and, 10, 131–35, 140; science and, 133, 135–40; security and, 130, 134, 136, 139, 142; Singh and, 276; Smiling Buddha test and, 129; Soviet Union and, 140; Standstill Agreement and, 141; strategy and, 140; superpowers and, 141; technology and, 132–33, 139–40, 142; United Kingdom and, 131–33, 137, 140; United Nations and, 113, 116, 126–27; uranium and, 137, 140; World War II and, 10, 130–35, 139, 142
Indian Army, 131
Indian Institute of Science, 138
Indian National Congress, 131
Indonesia, 109, 118, 121, 123, 125, 127, 204
Initial Period of War, The (Ministry of Defense), 82
Institute of Research on Nuclear Energy, 171
Inter-American Nuclear Energy Commission, 169
intercontinental ballistic missiles (ICBMs), 76, 79–84, 229, 233
Interim Committee, 21, 31–32, 38, 47
intermediate-range ballistic missiles (IRBMs), 76, 230, 233
International Atomic Energy Agency (IAEA), 94, 125–27, 142, 168, 173, 255, 289, 374n21
International Campaign to Abolish Nuclear Weapons (ICAN), 5, 384n61
international control: atomic bombs and, 12, 15, 22, 24, 26–32, 52, 74, 141–42, 302; China and, 223; discourses and, 247; India and, 141–42; nuclear weapons and, 12, 15, 52, 95, 138, 141–42, 176, 223, 247–48, 252, 259, 272, 278, 302; Roosevelt and, 24, 26, 28–32; Soviet Union and, 74; Truman and, 52
International Cooperation Agency (ICA), 118–19
internationalism, 264
international order, 9, 13, 15, 22, 25, 206, 262
International Physicians for the Prevention of Nuclear War (IPPNW), 194, 383n51, 384n61
international relations: 15–16; disarmament and, 259–60; discourses and, 245; historical perspectives and, 15–16, 294, 296, 307–9; India and, 130; politicians and, 2, 4, 7, 12, 15–16, 57, 63, 65, 67, 130, 245, 259–60, 294, 296, 307–9; race and, 7, 57, 63, 65, 67
Intondi, Vincent J., 58
Investigation Committee on the Use of Atomic Energy, 115
Iran: Bandung Conference and, 127; historical perspectives and, 295, 298, 307, 311; India and, 131; Japanese politics and, 96, 98, 100; nuclear energy and, 4; nuclear taboo and, 286, 289; nuclear weapons and, 165; Rouhani and, 165; South America and, 165, 176–77; Supreme Cultural Revolution Council and, 165
Iraq, 131, 225, 269, 281–82, 387n18
Ireland, 290
Iron Curtain, 3, 8
Irving, David, 187
Ishihara Shintarō, 103
Islam, 289

Israel, 172, 225, 277, 279, 289, 295
Italy, 127, 131, 295, 303–4

Japan: Allied Occupation of, 65, 90, 146, 207, 209; American Occupation in Japan and, 5; antinuclear movements and, 10, 92, 100, 110, 112, 116, 144–54, 161–62, 182, 191, 210, 277, 279, 342n1, 343n2; APEC and, 97; arms exports and, 94; Asian Nuclear Center and, 111, 118–25, 128; Atomic Energy Basic Law and, 152; Bandung Conference and, 109–28; banzai attackers and, 214; Black Panthers and, 56–57; Cabinet Secretariat and, 159–61; China's nuclear test of 1964 and, 154–56; civilians and, 3, 9, 13, 34, 40, 42, 45–46, 49, 54, 58, 60, 66, 74, 94, 115–16, 127, 202, 204, 208, 211, 214–15, 227, 239, 277, 303; defense budget of, 94; defense community and, 156–57; defense policy of, 95; diplomatic community and, 157–59; Dulles and, 90–91, 118, 207; as free rider, 97; Fukushima and, 13, 244, 247, 253, 256–57, 271, 275, 372n4; G-6 summit and, 95; Gulf War and, 103; incendiary raids and, 39; kamikaze bombers and, 214; Kokura, 39, 42, 44; Kyoto, 7, 35, 39–45, 48, 51, 54–55, 61, 319n31; Kyushu, 44, 325n88; labor camps and, 212; losses of, 89; *Lucky Dragon* incident and, 100, 109–10, 112, 144, 146, 148, 151, 207; Nanjing and, 11; National Police Reserve and, 90; National Research Council and, 248; Niigata, 39, 42, 44; nonnuclear policies and, 144–63; Nuclear Supplier's Group (NSG) and, 94–95; Official Development Assistance (ODA) and, 97; Okinawa, 92, 103, 144, 152–53, 210, 216; Pakistan and, 98; psychological strategies and, 38, 41, 50, 57, 268; race and, 56–62, 65–67, 69, 103; rearming of, 90; San Francisco Peace Treaty and, 90, 98, 112, 146; Science and Technology Agency (STA) and, 115, 124, 126, 128; Self-Defense Forces (SDF) and, 90, 95, 100, 104, 336n28; Signature Campaign and, 146–47; Stalin and, 65; Supreme Commander for the Allied Powers and, 248; three nonnuclear principles and, 151–54; Tokugawa Shogunate and, 208, 213; unconditional surrender of, 19, 21, 25, 32, 47, 65; U.S.-Japan Security Pact and, 90–91, 95, 98–100, 103–4, 146, 148–49, 158–60, 190, 210; victimhood and, 11, 181, 183, 185–87, 202, 213, 217–18; Yasukuni and, 11, 201–4, 213–18

Japan as Number 1: Lessons for America (Vogel), 95–96

Japan Atomic Energy Research Institute (JAERI), 124

Japan That Can Say No, The (Morita and Ishihara), 103

Japan Council against Atomic and Hydrogen Bombs, 147–49

Japanese Atomic Energy Commission (JAEC), 112–13, 127

Japanese Constitution, 90, 104

Japanese politics, 2; Abe and, 215–16; atomic bombs and, 89, 99, 103; atomic energy and, 94; Atoms for Peace campaign and, 9, 110–11, 114, 118, 120–27, 141, 165, 168–69, 172; civilians and, 94; Cold War and, 89–91, 96, 101–4; communism and, 90–91, 94; Defense Agency White Paper and, 92; Democratic Socialist Party and, 149–50; Diet and, 90, 94, 98–99, 101, 104, 116–17, 123, 152–53; diplomats and, 92–97, 105; economic issues and, 90–91, 95–105; Eisenhower and, 91; ethics and, 104; expanding diplomacy and, 95–98; First Review Conference and, 94; foreign policy and, 89, 91, 96–101; Fukuda and, 96; Hashimoto and, 215; Hatoyama and, 113–14; Hiroshima and, 89, 92, 95, 103; Hosokawa and, 105; Ikeda Hayato and, 91–92, 99; Ikeda Masanosuke and, 113; Iran and, 96, 98, 100; Japan Socialist Party (JSP) and, 113, 120–21, 123, 211; Kishi and, 91, 96, 125, 128, 345n28; Koizumi and, 215–16;

Liberal Democratic Party (LDP) and, 91–92, 94, 96, 99, 102–5, 119–20, 123, 125, 148, 154, 209, 211, 214, 217; Liberal Party and, 112; Matsumae and, 113; Matsunaga and, 93, 101; Miki and, 94, 125, 128; military and, 90–91, 94, 96–104, 333n5; Miyazawa and, 103–4, 215; morals and, 104; Nagasaki and, 89, 95, 104–5; Nakasone and, 92, 98–102, 113, 119, 215; National Liberal Party and, 112; North Atlantic Treaty and, 91; nuclear energy and, 92–95; Nuclear Nonproliferation Treaty (NPT) and, 92, 94, 129, 142, 144, 158–59, 172–73, 176, 210, 222, 262, 268, 271, 277, 281, 283–85, 290–91, 302–4, 333n5, 342n2; nuclear weapons and, 92–96, 99–101, 104; Ōhira and, 93, 97–98; Okinawa reversion treaty and, 92; Ozawa and, 105; pacifism and, 90, 94, 98–99, 104, 227; peace and, 9, 89–90, 93, 96–100, 104–5; plutonium and, 96; politicians and, 90, 92, 94, 101–3; postwar issues and, 8, 89–90, 97–98; public opinion and, 100; Reform Party and, 112–13; Satō and, 91–94, 146, 152–54, 156, 161, 209–10; security and, 8–9, 89–104; South Korea and, 94, 96, 104; Soviet Union and, 65, 89–90, 96, 98–102, 314n8; strategy and, 89, 92, 95, 98, 103–4; Suzuki and, 93, 98; Tanaka and, 93; technology and, 95–96, 99; Treaties Bureau and, 93; Treaty of Mutual Cooperation and Security and, 94; Treaty of Peace and Friendship and, 96; Truman and, 90; uranium and, 96; U.S. alliance and, 98–101; U.S.-Japan Defense Guidelines and, 94; World War II and, 89, 103, 115–17, 201–18; Yoshida Doctrine and, 89–95, 99, 101, 103–4, 113, 116, 209, 332n1
Japan Reform Party, 112–13
Japan Socialist Party (JSP), 113, 120–21, 123, 211, 337n6
Japan Youth Council, 149
Jasanoff, Sheila, 244
Jens, Walters, 190

Jervis, Robert, 16, 237, 304, 308
Jews, 179, 289
Jim Crow era, 70
Johnson, Lyndon B., 83, 226, 303
Joint Chiefs of Staff, 83, 87, 101, 325n91
Joint Commission, 249
Joliot-Curie, Frederic, 137–38
Jones, Matthew, 57, 63, 66
June 2 Movement, 188
Jungk, Robert, 182, 196

Kahn, Herman, 185–86
kamikaze bombers, 214
Kargil conflict, 236
Karnad, Bharat, 129–30
Kashmir, 236, 288
Katzenstein, Peter J., 152, 154
Kaya Seimi, 112
Kazakhstan, 71, 306
Keldysh, M. V., 86
Kelly, Petra, 191, 194
Kenkel, Wolfgang, 191, 192f
Kennedy, John F., 79
Kenzo Saito, 125
Kerry, John, 285
Khrushchev, Nikita, 75–79, 82–83, 228–29, 301, 344n23, 365n16, 367n23
Kike Wadatsumino koe (survivor accounts), 214
Kimball, Warren, 22, 25
Kim Jong Un, 286, 288–89
Kishi Nobusuke, 91, 96, 125, 128, 333n3, 345n28
Kissinger, Henry, 13, 65, 92–95, 99, 103, 173–74, 262
Koizumi Junichiro, 215–16
Kokura, 39, 42, 44
Korean War, 52–54, 90, 140, 207, 235–37, 280
Kort, Michael, 59
Kōsaka Masataka, 97
Kosovo, 269
Kosygin, Aleksei, 83, 231
Krishnan, K. S., 135
Krupar, Shiloh, 270

Kubo Takuya, 95
Kuboyama Aikichi, 110
Kuchinskaya, Olga, 255, 377n52
Kuklick, Bruce, 308
Ku Klux Klan, 63
Kuomintang rule, 212
Kurosaki Akira, 154
Kusuda Minoru, 161
Kuwait, 103, 269
Kyoto: as ancient capital of Japan, 35; military targets and, 7, 35, 39–45, 48, 51, 54–55, 61, 319n31; Truman and, 7, 35, 39–45, 48, 51, 54–55
Kyoto University, 97
Kyushu, 44, 325n88

labor camps, 11, 181–91, 194, 196–200, 212
Lafontaine, Oskar, 194
Laird, Melvin, 93, 99
La Rocque, Gene, 93
League of Nations, 24–25
Lebard, Meredith, 102
Lee, Christopher J., 340n41
legacies: Asian Nuclear Center and, 125; discourses and, 217; ethics and, 12–13; Hiroshima and, 1–16, 55, 71, 87, 104–5, 165, 177, 180, 188, 266, 280–81; morals and, 5, 7, 14; Nagasaki and, 1–8, 11, 13, 16, 55, 71, 104–5, 180, 188, 266, 273; Nazis and, 199; nuclear taboo and, 276–93; nuclear weapons and, 1–16; radiation and, 188
LeMay, Curtis E., 40, 320n36
Lenin, V. I., 76, 211, 213, 251
Levy, Daniel, 182, 352n12
Lewis, Jeffrey, 16
Liberal Democratic Party (LDP): antinuclear movements and, 148; Asian Nuclear Center and, 119–20, 123; Bandung Conference and, 119–20, 123, 125; discourses and, 209, 214, 217; Fukuda and, 96; Japanese politics and, 91–96, 99, 102–5, 119–20, 123, 125, 148, 154, 209, 211, 214, 217; Kishi and, 96; Nakasone and, 99; nonnuclear policies and, 148, 154; Ozawa and, 105; Policy Research Council and, 102–3; Watanabe and, 102–3
Liberal Party, 112
Lifton, Robert J., 193–94
Lilienthal, David, 53
Li Qianyu, 118
Little Boy, 1–2
Locke, Alaine, 70
London Suppliers Group, 302
Lucky Dragon incident, 100, 109–10, 112, 144, 146, 148, 151, 207

MacArthur, Douglas, 90, 238
machine guns, 328n34
MacLeish, Archibald, 47
Macmillan, Harold, 75
McNamara, Robert, 79–85
McNeill, William, 297
Maeda Maso, 123
Magsaysay, Ramón, 119
Malaya, 118, 125, 131
Malcolm X, 68
Malinovskii, R. Ya., 77, 83, 86
Malloy, Sean L., 7–8, 21, 56–70, 180, 271, 396
Manchuria Heavy Industries Development Corporation, 115
Mandlebaum, Michael, 15
Manhattan Project, 223, 365n9; early schedule of, 42; Groves and, 39–42, 44, 49; India and, 135, 140; Maud Committee Report and, 72; as response to Nazi bomb, 60; Roosevelt and, 19, 22, 26, 28, 32; secret committees and, 38; Stalin and, 20, 74–75; Truman and, 19, 32, 37–39; United Kingdom and, 140
Mansfield, Mike, 96
Mao Zedong, 224–29, 234–38, 241, 370n49
Marshall, Andrew, 305
Marshall, George, 30, 32, 39–40, 44, 49, 318n19, 321n57
Marshall Islands, 100, 268
martyrs, 203–4
Maruyama Masao, 112
Marxism, 113, 211, 213

mass murder, 11, 194, 201–4, 211–13, 215–18, 328n34
"Materials for Peaceful Uses of Atomic Energy" conference, 115
Matsumae Shigeyoshi, 113, 123
Matsunaga Nobuo, 93, 101
Matsushita Electric, 102
Maud Committee Report, 72
MCA, 102
medium-range ballistic missiles (MRBMs), 74, 83–84
Meinhof, Ulrike, 187
Messer, Robert, 31
metrocentricity, 261–62, 267–69
Mexico, 169, 171, 173, 268, 273, 290–91
Miki Takeo, 94, 125–26, 128, 334n11
military: Arnold and, 40, 42, 44; Bandung Conference and, 110–13, 116; China and, 221–30, 233, 235–41; conscientious objectors and, 184; Crowe and, 101; disarmament and, 269; discourses and, 207–11, 216, 244–54; genocide and, 11, 56–57, 70, 180, 182, 186, 189, 198–99, 263; Germany and, 185, 190; Groves and, 39–42, 44, 49, 324n76, 325n83, 327n16; historical perspectives and, 296–97, 301–3, 309–10; India and, 130–31, 136–39, 142; Japanese politics and, 90–91, 94, 96–104, 333n5; La Rocque and, 93; LeMay and, 40; MacArthur and, 90, 238; Marshall and, 30, 32, 39–40, 44, 49, 318n19, 321n57; noncombatants and, 35, 42, 50–51, 54, 205–6, 212; nonnuclear policies and, 149, 155–56, 160; nuclear taboo and, 276–79, 287–93; Pentagon and, 79, 85; race and, 59–61, 65–67, 70; Roosevelt and, 19, 23–24, 33; South America and, 165–66, 169–75; Soviet Union and, 72–88; Stackpole and, 103; Stone and, 44–45; strategists and, 4, 6, 12, 24, 38, 40–41, 67, 76–82, 85–88, 185, 193, 221, 224–25, 229, 233, 279, 288, 297, 301–2, 309–10; superpowers and, 3, 8, 72, 110, 140–41, 171, 173, 225, 229–34, 241, 262, 269, 271, 279, 300–301, 305, 308; Supreme Commander for the Allied Powers and, 248; Truman and, 7, 19, 34–54. *See also* specific war
Military-Industrial Commission, 80
Military Policy Committee, 60
military targets, 34, 67, 80–81; choosing Hiroshima and, 39–45; civilians and, 39–45; Groves and, 39–42, 44; Hiroshima and, 39–48; incendiary raids and, 39; Interim Committee and, 21, 31–32, 38, 47; Kyoto and, 7, 35, 39–45, 48, 51, 54–55, 61, 319n31; morals and, 39–44; Niigata and, 39, 42, 44; psychological impact of, 38, 41, 50, 57, 268; Reserved Areas and, 39; secret committees and, 38; Stimson and, 39–45, 318n19, 319n31, 321n54; Stone and, 44–45; Target Committee and, 38–39, 41, 61; Truman and, 7, 35, 39–45, 48, 51, 54–55
Ministry of Foreign Affairs, 158
Ministry of Medium Machine Building, 251, 331n42
Minuteman III ICBMs, 80, 84
MIT, 195
Mitsubishi Estate, 102
Miyazawa Kiichi, 103–4, 215
Modern War (Sokolovskii), 76
MOFA, 115–17, 124–28
Molotov, 73–74
monazite, 137, 140
Moon Jae-in, 289
morals: disarmament and, 272; discourses and, 212; ethics and, 104 (*see also* ethics); Germany and, 183, 185, 190; historical perspectives and, 302, 305, 310–11; India and, 129, 135; Japanese politics and, 104; legacies and, 5, 7, 14; nonnuclear policies and, 144; nuclear taboo and, 276, 279–80, 282, 285, 289, 291, 293; race and, 66–67; revolution in, 5; Soviet Union and, 78; targeting civilian populations and, 39–44; Truman and, 39–44, 51
Morgenthau, Hans, 259
Morita Akio, 103
Moses, Dirk, 199

Moynihan Report, 62
Mozzhorin, Yu. A., 80
Mufti, Aamir, 265, 378n5
Mukai Wakana, 10, 100, 116, 144–63, 180, 206, 227, 397
multiculturalism, 62–63
multiple independently targeted reentry vehicles (MIRVs), 80–83
Munnik, Len, 196
mushroom cloud, 4, 184, 186, 196, 250, 254, 360n115

Nagai Takashi, 209
Nagasaki: Bandung Conference and, 109–10, 124; Brodie on, 22–24; China and, 12, 222; demonstration effect of, 280; destruction of, 1, 3, 5, 8, 16, 22, 35, 71, 74, 89, 110, 130, 134, 183–84, 268, 297; disarmament and, 266–70, 273; discourses and, 202, 206–15, 243, 245, 248, 258; Fat Man and, 270; fiftieth anniversary of bombing of, 2; Germany and, 180–85, 188, 190, 194, 196, 198; historical perspectives and, 297, 307; India and, 130, 134; Japanese politics and, 89, 95, 104–5; Kyushu and, 44, 325n88; as last nuclear attack to date, 1; legacy of, 1–8, 11, 13, 16, 55, 71, 104–5, 180, 188, 266, 273; nonnuclear policies and, 144, 146, 162; nuclear revolution and, 3; nuclear taboo and, 277–80; orthodox/revisionist debate over, 7, 19–22, 58–59, 65, 177; race and, 56, 58–59, 68; radiation at, 162, 188, 194, 248, 267, 270; reason for bombing, 19–22; reserved list and, 39; Roosevelt and, 19–22, 31–32; scholarship on, 19; seventy-fifth anniversary of bombing of, 5; South America and, 166, 171; Soviet Union and, 71, 74, 88, 100; Truman and, 35–36, 39, 44, 49, 53, 55
Nagasaki child, 194–95
Nakasone Yasuhiro, 92, 98–102, 113, 119, 215, 335n18, 335n19
Nakazawa Kenji, 208
Nanjing, 11, 201–3, 211–13, 215–18

napalm, 187
Nasser, Gamal Abdel, 340n41
National Federation of Regional Women's Organizations, 149
National Institute for Defense Studies, 156–57
National Institute of Sciences of India (NIS), 133
National Liberal Party, 112
National Nuclear Energy Commission, 171
National Police Reserve, 90
National Press Club, 99
National Research Council, 248
national security doctrines, 10, 175
Native Americans, 67–68, 70, 269–70
NATO, 91, 100–101, 126, 189, 191, 282, 287, 291, 300–301, 309–10
"Natsu no hana" (Summer flower) (Hara), 207
Navajo people, 68, 269
Nazis, 184; Final Solution and, 186; Hitler and, 40–41, 166, 186–87; Holocaust and, 186, 190, 355n52; legacy of, 199; propaganda of, 198; race and, 60, 63; South America and, 166; Soviet Union and, 87
Nehring, Holger, 11, 151, 179–200, 281, 397
Nehru, Brijlal, 113
Nehru, Jawaharlal, 10, 113, 121, 129–30, 133–42
Nehru, Rameshwari, 113
neither confirm nor deny (NCND) policy, 93–94, 101
Netherlands, 290
neutron bombs, 188–89
New Delhi conference, 109, 111–14, 127
New Left, 187
newspapers: antinuclear movements and, 146; *Asahi shimbun*, 94, 212, 362n6; disarmament and, 263, 379n10; discourses and, 212, 362n6; Japanese politics and, 94, 99, 101–2; Nanjing massacre and, 212; *New York Times*, 101–2, 191, 275; public opinion and, 38, 44, 46–47, 57, 73, 94, 101–3, 121, 156, 180, 198; South America

and, 164; Soviet Union and, 250; *Wall Street Journal*, 263, 379n10; *Yomiuri shimbun*, 121, 146; *Die Zeit*, 198
New START Treaty, 283
Newton, Huey P., 56–57, 67, 69
New World, 11, 15, 23, 28
New York Times, 101–2, 191, 275
New Zealand, 100–101, 127, 290
Nicaragua, 67, 96
Niebuhr, Reinhold, 259
Nie Rongzhen, 224
Niigata, 39, 42, 44
Nike-X system, 82
Nintendo, 102
Nippon Kaigi, 216
Nishina Yoshio, 112
Nixon, Richard, 72, 84, 87, 92–93, 103, 153, 303, 333n6
Nixon, Rob, 274
Nobel Prize, 5, 93, 135, 383n51
no-first-use policies, 260, 282, 287–88, 293
noncombatants, 35, 42, 50–51, 54, 205–6, 212
nonnuclear policies: Anti-Ballistic Missile (ABM) Treaty and, 72, 279–81, 284; antinuclear movements and, 10–11, 16, 68, 92, 100, 110, 112, 116, 144–54, 161–62, 179, 182, 185, 189, 191, 207, 210–11, 217, 244, 246, 277, 279, 281, 290–92; atomic bombs and, 10, 146–52, 162; Atomic Energy Basic Law and, 152; Atoms for Peace and, 9, 110–11, 114, 118, 120–27, 141, 165, 168–69, 172; ballistic missiles and, 155; bureaucrats and, 145, 155, 159–63; Cabinet Secretariat and, 159–61; colonialism and, 149; communism and, 148–51, 157, 159; critique of deterrence and, 188–96; defense community and, 156–57; diplomats and, 149, 152, 156–61; economic issues and, 156, 158, 162–63; Eighteen-Nation Disarmament Committee and, 171; First World Conference against Atomic and Hydrogen Bombs and, 147; foreign policy and, 144, 157; ideologies and, 149; Japan and, 144–63; Liberal Democratic Party (LDP) and, 148, 154; military and, 149, 155–56, 160; morals and, 144; Nagasaki and, 144, 146, 162; North Korea and, 145; nuclear age and, 152; nuclear energy and, 152–53, 163; Nuclear Nonproliferation Treaty (NPT) and, 158, 277–78; nuclear weapons and, 144–47, 150–63; pacifism and, 144–45; peace and, 10, 146–53, 162–63; politicians and, 145, 159, 162; postwar issues and, 10; Presidential Directive 8 and, 96; public opinion and, 147; security and, 10, 144, 146, 148–49, 153–63; socialism and, 148–51; Soviet Union and, 145, 150, 158, 160; strategy and, 145–46, 151, 153, 155, 159–63; technology and, 161–78; three principles of, 151–54; Treaty on the Prohibition of Nuclear Weapons and, 5, 272; United Nations and, 155; World War II and, 145
North Korea, 368n32, 369n43; Bandung Conference and, 113; Black Panthers and, 56; brinksmanship of, 5; China and, 231; discourses and, 211, 216; historical perspectives and, 298; Kim Jong Un and, 286, 288–89; nonnuclear policies and, 145; nuclear energy and, 4, 16, 104; nuclear taboo and, 284, 286, 288–91; nuclear weapons and, 145; race and, 56
Nossack, Hans Erich, 198
nuclear age: Age of Hiroshima and, 1–3, 10, 12, 14–16, 178; China and, 12, 221, 227–28, 237, 241; disarmament and, 13, 67, 259, 263, 270; discourses and, 210–11, 244; duality of, 16; Germany and, 181, 186, 194, 200; great-power politics of, 7; historical perspectives and, 13–14, 294–311; India and, 10, 129–43; nonnuclear policies and, 152; nuclear taboo and, 285; race and, 64, 67–68; second, 263; South America and, 170–71, 178; Soviet Union and, 71; terms of engagement and, 6–7; Truman and, 6; unanswered questions of, 294–300, 304–11
nuclear club, 10, 223–25, 245, 262

nuclear energy: Asian Nuclear Center and, 111, 118–25, 128; Atoms for Peace and, 9, 110–11, 114, 118, 120–27, 141, 165, 168–69, 172; Bandung Conference and, 109–28; Brookhaven National Laboratory and, 118–23; cascades and, 172, 226, 247; Chernobyl and, 13, 243–44, 247, 252–57, 271, 377n48, 377n51; China and, 257; civilians and, 13, 110, 115–16, 127–28, 167–68, 175–76, 184, 244–56, 277, 297, 299, 303; disarmament and, 271, 275; discourses and, 243–46, 249–50, 253, 257; economic issues and, 246–48; France and, 257; fuel cycle and, 165, 168–70, 173–75; Fukushima and, 13, 244, 247, 253, 256–57, 271, 275, 372n4; Germany and, 184; historical perspectives on, 299, 303; India and, 135–39, 257; Iran and, 4; Japanese politics and, 92–95; Ministry of Medium Machine Building and, 251; nonnuclear policies and, 152–53, 163; North Korea and, 4, 16, 104; Pakistan and, 231; peaceful nuclear explosions (PNEs) and, 172–73, 176; peaceful use of, 4, 9, 15, 109–27, 141–42, 153, 163, 169, 172, 184, 194, 243, 245–46, 250, 253, 257; RBMK reactors and, 375n39; secret sites and, 249–53; South America and, 167–74, 177–78; Soviet Union and, 251, 375n39; Three Mile Island and, 247, 252, 271

nuclear harms, 13, 57, 67, 243, 261, 267–74

Nuclear Nonproliferation Treaty (NPT): Action Plan of, 290; Additional Protocols and, 176; Argentina and, 173; China and, 222, 278; disarmament and, 262, 268, 271; discourses and, 210; France and, 277; historical perspectives and, 302–4; India and, 129, 142; inspections and, 94, 176; International Atomic Energy Agency and, 94; Japanese politics and, 92, 94, 129, 142, 144, 158–59, 172–73, 176, 210, 222, 262, 268, 271, 277, 281, 283–85, 290–91, 302–4, 333n5, 342n2; legal asymmetry of, 291; nonnuclear policies and, 158; nuclear taboo and, 277–78, 281–85, 290–91; policy and, 144, 158–59; ratification of, 94; Russia and, 277; South America and, 172–73, 176; South Korea and, 94; United Kingdom and, 277; United States and, 277

nuclear order: discourses and, 12–13, 69, 244, 247–48, 252–53, 256–57; emergence of, 9; historical perspectives and, 294; India and, 140; nuclear taboo and, 289; South America and, 164–72, 176–78; United States and, 3, 9, 11, 13, 15, 68–69, 140, 165–70, 176–77, 294

nuclear posture review (NPR), 285–86

Nuclear Prohibition Treaty, 278, 289–90

Nuclear Proliferation International History Project, 390n4

nuclear revolution: China and, 12, 16, 221–22, 241–42; cultural fallout of, 15; destruction and, 8; disarmament and, 259–60; historical perspectives and, 14, 295, 297, 299, 306–7; India and, 10; Jervis and, 16; legacies of, 3; redefining power and, 9; Russia and, 16; South America and, 10, 164, 166, 168

Nuclear Suppliers' Group (NSG), 94–95, 167, 173

nuclear taboo, 13; ABM Treaty and, 279–81, 284; activism and, 281, 290–91; antinuclear movements and, 277, 279, 281, 290, 293; Argentina and, 281; arms race and, 277, 284; atomic bombs and, 279–80; atomic energy and, 289; ballistic missiles and, 279, 281, 284, 287–88; as belief about behavior, 277; biological weapons and, 278–79, 284–85, 288, 291; Brazil and, 290; challenge to, 276–77; chemical weapons and, 278–79, 284–85, 288, 291; China and, 288; civilians and, 277, 280, 286; Cold War and, 279, 281, 284, 288; Comprehensive Test Ban Treaty and, 291; contemporary status of, 284–86; disarmament and, 269, 279, 282–83; discourses and, 245; economic issues and, 276; Eisenhower and, 54, 277–78; France and, 277, 279,

291; future issues and, 292–93; Hiroshima and, 277–81, 285, 292; Humanitarian Consequences Initiative (HCI) and, 261, 272–74, 289–92; India and, 288; Iran and, 286, 289; legacy of, 276–93; military and, 276–79, 287–93; morals and, 276, 279–80, 282, 285, 289, 291, 293; Nagasaki and, 277–80; no-first-use policies and, 260, 282, 287–88, 293; nonproliferation regime and, 283–84; North Korea and, 284, 286, 288–91; nuclear age and, 285; Nuclear Nonproliferation Treaty (NPT) and, 277–78, 281, 283–84; nuclear order and, 289; Obama and, 282–85; Pakistan and, 279, 282, 288, 291; plutonium and, 288; postwar issues and, 279; public opinion and, 277, 279–80; radiation and, 290; rise of, 279–81; Russia and, 277, 279–88, 291–92; SALT and, 279–81; security and, 276–78, 281–82, 284, 287–88, 290–91, 293; South Korea and, 285, 288–89, 291; strategy and, 279, 283, 285, 287–93; superpowers and, 279; technology and, 277, 281, 283–84, 289, 293; Trump and, 285–93; United Kingdom and, 277, 279, 281, 291; United Nations and, 278–79, 283, 289–93; United States and, 276–92; World War II and, 276, 281, 283

nuclear waste, 261, 269–70, 272

nuclear weapons: antinuclear movements and, 10–11, 16, 68, 92, 100, 110, 112, 116, 144–54, 161–62, 179, 182, 185, 189, 191, 207, 210–11, 217, 244, 246, 277, 279, 281, 290–92; Armageddon and, 4, 8, 71–88, 308; arms race and, 9, 61, 74, 83–84, 134, 140–41, 195, 210–11, 269, 277, 284, 299, 305; assured destruction and, 79–81, 85, 232, 271, 280; assured retaliation and, 82, 86; Bandung Conference and, 109–17; Bikini Atoll and, 110, 112, 141, 162, 206–7, 211, 273; *Bulletin of the Atomic Scientists* and, 275; bunker-buster, 284; China and, 145, 154–59, 162, 221–42; civilians and, 7, 9, 36, 52–55, 60, 67, 94, 110, 184, 202, 206, 208, 224, 227, 245–46, 250–54, 280, 286; critique of deterrence and, 188–96; destruction from, 1, 3, 5, 8, 11, 16, 75, 80–81, 85, 88, 109, 113–15, 130, 134, 141, 147, 164, 178, 183–84, 189, 191, 196, 199–200, 207–8, 232, 238, 259, 264, 268, 271, 276, 279, 281, 292, 315n17, 316n19; disarmament and, 259–75; discourses and, 201, 206–12, 216, 243–58; *Enola Gay* and, 2, 103; fission and, 1, 3, 72, 135, 142, 247; France and, 3; future wars and, 3, 16, 73, 78, 83–84, 86, 116–17, 122–23, 127–31, 134, 141–42, 153, 157, 183, 189–95, 202, 206–12, 242, 257, 268–77, 280, 292–93, 299, 306, 308, 310; Germany and, 179–200; historical perspectives on, 294–311; Holocaust and, 8, 88, 188, 191, 202, 213; India and, 129–30, 134–35, 138, 141, 143; inspections and, 94, 175–76; international control and, 12, 15, 52, 95, 138, 141–42, 176, 223, 247–48, 252, 259, 272, 278, 302; international order and, 9, 13, 15, 22, 25, 206, 262; Iran and, 165; Japanese politics and, 92–96, 99–101, 104; Khrushchev and, 78–79; legacies of, 1–16; *Lucky Dragon* incident and, 100, 109–10, 112, 144, 146, 148, 151, 207; Malinovskii and, 77, 83, 86; Maud Committee Report and, 72; nonnuclear policies and, 144–47, 150–63; North Korea and, 145; Pakistan and, 231; plutonium and, 72, 74, 96, 142, 247, 251, 267–70, 288; preemptive strikes and, 77–81, 86, 225, 288, 297, 309–10; psychology and, 193–94; Pugwash movement and, 79, 85–86; race and, 57–60, 63–70; radiation and, 13, 75, 88, 110, 112, 162, 188, 194–95, 243–45, 248–49, 255–56, 267, 270, 279; reasons for pursuing, 302–4; Sakharov and, 88; SALT and, 84–85, 87, 279–81, 299, 304, 310; Sokolovskii and, 76–77, 82, 86; South America and, 165–78; Soviet Union and, 71, 75–79, 85–88, 145; superpowers and, 3, 8, 72, 110, 140–41, 171, 173, 225, 229–34, 241, 262, 269, 271, 279, 300–301, 305, 308; as taboo, 276–93; Treaty on

nuclear weapons (cont.)
the Prohibition of Nuclear Weapons and, 5, 272; Trinity tests and, 268, 273; Truman and, 36, 38, 52–54; United Nations ban of, 166, 272, 278, 289–93; United States and, 305 (see also United States); uranium and, 1, 5, 24, 68, 96, 121, 137, 166–68, 247, 261, 267, 269–71; uses of, 301–2; VNIIEF and, 75; warheads and, 3, 71, 76, 80–86, 157, 169, 210, 229–32, 247, 254, 285–88; weapons-free zones and, 100, 171, 173, 175, 278, 287
Nuclear Weapons Ban Treaty, 16, 216
Nuclear Weapons States (NWS), 262
Nunn, Sam, 262
Nuremberg War Crimes Tribunal, 191

Obama, Barack, 5, 67, 216, 276, 282–85, 290, 298, 394n37
Official Development Assistance (ODA), 97
Ōhira Masayoshi, 93, 97–98, 335n16
Ohta Hiroko, 207
Oka Ryōichi, 121
Okinawa, 92, 103, 144, 152–53, 210, 216
Olympics, 98
Omnibus Trade Bill, 102
Ootori Kurino, 126
Open-Ended Working Group (OEWG), 291
Oppenheimer, J. Robert, 47, 280, 323n67
Orientalism, 263, 379n12
Our Time (film), 114
Ozawa Ichirō, 105

Pacific theater, 3, 20, 38, 40, 49, 51, 96, 102, 104–5, 114
pacifism: discourses and, 206–13, 216, 218; Germany and, 182, 189; Japanese politics and, 90, 94, 98–99, 104, 227; nonnuclear policies and, 144–45; postwar issues and, 10
Page, Arthur, 45
Pakistan: atomic bombs and, 165; Bandung Conference and, 121, 125, 127; historical perspectives and, 295, 298; India and, 139, 142, 236; Japan and, 98; Kargil conflict and, 236; Kashmir and, 236, 288; nuclear energy and, 231; nuclear taboo and, 279, 282, 288, 291; nuclear weapons and, 231
Pax Christi, 188
peace: activism and, 2, 9, 180, 187–200, 207, 213, 281; antinuclear movements and, 10–11, 16, 68, 92, 100, 110, 112, 116, 144–54, 161–62, 179, 182, 185, 189, 191, 207, 210–11, 217, 244, 246, 277, 279, 281, 290–92; Atoms for Peace and, 9, 110–11, 114, 118, 120–27, 141, 165, 168–69, 172; Bandung Conference and, 9–10, 109–27; *Bulletin of the Atomic Scientists* and, 275; China and, 229, 233, 236, 238; conscientious objectors and, 184; détente and, 4, 16, 188, 310; disarmament and, 271; discourses and, 207–13, 216–17, 243–57; Geneva conferences and, 75, 113, 250, 303; Germany and, 180–84, 187–96, 199–200; Hiroshima Peace Memorial and, 5–6; historical perspectives and, 294–301, 305, 310; India and, 129, 133–34, 137, 140–42; Japanese politics and, 9, 89–90, 93, 96–100, 104–5; Liberal Democratic Party (LDP) and, 91–92, 94, 96, 99, 102, 104–5, 119–20, 123, 125, 148, 154, 209, 217; movements for, 10, 12, 15–16, 149–51, 162, 181–82, 190–91, 194–96, 199, 210, 211, 217; Nobel Peace Prize and, 5, 93; nonnuclear policies and, 10, 146–53, 162–63; Nuclear Nonproliferation Treaty (NPT) and, 92, 94, 129, 142, 144, 158–59, 172–73, 176, 210, 222, 262, 268, 271, 277, 281, 283–85, 290–91, 302–4; nuclear taboo and, 281; Nuclear Weapons Ban Treaty and, 16, 216; phony, 193; Roosevelt and, 20, 22, 31; SALT and, 84–85, 87, 279–81, 299, 304, 310; San Francisco Peace Treaty and, 90, 98, 112, 146; security and, 9–10, 12, 15, 89–90, 96–99, 104, 118, 134, 146, 149, 153, 169, 175, 193, 210, 229, 233, 245; South America and, 165, 168–69, 172, 175; Soviet

Union and, 75, 81, 250–51; Treaty of Mutual Cooperation and Security and, 94; Truman and, 47; UN Conference on Peaceful Uses of Atomic Energy and, 250; United Nations and, 16, 113, 116, 127, 250; U.S.-Japan Security Pact and, 90–91, 95, 98–100, 103–4, 146, 148–49, 158–60, 190, 210; world, 4, 31, 117, 210; World Peace Council and, 210; Yoshida Doctrine and, 89–95, 99, 101, 103–4, 113, 116, 209
peaceful nuclear explosions (PNEs), 172–73, 176
Peacekeeper missiles, 305
Peace Problems Symposium, 112
Pearl Harbor, 50, 59–60, 89, 102–3, 131
Pentagon, 79, 85
People's Conference on the Abolition of Nuclear Weapons and Building Peace, 150
Perkovich, George, 129
Perry, William J., 262, 287
Pershing II missiles, 189, 194–96, 305
Philippines, 65–68, 111, 119, 121, 127
Plaza Accord, 101
plutonium: disarmament and, 267–70; discourses and, 247, 261; implosion and, 72; India and, 142; Japanese politics and, 96; nuclear taboo and, 288; Soviet Union and, 72, 74; spontaneous fission and, 72
Plutopia (Brown), 251–52
poison gas, 187
Poland, 25, 27–28, 30–31
political science, 1, 4–6, 16, 57, 62, 95, 112–13, 222, 223, 295–96
politicians: Bandung Conference and, 109, 111, 113, 116, 119–28; brinksmanship of, 5; capitalism and, 25, 27, 63, 186, 211, 265, 296; discourses and, 209, 249; foreign relations and, 61–64; Germany and, 188–91, 194; imperialism, 62, 76, 149–50, 186, 229; India and, 132, 135, 139; international order and, 9, 13, 15, 22, 25, 206, 262; international relations and, 2, 4, 7, 12, 15–16, 57, 63, 65, 67, 130, 245, 259–60, 294, 296, 307–9; Japanese politics and, 90, 92, 94, 101–3; Leninism and, 76, 211, 213, 251; Marxism and, 113, 211, 213; nonnuclear policies and, 145, 159, 162; postwar issues and, 6, 9, 90, 135; South America and, 171, 173. *See also* specific politician

Politics of Invisibility, The (Kuchinskaya), 255
populism, 20, 203
Posener, Alan, 198
postwar issues: Allied Occupation of Japan and, 65, 90, 146; Bandung Conference and, 9; China and, 224; Cold War and, 2 (*see also* Cold War); diplomats and, 6, 9, 15, 68; disarmament and, 266; discourses and, 11–12, 205–6, 214, 218; Dulles and, 90–91, 118, 207; geopolitical hierarchies and, 9; Germany and, 11, 182; ideologies and, 11, 66; India and, 10, 131–35, 140; Japanese politics and, 8, 89–90, 97–98; nonnuclear policies and, 10; Nuclear Nonproliferation Treaty (NPT) and, 92, 94, 129, 142, 144, 158–59, 172–73, 176, 210, 222, 262, 268, 271, 277, 281, 283–85, 290–91, 302–4; nuclear taboo and, 279; pacifism and, 10; politicians and, 6, 9, 90, 135; postwar issues and, 35–44, 54–55; race and, 8, 68; Roosevelt and, 22–33; South America and, 165, 178; Soviet Union and, 23–28, 74; Treaty of Mutual Cooperation and Security and, 94; Truman and, 35–44, 54–55, 59, 65–66, 68; United Kingdom and, 23; United States and, 23; U.S.-Japan Security Pact and, 90–91, 95, 98–100, 103–4, 146; Yoshida Doctrine and, 89–95, 99, 101, 103–4, 113, 116, 209
Potsdam Conference, 20–21, 33–34, 39, 41–48, 51, 324n74
Potter, William, 284
poverty, 62, 135, 193
POWs, 50
preemptive strikes, 77–81, 86, 225, 288, 297, 309–10
Presidential Directive 8, 96

Protestants, 189–90
psychology: atomic bombs and, 38, 41, 50, 57, 268; bureaucratic studies and, 161; mass murder and, 194; militarization and, 193; nuclear weapons and, 193–94
public opinion: China and, 227; critique of deterrence and, 188–96; discourses and, 207, 216; Fukushima and, 372n4; Japanese politics and, 100; national security doctrines and, 10, 175; neither confirm nor deny (NCND) policy and, 93–94; newspapers and, 38, 44, 46–47, 57, 73, 94, 101–3, 121, 156, 180, 198; nonnuclear policies and, 147; nuclear taboo and, 277, 279–80; San Francisco Peace Treaty and, 90; South America and, 164; Stalin and, 26
Puerto Rico, 269
Pugwash movement, 79, 85–86
Putin, Vladimir, 74, 282, 285

Qian Xuesen, 224
Quadros, Jânio, 171

race: activism and, 57, 68–69; African Americans and, 56–57, 61–62, 67–79, 297, 326n5; antinuclear movements and, 68; arms race and, 61; atomic bombs and, 7, 19–24, 27–33, 56–70, 103; Bandung Conference and, 109; Black Panthers and, 56–57, 67–69; Chinese Exclusion Act and, 59; civilians and, 52, 58, 60, 66–67; Cold War and, 58, 63, 67–68; colonialism and, 8–9, 57–58, 62, 65–69; communism and, 58, 63, 65; diplomats and, 57, 59–60, 63, 65, 68–69; economic issues and, 62, 66, 70; Eisenhower and, 75; eugenicists and, 62; foreign policy and, 8, 58, 61–64, 69–70; Germans and, 56–57, 60; historical perspectives and, 57–61; Holocaust and, 8, 61, 180–86, 190, 198, 281, 355n52; ideologies and, 61–66, 69–70; international relations and, 7, 57, 63, 65, 67; Japan and, 56–62, 65–67, 69, 103; Jim Crow era and, 70; Ku Klux Klan and, 63; military and, 59–61, 65–67, 70; morals and, 66–67; Moynihan Report and, 62; multiculturalism and, 62–63; Nagasaki and, 56, 58–59, 68; Native Americans and, 67–68, 70, 269–70; North Korea and, 56; nuclear age and, 64, 67–68; nuclear weapons and, 57–60, 63–70; police brutality and, 56; postwar issues and, 8, 68; poverty and, 62, 135; science and, 57; security and, 63, 66, 69; slavery and, 56–57, 64, 67, 70, 267; Soviet Union and, 22–33, 59, 65–66; stereotypes and, 59; strategy and, 60, 66–67; suicide of, 75; Target Committee and, 61; technology and, 67; Truman and, 57, 59, 61–62, 65; Trump and, 62; white supremacy and, 59, 62–70; World War II and, 57, 61, 65–69
Radchenko, Sergey, 28
radiation: acceptable exposure to, 270; Aikichi and, 110, 112; Atomic Bomb Casualty Commission (ABCC) and, 270; Bandung Conference and, 110, 112; Cesium-137 and, 255; Chernobyl and, 13, 243–44, 247, 252–57, 271, 377n48, 377n51; discourses and, 243–45, 248–49, 255–56; effects of US arsenal, 75; Fukushima and, 13, 244, 247, 253, 256–57, 271, 275, 372n4; Geiger counters and, 2; health effects of, 13, 75, 88, 110, 112, 162, 194–95, 243–45, 248–49, 255–56, 267, 270, 279; Hiroshima and, 13, 88, 162, 188, 194–95, 244, 248, 267, 270, 279; industrial detection instruments and, 373n13; international standards on, 249; legacies of, 188; *Lucky Dragon* incident and, 100, 109–10, 112, 144, 146, 148, 151, 207; Nagasaki and, 162, 188, 194, 248, 267, 270; Native Americans and, 269–70; nonmilitary use of, 245; nuclear taboo and, 290; nuclear waste and, 261, 269–70, 272; nuclear weapons and, 13, 75, 88, 110, 112, 162, 188, 194–95, 243–45, 248–49, 255–56, 267, 270, 279; special interest groups and, 251; studies on effects

of, 195; Three Mile Island and, 247, 252, 271; zones and, 255
Radiation Exposure Compensation Act (RECA), 270
Radioisotopes School, 125–28
Radioisotope Training Center for the Asian Region, 125–26
Raghavan, Srinath, 10, 124, 129–43, 308, 397
Raman, C. V., 135
RAND, 308
Reagan, Ronald, 56, 98, 100, 193, 210, 298
Red Army Faction, 188
"Reflections before a Glass Cage" (Enzensberger), 185
Reischauer, Edwin, 92–93
religion, 157, 188–90, 203, 208–9, 214
Republicans, 2
Reserved Areas, 39
revisionism, 7, 19–22, 58–59, 65, 165, 177, 212, 216
Reykjavik conference, 307
Richter, Horst Eberhard, 193–94
Rising Sun (Crichton), 102
Robeson, Paul, 58
Rockefeller Center, 102
Rodong missile, 211
Romania, 295
Roosevelt, Franklin D.: Atlantic Charter and, 25; atomic bombs and, 6–7; bomb diplomacy of, 28–33; Cold War and, 7, 15, 33; communism and, 25, 30; death of, 32; declining health of, 27; economic issues and, 24–27; foreign policy and, 6, 26, 31–32; Four Freedoms speech and, 25, 30; Hyde Park deal of, 28–30, 316n32; international control and, 24, 26, 28–32; as the Juggler, 21–22; League of Nations and, 24–25; Manhattan Project and, 19, 22, 26, 28, 32; military and, 19, 23–24, 33; Nagasaki and, 19–22, 31–32; national advantage and, 15–16; orthodox/revisionist debate and, 7, 19–22; peace and, 20, 22, 31; postwar issues and, 22–33; secrecy of, 21–22, 29; security and, 23–31; Stalin and, 7, 15, 20, 25–32; strategy and, 20–24, 30–31; subordination of United Kingdom by, 25; technology and, 23–24, 28, 32; unconditional surrender policy of, 19, 25; Yalta Conference and, 26–32
Rosatom, 257
Rosenberg, David, 77, 309
Rosenman, Samuel, 47
Rothstein, Richard, 63–64
Rotter, Andrew, 179
Rouhani, Hassan, 165
Rōyama Masamichi, 112
Russell, Richard B., 47–48, 323n73
Russia, 4; deterrence and, 75–76; disarmament and, 270; discourses and, 211, 254–55, 257; Great Purge and, 74; historical perspectives and, 77–78, 86, 298, 310; nonnuclear policies and, 145; nuclear energy and, 72; nuclear modernization and, 16; Nuclear Nonproliferation Treaty (NPT) and, 277; nuclear revolution and, 16; nuclear taboo and, 277, 279, 282–88, 291–92; Putin and, 74, 282, 285; Truman and, 28, 42, 48, 51; VNIIEF and, 75
Russian Foreign Intelligence (SVR), 72
Russian Military Intelligence (GRU), 72

Sagane Ryōkichi, 124, 340n44
Saha, Meghnad, 133, 135–36, 138
Said, Edward, 13, 261, 264–65, 275
Sakata Shōichi, 113
Sakharov, Andrei, 88
Sakurauchi Yoshio, 103
San Francisco Peace Treaty, 90, 98, 112, 146
Sarney, José, 175–76
Sasaki Takuya, 8, 89–105, 397
Satō Eisaku, 91–94, 146, 152–54, 156, 161, 209–10
Saudi Arabia, 102
Savelyev, Aleksandr, 85–86
Schell, Jonathan, 13, 190, 261, 263–64, 273, 379n14, 380n16
Schelling, Thomas, 238, 306, 308, 364n6
Scherpe, Klaus, 196

Schily, Otto, 189–91
Schmid, Sonja D., 12–13, 243–58, 270, 384n59, 397
Schmidt, Helmut, 189
science, 155; Bandung Conference and, 109–15, 120–28; China and, 222–24; disarmament and, 266, 275; discourses and, 243–54, 258; Germany and, 182, 190; historical perspectives and, 295–96, 298, 307, 310–11; India and, 133–42; Japan and, 95; nuclear taboo and, 279–80; political, 1, 4–6, 16, 57, 62, 95, 112–13, 222–23, 295–96; race and, 57; social, 4, 266, 298, 307, 310; South America and, 164, 168, 173, 178; Soviet Union and, 72, 75, 79, 81, 83, 85–86; technology and, 2, 6, 10, 14, 83, 85–86, 110, 115, 120, 122–23, 128, 133, 139, 178, 222, 249–50; Truman and, 36–37, 53; VNIIEF and, 75
Science and Technology Agency (STA), 115, 124, 126, 128
Science Council of Japan, 112, 115, 122, 124
Scowcroft, Brent, 281
Scud missiles, 211
Seale, Bobby, 56
SEATO, 118–19
Seattle Mariners, 102
Sebald, W. G., 181, 198
security: atomic energy and, 8; Bandung Conference and, 118; Basic National Security Policy and, 76, 79; *Bulletin of the Atomic Scientists* and, 275; China and, 222–30, 233–34, 240; Comprehensive Test Ban Treaty and, 291; disarmament and, 259–62, 266, 274–75; discourses and, 209–10, 245; economic issues and, 8–9, 27, 66, 90–91, 97, 100–101, 104, 118, 139, 156, 163–64, 175, 225, 302; ethics and, 12–13; future wars and, 3, 16, 73, 78, 83–84, 86, 116–17, 122–23, 127–31, 134, 141–42, 153, 157, 183, 189–95, 202, 206–12, 242, 257, 268–77, 280, 292–93, 299, 306, 308, 310; Germany and, 182–84, 190, 193; historical perspectives and, 297–302, 311; India and, 130, 134, 136, 139, 142; Japanese politics and, 8–9, 89–104; nonnuclear policies and, 10, 144, 146, 148–49, 153–63; nuclear taboo and, 276–78, 281–82, 284, 287–91, 293; peace and, 9–10, 12, 15, 89–90, 96–99, 104, 118, 134, 146, 149, 153, 169, 175, 193, 210, 229, 233, 245; race and, 63, 66, 69; Roosevelt and, 23–31; South America and, 164, 167–77; Soviet Union and, 76, 79; Treaty of Mutual Cooperation and Security and, 94; Truman and, 52; U.S.-Japan Security Pact and, 90–91, 148–49, 158–60, 190, 210; weapons-free zones and, 100, 171, 173, 175, 278, 287

Security Research Commission, 156
Self-Defense Forces (SDF), 90, 95, 100, 104, 336n28
Semenov, V. S., 84
Sentinel system, 83
September 11, 2001 attacks, 196, 381n25
Serbia, 269, 307
Seventh World Conference against Atomic and Hydrogen Bombs, 150
Shigaki Mintō, 155, 346n40, 346n45, 347n61, 348n69
Shigemitsu Mamoru, 114–15
"Shikabane no machi" (City of corpses) (Ohta), 207
Shimizu Ikutarō, 98
Shimizu Kitarō, 112–13
Shingo Tanaka, 120
Shōriki Matsutarō, 121
Shultz, George, 13, 262
Signature Campaign against Atomic and Hydrogen Bombs, 146–47, 151
Singapore, 290, 306
Singh, Manmohan, 276
Sixth World Conference against Atomic and Hydrogen Bombs, 149
slavery, 56–57, 64, 67, 70, 267
"Slavery, Race, and Ideology in the United States of America" (Fields), 64
Smiling Buddha test, 129
Smith, Gerald C., 119
Smithsonian Museum, 103

Sneider, Richard, 120
Snyder, Glenn, 236
Social Democratic Party (SPD), 182, 186, 188–89, 191, 194–95
socialism: Bandung Conference and, 113, 117, 337n6; China and, 226, 235; discourses and, 209–11; Germany and, 183, 186–87, 191, 198–99; nonnuclear policies and, 148–51; South America and, 171; Soviet Union and, 87
social science, 4, 266, 298, 307, 310
Sokolovskii, V. D., 76–77, 82, 86, 330n27
Solingen, Etel, 162–63
Sölle, Dorothee, 191, 193, 358n92
Somalia, 269
Sommer, Theo, 198
Sony, 102–3
South Africa, 290
South America, 2; activism and, 171; Argentina, 10–11, 164–77, 281, 303; atomic bombs and, 165, 178; atomic energy and, 168, 172; Atoms for Peace and, 165, 168–69, 172; Brazil, 9–11, 164–77, 213, 290, 295, 303; Chile, 169; civilians and, 167–68, 175–76; Cold War and, 173; colonialism and, 166–71; communism and, 166, 171; Cuban Missile Crisis and, 171; diplomats and, 164, 168, 171, 173, 175; economic issues and, 164, 172, 175; Eighteen-Nation Disarmament Committee and, 171; Eisenhower and, 168–69; Falklands War and, 175; foreign policy and, 171; Hiroshima and, 164–67, 177–78; indigenous populations and, 167; inspections and, 175–76; Institute of Research on Nuclear Energy and, 171; Inter-American Nuclear Energy Commission and, 169; Iran and, 165, 176; Manhattan Project and, 42; military and, 165–66, 169–75; Nagasaki and, 166; National Nuclear Energy Commission and, 171; Nazis and, 166; nuclear age and, 170–71, 178; nuclear energy and, 167–74, 177–78; Nuclear Nonproliferation Treaty (NPT) and, 172–73, 176; nuclear order and, 164–72, 176–78; nuclear revolution and, 10, 164, 166, 168; nuclear weapons and, 165–78; peace and, 165, 168–69, 172, 175; politicians and, 171, 173; postwar issues and, 165, 178; public opinion and, 164; regional competition and, 169–72; science and, 164, 168, 173, 178; security and, 164, 167–77; socialism and, 171; Soviet Union and, 166, 169, 171; strategy and, 11, 177; superpowers and, 171, 173; Tlatelolco Treaty and, 173; United Nations and, 166; uranium and, 166–78; World War II and, 166
South China Sea, 216
South Korea: Bandung Conference and, 114, 127; discourses and, 257; historical perspectives and, 295, 303–4; Japanese politics and, 94, 96, 104; Moon Jae-in and, 289; nuclear taboo and, 285, 288–89, 291
Soviet Academy of Sciences, 86
Soviet Union, 2, 6; ABM systems and, 82–84, 87; Afghanistan and, 98; Anti-Ballistic Missile (ABM) Treaty and, 72, 279–81, 284; Armageddon and, 71–88; arms race and, 9, 74, 83–87; assured retaliation and, 82, 86; atomic bombs and, 72–74, 87; atomic energy and, 74; *Avrora* system and, 83; ballistic missiles and, 3, 71–72, 76–77, 82–84; Bandung Conference and, 110, 115, 118, 126, 128; Berlin Wall and, 196, 210; bombers and, 76–77, 80; Brezhnev and, 72, 81, 84, 87; brutality of, 26; bureaucrats and, 81; Central Committee and, 84, 87, 251; Chernobyl and, 13, 243–44, 247, 252–57, 271, 377n48, 377n51; China and, 210, 221–22, 225–41, 365n16, 365n17; civilians and, 74; Cold War and, 74–75, 77, 85; collapse of, 72, 202, 210, 307; communism and, 25, 76, 90; Cuba and, 4, 19, 71, 88, 171, 235, 300–302, 306, 308; Damansk conflict and, 237; deterrence and, 75–76; discourses and, 202, 207, 210–11, 218, 243, 249–57; economic

Soviet Union (*cont.*)
issues and, 77; Eisenhower and, 75–76, 79; espionage and, 72–73; First Chief Directorate and, 73; Germany and, 189; GOELRO and, 251; Gorbachev and, 283, 307; Gromyko and, 74; Hiroshima and, 72–75; historical perspectives and, 299–310; hydrogen bombs and, 3; India and, 132, 140; international control and, 74; Iron Curtain and, 3, 8; Japanese politics and, 89–90, 96, 98–102, 100, 314n8; Khrushchev and, 75–76, 78–79, 82–83, 228–29, 301, 344n23, 365n16, 367n23; Kosygin and, 83, 231; Lenin and, 76, 211, 213, 251; *Machtpolitik* and, 24; Malinovskii and, 77, 83, 86; Marxism and, 113, 211, 213; mass media and, 250; military and, 72–88; Ministry of Medium Machine Building and, 251, 331n42; Molotov and, 73–74; morals and, 78; Nagasaki and, 71, 74, 88; nonnuclear policies and, 145, 150, 158, 160; nuclear age and, 71; nuclear energy and, 251, 375n39; nuclear taboo and, 279–83; nuclear weapons and, 71, 75–79, 85–88, 145, 202; orthodox/revisionist debate and, 7; peace and, 75, 81, 250–51; plutonium and, 72, 74; postwar issues and, 23–28, 74; Pugwash movement and, 79, 85–86; race and, 59, 65–66; Reykjavik conference and, 307; Roosevelt and, 20–33; SALT and, 84–85, 87, 279–81, 299, 304, 310; science and, 72, 75, 79, 81, 83, 85–86; secret sites of, 249–53; security and, 76, 79; socialism and, 87; Sokolovskii and, 76–77, 82, 86; South America and, 166, 169, 171; Special Committee of the State Defense Committee and, 73, 329n8; Sputnik satellite and, 3; SS-20 missiles and, 100, 189, 310; Stalin and, 7, 15, 20, 25–32, 49, 65, 72–76, 82, 166, 222, 314n8; strategic arms policy and, 71–88; Strategic Rocket Forces and, 76, 80–81; strategy and, 71–72, 76–88; superpowers and, 72; technology and, 73, 83, 85–86, 88; Truman and, 21, 41–43, 48, 48–51, 73; TsNIIMash and, 80–81; Twentieth Party Congress and, 76; United Kingdom and, 26, 73, 78; United Nations and, 25; U.S. parity and, 71–72; World War II and, 76, 87; Yalta Conference and, 26–32

Spartan, 82
Spektor, Matias, 10–11, 94, 164–78, 397
Sprinker, Michael, 264
Sprint, 82
Sputnik satellite, 3
SS-20 missiles, 100, 189, 310
Stackpole, Henry, 103
Stalin, Joseph: Alliluyeva and, 72–73; arms race and, 74; brutality of, 26; China and, 222; death of, 222; First Chief Directorate and, 73; Gromyko and, 74; Hiroshima and, 7, 15, 20, 72–75, 166, 222; invasion operation of, 49; Khrushchev and, 82; Lenin and, 76; Manhattan Project and, 20, 74–75; Molotov and, 73–74; national advantage and, 15–16; orthodox/revisionist debate and, 7; postwar Japan and, 65; public opinion on, 26; Roosevelt and, 7, 15, 20, 25–32; South America and, 166; Soviet Union and, 7, 15, 20, 25–32, 49, 65, 72–76, 82, 166, 222; Special Committee of the State Defense Committee and, 73; Stimson and, 321n57; Truman and, 7, 15, 28, 49, 73, 314n8
Standstill Agreement, 141
START Treaty, 211, 285
States of Knowledge (Jasanoff), 244
Stimson, Henry, 319n23; civilian targets and, 40, 42–43, 48, 280; Harrison and, 325n83; military targets and, 39–45, 318n19, 319n31, 321n54; Page and, 45; Russell and, 323n73; Stalin and, 321n57; Truman and, 31–33, 35, 38–51, 54, 61, 280, 320n38, 321n53
Stoddard, Lothrop, 62
Stone, John N., 44–45, 322n57
Strategic Arms Limitation Talks (SALT), 84–85, 87, 279–81, 299, 304, 310
strategic bombing, 20, 23, 40, 60, 67, 89, 279

Strategic Integrated Operational Plan (SIOP), 79, 87
Strategic Rocket Forces, 76, 80–81
strategy: Anti-Ballistic Missile and Strategic Arms Limitation and, 8; assured destruction and, 79–81, 85, 232, 271, 280; assured retaliation and, 82, 86; Bandung Conference and, 118; China and, 12, 221–27, 229, 231, 233–34, 241–42; Cold War, 8, 67, 77, 85, 103–4, 140, 193, 222, 241, 288, 300, 302; diplomats and, 9; disarmament and, 259, 271; discourses and, 207, 255–56; Germany and, 180, 185, 191, 193, 199; historical perspectives and, 297–310; India and, 140; Japanese politics and, 89, 92, 95, 98, 103–4; Joint Chiefs of Staff and, 83, 87, 101; McNamara and, 79–85; military, 4, 6, 12, 24, 38, 40–41, 67, 76–82, 85–88, 185, 193, 221, 224–25, 229, 233, 279, 288, 297, 301–2, 309–10; nonnuclear policies and, 145–46, 151, 153, 155, 159–63; nuclear taboo and, 279, 283, 285, 287–93; preemptive strikes and, 77–78, 80–81, 86, 225, 288, 297, 309–10; psychological, 38, 41, 50, 57, 268; Pugwash movement and, 79, 85–86; race and, 60, 66–67; RAND and, 308; reasons for using atomic bombs and, 19–22; Roosevelt and, 20–24, 30–31; South America and, 11, 177; Soviet arms policy and, 71–88; Truman and, 3, 36–41, 44, 52, 54; U.S. Strategic Air Command and, 77
Strategy in the Missile Age (Brodie), 78
Strategy of Nuclear War, The (Malinovskii), 77
students, 118, 120, 125, 179, 184–88, 199, 208, 214, 216, 245, 353n20
submarine-launched ballistic missiles (SLBMs), 79–80
Suginami Woman's Council, 146–47
suicide, 75, 183, 214, 231
superpowers: Bandung Conference and, 110; China and, 225, 229–34, 240–41; disarmament and, 262, 269, 271; historical perspectives and, 300–301, 305, 308; India and, 141; military and, 3, 8, 72, 110, 140–41, 171, 173, 225, 229–34, 241, 262, 269, 271, 279, 300–301, 305, 308; nuclear taboo and, 279; South America and, 171, 173; Soviet Union and, 72
Super-Powers, The (Fox), 23
Supreme Commander for the Allied Powers (SCAP), 90, 248
Suzuki Zenkō, 93, 98
Sweden, 56, 113, 295, 303–4
Switzerland, 250, 257
Symington, W. Stuart, 53
Syria, 113, 131, 225
Sznaider, Natan, 182, 352n12

Taiwan, 114, 125, 127, 213, 224, 229, 235, 302, 304
Takaki, Ronald, 58–62
Takasaki Tatsunosuke, 115, 117
Taketani Mitsuo, 117, 120–21
Tanaka Kakuei, 93
Tannenwald, Nina, 13, 54, 177, 245, 269, 276–93, 318n12, 392n20, 397
Target Committee, 38–39, 41, 61, 324n77
Tata Institute of Fundamental Research, 138
Tate, Merze, 70
TDK, 125
technology: atomic energy and, 15 (*see also* atomic energy); Bandung Conference and, 110, 114–15, 119–23, 127–28; China and, 12, 221–23, 229, 233, 241–42; Cold War and, 185–87; cultural fallout and, 15; discourses and, 246–51; fuel cycle and, 165, 168–70, 173–75; Germany and, 179, 182, 185, 187, 190, 195–96, 200; historical perspectives and, 296, 302–3, 305; India and, 132–33, 139–40, 142; Japanese politics and, 95–96, 99; nonnuclear policies and, 161–78; nuclear order and, 9; nuclear taboo and, 277, 281, 283–84, 289, 293; nuclear weapons and, 3 (*see also* nuclear weapons); power of, 11; race and, 67; Roosevelt and, 23–24, 28, 32; *Sachzwänge* and, 187; science and, 2, 6, 10, 14, 83, 85–

technology (cont.)
86, 110, 115, 120, 122–23, 128, 133, 139, 178, 222, 249–50; Soviet Union and, 73, 83, 85–86, 88; Sputnik satellite and, 3; Truman and, 38; United Kingdom and, 73; victimhood and, 185–87

Teller, Edward, 280

terror, 56, 67, 187–88, 196, 223, 236, 241, 293, 300, 307, 381n25

Thailand, 98, 123, 125, 127–28

Third Bureau of International Cooperation, 115

Third World Conference against Atomic and Hydrogen Bombs, 148

Thompson, E. P., 189

Three Mile Island, 247, 252, 271

Tlatelolco Treaty, 173

Tōgō Fumihiko, 93

Tōjō Hideki, 91, 114

Tokai Mura, 96

Tokugawa Shogunate, 208, 213

Tomabechi Gizō, 119

Tominaga Gorō, 113–14

Tomotsugu Shinsuke, 9–10, 109–28, 141, 163, 398

trade unions, 148, 182, 186, 208, 210

Treaty of Mutual Cooperation and Security, 94

Treaty of Peace and Friendship, 96

Treaty on the Prohibition of Nuclear Weapons, 5, 261, 272

Trident missiles, 305

Trinity tests, 20–21, 41, 268, 273

Truman, Harry S.: Atomic Bomb Casualty Commission (ABCC) and, 249; atomic bombs and, 3, 6–7, 15, 19–22, 31–55, 59, 61–62, 65, 73, 249; Atomic Energy Act and, 54; Bandung Conference and, 120; bombers and, 50; Byrnes and, 20–21, 31–33, 43; civilians and, 34–36, 39–55; Cold War and, 15; discourses and, 249; disparate positions of, 34–37, 43–44, 47–55, 322n59; end-of-war strategy of, 3; foreign policy and, 7; Gridiron Dinner and, 51; Groves and, 39–42, 44, 49; historical perspectives and, 54–55, 298, 307; Interim Committee and, 38, 47; international control and, 52; Japanese politics and, 90; knowledge of Hiroshima by, 34–36, 39–55; Kyoto and, 7, 35, 39–45, 48, 51, 54–55; Manhattan Project and, 19, 32, 38–39, 42; military and, 7, 19, 34–55; morals and, 39–44, 51; Nagasaki and, 35–36, 39, 44, 49, 53, 55; national advantage and, 15–16; nuclear age and, 6; nuclear weapons and, 36, 38, 52–54; orthodox/revisionist debate and, 19–22; peace and, 47; populism and, 20; postwar issues and, 35–44, 54, 59, 65–66, 68; Potsdam Conference and, 20–21, 33–34, 39, 41–48, 51, 324n74; psychological strategies and, 38, 41, 50, 57, 268; race and, 57, 59, 61–62, 65; revisionist debate and, 19–22; Russell and, 47–48; science and, 36–37; security and, 52; Soviet Union and, 21, 28, 41–43, 48–51, 73; Stalin and, 7, 15, 28, 49, 73, 314n8; Stimson and, 31–33, 35, 38–51, 54, 61, 280, 320n38, 321n53; Stone memo and, 44–45, 322n57; strategy and, 3, 36–41, 44, 52, 54; Target Committee and, 38–39, 41; technology and, 38; unconditional surrender policy of, 21, 32, 47, 65; United Kingdom and, 51; World War II and, 34, 36, 38, 54

Truman Library, 45

Trump, Donald, 62, 76, 102, 285–93, 336n24, 391n8

Tsipis, Kosta, 195

TsNIIMash, 80–81

Tsongas, Paul, 102

Tsukishita Kiyoshi, 5–6

Tsuzuki Masao, 248

Turkey, 98, 126

Twenty-Fifth Special Committee for the Promotion of Science and Technology, 123

Ukraine, 255, 282

unconditional surrender, 19, 21, 25, 32, 47, 65

United Arab Republic (UAR), 126
United Kingdom: Bandung Conference and, 110, 118, 120, 127; Bomber Command and, 67; Churchill and, 28–30, 141; discourses and, 210, 257; historical perspectives and, 308; India and, 131–33, 137, 140; Macmillan and, 75; Manhattan Project and, 140; Maud Committee Report and, 72; Nuclear Nonproliferation Treaty (NPT) and, 277; nuclear taboo and, 277, 279, 281, 291; postwar issues and, 23; Soviet Union and, 20, 26, 73, 78; subordinate position of, 25; technology and, 73; Truman and, 51; United Nations and, 25; U.S. bases in, 78; Yalta Conference and, 26–32

United Nations, 389n57; Chernobyl and, 255–56; China and, 155; Conference on Peaceful Uses of Atomic Energy and, 250; disarmament and, 283; General Assembly and, 141, 291; Geneva conference and, 113, 250; India and, 113, 116, 126–27; League of Nations and, 24–25; MOFA and, 126; nonnuclear policies and, 155; Nuclear Prohibition Treaty and, 278, 289–90; nuclear taboo and, 278–79, 283, 289–93; Open-Ended Working Group (OEWG) and, 291; peace and, 16, 113, 116, 127, 250; Security Council and, 25–31, 52, 262; South America and, 166; total ban of nuclear weapons and, 166, 272, 278, 289–93; Treaty on the Prohibition of Nuclear Weapons and, 261; UNESCO and, 61, 125

United States: ABM systems and, 82–84, 87; African Americans and, 56–57, 61–62, 297; American Revolution and, 62; Anti-Ballistic Missile (ABM) Treaty and, 72, 279–81, 284; Argentina and, 172–77; arms race and, 9, 61, 74, 83–87, 134, 140–41, 195, 210–11, 269, 277, 284, 299, 305; Atomic Bomb Casualty Commission (ABCC) and, 5, 67–68, 248–49; Atoms for Peace and, 9, 110–11, 114, 118, 120–27, 141, 165, 168–69, 172; B-29 bombers and, 2, 103, 207; Basic National Security Policy and, 76, 79; Brazil and, 172–77; British bases of, 78; Carter and, 96–98, 174; Chinese Exclusion Act and, 59; Civil War and, 62; Clinton and, 104; Cold War and, 7 (*see also* Cold War); Cuban Missile Crisis and, 4, 19, 71, 88, 171, 235, 300–302, 308, 370n53; as debtor nation, 102–3; disarmament and, 262–63, 266–70, 273; Eisenhower and, 53–54, 75–76, 79, 91, 111, 118, 120, 125, 141, 168–69, 277–78, 309; *Enola Gay* and, 2, 103; Ford and, 93–94; foreign policy and, 22–24 (*see also* foreign policy); French bases of, 78; George H. W. Bush and, 103–4, 283; George W. Bush and, 284; German bases of, 78; globally projecting power of, 23–24; Gromyko and, 74; Gulf War and, 103, 105, 281–82; Hanford and, 251–52, 270, 273; historical perspectives and, 294–311; Hoover and, 39, 119–20; hydrogen bombs and, 3; incendiary raids and, 39; Japanese alliance and, 98–101; Johnson and, 83, 226, 303; Joint Chiefs of Staff and, 83, 87, 101; Kennedy and, 79; Korean War and, 52–54, 90, 140, 207, 235–37, 280; *Lucky Dragon* incident and, 100, 109–10, 112, 144, 146, 148, 151, 207; McNamara and, 79–85; Manhattan Project and, 19–20, 22, 26, 28, 32, 37–39, 60, 72, 74, 135, 140, 223; MIRVs and, 80–83; multibillion-dollar programs of, 305; Native Americans and, 67–68, 70, 269–70; NATO and, 91, 100–101, 126, 189, 191, 282, 287, 291, 300–301, 309–10; neither confirm nor deny (NCND) policy and, 93–94, 101; Nixon and, 72, 84, 87, 92–93, 103, 303; nuclear modernization and, 16; Nuclear Nonproliferation Treaty (NPT) and, 92, 94, 129, 142, 144, 158–59, 172–73, 176, 210, 222, 262, 268, 271, 277, 281, 283–85, 290–91, 302–4; nuclear order and, 3, 9, 11, 13, 15, 68–69, 140, 165–70, 176–77, 294; nuclear taboo and, 276–92; Obama and, 5, 67, 216, 276, 282–85, 290,

United States (*cont.*)
298, 394n37; Pacific theater and, 3, 38, 49; Pentagon and, 79, 85; postwar issues and, 23; Potsdam Conference and, 20–21, 33–34, 39, 41–48, 51; Pugwash movement and, 79, 85–86; race and, 59 (*see also* race); Reagan and, 56, 98, 100, 193, 210, 298; reason for using atomic bombs by, 19–22; Roosevelt and, 6 (*see also* Roosevelt, Franklin D.); SALT and, 84–85, 87, 279–81, 299, 304, 310; San Francisco Peace Treaty and, 90, 98, 112, 146; Sino-U.S. rapprochement and, 153; Soviet parity with, 71–72; Strategic Integrated Operational Plan (SIOP) and, 79, 87; Supreme Commander for the Allied Powers and, 248; Treaty of Mutual Cooperation and Security and, 94; Truman and, 53 (*see also* Truman, Harry S.); Trump and, 62, 76, 102, 285–93; unconditional surrender policy of, 19, 21, 25, 32, 47, 65; United Nations and, 25; Vietnam and, 8, 56, 58, 66, 127, 186–87, 195, 199, 236–38, 281; War Department and, 38, 46; Wilson and, 24–25, 27, 31; World War II and, 3 (*see also* World War II); Yalta Conference and, 26–32; Yoshida Doctrine and, 89–95, 99, 101, 103–4, 113, 116, 209

United States Information Agency, 114

United States National Security Council, 52, 118

United States Pacific Command (CINPAC), 101

University of Tokyo, 113

uranium: Bandung Conference and, 121; Congo mines of, 68, 270, 273; cornering market on, 24; disarmament and, 261, 267, 269–71; discourses and, 247; environmental destruction in mining, 5; fission and, 1, 247; India and, 137, 140; Japanese politics and, 96; Little Boy and, 1–2; monazite and, 137, 140; Navajo and, 68, 269–70; South America and, 166–78

U.S. Army Air Force, 1–2, 39–40, 67
U.S. Castle Bravo, 110
U.S. Department of Defense, 94, 103, 269
U.S. Department of Energy, 267, 269
U.S.-Japan Agreement Concerning Civil Uses of Atomic Energy, 120
U.S.-Japan Defense Guidelines, 94
U.S.-Japan Security Pact, 90–91, 95, 98–100, 103–4, 146, 148–49, 158–60, 190, 210
U.S. Marine Corps, 103
U.S. Navy, 79, 104, 191, 249
USS *Augusta*, 48
USS *Missouri*, 89, 101
U.S. State Department, 26–27, 92–93, 114, 118–19, 280
U.S. Strategic Air Command, 77
Ustinov, Dmitrii, 84

Venezuela, 126
victimhood, 11, 181, 183, 185–87, 202, 204–6, 213, 217–18, 222
Viedma Joint Statement on Nuclear Policy, 175–76
Vietnam, 8, 56, 58, 66, 127, 186–87, 195, 199, 236–38, 281
Villa, Brian Loring, 59
Vitalis, Robert, 68–69
VNIIEF, 75
Vogel, Ezra, 95–96

Wakaizumi Kei, 160
Walker, J. Samuel, 317n1, 318n14
Wall Street Journal, 263, 379n10
Walt, Steve, 391n8
Waltz, Kenneth, 235, 304
war crimes, 2, 65, 91, 181, 191, 204, 206, 212, 214, 217
Warsaw Pact, 87–88, 301
War without Mercy (Dower), 58
Watanabe Michio, 102–3
Watsuji Tetsuro, 112
weapons-free zones, 100, 171, 173, 175, 278, 287
Weil, Simone, 204–5

Weinberger, Caspar, 101
Wellerstein, Alex, 7, 34–55, 180, 398
West German Trade Union Federation, 186
White, Theodore, 101–2
white supremacy, 59, 62–70
Wicke, Jennifer, 264
Wilson, Woodrow, 24–25, 27, 31
World Health Organization (WHO), 127, 255
world peace, 4, 31, 117, 210
World Peace Council, 210
World War I, 24–25, 27, 131, 298, 307
World War II: Bandung Conference and, 115–17; China and, 222–23, 235; Cold War era and, 2; disarmament and, 266; discourses and, 5, 201–18, 249; Germany and, 11, 180–86, 191, 194–95, 198; historical perspectives and, 14–15, 103, 297, 309; Holocaust and, 8, 61, 180–86, 190, 198, 281; India and, 10, 130–35, 139, 142; Japanese politics and, 89, 103, 115–17, 201–18; nonnuclear policies and, 145; nuclear taboo and, 276, 281, 283; Nuremberg War Crimes Tribunal and, 191; Pacific theater of, 3, 20, 38, 40, 49, 51, 96, 102, 104–5, 114; race and, 57, 61, 65–69; Roosevelt and, 25; South America and, 166; Soviet Union and, 76, 87; terms of engagement and, 6–7; Truman and, 34, 36, 38, 54; Yalta Conference and, 26–32
World War III, 23, 76, 78, 194, 198, 200, 297, 300–301, 306

Xi Jinping, 368n37

Yalta Conference, 26–32
Yasui Kaoru, 147
Yasukuni, 11, 201–4, 213–18
Yomiuri shimbun newspaper, 121, 146
Yoshida Shigeru, 89–95, 99, 101, 103–4, 113, 116, 209, 332n1, 333n4
Yoshida Shingo, 95
Yuka Tsuchiya, 114
Yukawa Hideki, 120–21

Zakaria, Fareed, 289
Zakharov, M. V., 77
Zeit, Die (newspaper), 198
Zhenbao conflict, 237
Zwigenberg, Ran, 181

A NOTE ON THE TYPE

This book has been composed in Arno, an Old-style serif typeface in the
classic Venetian tradition, designed by Robert Slimbach at Adobe.

GPSR Authorized Representative: Easy Access System Europe - Mustamäe tee
50, 10621 Tallinn, Estonia, gpsr.requests@easproject.com

www.ingramcontent.com/pod-product-compliance
Lightning Source LLC
Chambersburg PA
CBHW051203300426
44116CB00006B/417